PRAISE FOR *LEADING THROUGH LEADERS*

"Jeremy asked me to review this book after he heard me speak at a business breakfast. I was flattered, and I was also hesitant – time is precious. However my attention was captured after reading just a few pages. What Jeremy has to say is intuitively sensible, clearly practical and well-proven, and much of it resonates instantaneously. Good leaders do much of what Jeremy says instinctively, it's not rocket science; but we often don't articulate it. Having it stripped of fads, then structured, simplified and explained so clearly – codified if you like – makes it possible not only to 'keep doing it better' but more importantly to have a framework for concurrently developing other leaders and your organization.

I love Jeremy's analysis of coaching and building teams – I have learned why certain things work and why others haven't in the past. I especially buy into Jeremy's exploration of morale and building confidence – it is so important to create both intellectual and emotional commitment, to be convincing and to create belief 'that it will be alright'. Not all leaders feel as I do, but in my case I have learned that in order to be convincing I need to be convinced. Jeremy shows how to achieve this for yourself and for those you lead. For 'action oriented' leaders prone to impulsive decisions, Jeremy provides the thought process which rather than slow things down, can speed things up.

I have the greatest admiration for the Army and I respect its approach to leadership. But more than that I am intrigued by how it develops individual leadership, yet systemically integrates it to get so many people pointing in the same direction, with such clear commitment, doing things so effectively in such short order. Execution is where so many organizations fall down. It has always been my experience that an OK strategy well executed delivers better results than a perfect strategy that is badly executed. By taking some military principles and changing the manner of their application, there are clearly lessons for all of us in civvy street to learn from the green machine.

I enjoyed reading Jeremy's manuscript; and you won't be disappointed with this book."

Fru Hazlitt, MD, ITV Commercial and Online

"Jeremy Tozer has done it again! Tozer's work on leadership, strategy and execution is rigorous, insightful and completely free of fads. His analysis is based on personal experience and careful observation of some of history's most outstanding leaders and the organizations that they have built. The book has a depth rarely found in other texts and applies to the simplest supervision of work through to the complex and sometimes morally challenging situations leaders find themselves in. Tozer's work is thorough and crystal clear in describing and showing how to be a better 'individual leader', while simultaneously developing the organization and its 'collective leadership capability' – the ultimate purpose of and systemically- and dynamically-aligned org usiness performance.

This is in my opinion the most complete and lucid work on leadership I have read. Instructive and compelling reading. It really is the best I have read, bar none."
Rob Anderson, Chief Executive, Best Western Australasia

"Translating the rigorous thinking behind, and practice of, military leadership, mission command and decision making into a civilian context is not easy. Yet these proven, robust and adaptable methods and principles – which focus activity and secure commitment – are equally relevant to business and public sector organizations when leaders adapt the style of their application. I commend the comprehensive manner in which Jeremy uses his experience in both the military and civilian work environments to generate intelligent analysis, and to provide effective and useful pointers to assist enterprises and their leaders in commerce, industry and the broader civilian environment to become more effective."
Lt Gen Andrew Graham CB CBE,
Director Research Foundation, General Dynamics
and former Director General Defence Academy of the United Kingdom

Leading Through Leaders

For Peter and for Christopher
Serve to Lead

Leadership is of the spirit, fortified by character,
enhanced by skill and refined by reflection;
its study a science, its practice an art, its impact a legacy.

May they learn from the
example of those Gallant Gentlemen

Leading Through Leaders

Driving strategy, execution and change

Jeremy Tozer

KoganPage

LONDON PHILADELPHIA NEW DELHI

Publisher's note

Every possible effort has been made to ensure that the information contained in this book is accurate at the time of going to press, and the publishers and author cannot accept responsibility for any errors or omissions, however caused. No responsibility for loss or damage occasioned to any person acting, or refraining from action, as a result of the material in this publication can be accepted by the editor, the publisher or the author.

First published in Great Britain and the United States in 2012 by Kogan Page Limited

Apart from any fair dealing for the purposes of research or private study, or criticism or review, as permitted under the Copyright, Designs and Patents Act 1988, this publication may only be reproduced, stored or transmitted, in any form or by any means, with the prior permission in writing of the publishers, or in the case of reprographic reproduction in accordance with the terms and licences issued by the CLA. Enquiries concerning reproduction outside these terms should be sent to the publishers at the undermentioned addresses:

120 Pentonville Road	1518 Walnut Street, Suite 1100	4737/23 Ansari Road
London N1 9JN	Philadelphia PA 19102	Daryaganj
United Kingdom	USA	New Delhi 110002
www.koganpage.com		India

© Jeremy Tozer, 2012

The right of Jeremy Tozer to be identified as the author of this work has been asserted by him in accordance with the Copyright, Designs and Patents Act 1988.

ISBN   978 0 7494 6619 0
E-ISBN   978 0 7494 6620 6

British Library Cataloguing-in-Publication Data

A CIP record for this book is available from the British Library.

Library of Congress Cataloging-in-Publication Data

Tozer, Jeremy.
  Leading through leaders : driving strategy, execution, and change / Jeremy Tozer. – 1st ed.
    p. cm.
  ISBN 978-0-7494-6619-0 – ISBN 978-0-7494-6620-6 1. Leadership.   2. Interpersonal communication.
3. Decision making.   4. Leadership–Moral and ethical aspects.   I. Title.
  HD57.7.T695 2012
  658.4'092–dc23
                                                                                                    2012010371

Typeset by Graphicraft Limited, Hong Kong
Printed and bound in India by Replika Press Pvt Ltd

CONTENTS

Foreword xiii
Acknowledgements xviii
About the Author xx

PART ONE Understanding Leadership and Its Context 1

01 The operating context, strategy execution and capability requirement 3

The operating context 4
Uncertainty and complexity 5
Exponential rate of change 7
Employee engagement, mobility and cynicism 7
Friction 8
Strategy to reality: the execution gap 9
Future agenda: the capability requirement 12
Leading through leaders: effects-based leadership (EBL) 16

02 Propositions about organizations, leadership, people and work 21

Organizational effectiveness: the corporate context of leadership 22
Leadership doctrine 23
Leadership, people and work 24
Clarity 27
Paradox: discipline and freedom 27
The pyramid of leadership learning 28
Differences and similarities in leadership 29
Leadership, leaders and teams 33
Impact of 'organization' on behaviour 34
The 'three-layer group' and its leader 35
People's expectations and desires 35

03 The role of a leader: Creating the ACE conditions for success 37

ACE as a leader's job description 38
ACE as an organizational and leadership effectiveness assessment and diagnostic tool 42

ACE as a leadership and organization effectiveness diagnostic tool 45
Organizational conditions: integrated leadership 48

04 Understanding leadership ability 53

Leadership and leader defined 53
Leadership and management 58
The leader and shared leadership 58
The relationship between leader and follower 59
The what of leadership: leadership knowledge and skills to perform functions 61
The leader's role in clarifying role relationships 67
Delegation of tasks 72
The how of leadership: leadership style and behaviour 76
Leader/follower relationships 87
Personal values and standards 88
Power, authority and leadership behaviour 92
Leadership thought: how people think and intellect aligned to level of work 95
Annex A: Leadership role profile 100

05 Communication – the lubricant of the leadership engine 106

Clarity and aligned communication channels 106
Formal and direct/conscious communication 107
Informal and direct/conscious communication 108
Formal and indirect/subconscious communication 109
Informal and indirect/subconscious communication 109
Communication in an organizational structure 110

06 Leading transformation and change 113

Roadmap to change 116
Emotional responses during change 122
The change paradox 125

PART TWO Developing the ACE Conditions for Success 127

SECTION ONE Developing Ability 127

07 Introduction to developing ability 129
Education and training 130
Experience 131
Exposure 131

08 Understanding people, behaviour and emotional intelligence 133
Basic psychology – the study of the mind and behaviour 134
What is personality? 140
Human nature: collaborate and compete 142
How the brain works 146
Human behaviour and emotional intelligence 153
The core identity 174
Perception 180
Emotional intelligence: the enabler of adaptable and appropriate leadership style 186

09 Interpersonal communication: the currency of leadership 200
Leader–team communication 201
The communication process 202
Building rapport 207
Listening 208
Questioning 211
Inferences 214
Style of communication and assertiveness 214
How to assert yourself 217
Non-verbal communication 218
Eye accessing cues 221
Assertive communication 223

10 Coaching 229
Introduction to coaching 230
The coach's position 233
Coach's toolkit 235
Path to mastery 236
Coaching conversation agenda 241

Developing behaviour   247
Changing attitudes   251
Building skill   253
Promotion and maintenance of the desire to learn   256
Confirmation that training has been assimilated   257
Question technique   258
Fault checking   259

11 Influence, persuasion and conflict resolution   260

Means of influence   260
Persuasion   262
Conflict   268
Conflict resolution   274

SECTION TWO Clarity and Engagement at Every Level   283

12 The leadership work of creating clarity and engagement: problems, decisions and plans   285

Problems to solve, decisions to make   285
A trio of recurring, cascading and iterating processes   289

13 People, personality and decision making   295

Cognition   296
Ways of thinking   297
Decision-making biases   298
Cognitive dissonance   298
Group dynamics   299
Understanding   300

14 Decision making: the appreciation   302

Introduction   302
The appreciation in detail   309
Task and time schematic plan   320
Appreciations at the strategic level   325
Contingency planning   335
Other problem-solving tools and techniques   336
The appreciation and personality types   337
Summary   338
Examples of appreciations   340
Annex A: Standard Operating Procedure (SOP) for meetings and minutes   363

Annex B: Appreciation template 366
Annex C: Project/task outline plan template 370
Annex D: Strategic plan and second-order task tracking document template 372

15 Planning and briefing 375

Planning 377
Detailed plan format 377
The briefing 379
Early warning 384
Communication: routine briefing and updates 384
Project management and routine leadership 385
Other common tools 385

16 Cascade of planning and briefing 387

Tasking procedure 387
Leadership structure 390
Extraction of relevant information 390
Communication in an organizational structure 392

17 The intelligence system to inform decision making 395

The intelligence cycle 396
Intelligence and planning 400

18 Directing, coordinating, controlling and evaluating progress 403

Directing 404
Coordinating 405
Control (and influence) 407
Evaluating progress 408

SECTION THREE Shaping the Environment 409

19 Introduction to shaping the environment 411

20 Teams and groups 412

Characteristics of groups and teams 412
Types of teams 416
Group dynamics 418

Stages of team development 422
Maintaining the team 431
Advice to leaders 432

21 The essential intangibles: morale, loyalty and trust 434

Morale 434
Loyalty 443
Trust 444

22 The role of organization and structure in leadership 447

Principles of organization 450

23 Organization ethos and culture: built to adapt and to last 466

Core identity 469
Business doctrine 472
Mythologies 476
Cultural norms 476
Envisioned future 477

24 Conclusion 479

Glosssary 481
Index 487

FOREWORD

There is a popular misconception, perpetuated by Hollywood, that armies are machines that are full of robots and that officers lead by simply ordering people to do things. As far as the British Army is concerned, nothing could be further from the truth in my experience. It is true that an officer has the legal authority to give orders to soldiers, and one might get away with doing that in barracks. But if that is an officer's approach to leadership, he will find that when his platoon is being shot at, he will not have the relationship of mutual trust and confidence that is necessary for both personal survival and military success on the battlefield. That relationship-building process is seldom a feature of movie blockbusters.

The British Army certainly has an emphasis on the creation of 'clarity' – what, why, how, who, when and where – the result of effective decision making, planning and briefing, and it tends to be very good at it. The Army also has a deep understanding of the value of the intangible aspects of leadership such as morale, loyalty, trust and confidence and how those things are built – it has learnt that the hard way over several centuries, and its understanding of those 'soft' areas is greater than in most businesses and public sector organizations that I have encountered.

So if I have dispelled the popular misconception that I opened with, or at least persuaded you to question it, then read on.

Elizabeth the Second by the Grace of God of the United Kingdom of Great Britain and Northern Ireland and Her other Realms and Territories Queen, Head of the Commonwealth, Defender of the Faith.

To Our Trusty and well-beloved Jeremy Ian Tozer Greeting!

We, reposing especial Trust and Confidence in your Loyalty, Courage, and good Conduct do by these Presents, Constitute and Appoint you to be an Officer in Our Land Forces from the Second day of September 1983. You are therefore carefully and diligently to discharge your Duty as such in the Rank of Second Lieutenant or in such other Rank as We may from time to time hereafter be pleased to promote or appoint you to, of which a notification will be made in the London Gazette, or in such other manner as may for the time being prescribed by Us in Council, and you are in such manner and on such occasions as may be prescribed by Us to exercise and well discipline in their duties such officers, men and women as may be placed under your orders from time to time and use your best endeavours to keep them in good order and discipline.

And We do hereby Command them to Obey you as their superior Officer, and you to observe and follow such Orders and Directions as from time to time you shall receive from Us, or any your superior Officer; according to the Rules and Discipline of War; in pursuance of the Trust hereby reposed in you.

This is the wording from my Commission, which I am still proud to have hanging on my wall more than 30 years after I was granted it. A Commission is the document signed by the Sovereign that gives you legal *authority* over soldiers and legal *responsibility* for their conduct. The Commission does not mention decision making or planning; it talks of trust, confidence, loyalty and duty.

While half of this book is given over to the essential 'hard stuff' of creating clarity – decision making, planning and organizing – half of it is given over to the 'soft stuff' (which is actually the hard stuff to do well) that enables you, the leader, to build the trust and confidence that your people need to have in you if you are to succeed. These are lessons I learnt well at Sandhurst, which are encapsulated in the Academy's motto: 'Serve to Lead'.

From the age of 8 I wanted to be a soldier, and I thought I would be a soldier for all my working life. After school and university, I swore my oath of allegiance, took the traditional Queen's Shilling (an Officer Cadet's day's pay, which back then was £8.35 if my memory is correct) and started my training at The Royal Military Academy Sandhurst, eager to join the ranks of those Gallant Gentlemen whom ES Turner had written about. It was hard, but provided you maintained your sense of humour it was quite enjoyable and it taught me more than I realized at the time; indeed it was probably another 15 years or more until I fully appreciated what I had gained.

I served for almost 10 years in The Intelligence Corps and The Duke of Edinburgh's Royal Regiment (Berkshire and Wiltshire). After the reunification of Germany in 1990, it was clear that the government was going to declare the world 'safe' and disband a large part of the Army and spend 'the peace dividend' on election inducements. I knew that it would be a far from stable world that emerged, and that an overstretched, under-equipped and under-supported Army would be committed to unforeseen emergencies (there had been around 70 unforeseen emergencies involving the deployment of British troops outside the NATO area since 1945), and frankly I thought that I had done my bit and that I would move on while I was still young enough to do something else!

After a year of looking for suitable employment in the UK, I decided to try somewhere else and ended up in Sydney where I spent the next 14 years. I started my business life working in the fast-moving consumer goods industry, where I was told that I would have far more freedom than I had had in the Army. They couldn't have been more wrong. I had more freedom as a young platoon commander patrolling the streets of Northern Ireland than I would have until I was the global chief executive of that business! I was very successful in my job, but after two months I was bored and I found little obvious and compelling meaning for me in the work that I was being asked to do (the company and the leaders that I met, never provided or created meaning, perhaps they had never thought about it, nor did they meet the expectations that they had set for me on recruitment about promotion and responsibility after 6 months of meeting objectives). Remember that a mind stretched by a new experience can never go back to its old dimensions and the Army had certainly stretched mine. It now needed more than that company could give me.

At this point I started thinking about leadership and why this company was so different to the Army, and about what had I learnt in the Army that would work (perhaps if done differently) and what was totally irrelevant. After all, they were both stuffed full of people who needed to know what they should be doing and be committed to achieving their tasks.

From there I fell into headhunting for a couple of years, and again found myself to be very good at building business and assessing 'character' – one of the things most soldiers do very well is to 'size people up'. You live and work in such close proximity to people, and depend upon them for your life, so you learn to do this unconsciously. While I was recruiting, leadership started to be a subject that corporations were talking about and I saw many 'consultants' – some of whom I considered to be charlatans, who had never led a horse to water let alone forged a group of people into a cohesive unit – make a lot of money from spouting nonsense. Rather than simply get angry, I decided to channel my energy into writing a book and starting a leadership consulting business. Between late 1995 and mid-1996 I wrote my first book which was published in 1997. I decided to write it because, according to my simple logic, author was short for authority on the subject so you couldn't be wrong, and it would help me clarify my thoughts and define the consulting offer. So I wrote the book, based entirely on my experience of what worked in the Army and what I thought would have worked in the consumer goods company that had employed me, and in the clients that I had recruited for. The idea behind that book was to filter out the totally inappropriate military ways, to adapt the remaining relevant military principles and practices and change the style or manner of their application, and to integrate some other good ideas that I had seen or read about since leaving the Army, and add some original thought. A substantial part of that book focused on the primary tools for creating 'clarity, alignment and engagement' with people: the iterating, recurring and cascading mission-focused and effects-based leadership tools of mission analysis, the appreciation (decision-making), planning and briefing. That book was quite successful, especially since I had not undertaken any leadership consulting work when I started to write it!

Since then I have been privileged to work extensively with companies such as Cisco Systems, Pfizer, Philips and ABN Amro across Asia, the United States, Australasia and Europe. It is to ABN Amro (or BZW as they were in Sydney when I first worked with them) and to Cisco Systems to whom I am most grateful, because given the scope and duration of the work that my colleagues and I undertook for them around the world, wittingly or unwittingly, they were the organizations in which I applied, adapted and proved most of what is written about in this book.

Fifteen years after the publication of my first book, I have managed to produce this sequel. It takes the core of the first book (now proved with some qualitatively and 'financially' impressive case studies and hopefully much better explained), and integrates it into what is a much bigger picture of leadership development, strategy development and execution, and organizational design and capability development (which are all inextricably linked). All of it is based on a combination of practical experience, deep reflection and research.

I have endeavoured to produce a book that may be used in two ways:

- as a total system for defining strategy and enabling its effective execution – based on the development of integrated leadership and organizational leadership capacity, and the design of structure, systems and processes that enable a leadership and performance culture.

- as a collection of discrete components that may be used independently of the others by individual leaders, each of which will add value in its own right, but which will add more value as other components are added to it and as more leaders use the same methods.

We are all, to some extent, creatures of habit and victims of our experience. Some of these ideas may feel quite alien to some readers, for others they will resonate instantaneously. If you are in the former camp, don't let this reaction close your mind to thinking about new ideas. They have all been proved to work consistently, and you should explore the reasons why they don't resonate with you. These ideas are also both scaleable and transferable – how they are introduced and with what common 'language' is what differs from organization to organization and that may be determined by making an appreciation of that problem (see Chapter 14).

A word on language. Part of the problem with leadership is that in most organizations a plethora of leadership terms are used, with as many different meanings as there are people using them. I use leadership terminology quite precisely in this book; a mission is not confused with an objective – they are different. To assist you, I have written a glossary of terminology. If you don't like the word I use, change it – but it facilitates clear communication in your enterprise if you are consistent with the terms that you do use.

In Part I of the book, the scene will be set with an examination of:

- the operating context and the capability requirement of effective organizations;
- core propositions about people and the nature of work;
- the ACE conditions for business success: Ability, Clarity and Environment;
- the role and responsibilities of a leader, and the nature of leadership;
- communication as the lubricant of the leadership engine; and
- the leadership of change.

The intent of Part I is, in very basic terms, to suggest what it is that leaders should actually be doing, and why and how they should be doing it.

Part II provides you with the necessary conceptual tools (in detail), the application of which will enable leaders to create the ACE conditions for success:

- to develop people's Ability, the realm of coaching and feedback and a means of creating emotional engagement.
- to create Clarity, the intellectual basis for decisions and plans and the alignment of activity, in a way that engages people.
- to shape the Environment, the foundation of both emotional engagement and material and structural support.

While it is always useful to have the precedent of experience to fall back on, there are circumstances when faced with the new or unexpected where experience cannot help you. Often, as a leader, you must rely on your knowledge and understanding of yourself, your team and their capabilities and limitations to ensure the success of your leadership.

To this end, I hope that this book will equip you to think and act for yourself more successfully. But besides all this, you must genuinely want to lead. If you have no desire or motivation to lead and to be responsible for the performance and conduct of others, it will be difficult for others to follow you – your lack of authenticity will show.

****

Early in the adventure of *Through the Looking Glass*, Alice meets the infamous Red Queen. Taking her by the hand, the two survey a chessboard stretching across the landscape and Alice muses on how nice it would be to play the part of a pawn (though she would like to be Queen best!).

The Red Queen obliges and sets off at a run towards the chessboard. 'Faster! Faster!' the Queen urges Alice, who follows her panting, with the wind whistling through her hair. Alice notices, however, that no matter how hard they run, nothing seems to change places. Eventually, breathless and giddy, they stop.

'Why I do believe we've been under this tree the whole time! Everything is just as it was!' Alice cries.

'Have a biscuit?' the Red Queen replies.

Like the world of the Red Queen, we live in a dynamic landscape. We may run, like Alice, but find the landscape is moving with us, and so end up on the same spot, despite all our exertions. Our landscape is dynamic, because people and our operating contexts are dynamic. For a leader, the last sentence should provoke excitement and a sense of challenge.

The Red Queen later explains that to get anywhere, you have to run 'twice as fast'.

By applying the leadership practices of effects-based leadership (EBL) – mission analysis and back briefing, deductive appreciations of problems, planning and briefing – with social process and emotional intelligence, you will develop the speed to overtake the moving landscape. It's less about effort, and more about wisdom.

ACKNOWLEDGEMENTS

This is the section of the book that I have struggled with most because of the possibility of causing offence through an unintended error or omission. I hope that I have got it right!

There are very many people I need to thank for their support, advice and assistance in writing this book, and/or for helping me to learn about leadership, people and organizations over the years.

In no particular order, may I thank the following:

- Clients past and present, who have provided the laboratory in which I have developed, refined and proved the concepts and ideas in this book.

- Rob Anderson (CEO Best Western Australia), Fru Hazlitt (MD ITV Commercial & Online), Lt Gen Andrew Graham, Janet Ramey, Mawgan Wilkins, Kirby Grattan and Brad Cook (Cisco), Mike Begg (HBOS Australia), and David Lawson (ABN Amro).

- My consulting colleagues at Tozer Consulting and especially Ann Rennie, Amanda Larcombe, Sergio Miller, Mark Oliver, Steve Balm, Amanda Murray, Annie Broadbent and Emma Brown.

- Dolores Knox at the Union Street Studio in Sydney for helping to turn my leadership ideas into meaningful graphics for over a decade.

- Matthew Smith, Sarah Cooke, Shereen Muhyeddeen and Ashley Simon at Kogan Page.

- The late Dr Elliott Jaques who was an early inspiration for me to think long and hard about leadership as an organizational capability and with whom I enjoyed discussion.

- Peter, my teenage son, who has just found his first weekend job and who is already experiencing and assessing the quality of leadership in a large retail chain and considering which examples he should follow, and what should be avoided at all costs!

- Charlotte for giving me the space and emotional support to write this book while also looking after baby Christopher and for all her other help and support.

- All the instructors at the Royal Military Academy Sandhurst, who left such an impression on me many years ago.

- My first Commanding Officer, Mike Constantine, for giving me such confidence when I arrived to join his battalion in Londonderry, fresh from Sandhurst.

My first platoon sergeant, Jim Duncan, whose professionalism eased my induction to operations in Londonderry and with whom I developed a superb working relationship which enabled us to read each other's minds when radio communications failed.

The Officers' Mess, 1st Battalion, The Duke of Edinburgh's Royal Regiment (Berkshire and Wiltshire) (1DERR) for producing lifelong friends.

The Warrant Officers' and Sergeants' Mess, 1DERR, for producing such a superb backbone for the battalion as well as numerous regrettable hangovers.

...And if you're reading this and you think that you should be on the list, then I apologize profusely for this discourteous and unintentional error and hope to correct it for the next edition – providing that you let me know!

ABOUT THE AUTHOR

Since 1995, Jeremy and his colleagues have provided leadership assessment and development, strategy and execution, and organizational change consulting services to clients in the private, public and third sectors across the UK and the EU, Asia, Australasia and the United States. He is an Executive Fellow at Henley Business School.

Jeremy has designed and led large-scale projects in the UK, the United States, Japan, Hong Kong, Singapore, Australia and Tanzania with clients such as Cisco Systems, MCI, Pfizer, Philips, ABN AMRO, Best Western, Capital Finance/HBOS, Rothschilds, The Tanzanian Civil Service, BZW, St George Bank, Roche, and Colgate Palmolive. He has provided leadership advice to the Royal Military Academy Sandhurst and to The Joint Services Command and Staff College.

Prior to 1995, Jeremy worked as an executive search consultant and as a sales executive with Procter & Gamble in the fast-moving consumer goods industry. His formative years were spent as an officer in the British Army. During his 10-year military career, Jeremy served in Northern Ireland, Hong Kong, Brunei, Berlin, Cyprus, Norway, Turkey, Denmark and Italy. His military career includes the leadership of 180 soldiers in an infantry company group of 1st Battalion The Duke of Edinburgh's Royal Regiment (Berkshire and Wiltshire) – now amalgamated into The Rifles – and the leadership of small teams of specialists in The Intelligence Corps. During his military career, Jeremy was responsible for briefing Cabinet Ministers and four-star officers.

Jeremy's best-selling book, *Leading Initiatives: Leadership, teamwork and the bottom line*, published in 1997 (and written in 1995/96) effectively launched his leadership consulting career. That blueprint has been honed and developed with 16 years' worth of practical application, research and reflection and became the foundation of an MSc in Leadership and Organization that Jeremy designed.

Jeremy was born in Devon, educated in the UK at Churston Grammar School, Welbeck College, The University of Warwick (BSc Hons in Engineering Electronics), The Royal Military Academy Sandhurst, and Junior Division, The Staff College. He is married with two sons and his personal interests include sailing (he completed the 1995, 1996 and 1998 Sydney-Hobart races), traditional English music and dance (he organizes festivals), playing melodeon (he has an English ceilidh band that you can book called Monty's Maggot!), shooting, his dogs, fencing, mountain walking, traditional cider, perry and real ale, sea shanties (he founded a group in Sydney that performed at several classic boat festivals while he was living there), and traditional New Orleans Jazz (he has produced one CD).

PART ONE
Understanding Leadership and Its Context

01
The operating context, strategy execution and capability requirement

The operating context

Uncertainty and complexity

Exponential rate of change

Employee engagement, mobility and cynicism

Friction

Strategy to reality: the execution gap

Future agenda: the capability requirement

Leading through leaders: effects-based leadership (EBL)

In this chapter we will set the scene for the book and briefly examine the context and conditions in which organizations function, because these conditions are forcing organizations to develop more effective approaches to leadership, strategy development and its effective execution – whether that strategy execution involves change and transformation, merger and acquisition, strategic partnerships or anything else.

The operating context

ICT, information and the compression of time and space

> *Leadership in the age of almost instantaneous messaging is more difficult than it was 30 or 100 years ago. Before mobile telephones, e-mail and high quality battlefield radio networks, military leaders were unable to interfere with junior leaders and had no alternative to delegation and trust. So more thought had to be given to providing clarity of strategic direction and intent.*

I wrote this over a decade ago, it is even more true today.

Information and communications technology (ICT), in some respects, is a double-edged sword. The positives are well known and well documented and it is not the intent of this book to explore them. On the downside it has led to a proliferation of data and information (some of dubious provenance) flowing beyond normal 'role' boundaries, blurring relationships and 'meaning' in the process. Some of this data is useful, but some (much?) of it is useless, serving only to cloud the real issues, adding to the 'fog of war', and some of it is simply untrue or inaccurate – creating 'information anarchy'. We are also witness to the increasing quantity combined with reduced substance and depth of meaning of information – 140 or less Twitter characters (which seems to be both a reflection of and inducer of shallow thinking).

The ability to gather and transmit data often raises expectations and demands for even more (creating unnecessary administrative bureaucracies), compounding the problem. Yet this volume of information rarely enhances understanding or improves decision making. A perceived need to integrate a multitude of sources each producing a large volume of data easily results in information overload and indecision – leadership paralysis. Meanwhile poorly led and badly organized organizations, especially those that are cavalier with their investors' cash (taxpayers' money in the public sector), create self-serving bureaucracies that compile and circulate reports that no one wants, needs or reads in order to justify their existence (this is all too frequently observed within the public sector).

The ease with which e-mails may be transmitted, combined with unclear role relationships typical of matrix structures (and other forms of organization), organizational politics, and poor 'e-mail discipline' (especially in understanding the difference between a 'To' (action) and 'cc' (for information) addressee) has helped to damage any form of 'integrated leadership' in many organizations. Too often executives and senior managers bypass subordinate leaders when requesting information (invariably this creates research work and conflicts with other priorities), delegating new tasks (that the intermediate leader is unaware of), and otherwise interfering with decision making and planning. This is often done with little regard for their subordinate leaders and their credibility that is being undermined and the confusion that they are adding. Additionally, this micromanagement adds to the complexity that executives face, slowing down decision cycles and timely action and further disengaging people.

- Google processes 1,000,000,000 searches per day as of 5 March 2011.
- There are 2 billion e-mail users worldwide, September 2011.
- Facebook is used by one in every 13 people on earth; over half its 500 million users log in daily and spend 700 billion minutes a month on the site.
- Over 294 billion e-mails are sent a day (2.8 million per second); it was 247 billion in 2009.
- 77 per cent of the world's population are mobile subscribers.
- Half a billion people accessed the mobile internet in 2009; this is expected to double in five years.
- The NYSE can process 10 billion shares per day.

It has also led to a dependency on technology for information and reduced the time senior executives spend on the front line, learning what real conditions are like and comparing what is strategically desirable with that which is tactically possible. Techno-centric decision making is being applied to complex problems where a grasp of the 'unmeasurable human factors' is required – many an acquisition or merger has failed to deliver the expected return for 'people and culture reasons'.

Data proliferation, and the ease with which data now flows and people communicate (not always clearly, concisely and accurately!) has meant that work in all spheres of activity has become increasingly complex and increasingly fast. As a result operating contexts become ever more dynamic and the working world ever smaller. All of this may be summed up in the phrase: 'confusion amid the compression of time and space'.

Yet with this globalization, there is the paradox of increasing fragmentation. This is due in part at the macro-level to the growing streak of (national) individuality in the face of relentless homogeneity, combined with disparities and imbalances, such as the rich–poor divide both within and between countries. At the organizational level, this fragmentation is exacerbated by the increasing divide between executives, their global strategies (and very probably their remuneration packages) and the work that is actually done at the tactical level.

Uncertainty and complexity

At the global level, the recent financial crisis (with its roots in 'corrupt' and/or ineffective leadership, ineffective governance and regulation, and cavalier and greedy decision making) and the problems of the Eurozone (with its roots in the lack of a single, democratically elected and binding authority) has decreased the resilience of economies, countries and organizations. Meanwhile the risk consequences of globalization – economic disparity and governance failures – and geopolitical and

Understanding Leadership

societal tensions highlight the inability of many leaders and their organizations to cope with these challenges. This is being compounded with global risks:[1]

- Economic risks – global imbalances and currency volatility, fiscal crises and asset price collapse within and between countries.
- Illegal economy risks – illicit trade, organized crime and corruption.
- Water-food-energy security risks.
- Climate change risks.
- Demographic change risks.

Customer and financial pressures, and the sheer span of activity in some major conglomerates are forcing competitors (complex organizations in their own right) to work together in complex partnerships. For example, Samsung is both competing with Apple (and pursuing legal action) and supplying components to the latter, and pharmaceutical companies are moving from the era of 'block buster' drug manufacturer and marketer, to Pharma 3.0[2] information aggregator/miner and key partner in an infinitely more complex 'health outcomes ecosystem'. Global companies, political parties, the civil service and armies all operate in ambiguous and complex circumstances and in the spotlight of the world's ever watchful and ever critical media waiting to spot that bad decision. At the tactical level, work is made more complex by the need to leverage expertise across diverse teams, groups and locations in order to seize opportunities, maximize productivity and add greater value to the product or service offered.

- In 10 years, China will be the largest English-speaking nation.
- Chinese skilled labour is 40 per cent of the OECD total.
- By 2050 the four BRIC economies with 25 per cent of the globe's land area could eclipse the G6 combined economies (G7 less Canada).

Organizations themselves are more complex than ever, spanning cultures, continents and an array of internal functions and business units spinning around and along their direction of travel. (However, many organizations are unnecessarily complex and difficult to work in because they have not been carefully designed according to scalable principles in the first place – this is the subject of a later chapter.) This picture is best described by the currently fashionable acronym 'VUCA':

- *Volatility.* The nature, speed and dynamics of change and its drivers.
- *Uncertainty.* The lack of predictability, and the need to be ready for the unexpected.
- *Complexity.* The multiplicity of factors and their impact on work and achieving objectives, and the chaos and confusion that surround an organization drowning in data.

- *Ambiguity.* The lack of clarity in the meaning that may be attributed to information, and cause-and-effect confusion.

Exponential rate of change

The only living thing that survives, is that which adapts to change.
(Field Marshal Viscount Slim)

Any observer of life in the last two decades will probably agree with the statement that the rate of change is increasing. And it is not just the rate of change that is speeding up: its scope and impact is increasing with it, challenging some fundamental norms and expectations.

Evidence may be seen in e-mail and mobile phone activity, transistor speeds (which enable so many 'machines'), miniaturization, patents filed, product lifecycles, company mergers, acquisitions and failures, population growth and demographic changes. Indeed it has been estimated that progress in the whole of the 20th century is equivalent to 20 years of progress at today's rate, and that the world will make another 20 years of progress at today's rate in the next 14 years, and the same again seven years after that.[3] In other words, change is not increasing in a linear fashion, but exponentially. And it is not going to ease up.

Human unpredictability, stress and emotion

People are now working longer and harder (intellectually, if not physically) than ever before. However, what remains the same is that one of the few predictable things about people is that they are unpredictable in their behaviour. People have their own motivation and needs, beliefs and values and so on, all of which influence how they perceive information and problems. People also suffer from stress, which gives rise to emotions and emotions need to be expressed. Part of that expression is the influence of emotion and perception on decision making.

The psychology of behaviour and decision making is explored in Chapters 8 and 13, but suffice it to say here that despite our best efforts to remain objective in decision making, our emotions often conflict with logic, resulting in flawed decisions and the inevitable consequences.

Employee engagement, mobility and cynicism

Over recent years, many employees have learnt, as a result of their own experience or that of their peers, that the loyalty typically given to employer organizations in the past is unlikely to be matched when economic times are tough or mergers and acquisitions loom. Also, the only person really concerned with their own interests, aspirations, development needs (personal, professional and career) and desire to use their capability to the full is the individual him or herself.

Recently commentators have noted the increasing gap in remuneration between board room and front-line staff (as a multiple of the lowest paid employee), and the clear discrepancy in some organizations between 'executive impact' and remuneration. It is therefore not surprising that loyalty and attachment to the employer organization, which is represented in the form of disconnected executive leaders, is much reduced. Indeed in organizations subject to repeated restructures, such as public sector entities which are political footballs, cynicism abounds – 'Sit out this change and do nothing, another will come along in a year and we will be back to last year's operating model.'

Clearly engaging staff to harness their discretionary effort is much harder than in the past. Yet in this dynamic, complex environment that we all occupy it is even more necessary to do it if organizational agility and effectiveness are to be developed. This employee cynicism is matched by public unease with 'big business', 'public services' and 'politics':

- 'corporate excess' (in the UK, bankers are taking the brunt of public anger);
- unethical and unsustainable business practices;
- greedy, self-centred, seemingly 'untouchable' and 'unaccountable' incompetent and/or dishonest senior executives (in both the corporate and public sectors) and politicians.

Friction

Everyone has experience of 'wading through treacle' to get anything done in their organization. It is often more difficult to move things internally than externally – the friction that inhibits forward progress can be quite incredible, especially in public sector organizations. Clausewitz[4] was probably the first person to provide an analysis of the sources of friction and its unpredictable effects. Although he was writing about war at the start of the 19th century, he might just as well have been writing about business or war today. Clausewitz[5] cited:

- insufficient knowledge of the enemy (or business competitors and the market);
- rumour and exaggeration in communication;
- uncertainty or over-estimation of one's own real capability and disposition;
- the difference between expected actions and outcomes, and reality;
- the tendency to change plans when confronted with vivid battlefield images and the perceptions that they create;
- the need to change plans in response to enemy reactions (or in business terms, competitor actions and reactions, and market dynamics), and actual progress, complexity and chance.

In considering these sources of friction, much of it may be reduced to decisions resulting from imperfect information (situations are dynamic), or actions or decisions resulting from the imperfect transmission and imperfect interpretation of information (each human is unique).[6]

In essence friction stems from the effects of time, space, people and human nature – it is the force that makes the reality of war (or business) and the leadership of large organizations different from the conceptual and abstract models used in its study. Every individual person is a friction-producing part in the machine of business, producing a delicate system of endless complexity and unreliability in which the simplest things become difficult to do.

Strategy to reality: the execution gap

Most organizations have strategies ('most' because we have encountered some without). These might exploit new technologies, leverage the brand, focus on the customer or on business partnerships that reach the end-user, and/or include a series of internal people, culture and organization development programmes to increase the pace of activity and productivity and so on. In some companies, these are simple and clear and may be recited by the most junior of employees who have read the wall poster or coffee mugs that are issued to go with the new strategy. In some organizations they are far from simple or clear; and some are not much more than statements of hope and aspiration.

In many organizations that we have encountered, there is a gap between the desired goals as articulated in the strategy, and the actual results that execution delivers, as shown in Figure 1.1. I have seen this in younger more decentralized but still large internetworking, mobile telecommunications, and IT companies and in 'older',

FIGURE 1.1 The strategy to reality performance gap

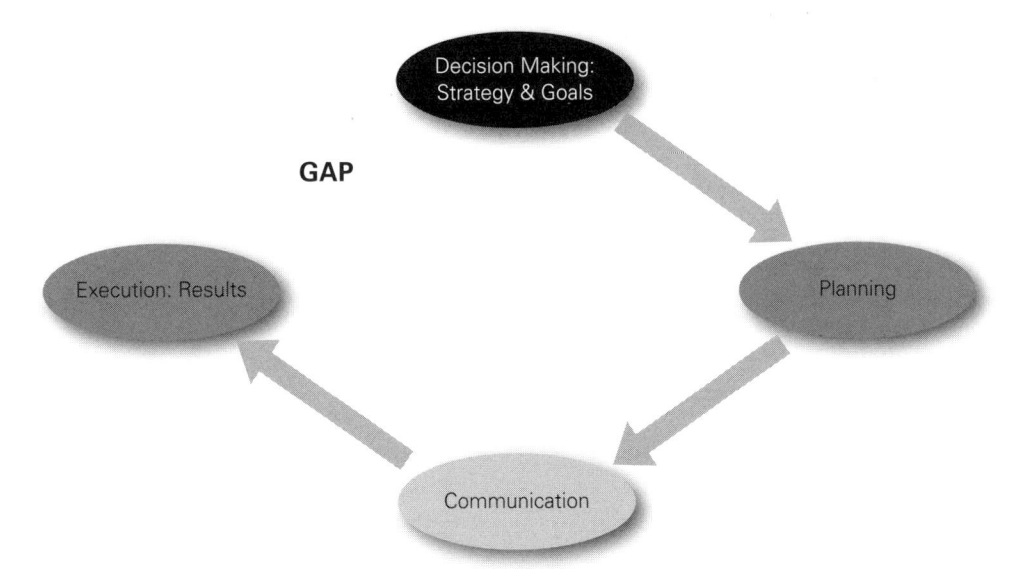

© Jeremy Tozer, 1997–2006

more 'mature' organizations such as pharmaceutical and consumer goods companies, and in public sector health and higher education organizations.

Before we look at the reasons for this gap in more detail, let us be clear on what a strategy is. Strategy articulates a decision to pursue a course of action, to do 'work' (to complete an organizational-level task, or achieve a defined end-state and objectives), together with the reason for doing that (purpose, which gives meaning to the work). It provides coherence between actual capability and the objectives that have been defined, and addresses in outline how the strategic objectives will be achieved, which includes exploiting your centre of gravity.[7] It provides a rationale and framework for operational and tactical actions.

In this respect, strategy is a statement of 'higher intent' but is not a detailed plan in itself. A strategic plan may outline the preferred course of action at the outset of implementing the strategy – provide direction – but this will inevitably evolve. If planned in detail as far ahead as 'the end state', an awful lot of planning time and effort will be wasted, for reasons explained below.

Figure 1.2 shows the four gaps caused by internal friction which leads to the performance gap:

1 There is a gap that results from using imperfect information and/or an imperfect decision-making process.[8] Information may be imperfect because situations are dynamic and VUCA: there is an excess of information quantity and a lack of information quality. This imperfect information may then be used in an imperfect and/or irrational decision-making process in 'undisciplined' organizations which fails to ask the right questions and

FIGURE 1.2   The strategy to reality gaps

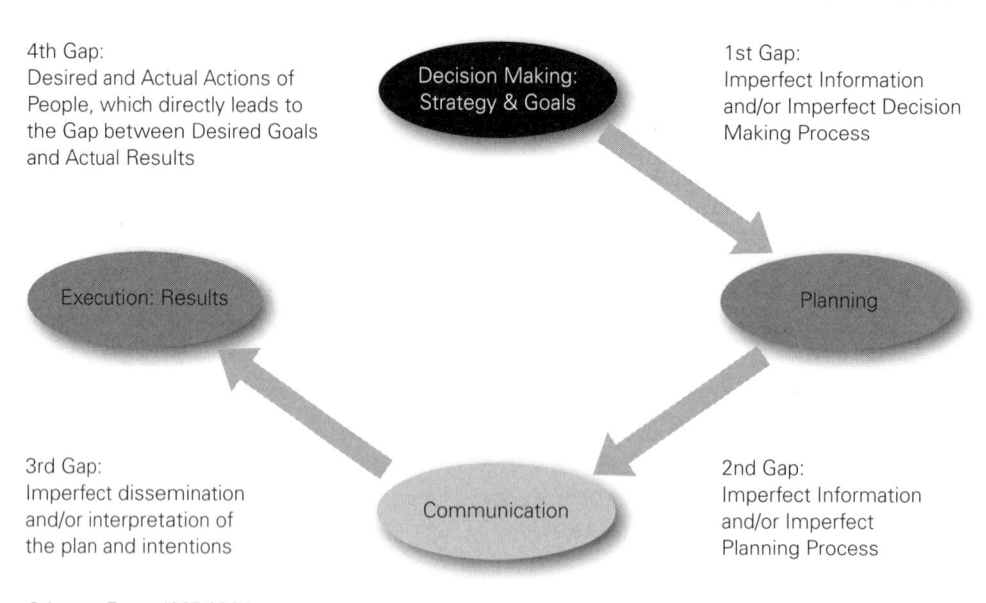

4th Gap:
Desired and Actual Actions of People, which directly leads to the Gap between Desired Goals and Actual Results

Decision Making: Strategy & Goals

1st Gap:
Imperfect Information and/or Imperfect Decision Making Process

Execution: Results

Planning

3rd Gap:
Imperfect dissemination and/or interpretation of the plan and intentions

Communication

2nd Gap:
Imperfect Information and/or Imperfect Planning Process

© Jeremy Tozer, 1997–2006

correctly interpret the information – a process that may also be distorted by strength of executive personality (in governments, there is the additional distortion of political dogma).

2 Similar to the above, imperfect information and/or an imperfect detailed (action) planning process – in some organizations, decision making is thought of as planning with no distinction between what happens in the decision-making process (eg the clarification of aim, objectives, purpose, outline plan options and the selection of one option), and in detailed planning (the conversion of the selected option into a workable plan).

3 There is a gap that results from the imperfect communication and/or the imperfect interpretation of the plan as communicated.[9]

4 There is the gap between desired actions and the actual actions of people at the front line. Since the actual actions of people are what lead to organizational outcomes and results, if there is a difference between actual and desired actions (especially in a dynamic environment), it is not surprising that there will be a gap between actual and desired results.

People may 'know' the information given in the strategy, but what they lack is the effective understanding of that information to the point that they may articulate clear priorities and desired effects for their work and that of their teams, and particularly a way of making sense of the strategy in a dynamic environment. The business unit leader can recite the strategy, but still asks the question, 'What do you really want me to do?'[10] We have witnessed frustrated organizational leaders from the business CEO to the Vice Chancellor – reply to similar questions with words to the effect that, 'The strategy provides sufficient direction, you are all competent senior people, you don't want or need me to tell you exactly what I want you to do.'

The key point is that too many strategies do not actually provide clear direction, nor do leaders (at any level) have at their disposal a mechanism for translating 'higher intent' into genuine understanding – meaningful effects, objectives and priorities for their work. The result is that new initiatives and new work streams are piled on top of pre-existing workloads with no sense of priority, precious time is wasted in an endless stream of meetings that attempt to solve both new and pre-existing problems related to this combined activity. These meetings, in turn, create even more work for people. This is compounded with the fact that when priorities are unclear for people, they default to work defined by past habit, personal interest, personal gain and/or personal preference. The net result is the sense of 'wading through treacle':

- an inability to build momentum and increase the tempo of operations;
- a waste of time, emotional energy and other resources invested in work which, while it may be well executed in itself, is unaligned to the bigger organizational picture;
- the burnout of people;
- a sluggish and cumbersome organization that is not sufficiently agile to thrive and survive in the modern world.

A common reaction to this separation between desired and actual actions – of change not going according to plan – is to increase and centralize management controls and the measurement of progress and results, and to interfere with lower level planning and delegation, or to lead by micromanagement. This puts additional stresses on leaders, disempowers junior leaders and staff, and builds a dependency culture in which people are unwilling to use their initiative and do anything unless explicitly told to do so by a senior person.

Future agenda: the capability requirement

A new approach to leadership is required to succeed in a world in which:

- exponential change makes life more difficult for organizations that are generally not very adept at changing anyway;
- data proliferation, the compression of time and space and VUCA abound;
- expertise needs to be leveraged across complex organizations;
- more people are more cynical about their employers and their intentions and more concerned with taking charge of their own destiny;
- information used in decision making will be imperfect;
- 'the public' are increasingly concerned about 'corporate excess' and 'ethical business';
- the impact of individual personality on thinking, interpretation, decision making and communication clearly presents challenges (risk?) to organizations.

Such an approach must satisfactorily answer 'the big questions'. How should we most effectively:

- Anticipate or predict the future and identify 'the big issues' on the horizon?
  - Identify what we don't know but should know?
  - Identify vulnerability to externally driven change in our markets and adjacent sectors?
- Develop and maintain sources of competitive advantage?
  - Exploit existing capabilities and new technology to create new sources of value?
- Cope with unexpected situations, new realities and new opportunities?
- Develop organizational agility?
  - Process available information and extract meaning in a timely manner?
  - Make quick and effective decisions when plans clearly need to be changed?
  - Ensure clarity and accuracy in communication (during transmission and in interpretation on reception)?
  - Ensure that activity is aligned in dynamic environments, which by its complexity requires integrated leadership from more leaders in more places?

FIGURE 1.3 Aligning complex organizational activity to a clear aim and purpose

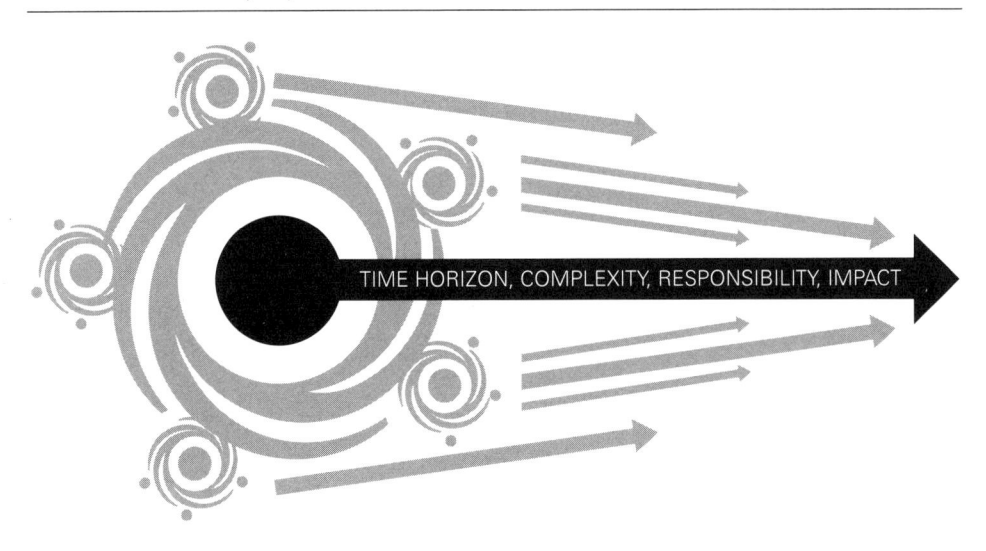

TIME HORIZON, COMPLEXITY, RESPONSIBILITY, IMPACT

© Jeremy Tozer, 2010

- Ensure scalability so that the approach works as organizations change size and shape?
- Enable the approach to work across borders, boundaries and cultures?
- Engage and gain the support of stakeholders in our future?
    - Maintain and build our reputation and brand?
    - Harness employees' energy, discretionary effort, talents and loyalty?
    - Influence new international standards?
    - Influence regulatory change?
    - Match global and local operations to changing legal frameworks?

This context requires organizations and the teams and groups that comprise them to be perpetually change-ready and agile. And this context requires leaders at all levels to align activity in dynamic circumstances and secure the engagement of people in order to harness their initiative, commitment and innovation and deliver optimal results.

These leaders, of divisions, business units and teams that make up the organization are primarily differentiated by the time horizon and complexity of their work, their responsibility and the scope of their impact over time (and by the size of remuneration packages!). Yet they all must solve problems, make decisions, produce plans – create clarity – and take people with them while that clarity is created. So the essence of what follows is as applicable to the junior team leader as it is to the CEO. Indeed if clarity is not created at the top, then it will only get foggier as it trickles down; but this does not mean the CEO doing the work of leaders at tactical levels to create that clarity.

Leaders must learn to cope with problems and situations that are less structured, less bounded and less predictable than previously existed: 'wicked problems'.[11,12] Indeed in the past, what has passed for problem solving in some areas has actually been a consistent approach based on precedent or rote process. Change, if it has succeeded (75 per cent of change fails in its own terms),[13] has often been planned to take organizations from one static and predictable state to another.

This context requires a new mindset for all organizations. Dynamic situations in which a myriad of factors and participants interplay require leaders at all levels to ask the right questions and facilitate time-effective incisive discussion on the answers to those questions, rather than simply 'telling people the answer to past problems'. Dynamic situations require organizations to have a dynamic approach to creating clarity.

Traditionally, large organizations have kept information and control of people centralized, and only required people to do what they were told to do. This command and control system seemed to work in the slower, steadier world of yesteryear. Other fads and panaceas have been tried since then, such as self-directed work teams, quality circles, overlaying matrix structures with a plethora of dotted lines and ill-defined role relationships, finding talent and paying them obscene amounts of money and hoping that would do the trick (the Enron approach), and so on.

How have these fads and ideas assisted the optimal execution of strategy? If the phrases 'unclear delegation, lack of delegation, lack of authority, poor decisions, indecision, inertia, duplication, lack of trust, rigid silos, inertia, poor communication, unclear responsibilities, excessive meetings, excessive control, lack of freedom, pointless meetings, lack of alignment, lack of engagement, lack of ownership and accountability' are mentioned, too many people (if they are honest) would recognize them as present in their organization. Given these 'execution inertia symptoms' that so many organizations have (how many strategies have you seen presented which remain little more than unused documents a year or so later when they are superseded with the next grand 'strategy' or big idea?), these fads clearly all fail in today's faster, more uncertain, more complex, more ambiguous, more dynamic digital information era.

Imagine working in an organization in which your boss routinely gave you:

- clear direction about the higher level aim and purpose, desired end-state and strategic objectives;
- defined objectives for you (and your team) to achieve and their place in the higher level plan;
- a clear definition of your framework for work such as your operating context, boundaries to the discretion you may exercise, your freedom of action and constraints and limitations (the minimum needed consistent with cooperation and collaboration with other groups);
- the resources and authority necessary to achieve your objectives.

And before you initiated activity, you confirmed your understanding of direction by 'back briefing' to your boss, your intentions, tasks, priority of work, desired effects and outcomes (and in the process your boss learnt more about the implications of his or her direction, and you ensured lateral and vertical alignment).

Imagine you and your boss being well-trained in your respective leadership roles and especially in the thought and social processes of decision making, planning and briefing. Imagine then being trusted to get on with it – to confirm understanding of 'higher intent', to work out, with your team members, how to achieve that which needs to be achieved for the organization of which you are part, to produce a plan, brief those involved in the execution, and then execute the plan (and change the plan as the situation dictates but always with the higher intent and alignment in mind) – all this within a cycle of dynamic review and feedback up and down the organization. Clear direction together with the freedom and trust to get on with the job. Can such a systemic approach to distributed leadership exist? More to the point, can it actually work?

Well it does exist in places and it works extremely well. This is the British military doctrine of Mission Command. In the business world this might be better described as the philosophy of effects-based leadership (EBL), given the connotation usually given to the word 'command'[14] and the lack of understanding of its military definition and the 'stakeholder engagement and commitment' that the Army develops. The army has been 'leading' and 'organizing' within the compression of time and space and amongst uncertainty for a lot longer than any other sphere of endeavour. This is primarily because the nature of war compresses time and inures leaders to living with uncertainty and the consequences of decisions (or indecision). These consequences are rapidly evident and potentially devastating. While imitating an army in its entirety is probably not the best way ahead for most other organizations, some of the principles and processes it employs hold good – albeit processes and principles employed in a different style or manner.

EBL provides a very effective answer to the four 'strategy to reality execution gap' problems of imperfect decision making, imperfect planning, imperfect transmission and interpretation of information, and desired and actual activity and outcomes. It addresses the alignment and agility challenges that organizations have in the execution of strategy, and a large part of the 'engagement and commitment' challenge (day-to-day commitment to and accountability for the task at hand). It focuses on the 'effects' that leaders wish to have at every level – on 'task', 'the context' and people. It incorporates 'higher intent' and 'changes to the situation', and results in dynamic alignment and prioritization of delegated activity with a unified, committed team (rather than simply piling new work on top of current work).

However, the philosophy of EBL does not directly address the structural framework within which people work, and which can facilitate easy working relationships or be the cause of excessive and unnecessary stress, confusion and waste. Nor does EBL directly incorporate some of the essential aspects of leadership and organizational capability such as emotional intelligence, coaching ability, ability to define role relationships and so on. A substantial portion of this book is devoted to the leadership processes of effects-based decision making, planning and briefing – which are the core leadership practices of EBL, and which, as leadership tools, are still extremely effective even when EBL or effects-based leadership is not adopted as an organizational philosophy. However, this book is not devoted exclusively to EBL, but also incorporates those other aspects of leadership and organization design that enable leaders to drive business success, and build sustainable organizations.

Mission command or EBL is not new. Its roots are to be found in the Prussian Army and its analysis of its woeful performance in fighting the French in the early

19th century, and it has had considerable evolution in the counter-insurgency warfare of more recent times. Dynamic operating contexts in which quick and effective local decisions grounded in an understanding of the higher intent are essential if one is to be successful in killing or capturing the terrorist, preventing (or minimizing) your own casualties, while also winning local hearts and minds – decisions made under conditions of extreme physical and mental stress, in the glare of the media, and with truly awful and immediate consequences when the decision is wrong.

> *The concept of Auftragstaktik or 'mission tactics'... made it the responsibility of each German officer and NCO... to do without question or doubt whatever the situation required, as he personally saw it. Omission and inactivity were considered worse than a wrong choice of expedient. Even disobedience of orders was not inconsistent with this philosophy.*
>
> (Lt Col John English, 1981, *A Perspective on Infantry*, Praeger)

My formative years in the British Army and consulting experience and research of the last 15 years can provide some useful insights into building leadership capability and organizational agility. The primary requirement is to embrace the paradox of discipline and freedom. The discipline of intelligently applying effective principles and processes as a matter of routine, such as a problem-solving process that exploits the collective experience, creativity and energy of the team, will create freedom of choice (more options will be identified, for example) and freedom of action within defined boundaries. This is the autonomy that so many people crave.

This is acknowledged in many professions – the discipline of science, R&D, accountancy, orchestral music, high performing sports teams and so on – but rarely in the constructs used by organizations in their approach to leadership, management, organization design and the development of those elements. The relationship between this paradox and creating clarity is explored in the next chapter.

Leading through leaders: effects-based leadership (EBL)

Effective execution of plans requires two elements at the start: more robust and rigorous development of plans that are inherently adaptable in the first place, and faster decisions and more agile organizations to cope with the fact that 'no plan survives contact with the enemy'[15] and the chaos faced on a daily basis – decentralized decision making, with authority given to the lowest level at which capability exists is of paramount importance.

The philosophy of EBL is an approach to operating in fast-moving, complex, uncertain and changing environments which demand high-quality decisions quickly, and responsive organizations able to act in concert and at speed with full commitment and ownership if they are to be successful. Academics sometimes refer to this as 'systemic distributed leadership'. The effect of EBL is to overcome inertia, and make or do more and better from less more effectively. EBL produces a flexible, agile and aligned organization able to rapidly refocus, realign and reorganize as and when needed, which works at a higher tempo, and which has greater propensity to take

FIGURE 1.4 The cycle of effects-based leadership processes

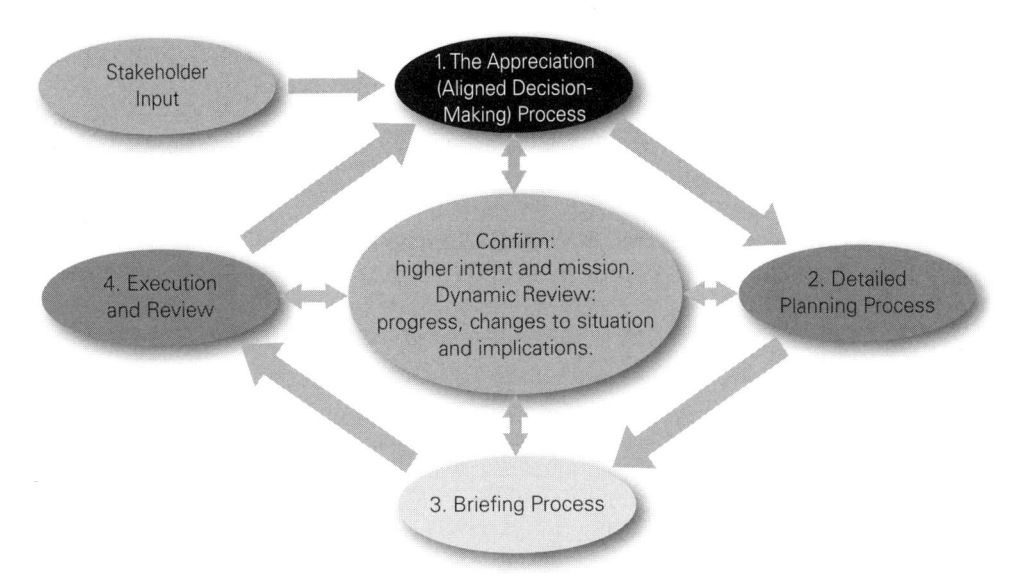

[Diagram: Stakeholder Input → 1. The Appreciation (Aligned Decision-Making) Process; central node "Confirm: higher intent and mission. Dynamic Review: progress, changes to situation and implications." connected to 1, 2. Detailed Planning Process, 3. Briefing Process, and 4. Execution and Review, arranged in a cycle 1→2→3→4→1]

© Jeremy Tozer, 1997–2007

calculated risks (Who Dares Wins). Mission command is a force multiplier on the battlefield. EBL is a source of competitive advantage in business.

The dynamic EBL processes, shown in Figure 1.4, consist of mission analysis and the appreciation (or aligned decision making), detailed planning and briefing (these are examined in detail in Chapters 15 and 16). In reality, these processes actually have two parallel processes running within each of them: 1) the thought process or steps to follow, which are a handrail to guide the sequence of thought, not a rote process to be the slave of, and 2) the social process with which the thought process is applied to secure engagement and ownership – the use of the leader's emotional intelligence.

This approach is not an academic theory but a set of intellectually rigorous, dynamic, iterative, intelligently applied leadership processes which by their nature self-check and self-adjust. Leaders at all levels regularly brief their 'subordinate' leaders to keep them 'in context': to ensure awareness of the current situation, provide direction, delegate objectives and tasks and define the purpose of these, define constraints and limitations on action, and allocate resources (briefing 'the what') – to ensure people understand their part in higher level plans. Subordinate leaders then develop their understanding of this through a process of mission analysis: the consideration of higher intent, the effects that they should achieve, their specified and implied tasks and priority of work, which is confirmed through a back brief to their immediate leader, providing circumstances allow this. This back briefing provides an opportunity for dialogue to confirm your intentions, tasks, effects, priorities and outcomes; and in the process your leader may learn more about the implications of the direction given, and you will also ensure lateral and vertical alignment. Should circumstances prevent the opportunity for a back briefing, subordinate leaders will still be trusted to get on with meaningful work because their boss will know that they have gone through the thought process of mission analysis.

Once the mission analysis is complete, the leader will then determine the best plan to achieve those objectives (the how). The mission analysis and subsequent stages of planning may each be conducted by the leader alone, facilitated as a focused and collective discussion with key individuals and/or the team, and completed in one or several meetings with the output briefed to those involved or affected – an iterative, non-linear process. This is a choice for the intelligent leader to make and some guidance is provided in later chapters. The result is a robust plan, owned by all, the final draft of which is briefed to the team prior to the start of execution.

The time spent in the decision-making process will reflect the urgency of the situation and the complexity of the decision being made. If the problem being analysed is relatively simple, or the situation is urgent, then the thought process of mission analysis and the appreciation may be very quickly conducted on the spot in one's mind – 'the combat appreciation'. If one is defining the organizational strategy, then it will take considerably longer and involve a number of people.

It is the social process (emotional intelligence) with which the conceptual process steps are applied that makes this military concept both practical and effective in non-military organizations. This has been proved in sectors such as technology and IT, leisure, consumer goods, pharmaceuticals, banking and finance, higher education and local government.

EBL, illustrated in Figure 1.4, requires timely and effective decision making by junior leaders who apply 'mission analysis' to understand the context, the 'higher intent', the objectives, effects and specified and implied tasks that they should achieve, the purpose of these objectives, tasks and effects, and the constraints and limitation on their freedom of action. This ends with junior leaders defining their mission (overall aim and its purpose) and back briefing their mission analysis to their boss to check clarity. EBL also requires junior leaders to have a clear responsibility and desire to fulfil that intent and not 'delegate the job back up the chain' (this has implications for structural clarity and the selection and training of leaders); equally it requires senior leaders to be clear in their intent and not interfere with junior leaders' work. There is a built-in failsafe that enables junior leaders to help senior leaders be clearer in their own minds – the back brief already mentioned.

The thought process used reduces complexity to simplicity, for without simplicity there is no clarity, and without clarity there is little or no progress or action on the ground and momentum is lost. The thought process makes 'higher intent' meaningful and enables people to maintain alignment; people therefore know that they are making an important contribution, which is motivating in itself.

These practices iterate (hence they self-monitor and self-adjust as progress is assessed and situations change), they recur, and they cascade through the organization, as shown in Figure 1.5. This connects the CEO with the front-line operator and provides line of sight from corporate strategic objectives to the actions of the most junior individuals. It breaks strategy into smaller more manageable parts, and through back briefing and reviews it reintegrates these small chunks into the whole. The philosophy balances control and alignment with freedom and autonomy, and this common operating platform builds mutual trust and confidence.

FIGURE 1.5   The cascade of effects-based leadership processes

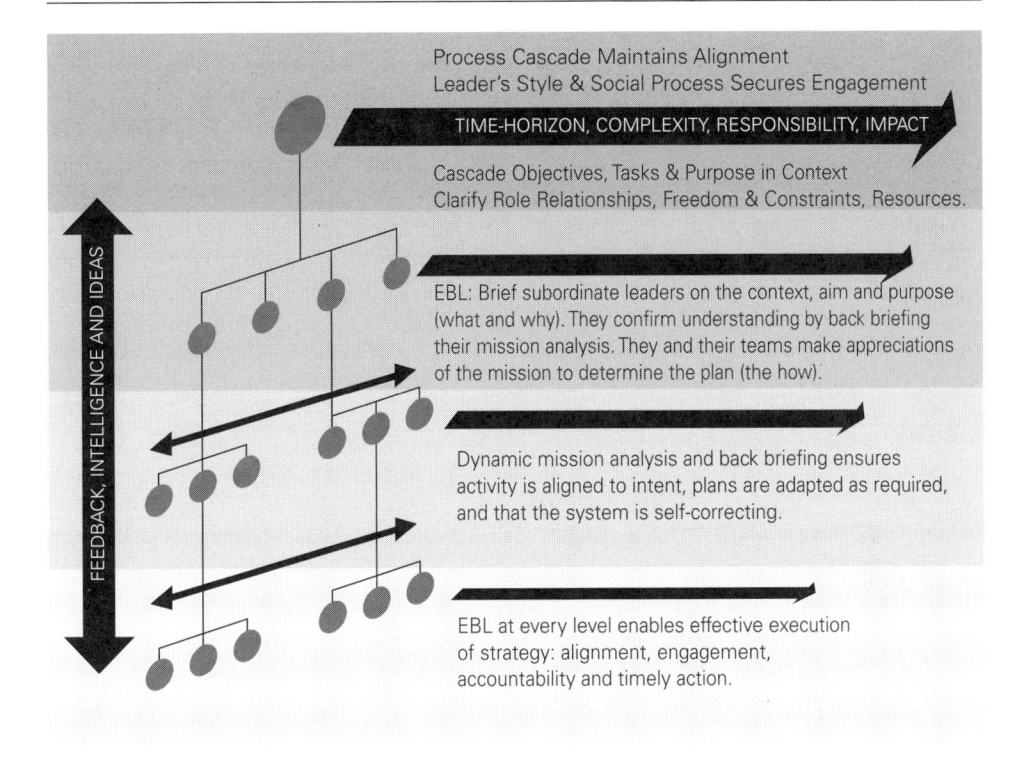

Process Cascade Maintains Alignment
Leader's Style & Social Process Secures Engagement

TIME-HORIZON, COMPLEXITY, RESPONSIBILITY, IMPACT

Cascade Objectives, Tasks & Purpose in Context
Clarify Role Relationships, Freedom & Constraints, Resources.

EBL: Brief subordinate leaders on the context, aim and purpose (what and why). They confirm understanding by back briefing their mission analysis. They and their teams make appreciations of the mission to determine the plan (the how).

Dynamic mission analysis and back briefing ensures activity is aligned to intent, plans are adapted as required, and that the system is self-correcting.

EBL at every level enables effective execution of strategy: alignment, engagement, accountability and timely action.

FEEDBACK, INTELLIGENCE AND IDEAS

© Jeremy Tozer, 1997–2007

Because the emphasis of this approach is on 'initiative' – timely action and alignment of activity in context – it is tempting to think that EBL does not focus on engaging people in the process. The 'social process' – the facilitated application of the thought process for problem solving, decision making and planning – rather than the leader telling, is what secures ownership, commitment and engagement. Naturally, on the battlefield there is no time for facilitated discussion so under fire the military leader is required to be more directive, but the same conceptual tool *applied in a facilitated manner* succeeds and can endure in business, as has been proved (since I first wrote about this in 1997) with clients in companies such as Cisco Systems, Pfizer, Philips, and in the public sector (civil service, local government, National Health Service and higher education) and the voluntary sector. A facilitated approach also enables the soldier to work with the civilian agencies that are frequent business partners in operations other than war.

The discipline of using EBL processes, as with any new tool, may feel cumbersome at first. But very quickly you will find that your confidence builds as its benefits are seen (and they are seen very quickly) and as your confidence builds, so does your flexibility and dexterity in the use of these tools. The clarity that is created, combined with the social process that is used, builds trust. Trust is also built throughout the organization because leaders at all levels know that other leaders will all apply the same methodology and therefore that decisions will be made, plans will be created and all of it communicated more 'holistically', clearly and effectively. The discipline of EBL is liberating – it creates freedom of thought and action for people, tempered only by the minimum constraints needed for coordinated activity between groups.

It is not essential that an entire organization embraces the concept of EBL simultaneously. Individual work teams or distinct business units might adopt such an approach which may then be expanded across an organization when its benefits are seen.

This book explores not only the core leadership processes associated with EBL, but also the social process and human side of leadership (equally important in taking people with you on the journey), and the design of the framework in which people operate together – organization structure.

Notes

1. *Global Risks 2011*, 6th edn, World Economic Forum.
2. Ernst & Young Global Pharmaceutical Industry Report, 2011, *Progressions: Building Pharma 3.0*.
3. Ray Kurzweil, 2003, *Perspectives on Business Innovation*.
4. Carl von Clausewitz, Prussian officer and German military theorist who stressed the moral and political aspects of war, author of Vom Kriege (*On War*).
5. Barry D Watts, 2000, *Clausewitzian Friction and Future War*, McNair paper 52, Institute the national strategic studies, Washington, DC; National Defence University, revised edition.
6. Stephen Bungay, 2011, *The Art of Action*, London: Nicolas Brealey.
7. That characteristic, or capability, from which a competitor derives its freedom of action, or corporate power and competitive advantage. A centre of gravity may not always be tangible and may be an abstraction such as morale, confidence or brand and may change.
8. See Note 6 above.
9. See Note 6 above.
10. See Note 6 above.
11. Rittel, H and Webber, M, Dilemmas in a general theory of planning, *Policy Sciences*, 4.
12. Grint K, 2010, *Wicked Problems and Clumsy Solutions: The role of leadership in the new public leadership challenge*, in Brookes, S and Grint, K (eds), Basingstoke: Macmillan.
13. Marvin Washington and Marla Hacker, Why change fails: knowledge counts, *Leadership & Organization Development Journal*, 26, 5, pp 400–11.
14. Command in the Army is the combination of legal authority to issue orders, the legal responsibility for the actions of those under command, together with responsibility for the training, administration, deployment, leadership and management of those under command.
15. Moltke, Helmuth Graf Von, 1892, in *Militarische Werke*. Von Moltke was another Prussian officer and follower of Clausewitz.

02
Propositions about organizations, leadership, people and work

Organizational effectiveness: the corporate context of leadership

Doctrine

Leadership, people and work

Clarity

Paradox: discipline and freedom

The pyramid of leadership learning

Differences and similarities in leadership

Leadership, leaders and teams

Impact of 'organization' on behaviour

The 'three-layer group' and its leader

People's expectations and desires

Whoever wishes to foresee the future must consult the past; for human events ever resemble those of preceding times. This arises from the fact that they are produced by men who ever have been, and ever will be, animated by the same passions, and thus they necessarily have the same result.

(Machiavelli)

This book has been written to outline a proven and effective approach to leadership that was touched on in the last chapter: both to aid individual leaders and to provide the basis for building 'integrated leadership'[1] and 'organizational leadership capacity'.[2] The concepts described in this book enable different levels of leadership in organizations to be integrated by identifying the features common to all levels of leader while also allowing level-specific features to be studied 'in context'. It is based on an understanding of people in general and of the exercise of leadership in the real world in particular. Fads and panaceas are not presented. Rather, only timeless and proven principles are outlined for you to assimilate and apply with common sense, sound judgement, quick wits and wisdom.

It is not possible for this book to develop the reader's expertise in the use of these concepts, or to develop the leader's personal qualities of leadership – that can only be done with practical experience, challenging training and honest feedback and reflection. However, given the fact that you are reading this book it is reasonable to infer that you value leadership and have the will to lead. Assimilation of the knowledge and skills presented here can only increase your capacity to lead, and therefore your success.

Before the role of the leader, the nature of leadership or any leadership tools, processes and concepts may be examined, it is necessary to agree on some fundamental assumptions and principles. These assumptions and principles are the foundations upon which all the following chapters are based.

Organizational effectiveness: the corporate context of leadership

All organizations are judged by their effectiveness, no matter what business they are engaged in. What gives an organization its effectiveness is its capability to be effective; which has the three components shown in Figure 2.1.

The physical component

This provides the means to operate. It includes capital and cash flow, people and their training, logistics, equipment, products, facilities and the distribution system. In short, anything that can be bought or hired to enhance capability.

FIGURE 2.1 Organizational effectiveness

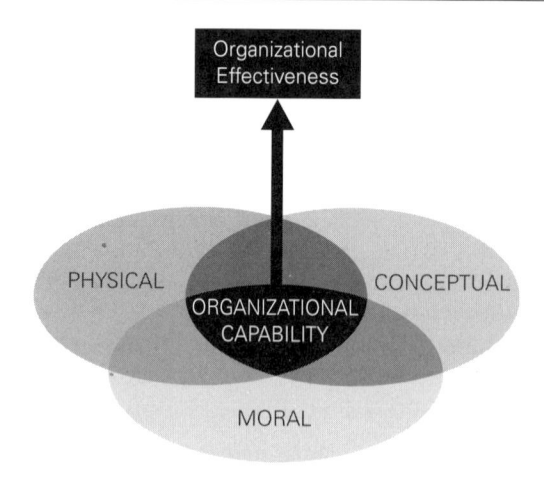

© Jeremy Tozer, 1997–2007

The moral component

The moral component is the ability to get people to work together effectively to achieve organizational objectives. It is based on the leadership that provides direction, delegates tasks and responsibility (with commensurate authority, resources and clear 'parameters and boundaries'), creates a sense of purpose, and shapes an environment in which people may give of their best. An ethical foundation, motivation, pride, esprit de corps, 'fighting spirit' (if you are a soldier or rugby player) and morale are all essential parts of the moral component and are largely a reflection of the quality of leadership within the organization.

The conceptual component

This is the thinking behind what an organization does. It includes the fundamental principles, concepts and models that are the basis of an enterprise's operations and development. It spans high level principles and concepts, operational practices and procedures, and understanding of the operating context. It also includes the 'leadership doctrine' of any enterprise that enables the 'moral component' to be developed, deployed and leveraged throughout the organization to provide competitive advantage.

Leadership doctrine

Dogma is 'what to think'.
Doctrine is 'how to think' effectively.

The guidance of doctrine is not to be confused with slavish adherence to dogma. In this context, a 'leadership doctrine' contains the fundamental principles, concepts and tools that guide how people are organized (structure and role relationships) and led (aligned, engaged, inspired and developed) to achieve objectives. It provides a foundation for common understanding and sets common expectations for leaders and the led throughout an organization. It thus enables the alignment and integration of the work of diverse teams and units throughout an enterprise with people engaged in their work and engaged with the organization and its purpose and identity.

It should inform and be reinforced by the 'people' policies, processes and systems relating to recruitment, selection, training and development (personal, professional and career), performance management, and reward and recognition. Everything then becomes mutually supporting.

Such a doctrine must be an intellectually rigorous, clearly articulated and experience-based understanding that gives competitive advantage to an organization and its partners. This common understanding is designed to guide and requires intelligent application by leaders who exercise their discretion and judgement to suit the local conditions; it is therefore elastic and adaptable, and will evolve through trial, exercise, the advance of technology, availability of resources and (if it ever happens) developments in human nature – as one of our clients says, 'It is a tight-loose fit.' It is not intended to reduce risk for managers by providing rote recipes for predictable and unthinking action, nor is it there to constrain. This book is a leadership doctrine which may be selectively used.

This doctrine's components are:

- philosophical and intellectual, drawing from enduring lessons of the past;
- practical, based on an analysis of the present thus making it relevant to contemporary work; and
- predictive, accounting for future developments as far as they may be anticipated.

Anything that you do repeatedly that works well every time must have a sound theory behind it; and if you eschew theory favouring purely practical action then you just do not know what the theory is. This book is based on ideas and concepts repeatedly proven to work in different sectors (private, public, voluntary) and in different countries and cultures. It provides the basis of the conceptual component of organizational effectiveness relating to leadership, which in turn enables the moral component to be exercised: by aligning work and creating 'follower engagement' to release people's maximum discretionary effort. It is through this that success may be enjoyed on a sustainable basis.

A leader has got to learn to dominate events which surround him; he must never allow these events to get the better of him; he must allow nothing to divert him from his aim; he must always be on top of the job and be prepared to accept responsibility. He must endeavour to produce, on every level, commanders with the qualities of leadership which inspire confidence in others. These qualities are possessed in some degree by all men chosen as leaders but they need to be developed and trained.

(Field Marshal Montgomery)

Leadership, people and work

People do things for one of two reasons: either because they are forced to, or because they want to. If compulsion is to be replaced by inclination, then working effectively to achieve organizational objectives can only happen as a result of inspired personal leadership supported by an enabling environment. There are often many people in organizations who know or who can see what needs to be done and have the desired inclination, but they are unable to 'connect' with people collectively (rather than individuals) to engage a unified and collective effort, and/or they lack the confidence or motivation to lead, to take responsibility.

Leaders realize the potential of the existing inclination. Leaders create cohesive and effective teams and are vital members of those teams. This last point needs emphasizing – leaders are not outside their teams, they are very much part of their team but have a relationship that others do not have with the team, for whom they are responsible as a collective entity.

The late Dr Elliott Jaques,[3] with whom I was privileged to discuss parts of my first book, and who is eminent in the field of organization, structure and hierarchy, points out that a leader does not exist per se, but exists in the context of a purpose – commercial, political, sporting, military or social. A leader may formally be head of a team of direct reports, or may have an ad hoc role of leading a 'flat structure' project team. While the context may change, the essential responsibilities and prerequisites for success differ very little. The word 'leader' is not qualified here as managerial, military, political, sporting or whatever since the concepts outlined here are relevant to any type of organization – as has been demonstrated through their adoption in public, private and voluntary/third sector organizations in the UK, United States, Europe, Africa and Asia.

Leadership is one of the most observed and least understood phenomena on earth.

(J M Burns)

Leaders and the people who follow them represent one of the oldest, most natural and most effective of all human relationships. Yet the function of leadership cannot be discharged on one side without a requirement to be led on the other. Unless people recognize and feel a need to be led, it is near impossible to move them in one's favoured direction. As General Sir John Hackett, a Professor of Classics, King's College, London, wrote:[4]

The leader has something which the others want and which only he can provide. The man who can show the tribesmen where the water-hole is has a special knowledge: he can direct those in need to the place where their need can be satisfied. But you would call him no more than a guide and not a leader unless something else were present. This something is partly the ability to find an answer to a problem which the others cannot solve. But there is also the power, when difficulties have to be overcome, to help people over them. A capacity to help people in the overcoming of the difficulties which face them in a joint enterprise is one of those things which distinguish the person who is a leader from the person who is no more than a guide. What the leader has to give is the direction of a joint effort which will bring success. That is what he is there for, and he must have sufficient mastery of the techniques involved to do what is demanded of him by those he leads.

The nature of leadership is to make things happen, to make or do more – and better – from less, with people who are happy with their part in doing that. To improve means to challenge, to change, to innovate and to learn on a daily basis. Sir John Harvey-Jones,[5] the former chairman of ICI, rightly said that leadership is 'not about maintaining the status quo, but maintaining the highest rate of change that the organization and the people within it can stand'. It is the leader's job to ensure that continuous questioning, clarifying, improving, sharing, innovating, coaching, learning and adoption is integrated into day-to-day life. It is then part of the culture and becomes habit-forming in a most positive sense. It is in this way that the leader 'adds value' and justifies his or her presence.

Therefore, the organizational holy grail of 'optimized commercial capability' – a culture of drive, teamwork, delegated and timely decision making, dynamic alignment of activity and resource allocation, staff engagement, ownership, performance improvement, innovation, customer focus, sustainability and increasing shareholder value – are all underpinned by one thing: effective leadership at all levels – 'organizational leadership capacity'.

The art of leadership cannot be learnt from a book or in a classroom and then practised in a mechanical fashion. Whilst leadership and organization concepts and principles can be studied and give an essential insight into the subject, science suggests exactness and reproducibility – and anyone who has worked with people will know that they can be most unpredictable, which is probably why so many people are frightened of taking a leadership role! The practice of leadership is an art.

Leadership is an individual and personal ability that is born and is evident in some, but can be developed in others who have the will and potential. It is an individual expression of long-established principles that have not changed as human nature has not changed over the millennia. Leadership is not a skill in itself, but a combination of skills and personal qualities and the use of 'tools' that can be developed and applied with thought and common sense.

If you would define the future, study the past.
(Confucius)

There are many great lessons to be learnt from the study of business, political and military history. Whilst technology and the employment of systems and processes has changed out of all recognition and leaders in different periods of history may be isolated by time, all leaders are united by the consistent themes of human nature and the responsibility they have shared and the principles they have employed. Most great leaders have studied the campaigns and personalities of other great leaders in history and have learnt much from doing so. De Gaulle was always aware of the links of leadership throughout history, and in 1934 he wrote[6] that whatever the time and place there is a philosophy of command as unchangeable as human nature. When Charles XII wept at the recital of Alexander's exploits, when Napoleon poured over Frederick the Great's campaigns, when Foch taught Napoleon's methods, it was because they were aware of this feeling of this permanence. In 1905 Henderson[7] wrote:

> *military history offers a more comprehensive view of those processes than even active service... the art of war is crystallized in a few great principles and it is a study of history alone that makes such principles so familiar but to apply them becomes a matter of instinct... The study of history results in the accumulation of facts and the understanding of knowledge and facts however wide constitutes experience* (sic).

Any initiative to institutionalize 'leadership at all levels' must be based on sound principles and pursued with vigour, and sustained over time by the organization's leader and executive leadership team. All leaders need to set clear expectations and the example for more junior leaders to follow. 'Do as I do' has to be the rule, not 'Do as I say while I do as I've always done.' Over-simplified solutions, fads and panaceas become expensive. Each failed attempt and need for 'another change' will further erode the morale of staff within the organization and will breed more cynicism (just ask anyone in the NHS!).

For any leadership model to be used in organizational development, some basic propositions about the 'nature of human nature', people at work and organizational development initiatives must be agreed.

Clarity

Many books stress the need for clarity of vision, task, role, values and so on; but frequently no clarity of meaning is established for the words used in that book – nor in any organization's daily use of language and terminology, come to that. If 10 different managers were to define words like 'mission', 'objective', 'task', etc there would probably be 10 different answers. The 'science' of leadership and organization has no universally agreed terms, unlike other sciences such as physics, chemistry and so on. Yet without the clarity of common terminology, we cannot discuss concepts and ideas effectively for we will always assign our own meaning and therefore have different interpretations and understanding from those with whom we work. It is therefore worth persevering with what might appear to be pedantic at first glance.

Throughout this book, key words are used in a consistent sense, and that sense is given in the Glossary. So words like 'mission' and 'objective' are not to be confused by the reader. For example, in this book, a *mission* is a clear, concise and unequivocal statement of overall intent and the purpose it is designed to fulfil, best expressed as 'to do (something) in order to (achieve something)'. An *objective* is a precise statement of a measurable, defined goal that needs to be attained if the mission that gave rise to the objective is to be achieved. It is usual for a number of objectives to be essential to achieving a mission. So a mission is not the same as an objective.

You do not necessarily need to adopt the same terminology that I use within your organization, but it aids clarity and effective strategy development and execution if you do use a consistent and commonly understood set of terms.

Paradox: discipline and freedom

There is a paradox that needs to be embraced between discipline and freedom, and it is inextricably linked with clarity. For scientists to conduct research and to have meaningful discussions with other scientists, they need to talk in terms that other scientists understand, and be guided by sound scientific principles. They need to employ the discipline of effective process and common terminology, to have the freedom to create new understanding. The same applies to musicians in jazz and traditional folk bands. Without the discipline of practice to understand both one's instrument and a particular tune and to know them both inside out, it is almost impossible to add the spontaneity and improvisation into one's playing that is needed to make a tune sound interesting. The discipline of structuring this book in terms of chapter, section and paragraph headings has created the freedom to fill in the blank spaces with what needs to be said in the right place. The discipline of an actor rehearsing gives that actor the freedom to move smoothly and with elegance across the stage.

Alistair Mant,[8] when considering an agreed arrangement in organizations about how people will relate to one another (a 'constitution'), wrote:

> *The more formal it is, the clearer it can be and, again somewhat paradoxically, the easier it will be to change. If you are clear about something in the first place, it is possible to know which bits to change. If you are unclear, you don't know where to start, or indeed,*

FIGURE 2.2 The path to freedom

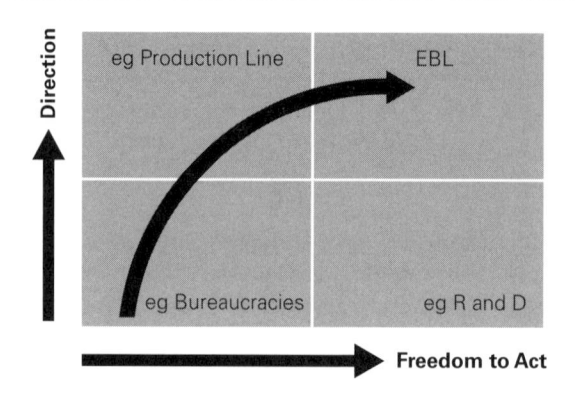

(Figure: A 2x2 matrix with vertical axis "Direction" and horizontal axis "Freedom to Act". Top-left: eg Production Line; Top-right: EBL; Bottom-left: eg Bureaucracies; Bottom-right: eg R and D. A curved arrow sweeps from bottom-left up to top-right.)

© Jeremy Tozer, 1997–2007

what people think the existing arrangements are. To be free, paradoxically, you must be bounded. To attempt to do without boundaries is to become entrapped in a power web of covert and subtle accommodations.

Change is aided by stability – clarity provides a form of stability and security; without this, people pursue survival.

The 'path to freedom' is illustrated in Figure 2.2. Organizations in which people have both little freedom to act (perceived or real freedom) and little clarity about what they are trying to achieve, how, why, their authority and accountability and so on, are characterized by bureaucracies. Production lines in factories give very clear direction to people – typically it is so clear that it ceases to be direction in the sense that we will use direction in later chapters, but rather a rigid set of standing instructions and standard operating procedures, with little scope for initiative. This might enable a factory to consistently produce products of the same quality and at the same rate, but it is probably not the best approach to take in a service industry in which the customer expects the customer service representative to solve his or her problems.

The concept of effects-based leadership (EBL) that was introduced in Chapter 1 provides leaders at all levels with autonomy and freedom to use their initiative – but that is bounded by clear direction, which incorporates higher level intentions and purpose, defined role relationships and delegated authority, accountability and resources.

The pyramid of leadership learning

The principles used to lead a large group are the same as those used to lead a small group. It is a matter of appropriate organization.

(Sun Tzu)

If the pyramid of learning is to work (leaders at one level developing the leaders at the level below them), then a leadership doctrine must be developed that enables a common understanding and language (the currency of leadership) across the organization. However, the model adopted must also enable different aspects of leadership to be examined at different levels within the structure, within different business functions, and across different national cultures in global enterprises.

Some managers race into studying aspects of strategic leadership which they fail to use successfully because they lack the basic understanding of what leadership is all about. The 'nuts and bolts' of leadership will be the focus of much of this book, since the 'big picture' is simply a grouping of many 'little pictures' – what should be applied to the few can be applied to the many if the concept is grounded in first principles.

Differences and similarities in leadership

Large organizations are systems for defining and achieving tasks to fulfil a purpose. The only way that they may operate effectively is when some people are held accountable for the work outputs of other people. This means hierarchy. It may not be PC to say so for those devotees of delayering and leaderless group working, but it is a fact of life. What matters is that the hierarchy is carefully designed and is populated with leaders whose capability and authority is matched to their level of work complexity, which is one quantum step greater than the people working for that leader. In that way, leaders may keep their subordinate leaders in context, while working sufficiently far enough ahead that they remove obstacles and pave the way for their subordinates and are also prevented from interfering in their subordinate leaders' work.

The functions that effective leaders perform (or should perform) vary little between levels, organizations and industries. All leaders at all levels:

- solve problems and make decisions;
- plan and brief;
- control, organize and coordinate;
- support, resource and coach;
- inform and report;
- monitor and evaluate.

How they do this does differ, however. This is partly due to the need to display an appropriate style (individual leadership behaviour and emotional intelligence) for the situation, and is partly based on the level of work undertaken (a function of organization).

What separates the junior leader's work (the supervisor or the corporal) from the senior executive's work (the director or the general) is:

- the level of complexity of the work faced;
- the degree of ambiguity or uncertainty and its implications;
- the time horizon required in the leader;

FIGURE 2.3 The hierarchy of 'complexity' and 'level of leadership work'

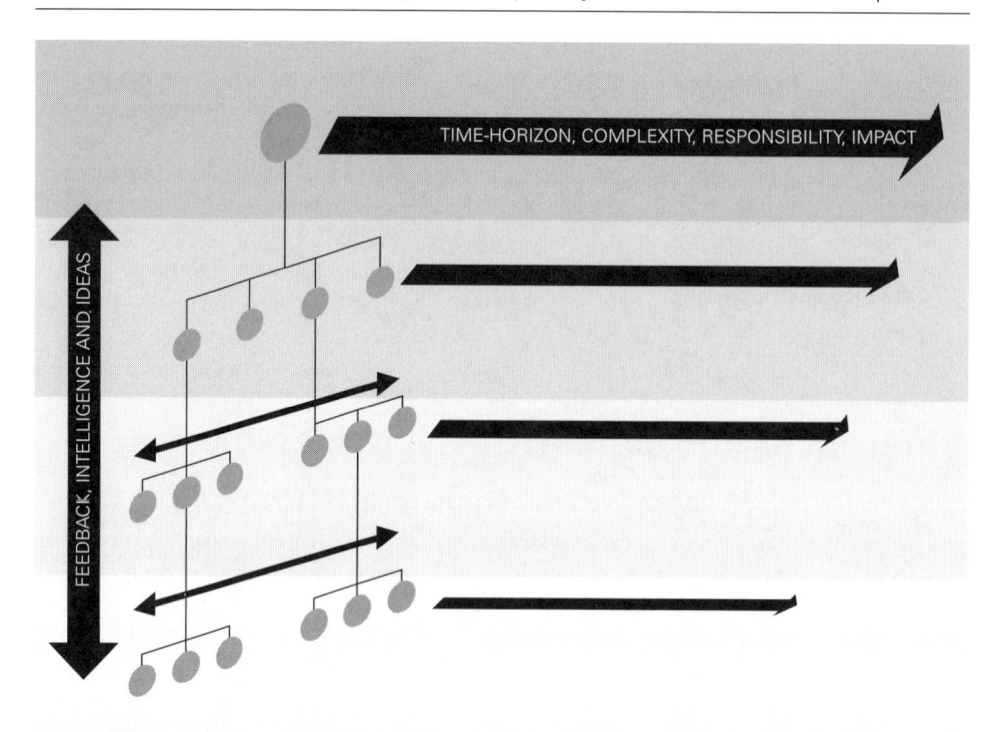

© Jeremy Tozer, 1997–2007

- the level of responsibility felt by the (psychologically well-adjusted) leader; and
- the leader's impact, including the attention paid by the organization to 'behaviour and signal actions'.

This is shown in Figure 2.3.

In brief, many of the functions performed by leaders remain the same at all levels, as does the requirement for behavioural flexibility and emotional intelligence (leadership style). What changes is the level of complexity faced and the 'time horizon' and cognitive capacity required of the leader, the leader's 'felt responsibility', power and influence and impact over time.

Recognition of this enables a common philosophy or doctrine of leadership to be used across an organization. A doctrine based upon a common understanding of the leader's role and common leadership methods (and language) aid the 'clarity creating, aligning and engaging' functions of decision making, planning and briefing which may be used at different orders of complexity. Alignment is created through a cascade of tasks and objectives set in context and the recipient understanding that context and higher intent. Engagement is secured by delegating authority, resources and defining boundaries and constraints on action and, within this, allowing the recipient leader and his or her team to determine how best to achieve objectives and complete tasks –

decentralization of decision making. These methods or leadersh
be intelligently applied and should be designed to cascade, recur, it
the leadership structure – across levels, locations and departmei.
alignment, ownership and trust and an agile, mission-focused organ.

Caveat: Figure 2.3 is not intended to convey any senses of 'top-dov
it is intended to show structure based on levels of work complexity v
people working in alignment to execute strategy and achieve organizati.
tives. To do this they have delegated authority, resources and responsibility

Leadership vs leader

If leadership is something that everyone in the organization can demonstrate if they choose to, then the concept of 'leadership' needs to be separated from that of 'a leader'. That difference is in the nature of responsibility and is highlighted in the two working definitions below:

> **Leadership:** *the capacity and will to rally people to a common purpose willingly, together with the character that inspires confidence and trust.*
>
> (Adapted from Field Marshal Montgomery)

We may amplify Montgomery's[9] definition for our purposes by saying that 'capacity' means skills and knowledge that may be learnt; 'character' means behaviour and attitude that may be developed if people choose to. The will to lead, however, has to be innate.

> **Leader:** *a person responsible for achieving organizational objectives through the work of others, and for building and maintaining the team that he or she is a member of by creating the conditions for their success.*
>
> (Tozer)

All leaders would do well to remember a maxim of Napoleon's that 'there is no such thing as a bad soldier, only a bad officer'. He understood this aspect of leadership responsibility. Since both individual leaders and the teams of individuals whom they would lead are unique, leadership must be considered to be individual in its application. These definitions allow for the concept of 'shared leadership' (discussed in the next chapter) and also provide the foundation for the effective selection and development of leadership.

Leaders vs managers

One of the most counter-productive approaches in the institutionalization of leadership is the view that leaders (with vision and charisma) exist only at the top of an organization and that everyone else responsible for people is a manager (responsible only for unthinking work allocation). This immediately prevents the application of a universal leadership model, and introduces an artificial boundary that creates 'them and us'. No matter what their level is, anyone who is responsible for other people and their outputs must be viewed by themselves and by the organization as a leader, and treated and developed as such. Failure to do this creates a leadership vacuum and a culture of dependence, complacency and risk avoidance. Supervisors junior leaders are too often given the accountability of a leader but with neither the recognition nor the authority; they are thus in an untenable position, forced to rely on goodwill and influence.

Unless managers have had their leadership skills developed throughout their careers, how can they assume a senior role and be effective in that role? How much damage have we all witnessed ineffective leaders do to organizations by failing to seize opportunities, initiate change when it is needed, and perhaps most notably, by failing to listen to and be responsible for their employees' best interests? What does this lack of leadership ability cost organizations through staff turnover, retraining, lost opportunities, poor motivation, unwillingness to change, etc? Has there ever been a climate and attitude survey that has not highlighted the fact that most employees feel that they are not working at a level even close to their full potential?

In the dictionary, definitions of manage, manager and management are usually associated with control, administration, precision, continuation of unchanging processes, regulation, etc. Lead, leader or leadership, however, are associated with showing the way, guiding, taking to a certain destination, inspiring others to follow. We must differentiate the concept of leadership and management. People are willing to be led because leaders provide security by creating clarity, by building belief that the difficult is possible, by building confidence and lightening people's burdens. All experience suggests that people are not so willing to be managed – one may manage tasks, time, material and other inanimate resources, but not the people who must complete those tasks. The etymological roots support this – 'leader' comes from the old Anglo Saxon *leaden*, which means to cause to go with one. On the other hand, 'management' is derived from the Latin *manus*, meaning hand, a hand that manipulates.

Continued use of the word 'management' reinforces the management myth that determines the cost of everything and the value of nothing. To position leadership as part of management is to immediately devalue leadership and to fail to recognize the power of effective leadership. Nor is 'leadership' a separate activity to 'management'. To lead people effectively requires a leader to also be able to manage those things that need to be managed. So for the purposes of this book, we will pursue the notion that management – the ability to allocate, monitor and administer – is the organizational and rational aspect of leadership and a subset of leadership, not something separate.

As Professor Warren Bennis writes:[10]

The manager administers; the leader innovates.
The manager is a copy; the leader is an original.
The manager maintains; the leader develops.
The manager focuses on systems and structure; the leader focuses on people.
The manager relies on control; the leader inspires trust.
The manager has a short-range view; the leader has a long-range perspective.
The manager asks how and when; the leader asks what and why.
The manager has his eye on the bottom line; the leader has his eye on the horizon.
The manager imitates; the leader originates.
The manager accepts the status quo; the leader challenges it.
The manager does things right; the leader does the right thing.

Leadership, leaders and teams

With regard to teamwork, effective teams are the result of effective leadership (from the team's leader and others within the team). If people are to have real confidence in the organization, effective leadership must be provided by the appointed leader of a team and not abdicated to others (the leader need not provide all the leadership, but the team's leader must be an effective leader). The concept of self-managed or self-directed work teams can be misleading. No team that is part of a bigger organization can be totally self-directed; it has to be aligned to the wider organization. What is intended by this concept is that low-level decisions that should have been delegated to team members from the outset are actually delegated and that is part of effective leadership. Also, every team requires a leader to build the team's identity, to champion the team's interests, and to take responsibility for the team, its outputs and its development. Since organizations have contracts with individuals and hold individuals and not whole teams accountable for results, again the concept of self-directed leaderless teams as a panacea for all ills is flawed.

The size of any team has to be determined by several factors. They are:

- the geographical location of the team members;
- the complexity of their work and therefore the time that a leader needs to spend in clarifying and supporting that work;
- their ability and the need for the development of team members (so, not too many in a team); and
- the removal of stifling over-supervision (so, not too few people in a team).

Being a leader is a full-time job

Providing effective leadership to a team is a full-time role in itself, and no leader who is required to invest excessive time in selling, researching or designing products or services can be expected to provide effective leadership to the team as well. This is particularly so when part of a leader's remuneration is based on his or her own 'functional productivity' (eg, sales activity) rather than solely on the leadership of the team and their resulting outputs (eg, sales revenue). Organizational structure must be designed to enable leaders to lead, and people policies, processes and systems (performance management, recruitment and selection, learning and development, reward and recognition) must support them. Examination of the 'functional leadership checklist' in Chapter 4 is alone proof of this.

The power of personal example

Too many senior executives seem only to consider 'strategic leadership' to be their role. Yet most if not all have their own team of direct reports to lead and all too often the power of personal example is forgotten – the thoughtless executive who passes a ringing telephone and ignores it is not setting the example of customer service that she or he would like their followers to adopt. The message, 'It doesn't really matter' has been clearly sent, and will be understood to be the behaviour that is acceptable in the company.

The personal example of senior leaders has strategic impact internally because the organization pays attention to that behaviour: 'people at the top are successful, their behaviour has contributed to their success, it is behaviour to be imitated', is what the organization believes to be true.

Impact of 'organization' on behaviour

The impact of 'organization' – structure, leadership and business processes, HR and other systems – on collective behaviour and the basic principles underlying effective organization design must be appreciated. Part of this is the understanding of the paradox of 'clarity and discipline of structure and process' creating 'freedom and agility to act'. By applying first principles, leaders can construct a framework within which people can cooperate, and which is trust-inducing. In the absence of a clear framework, the 'rules of the game' will be made up as people go along: this will inevitably lead to unnecessary conflict and a waste of time, money, effort and emotional energy. The 'dotted lines' in matrix structures need to be clarified in order to define lateral role relationships and to align accountability with authority (eg, authorities to inform, be informed, start, delay, stop, audit work and to receive service) – this does not mean the same as the creation of unnecessary layers with vertical authority (meaning hiring, firing, deciding work priority, holding to account and being accountable for subordinates' outputs). This issue is explored in greater detail in Chapters 4 and 22. Role 'un-clarity', and misalignment of accountability and authority, is usually the single biggest source of stress for people in large enterprises that hold them responsible for their performance.

This approach to organization will include a system of common leadership processes (already referred to) that give the organization capability to change and react with far greater agility. These processes include the problem solving – decision making – detailed planning – briefing sequence of cascading; recurring processes that enable 'strategy' to become 'reality' and which include context setting and just-in-time task assignment, coaching, personal effectiveness appraisal, reward and recognition. When embedded into the organization, these processes enable continuous change and innovation, and optimal performance; they also help to perpetuate a culture of leadership as they remain long after people have moved on.

Trust

People do not have to like each other to work together effectively, but they do need to respect and trust each other. Trust is what holds organization together. When structures, systems and processes are designed they should all be tested against the question: does this induce or directly build trust?

The 'three-layer group' and its leader

It is important to recognize the role of the 'three-layer group' leader's role; that is to say the leader of a team of 'subordinate leaders' who each have their own team of 'subordinate team members'. Dr Jaques[11] called this a 'Mutual Recognition Unit' (MRU) and gave guidance on its size, which should allow the 'leader-once-removed' (LoR) to know all the 'subordinates-once-removed' (SoRs) by name and face. The LoR (or your boss's boss) is the person best positioned to:

- ensure equilibration of the quality of leadership provided by subordinate leaders to their teams (ie the same deal across the organizational unit);
- conduct talent pool analysis of SoRs (subordinates' subordinates) with a detached and holistic view (since those subordinate leaders may be threatened by capable team members); and
- enable timely career development.

This is explored in greater detail later in this book.

People's expectations and desires

People in organizations generally:

- Find work that allows them to use their ability to the full satisfying.
- Do not have to be motivated to do satisfying work.
- Seek fair differential remuneration for that work (the concept of felt-fair pay based on level of work complexity rather than the 'number of direct reports' which is sometimes the case).
- Seek opportunity for personal growth and, where appropriate, participation in policy and planning development (via feedback and 'questioning and listening' systems) – they are not responsible for policy, decisions and plans.
- Require mutual trust and confidence between people.
- Believe in meritocracy; seek fairness in all interaction and respect for the individual.
- Expect clear accountability with authority to match that accountability, both laterally and vertically.
- Require accountable, competent leaders and frequent interaction with their leaders.
- Pay careful attention to the example of leaders, especially senior leaders, and imitate 'successful' people's behaviour.

The above points are usually implicit in the lists of values that are seen in most organizations with references to integrity, mutual respect, customer-focus, sustainable shareholder value, and so on. (Such lists vary little because all organizations are full of things called people and these values reflect human nature which has changed little in thousands of years and is not likely to change any time soon.) These points should be explicitly reflected in an effective organization's systems, policies, processes, stated expectations and leaders' example and behaviour.

Notes

1. The capability that results from integrating leadership between and within levels, business units and locations through common methods for communicating, enabling timely decisions by those best placed to make them, and aligning activity in a manner that engages people and encourages the display of initiative, and by aligning accountability with authority both laterally and vertically to define role relationships.
2. The collective leadership capability that results from developing leadership in depth and breadth within an organization primarily through embedding common methods for communicating, enabling timely decisions by those best placed to make them, and aligning activity in a manner that engages people and encourages the display of initiative.
3. Elliott Jaques, 1996, *Requisite Organization: A total system for effective managerial organization and managerial leadership for the 21st century*, Arlington, VA: Cason Hall.
4. General Sir John Hackett, 1983, *The Profession of Arms*, London: Sidgwick & Jackson.
5. Sir John Harvey-Jones, 1988, *Making It Happen*, London: HarperCollins.
6. General De Gaulle, 1934, *The Army of the Future*.
7. Col G F R Henderson, 1905, *The Science Of War*, London: Longmans.
8. Alistair Mant, 1983, *Leaders We Deserve*, Martin Robertson & Co.
9. Field Marshal The Viscount Montgomery of Alamein, 1961, *The Path to Leadership*, London: Collins. (I have added the words 'and trust'.)
10. Warren Bennis, 1989, *On Becoming a Leader*, Sydney: Century Hutchinson.
11. Elliott Jaques, 1996, *Requisite Organization: A total system for effective managerial organization and managerial leadership for the 21st century*, Arlington, VA: Cason Hall.

03
The role of a leader: Creating the ACE conditions for success

> ACE as a leader's job description
>
> ACE as an organizational and leadership effectiveness assessment and diagnostic tool
>
> ACE as a leadership and organization effectiveness diagnostic tool
>
> Organizational conditions: integrated leadership

Think of a team, any team, in any sport. For the sake of example, choose the 2011 English Rugby World Cup (RWC) team. If you ask the question, 'What are all the things that affect the team's success?' the answers will probably include those shown in Table 3.1.

If you think about these factors that affect the team's ability to succeed, they may all be separated out under the headings of:

Ability,

Clarity, and

Environment.

These are the ACE conditions for success which are optimized for sustainable performance.

What about things like motivation, communication and empowerment – they are missing from Table 3.1. Motivation is a word that can have broad meaning. Leaders cannot simply 'motivate' people. Motivation results from: a clear, stretching yet attainable objective, confidence in one's ability and in one's leaders, an innate desire 'to do the job', and a supportive environment. Motivation has components in all three ACE areas.

Understanding Leadership

TABLE 3.1 Factors affecting (RWC) team success

• Fitness • Passing and kicking skills • Rules of the game • Rules of the competition • Knowledge of competitors • Quick thinking • Fighting spirit • Cooperation • Drive • Determination • Optimism • Confidence • Teamwork • Self-discipline	• A clear, shared aim and purpose • RWC competition strategy • Game plan for each match – Tactics • Understanding of roles in the team • Clear expectations	• Leader (team manager or captain) and leadership (from all) • Team identity • Morale • Training • Coaching • Facilities to train • Equipment • Money • Rewards and recognition • Team discipline and cohesion • Supporters

Similarly effective business communication has ACE components. It is spoken with confidence and conviction matched with 'appropriate body language' and/or written and disseminated through various forms of media in a clear, recognizable, brief and structured format.

Empowerment again has all three ACE components. It results from being trusted by your boss, having the resources that you really need, being confident in your ability to do the job (including having an effective thought process for problem solving and aligned decision making at your fingertips), knowing what you are trying to achieve, why and how, and having clear guidelines and authority for decision making.

ACE as a leader's job description

All experience and extensive research suggests that there are three universal and fundamental preconditions that must be satisfied for any organization, team or individual to enjoy success: Ability, Clarity, and Environment (Figure 3.1), and it is the leader's responsibility to shape, develop or create these conditions.

This concept applies at any level in any activity, and it is a basic job description for any leader. Effective leaders at all levels create the clarity, shape the environment and develop the ability of their people to succeed. Politicians take note!

FIGURE 3.1 The ACE conditions for success

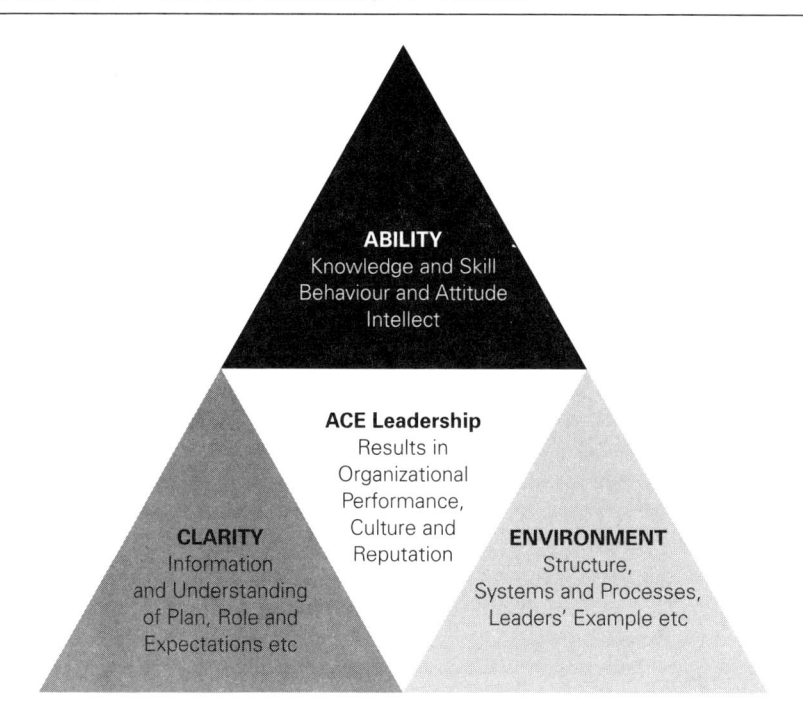

ABILITY
Knowledge and Skill
Behaviour and Attitude
Intellect

ACE Leadership
Results in
Organizational
Performance,
Culture and
Reputation

CLARITY
Information
and Understanding
of Plan, Role and
Expectations etc

ENVIRONMENT
Structure,
Systems and Processes,
Leaders' Example etc

© Jeremy Tozer, 1997–2007

It may also be deployed as a diagnostic tool when analysing reasons for high performance that you wish to repeat (England in the 2003 RWC), or failure that you don't (England in the 2011 RWC). The presence of these conditions is evidence of leadership – creating these conditions is the leader's inescapable responsibility.

Ability

Ability is a function of process, knowledge and skill, applied with the appropriate behaviour and attitude (which, for leaders, you may call 'flexible leadership style' or 'emotional intelligence'), together with the right level of intellect for the level of work and complexity faced. Leadership ability and developing people's ability is the focus of Chapters 4, 8 and 10.

Clarity

Clarity is a function of two factors: the right information and the effective understanding of that information to enable aligned action that contributes to achieving the higher intent. Such clarity includes the creation and clear communication of expectations, desired end-state, aim, purpose and intent (purpose creates meaning which aids motivation as well as enabling alignment), strategic and tactical plans, team and individual roles and objectives, authority and accountability and so on.

In an organizational context, this 'clarity' is best created through cascaded, integrated and inclusive leadership processes for problem solving and aligned decision making, planning and briefing. These flexible and adaptable processes will enable feedback and questioning and will, through the style of their application, create the foundation of accountability, ownership, engagement and trust. This is examined in detail in Chapters 12 to 18; some key aspects will be examined briefly in this chapter to assist in setting the context for the rest of the book.

Clarity versus order

In a recent discussion about leadership and organization development in pursuit of Pharma 3.0[1] with the Vice President of Learning and Development in one of the world's largest pharmaceutical companies, one of the questions asked was:

> Frankly we have a degree of chaos. There is little common understanding or interpretation of plans, or of leadership roles, expectations and language, which results in people not aligning their work to strategy, going off at tangents, and not fully cooperating. We're not agile enough. You've emphasized creating 'clarity' rather than 'order'. Why is that?

This provoked some quick thinking and with the benefit of hindsight, the response still holds good!

> Clarity enables you to have order, but any effective means of creating clarity in dynamic environments – effective meaning both alignment of and engagement in work – also embeds collective agility and adaptability, the means to thrive in changing environments. If order alone is pursued, then chaos may be replaced with excessive 'organization' resulting in inflexibility and the problems associated with a bureaucracy. It was the German love of order in the last war that enabled the 'cork screw minds' in British Intelligence to run German Intelligence. *Deutsches ordnung* made their intelligence service both predictable and inflexible.

Environment

Environment comprises the infrastructure of the workplace – its systems and processes, structure, facilities, and its 'philosophy' or approach to its business – and importantly the example of its leaders, which all influence culture:

- Leaders' example of values in action, trust, delegation, accountability and learning (which starts at the top) – leaders' style and behaviour.
- HR policies, processes and systems that are used by leaders to recruit, select, develop, incentivize, manage, recognize and reward the desired 'ability' (behaviour and attitude and intellect, not simply skill and knowledge which may be assessed and 'trained' easily).
- Organization structure (accountability aligned with authority both vertically and laterally, with defined role relationships – this is trust-inducing and in general the least understood aspect of organizational leadership).
- Business processes and systems.
- Workplace layout.
- Allocated resources.

- Products and services that staff have confidence in.
- Beliefs and myths about the way in which things are done and which in turn influence how people react and behave.
- Embedded leadership processes for integrating leadership, and creating clarity, alignment and engagement – processes applied with appropriate behaviour.
- The external 'market' and/or 'geopolitical climate' are part of environment. These may be influenced by large 'players' but not directly controlled.

In organizations with poorly designed and 'unaligned' or dysfunctional structure, systems and processes which induce 'dysfunctional behaviour', good leaders can do much to insulate their teams from 'organizational nonsense' rather than play victim to the 'unbeatable system' through their personal leadership. This, however, does add to the stress under which such leaders work and is unnecessary and a significant impediment to optimal performance. The environment is examined in Chapters 19 to 23, and again some key aspects will be addressed in this chapter.

Danger in the comfort zone

Clinical professor of psychiatry Judith Bardwick[2] has shown that people's optimum level of performance is reached when there is a degree of stress; the effective conditions are shown in Figure 3.2. Excessive stress (worries about job security, change, consequences of actions and so on) leads to the paralysis of fear; the complete absence of stress leads to complacency and an entitlement culture. This may occur at the individual, organizational and national levels: at the time of writing, the British government's review of the welfare and benefits system is recognition of this on a grand scale.

What the leader must bear in mind is that what is stressful for one person may not be stressful for another. So while a number of organizational conditions may be designed for everyone to work within, the leader must also adapt how he or she leads individuals to get the best out of that individual. We all know that there are those who need a degree of mollycoddling and nursing to perform to their optimum level;

FIGURE 3.2 Effective ACE conditions

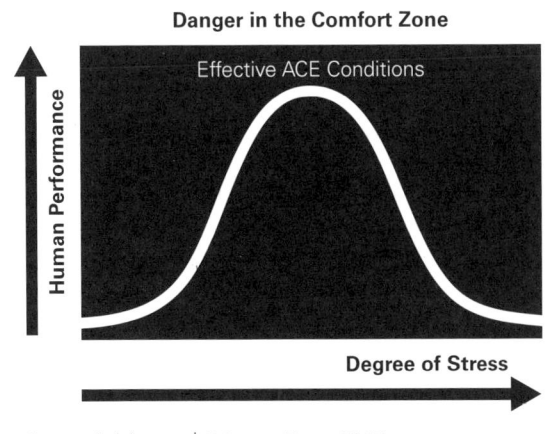

After Bardwick, 1995 | © Jeremy Tozer, 2007

equally, there are others who just need to be pointed in the right direction and let go and then brought back into line when they deviate from the desired path.

Other essential points to note

To fully grasp this ACE concept, you must appreciate the following points:

- The combination of all these ACE conditions shapes the organization's 'culture', levels of performance, and reputation or external image.
- A leader's own leadership ability enables the leader to create and shape the clarity and environment for his or her team members, as well develop team members' ability. This applies at all levels.
- Clarity must be created first as it dictates the requirements of the environment and the ability needed in the workforce. In my experience, 95 per cent of performance improvement comes from increased clarity, not more training or more expenditure on resources. How a leader 'creates clarity' plays a significant part in shaping 'culture', 'ownership' and the immediate working environment.
- ACE provides a diagnostic tool at both collective and individual levels to assess why high performance is or is not being maintained and how good performance may be repeated and poor performance improved.

When things go wrong, the private sector and politicians often tend to blame someone else's ability for failure, while in the public sector, civil servants, council and NHS staff tend to play victim to the environment. Yet it is all too often clarity (or the lack of it) that is to blame. The creation of clarity is the leader's responsibility at every level. If the boss doesn't create it, then more junior leaders need to ask the questions that establish clarity. Having said that, the near impossibility of permanently ending the tax-payer funded career of even the most incompetent public sector employee does little to induce achievement. (There are examples of public sector CEOs who have presided over regimes that have ensured that hospitals remain in tens of millions of pounds worth of debt, have unexpectedly high mortality rates or consistently failed to make any tangible progress in council local strategic partnerships, who have been sacked from one organization, recycled and appear within months as the salvation of another organization in trouble.)

ACE as an organizational and leadership effectiveness assessment and diagnostic tool

The dynamics of the quarks and gluons is controlled by the chromodynamics Lagrangian equation:

$$L_{QCD} = \Psi_i(i\gamma^\mu(D_\mu)_{ij} - m\delta_{ij})\Psi_j - G^a_{\mu\nu}G_a^{\mu\nu} = \Psi_i(i\gamma^\mu\delta_\mu - m)\Psi_i - gG^a_{\mu}\Psi_i\gamma^\mu T^a_{ij}\Psi_j - G^a_{\mu\nu}G_a^{\mu\nu}$$

For a long time scientists tried to measure the presence of quarks. Then they realized that that was simply too difficult, so they looked for evidence of the existence of quarks and satisfied themselves with measuring that. The same idea may be extended to measuring leadership and organizational effectiveness.

It is the responsibility of leaders at all levels to create the ACE conditions in which their people may be successful in achieving organizational objectives. When aggregated across the organization, the presence of these ACE conditions is 'organizational effectiveness' or 'organizational capability'. These conditions may be assessed and measured and used as a performance diagnosis. While leadership cannot be 'measured' per se, the presence of the ACE conditions is evidence of leadership; so this powerful mechanism is also a measure of the organization's quality of leadership and its leadership capacity.

To aid assessment, the three ACE elements have each been broken into nine smaller component parts to enable detailed understanding and assessment of internal ACE conditions. Questions for each of these 27 parts may be developed to assess both the importance of that element to the respondent, and the degree to which that element is present in the respondent's work. While analysis to individual question level may be useful, experience shows that a traffic light map of the organization such as Figure 3.3 is most useful.

FIGURE 3.3 ACE Insights assessment of the conditions for success

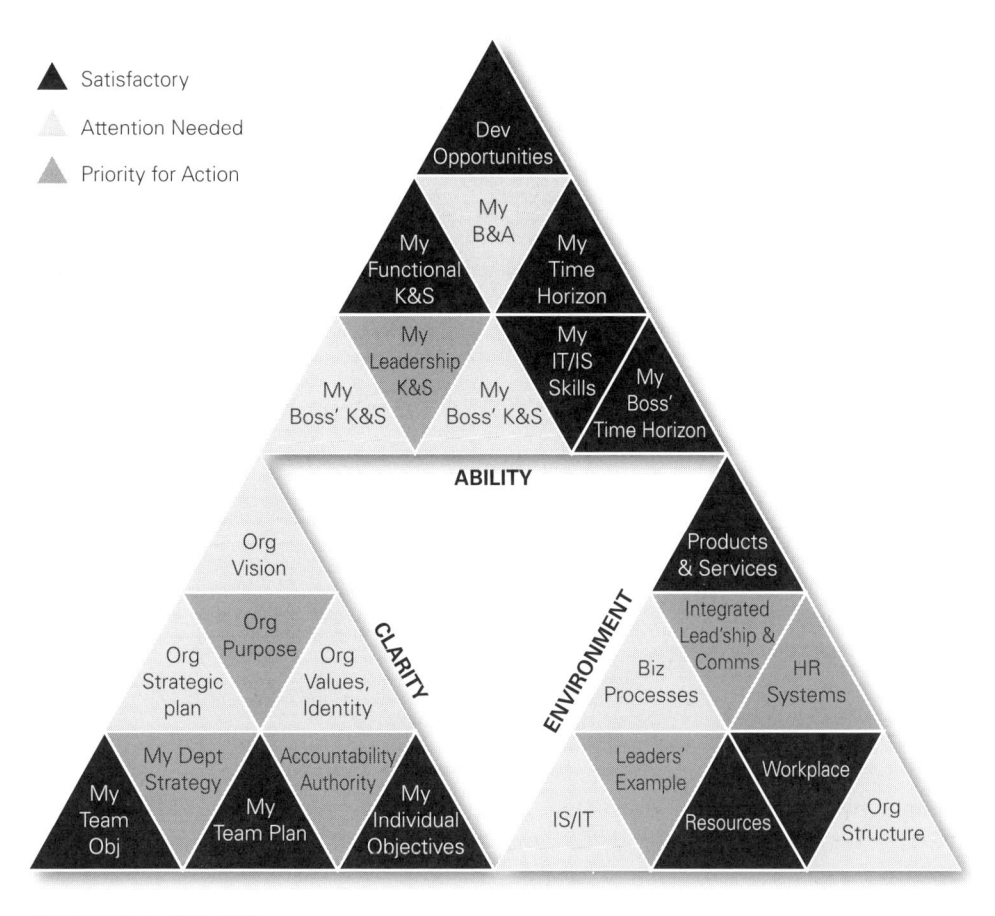

© Jeremy Tozer, 1997–2007

Understanding Leadership

The generic 27 question areas (which may, of course, be tailored to suit individual organizations and their circumstances) are shown in Table 3.2.

Typically around 100 questions are used in the online version of the ACE audit, whereas in the workshop version the definition of each of the nine elements may be

TABLE 3.2 The generic question areas

ABILITY
1. Your behaviour and attitude/emotional intelligence
2. Your 'leadership' knowledge and skill
3. Your 'functional' knowledge and skill
4. Your time horizon-ability and time to anticipate and plan ahead
5. Your opportunities for development (career, personal and professional)
6. Your IT/IS skills
7. Your boss's knowledge and skill (leadership and functional)
8. Your boss's behaviour and attitude
9. Your boss's time horizon-ability and time to anticipate and plan ahead

Clarity
10. Vision
11. The organization's purpose – its reason for existing
12. The organization's values and identity
13. Vision, strategic objectives and strategic plan
14. Division or department strategy (role, objectives and plan)
15. Team role, tasks, objectives and priorities
16. Team plan to achieve objectives
17. Individual role: accountability and authority (aligned to accountability)
18. Individual role: personal tasks, objectives and priorities

Environment
19. Organization structure that enables effective working relationships
20. Workplace layout conducive to effective working practices
21. HR policies, processes and systems integrated to induce desired behaviour
22. Integrated leadership and communication to ensure alignment of and accountability for activity
23. Leaders' example and behaviour congruent with organization vision and values
24. IS/IT systems – integrated, robust and user-friendly
25. Business processes and procedures – effective and efficient
26. Resource allocation minimum required to meet accountability
27. Products/services that staff have confidence in

more useful. The responses to these questions may be reinforced by gathering evidence of examples to support the overall assessment of a 'question area'. It is also useful to ask staff to identify areas for quick wins – which may be used to build confidence.

Any leader's perception of these conditions is, in our experience, very unlikely to be the same as those of the people above or below that leader, or indeed outside of the organization. If an ACE Insights survey is conducted at each level of leadership or employment band in the organization, it is quite usual to see more green in responses at the top of the organization and more red at lower levels – things deteriorate as you work your way down the business. It is also possible to see a 'bounce level' – this is the level at which everyone below is frustrated (usually because of lack of clarity), and everyone above is frustrated because every decision is delegated upwards, but the bouncers are fairly happy with everything.

If there is a perception gap between levels, and since perception is reality, you as a leader have a problem to solve – if only one of perception (which is unlikely: people in organizations are quite often more aware of its faults and development needs than its executive leaders). In this regard, a comparison of traffic light maps (by level, function, business unit and location) is helpful.

Such an audit or assessment provides an evidence base to create awareness of the need to change (and this is referred to in Chapter 6) and also to identify the priorities for organizational development (and this is again referred to in Chapter 14). It also provides an understanding of how your leadership structure facilitates the achievement of objectives (or not), and also may assess the quality and depth of leadership within the organization. Once such an audit mechanism is created (and it may include your other regular internal survey questions), it can track and compare development over time.[3]

ACE as a leadership and organization effectiveness diagnostic tool

ACE Insights is as relevant in assessing the drivers of organizational effectiveness for a commercial organization as it is for a university, a National Health Service Trust or any other public sector organization.

For example, within one NHS Primary Care Trust (PCT) in the South West of England, it was used very rapidly to define the organizational development plan for that trust to meet its World Class Commissioning obligations. The engagement of the workforce in this process, combined with the quick wins that the survey identified, resulted in the trust being placed in the top quartile of PCTs in the Department of Health staff survey (particularly in 'staff sense of value'), and being nominated for the *Health Service Journal*'s 'Primary Care Organization of the Year'. With the same PCT, the output of the survey also informed the full, deliberate appreciation (see Chapter 14) that was initiated simultaneously to shape a holistic, integrated plan to deliver the most efficient and effective health services for the people of that county – all that is needed now is development of the leadership capacity to execute the plan, a key task on the plan itself.

CASE STUDY

Several years ago I was approached by a supermarket chain. It had been a very profitable discount chain, retailing branded products and its 'own brand' goods, which were basically cheap ingredients in plain packaging, stacked in cluttered aisles creating 'a feeling of plenty' – but with a huge margin attached. To quote the company HR Director, it was 'going down the tubes, it was the store managers' fault – they were not good leaders, how could they be fixed?'

I spent a couple of days nosing around some supermarkets talking to people. Then I assembled 24 store managers, used an exercise to teach the ACE concept, and asked them what needed to be changed using ACE as a diagnostic. This is a précis of what they said.

Ability

- Too many people in the whole chain lack the ability for their role, eg Category Managers lack retail experience (too many 'un-blooded MBAs and graduates', many middle and senior managers are not seen as effective leaders). Selection is often based on technical skill rather than behaviour and skill combined.

- Store managers and supervisors all need leadership development; specifically they felt they lacked the ability to:
  - think clearly;
  - facilitate problem solving;
  - brief people clearly about plans, objectives and individual tasks and roles;
  - give feedback, coach and develop;
  - perform these leadership functions in an appropriate manner or style.

- The training system builds in differences rather than ensures consistency. Lack of a real training centre combined with the stores' system of paying part-time staff on training out of a store's budget while measuring the store manager on his P & L sheet, means induction and role-related training is either not conducted or only partially completed.

Clarity

- There is no common or meaningful understanding of the company vision, nor a sense of purpose, nor of the strategy and tactics to achieve this.

- There is no common understanding of the intended difference or similarity – and its rationale – between the three types of store in the chain (one for dry and canned goods, one with a limited range of fresh produce, and a third with a wide range of fresh produce).

- A newly launched 'premium' home brand range sends a very different message to the no frills, cheap home brand – what are we now trying to be?

- There is no clarity of decision-making authority constraints or freedom of action. As a result it is assumed that no freedom of action (or initiative) is permitted.

- The ground rules change weekly because of unclear thinking and poor planning (eg, wage control, sales, receivables policy and process). Because 'the reasons why' are often poorly explained or not explained, compliance is a problem.

Environment

- Store managers are not allowed to order stock, stock is allocated centrally. The result is either 'out of stocks' or inappropriate stock for stores' local demographics, which remain unsold.
- The stock system is reactive and allows no flexibility to order in anticipation of local events, weather and so on.
- Procedures do not allow store managers to make best use of space for displays and align merchandising to local customers' needs and preferences. There is no freedom to merchandise excessive stock allocations.
- There is little or no advance warning of the amount of stock due to be delivered, consequently it is impossible to have the right amount of staff available for unloading, etc. Any notice about stock quantities is generally incorrect.
- Senior managers should be more visible in the stores more often (not just the store closest to head office), and take a genuine interest in people.
- A few of the new senior executives are excellent, but most middle managers hide behind voicemail or secretaries, have little sense of accountability and practise 'buck passing'.
- There is little or no recognition or use of basic courtesies above store level (no use of please and thank you by leaders). For example, instead of a 'Well done, losses have been cut by X per cent, what are the reasons for this and how can we improve it' remarks are along the lines of 'Do better.'
- Most training is left to the individual stores. It is either not conducted or is done badly. Employees who are sent away on training remain on a store's payroll budget, and training is often cut short because the store budget does not allow training to be finished.
- The performance management system does not encourage leaders to fulfil their leadership responsibilities, it is geared simply to cost-cutting and budgets and not 'people measures'.
- People who care about the company and offer suggestions about improvements are regarded as 'whingers' and ignored, whereas those doing real damage (quiet survivors who do not care) are regarded as better performers.

Clearly the store managers recognized their own lack of leadership ability, but they were not being set up for success. 'Fixing their ability' would be a waste of time until the organizational clarity and environment issues were addressed – which meant 'fixing the senior leaders'! My report sent shock waves around the top team. Shortly after I started work on the project, the board sold off half of the company and realized the value of their property portfolio!

Organizational conditions: integrated leadership

> **Integrated Leadership**
>
> Leaders at every level learned the ACE agenda and common processes for decision making, planning, briefing and coaching that build alignment, trust and flexibility. Results include:
>
> - Change Time halved: A planned two-year change project has been implemented in 12 months with constant headcount reduction and minimal angst.
>
> - Metrics doubled: Applications processed within service level agreement turnaround times have risen from 40% to 80%.
>
> - Metrics doubled: A fully functional quality control system is in place – Vetting from 37% to 100%.
>
> - Leaders are able to lead their teams in difficult times, and they take change easily in their stride.
>
> - A full multi-skilling programme has been implemented in the last 6 months across all disciplines.
>
> - Morale is high and retention increased.
>
> - 'Best Practice' procedures implemented and enhanced.
>
> (Mike Begg, National Manager, Capital Finance HBOSA)

Within every organization there is a leadership environment that tends to vary with the organization, but it is usually possible to identify three levels of leadership; and the larger the organization, the more distinct these layers may become. This is shown in Figure 3.4.

'Tactical' (or episodic) leadership is the level at which junior and front-line managers and supervisors operate. They exercise leadership to solve a series of 'local problems' that require relatively quick solutions – leadership episodes that are usually bounded by time and resources. Tactical work is the day-to-day delivery of business processes and their outputs, some of which may be defined by standard operating procedures (SOPs) the extent of which will be determined by the nature of the business (a retailer may need more defined SOPs to provide consistent (tactical) customer experiences than a consultancy solving strategic problems). It is these leadership episodes that provide the opportunities for the leader to build the respect, confidence and trust that the team has to have in the leader if he or she is to be an effective leader.

It is the function of what used to be called 'middle management' and the staff in head offices to provide 'operational' leadership. They interpret policy and make strategy and objectives meaningful for more junior leaders, and assist in shaping

FIGURE 3.4 Integrated levels of leadership

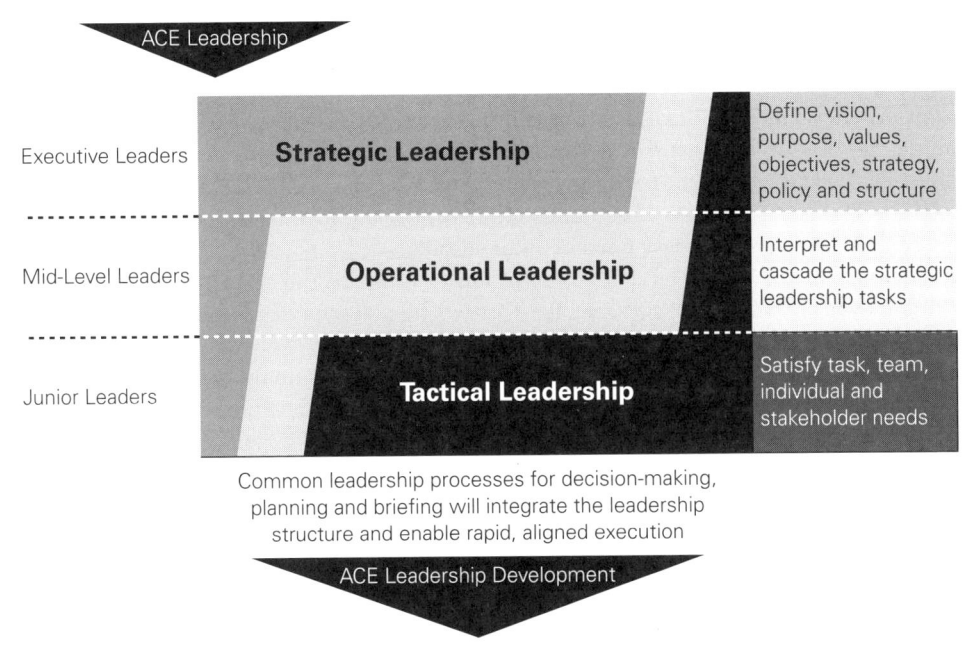

```
                    ACE Leadership

Executive Leaders    Strategic Leadership        Define vision,
                                                 purpose, values,
                                                 objectives, strategy,
                                                 policy and structure

Mid-Level Leaders    Operational Leadership      Interpret and
                                                 cascade the strategic
                                                 leadership tasks

Junior Leaders       Tactical Leadership         Satisfy task, team,
                                                 individual and
                                                 stakeholder needs

        Common leadership processes for decision-making,
        planning and briefing will integrate the leadership
          structure and enable rapid, aligned execution
                    ACE Leadership Development
```

After Dr John Potter & RMAS | © Jeremy Tozer, 1997–2006

a climate in which effective leadership is taken for granted. They create an environment where leadership episodes may take place successfully on a day-to-day basis and they are likely to have responsibility for several leadership episodes or tasks executed both sequentially and in parallel. Their work also involves creating and promoting a day-to-day culture in the organization that makes clear which behaviours are desirable and which are not. Where the nature of the business requires increased agility and flexibility in developing, implementing and adapting plans, this level may require relatively more leaders than a business that requires greater uniformity (or conformity). Unfortunately (and to the detriment of organizational effectiveness), in many businesses these two levels tend to be confused, merged, muddled and referred to variously as 'operational', 'tactical' or the execution level with no distinction between the leadership work conducted in these levels.

The 'strategic' leaders define the vision or end-state and long-term objectives of the enterprise and the strategic plan for achieving that end-state; they lay down policies that give direction to behaviour; define the framework in which others work (structure, systems and processes); and represent the organization externally. This level should also be defining the conceptual component of corporate or commercial effectiveness described in Chapter 2. Their views and personal example set the tone and direction for others to follow – as senior people they are successful, and their behaviour is to be imitated. They influence all, especially the middle managers and their staff, by their decisions and actions.

These three areas of leadership within organizations are not discrete, which is why each level reaches into the other two. If we consider the work of senior executives in more detail we can appreciate that they can and do lead others in accomplishing short-term tasks; they also have their own teams of 'subordinate leaders' to build and maintain, to coach and develop, to make decisions and create plans with and to brief. The CEO's job includes (but is not limited to) the same leadership responsibilities for his or her team that the front-line team leader has – only complexity, unknown variables, level of responsibility, authority and time horizon differ in this respect. The CEO will also have additional responsibilities to the board, to shareholders, to strategic business partners and so on.

Senior executives also have a contribution to make to the operational leadership climate even if their main energies are focused on strategic leadership, by checking that operational leaders 'are clear' and by ensuring that the organizational values are adhered to and demonstrated in their behaviour. Values dictate the code of acceptable behaviour and should underpin decisions (although too often values are merely something to be printed on mugs and hand-outs in HR offices). The example has to be set at the top because it is interpreted as the behaviour that leads to personal success within the company and thus may be imitated down through the organization.

Organizational leaders should not rely purely on information fed upwards – they need to 'get out onto the ground' and talk to front-line employees to form an appreciation of how information or plans have really been interpreted and executed. They also demonstrate their concern for people by such visits – providing that they show a genuine interest during conversation, and take appropriate follow-up action based upon what they hear.

The operational level has considerable contributions to make in both directions by interpreting policy and providing the day-to-day framework for tactical leadership to occur while keeping the strategic leaders informed of developments, issues, areas of concern, actual progress and so on which influence future decisions.

Leaders at the tactical level, where energies are concentrated on solving short-term problems and carrying out short-term tasks, need to align themselves to strategy and have contributions to make to strategy, possibly from research and development findings or the lessons of newly tried techniques and processes, or from access to 'market intelligence' and knowledge of customer needs.

As an FMCG (Fast Moving Consumer Goods) sales account manager, I was required to 'sell in' a brand of nappies on their launch in Australia. Since we were in the company's Asia Pacific region we received the APAC packaged variant – with Japanese, Malay, Mandarin, Thai on it – just about every Asian language was prominent, but the English text was hard to spot. Immediately the sales force said this was unsellable in Australia because, unsurprisingly, most Australians speak English! However, we were in APAC and the sales force was not something to be listened to, so off we went to sell the unsellable. In most parts of the world, the product had huge market share; it was a very efficacious product. However, it failed in Australia. For a year we had to sell the unsellable (demoralizing), which was eventually replaced by the US packaged variant; but we never reached the same share as other countries.

How well strategic leaders listen, how actively they talk to people at the front, how effective the front-line staff are at gathering intelligence, and how effective the formal upwards feedback systems are, dictate the extent to which tactical leaders may inform strategy. Strategic leaders need to check that what is strategically desirable is tactically possible – this is why Generals have helicopters to visit front-line units, job descriptions that are pure leadership roles, and have headquarters staff that allow leaders to lead without getting caught up in 'niff naff and trivia'.

Tactical leadership at every level is the means for cascading strategic plans and enabling execution, and the lack of it by strategic leaders, and the lack of any organizational system for it, is often the cause of organizational failure to achieve strategic aims. Tactical leadership is primarily concerned with individual leaders' personal leadership ability – their actions and behaviour (or style or emotional intelligence, whichever language you prefer). Leadership ability is explored in detail in the next chapter.

One way of looking at work is to describe any work as a series of layered, concurrent and consecutive problems to solve and decisions to make (some problems are called 'challenges' or 'obstacles', others 'opportunities', 'projects' or 'change initiatives'). Developing effectiveness in these areas is the core to building organizational capacity and the foundation for learning other skills (negotiation, conflict resolution and so on). When leaders are clear about their actual role (and so many have ineffective beliefs about leadership) and know 'what to do' (the steps of a process), all experience shows that they are better able to develop 'how they do it' (flexible and appropriate style) as their confidence in the use of the tools of their trade is built.

As we have said, the work of leaders at all levels involves performing the functions of:

- problem solving and decision making;
- detailed planning and briefing;
- controlling and coordinating;
- supporting, enabling and coaching (providing resources and moral support, removing obstacles);
- informing and updating;
- evaluating and reviewing progress.

The principles used to lead a large group are the same as those used to lead a small group. It is a matter of appropriate organization.
(Sun Tzu, *The Art of War*)

Both the supervisor and the chief executive need to facilitate problem solving, provide briefings for and coach their immediate teams and so on. The key differences in level of leadership are complexity, the time-horizon required in the leader by the role, the leader's personal impact over time, and the leader's level of felt responsibility.

Common 'intelligent' methods or processes can be introduced for much of this leadership work, especially the clarity and engaging steps of problem solving, decision making, planning and briefing ('intelligent' because they are universally applicable hand rails to be applied with thought and discretion, not rote methods to be slavishly and blindly adhered to, creating processes behind which ineffective leaders may hide). The steps in a process can remain the same at each level, only the number of variables or complexity in the process changes by level as does the appropriate style with which a leader 'intelligently' performs these functions.

Tactical leadership is therefore the basis for a common organizational understanding of the role of leaders and the language of leadership, and for building organizational capability. This enables a common framework using a common language, and creates a systemic means of rapid alignment and engagement of diverse units, teams and individuals with a built-in means of continuous learning and adjustment. This is another intellectual route that 'justifies' the effects-based leadership (EBL) approach outlined in Chapter 1, the tools of which are explained in detail in Chapters 14, 15 and 16.

Notes

1 Ernst & Young Global Pharmaceutical Industry Report, 2011, *Progressions: Building Pharma 3.0*.
2 Judith M Bardwick, 1993, *Danger in the Comfort Zone*, AMACOM.
3 A sample spreadsheet of ACE Insights questions that colour codes itself depending upon input may be found at **www.tozerconsulting.com**.

04
Understanding leadership ability

- Leadership and leader defined
- Leadership and management
- The leader and shared leadership
- The relationship between leader and follower
- The what of leadership: leadership knowledge and skills to perform functions
- The leader's role in clarifying role relationships
- Delegation of tasks
- The how of leadership: leadership style and behaviour
- Leader/follower relationships
- Personal values and standards
- Power, authority and leadership behaviour
- Leadership thought: how people think and intellect aligned to level of work
- Annex A: Leadership role profile

Leadership and leader defined

If we are to select leaders and develop leadership, it helps to have a clear understanding of those two terms. In recent years, more books have been written about leadership than about any other business or professional subject. Some authors have provided their own definitions of leadership, while many more have quoted others. Here is a selection of definitions of leadership:

> *Leadership is getting somebody else to do something you want done because he wants to do it.*
>
> (President Dwight Eisenhower)

> *Leadership is a psychological force that has nothing to do with morals or good character or even intelligence: nothing to do with ideals or idealism. It is a matter of relative will*

powers, a basic connection between one animal and the rest of the herd. Leadership is a process by which a single aim and unified action are imparted on the herd. Not surprisingly it is most in evidence in times or circumstances of danger or challenge. Leadership is not imposed like authority. It is actually welcomed and wanted by the led.

(Corelli Barnett, historian)

Leadership – that combination of example, persuasion and compulsion that makes men do what you want them to; it is an extension of personality. It is the most personal thing in the world for the simple reason that it is just plain you.

(Field Marshal Viscount Slim)

Leadership is the ability to elicit extraordinary performance from ordinary people.

(Sir John Harvey-Jones)

Leadership – The capacity and the will to rally men and women to a common purpose, and the character which will inspire confidence.

(Field Marshal Montgomery)

Leadership – the process that goes on between leader and follower (which is mainly emotional, although there is an intellectual aspect as well); and the context of the leadership (this concerns the destination towards which the leader points, which is usually rational but may contain highly emotional elements too).

(Alistair Mant)[1]

Current Actual Capability =
   f(Cognitive Power . Values . Skilled Knowledge . Wisdom) – Temperamental Defects.

(Jaques and Clement)[2]

All of these are valid, but perhaps the most useful are those given by Montgomery, Mant, and Jaques and Clement. Montgomery provides his hallmark clarity, together with a working definition with which it is hard to disagree and which facilitates practical application. Mant splits leadership into the social process (which must be based upon a relationship of mutual trust and confidence if it is to work), and the purpose of the leadership. If this purpose is clearly 'noble' or useful, (as charitable or public service work is), then there is usually less demand on the personal aspect of leadership (the persuasion or rallying), because the purpose is itself persuasive.

Jaques and Clement take an approach that is quite different to many others. They view leadership as a matter of competence in a specific role that carries with it leadership accountability. They provide a formula that defines capability as a function of cognitive power (capability to do a particular kind of work at a given level), the value that person attaches to their (leadership) work, the skilled application of knowledge, wisdom (the soundness of a person's judgement about people and the ways of the world) less the impact of personality (and an absence of any dysfunctional personal characteristics). In comparing these two definitions, 'will' may be equated with 'value attached to leadership work', and 'capacity' may be equated with 'skill, knowledge, wisdom and cognitive power'.

Where they differ, and where most soldier authors differ from Elliott Jaques' view (as became clear in discussions with Dr Jaques), is in the requirement for character, or notable traits. Jaques stated that only the absence of dysfunctional characteristics is necessary. The view that this book will pursue is that an absence of dysfunctional characteristics in the presence of the other elements of capability will enable the leader to exercise an adequate quality of leadership, but that teams and organizations wishing to excel in their performance, particularly in turbulent times, require leaders to have 'that bit more'.

There is nothing in life like a clear definition.
(The Duke of Wellington)

We shall return to these themes shortly, but for now let us re-examine the definitions that were provided in Chapter 2; their usefulness will become clear as we progress:

Leadership: the capacity and will to rally people to a common purpose willingly, together with the character that inspires confidence and trust.
(Adapted from Field Marshal Montgomery)

Leader: a person responsible for achieving organizational objectives through the work of others, and for building and maintaining the team that he or she is a member of by creating the conditions for their success.
(Tozer)

Leadership

The word 'willingly' has been added to Montgomery's definition to emphasize the point that people must want to do something if they are to perform to their best. Whilst confidence is dependent on trust, it also has been emphasized because all too often there is a 'them and us' syndrome in organizations that is due to a lack of trust which, to quote James Strong, a former CEO of Qantas, 'gives rise to cynicism and suspicion at the motives and intentions of the company at every development'. Building trust takes time, consistency and hard work; it is maintained by a balancing act often on a knife-edge and it is all too easily destroyed by a thoughtless word or action. Since both individual leaders and the teams of individuals whom they would lead are unique, leadership must be considered to be individual in its application. This is reflected in the use of the word 'character'.

It's not about being nice. If you want to be a popular boss, the trick is to take responsibility.
(Alistair Mant)

Leader

A separate definition has been considered and articulated to define 'leader' for several reasons:

- To recognize the fact that anyone may display leadership if they choose to.
- To allow the concept of shared leadership to operate.
- To emphasize the point that leaders have responsibility.

This responsibility has three parts:

1 to the people that you lead for their development, welfare, administration and so on;
2 to your organization for their tasking and deployment; and
3 for the performance and actions of the people that you lead.

This book will pursue the view that there are three elements involved in the development and exercise of leadership, two of which are concerned with your relationships with people above, below and beside you in your organizational structure (technically speaking your superiors, peers and subordinates – terms I shall use for the sake of clarity).

On one hand there is the practical side of demonstrating leadership, acting out its functions and showing that you – the leader – have the capacity to lead using various skills, processes or concepts – the 'tools'. Much of this activity can be reduced to 'first principles' and 'standard operating procedures' that have universal application and which may be applied with discretion, common sense and intelligence. This is an approach that can leave effective 'ways' embedded in an organization and transcend the movement of people into and out of the organization. Skills and knowledge are trainable and learnable.

On the other hand, there are those behaviours and qualities you need to display so that others may recognize them in you and be moved to follow you – this is the character that inspires confidence and trust. This may also be called 'emotional intelligence', or flexible or appropriate leadership style. It is more easily developed when aspiring leaders are confident in knowing what to do (ie, they have the understanding derived from experience in applying concepts, processes and skilled knowledge). Behaviour (and the attitude or behavioural intention that gives rise to it) is not so much trained as nurtured and developed over time.

More on behaviour (or personal traits and values that are reflected in choices and behaviour) in Chapter 8, but in brief these are not developed in comfortable, easy and challenge-free conditions but by placing demands on leaders that produce spontaneous behaviour – behavioural evidence. To develop such qualities, personal limits must be extended and stress and pressure are necessary to do this. In this way, confidence, self-esteem (amongst other qualities) and personal attitudes are developed; and individuals learn about themselves and others' perception of them from the behavioural evidence. This might be termed 'personal development', concurrent with the assimilation of skills and knowledge.

The third element relates to how one thinks and one's intellect or cognitive power. That is to say, thinking is governed by purpose (which legitimizes the leader) and by having the intellectual horsepower to organize and process information to cope with the level of complexity of the work that one faces and the time span over which one's work has impact and downstream consequences. This matures over time with stretching experiences. This view of leadership is illustrated in Figure 4.1.

There is a fourth element that is required if one is to demonstrate effective leadership; this also appears in Montgomery's definition of leadership as 'the will', and Jaques and Clement's definition as motivation to lead or the value attached to leadership work. Leaders must have an innate and genuine commitment to the organization's purpose and a desire or motivation to lead people, and be responsible for those people, their performance and for helping them overcome obstacles in their path if they are to be successful – they must value being a leader. As a recruitment consultant, I observed that many people pursuing higher level roles wanted the status and pay associated with 'a bigger job' and the functional growth and responsibility, but rarely wanted full responsibility for people and their unpredictable actions. If a person does not place value on the leadership role, and does not have a genuine desire for

FIGURE 4.1 The components of leadership ability

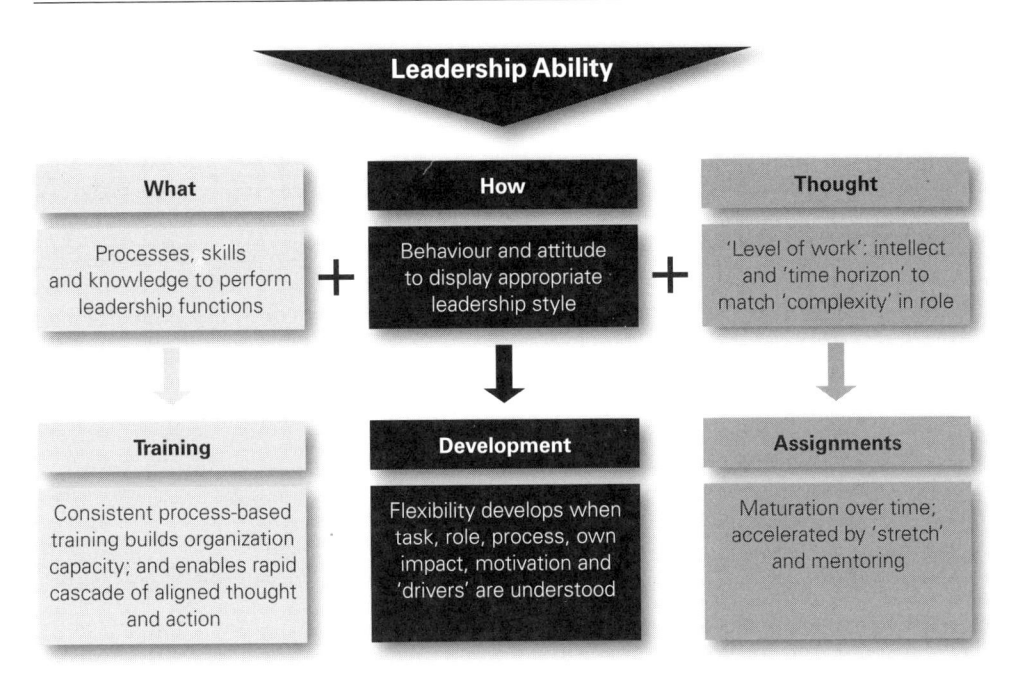

```
                        Leadership Ability

        What                    How                   Thought

  Processes, skills       Behaviour and attitude    'Level of work': intellect
  and knowledge to  +     to display appropriate  + and 'time horizon' to
  perform leadership      leadership style          match 'complexity' in role
  functions
       ↓                       ↓                         ↓
     Training              Development               Assignments

  Consistent process-based   Flexibility develops when   Maturation over time;
  training builds organization   task, role, process, own   accelerated by 'stretch'
  capacity; and enables rapid    impact, motivation and     and mentoring
  cascade of aligned thought     'drivers' are understood
  and action
```

© Jeremy Tozer, 2007

the responsibility that is part and parcel of being a leader, then that person is unlikely to be successful. Indeed, when people hold jobs that they do not really want or enjoy, particularly if responsibility for results, outputs, people's behaviour, creating clarity, resolving conflict and so on are features of that job, they will never be entirely successful and will very probably have a constant sense of discomfort and suffer from stress. It is unfortunate that in many organizations advancement and increases in pay are very often associated with responsibility for people, rather than for functional expertise and working as an 'individual contributor' operating at higher levels of complexity on projects requiring a long time horizon. Selection must start with identifying motivation and the desire to lead and be responsible.

The beauty and strength of the template at Figure 4.1 is fourfold:

1. It is simple, easy to understand and relate to, and implement.
2. It is not a slave to any one theory of leadership; many theories are valid but few are complete and holistic.
3. It may be applied universally to any level within any enterprise, with the appropriate level of learning and development support provided.
4. It is derived from the definition of leadership already presented, and when applied to recruitment, selection, learning and development, performance management and reward and recognition will give the benefits of consistency and congruency in practices, policies and procedures throughout the organization.

Leadership and management

> Leadership – People, Confidence and Turbulence
>
> Management – Spreadsheets, Stuff and Numbers

Here we will take the view that management involves the allocation, organization and control of resources to achieve objectives and the measurement of progress. Management requires the capability to deploy a range of task-focused techniques and skills to enhance and facilitate planning, organizing, monitoring and measuring. A manager need only have 'management skills' if he or she does not have to interact with people. As soon as people are involved then management alone is insufficient. We all use the expression that 'soldiers are led into battle'; I have yet to read or hear of soldiers being 'managed into battle'. It seems to me that management is an essential part of being an effective leader, but leadership is not part of management.

> *There is a difference between leadership and management. Leadership is of the spirit, compounded of personality and vision; its practice is an art. Management is of the mind, more a matter of accurate calculation, of statistics, of methods, timetables and routine; its practice is a science. Managers are necessary. Leaders are essential.*
>
> (Field Marshal Viscount Slim of Burma)

To view leadership as an aspect of a manager's role is to downgrade the importance of leadership and therefore the priority afforded to it. This can be a recipe for disaster. Sadly many organizations unwittingly perpetuate a misplaced view about leadership by the unconscious and habitual use of the term 'manager' in the titles on business cards and the separation in some organizations of leadership development from management development.

Successful management is readily measured against objective criteria but managers and executives are not leaders until their position has been ratified in the hearts and minds of those whom they would lead.

The leader and shared leadership

The reason that the definitions of leader and leadership that I use are differentiated is that it allows for the concept of 'shared leadership', but recognizes that someone has to be responsible.

For example, imagine you are in the crew of the yacht 'Mark Twain' (as I was for several years). There are times, such as rounding a downwind sea mark (a buoy marking the course and around which yachts must turn) when you are racing, that shared leadership is evident. In such a manoeuvre one wants to keep going as fast as one can for as long as one can, which means keeping the spinnaker hoisted for as long as possible. But for the next upwind leg, the spinnaker has to be replaced with the genoa (a different sail).

As you close with the mark, the skipper is likely to lose sight of it so authority is delegated to the foredeck hand to call for the genoa to be hoisted, then for the spinnaker halyard, sheets and braces (ropes at the three corners of the spinnaker) to be run to take the spinnaker in. Then the mid-deck takes over to clear the spinnaker pole and set the genoa.

Eventually when the mark is rounded and everything is once again 'shipshape and Bristol fashion', leadership returns to the skipper. Leadership is rotated because it has to be, but the one thing that does not rotate is the fact that at all times the skipper remains responsible for the safety of the yacht and her crew (as the helpful race committee reminded us by radio during the fateful 1998 Sydney Hobart race!). Leadership rotates in all effective high-performing teams, but not responsibility. So leadership is both a cause and an effect or outcome. Leadership at lower levels is the outcome of good leadership at higher levels, whether on a boat or in a business.

As a leader you are a member of the team, but somewhat removed from it. This has to be the case if you are to view the team in the context of the 'bigger picture', build the identity of the collective team entity, take the hard decisions that inevitably arise as well as take full responsibility – for performance, people's development, administration and welfare. The inexperienced leader may try to be liked by his or her team; this is a serious error – the leader needs to be respected (and respect has to be earned), but the effective leader does not need to be liked. Part of leadership is about relieving other team members of the burden of decision and of responsibility. This can never be given away nor shared, and it is one of the factors that differentiate the leader from the led.

One of the objectives and outcomes of good leaders is to make themselves redundant in operational terms, so that desired actions (to achieve 'higher intent') and behavioural norms continue whether or not the leader is present. The leader's coaching and briefing should result in a team of followers who are so competent, confident and 'clear' that day-to-day situations can be managed by them without the direct involvement of the leader. This involves adapting to change and then actively seeking opportunities to improve things. This frees the leader from routine tactical issues and enables him or her to pay attention to bigger issues and to remove obstacles before the team gets to them.

The relationship between leader and follower

General Sir John Hackett[3] has some very interesting things to say about the relationship between the leader and follower. To discern his key points, you will need to separate the message from what might be termed the 'contemporary and politically correct' aversion to some of the words that were in common use when this was written. It has implications for both 'the doing' and 'being' of leadership:

> For the discharge of the function of leadership the establishment of a dominant position for the leader over the led is indispensable. How does this come about?
>
> In the archetypal leader/follower relationship it happens of its own accord. I do not mean here the establishment of dominance by brute force and fear. In all I have to say here I am concerned exclusively with subordination by consent.
>
> The leader has something the others want and that only he can provide. The man who can show the tribesmen where the water hole is has a special knowledge: he can direct those in need to a place where their need can be satisfied. But you would call him no

more than a guide and not a leader unless something else was present. This something is partly the ability to find an answer to a problem which the others cannot solve. But there is also the power, when difficulties have to be overcome, to help people overcome them. A capacity to help people in the overcoming of the difficulties which face them in a joint enterprise is one of those things which distinguish the person who is a leader from the person who is no more than a guide.

In the more complex leader/follower relationship which you find in a modern army the leader is still giving something which the led require. All are bound together in a common undertaking whose success is of common concern. ... What the leader has to give is the direction of a joint effort which will bring success. That is what he is there for, and he must have sufficient mastery of the techniques involved to do what is demanded of him by those he leads. Very early on in the inquiry, you will notice, there emerges the suggestion that the function of leadership cannot be discharged on the one side without a requirement to be led on the other.

To make a commanding position over other men acceptable to them it is also necessary for the man holding it to possess in a higher degree than they do qualities which they respect.

You have in fact, as it seems to me, to be good at what is done by the professionals under your management if you are to exercise effective leadership over them, especially where the leader/follower relationship comes under considerable strain. It is not good enough to be able simply to coordinate... and the heavier the stresses the more clearly this emerges.

Of course people set in authority at all levels in an army can be carried along by the machine itself, caught up in its rank structure. But when this happens the relationship between leaders and led may be too weak to withstand strain. It is very likely to break down when stress is heavy.

Can we distinguish between the qualities required in any leadership situation and the qualities required in specific situations... Knowing what it is best to do is important but knowing how to get things done seem to me clearly more so... In fact, the heavier the stress on a group the higher the importance of what I might call personal qualities as distinct from professional competence.

The essential leadership situation does not arise unless there is a recognised requirement by someone to be led. Leadership is, in fact, a response on one side to an awareness of need on the other.

It is just worthwhile, perhaps, pointing out here that the relationship between a leader and those led is essentially different in one important respect when looked at from different ends of the nexus. The leader leads a group. However much he seeks to bind the members together in it by individual treatment his responsibility is over the group and to them as a whole. The member of the group, on the other hand, however much he may be bound together with the other members, responds to the leader essentially as an individual.

The power of example is very important to people under stress. For one thing it affords an outlet for hero worship, to which there seems to be an important and deep-rooted inclination in men. The person under stress is aware of inadequacies. He sees someone else apparently less burdened in this way. To some extent he identifies with that other person. This gives him some release. He is then likely to be grateful and become even more biddable. He will be even more open to the influence of suggestion and example than he was before.

One important thing in the leader/follower relationship, it has always seemed to me, is that you get what you give, and no more. You are only really entitled to ask from below what you are prepared to give to those above. Beginners in this game have sometimes thought to acquire prestige with their subordinates by affecting a fine disregard of their superiors. But buying compliance by disloyalty is a short-term expedient which is in the highest degree dangerous.

The what of leadership: leadership knowledge and skills to perform functions

The purpose of this section is to give you a real understanding of what an effective leader does – the leader's real role and full range of responsibilities for which skills and knowledge are required to undertake the core functions. This will help you to develop yourself, increase your own confidence, and develop further your own leadership potential.

Leadership knowledge

An effective leader's knowledge comes in four parts. First, there is knowledge of the organization and the business it is in, and of the team's functional expertise (such as sales, marketing, accounting, manufacturing and so on). This enables them to network around the organization, leverage support and assistance when it is required, and it contributes to effective decision making. That lies outside the realm of this book.

Second is knowledge of your team members. Any leader must know his or her team, both as individuals and collectively. To be able to guide their thinking, to know what will inspire and what will engage, a leader must know how and what they think about the challenges and work that is set for them. If leaders know this, they are more likely to be able to predict and anticipate their team members' reactions. To get the best from teams, leaders have to direct them like an orchestra, using their knowledge of each to best advantage in pursuit of the common purpose. All Officer Cadets at Sandhurst are taught that on assuming command of their first platoon, if they do not take over the previous platoon commander's notebook they need to create one with a section for each individual soldier under their command. This notebook should contain essential information such as date of birth, blood group, next of kin details and so on, but its real value is in the comments section. Every time the platoon commander learns something about one of his soldiers he adds to it – the soldier's upbringing and home life, his wife or girlfriend's name, his children's birthdays, favourite football team, aspirations and ambitions, quirks and foibles, and the motivators. This knowledge is invaluable in getting the best from your people, as I found in Northern Ireland throughout the 1980s.

Third is knowledge of yourself – what has shaped you, why you perceive and react in the way that you typically do. This knowledge, or intrapersonal intelligence, is dealt with in Chapter 8.

Fourth is knowledge of leadership concepts, processes, methods and principles. The application of these tools may be called the 'skills of leadership'. While this book cannot develop your skills per se, it will add to your knowledge and if you apply this intelligently, and seek feedback to adjust and develop how you use these tools, you will develop skill and grow in confidence. Arguably the starting point in developing the knowledge required in a leader is to understand something that many leaders' job descriptions overlook, and that is an understanding of the leadership role – the leadership functions that you are employed to perform. From an understanding of the functions that leaders need to perform, flows a list of knowledge that needs to be assimilated and the skills that need to be developed.

The functional approach provides you with a method of observing other leaders' performance critically and measuring your practical leadership ability against theirs. It provides a model against which skills and knowledge may be learnt, while your leadership behaviour and appropriate style may be developed by seeking feedback about how you perform your leadership functions and the impact of your behaviour.

Here is some of the background to the model. The ideas that go to make up this approach to the subject were developed at The Royal Military Academy, Sandhurst (RMAS) in the UK in the 1960s as a result of studies carried out on the leadership course that was being conducted at that time by Professor John Adair[4,5] and senior RMAS instructors. That study revolutionized the understanding of leadership. Until that time, leadership was almost universally developed by studying and trying to emulate lists of leadership qualities. This was not too helpful, because no two organizations used the same lists of qualities despite the leaders in those organizations having identical roles. And in military academies, which at that time were more concerned with leadership than any commercial organization was, few senior officers would agree on the qualities that should gain a place on the list. The ideas spread worldwide, and were adopted by many military academies, business schools and corporate organizations. In the UK it was adopted by the Industrial Society and renamed 'Action-centred leadership'.

Additionally, during the past 50 or so years there have been many studies of the behaviour of people who are grouped together, both voluntarily and compulsorily. Within this framework of group behaviour certain patterns repeat themselves. It seems that people in a group need a leader and there is always someone who, to some level or other, emerges to perform the necessary functions to satisfy the group at the time. It was with the identification of these leadership functions that John Adair produced his theory.

Adair proposes that working groups are like individual people in that they develop their own unique character and have some specific needs in common. He also states that there are three main areas where a leader has to act to satisfy the requirements of a group for leadership. These three areas coincide with the pattern of needs generated by the group and are shown in the Venn diagram created by the three inner circles in Figure 4.2.

Task needs

First, a group needs an external focus, normally a task to complete that, unsurprisingly, should be successfully achieved. Failure introduces pressures that, in a group with no formal or disciplined structure, can lead to members leaving or, in the worst case, the complete disintegration of the group. If opportunities to leave do not exist

FIGURE 4.2 The areas of need for a leader to satisfy

A leader satisfies four 'circles of need' by performing the functions of:

- Problem Solving and Decision-Making
- Planning and Briefing
- Controlling and Coordinating
- Enabling, Supporting and Coaching
- Informing and Updating
- Monitoring and Evaluating

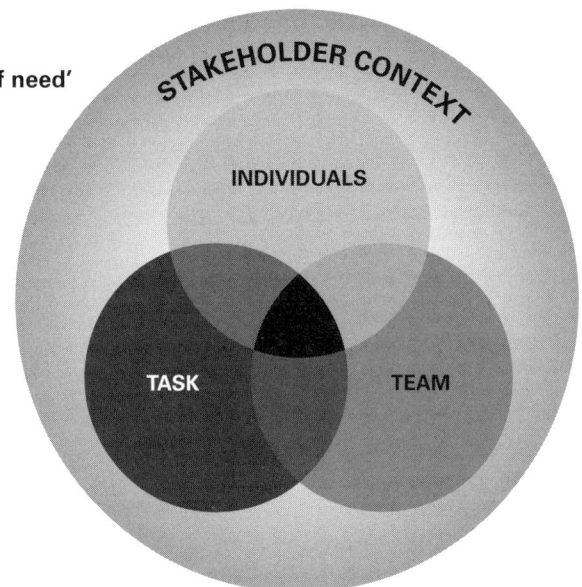

STAKEHOLDER CONTEXT

INDIVIDUALS

TASK

TEAM

After Adair and RMAS | © Jeremy Tozer, 1997

you get an increase in personality conflicts within the group, a decline in general morale, and a falling-off of efficiency. You do find that both the team and individuals' real strengths and weaknesses – their true character – are more vividly seen in conditions of adversity than in good times. The leader's function, your function if you are reading this book, is to ensure that each task given to the team to complete is successfully completed.

Team needs

Second, a team has certain needs if it is to survive as a cohesive social entity. In the first place, once a group has formed, the dynamics of the situation operate to hold it together. You might be aware of the strong bonds of loyalty that have begun to hold your own team together at work. Do you really, voluntarily, have much to do with the people in other work groups in your lunch breaks or do you remain with your own team (unless you need to network!)? If you are honest, you will probably admit that actually it is 'just that I seem to be happier getting on with the people in my team'. You see, group dynamics are at work in your life. Thus, the leader has to satisfy the needs of his or her group: it is the leader's task to ensure its survival.

In realistic terms this means helping it to develop a corporate identity, to forge it into a winning team. If there is a lack of unity or poor relationships within the team then, again, individual satisfaction and task performance suffer. Uniting to face a common external threat or to extinguish internal disruptive behaviour that contravenes 'the norms' is commonly seen as a way of a team maintaining its cohesion.

Individual needs

Third, you must remember that a team is composed of a number of individuals and that each of those individuals has his or her own particular needs in addition to those generated by the team. The task, remember, has to be completed by a group of individual team members and they each need to feel that their contribution to the group is recognized and is important. Their individual need for status and responsibility, their aspirations, ambitions, motivational and development needs – physical, emotional and psychological needs – have to be met by the leader.

I have added a fourth circle has been added around Adair's model. What the team does takes place within a stakeholder context. Within an organization, any team's actions will impact on other teams, groups and individuals, either inside or outside the organization. Also, these actions all take place within a national and organizational culture, and within the operating context such as that described in Chapter 2.

That the three inner circles overlap indicates their interdependence. If you cover the task you can see that sections of both team maintenance and individual needs are also covered. In short, lack of a task, failure to achieve it, or an excessive and continuous emphasis on task-related activity lead to increased disruptive tendencies within the team, and a decrease in individuals' satisfaction with membership of the team – they will leave the team when they find opportunities to work elsewhere.

Thus morale, motivation and discipline deteriorate if this situation is allowed to continue. The converse is also true. When a team successfully completes a task, the degree of group cohesiveness and identity increases, as does the level of individual satisfaction with membership. The moment of victory closes the gaps, emotionally and psychologically, among people and it always generates a rise in the level of morale, pride and esprit de corps. Therefore, when past success has raised the sustained level of morale and team spirit, the momentum that has been generated probably makes future success more probable. This also provides a healthy climate in which individuals can work.

The three areas of need must be balanced against each other; to satisfy one completely will probably be to the detriment of the other two. If this happens, a short-term focus on, say, task needs, must soon be balanced by a focus on satisfying the individual and team needs. The negative effects of excessive task orientation are shown by staff turnover, loss of knowledge and expertise, lack of individual satisfaction or team cohesion. The leader, then, must perform certain functions if he or she is to satisfy all the areas of need that exist; in short the leader must be continuously aware of the real scope of the leader's role and its responsibilities.

The majority of any leader's work comes under the six sequential and cyclic functional headings of problem solving and decision making, planning and briefing, controlling and coordinating, supporting and coaching, informing and updating, and lastly, monitoring and evaluating.

The functional leadership checklist

The functional leadership checklist in Figure 4.3 is a simple matrix that has on the horizontal axis the four areas of need (task, team, individual and stakeholder context), and on the vertical axis the six core leadership functions. Within each 'box',

Understanding Leadership Ability 65

FIGURE 4.3   Functional leadership checklist

Leadership Functions/Area of Need	Achieve TASK	Build and Maintain THE TEAM	Satisfy and Develop INDIVIDUALS	Satisfy STAKEHOLDERS
Problem-Solving and Aligned Decision-Making	• Mission Analysis: Define higher intent, desired effects, clarify aim and purpose, back brief • Identify factors, make deductions, identify and compare courses of action open • Decision	• Select and induct • Establish communication • Clarify ground rules and use of process • Involve team including remote members – facilitate • Detail sub-groups and leaders • Clarify team's mission	• Assess skill level of each person • Use expertise of individuals	• Identify other stakeholders, needs and measures of success • Lobby stakeholders • Establish working 'contracts'
Detailed Planning and Briefing	• Plan: Situation 2 levels up, Mission, Execution (Outline, Tasks/Phases), Admin and Logistics, Control and Comms • Rehearse: accuracy, brevity, clarity and simplicity • Give personal verbal brief where possible	• Give clear enthusiastic briefings • Explain the 'reasons why' and outline plan • Set standards and priorities • Take people into your confidence • Questions from and then to the team	• Check remote people are briefed • Check people know plan in outline and their role in detail • Ask confirmatory open questions • Use expertise of individuals to form plan	• Explain the 'reasons why' and outline plan • Ensure all stakeholders are informed
Controlling and Coordinating	• Direct all activity towards achieving the aim • Provide resources • Agree measures • Monitor progress; re-plan and rebrief if needed	• Coordinate • Maintain standards • Use team dynamics • Review activity	• Maintain standards • Ensure visits and reviews happen • Address individual and stakeholder needs • Offer and seek feedback	• Ensure visits and reviews happen with all stakeholders • Address individual and stakeholder needs
Enabling, Supporting and Coaching	• Ensure continued provision of resources • Build internal and external networks • Anticipate and remove obstacles	• Coach: Aim and Objectives, Situation/Factors (feedback – (example, impact, commit), ACE reasons, deductions), Options, Decision • Learning environment • Maintain team spirit • Build team identity	• Coach • Encourage initiative • Motivational needs • Seek/give feedback • Build self-confidence • Ensure sound administration	• Elicit stakeholder feedback • Lobby for support
Informing and Updating	• Be aware of progress, and of the 'big picture' 2 levels up • Situation Report (Sitrep) briefs up and down the chain	• Recognize and be grateful for team efforts • Keep team informed • Communication	• Thank and praise • Give recognition • Identify and address causes of demotivation	• Keep stakeholders informed of progress
Monitoring and Evaluating	• Debrief – reasons • Mission achieved? • Evaluate success against measures • Mission Analysis, re-plan and re-brief as needed	• Recognize success • Debrief ACE diagnostics – learn from experience • Share learning, ensure adoption • Address team development needs	• Debrief • Listen to feedback • Assess performance, recognize and reward • Address development needs	• Build and manage partnerships for the future in line with the vision/aim and purpose

After Adair and RMAS | Excerpted and updated from the book *Leading Initiatives*, by Jeremy Tozer there is a bullet point summary of the discrete leadership actions that need to be taken to satisfy that area of need, while forming that particular function. To keep this checklist as short as possible, leadership actions have not been repeated in multiple boxes; common sense will tell you when an action is as relevant to 'one box' as another.

For a one-off project that is small in scope this is the essential project management tool; for an ongoing task the checklist becomes cyclical. As soon as you have evaluated a result you may need to re-plan, re-brief, and so on. As a leader in business, you will probably have a whole series of concurrent projects and tasks ongoing. Most of these will be in different phases of completion, and what you might call operational work may be thought of as a never-ending project. Whatever the nature of your leadership work, you will find this a useful checklist to ensure that you are doing all that you should be doing, something which few leadership job descriptions ever make clear.

Processes may be introduced for some of these key functions, especially those relating to decision making, planning and briefing, which are the core tools that ensure alignment within a large organization. As has been said, the same process may apply at every level; all that changes at higher levels is complexity, time span, impact and felt responsibility. This is the basis of building organizational capacity.

At the lowest level of leader in an organization, familiarity with this checklist does much to improve the aspiring leader's ability. A common use of this approach assists in closing the gap between management and supervisors. The checklist is also the foundation for all further leadership development since almost every other subject that may be studied has application in one or more of the checklist boxes.

Few leaders will be naturally inclined and/or able to perform all these functions in equal measure, and many organizations have not been designed to allow leaders to lead, so the leader does not have sufficient time to exercise all these functions. Nor is it desirable for him or her to do so – delegation is an effective mechanism for involving, motivating and developing; it is also essential in freeing up the leader's time to concentrate on more important matters. Aspects of the leader's role may be delegated, such as the task-related/monitoring work of measuring progress and comparing it to anticipated progress, or drafting situation reports and disseminating them after they have been approved by the leader. The leader has to accept and to exercise responsibility, however, for ensuring that all these functions are completed.

Why not assess your functional leadership ability? Read the checklist in Figure 4.4, be honest with yourself, and rate yourself out of 10 in each box – what are your strengths and how can you best play to them? What are your weaknesses and how will you overcome them? Is there a vertical or horizontal line that is consistently weak? What does this mean? (In leadership development programmes, we have often observed a consistently weak self-assessment throughout the individual or stakeholder columns, or the decision making and briefing lines.)

FIGURE 4.4 Functional leadership checklist self-assessment

Function/Area of Need	Task	Team	Individual	Stakeholders
Problem-Solving & Decision-Making				
Planning & Briefing				
Controlling & Coordinating				
Enabling, Supporting & Coaching				
Informing & Updating				
Monitoring & Evaluating				

The leader's role in clarifying role relationships

Executive leaders are responsible for designing organizational structure at the macro level. However, leaders at all levels are responsible for clarifying the role relationships that exist between their team members, and that part of organization structure is introduced here.

In most organizations, a major cause of unnecessary stress, duplication of effort or gaps in the execution of plans, time wasted in meetings, and so on is the lack of clarity that individuals have about how their role relates to their peers around them. This is especially so in ill-defined matrices with their multitude of dotted lines that permeate many organizations. This allows people to hide by creating places where no one anywhere is accountable for anything. Or this creates avoidable conflict when people try to establish the authority they need to meet their accountabilities to their bosses. If structural ground rules are not established, people will naturally invent their own to best advantage causing unnecessary conflict and generally resulting in a huge waste of time at meetings. There are few organizations that do not need to operate some form of matrix structure; a matrix is not inherently wrong. What is wrong is leaving them as unclear as they tend to be.

One telecommunications company that I was associated with went through three restructures in as many years, from a product-based structure (long-distance, mobile, and so on), to a customer-based structure (consumer, corporations, government, etc), and then back to a product-based structure. The fundamental reason why their structures failed them was not that either approach was wrong, but the lack of clarity that was created in role relationships.

As another example, a buyer in retailing organizations is usually accountable for the sales revenue generated for the range of goods that she or he has purchased. The buyers typically are the 'creative lead' in the buying team (the team has both buyers and merchandisers). They design, develop and create the range of goods to be offered to consumers, and work with strategic suppliers in doing this, and they negotiate prices with suppliers. The other half of the buying team are the merchandisers, who are essentially accountants who 'run the numbers': detailed sales analysis, forecasting, planning and budgeting, and order placing. If the merchandiser who supports the buyer is not accountable to the buyer, but to another person working to a different agenda, how can that buyer legitimately be held accountable for the sales of that buyer's range if the merchandiser does not perform adequately, or disagrees with the buyer and does not place the orders that the buyer has requested?

The problem is a lack of alignment between the accountabilities that people have to their boss and the authority that they have to meet those accountabilities. All too often people are told to use their influence to get things done, which is usually their boss's excuse for failing to properly consider the framework in which their people are being forced to work. While authority should be the last resort to make things happen, if a person's role is not legitimized by the clear delegation of authority, his or her role is fundamentally untenable. Authority is usually considered only in the vertical hierarchical sense, with little attention paid to lateral role relationships. Equally, little attention is paid to the role of the 'leader-once-removed' in any organizational structure, which is where we shall start to explore this aspect of structure.

Compare this to my experience as an Intelligence Officer in the Army. As the intelligence officer in 5 Airborne Brigade Headquarters, I worked in a matrix structure. The matrix included my internal peers who worked in operations (plans and deployment), logistics, personnel administration and so on. Externally, the matrix included my team of five NCOs, the sources and agencies providing the material that I worked with (which I had authority to task), and the Intelligence Corps (responsible for my intelligence training, postings and career, and the intelligence policies and processes with which I worked, which I was able to influence through the chain of command). However, my day-to-day role was to meet the intelligence requirements set for me by my Brigade Commander, and in this respect my priority of work and tasking came from the Brigadier via the Chief-of-Staff. In outline, what I had to do was determined by the Brigadier, my approach to doing that was determined by my parent Corps, and how I did that in detail determined by me. This is effective matrix working, a complex network of relationships but with the roles clearly defined by their relationships to each other.

In considering role relationships, too many people and too many HR departments are obsessed with who reports to whom. One can report to many different people about many different things, but from the perspective of making sure that things happen, only one person can give any other person a priority of work and then be held accountable for their outputs. And if no leader is held accountable for the work of others, then there is no leadership structure and nothing will ever get done. This is where the design of structure needs to start, with the recognition of the fundamental principle of 'unity of leadership': only one leader can define a subordinate's priority of work if that leader is to be held accountable for the work of that subordinate.

We shall now consider some basic principles, which intuitively make sense to most readers who have endured the pain of being held accountable for work which they had no authority to influence. These principles embody the paradox of 'discipline creating freedom' described in Chapter 2. While they will make sense almost immediately to many people in the private sector, one may be forgiven for thinking that the public sector might resist this sort of approach. These principles were successfully introduced to a group of people who at first thought were the antithesis of a disciplined approach to leadership and structure: the deans and heads of school found in the faculties of a university, and its supporting directorates. Having understood the value of clarity through various exercises and activities, rational discussion of these principles led to them very quickly being assimilated. Indeed, the only resistance observed was from three or four heads of school out of a population of almost 30, whose leadership performance was ineffective at best.

In most organizations of any size, three-layer hierarchical groups will be seen at the same level across the organization and/or recurring down from the top of the organization. A three-layer group consists of a leader (the Leader-once-Removed (LoR)), a team of peer leaders, and their team members (who are the 'Subordinates-once-Removed (SoR) from their leader's leader). This is represented by levels ABC and BCD in Figure 4.5. Ideally, the number of people involved in such a grouping permits everyone to know everyone else by name (to create what Elliott Jaques[6] calls a 'Mutual Recognition Unit' (MRU)).

FIGURE 4.5 A leadership hierarchy based on levels of work complexity

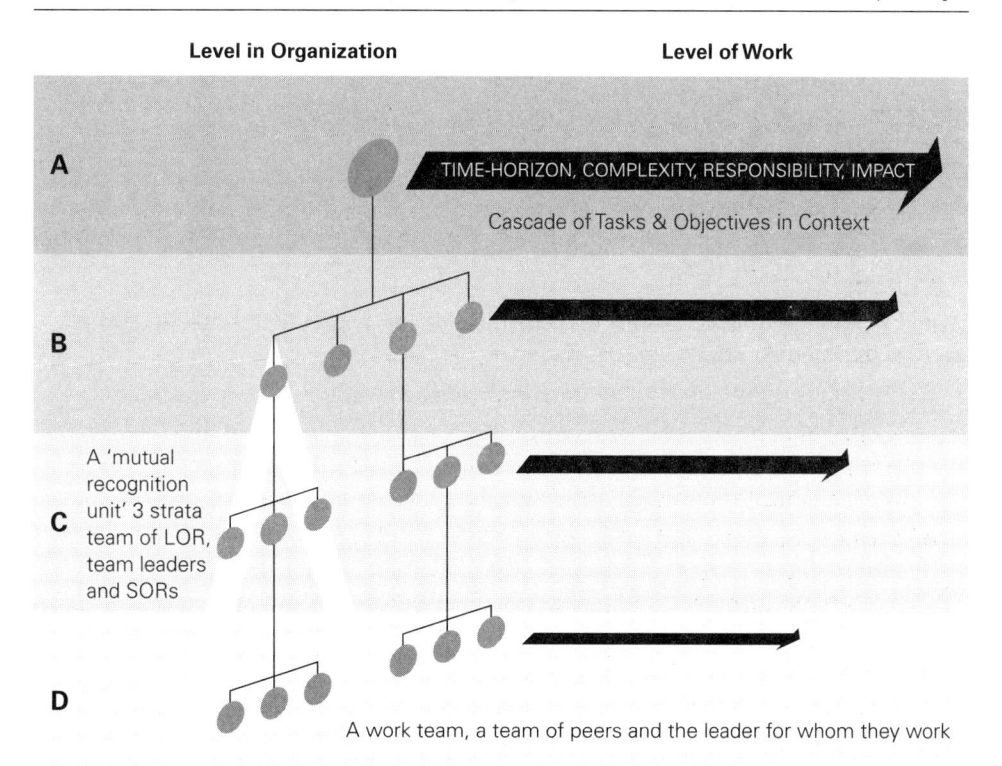

LOR = Leader Once Removed, SOR = Subordinate Once Removed

After Dr Elliott Jaques 1988/1996 | © Jeremy Tozer, 2008

In this structure, the types of role that need clearly defined accountability and authority include the following:

- the leader of a team;
- the leader of an MRU (the LoR in a three-strata grouping);
- lateral role relationships among peers at the same level within an organization.

Vertical authority: the leader of the team

If Senior Leader A holds a Leader B accountable for the outputs of subordinates C1, C2, etc, then Leader B must have the authority to:

- Veto any new appointment of a subordinate to the leader's team.
- Induct and set work context for team members.
- Delegate clear tasks, accountability and authority to team members C1, C2, etc.
- Clarify the role relationships between members of the leader's team.
- Coach and provide regular feedback to team members.
- Provide recognition for performance and verbal appraisal.
- Contribute to performance appraisal and recommend any grade awarded.
- Initiate or recommend removal from role of team members who are not performing to the level required for which expectations have been set.

Vertical authority: the leader-once-removed

While the Leader A at the top of a three-strata MRU has the same responsibility to develop and create the ACE conditions for success for his or her immediate team of peer leaders at B as they do with their teams at C, she or he also has additional responsibilities as the LoR:

- Ensuring that a consistent quality of leadership is provided to the teams of SORs by their leaders across the group.
- Ensuring equality of opportunity and work conditions across the group.
- Establishing clear working relationships between all teams of SoRs across the group. In cases where the SoRs' immediate team leaders have been unable to agree amongst themselves, this is escalated to the LoR.
- Talent pool analysis, development of SORs and succession planning for subordinates. This is because only the LoR has the broader perspective of levels of performance and potential across the group, and it eliminates the effects of conflicts of personality that may occur between a competent team leader and a competent SoR.
- Final decision making in relation to dismissal, removal from role, promotion, transfers, appeals and pay reviews (the SoR's immediate leader may recommend but should not decide).
- Building and sustaining the three-strata MRU team.

FIGURE 4.6 Vertical authority and accountability

	Leader - Subordinate	Leader Once Removed – Subordinate Once Removed	Supervisor – Subordinate	Project Team Leader – Subordinate	Project Leader – Peer Colleague on Project
D = Decide, **R** = Recommend					
Veto appointment	D	D	R	D	D
Induct and set work context	D	D	R	R	D
Determine task type	D	D	R	R	D
Assign task		D	D	D	D
Coach		D	D	D	D
Verbal appraisal (recognition)	D	D	D	D	D
Recorded appraisal (recognition)	R	R	R	D	R
Pay change and bonus within band				D	R
Transfer from role	R	R	R	D	R
Assess potential and career counsel			R	D	R
Change pay band			R	D	R
Promote/Demote			R	D	R
Dismiss			R	D	R
Appeal				D	

After Dr Elliott Jaques 1988/1996 | © Jeremy Tozer, 1997–2006

In addition to the LoR, leader and SoR authority and accountability relationships described above, there are the relationships between a supervisor or a project team leader and their team members to consider, and the relationship between a project leader and a peer colleague on the project. All of these accountability and authority relationships are suggested in Figure 4.6.

Lateral role relationships

Lateral role relationship occurs when C1 has accountability to his or her leader for causing C2 to take action, but C2's leader is accountable for the C2's output. Here is a summary of the types of lateral role relationships that exist:

- *Collateral.* Collateral relationships exist only between a leader's immediate peer subordinate team members.
- *Adviser.* All team members have advisory relationships with their leader; the adviser must use his or her initiative to freely offer advice.
- *Service receiver.* A service receiver must know what services he or she is authorized to receive and from whom (eg support for their PC).
- *Coordinator.* Coordinative roles exist when people not subordinate to each other need to work in concert with one another to get things done.
- *Monitor.* Monitors ensure standards are adhered to.
- *Auditor.* Auditing is a stronger form of monitoring; prescribing is the strongest.
- *Prescriber.* Prescriptive roles (eg safety roles) need to have stop/start type authorities delegated.

When a person, C1, has had the nature of his or her role relationship with their peers clarified, then C1 requires the lateral authorities shown in Figure 4.7 to meet his or her accountabilities to the leader, and the other people at level C need to know that C1 has been delegated these authorities. If a level B leader cannot agree the lateral authorities for his or her Cs among peer level B leaders, then he or she needs to escalate the decision to their LoR, Leader A.

Delegation of tasks

The delegation of tasks is an essential feature of being an effective leader, yet all too often this apparently simple function of leadership is done badly or not at all. You will all have experienced, and suffered from, the frustration at the waste of time, effort, resources and emotional energy that result from unclear tasks and misunderstandings. This often leads to blame, unhelpful sets of beliefs and mythologies within the organization and a negative impact on morale and confidence. People are spontaneously energetic about things that interest them or that they care about; the leadership challenge is not to encourage by incentives but to create work that has inherent meaning and value that allows people to release their energy.

What is a task? A task is an intention to turn an idea into reality through work. As Macdonald[7] has made clear, a machine may be programmed to carry out a task in terms of quantity and quality (within tolerances), time to completion and resource inputs. But people are not machines and if they have no opportunity to exercise discretion in the path followed to complete the task, then the organization will not realize the potential value that they can add by understanding the purpose of their work, how it relates to the work of others, and adapting their work by exercising

FIGURE 4.7 Lateral authority and accountability

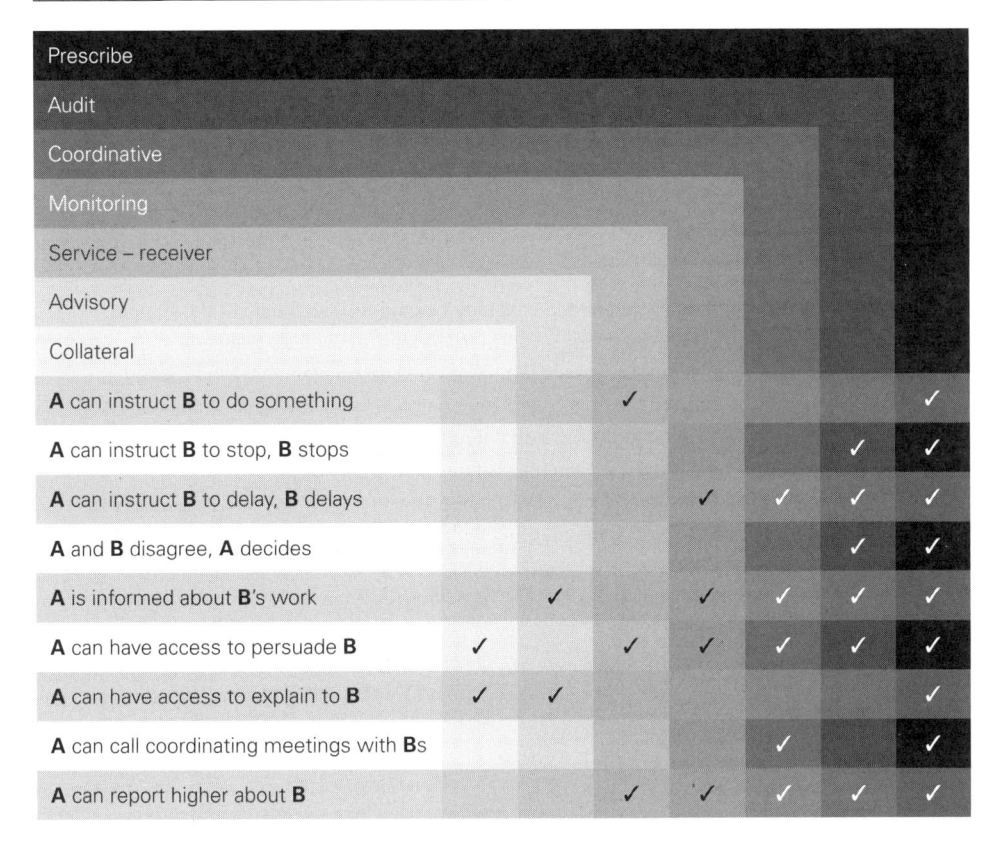

Prescribe							
Audit							
Coordinative							
Monitoring							
Service – receiver							
Advisory							
Collateral							
A can instruct B to do something				✓			✓
A can instruct B to stop, B stops						✓	✓
A can instruct B to delay, B delays				✓	✓	✓	✓
A and B disagree, A decides						✓	✓
A is informed about B's work		✓		✓	✓	✓	✓
A can have access to persuade B	✓		✓	✓	✓	✓	✓
A can have access to explain to B	✓	✓					✓
A can call coordinating meetings with Bs						✓	✓
A can report higher about B			✓	✓	✓	✓	✓

After Dr Elliott Jaques, 1988/1996 | © Jeremy Tozer, 1997–2006

judgement as circumstances change and by conceiving innovative and improved ways of achieving the same or better outcomes.

So when the leader delegates tasks, he or she must make clear the context and purpose of the task (the reasons why it is important), how it relates to the work of others, the outcomes or effects that are expected, and the priorities of those effects. The other components needed to define a task include the quantity or quality of the output, the resources available, the date by which the task must be completed, and the freedom of action (or the boundaries limiting freedom of action) that exists for the person to whom the task has been delegated. If a person is to exercise discretion in achieving a task, then at least one of the elements of quantity/quality, resource use or time should be left open or given with an upper or lower limit. Allowing people to exercise discretion not only engages people but provides leaders with the mechanism for assessing performance in a meritocracy.

Let us consider the reasons for delegation. They are:

- To lighten the leader's load. All leaders have too much to do and too little time to do it in, and some of it is best done by others.

- To devote time and energy to thinking about bigger issues, and for anticipating and planning the future. Undisturbed incisive thought is an undervalued yet essential activity for which time and space are required by the leader.
- To 'stretch' and develop team members and to help them implement their personal and career development plans and prepare them for other appointments.
- To meet their individual motivational needs, thus increasing their engagement with the company and releasing additional discretionary effort.

> As a recently arrived and newly appointed company second-in-command in 1st Battalion The Duke Of Edinburgh's Royal Regiment in Northern Ireland, and with a company commander on loan from another regiment (The Staffordshire Regiment) to whom I was an unknown quantity, I relished the operational accountability that was rapidly delegated to me in the first month in addition to the 2IC's admin role.
>
> It not only rapidly established a close and trusting relationship between my boss (Major Jim Tanner) and I, but stretched and challenged me in a way that was truly satisfying. It was as if I were the company commander (but without the pay!).
>
> It prepared me so well for the next rung up the ladder that, as a fairly junior Captain, I was appointed acting company commander and left to my own devices for four months or so in the province while the boss was away on a career course. That acting appointment in an operational theatre again was the most wonderful opportunity for personal development. It was sad to learn through experience that that aspect of leadership would be so lacking in my first corporate employer.
>
> (Tozer)

What sort of tasks should the leader delegate? Usually they will be routine tasks, minor tasks and tasks that others can do as well as or better than the leader. It is important to understand what should not be delegated by the leader:

- Matters that are exceptional to normal policy, and which may be setting a precedent.
- Possibly matters with serious consequences (but define 'serious' – this is a relative term. If all matters are considered serious nothing will be delegated, so this is another leadership judgement).
- Tasks requiring your 'status' as a leader. One of your team members may be as able or better able than you to perform the task, but if he or she is not perceived as credible (at least initially) by others who will be encountered during completion of that task, then you must at least start work on that task.

When delegating tasks, consider to whom you should delegate:

- Your direct subordinates, not to theirs – bypassing a subordinate leader and tasking one of their subordinates directly is disrespectful, discourteous, causes confusion and undermines the subordinate leader's position.

- Those with most spare capacity and time. Avoid delegating to the busy person who always gets things done; eventually you will add the straw that breaks the camel's back.
- Those needing experience and growth – if this is the case, then you may need to give additional guidance on how they might approach the task or ask them to discuss options with you before they implement one.
- To the lowest level at which capability exists – and this is most effectively and most easily done when everyone who may need to solve problems and make decisions uses the same fundamental thought process of mission analysis and appreciation. This process is explained in detail in Chapter 14. If you are confident that your people will look up before they look down at a problem and understand your intentions and where they fit into your plan, you may be confident that whatever they do will be aligned to your main effort.

At this point it is worth mentioning the main reasons why some leaders do not delegate tasks:

- They are insecure – they avoid risk by retaining control (while also imposing a heavy workload on themselves).
- They feel more competent than others.
- They cannot define clear objectives and parameters.
- They fear being thought incapable.
- They fail to realize that 'trust' and 'risk' are linked. To build trust as a leader, you must first extend trust to others, which means taking a risk.

The corollary to the reasons for leaders not delegating tasks is to ask why some people do not wish to be delegated responsibility:

- They fear criticism if they fail.
- They lack self-confidence.
- They feel that it is easier to be given a solution.
- They think leaders are paid to be responsible and not to delegate.
- They believe that they do the work and the leader takes the credit.
- They lack identification with the organization.
- The work provides no meaning for them.

If you have problems with delegating to people you need to understand why; there may be a conversation you need to have.

> *Whitelaw (The Home Secretary) then turned to me and said: 'Peter, I want you to understand two things. The first is that if and when the operation is launched, I will not interfere in any way; the second is that if anything goes wrong, I will take the responsibility afterwards.' The fact that the Home Secretary spoke up like that, in front of everyone else, impressed me a great deal: here was that rare being, a politician who was not trying to protect his own career, but was prepared to shoulder responsibility.*
> (General Sir Peter de la Billière as commander of the operation to assault the Iranian Embassy in London, 1980. General Sir Peter de la Billière, 1994, *Looking for Trouble*, Harper Collins)

As a leader, you will be delegated tasks by your own leader. Some of them you will wish to carry out personally, others you will wish to delegate to your team members – but you cannot escape or abdicate your responsibility for completion of the task. As a leader of a team you have responsibility for everything done by members of that team, including the complete outcomes and results of their combined work. Individual team members can only be accountable for areas under their direct control. This acceptance of responsibility by leaders is the key to building trust, confidence and loyalty. The buck therefore stops with the leader.

The how of leadership: leadership style and behaviour

With regard to character or personality – the trait theory of leadership stresses the need for 'personal qualities' but how do you define the list of essential qualities and then use them as part of selection and development? As we have discussed earlier, no two leaders will agree on the same list of essential and desirable traits which, de facto, discounts the situation or context in which leadership is occurring and the nature of the people in that situation. Even if you defined a list, not every effective leader has them all in the same ratio. Perhaps part of the answer lies in having enough strength in a sufficient number of desirable attributes to make one acceptable to one's followers and, more importantly, not having any dysfunctional characteristics and psychological damage that gives rise to tyrannical, cowardly and deceitful behaviour.

However, it is easier and more useful to define essential and desirable leadership behaviours – because effective leadership behaviour will indicate the presence of a cluster of leadership qualities or traits. Since both behaviour and its impact, on people and task, may be observed, it may also be used in selection and development.

> *A leader is best when people barely know that he exists, not so good when people obey and acclaim him, worst when they despise him: Fail to honour people, they fail to honour you: But of a good leader, who talks little, when his work is done, his aim fulfilled, they will all say, 'We did this ourselves'.*
>
> (Lao Tze 600 BC)

Leaders (whether they were leaders for good or ill) all have a readily recognizable and distinguishing 'style', or personal qualities. At the highest level one need only think of politicians, such as Winston Churchill, Margaret Thatcher, George W Bush or Gordon Brown, or businessmen like Richard Branson or the late Steve Jobs, or servicemen such as Montgomery, Patton, Slim, Nelson or the Duke of Wellington to prove this. That we think of the highest levels of leadership in this context is probably due to the fact that these leaders are recognized by most of us and their lives are well documented. It does not diminish the necessity for these qualities at lower levels where the raw material of their profession remains the same – people. But occupying a strategic leadership appointment does magnify the effect of character or personality in the exercise of leadership, as will be discussed later. Personality impacts on thinking and decision making (Chapter 17) and the behaviour of senior people sets the tone for everyone else in their organization. We have to remember that the lower levels of leadership are the training ground in which the seeds of our future success are laid as leaders develop and prepare themselves for higher office.

Historically, leadership has been virtually the exclusive domain of the services, and its leaders (for which we can substitute the word 'officers') were expected to be 'gentlemen'. Indeed the UK Army Act 1955, which governed my military service, prescribes the penalties for 'conduct unbecoming the character of an officer and a gentlemen'. Wellington insisted that his officers were gentlemen – 'The description of gentlemen of whom the Officers of the Army were composed made, from their education, manners and habits, the best Officers in the world...', because, I suggest, inherent in the accepted meaning of that word were many of the attitudes and behaviours that will be discussed in this book.

The problem with studying the qualities of leaders is that while all leaders have certain attributes that one can list, few leaders if any have the same qualities developed to the same level. But they usually reflect and exemplify those things that are expected by those within their team and which are demanded by the situation or context within which work is done. Hence the earlier assertion that leadership is individual in its nature and application.

However, a base level of certain attributes (which may be more usefully described in terms of 'preferred behaviour' – that is to say the behaviour that person typically displays, particularly when under stress) is common among virtually all effective leaders. What varies is the strength of each component in the final blend. It is these attributes that leaders need to grasp the importance of and seek to develop by gaining an understanding of their own strengths and weaknesses. To develop such qualities and behaviours is not easy without objective assessment, specific feedback about actions and impact from one's followers, peers and 'superiors', and deep personal reflection.

Style is a very difficult thing to discuss since there are at least two views of what style is. Do we mean the manner in which we choose to handle a specific situation (being adaptable and displaying an appropriate leadership style) or our general approach to leadership, based on the extension or projection of personality – our own personal style that makes us who we are? This style will reflect our own ethics, beliefs and personal value system and will inevitably vary from person to person. We cannot change our personality easily and to try a chameleon approach to interpersonal dealings reeks of insincerity and that leads to a breakdown of trust and confidence.

The most effective leaders will be consistent in terms of their personality and character yet flexible in terms of decision making and motivational influence and context-appropriate behaviour. However, the pillars of leadership that underpin an individual's leadership style ought to include integrity (a mix of honesty, authenticity, reliability, 'being straight with people', unselfishness and loyalty upwards, downwards and sideways), moral courage, initiative, willpower, confidence, judgement, flexibility of mind, empathy, humility, enthusiasm, 'realistic optimism', energy and the ability to communicate effectively at all levels.

Leadership style, the how of leadership, is about working effectively with people to obtain their confidence, trust, respect and loyalty and willing subordination of self to the leader's (and therefore the team's) aim and objectives. It involves displaying a mix of collaborative and directive behaviour while enabling the team to achieve the desired results.

Let's consider the first definition of style – the manner in which we exercise leadership. Many people will be familiar with the two-dimensional concept of situational leadership. In essence this model suggests that if the leader has highly able and highly willing team members then the leader should delegate work and decision-making authority, and with less willing and less able people the leader should 'tell' (or direct). This model is valid in what might be called 'normal' situations in which there are no external factors affecting the situation and no specific and 'correct' course of action. In a crisis, or mission-critical or 'safety' situation, no matter how able the team is the leader needs to be directive and create clarity of the plan of action very quickly rather than delegate work by saying 'over to you' (which in this case amounts to abdicating responsibility!). This is where the situational model has limitations on its use and why the concept below is offered as a leadership style model which has no caveats to limit its use.

> *The modern fashion is to be very rude indeed about management by 'command and control' as if it were a bad thing in itself. The truth is it works beautifully if the boss is any good; that is, clever, decisive and humane. The military has always known this. If you're stuck with lousy bosses, you can see the dangers of a command and control regime.*
> *It will show up every weakness in every boss: the hesitancy, the cowardice, the deceit and especially the bullying. We learn this very early on from experience of family life.*
> (Alistair Mant)[8]

Effective leaders at every level display personal leadership in an appropriate style on a continuum that has at its extremes 'directive' leadership (authoritatively making decisions and delegating well-defined tasks and actions to take – but always explaining the reason why); and 'collaborative' leadership (inclusive and participative to engage people; delegating authority and decision making is a prime feature). Along the continuum exist consultative (followers have input but the leader decides) and consensus (followers and leaders jointly agree) styles.

Now there are many occasions where directive leadership is required – such as crises, mission-critical processes that have a defined right way to do things, and the need to create clarity when there is confusion. Quite often people just want a decision made – any decision – so that they can get on with their work. Directive leadership has had such a hammering in much 'popular leadership literature' in favour of the other extreme that it seems that many corporate managers are now frightened to provide it when it is what people want, expect and need. What is less understood is that one can be directive in both an effective and ineffective manner – there is a world of difference between saying 'Do XY and Z!' and 'I need you to do XY and Z please because…', yet both are directive statements containing some of the same words.

It seems that, quite often, people confuse directive and autocratic leadership. Autocratic control freaks usually tell people both what to do and how to do it while withholding information, providing no feedback and preventing any two-way flow of communication. The autocratic style is not sustainable and seldom effective. Effective directive leadership means explaining to people what they must achieve and why while imposing the minimum constraints on the way in which they will do that consistent with the need for speed and coordination.

Collaboration and participation will ensure people's buy-in to what is happening as well as tapping into expertise, encouraging innovation and stimulating the sharing of knowledge. However, ground rules need to be clarified, especially with regard to decision making. For example, people might participate in defining a problem, discussing factors affecting its resolution and discussing the pros and cons of options; but it may or may not be appropriate for them to make the final decision on which option to adopt (whether by consensus or simple majority) – because ultimately that is the leader's responsibility. Management of expectations is the key to involving people in decision making – the decision might finally be made by the leader alone, by the leader bearing in mind advice and recommendations of others, by consensus, or the decision might be delegated; yet everyone may be involved in all the discussion leading to the actual decision being taken.

Strategic (or transformational) leaders align people to a shared, transforming vision of the future. While it is the organizational leader's responsibility to formulate and articulate the organizational vision, all other leaders share the responsibility of ensuring that it is clearly understood by everyone. However, to transform it is necessary to plan and follow through, which means attending to detail (important detail, not all detail!), the realm of transactional or tactical leadership.

These two axes formed by directive/collaborative and strategic-transformational/tactical-transactional create four leadership style quadrants[9], shown in Figure 4.8.

FIGURE 4.8 Leadership style quadrants

Strategic Leadership
Purpose, Values, Vision, Meaning and Belief, Step Change

Directive — Clear, firm, overcome inertia

Collaborative — Bring out the best in people

PURPOSEFUL | INSPIRATIONAL
ORGANIZED | CONSIDERATE

Tactical Leadership
Monitor important detail, incremental improvement

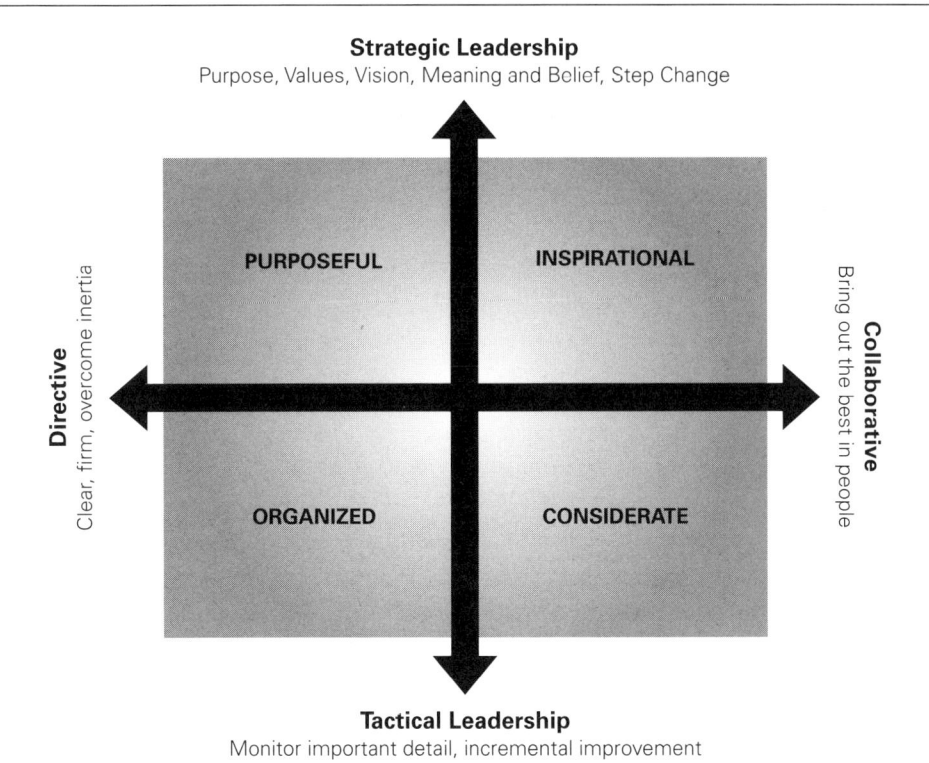

After Farey | © Jeremy Tozer, 1997–2006

FIGURE 4.9 Leadership style quadrants in detail

Purposeful	Inspirational
• Sets clear aim and intent • Readily asks the 'why' question • Has past, present and future orientation • Is a catalyst or trigger for change • Values competence (especially intellectual competence) • Challenges norms, anticipates and removes obstacles • Focuses on inventing more than improving • Makes sure results are effective • Can be decisive and take risks	• Leads by example – 'signal actions' • Readily asks the 'what if' or 'why' question • Has a largely future orientation • Champions the team • Values making a difference • Builds networks, shows insight and credits others • Communicates with enthusiasm • Focuses on helping people grow • Ensures results are in line with values
Organized	**Considerate**
• Disciplined and efficient approach • Readily asks the 'what' question • Has largely a past or present orientation • Clear objectives, procedures and measures • Values logic and physical competence • Challenges illogical thought • Is productive • Focuses on continuous improvement • Takes responsibility for results	• Shows concern for individuals' welfare • Readily asks the 'who' question • Has largely a past or present orientation • Builds friendships with team members • Values the individual • Is quick to praise, thank and reward • Genuinely interested in others • Focuses on listening and on sharing information • Ensures that results help people

After Farey | © Jeremy Tozer, 2008

At higher levels of leadership, more time may be spent on strategic activities to enable quantum increases in performance, rather than on tactical activities that lead to incremental improvements. However, many a strategic initiative has failed due to lack of sustained attention to important detail and follow through. This combination of strategic and tactical leadership enables leaders to transcend current situations. Figure 4.9 illustrates these four style quadrants in more detail.

Selection of appropriate leadership style

The selection of style depends upon not only the ability of followers but also on the nature of the situation or context in which the leader and team are operating. For example, a leader may have a team of highly willing and able people who in quiet

Understanding Leadership Ability

times would expect a participative style; but in crisis the context has a higher priority therefore a directive style is required.

Effective leadership depends more on knowing how to get things done than on being good at knowing what it would be best to do. What the leader needs to have at his or her fingertips is an effective thought process for problem solving and decision making (the former is the activity, the latter is the result), which the leader can apply with appropriate social process (leadership style) to harness the team's expertise and secure their engagement in developing innovative solutions to problems, tasks and opportunities. This is arguably the most important leadership activity, and as such receives considerable attention in Chapters 14 to 16.

Under pressure, a group of people can often be dominated by the one person who sees (or thinks he or she can see) most clearly and can best explain the issue (this is where subject matter experts may demonstrate leadership). Bewildered people turn towards anyone who can help to clear the confusion in their minds. Even creating in confused people the illusion that their minds have been cleared can have a similar effect. When effectively done, the clarification of an issue can act upon people under pressure like a magnet.

Generally, a *directive style* is more appropriate when the leader:

- needs to create clarity where there is confusion to get things happening;
- needs to make a decision and time is short;
- is faced by a dangerous situation with safety and risk management issues;
- is faced with specific, simple tasks to be achieved in a limited time frame;
- is required to trigger conditioned responses developed during training; and
- has to organize and direct large numbers of people.

Leaders who adopt a directive style want or need immediate compliance or the quickest response to a given situation. They are focused on task goals, possibly at the cost of team and individual needs. This approach, if it is used to the extent that it becomes the norm, risks negative consequences such as the stifling of initiative, inducing low commitment, increasing staff turnover and – most dangerous of all – developing a dependency culture in which no one does anything unless they are specifically told to do so by the leader, and in which the lowest level of decisions is delegated upwards.

Participative or collaborative behaviour reflects the high end of the participation scale where the leader consciously chooses to involve the team in problem solving and decision making. The leader may encourage work as a group towards a joint decision or maintain a stronger level of control over the actual decision-making process, yet, through consultation, utilize the combined wisdom of the team to scope problems and develop options.

Collaborative leadership behaviour is suitable when the leader:

- is teaching complex skills and knowledge;
- is problem solving in a complex, dynamic and uncertain environment where time is not a major concern and the experience in the team needs to be harnessed fully;
- wants to develop trust and team communication norms;

- knows that the team's understanding of, and commitment to, a decision is important;
- wants to encourage personal development by allowing followers to determine their involvement in work and to exercise leadership within a group of peers;
- acknowledges that certain team members are subject-matter or technical experts; or
- is required to work with peers on tasks requiring joint problem resolution.

The practical experience of most leaders would support Vroom's[10] conclusion that if you:

Place a group with strong independence drives under a supervisor who needs to keep his men under his thumb the result is very likely to be trouble. Similarly, if you take docile men, who are accustomed to obedience and respect for their supervisors and place them under a supervisor who tries to make them manage their own work, they are likely to wonder uneasily whether he really knows what he is doing.

In general, leaders can give their team members greater freedom of action when the following conditions have been met or exceeded:

- Clarity has been created about roles, tasks, plans and their purpose and the context in which they are set. (This means effective understanding of information, not simply the rote learning of information.)
- Team members have a relatively high need for independence and a readiness to accept accountability for their decisions and actions.
- Team members are interested in the job at hand and believe it to be important to their own success as well as that of the organization.
- Team members identify with the organization's objectives and values.
- Team members have been sufficiently well trained to cope with the problem faced or the type of task undertaken; their reactions are then likely to be, if not entirely predictable, at least aligned to the main effort.

Style should change as the situation with the same group of people evolves. For example, during a business merger or major change, a leader may need to be directive to create clarity of aim and purpose to align thought and action; but as people's understanding of aim, purpose and strategy develops, so the leader may move to a more collaborative style. The faster the leader is able to create clarity, the sooner the leader can afford to be less directive in his or her style.

It is also possible for a leader to be seen as several or even all four styles simultaneously: having an effective problem-solving and decision-making process that you can facilitate at your fingertips means that you are organized. Directing or influencing the process sequence or flow means that you are purposeful; facilitating the application of the process by asking open questions to gain input means that you are seen as considerate; and doing this with enthusiasm and agreeing actions based on the team's deductions means that you can be seen as inspirational. Equally style can appear to change; for example, what may initially have been consultation can become a joint decision when it becomes evident that the followers agree with the leader's preferred choice; alternatively, what was initially a group decision may become only consultation, where the collaborative team becomes deadlocked and the leader has to make the final decision.

It is my personal experience that when the leader has developed a relationship of mutual trust and confidence with the team, when dealing with low-level trivial matters, it is possible for the leader to be less collaborative and more directive. The team usually welcomes this because, like the leader, they are busy people. This is clearly more time-efficient for both team members and the leader, but it requires that relationship of mutual trust and confidence to exist – which means displaying almost an excess of collaborative behaviour early on in the relationship.

Business leadership in the past has also encompassed 'incentive-based' leadership using the 'stick and carrot' (rewards and punishments) to gain compliance towards a desired objective or adherence to organizational norms and values. Formal means include financial bonuses and public acclaim in journals, 'news bulletins', awards ceremonies and so on. Informal rewards can include verbal recognition for a job well done and inclusion in team activities. Similarly, 'punishments' may involve reprimands, being overlooked for a project or being ignored by the leader in favour of other team members. This incentive-based approach is characterized by the self-interest of the follower – the lower order needs in Maslow's hierarchy (see Chapter 8 for more on Maslow). Incentive-based motivation requires the leader to clarify the role and task requirements and relate these to personal safety, security, welfare and social affiliation needs.

Incentives (and disincentives) only influence follower performance up to a point. When this point is reached, the follower decides the value of the reward and the individual importance of continuing to perform as the leader desires. This approach is generally only reactive to present issues and not oriented to the future and does nothing to institutionalize effective behaviours, and carries the danger of the leader being seen to lead solely through bribery or threats of punishment.

Indeed Dan Pink[11] has a very different view of incentives, based on research funded by the US Federal Reserve Bank and conducted at the Massachusetts Institute of Technology. In a nutshell, it showed that financial incentives only work for very basic, mechanical tasks, and that when work requires anything more than the most rudimentary cognitive skills – such as conceptual thought and creativity – the larger the reward the lower the level of performance. This research suggested that money is best used as an incentive when it is taken off the table – when people are paid sufficiently well that they do not think about money at work, so that they think about the work instead. The research showed that the motivational drivers for people engaged in work requiring any form of cognitive processing were autonomy, mastery (getting better at something), and having a meaningful sense of purpose (making the world a little better while also making profit). The stick and carrot approach is perhaps best suited to leaders who are unable to build any sense of mutual trust and confidence with their teams, in which case they can hardly be termed effective leaders!

Transforming behaviour happens when the leader inspires followers to sacrifice their own self-interest for the sake of the team – a graphic example is when a soldier in battle rushes an enemy position knowing that the chances of personal survival could be low. The action is not performed for the sake of reward, but for the good of the team. Followers of a transforming leader feel trust, loyalty and respect towards the leader and the team and, being aware of the importance of the task purpose, they are motivated to do more than was originally expected of them. Transforming behaviour appeals to higher ideals and shared leadership values. In war these might be freedom, justice, a lasting peace and humanitarianism together with a sense of duty and loyalty to one's comrades and one's regiment and its history. In the pharmaceutical industry, these might be improving people's quality of life, finding cures to diseases and illnesses and so on. In terms of Maslow's hierarchy of needs, transforming leaders activate the higher order needs of followers.

As in all aspects of leadership, one's style must be kept in balance to avoid being perceived as fanatical, gullible and so on. It is not a question of being purposeful or considerate, inspirational or organized, but being perceived as being 'just right' in all four quadrants. This means being seen as not too much nor too little of any of the quadrant styles (see Figure 4.10). For development of style to occur, self-awareness and the will to develop are prerequisites. This self-awareness can only be generated by dispassionate personal reflection, by receiving feedback on behaviour and its impact and effectiveness, and by perceiving feedback that may exist in the system,

FIGURE 4.10   Too much and too little of the four styles

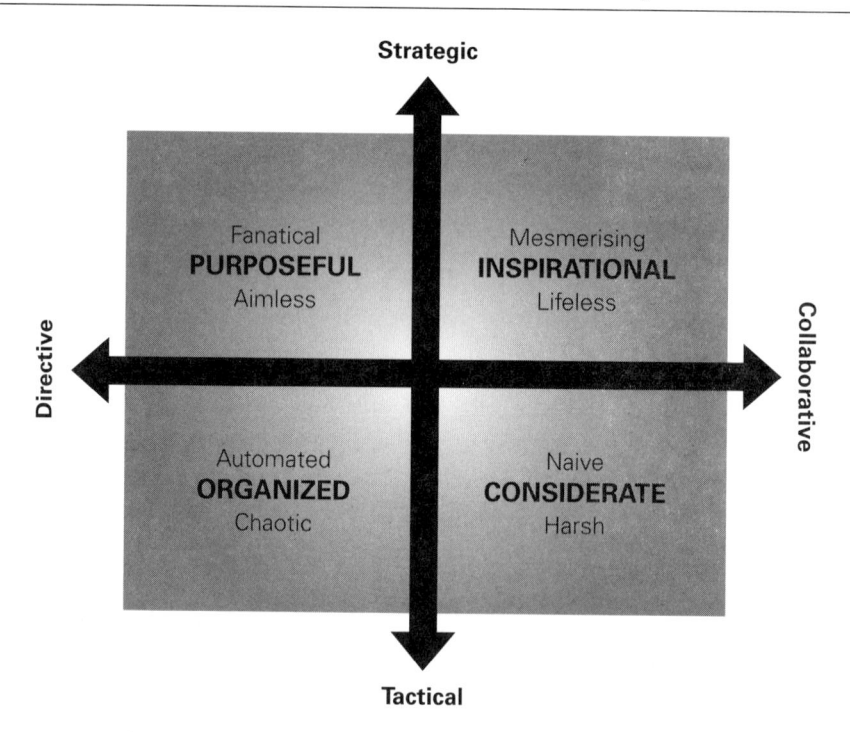

After Farey | © Jeremy Tozer, 1997–2006

FIGURE 4.11 Follower level and leadership coaching style

Low	Follower Ability		High
Low Skill & Low Will	High Skill & Low Will	Low Skill & High Will	High Skill & High Will
Directive	Leadership Style		Collaborative
Direct	Excite	Guide	Delegate

After Landsberg | © Jeremy Tozer, 1997–2006

but which is not offered. For example, in an investment banking client, the receptionist controlled the allocation of meeting rooms. Some of the rooms were very well appointed with wonderful views that were conducive to effective deal-making, others were less so. One banker always wondered why he was allocated the worst rooms for his client meetings, and never made the connection to his rude and off-hand manner with the receptionist. If he cared to open his eyes, there was feedback in the system for him.

We can adapt this leadership style model for coaching, and draw on the work of Max Landsberg.[12] The 'coaching' style is chosen by first assessing the ability level of the follower(s) in relation to the task that is being performed. In Figure 4.11 'skill' should be read to mean skill and knowledge, and 'will' should be read to mean behaviour and attitude – 'skill and will' is merely a neat form of shorthand. In Figure 4.11, I suggest that people with a lower level of skill but a 'better' attitude are more able than people with a higher skill level but a poor attitude. It is relatively simple to train people in skills and knowledge; it is less easy to shape their behaviour. The appropriate leadership style is then selected by locating the position of the person being lead within the skill/will matrix – but in real life the choice may need to be made instantaneously.

For example, let's assume you are leading a team of call centre customer service staff and need to improve the general level of performance. One of your team has several months' experience in the job and has worked in several call centres before. However, he clearly does not enjoy the role and is unwilling to always put himself out to assist customers. You might best start by understanding his (motivational) needs, exciting him about the role, the reasons why his work is necessary and why the role needs to be performed and the opportunities open. You might also do what you can to prevent boredom and provide additional responsibility.

The four coaching styles that relate to the four 'follower ability' levels are shown in Figure 4.12.

FIGURE 4.12 The four coaching styles

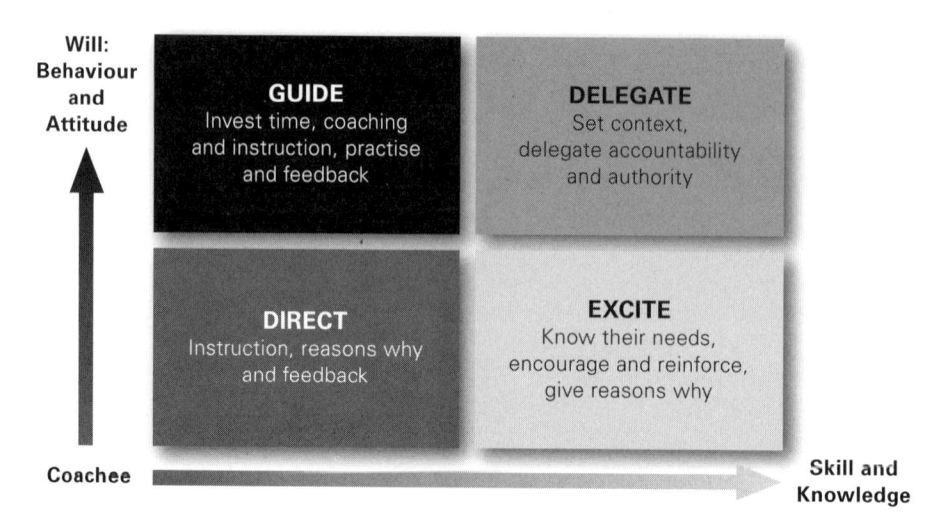

```
Will:
Behaviour
and           GUIDE                    DELEGATE
Attitude      Invest time, coaching    Set context,
              and instruction, practise delegate accountability
              and feedback             and authority

              DIRECT                   EXCITE
                                       Know their needs,
              Instruction, reasons why encourage and reinforce,
              and feedback             give reasons why

Coachee                                          Skill and
                                                 Knowledge
```

After Landsberg | © Jeremy Tozer, 1997–2007

The *direct style* is characterized by explaining, demonstrating and giving feedback on performance – structuring, informing, describing, establishing. Support consists of setting positive expectations and providing enough two-way communication to ensure that directions are clear and feedback is understood. The leader will:

- Build the will (by providing clear briefings, creating small 'wins', demonstrating confidence in the person's ability to reach the required standard and developing a vision of future performance), build the skill (through structured tasks, coaching and training).
- Sustain the will (by raising the bar, trusting, providing frequent feedback, praise and recognition).
- Closely supervise within clear parameters.

The *excite style* is characterized by encouragement and reinforcement – facilitating, committing, involving, motivating. The leader does not tell or direct the other person. Instead, the leader shares responsibility for decision making. The leader will identify reasons for low will (discover what the person's hot buttons are; where the employee really wants to go and how this task/job helps), give good reasons why the task/job is important, monitor and give feedback.

The *guide style* is characterized by formal coaching and training – teaching, explaining, practising and providing feedback. There is a higher amount of supportive behaviour provided by the leader to develop in-depth understanding, and skills practice with feedback. The leader will invest time to train, coach, explain, answer questions, and create a risk-free environment to allow learning. Constraints are relaxed as progress is made.

The *delegate style* is characterized by a more hands-off approach that gives the other person room to make and implement decisions – entrusting, monitoring, observing, assigning. Of all the styles, this is the most unstructured – except for the need to provide clarity of context, desired outcome, authority and constraints. Supportive behaviour is used to reinforce and reward the person for achieving intended results. The leader will provide freedom to do the job (by setting objectives not methods, and by giving praise), encourage people to take responsibility by involving them in decision making, and by taking appropriate risks (delegating stretching tasks). Arguably this is not coaching at all, but the leader merely trusting people to get on with their jobs, having set the direction and context. This is the doctrine of 'effects-based leadership (EBL)' introduced in Chapter 1 and explained further in Chapter 12.

This is really all you need to know about what your followers will observe – your leadership style. The drivers and influencers of human behaviour and emotional intelligence that underpin your style are discussed in Chapter 8 – and that does require some thought!

Leader/follower relationships

Leadership implies control of, and/or influence over, other people. This influence and control is, naturally, greater if the leader has the support, confidence and trust of the team members. If you are accepted by your team as its leader you obviously have considerable control. As a leader you only have authority by virtue of your appointment and your position. Power is derived from the willingness of your subordinates to accept you; when your leadership is accepted they give you power.

Sometimes it is difficult to tell just how much support and backing a group is giving you. We tend to be unrealistic – often believing that our relationships are better than they are. Be aware of this trend and beware of it.

Pointers to the existence of good relations with your team include:

- Do members of your team try to keep you out of trouble?
- Do they warn you of potential difficulties?
- Are they conscientious about tasks that you have allotted them?
- Do they do what you want, rather than just what you ask them to?
- Do they behave as you would wish when you are not present?
- Do they include you in 'small talk'?
- Do they seem genuinely friendly and eager to please you?

I knew I had succeeded as a platoon commander, when, after a few refreshing ales on my last night out with the platoon, I was invited to depart the nightclub for talking to the manager's girlfriend (a barmaid) and the entire platoon suggested that they might redecorate the club if the bouncers did not retreat. It was a heavy night, and we went on to win the 8 mile inter-platoon race with full kit the next morning.

(The author)

If you can honestly answer 'yes' to these questions then your relations with your team are probably good. The ideal leader, at any level, achieves the loyalty and affection of his or her team by inspiration, rather than by coercion and through wielding his or her authority.

It is of great importance to your team that you are seen to be getting on with your boss. When your superior supports you and works with you, you are held in esteem by your team members. If it can be seen that your suggestions and recommendations are accepted by the superior then the team grows in trust and confidence in your ability to lead them successfully.

Personal values and standards

Having said that there are limitations to the effectiveness of a qualities or traits approach to leadership, there are certain attributes that an effective leader should hold dear – perhaps better termed as 'core leadership values'. How values and beliefs are shaped is dealt with in Chapter 8; here we will only consider what those leadership values are.

Moral courage

> *Courage is rightly esteemed the first among all qualities; it is the quality that guarantees all others.* (Winston Churchill)

> *The daily choice of right instead of wrong.* (Aristotle)

Courage, in the sense of moral courage, is an essential leadership value. It is important that we know what the differences are between moral and physical courage. Physical courage drives someone on to achieve a purpose at the risk of death or injury. Lord Moran[13] (an adviser to Churchill) likened courage to a bank balance: you can draw on it, but if you overdraw, you break down – the strain has been too much.

Moral courage stems from a cool, thinking approach that makes one do something because it is the right, correct and necessary thing to do, even if it is difficult, unpopular or distasteful to implement. It is therefore very closely related to the concepts of self-discipline and sense of duty. Every time leaders display moral courage, their characters are strengthened and it becomes easy to repeat a display of moral courage in the future. However, when leaders fail to exercise that quality, perhaps thinking that little things do not matter, they are less capable of displaying it when it is really needed – the stock of moral courage has not built up. Displaying moral courage is a deliberate and calculated decision.

> *To teach moral courage is another matter. And it has to be taught because so few, if any, have it naturally. Young men can learn it from their parents, from school... from other early influences, but to inculcate it in a grown-up who lacks it, requires not so much teaching as some striking emotional experience – something that suddenly bursts upon him; something in the nature of the vision. That rarely happens, and that is why you will find most men with moral courage limited by precept and example in their youth.*
> (Field Marshal Slim)[14]

Junior leaders need moral courage, particularly:

- When dealing with older team members who are not performing adequately and who often have strong personalities.
- Maintaining standards in a new team, despite what the previous 'boss' used to allow.
- In taking responsibility for passing on unpopular decisions.
- Speaking out in meetings when experienced managers, specialists, or senior executives are present.

Moral courage is not the peculiar prerogative of business, political and military leaders: indeed, the need for it constantly arises in any walk of life that demands acceptance of responsibility. The greater the responsibility, the greater the degree of moral courage demanded.

Leaders must have the moral courage to take unpopular, difficult but necessary decisions and implement them if they have been given from above as if they were their own. Of course, the reasons must be explained, but one must pass on all decisions as if they were one's own and one must support them as a leader. To do otherwise is to display a lack of loyalty to your organization and to your leader. To try to pass responsibility for arriving at and/or implementing unpopular decisions does nothing to convince your team of the rightness and the necessity for that decision. Instead it shows that you, as a leader, lack willpower, loyalty to your superiors, and self-confidence. It is also a breach of your integrity and this will therefore lead to a loss of respect among your followers; the result is a breakdown of trust between you and your team. Leaders must have the courage of their convictions, stand their ground and fight the case; but when discussion is over and a decision is made, then leaders have a duty to act on that decision. That is why leaders are paid more. And it is their responsibility to shoulder!

Integrity

Integrity can be a tricky area to consider because of the nebulous and intangible nature of the concept. It is simple enough to look up the definition of the word:

- *Webster's* suggest it is 'adherence to a moral code, artistic or other values'.
- *Chambers* reads: 'the unimpaired state of anything, uprightness, honesty, purity.'
- *The Oxford English Dictionary* suggests 'freedom from moral corruption, innocence, selflessness, soundness of moral principle, the character of uncorrupted virtue, uprightness, honesty, sincerity.'

'Integrity' is derived from the Latin *integer* meaning whole or untouched. We will use it in the sense that it embraces a combination of the values or virtues of honesty, sincerity, reliability, unselfishness, loyalty, honour, fairness, consistency and 'being straight' without which it is impossible to gain the trust and respect of people around you. Most of these virtues are self-explanatory, but several deserve a few more words:

- *Sincerity.* Be entirely yourself; do not try and be someone you are not – it will be seen through.
- *Reliability.* Ensure that you keep to your word, honour any promises or guarantees that you have made, and ensure that you meet the expectations that others have of you. Be accountable for your work – the maxim 'follow-up, follow-through' is worth observing.
- *Consistency.* Consistency applies both to standards that you set and the way in which you typically work – the example that you set in behaving in line with espoused organizational values. Inconsistency should not be tolerated for the sake of expediency. The world is a changing and uncertain place, and one of the few things that can give people security is consistency in the nature of their working relationships and daily expectations.
- *Being straight.* This means saying what you mean, meaning what you say and not implying things which you know not to be true in an attempt to mislead, avoid conflict or divert attention.

Loyalty

Loyalty is being faithful or true to allegiance, and is an essential part of integrity. As a leader, your loyalty extends upwards, downwards and sideways.

Upwards, it is to both your own leader and your employing organization. This means implementing decisions with which you disagree, as if they were your own. By all means share your concerns and discuss matters with your leader and influence the decision before it is made (you might find that your boss knows more about a situation than you do, and he or she is making the right decision). But once the decision has been made, you must support it both in the letter and in the spirit, which you must implement without criticism of your superiors. If you do not demonstrate loyalty to your leaders you will be in no position to expect your team members to demonstrate loyalty to you. This is personal example in action! While you must demonstrate loyalty upwards, do not hide behind your superiors – you will be seen to be weak.

Downwards, your loyalty should extend to your team members; you are the team's champion. Although your first loyalty must be to your organization and then to your own leader, you are responsible for and must be loyal to the people that you have the privilege to lead. Accept the responsibility for your (and, where appropriate, their) errors, and never let blame fall unfairly on your team members. Protect their interests and state their case; however, do not try to protect the team member who is to blame and deserves the consequences. Equally, when the team is performing well and is enjoying success that is recognized, the wise leader will not claim the glory but say that the success is the team's success, and then quietly bask in the reflected glory!

Sideways, your loyalty is to your peers. Support them, look after their interests, and do not imply criticism or apportion blame. Playing corporate politics and jockeying for position is an act of disloyalty.

> There's a great deal of talk about loyalty from the bottom to the top. Loyalty from the top down is even more necessary and is much less prevalent. One of the most

frequently noted characteristics of great men who have remained great is loyalty to their subordinates.

(General George S Patton)[15]

Self-discipline

Self-discipline is explored in more detail in Chapter 21; suffice it so say here that leaders need to value and maintain the highest standards of self-discipline. This helps leaders continuously to display the personal example that inspires others and maintains the relentless pursuit of excellence (with implications for innovation and continuous improvement within the team). It ensures that the leader, especially when working under conditions of stress and high pressure, does not cut corners, miss important detail, bypass effective and efficient processes, or overlook the needs of the team and individuals within the team. Self-discipline enables a leader to act on feedback and change behaviour when that is required.

When pressure and stress abound, and when things look bleak, tricky or uncertain, it reinforces one's self-confidence. Self-discipline helps leaders to face new challenges undaunted, and to set the example that others will follow; it also underpins consistency.

I never cease to admire his calmness and courtesy; the strain of a touch and go situation for long periods on end must've been well-nigh unbearable. His imperturbability did not stem from insensitivity, but rather from a superhuman self-discipline.

(Subordinate describing Slim)[16]

Humility and respect for others

A leader may be superior by virtue of the appointment or role that he or she occupies within the leadership structure, but this does not make that person a superior being! Without humility to hold it in check, the power of authority, and 'excessive' pride in one's organization, excessive pay may build arrogance, vanity and an inflated notion of self-worth that induces the leader to not respect other people. This is dangerous, both in terms of its impact on your decision making and in the nature of the relationships that you will have with people. Few of history's great leaders have lost the personal touch: they retain the ability to talk and relate to the lowest level of employee one-to-one, away from the trappings and splendour of 'high office'.

Selfless commitment

Success in an organization's endeavours requires commitment, which in turn imposes the stress of responsibility and demands on a leader's time and emotional energy. This is particularly so with respect to providing coaching and emotional (or confidence-building) support to individual team members. This requires a degree of selflessness and self-sacrifice in discharging your leadership duties to your organization and to the people you are privileged to lead; you must put their interests well ahead of your personal interests. This is something that young officers learn very early on at Sandhurst: you don't consider feeding yourself until you have ensured that all your soldiers have been fed first! The energy that fuels selfless commitment comes from caring (being passionate) about outcomes and the contribution that organizations make to society.

Charisma

It would be wrong to conclude this section on leadership style and behaviour without briefly addressing charisma. Charisma here is used in the sense of 'an excessively strong blend of personal attributes that induces people to assign godlike status to the charismatic leader and follow his wishes without question'. Aristotle says that virtue rests somewhere between two extremes. Like most things in life, anything that is done or possessed to an extreme can become a liability and needs to be counterbalanced by something or someone else. It is the same with the charismatic leader: such strength of personality often develops an ego that ensures that that person remains blind to reality or indifferent to advice that conflicts with his or her own preconceived ideas. Many charismatic leaders generate a band of sycophantic followers. If sycophants and cult worshippers are prevalent within a leadership team, the charismatic leader has nothing to balance out his or her own excesses.

Charismatic leaders certainly inspire their followers, but inspiration does not rely on charisma. Inspiration, in our context, contains an intellectual component (the plan and its rationale) as well as the leader's personal (behavioural) example and ability to communicate. Thus it differs from the raw emotion of charisma. If followers are drawn to a leader's purpose, the leader is inspiring; if followers are drawn to the leader personally, he or she is charismatic. Which appeals most to a follower must depend to a large extent on the individual follower. No doubt there are some successful charismatic leaders, but few have endured over time.

The key point about charisma is that it is not essential to be charismatic to be an effective and successful leader, nor is charisma a prerequisite for the ability to inspire people.

Power, authority and leadership behaviour

I shall desire every Officer by love and affable courage to command his soldiers, since what is done by fear is done unwillingly and what is unwillingly attempted can never prosper.
(The Earl of Essex addressing the Parliamentary Army in 1642)

The terms 'power', 'authority' and 'influence' are often used interchangeably, but in common with everything else in this book, there is a need to establish some clarity about these terms. Influence is simply the effect that someone or something has on someone or something else. With respect to people, the outcomes of influence may be seen in terms of commitment (discretionary effort exerted), compliance (doing the bare minimum), and resistance (obstructing progress). Power is the ability of someone to exert influence, and it has a number of sources, one of which is legitimate role authority. Figure 4.13 illustrates the sources of power and the results that they may achieve.

FIGURE 4.13 Sources of power and results obtainable

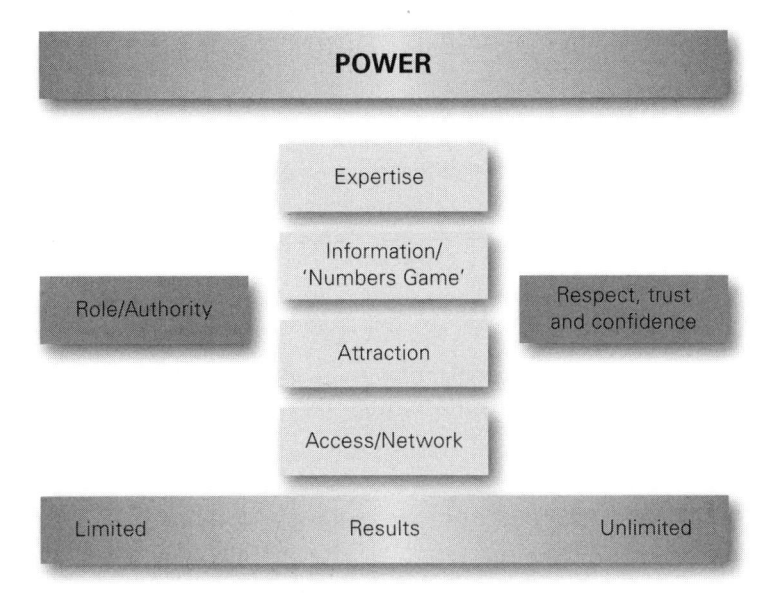

```
                        POWER

                       Expertise

                    Information/
                    'Numbers Game'
    Role/Authority                      Respect, trust
                                        and confidence
                       Attraction

                    Access/Network

    Limited            Results             Unlimited
```

© Jeremy Tozer, 1997–2007

The power of role or authority

This is sometimes called 'legitimate' or 'position' power. It is the legitimate authority by virtue of the role that a leader occupies to direct and deploy people, make decisions, allocate resources, control rewards and punishments and so on. If one is held accountable for the outputs of others, then this is the authority that makes one's leadership role tenable by underwriting it with sufficient minimum authority to get the job done. Authority also includes the ability to exert coercive power through punishment for non-compliance, and incentives (bribes) for compliance. Incentive-based power is only effective if individuals value the rewards being offered. If the leader relies on authority, he or she will be seen as excessively directive and will find it difficult to develop strong leader–follower relationships.

The power of expertise

This form of power is derived from having particular expertise, knowledge or skill in a subject area to which other people defer (sometimes because it is easier than developing a genuine solution or range of options). Thus a person may use the power of expertise to influence decisions and actions in that particular subject area. The downside to this is that, very often, people use solutions to past problems to solve current problems. Most problems are unique and require a unique solution, so while a recycled solution might work, it will often not be the most effective or elegant solution, and it could fail miserably.

In highly technical or specialist areas subordinates may possess more expert power than their superiors. Influence is gained through rules and procedures.

The power of information

This form of power is derived from having information, access to information or control of information that is not generally available. People may be able to influence others because they possess some information that is needed to achieve a certain outcome. Often it may be used together with expert power, but the specific information may not be the result of expertise. The person using this form of power therefore has inside knowledge which may be used to the person's advantage, or information which may be denied to other people, thus keeping them in the dark and disadvantaged. A person who relies on this form of power and his or her network may well be perceived by others as untrustworthy or a 'politician'.

Power of attraction

The power of attraction (aka personal or referent power) relies on liking. It is the power of charisma, which is a personality-based form of dominance. Influence is gained through persuasion and people's desire to identify with the qualities displayed by the individual with 'attraction' power. People may appear to be in awe of the charismatic person and paying close attention to him or her, but when that person departs, if there is no substance behind the charisma then a vacuum is left behind.

The power of access and the network

This form of power is derived from someone's personal relationships with people in their network who hold other forms of power. An ability to network is essential in most if not all leadership roles, but when this is used to excess it may be seen to be playing politics and/or abdicating responsibility for the team and its tasks. Deriving power from strong personal relationships with others who have power may also result in one being seen to be weak.

The power of respect, trust and confidence

The power of respect, trust and confidence can be the most effective form of power (especially if it is underwritten by authority). It is based on the individual leader being a known quantity within the organization – known for professional competence, effective decision making, effective communication, genuine concern for people and all the other 'good things' that are part of being an effective leader.

Each leader will use all of these forms of power and methods of influence at various times. Arguably, the most effective leaders use a combination of power sources simultaneously to influence events and outcomes.

Leadership thought: how people think and intellect aligned to level of work

Having considered 'the what' of leadership (skill and knowledge to perform functions), and 'the how' of leadership (behaviour and attitude), let us now move on to consider the third element of leadership ability: how leaders think and their cognitive power or intellectual horsepower to organize information, derive meaning and manage complexity.

How leaders think

Alistair Mant[17] observed that there were two primary ways of thinking. He called one the 'binary mode', which is characterized by leaders needing to prevail over or to avoid domination by other people, to use their power to ensure that the question 'Will I win or will I lose' is answered in their favour. It is a manifestation of the fight or flight instinct and people who display tyrannical, cowardly and deceitful habits are generally people with a very strong binary orientation. The other type he called the 'ternary mode'. In this mode, people keep in mind a 'third corner' rationale or purpose for any action or decision. Leaders ask questions such as 'What is it for' and 'Why?', and use the purpose of the organization as their reference point in decision making. (Ternary thinkers take a step backwards to make sense of events, are more dependable and tend to be safer to promote to higher rank.)

The ternary thinker focuses on outputs, derives legitimacy from the 'third corner' organizational purpose, and is not 'the boss of people so much as slave of the purpose'. The ternary thinker creates fair constitutional structures and institutionalizes some way for people to have a stake in constitutional change. In this respect, decisions and behaviour have either a selfish or selfless focus – and this is reflected in several theories and models of motivation (see Chapter 8).

Howard Gardner[18] believes that there are at least seven distinctive intellectual capabilities, most of which are ignored in both school education and the world of work. Those seven 'intelligences' (Gardner's term) may be described as:

1 *Linguistic* – this involves sensitivity to spoken and written language, the ability to learn language and effectively use language to express oneself. It includes reading, writing, telling stories and so on.
2 *Logical-mathematical* – this is the ability to analyse situations and investigate problems scientifically. It includes detecting patterns, reasoning deductively and thinking logically.
3 *Musical* – this is an ability to perform, compose or appreciate music, and the patterns of musical notes. It includes the ability to identify pitch, tone and rhythm.
4 *Bodily-kinaesthetic* – this is controlling one's body, or parts of it, to manipulate objects and perform physical tasks. It includes a sense of timing, the purpose of the physical action and training responses so they become reflexes.
5 *Spatial* – this is the recognition and use of patterns of wide space and confined areas, and visualizing with the mind's eye.

6 *Interpersonal* – this is the ability to understand the intentions, motivations, desires and emotions of other people. This understanding stems from both 'awareness' and the derivation of meaning from that which has been observed. There is more on this in Chapter 8.

7 *Intrapersonal* – this is the ability to understand one's own triggers and drivers of thinking and behaviour, perceptual filters, motivation and personal sense of purpose and so on, and to apply self-control so that behaviour helps instead of hinders in developing relationships. This is also examined in Chapter 8.

If this is the case, then there are obvious implications for how people are educated, trained, developed and led. By focusing on people with linguistic and logical-mathematical intelligences it is possible to over-promote people who are too narrow in their thinking. Those of you who read about 'leadership' will no doubt be familiar with the work of Daniel Goleman and his exploration of emotional intelligence (EI), which concentrates on the interpersonal and intrapersonal intelligences mentioned above. If Gardner is right, then the focus on EI limits the development of broad-band intelligence.

Many of the most successful leaders are high in broad-band intelligence – certainly all of those identified by Mant. This enables them to be versatile because their minds have access to every possible way of thinking or doing. This gives them versatility at work because they find it easy to make connections and relate to so many things; and it gives them social versatility because they can get inside the minds of and relate to so many different types of people.

Mant, Jaques and others have also identified the need for leaders to be good at 'systems thinking'. In outline this is the ability to study activity and move backwards and forwards along the chain of cause and effect, to identify and understand systems (which are patterns of inputs and outputs) and to recognize activities that are subsystems of larger systems. This sort of thinking requires the organizing and processing of large volumes of data, which becomes increasingly complex and needs to be processed at speed. Mant calls this 'intellectual firepower'; Jaques calls it 'cognitive power'. It is very different to narrowly focused subject-specific academic intelligence, but it enables judgement.

Judgement is what you do when you don't (and can't) know what to do (but you sense you have to do something – fast)!

(Alistair Mant)

Cognitive power and level of work

It has already been suggested that leaders and others need to have the intellectual firepower or 'cognitive power' to cope with the level of complexity of the work that they face. This concept is fully explored by Elliott Jaques,[19] and his work on 'Requisite Organization' is essential reading for senior executives. His research spans human capability (time-horizon[20] and the mental processes to manage complexity), and effective hierarchy (levels of work[21] defined by role time span[22] and complexity). A summary of over 55 years of research by Jaques and his colleagues is given in Chapter 22.

The point to make in this chapter is that human cognitive power may be measured in terms of levels of abstraction, or 'time-horizon'. That is to say the maximum time period into the future that a person is able to anticipate, organize thoughts, plan for and achieve an aim. These quantum steps can be addressed by considering cognitive processes (the mental processes that enable a person to reorganize information and use it) and the level of information complexity encountered (essentially concrete or abstract information); they have discrete boundaries that exist at time horizons of:

1 day	3 months
1 year	2 years
5 years	10 years
20 years	50 years

Human cognitive power follows a predictable pattern of growth or maturation, although people do not mature at the same time – the pattern is consistent, but not the age at which people 'grow' to the next level. Maturation is accelerated with stretching experiences and responsibility. This is the key point for leaders and HR executives concerned with succession planning and talent management.

Roles may also be assessed in terms of time span. Time span is the target completion time of the longest assignments (tasks or projects) that may be encountered in a role. 'Real' boundaries of leadership roles in the most effective hierarchical pyramids exist within organizations at time spans that coincide with the time horizons described above. These boundaries coincide with the desired number of strata or levels in any large organization. The greater the time span of a role – or level of work – the greater the level of responsibility felt by the incumbent and the downstream impact of decisions – the role's scope.

Implications for structure

The implications of level of work and requisite hierarchical structure in organizations are described in Chapter 22. However, they are highlighted here because they are so intimately connected with a leader's cognitive power:

- Human cognitive capability, which defines a person's time-horizon, follows a predictable pattern of growth or maturation of one day, three months, one year, two years, five years, 10 years, 20 years and 50 years. This is based on a person's cognitive processing of information of different orders of complexity. The pattern is predictable but people do not mature at the same time or age.
- Real boundaries of managerial hierarchical layers or 'strata' exist in the most effective organizations at time spans that are also one day, three months, one year, two years, five years, 10 years, 20 years and 50 years. These time spans coincide with the desired number of strata in any large organization and these hierarchical strata reflect the stratification of human cognitive capability, which may be measured in terms of levels of abstraction and time-horizon.
- The levels of work or strata of an organization, measured by time span, are based upon the level of task complexity (itself affected by the level of

information complexity), with each strata containing roles of the same level of work faced by leaders and individual contributors within it.

- The greater the time span of a role – or level of work – the greater the level of responsibility and the greater its felt level by the incumbent and subordinates – the role's scope. To be effective, the occupant of a role needs to have the time-horizon and cognitive capability to match the time span or level of work in that role. This assists in defining selection criteria.
- These quantum steps can be addressed by considering cognitive processes, information and task complexity.
- A leader at every level or stratum within an organization must be sufficiently more capable than his subordinates to add value, set context for the work, have the wisdom to judge the effects and implications of subordinates' proposals, and be sufficiently self-assured to get on with his or her own job whilst leaving the subordinates to do theirs without breathing down their necks. To do this effectively, the leader must be one quantum step higher in cognitive capability, and managing work one strata of complexity higher than his or her subordinates.

(Note that these strata are defined levels of work, they are not pay grades; there may be more pay grades than strata.)

Notes

1. Alistair Mant, 1997, *Intelligent Leadership*, Sydney: Allen and Unwin.
2. Elliott Jaques and Stephen Clement, 1991, *Executive Leadership*, Arlington, VA: Cason Hall.
3. General Sir John Hackett, 1983, *The Profession of Arms*, London: Sidgwick & Jackson.
4. John Adair, 1973, *Action Centred Leadership*, Maidenhead: McGraw-Hill.
5. John Adair, 1983, *Effective Leadership*, Aldershot: Gower.
6. Elliott Jaques, 1996, *Requisite Organization: A total system for effective managerial organization and managerial leadership for the 21st century*, Arlington, VA: Cason Hall.
7. I Macdonald, C Burke and K Stewart, 2006, *Systems Leadership: Creating positive organizations*, Aldershot: Gower.
8. Alistair Mant, 1983, *Leaders We Deserve*, London: Martin Robertson & Co.
9. Peter Farey, 1993, 'Mapping the Leader Manager', *Management Education and Development*, vol 24.
10. V H Vroom, 1959, 'Some personality determinants of the effects of participation', *Journal of Abnormal and Social Psychology*, pp 322–27; also published under the same title, 1960, Englewood Cliffs, NJ: Prentice Hall.
11. Dan Pink, 2009, *Drive: The surprising truth about what motivates us*, Harmondsworth: Riverhead Books (Penguin).
12. Max Landsberg, 2003, *The Tao of Coaching*, London: Profile Business.
13. Lord Moran, 1945, *The Anatomy of Courage*, London: Constable.
14. Field Marshal Sir William Slim, 1957, *Courage and other Broadcasts*, London: Cassell.

15 Gen George S Patton Jr, 1947, *War as I Knew It*, Boston, MA: Houghton Mifflin Co.

16 Ronald Lewin, 1976, *Slim: The Standard Bearer*, London: Leo Cooper.

17 Alistair Mant, 1983, *Leaders We Deserve*, London: Martin Robertson & Co.

18 Howard Gardner, 1993, *Frames of Mind: The theory of multiple intelligences*, New York: Basic Books.

19 Elliott Jaques, 1996, *Requisite Organization: A total system for effective managerial organization and managerial leadership for the 21st century*, Arlington, VA: Cason Hall.

20 Time-horizon: the maximum period that a person is able to anticipate ahead, to plan, organize and achieve his or her task.

21 Level of work: the weight of responsibility felt in roles as a result of the complexity of the task and information relating to the task, and measured by the time span of the role.

22 Time span: the targeted completion time of the longest task or task sequence in a role. Time span measures level of work.

Annex A: Leadership role profile

Most of the clients with whom we have worked over the years have developed various leadership role profiles. Some of these have been inadequate for a variety of reasons:

- Skills, knowledge and/or behaviours that should apply to leaders at all levels have been 'allocated' only to leaders at or above a certain level.
- They have ignored the role of process in certain aspects of leadership work.
- They have assumed that leaders already have certain attributes (for example one technology client assumed people knew how to make decisions), and the profile has not addressed that ability.
- The approach to creating the profile has not allowed it to be used for multiple purposes – recruitment, selection, training and development, performance management, reward and recognition and talent management.

Should readers wish to review the profiles used in their own organizations, the profile below is an attempt to combine both the 'what' and the 'how' of leadership. This profile may then be overlaid with Jaques' approach to assessing a leader's time horizon and cognitive power based on the fact that it is complexity that varies with level of leadership (rather than the 'bullet point' description of the work that a leader needs to do and the behaviours that a leader needs to display).

Problem solving and aligned decision making

Solves problems and makes sound decisions in a timely manner using rational thought, in order to achieve a defined aim and purpose and to align work activity.

Critical behaviours

- Defines the 'higher intent' and sets the decision in the wider context and purpose.
- Clarifies the desired effects a decision is intended to achieve with stakeholders and sets this in the wider context.
- Anticipates future requirements.
- Defines a clear, unambiguous aim and purpose (or mission) of a decision before identifying options.
- Identifies the key factors that affect achieving the aim and purpose.
- Considers each factor and makes valid deductions.
- Checks and questions assumptions, and separates assumptions from deductions.
- Explores overall courses of action and identifies creative possibilities.
- Compares and evaluates courses of action, weighing the practical consequences and the impacts on people as well as the task.

- Regularly reviews what is happening and considers the implications of changes.
- Increases understanding of problems and secures engagement by facilitating the process or steps of the process with stakeholders and by back briefing them to keep them informed and engaged as matters progress.
- Flexible in applying the decision-making process; uses it routinely:
  - 'on the spot' for quick decisions, or
  - in a deliberate (documented) manner for major decisions and/or recommendations;
  - individually, or
  - collectively at meetings (or over a series of meetings) as appropriate.

Planning and briefing

Organizes and coordinates people and resources and keeps people informed, in order to achieve a defined aim in the most efficient and effective manner possible within given constraints.

Critical behaviours

- Adheres to the defined outline sequence and structure for plans and briefs and ensures that plans are the result of effective decision making.
- Ensures that plans contain clear and concise delegated tasks (and reasons), objectives, authority and constraints, and allows people to use their initiative within this framework.
- Ensures that plans contain the minimum detailed instructions required for coordinated action.
- Organizes resources effectively with clear milestones, leading indicators of success, and standards.
- Arranges regular face-to-face briefings and visits to confirm understanding of key messages and to assess progress.
- Shares information, ensuring people understand the reasons for decisions.
- Checks that people 'two levels down' understand plans in outline 'two levels up', and their role, task/s, accountability and authority in detail.
- Uses the briefing and reporting system to share clear, accurate and timely information.
- Modifies/adapts plans in a positive manner in the light of changing circumstances.

Coaching and developing others

Guides and develops others and provides training, in order to enhance their applied potential.

Critical behaviours

- Continually assesses and agrees training and development needs.
- Ensures that people understand the performance standards and purpose of their work.
- Ensures that people understand their specific tasks, accountabilities and authority.
- Utilizes the skills training lesson cycle of explanation, demonstration, imitation, practice, feedback in training sessions for skills within the leader's field of expertise.
- Gives regular, timely and objective feedback supported with specific examples of behaviour and its impact – both developmental feedback (poor to adequate performance) and reinforcing feedback (maintaining good performance).
- Seeks to develop people by understanding the reasons for their performance (ability, clarity, environment) including their needs and aspirations.
- Listens and asks probing questions to understand people's concerns and issues relating to performance standards.
- Encourages initiative and builds confidence by trusting people to use their judgement to solve problems.
- Asks open questions to prompt thinking and help others solve problems for themselves.
- Is assertive and displays moral courage when dealing with poor performance: 'hard on the behaviour' but open on the reasons for it.
- Recognizes good performance and celebrates success to maintain performance levels.

Monitoring and evaluating

Is aware of activity, progress, resource deployment and future challenges, in order to take anticipatory action to ensure that performance is optimized.

Critical behaviours

- Checks administrative arrangements and the effective use of resources.
- Visits the front line and explores practical, operational issues with the people who are doing the work.
- Seeks and gives regular and specific feedback in discussions with individuals and teams.
- Ensures that 'strategic goals' are translated into practical, realistic objectives.
- Regularly reviews milestones, measures, standards, progress and processes, taking appropriate action.
- Ensures that all stakeholders are kept informed of progress, changes to plans, and the implications of changes.

- Reviews activities and ensures that lessons are learnt, shared, adopted and embedded.

Building relationships and influencing

Builds and maintains strong personal relationships (internally and externally) and persuades others to embrace a task and its purpose, in order to secure favourable decisions and actions.

Critical behaviours

- Appears confident and relaxed with people, effectively building rapport.
- Actively listens, displaying authenticity, attentiveness, warmth and empathy through body language, words and voice tone.
- Asks open questions to understand others' needs, wants, expectations and concerns, leading to proposals for action.
- Explores issues and discusses opportunities to add value.
- Communicates clearly, accurately and sensitively, adapting his or her approach to match the situation, the people and/or the culture.
- Clarifies expectations and understanding, and follows-through with commitments in a timely manner.
- Maintains a flow of useful and timely information.
- Is an ambassador for the organization and his or her part of the organization externally.

Teamwork and team development

Works and interacts effectively with others, in order to achieve a common aim and purpose while building team cohesion and unity.

Critical behaviours

- Builds team identity by uniting the team around a common purpose.
- Ensures regular team briefings and a 3D flow of useful information and ideas.
- Establishes clear expectations, roles, working relationships, standards and priorities for all in the team.
- Anticipates and clarifies task, team and individual team members' needs, showing commitment and initiative.
- Praises, recognizes and encourages team members.
- Appears cooperative and collaborative when appropriate.
- Shares thoughts, feelings and information with other team members.
- Resolves conflict in a timely manner and prevents reoccurrence by addressing the root cause(s).

- Takes responsibility for both people and results and avoids blaming team members.
- Makes statements and gives briefs in an optimistic, confident and articulate manner while demonstrating loyalty upwards.
- Shapes the environment people work within – reviewing and streamlining business processes, clarifying role relationships, removing unnecessary constraints and challenging unhelpful norms and habits, setting the example of behaviour for others to follow.

Determination and drive for performance

Demonstrates high levels of focus, persistence, enthusiasm and resilience, in order to achieve a defined aim and to raise performance levels.

Critical behaviours

- Maintains a sense of urgency, prevents unnecessary delay and overcomes inertia.
- Encourages continuous improvement, innovation and openness to change.
- Treats an unanticipated mistake as a learning exercise not a blaming exercise.
- Displays moral courage and deals promptly, consistently and fairly with low levels of performance and ineffective behaviour.
- Celebrates success and recognizes others' efforts.
- Actively works to achieve the aim despite barriers or difficulties.
- Displays emotional resilience when under pressure and/or facing setbacks.
- Demonstrates clarity of purpose in pursuing a course of action.
- Demonstrates persistence, enthusiasm and optimism in pursuing a course of action.
- Actively engages in knowledge management and the sharing and adoption of better ways of working.

Personal example

Is conscious of the impact of and signals sent by personal behaviour, and strives to set the example that others should follow, in order to earn the respect, confidence and trust of people.

Critical behaviours

- Upholds organizational values and reflects this in decision making and choices.
- Is fair, 'straight' and consistent in interaction with others and avoids sending ambiguous or 'tangential' messages.
- Trusts colleagues to meet expectations.

- Displays moral courage and does not hesitate to do or say 'the right thing'.
- Displays loyalty to the organization and superiors, and supports decisions and actions as if they were his or her own.
- Displays loyalty to peers and does not criticize them openly.
- Displays loyalty to staff and subordinate team members; passes credit downwards, recognizes others' efforts and avoids blaming subordinates for team failure.
- Takes a genuine interest in staff, their hopes, aspirations, development needs and background.

Self-development

Understands the experiences and beliefs that shape own values, motivators, typical behaviour and reactions, strengths and development areas, and takes action, in order to improve behaviour over the long term.

Critical behaviours

- Actively seeks feedback on behaviour and its impact on both people and task to identify strengths and development needs.
- Is not threatened by or closed to feedback.
- Questions and reflects on own experiences, beliefs, motivations and their impact.
- Asks a range of questions to enhance learning, asking 'why', 'what', 'what if' and 'how does this work'.
- Takes responsibility for what happens to self, avoids blaming others or the situation.
- Leverages own strengths, applying abilities appropriately and engages others to ensure that personal weaknesses or work preferences do not negatively impact team performance.
- Treats mistakes as opportunities to learn and improve, practising in areas of weakness and changing how things are done.
- Open-minded when receiving new information or ideas.

05 Communication – the lubricant of the leadership engine

Clarity and aligned communication channels

Formal and direct/conscious communication

Informal and direct/conscious communication

Formal and indirect/subconscious communication

Informal and indirect/subconscious communication

Communication in an organizational structure

There are many experts in communication and many excellent books on the subject, and it is not the aim of this book to compete with or to try to replace them. However, since communication is the lubricant of the leadership engine, it would be remiss to produce a book with no reference to the essential features of communication from a leadership perspective. In this chapter we will look at the four channels of communication; interpersonal communication will be considered in more detail in Chapter 9.

Clarity and aligned communication channels

As was stressed earlier in Chapter 3, 'clarity' is the ACE condition that must be created first. Nothing can be too clear at the outset because organizations have a tendency to add 'fog' as messages are disseminated and as time progresses – those in the chain frequently alter the message by colouring it with their own agenda, perceptions and filters. This causes confusion, wastes time and resources, induces frustration and

FIGURE 5.1 Communication channels in organizations

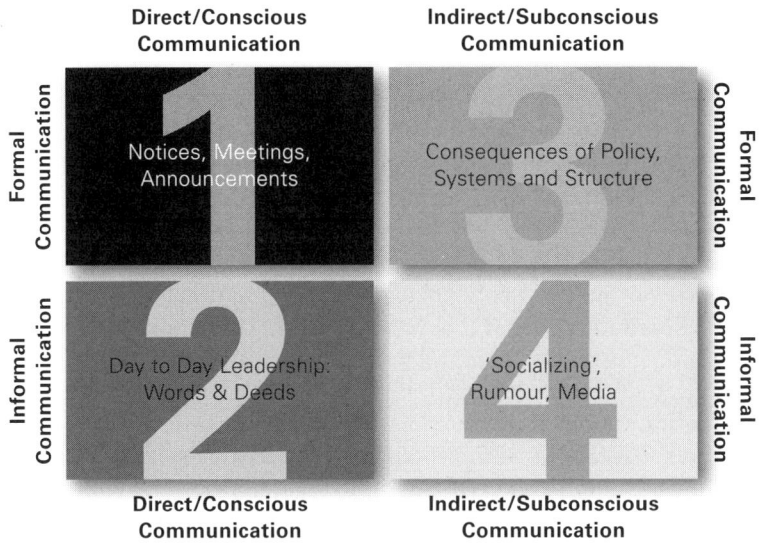

	Direct/Conscious Communication	Indirect/Subconscious Communication	
Formal Communication	1. Notices, Meetings, Announcements	3. Consequences of Policy, Systems and Structure	**Formal Communication**
Informal Communication	2. Day to Day Leadership: Words & Deeds	4. 'Socializing', Rumour, Media	**Informal Communication**
	Direct/Conscious Communication	Indirect/Subconscious Communication	

© Jeremy Tozer, 1997–2006

stifles initiative and performance. It is frequently seen in large organizations going through change, with senior executives putting different interpretations on the CEO's proclamations to produce mixed messages, or mixed messages being created by executive words not being matched by executive deeds, or CEO words being undermined by systems and structure that induce behaviour that is different to the behaviour that the CEO wishes to see.

Anything that is important must be explicit not implicit unambiguous and not open to misinterpretation – messages cannot be too clear, and important messages cannot be repeated too often and leaders must not worry unduly about repeating themselves. Perhaps the word 'restate' should be used instead of 'repeat', because if people do not hear the message first time, it may be because the words or form of media used do not resonate with them. So the intent of the message must remain the same, but not necessarily the words used, when the message is driven home and emphasized.

Communication is a very broad subject. From an organizational leadership perspective, it should be viewed as having four different components or channels, all of which must be in alignment if messages are to be clear and not mixed or confused. These communication channels are illustrated in Figure 5.1.

1 Formal and direct/conscious communication

Formal and direct or conscious communication tends to be the method that many organizations rely on. It can take the form of e-mail, notices, announcements in meetings, in-house publications and video recordings of 'state of the nation' addresses.

However, it is not usually the means that is most listened to – that is method 4! E-mail is a wonderful tool, which is horribly abused: people write as if they were having a conversation but without the other person having the means to interpret non-verbal communication and to check understanding. The result tends to be long-winded and vague e-mails that are misinterpreted (sometimes causing great offence unintentionally), and a very large volume of unnecessary e-mail.

A formal form of communication that is very evident in many public sector offices that I have visited is the tatty announcement or new guideline with dog-eared corners that is stuck on the wall in whatever space is available with yellowing tape peeling away from the wall on old notices. There is no sense of order to this vast array of notices, nor do they appear to be read by any of the staff, only by bored council taxpayers or hospital patients waiting for attention. Such notices even find their way into operating theatres (I have seen them), which I find amazing given that they provide hiding places for dirt and germs!

Formal collective team briefings, followed by question-and-answer sessions are essential to the continuous creation of clarity for people. Unfortunately, e-mail tends to be used as a substitute for things that really need to be said face-to-face, so that the leader can check both collective and individual understanding and address any concerns. The ideal combination is for the formal face-to-face briefing to be followed up with explanatory notes that are distributed by whatever other appropriate means.

2 Informal and direct/conscious communication

The informal and direct form of communication is really the preserve of day-to-day leadership. In simple terms, the leader informally checks for understanding of messages delivered in 1 above. This involves the leader setting the example for others to follow and behaving in alignment with whatever direction he or she has given to the team. It also involves the leader having regular, informal conversations with team members individually, during the course of which the leader will check for understanding of whatever formal messages and direction have been given. It is not only acceptable, but it is essential, that leaders-once-removed (LoRs) visit and talk with their subordinates-once-removed (SoRs) periodically; that is to say the leader of a three-strata mutual recognition unit should be talking to subordinate leaders' own team members (the MRU was introduced in Chapter 2). This is not to bypass the chain of command, but to ensure that the direction that has been made clear to the subordinate leaders has been passed on in meaningful terms and without distortion by those subordinate leaders. If during such informal conversations it becomes apparent that those SoRs are not clear, the LoR can seize the opportunity to create clarity. That LoR will then need to analyse the reasons for the misalignment occurring. Is it due to the LoR being unclear to the subordinate leaders, or is it due to a subordinate leader's inability to create clarity for his or her team members and check their perceptions, or for other reasons?

It is through these interactions between the LoR and SoRs that the LoR may assess the quality of leadership provided by subordinate leaders in the MRU, and may add to his or her knowledge of all the people within that MRU. This is particularly useful in assessing talent and potential.

3 Formal and indirect/subconscious communication

The formal and subconscious or indirect communication channel is made up of the policies, processes, systems, organizational structure/role relationships (accountability and authority) and symbols which give rise to behavioural and cultural consequences. This is usually the preserve of organizational leaders and the HR department – which usually has within its remit the levers of policies and processes relating to recruitment and selection, performance management, learning and development, and reward and recognition. All too often policy and process are conceived and designed at too low a level without a full appreciation of their behavioural consequences or how they should be integrated with the rest of organization design.

For example, a major technology company wanted its corporate and government sales force to sell solutions (comprising new product, spares, service and system design as appropriate), but the financial incentives (which were very high) focused on and incentivized the sales of new product. Other partners in the supply chain were allowed to develop the spares and service business, which was seen as secondary in the face of historically high growth in new product sales. This meant that the original equipment manufacturer lost control of relationships with customers. A few years ago, the combination of the technology bubble bursting and shrinking the market, and its equipment having an operational lifetime far in excess of that which was predicted, resulted in efforts to build the spares and service business, which had been taken over by channel partners.

Organizational leaders should take great pains to ensure that all these channel 3 communication levers are integrated with the same language and terminology, set the same expectations for people, and induce the same desired behaviours.

4 Informal and indirect/subconscious communication

The informal and indirect communication channel is that of rumour, gossip, social chitchat and information in media sources external to the organization. People love rumour, gossip and intrigue; they listen to it and spread it. It is the leader's task to ensure that the grapevine carries messages that are completely in alignment with the messages disseminated via channel 1. Whether it is done during tea-breaks during the working day or with drinks in the local pub after work, wise leaders ensure that social conversation is well-informed, accurate and helpful.

One of the best-networked factory general managers that we have encountered was a chap who took up smoking cigars. He did this (professing not to inhale) so that he could engage in social conversation during the day with the company's other smokers on 'neutral ground'. Not only was he remarkably well-informed about what people were thinking in the organization, he selectively used this route to pave the way for or to reinforce other forms of communication.

Communication in an organizational structure

Again, it must be stressed that the diagrams presented here to illustrate organization structure are a hierarchy of levels of work complexity. They are not meant to promote the archetypal command and control, rigid and inflexible organization that has characterized many organizations to date.

Most organizations have some form of structure of leadership accountability, and it is this structure which should be used to facilitate the passage of information up, down and across the organization. Figure 5.2 illustrates how communication may

FIGURE 5.2 Communication between a leader and his or her team

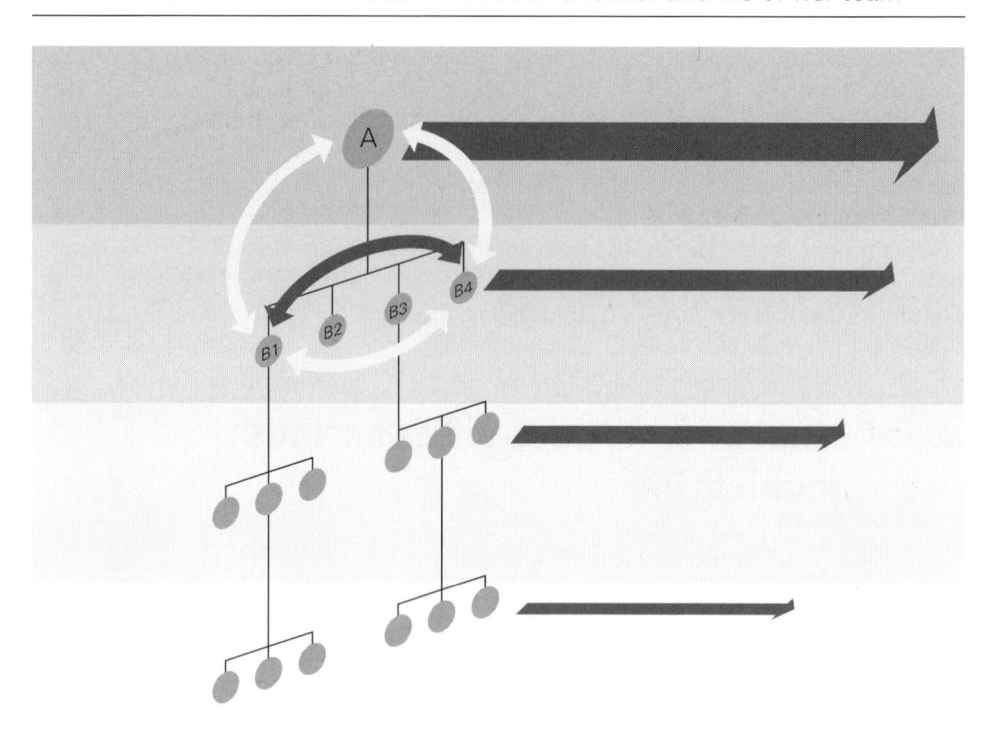

© Jeremy Tozer, 2008

flow within a work team which, by definition, has two levels of work within it – that of the leader and that of the team members. The leader A may, quite obviously, talk to any of his or her team members as individuals, or to the team (or a group within the team) collectively. The team members (B1 – B4) will, quite naturally, talk to each other. In this example, the leader and team in question are at the top of the organization, and this pattern of relationships repeats – B1 and B3 are both leaders of teams, and similarly, some of their subordinates are also team leaders.

The circle of communication shown in light shading indicates the leadership communication between the team leader and either individual members of the team, or the whole team. The dark arrow indicates the communication among peer team members. The 'clarity' created by leader A will determine how much time the leader needs to spend in resolving minor differences and clearing up misunderstandings, which is time wasted in unnecessary 'light' communication. If sufficient clarity is created, the peer team members can get on and do their jobs without delay communicating at the 'dark' level without having to escalate issues to the leader, thus freeing up the leader's time.

A three-level grouping is shown in Figure 5.3 – it shows leader A of a team of subordinate leaders B1 – B4, who have teams at level C (for simplicity only two

FIGURE 5.3 Communication between a leader of a team of leaders and their teams

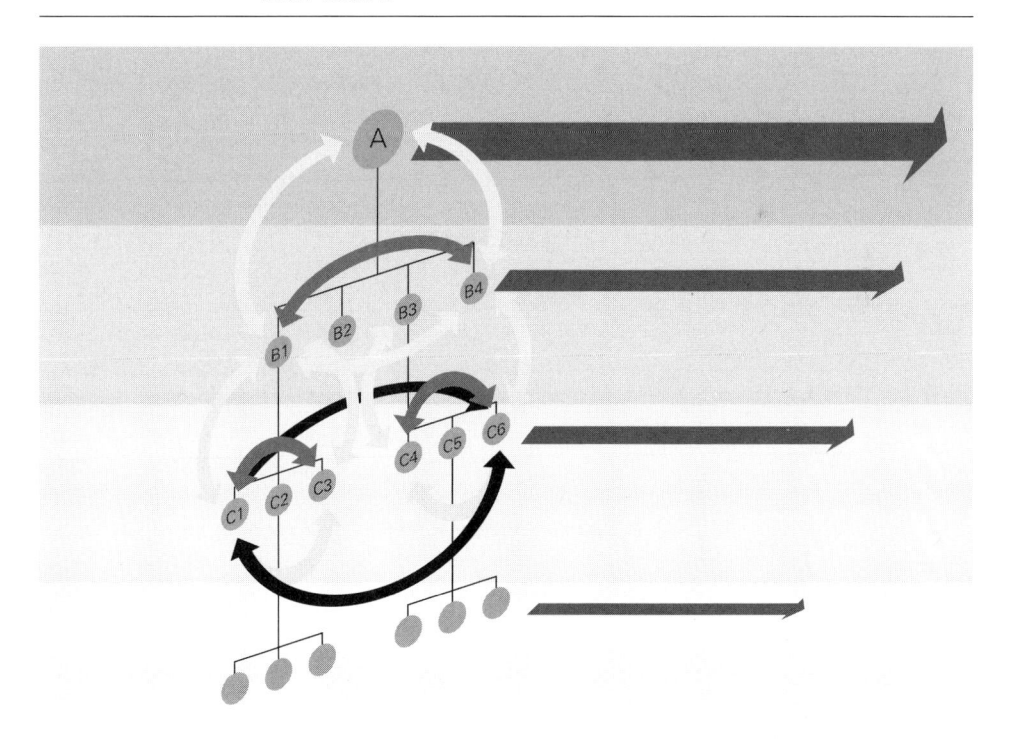

© Jeremy Tozer, 2008

teams are shown, C1 – C3, and C4 – C6). The pattern of communication relationships of Figure 5.2 is repeated, and an additional communication loop is added. The black communication loop illustrates communication between peers in different teams working across the organization.

The same comments apply to the 'light' and 'dark' communication as before. Where peers in different teams at level C are unable to agree or clarify misunderstandings, they escalate matters to their respective leaders at level B. If the leaders at level B are unable to agree things between themselves, they in turn escalate the matter to the leader at level A, who is the final arbiter. However, the leader at level A will not be expecting trivial matters to reach his or her level of escalation. This shows that if the leader at level A has been really clear, she or he will minimize the amount of unnecessary time that has to be spent in extra conversations and in dealing with 'niff naff and trivia'.

This pattern of three-level groups also recurs in any large organization structure, and the leader of a three-level group adds some checks and balances to the work of their subordinate leaders. This is explored in Chapter 22.

06
Leading transformation and change

> Roadmap to change
>
> Emotional responses during change
>
> The change paradox

To change organizations and their cultures (the collective behaviour of people), leaders have four tools at their disposal:

1 Their personal example.
2 The structure of the organization.
3 The Policies, systems, processes and standard operating procedures (SOPs).
4 Symbols that signify change.

Personal example is discussed in Chapters 4 and 8, and the structure of the organization in Chapter 22. Policies are statements of intent that give direction to desired behaviour in specific subject areas, such as reward and recognition. Policies should be drafted at board level, and all policies should be coherent and directed at developing the same pattern of collective behaviour.

It is the systems, processes and SOPs of the organization through which these policies are enacted. As I said in my 1997 book, systems drive behaviour and need to be carefully designed and aligned to the desired collective behaviour and culture. Macdonald, Burke and Stewart[1] identify two types of system: systems of equalization and systems of differentiation.

A system of equalization does not differentiate between people, whether the person is a CEO or a forklift driver – it applies to everyone. Common systems of equalization are health and safety, and equal employment and opportunity. Systems of equalization are usually perceived to be fair when they relate to matters not directly connected to work undertaken.

A system of differentiation does distinguish between people, and it is not inherently bad. The obvious example is compensation and benefits based on roles, level of work, contribution and performance. What matters is that the system is designed around a clear intent: if the system is to differentiate what is the business reason for doing so? Returning to our example of symbols, having a parking space is a symbol. The allocation of parking spaces is a system that can differentiate (unless perhaps it is designed to allocate insufficient parking spaces by lottery!). Macdonald, Burke and Stewart also analyse systems on two axes: authorized and unauthorized, productive and counter-productive:

- Authorized and productive are well designed, implemented systems.
- Authorized and counter-productive systems generally include restrictive practices that have been adopted (possibly at trade union insistence).
- Unauthorized and productive involve people cutting corners or bypassing processes to get things done.
- Unauthorized and counter-productive involves leadership based on intimidation and threats, stealing, work quotas and so on.

The appreciation process described in Chapter 14 is the ideal mechanism for designing new systems, processes and SOPs or reviewing current ones. The question of intent (equalization, differentiation and so on) features in mission analysis; factors will include core concepts, measures, benefits, integration and coherence of other systems, checks and balances, authorities and accountabilities, audit trails, communication, piloting and trials, acceptance and implementation.

The importance of symbols increases with the distance between the level of the leader and the level of the followers in the organization. Clearly the example of an individual leader is symbolic itself; for example the factory general manager in Sydney with whom we worked, who ceremonially ripped the Bundy (time recorder) clock off the wall to initiate cultural change. Other symbols include things like named parking spaces, uniform and insignia, titles, executive dining room privileges, 'rights' to attend corporate parties and events (which might be restricted to people of a certain level) and so on.

The leadership processes for leading change – both the intellectual thought process and the social process for creating alignment together with commitment – are the same as those that are required for effective execution of any plan, and are examined in detail in Chapters 12 to 18. Leadership style and behaviour was introduced in Chapter 4 and the drivers of both the leader's behaviour and behaviour of other people is examined in Chapter 8; changing the behaviour of individuals is considered in Chapter 10. The organization's 'environmental' levers of change are examined in Chapters 19 to 23. When these methods and concepts are embedded in the organization, agility and adeptness at anticipating and implementing change are magnified beyond measure. Given that most of this book is given over to the tools for leading and enabling change, this chapter will have a narrow focus on some of the challenges posed by change.

Leading Transformation and Change

The only living organism that survives is that which adapts to change.
(Field Marshal Slim)

Change may be incremental over time, or cataclysmic, occurring in a short time frame – revolution is just evolution that is happening very quickly! If change is to be steered and monitored then it must be planned. If unplanned change occurs as a result of external forces and drivers, then you are reacting to change and not leading it. If you do not lead change, it will lead you – as Eurozone leaders are currently discovering. The complexity of change can induce leaders to match its complexity in their plans. Success is usually found in simplicity – the completion of many simple tasks, all of which are aligned to the overriding and defined higher intent.

Many attempts at transformation or change fail. Each new failure adds to cynicism, change exhaustion and a reduction in the energy and commitment to the next change programme – constant restructuring in the NHS is a prime example. The reasons for failure are many, and generally include the following elements:

- Failure to establish a genuine awareness of the need for change and a sense of urgency. Complacency remains and inertia is not overcome. Instead of developing a sense of urgency, anxiety is heightened instead and people react by 'taking cover'.
- Managers overestimate their ability to impose change on their organization and its people. Change is done to people rather than effected with people – and they don't like it. The ability of people to change when well led is often underestimated, while leadership capability is overestimated.
- Confidence is not built and maintained, and quick wins and minor successes are not recognized and celebrated. If people do not see progress being made, they will become disheartened.
- Clarity has not been achieved. Either the vision or strategic plan is unclear, or it is understood at a high level, but people are unclear what they actually need to do and what the priorities of work are for them – there is no ability to translate strategy into reality via effective execution (which means there are problems with the whole approach to decision making, planning, briefing working in a cascading, recurring and iterating fashion). This is seen in interminable discussion about every decision at every level. Either paralysis results or new tasks and projects are added to an existing high operational workload and nothing gets done particularly well and stress is increased.
- Change becomes an activity in its own right, becoming the focus in place of business performance.
- Wider communication fails, with an insufficient or ineffective flow of communication (possibly coming solely from the CEO, and not from other leaders), and/or executive behaviour failing the test of congruency with the vision.
- The environment to help change take place does not exist. Momentum is not maintained, and psychological, physical obstacles are not removed by leaders.
- Leaders take their eye off the ball too soon. They may see progress being made, think that the change has been completed, and take their foot off the pedal when they are distracted by new challenges.

- Influential people who are 'blockers' and have a corrosive effect, are tolerated.
- The change is not properly embedded by aligning all organizational policies, processes, systems, symbols, structures and the expectations set for leaders and people at every level. This especially includes all HR activities related to recruitment and selection, learning and development, performance management, and reward and recognition.

The words 'change' and 'transformation' have made many consultants very rich, and some authors have helped to make this subject overcomplicated and unnecessarily daunting. This furthers the belief that change is a complex subject in its own right, divorced from day-to-day leadership. It is not. In the private, public and voluntary sectors change tends, or has tended until now, to be viewed in the sense of a move from one defined static state to another defined static state, and it is something that seems to strike fear in the hearts of many people.

This is diametrically opposed to my experience of change while soldiering. In that organization, change – whether a transformational step-change (eg amalgamation of old Regiments with long, proud histories) or an incremental improvement (minor change in tactical doctrine) – is generally viewed as simply another leadership task to be planned and led. Leadership is all about making more and better from less, so continuous improvement, learning, innovation and major change are taken in the organization's stride. What enables change in the Army is its ability to embrace the paradox of 'discipline and freedom' reflected in both its approach to leadership processes and its approach to clarifying role relationships, made human by the behaviour of carefully selected and trained leaders at every level.

There is a difference between change management and leading change: the former attempts to control every aspect of change and make it entirely predictable. As we have already said, no plan survives contact with the enemy, and the friction of getting things done requires managers to let go of their micromanagement tools and behaviour, and to start leading change and releasing the talents and energy of the organization.

Leading change is in essence an appreciation of the situation, and the development and execution of a well-communicated plan by people who understand and own their part in it. The tools for this are no different to the tools that enable effective leadership to be exercised on a daily basis, and change being thought of as a separate subject perhaps reflects poor understanding and development of both individual leadership and organizational leadership capacity.

Routecard for leading change

John Kotter[2] in his work *Leading Change*, presents an eight-stage roadmap to follow. For historians, this is remarkably similar to Slim's[3] approach to turning defeat into victory in the jungles of Burma and Templer's[4] approach to leadership in Malaya. These thoughts have been combined and further developed in Table 6.1, and linked to the tools included in this book.

TABLE 6.1 Route card for leading change

What The Leader Does	How The Leader Does It
1 Get clear on the problem: Frame the context to create awareness of the need to change and to instil urgency.	What is the current situation, and what are its features? Enable understanding of the actual situation that your organization is in and of your organization's actual capability and effectiveness (ACE as a diagnostic). Expect unpalatable answers to hard questions.
2 Get the right team and build a powerful guiding coalition.	Form a team of committed and effective leaders, who are 'underwritten' with authority. They must be sufficient in number to form 'critical mass'.
3 Get the priorities right: Frame the problem to define the vision or end-state and its purpose.	How should a more favourable situation be described? Involve stakeholders in 'Mission Analysis' to define 'higher intent' and desired effects. Distil to define vision/aim and its purpose (= Mission).
4 Get the priorities right: Frame the problem and define and brief the strategic plan to achieve the mission.	How will we achieve this change? Involve stakeholders in an Appreciation of 'factors affecting' achievement of the mission, the courses of action open (CoA), and the decision on the selected CoA in order to define the strategic plan. Cascade brief the strategic plan. Cease all unaligned activity.
5 Get the organization right and empower others to act.	Reflect the plan in structure and align accountability with authority vertically and laterally. Use leaders' example and the effects-based leadership (EBL) cascade of briefings, mission analysis, and planning to define priorities, align activity, and engage people in execution at all levels – trust them. Develop or replace ineffective leaders quickly.
6 Get the right spirit into the people, build confidence and trust them to get on with it.	Plan for quick wins and ensure progress in tracked. Recognize, reward and celebrate success. Build and leverage organizational identity – create stability or predictability that does not detract from the change.
7 Consolidate improvements and maintain momentum.	Use knowledge management, and the EBL system to share, celebrate and adopt best practise.
8 Embed and institutionalize the change.	Reinforce success by aligning all related leadership expectation, policies, process, system, structural, symbolic & HR 'levers'. This 'environmental work' may be done concurrently with 5, 6 & 7.

After Templer, Slim & Kotter   © Jeremy Tozer 2012

Frame the context

> *It is impossible to change organizations which do not accept the dangers of their present way of doing things. The task of leadership is to make the status quo more dangerous than launching into the unknown.*
>
> (Sir John Harvey-Jones, formerly Chairman ICI)

Before any change or development can take place, a prerequisite is the understanding of the need for change – if there is no understanding there may be no commitment. This provides 'the reason why', and contributes to creating the sense of urgency that is necessary to overcome the inertia found in all organizations.

In doing this it is necessary to have a grasp of the operating context or situation in which you and your organization exist, and of the drivers that influence the dynamics of that context. This is not the situation that you would like to be in, or hope to be in, but the situation that you actually are in. There is both an external component to this (geopolitical, market, competitors and so on), and an internal component that consists of your organization's assets and resources, and its capability – a key part of which is dictated by the breadth and depth of leadership within the organization, and its culture.

To have a firm grasp of the context means asking questions and digesting the answers – and some of those answers may include unpalatable and unwelcome news (particularly with regard to internal capability, leadership and culture). External consultants who are outside of the internal political system generally have a more objective view of an organization's capability than that organization's leaders. 'ACE Insights' introduced in Chapter 3, can be a useful tool in helping senior leaders come to grips with reality. An internal 'intelligence function' using the sorts of ideas that are introduced in Chapter 17 should be able to provide information to enable executive leaders to anticipate major changes to the external operating context.

The leader who dismisses an objective assessment of reality, preferring to substitute his or her rosier view of life inside the organization, is immediately hamstringing the organization. This is particularly prevalent when CEOs or boards of directors lack self-confidence and self-assurance. The ego's defence mechanism kicks in, refusing to accept the objective assessment of the organization's effectiveness because this is also an assessment of the leadership ability of that CEO or those directors. Loud and superficially confident assertions follow to the effect that 'this organization is perfect, and so is my leadership'.

If you wish to be instrumental in the rate of change that is greater than the organization is used to, it is worth remembering that change comes from dissatisfaction with the present, and fear of change comes from the unknown. So the task of leadership, in one sense, is to make the status quo seem more dangerous than the new: you are selling to people's fears.

Build a powerful guiding coalition

Organizational transformation has to be led by the CEO with a unified, committed and aligned executive leadership team. If consultants assist the CEO and top team they must have the strength of relationship to be candid and frank, and they must also be able to work with the business' internal organization development team.

Change needs to be driven by leaders at every level, for no leader can do everything by him or herself. The leadership structure, staffed with effective leaders, provides the backbone for this, but they will need particular support, which may come from a coalition of change champions. The key is to have a critical mass of committed and effective change leaders drawn from whatever part(s) of the organization the change is being focused on, who are actively engaged in supporting the change process.

Frame the problem: define the end-state

The end-state is the destination of the journey of change; it may also be called the 'vision'. The term 'end-state' is used in preference as it implies a more precise description.

The mission analysis found in Chapter 14 is particularly useful in defining the end-state and organizational mission. When undertaken by key stakeholders, with their output being collated, integrated, clarified (and reduced in volume – there will always be too many words initially) and then played back to those stakeholders, their commitment will be ensured.

Frame the problem: define the plan

Now that the end-state and mission have been defined, it is necessary to produce the outline strategic plan, which forms the basis of work to achieve the end-state. The appreciation is the ideal process of doing this (explained in detail in Chapter 14), and the comments about stakeholder involvement in mission analysis also apply to this. It is important that when new priorities are taken on the old ones are dispensed with – very often large organizations take on new priorities and initiatives but do not let go of the old to create space for them.

We do not accept change readily and until we change, the organization cannot change. So, in planning change we need to take into consideration the people and emotional factors that may limit progress, other likely obstructions to change – and the speed and extent of change, and its 'stickiness'. This inevitably means overcoming many ill-founded perceptions and the fear of change.

Change planning must also be holistic in that policy, process, systems, symbols and structure and the expectations set for people must all be in the alignment. Without this, change may result in the sort of nonsense we witnessed in one bank: a paper-free organization merged with a paper-driven organization, and after the merger change resulted in electronic documentation, much of which was then printed and filed. Beware of the tendency to over-control – the less a change programme works, the more controls, measurements and reports are introduced – often of the change plan, rather than the desired outcomes of the change. Given that many changes are aimed at 'empowering people', there is an obvious contradiction in this!

If the change involves using and embedding concepts such as those found in this book (possibly 'translated' into the organization's own language), then it is essential they are integrated with any other models in use and that all executives understand and fully embrace them – they will not own the change otherwise. Such a change will probably include leadership assessment and development – and effective leadership development is the key to making the change reality: internal leaders lead the change, not external consultants. It is quite probable that some leaders will not wish or be able to adopt the changes required to their role and behaviour. In which case, changes will need to be made in who occupies certain leadership roles. We have seen this on many occasions, usually as a result of assessment centres – in which people often make the call themselves, and a mutually respectful and dignified change is easily facilitated.

Empower others to act

An iterating, recurring and cascading suite of leadership processes for decision making (the appreciation), detailed planning and briefing enable the clarity (information and understanding) to be created that ensures alignment. The clear delegation of tasks, authority and resources, together with the removal of interference and any executive bypassing of 'the chain of command', and exemplary leadership behaviour (re-read leadership style in Chapter 4) will create an environment that empowers people to act. Concurrently with this, the systemic drivers of an empowering environment (for example, HR policies, systems and processes for performance management, reward and recognition, etc) may be addressed.

Do not underestimate the power of emotional intelligence in creating the climate for change and growth: warmth, empathy and genuineness. Emotional intelligence is examined in detail in Chapter 8.

Build confidence

Confidence is the single most important ingredient in any endeavour, as Eurozone leaders are now discovering with market reaction to their plans (which arguably have no basis in sound economic concepts, democratic principles or a predictable bank balance!). When leaders (at all levels) feel a sense of insecurity and a lack of confidence in their ability to 'do the job', the less prepared they tend to be to involve others – lowering commitment and engagement.

In 1942, when Slim assumed command of the 15th Army in Burma, he took command of an army that had experienced nothing but defeat and withdrawal, that had been forced out of Malaya and was steadily moving back through Burma in the direction of India – an army with very low morale, convinced of the superiority and invincibility of the enemy. Building confidence was a key feature of his plan to rebuild the army, and having invested in rigorous jungle warfare training, he deployed units on relatively simple operations in which success was as close to being guaranteed as it may be in war. With success, confidence grew, and as confidence grew, operations became bigger and bolder. Slim forged 'the forgotten army' into a thoroughly effective fighting force, and in September 1945 he sat beside Mountbatten and accepted the formal, unconditional surrender of the Japanese forces in Southeast Asia.

Starting slowly might be the only way to gain acceptance and instigate change. The conviction of the leader must become your team members' conviction, through their trust in you. Symbolic acts from the top can be the catalyst that really initiates change and sets the tone for the future. Change needs to be seen from the top down, with leaders setting the example and changing faster than others. Leaders need to be seen as initiating the change rather than working at the same pace as other staff (or, worse still, following others or practising the 'do as I say, don't do as I do' approach to management!).

During change, direction needs to be especially clear – leaders cannot make expectations too clear too often! To unleash energy and organizational potential by freeing people from the shackles of bureaucracy and ineffective processes, which may well have been ingrained over many years, requires people to think and act in a very different way. They will need to start taking responsibility for the sorts of decisions they may never have made in the past – decisions they have delegated upwards! Leaders must drum home that that is the expectation, and if people make mistakes, which they inevitably will, they must be treated as learning exercises not blaming exercises.

Inevitably, some people do not change or cope with retraining, and separation is necessary. This must be handled sensitively and with dignity or organizational confidence will be damaged. And when separation occurs, the most important aspect is the preservation of individuals' self-esteem and dignity. An employer has a moral obligation to take care of those whose lives it is changing dramatically by throwing them into turmoil and uncertainty. And a mentally scarred group of former employees does nothing to give confidence to those that remain or those you may wish to recruit in the future.

Consolidate improvements and maintain momentum

As success is enjoyed, and new and better ways of doing things are proven, it is vital that the successful experience is exploited. This means maintaining momentum and continuing to seek out improvement and innovation, sharing knowledge and experience, ensuring its adoption in other parts of the organization and institutionalizing such approaches. All of this is the task of leadership.

Embed and institutionalize the change

The institutionalization of the change is really the responsibility of executive leaders, who are ultimately accountable for the design of the organization and its processes and systems and the development of its culture. The HR department has an important role to play in this. It may assist in embedding organizational learning by incorporating recent experience into the training and development system in real time, and it may assist with the celebration of success through the design of the performance management and reward and recognition systems. The Army ensures that the most recent experience is reflected in training by extracting officers and NCOs from units that have just returned from operations, and posting them to training and 'concepts and doctrine' development roles. Training is not conducted by people far

Emotional responses during change

> *Dealing with change is all in the mind. Once you have people working in the same direction as real members of real teams, change becomes part of everyday life. Leaders need to start the process which ultimately the team will complete.*
> (John Quinn, former Managing Director, Thorn Lighting Pty Ltd)

Change can be chosen and voluntary, emergent and evolutionary, or imposed by authority or force of circumstance. The different stages of emotional response to imposed change are illustrated in the well-known transition cycle of Figure 6.1, which is derived from the 'grief cycle' work of Elizabeth Kübler-Ross.

It is important that leaders are aware of this, so that they may recognize the phase that individuals and groups are in, and meet people where they are at in the appropriate manner. For example, if people are in the first phase of shock and denial, it probably will not be too useful to talk in detail about what is going to happen – rather people need to understand why things are happening.

Shock and denial

The first stage that people go through is that of shock and denial. When we are faced with trauma or bad news, we often experience initial disbelief or denial that we now have to live in a new reality. We think there must have been some mistake, that

FIGURE 6.1 Emotional responses in change

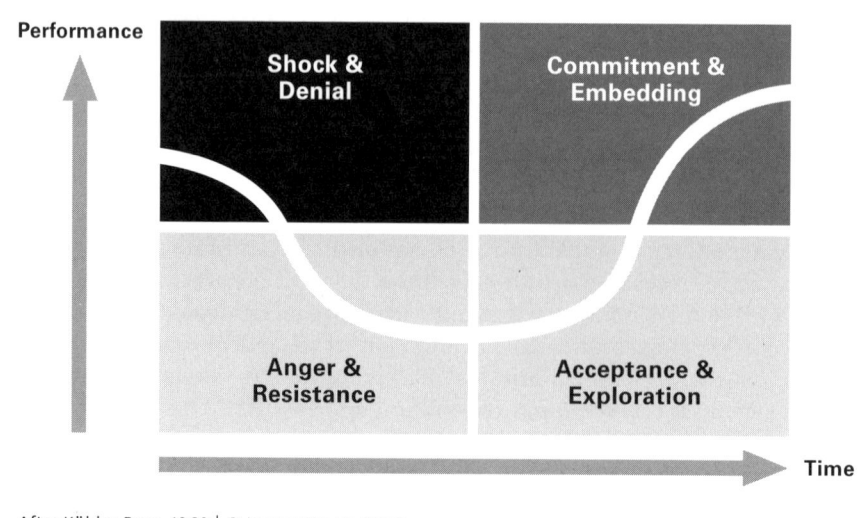

After Kübler-Ross, 1969 | © Jeremy Tozer, 2007

what we are told is going to happen is not actually intended and can't happen. Denial is a defence mechanism used to protect the ego. Denial does not last long, and if leaders have been regularly briefing their teams, taking questions and checking for understanding about the 'drivers of the operating context' and the organization's intentions, then most of these reactions can be minimized or eliminated because there will be no surprise that something has to change.

Anger and resistance

From shock and denial people move into the stage of anger (the emotion) and resistance to change (emotion reflected in behaviour). This might take the form of passive resistance or overt 'acts of sabotage'. Within this phase there may be bargaining in which there may be suggestions for doing things differently but which often amount to leaving everything as it was. Depression might also be observed in this phase in which people give up, or become lethargic, uninterested or melancholy – they feel sorry for themselves. Organizationally this is reflected in a drop in morale, and probably a loss of productivity.

Maslow's hierarchy of needs (see Chapter 8) indicates the need people have for security. Change threatens their level of security. Change takes people out of their comfort zone and may induce defensive actions from real or imagined threats. Some of the common barriers and hindrances are outlined below.

Perceptual blocks

The nature of perception and the problems it causes generally are discussed in Chapter 13. In relation to change, people may be inclined to stereotype, look for ulterior motives in all leadership decisions and behaviour, encounter difficulty in defining the exact nature of a problem, limit the scope of a problem's examination, and so on.

Emotional blocks

Emotional blocks to change include the fear of failure (largely based on low self-confidence and self-esteem), lack of trust and confidence in others, the inability to cope with apparently conflicting information, a predisposition to be judgemental and to reject ideas without consideration, and the inability to devote time to considering problems and situations dispassionately. The lack of confidence in plans for the future is an emotional block, itself caused by a cognitive block.

People fear change, and fear underlies much resistance. It is not really a fear of change, per se, but rather a fear of anticipated or potential loss associated with the change. This may include:

- Loss of security as previous certainties end and the future is seen as uncertain.
- Loss of confidence as people worry about their capacity successfully to learn new skills and new ways.
- Loss of relationships due to restructuring and the resultant change in working relationships, and possibly friends being made redundant.

- Loss of direction as people seek clarity in the organization's aim, purpose and objectives, and the direction their own career will take.
- Loss of territory and/or status, which may be due to a change in physical space (for example losing an office to move into an open-plan space) or a change to the 'perks' that accompany status.

Organizational blocks

A common organizational block is lack of clarity – people may be able to recite the vision, but they lack understanding of what it means for their day-to-day activity and priority of work. Another clarity block is the oft-seen lack of consistency in messages, or mixed messages, that come from different senior executives – a reflection of their own lack of understanding. Cultural blocks to change may include historical precedent, ingrained habits and norms, taboo subjects that are never discussed, the conflict between reason based on logic and facts and reaction based on experience and feelings, and the effect of inflexible tradition. Environmental blocks to change include a lack of support for individuals within the organization, the inability of leaders to cope with constructive criticism, and leaders failing to listen to their people and their ideas.

Cognitive blocks

The cognitive blocks to change being implemented include the use by leaders of inappropriate or imprecise language and terminology that is not commonly understood, mental inflexibility in the use of new methods, processes and procedures, and insufficient or inadequate information and understanding of 'what, why and how'. Unless these barriers are removed by effective leadership and communication, programmes and priorities can easily become derailed without apparent cause. Attitudinal shifts can only be created through positive, consistent and frequent articulation of direction and its benefits by leaders in language that is understood by all, meaningful two-way conversation and feedback, and by the example of leaders' behaviour.

Exploration and acceptance

Next people move into the phase of exploration and acceptance. People emerge from depression, explore new ideas and new ways and, accepting that change is inevitable, look towards the future with a positive attitude. Deciding to accept and explore change is one thing. However, it takes lots of self-discipline and support to adjust and to 'solve problems' and change habits that have been shaped over a long period of time.

Commit and embrace

The support of the leader and others that the individual respects will help build commitment. Finally, as the new order is seen to be more effective, best practice is shared and success (individually and collectively) is recognized (reinforcing feedback) and rewarded, people commit to and embrace the new.

The change paradox

For change you need stability; without stability people pursue survival and, after ructions, return to square one or worse.

(Alistair Mant)

There is an apparent paradox here. People may become bored surprisingly quickly, and experiments on sensory deprivation and solitary confinement have shown the need for the stimulation of change. If that is the case, you would imagine more people would not merely enjoy change but actively seek it out and promote it. It is the areas of change, the depth or extent of the change in those areas and one's immediate leader's 'quality of leadership' that limit this readiness to change. In simple terms, we like both change and stability at the same time.

This is reflected in Collins and Porras' work on companies, *Built to Last* (see Chapter 23). Human beings seek change and stimulation, but not too much at the same time. So the task of leadership is to initiate change, then build up the tolerance and capability to work with, lead and embed change – and increase the pace and scale that the organization or team can cope with. The art of leadership during times of change may well be as much to do with creating stability zones as with areas for change and development.

In some quarters, change planning involves an examination of 'driving forces' and 'restraining forces'. The leader may influence or harness some (or all) of these in order to create change. Where some organizations can go wrong is in trying to shift from the present state to the future state by simply stepping up the driving forces. People inevitably become trapped in comfort zones, and an increase in driving forces frequently results in more resistance being created by the restraining forces, manifested in resistance to change. What the leader needs to do is to concentrate on removing one or more of the restraining forces so that the natural balance of the status quo is altered. This allows the driving forces to move the situation towards the desired one in a natural way. Thus, there is a requirement for thorough, objective and dispassionate self-assessment by the leader, and of the organization's effectiveness and its culture (perhaps using the ACE model as a diagnostic). This may provide unpalatable results but they will need to be digested if progress is to be made and change realized.

Notes

1. Ian Macdonald, Catherine Burke and Karl Stewart, 2006, *Systems, Leadership: Creating positive organizations*, Aldershot: Gower.
2. John P Kotter, 1996, *Leading Change*, Boston, MA: Harvard Business School Press.
3. Field Marshal Sir William Slim, 1956, *Defeat into Victory*, London: Cassell.
4. John Cloake, 1985, *Templer, Tiger of Malaya: The life of field marshal Sir Gerald Templer*, London: Harrap.

PART TWO
Developing the ACE Conditions for Success

Section 1: Developing Ability

07
Introduction to developing ability

The next point... is the selection of commanders. Probably a third of my waking hours were spent in the consideration of personalities... Merit, leadership and the ability to do the job were the sole criteria; I made it my business to know all commanders and to insist on a high standard... Good senior commanders, once chosen, must be trusted and backed to the limit... Every officer has his ceiling in rank above which he should not be allowed to rise... The judging of a man's ceiling... is one of the great problems which a commander must solve and it occupied much of my time.

(Field Marshal Montgomery)[1]

In Chapter 3 the point was made that a leader is responsible for creating or developing the ACE conditions for success for his or her team. This includes responsibility for developing (and/or ensuring the development of) the leader's team members. The purpose of this section is to help you to meet that responsibility.

A psychologist might say people may only do three things – think, feel and act. This explains our three elements of ability shown in Figure 7.1:

1 *Skills and knowledge.* Skills are most effectively developed and knowledge most effectively assimilated, initially, through formal training (which may be collective face-to-face programmes, or individual self-study and e-learning).

2 *Behaviour and attitude.* Behaviour is most effectively developed through continual feedback, coaching and reflection. Attitudes may be shaped as a result of developing new behaviour, or by challenging the system of beliefs that underpin behaviour. This is explained further in the next chapter.

3 *Intellect and mode of thinking.* Intellectual horsepower (or cognitive capability) matures over time, and the maturation may be accelerated with stretching assignments, projects and tasks, and exposure to 'thought leaders'.

We find it useful to think of development as having three main routes: education, experience and exposure.

FIGURE 7.1 The elements of ability

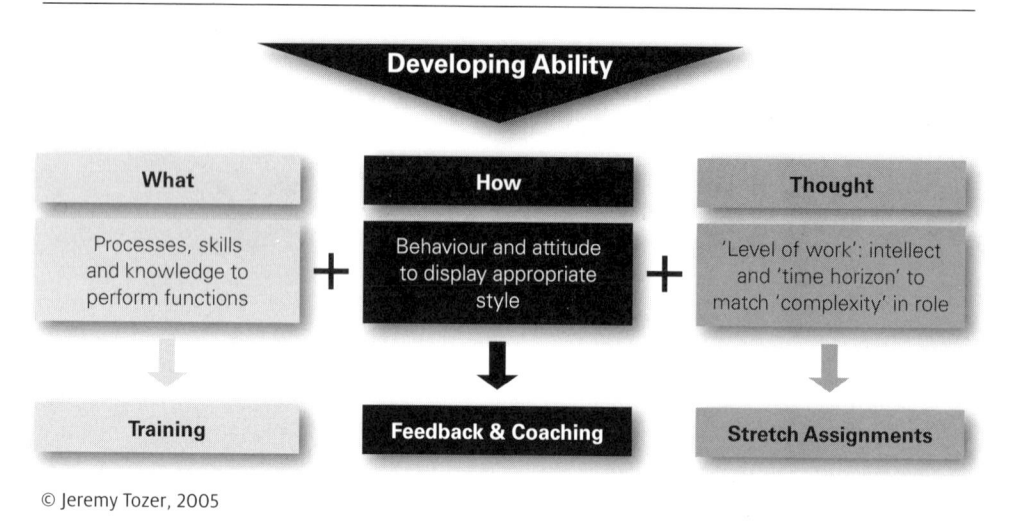

```
                        Developing Ability

    What                      How                      Thought

Processes, skills      Behaviour and attitude     'Level of work': intellect
and knowledge to    +  to display appropriate  +  and 'time horizon' to
perform functions         style                    match 'complexity' in role

    ↓                       ↓                           ↓

   Training            Feedback & Coaching        Stretch Assignments
```

© Jeremy Tozer, 2005

Education and training

Education and training is the formal and planned assimilation of skills and knowledge. Skills training (doing) and knowledge training (understanding facts and concepts) differ. The former requires practice and feedback to be effective, and is best tested by putting the skills into practice. If the skills relate to 'people', then they may only be effectively developed in a face-to-face environment and a person's effectiveness in such skills is best assessed by observation of the skills in action. Knowledge may be learnt through collective programmes and workshops, or individual e-learning and self-study programmes but discussion and application (coaching on the job?) is required for understanding and adoption.

Formal education and training is usually the responsibility of HR departments and their learning and development divisions, but it is a leader's responsibility to ensure that his or her people receive the formal training and education that they require.

While leaders do not usually have a formal requirement 'to be a trainer' within their leadership role, it can only assist every leader to understand the basics of delivering effective training. It is perfectly possible that you will need to conduct some low-level training yourself, possibly to induct a new team member or to pass on training you have received that you know your team will benefit from. To this end, there are some notes on basic methods of facilitation and training included within Chapter 10.

Experience

Experience means providing your team members with development 'on the job'. This may be deliberate and planned, in that you delegate specific tasks to individuals who you support with preparatory coaching before they undertake the task, coaching during the task, and coaching and debriefing on completion of the task. Equally it may be ad hoc, when you provide real-time feedback and possibly coaching to an individual on the spot. (In our language, feedback and coaching are not the same: feedback is part of the coaching conversation, but may stand alone. This is explained in Chapter 10.)

Experience may be gained from cross-functional programmes, projects and assignments. Development through experience may also extend to high-profile programmes, projects and assignments undertaken with peers from partner organizations – supply or value chain partners, or partners in a learning consortium. These may be designed to be intellectually stretching as well as to develop skills and behaviour, so that the full range of ability is developed.

Exposure

Exposure includes opening the mind to new possibilities, ways, means and ideas. This may be done through a number of mechanisms, some of which may also be targeted at developing cognitive capability:

- Shadowing other people in the organization, particularly strategic leaders to understand what is important at that level of leadership.
- Researching and analysing the 'operating context' – the market and its drivers, competitors, technology and product development issues, and so on (see Chapter 1, and the strategic appreciation section of Chapter 14) and, importantly, determining the implications for the organization.
- Involvement in strategic planning activity that follows on from the above research. Conducting strategic mission analysis (Chapter 14), usually lifts a person's level of thinking by a quantum step.
- 'Intellectual stimulation' provided by 'thought leaders' – who are usually consultants or business school academics, and recognized experts in their subject area.
- A method favoured in junior officer training, but rarely seen in other organizations, is the requirement for leaders to write essays for publication in in-house journals, and papers to be presented to executive panels and to wider audiences.
- Attachments to other external organizations, possibly partners in the supply chain or partners within a learning consortium. This might include exchange postings where people from two organizations swap jobs for a period of time.

In Chapter 8, we examine the drivers of human behaviour and the nature of emotional intelligence. This will assist you to both understand and develop your people, and to understand and develop yourself as a leader. Chapter 9 moves on to the essential components of interpersonal communication. Then in Chapter 10 (coaching), basic leadership psychology and leadership communication are combined with a coaching conversation framework, to help you to develop your ability in this key leadership activity. Chapter 10 concludes with some aids to assist you in providing basic training to your people, should you be required to do that. Chapter 11 then adds some further thoughts on persuasion, influence and conflict resolution.

Note

1 *The Memoirs of Field-Marshal Montgomery of Alamein, K G*, 1958, London: Collins.

08
Understanding people, behaviour and emotional intelligence

Basic psychology – the study of the mind and behaviour

What is personality?

Human nature: collaborate and compete

How the brain works

Human behaviour and emotional intelligence

The core identity

Perception

Emotional intelligence: the enabler of adaptable and appropriate leadership style

The only predictable thing about people is that they are often unpredictable.

Why do individuals often act so differently in similar circumstances?

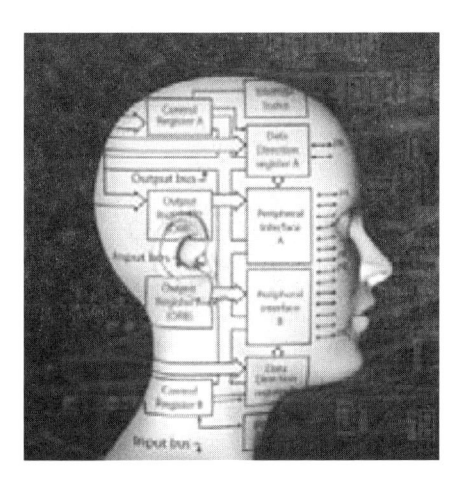

Because they think differently.

This chapter is designed to give an overview of the psychology of personality, motivation and behaviour in order to assist leaders to better understand and hopefully anticipate the reactions and behaviour of others and to develop their own 'emotional intelligence'. I am particularly grateful to my friend and brother-in-arms Sergio Miller for his invaluable assistance in writing the first half of this chapter, and to my friends and colleagues Amanda Larcombe and Mark Oliver for their help in developing the model of the drivers of behaviour and emotional intelligence, and sanity checking this chapter. I am particularly grateful to Amanda for showing me how Transactional Analysis (TA) may be used as a development tool and for contributing the section on TA, and to Mark for providing the section on the universal hierarchy of motivation.

First, we will explore basic psychology, its roots and common models, the concept of personality, human nature's basic drives and mechanics of the brain. Then we will look at what this means for the leader, with a simple and holistic model of the drivers of human behaviour. Finally we will discuss emotional intelligence – what it is, its relationship to the drivers of behaviour, and how the leader might develop this in himself or herself.

The leader is responsible for creating the ACE conditions for success, which includes shaping an environment in which people can perform at their peak level of ability – doing, being and thinking. There are many tools and processes that support the doing of leadership – the leadership functions. However, the most effective tool in creating the optimal immediate environment for a leader's team is the leader him or herself – by creating an environment of warmth, empathy and genuineness, the environment for growth.

To facilitate a climate of optimal 'being', the leader must understand others, the meaning of their behaviour and their attitudes and motivations. The leader with high emotional intelligence has an ability to respond and interpret rather than react, to appreciate others and their behaviour in the same way that an art critic appreciates a fine painting.

To understand others more effectively the leader must first be aware of him or herself. 'Know thyself', the ancient Greek aphorism, or self-awareness, is the foundation of emotional intelligence and a critical element of an environment conducive to optimal 'being'. In other words, the leader needs personal clarity.

Know Thyself.
      (Attributed to various ancient Greek sages)

Basic psychology – the study of the mind and behaviour

We are all amateur psychologists. From an early age we are equipped with a set of inherent skills that eventually allow us to interact with and influence our fellow adults. We hold jobs, marry, and play games, more or less successfully, because we have these skills. We can tell that someone has a different mind to us, and we can make interpretations on what thoughts and feelings may be passing through that mind. Accordingly, we adjust our behaviour.

Interest in the study of the mind dates back to the ancient civilizations of Greece, Egypt, China and India. Islamic physicians performed psychotherapy in psychiatric hospitals as early as the 8th century, and arguably the world's first psychology experiment was conducted in China in the 6th century AD by Lin Xie when he asked people to draw a square with one hand while drawing a circle with the other. While no doubt these early pioneers have their own theories, much early 'psychology' was influenced by or derived from philosophical thought.

Psychology as we know it today started to develop in the mid to late 1800s in the West – notably in northern Europe and the United States – when the transition was made from psychology as a branch of philosophy, to psychology as a science. This has now influenced the East, with many Asian practitioners studying in the West, and returning to the East to continue their research, practice and publishing.

The midwife to the permeation of psychology in our everyday lives, curiously, was war. After the First World War – The Great War – a war of unimagined destruction, nothing was ever going to be the same again. For two millennia, Western culture built on Judeo-Greek foundations, was transmitted through the Roman Empire and became the world our forefathers knew. The Great War cracked those foundations, which were further eroded after the Second World War.

The 20th century, in many ways, was the US century, and the *Pax Americana*, like its imperial forefather the Roman Empire, has transmitted modernity to the world. Instantaneous, global communications have provided the conduit for the process we call 'globalization'.

With the new has come psychology. But why did military men, stereotypically blockheads demanding obedience and self-sacrifice, embrace the new-fangled science ahead of their peers? Actually, soldiers have commonly been at the forefront of new ideas and have frequently promoted change in the quest for operational effectiveness. But the challenge facing the armies in The Great War was of an altogether different order to that faced by commanders in the previous years. Mechanical war, modern industrial production and mass mobilization were new.

How do you discriminate, select and apportion thousands of recruits into your army? A medical examination was not enough in an age when intelligence also had to be measured, and so the IQ Test was conceived, from which every intelligence test sat by every nervous student has followed. How do you provide 'motivation' for individuals – by training their minds more than their bodies? How do you align the interests of that individual with those of the organization – by threats or incentives? How do you lead? Was the conscripted soldier likely to display the obedience of a 'working dog', or would the officer class need to use a wider spectrum of leadership skills, to gain the confidence and obedience of subordinates? More than any other factor, it was the proportion of 'psychological casualties' – as many as a quarter of the total – that raised the profile of psychology on the battlefield. Clearly a pump haemorrhaging 25 per cent of its circulating fluid needed fixing.

The ebb and flow of civilians to and from mass conscription did not happen once, but twice in the 20th century. The means and extent of industrial production have not decayed, they have boomed. And service industries have followed. Capital markets, telecommunications and the internet astonish. In this landscape, shifting like a view from a train window, psychology has also taken a seat in the civilian workplace.

This should not surprise. The challenges facing a civilian leader are not materially different to those facing a military leader. Motivating, encouraging better performance, or breeding loyalty, are semantically identical, whether you find yourself sitting at the gunner's station of a tank, or in front of a PC. If the traffic in psychology flowed from military to civil society at the beginning of the century, by the end of the century it has become a variegated and expansive delta. We are interested in 'personality' to achieve an end. This is what this chapter will explore – a middle ground of psychological knowledge from which you can draw exciting insights and better ways of working. It is open to anyone with an interested mind and a willingness to change – this might be called a psychology of success. We will start by delving into the major influences on the development of psychology in the West.

Greek philosophy and beliefs remain one of the principal foundations of Western culture (the other is Christianity). Greek beliefs about human nature were many. The most popular – which was transmitted by the Romans throughout medieval and Renaissance Europe – was that human nature depended on the balance of fluids in the body – 'the humours'. There were four:

Phlegm	**Phlegmatic**	(calm, placid)
Yellow bile	**Choleric**	(hasty, hot-tempered)
Black bile	**Melancholic**	(gloomy, serious)
Blood	**Sanguine**	(cheerful, outgoing)

The other popular analogy for human nature was the charioteer. Attributed to both Plato and Galen, it proposed that human nature was like a charioteer driving two horses. One horse represented intentions, the other emotions, and the charioteer represented the rational mind.

The Greek contribution went further: the many strands of Greek philosophy established an understanding of human nature and schools of 'right' behaviour, based on this understanding. Aristotelianism, Platonism, Pythagoreanism and others were Greek 'approaches to life' that are still recognizable today. The Greeks illustrated their beliefs through theatre and the myths. Key concepts included opposition, change, eternal motion, mortality and immortality, the ideal and the real, theory ('passionate, sympathetic contemplation'), and the pursuit of truth.

Medieval and Renaissance theories about human nature were derived from the classical world. Christian and pagan beliefs provided the spiritual foundations for Western society. The Enlightenment dislocated Western culture and began the modern age. Foremost in this development was the idea of 'self'. This began a process that transformed Western societies, their economic assumptions, their expressions, even the way they looked. In many ways, we are still living out the implications of the Enlightenment. Key philosophers who influenced psychological thinking include:

Descartes – Meditations ('Thoughts') 'Cogito ergo sum' ('I think therefore I am').

Locke – An Essay on the Understanding of Human Nature – empiricism.

Hobbes – Leviathan: 'Life is nasty, brutish, and short'.

Rousseau – The noble savage.

Newton – Principles of Natural Philosophy.

The Victorian period began with a mix of beliefs about human nature, most of them quasi-scientific. Phrenology was very popular, mesmerism (hypnotism) was also practised. Then came the big thinkers of the century like Darwin, Freud and Jung.

It is worth spending some time on Freudian ideas because of the impact that he has had in both professional literature and our everyday conversation. He has helped us to question and understand ourselves – our experiences, our social conditioning. He has helped to overcome the myth of the 'rational man', and has helped us to confront the reality of our irrational inner selves.

Austrian Sigmund Freud (1856–1939) based many of his beliefs on the following premises:

- Humans share with lower animals certain powerful instincts – the libido.
- Unlike lower animals, humans must learn to control, frustrate, direct and sublimate these instinctual energies.
- While by far the largest part of this learning occurs in early childhood, its effects on the adult personality are profound and long-lasting.
- Residues of this early learning, and in particular unresolved conflicts between infantile desires and the demands of adulthood, may remain wholly unconscious yet provide a source of inexhaustible anxiety.
- This anxiety can become the driving force of one's lifetime endeavours.

Freud[1] developed a model of personality based on the id, the ego and the super-ego. The id is the set of uncoordinated instinctual trends and drives:

> *It contains everything that is inherited, that is present at birth, that is laid down in the constitution – above all, therefore, the instincts (drives)... It is the dark, inaccessible part of our personality... We approach the id with analogies: we call it a chaos, a cauldron of seething excitations... it is filled with energy reaching it from the instincts, but it has no organization... but only the striving to bring about the satisfaction of instinctual needs subject to the observance of the pleasure principle.*

The ego represents reason and common sense in contrast to the passions of the id; it seeks to please the id's drive in realistic ways that will benefit in the long term rather than bringing grief. The ego helps us to organize our thinking and make sense of the world around us. The ego is the organized part of personality and includes defensive, perceptual, cognitive and executive (control) functions. While the ego contains conscious awareness, not all of the ego's operations are conscious. The ego can prefer to gloss over the reality of the consequences of behaviour driven by the id, while pretending to have regard for that reality. It is watched over by the super-ego, which punishes the ego with feelings of guilt anxiety and inferiority. To overcome this, the ego unconsciously uses defence mechanisms that are subconscious, self-deceptive and distorting. In the short term they protect the mind from being overwhelmed by threat; in the long term they are often unhealthy and undesirable. Those defence mechanisms include:

- *Repression.* Forcing a threatening memory, idea or thought out of the conscious mind and making it unconscious.
- *Denial.* Refusing to acknowledge a certain aspect of reality.
- *Displacement.* Choosing a substitute object for the expression of your feelings because you cannot express them openly towards your intended target ('cathecting').
- *Identification.* The introjection of an external object or person into one's own personality.
- *Reaction formation.* Consciously feeling/thinking the very opposite of what you truly (unconsciously) feel/think.
- *Projection.* Displacing your unwanted feelings and characteristics onto someone else.
- *Regression.* Engaging in behaviour typical of an earlier stage of development. We usually regress to the point of fixation.
- *Rationalization.* Finding an acceptable 'excuse' for that which is generally unacceptable.
- *Isolation.* Separating contradictory thoughts into compartments so that no conflict is experienced.
- *Sublimation.* A form of displacement in which a substitute activity is found to express an unacceptable impulse.

The super-ego is associated with conscience, reward and punishment, and it plays a critical and moralizing role. It takes the role of parent or teacher and strives for perfection, and to act in a socially appropriate manner in contrast to the id and its pursuit of self-gratification.

For Freud, human behaviour is based on conflict and compromise manifested typically in three forms: neurotic symptoms (when the id's demands overwhelm the ego); defence mechanisms (when the id's demands are 'controlled'); and dreams (when the id's demands are 'rehearsed' in sleep). Freud believed that adult behaviours (and hence neuroses, perversions, etc) are the result of inadequate solutions to stages of infantile and childhood development. Each stage involves a particular way of achieving gratification and the degree and manner in which that gratification is achieved can produce permanent consequences for the individual ('fixation').

Swiss psychiatrist Carl Jung (1875–1961) has had a similar impact on psychology to that of Freud. The premises of Jungian psychology, in brief, are:

- Unlike lower animals, a human's libido (life force) has non-sexual (spiritual) as well as sexual aspects.
- We do not 'acquire' personality and behaviour through learning and experience; we are 'whole' almost from the moment of birth.
- Our aim in life is to maintain 'wholeness' and to achieve 'individuation', to prevent dissociation of the psyche into conflicting parts.
- Failure to achieve 'wholeness' ('congruence') and non-acceptance of life 'as it is' is the basis of mental illness ('all neuroses are an excuse for legitimate suffering').

In the Jungian[2] structure of personality, the psyche has three parts: consciousness, personal unconscious and collective unconscious. Jung's consciousness incorporates four functional modes:

1 Thinking, comprehension through cognition.
2 Feeling, evaluation through feelings (pleasant – unpleasant).
3 Sensing, perception through the senses.
4 Intuition, perception via the unconscious.

Each individual has a predisposition and balance of these four functions. In addition, there are two attitudes that determine the orientation of the conscious mind: extroversion and introversion. (Many readers will be familiar with the Myers-Briggs Type Indicator (MBTI) which is frequently used in 'team-building workshops', and which is based on Jungian psychology.)

The personal unconscious is the individual's particular and unique experiences. A major feature of the personal unconscious is that clusters of thoughts, feeling and sensations form complexes. The collective unconscious consists of inherited characteristics, 'primordial images' known as 'archetypes'. Jung emphasized four principal archetypes:

1 The persona (mask), the outward face we present to the world.
2 Animus/anima complex. Anima is the unconscious feminine component in men and the animus is the unconscious masculine component in women. Often, when people ignore one of these complexes, it vies for attention by projecting itself on to others. According to Jung, this is sometimes why we are attracted to certain strangers. We see our anima or animus in them.
3 The shadow, Freud's id, either the source of our greatest creative impulses or of our destruction.
4 The self, the 'central' archetype – 'individuation'. Jung's definition stressed an almost mystical self, the perfect state of selfhood being a Buddha-like state.

Modern psychology has several schools of thought. These are behavioural, cognitive, neurological, humanistic and evolutionary and are briefly described below:

- *Behavioural psychology.* Human behaviour is shaped by our environment and is a collection of learnt responses to stimuli (conditioning). Psychological wellbeing is having an appropriate repertoire of adaptive responses.
- *Cognitive psychology.* Human beings are information processors, selecting information, coding, storing and retrieving it when needed. Memory, perception and language are central. Psychological wellbeing is having properly functioning cognitive processes and the ability to use them to control behaviour.
- *Neurological psychology.* Human beings are determined by physiological and neurobiological factors. Understanding the central nervous system is key. Psychological wellbeing is having a properly functioning nervous system.
- *Humanistic psychology.* Human beings are unique, free and self-actualizing, we are not animals. Psychological wellbeing is accepting oneself, realizing

one's potential, achieving intimacy with others, and finding your own meaning to life.
- *Evolutionary psychology.* Human beings are gene machines – carriers of 'selfish genes'. Human behaviour is determined by the need for gene replication. Psychological wellbeing is fulfilling the interests of your genes.

What does this all mean? Whereas human behaviour has remained remarkably consistent through the millennia, as far as anyone can tell, explanations for human behaviour have changed. We are in a better position today than ever before to make informed, discriminating judgements about our fellow human beings. As leaders, you should find this exciting and intellectually intimidating.

What is personality?

To say that someone has 'a lot of personality' is meaningless in psychology. 'Personality' – in mainstream psychology – remains an abstract and much debated concept. This is because it is not a 'thing' we all have, in the same way that we can all be said to possess a nose. We have to infer personality from behaviour and the two are not the same. This raises a question – how then can we talk sensibly of something that can only be observed indirectly through the prism of behaviour?

There are two broad churches in the study of personality, both of which have attracted colourful and persuasive preachers. One stresses the uniqueness of the individual and is called the idiographic approach. To sit and listen at this pulpit is to find oneself being asked to believe in constructive alternativism, personal construct theories and fundamental postulates. If this wearies you, the church over the road offers the nomothetic approach, which includes factor analysis, psychometric tables and fundamental attributions. And gathering large numbers of followers on the fringes are the pedagogical giants of psychoanalysis, Freud, Jung and Adler, preaching ids, egos, personas and animas. Some of their beliefs fall in the idiographic school, and some in the nomothetic, but ultimately they are distinctive philosophical branches.

For the potential leader in the corporate world, these scholarly digressions may be interesting, but which is helpful? Fortunately, psychology does offer assistance, and it is to be found in the nomothetic approach to personality. This is not to say that the other schools are mistaken, rather that they offer less practical guidance to the leader on the ground.

The key to nomothetics is comparison: we may not be able to define 'personality' in its own right, but we can compare people. We can say that Robert is more persistent than Jane, Jane is more controlled than Ann, and that Ann is more impulsive than Fred. When we do this, we are invoking traits. It is these traits that provide us with the necessary cues to make judgements on our employees. In turn we can exploit these to best 'fit the person to the job'. If this sounds familiar, so it should – it is the basis of the psychometric assessment, which most of us have experienced in our adult life.

Where did this classification of human personality begin? The timeline is extremely long. As we have seen, the ancient world bequeathed the 'four humours', which remained the staple of Western culture for two millennia. In Eastern traditions, a very different approach to the human condition emerged. What Western culture might call 'types' appears to be of universal fascination in all cultures. You will find the portrayal of the fool, the wise man, or the timid virgin in a Japanese Noh play and in a play by Sophocles. But in Eastern cultures, the exploration of 'personality' was extruded from philosophy and religion, and thus ultimately debarred from the science of psychology, which has European origins.

From the area of modern-day northern India emerged a kaleidoscope of religious and philosophical beliefs, which would form the basis of the non-Judeo Christian religions such as Taoism, Buddhism and Hinduism, and the subtle philosophy of Tao (or 'the way'). These would stress the importance of self-control, tranquillity and detachment from self and things. 'Tao' remains a difficult and paradoxical concept for the Western mind to understand, and represents a best interpretation – in the English language – of a compound of ideas. *The Way of Chung Tzu*, a classic 6th century Chinese text, summarizes this difficulty, and its continuing fascination, in this simple quatrain:

> *Tao is beyond words*
> *And beyond things.*
> *Where there is no longer word or silence,*
> *Tao is apprehended.*

From Western traditions, the tendency to classify into four parts remains to this day – it is evident in the respected MBTI, Marston/Geier's DiSC, Eysenck's four types, and so on.

In the modern era, the grandfather of classification is undoubtedly Gordon W Allport (1897–1967). Assisted by researchers, Allport collated 18,000 words describing traits! Reducing these to a more a more manageable 4–5,000, Allport proposed a theory of cardinal, central and secondary traits, leaving room for individual traits that are idiosyncratic to an individual. Although this great work was started in the 1930s, it was not until the 1960s that it was gifted with an appropriate title. Today it is known as 'Allport's Trait Theory' and it is one of the foundations on which modern-day psychometrics is built.

Allport's drive was classification, not comparison. To pursue the latter, statistical enquiry was required. The psychologists Eysenck and Cattell, used 'Factor analysis' to distil 'personality' in a manageable way. Factor analysis, as the term suggests, attempts to correlate large amounts of data (the questions in a personality questionnaire) by identifying correlations (or factors) to define a person against a scale of different traits (such as introverted and extroverted).

The first questionnaire, it is generally acknowledged, was the Maudsley Medical Questionnaire (MMQ), used in 1952. The Eysenck Personality Inventory (EPI) and Cattell's 16PF (Primary Factors) Questionnaire both date back to the 1960s. All have since been refined and joined by many more variants. Probably the most successful – in terms of popularity in the corporate world – is the MBTI. Ironically, this was not the work of a professional psychologist. Mother and daughter team Katherine Cook Briggs and Isabel Briggs Myers became interested in the work of Carl Jung, and exploited the Jungian structures to create the well-known MBTI matrix of 16 psychological types based on:

- Extroversion/Introversion.
- Sensing/Intuition.
- Thinking/Feeling.
- Judgement/Perception.

With so many choices and competing views, where does the potential corporate leader stand? It is a matter of common sense that some people are better suited to certain roles than to others. It is also a matter of experience that we naturally compare and classify our friends and colleagues, while also remaining cognisant of their unique qualities. Psychometric assessments aid this process, bestowing both independence and objectivity to what would otherwise be 'opinion'. The key is to remember that such assessments are aids to understanding people; they are not in themselves decision-making tools – although sadly they are inappropriately used as such.

A last word on the idiographic school of personality study: you may find the notion that you can be 'described' by a psychometric assessment vexing. So may your employees. We transcend categories because we are – in the end – unique. Respect and interest in what makes each of us unique – not just better or worse – is also a characteristic of a great leader. So remember:

- There is no such thing as 'having a lot of personality'. Personality is inferred from behaviour and may be described as the sum of those aspects of individuals that distinguish them from others.
- Psychology broadly approaches the study of personality by focusing on individual uniqueness (the idiographic approach), or by comparison of traits (the nomothetic approach).
- Psychometric assessments offer a tool to highlight traits that you might wish to examine (through observation of behaviour and through dialogue), or develop (through practice, feedback, reflection and coaching).
- We are all unique!

Human nature: collaborate and compete

Human nature rests between the two poles of 'collaboration' and 'cheating', or cooperating and competing.

Defining personality does not bring us any closer to understanding people. It may provide us with a scale of adjectives; but unless you made the context clear you could be describing your pet dog, not your colleague. If it is beyond debate that we are fundamentally different to our pets, then we may wish to ask: what is 'human-ness' as opposed to 'dog-ness'? For this we must turn to biology and the process of evolution. Everything – it has been commented – can be inherited, apart from sterility. We are products of evolution and our inheritance is 'human nature'.

Is this inheritance – our 'human nature' – a benefice or a debt? Is human nature intrinsically good or bad? Debating this question may pass an entertaining hour at a dinner party. Equally it may determine the human resources strategy of a blue-chip firm. Certainly it vexed strategists during the Cold War, and the metaphor they fell upon was based on a game called the Prisoner's Dilemma. It does nothing less than try to explain the core of human nature and it is worth telling.

The story behind the game the Prisoner's Dilemma is apocryphal. Two prisoners hatched a plot to escape. The plot had one flaw. At one point in the escape route, neither prisoner could see the other. This point was the critical decision-point in the escape plan. Both prisoners had to carry out their part of the plan independently, out of sight of each other, if the plan were to succeed at all. But there was a catch. If one of the prisoners cheated on the other, the cheater had a much better chance of escaping than if he continued with the agreed plan. If both prisoners decided to cheat on each other, they had no chance of escaping – the plan would fail. And if both prisoners executed the agreed plan of escape they had a fair chance of escape.

The Prisoner's Dilemma is therefore this: should I trust my fellow prisoner? If I trust him and he cheats, I will be captured and he will have a good chance of escaping. If I trust him and he carries out the agreed part of the plan, we both have a fair chance of escaping. If we both cheat at the same time, then we will both be caught. But if I cheat first, he will be caught and I will have a good chance of escaping. What should I do? The other prisoner is, of course, thinking on exactly the same lines.

The Prisoner's Dilemma was used for war-gaming by US political scientists, who were working for the Pentagon at the height of the Cold War. The scientist usually associated with the game in this context is Robert Axelrod. The fear that besieged the Pentagon was *escalation*. How do you win (or even successfully conclude) a war when both sides have the capacity to destroy the other? Do you fight a limited war and trust that your opponent won't go nuclear? Or do you press the button first and annihilate your opponent? Or will both sides press the button simultaneously and annihilate each other? Or will you annihilate just one city on either side of the Atlantic? When warfare has the potential of becoming a 'zero sum game' (both sides lose completely), how do you avoid this fate?

Two biologists – Robert Axelrod and William Hamilton – collaborated to solve this puzzle. Hamilton was struck by the possible application of the Prisoner's Dilemma to explore issues in evolution. By the 1950s Darwin's theory of evolution had been refined in one major way: the popular idea of competition between the species had been overtaken by the concept of competition intra-species. In other words, the answer to the question: 'How fast do I have to run to avoid being eaten by a bear?' is: 'Faster than the person beside me.' The most significant arena for competition is between animals of the same species, not between different species. But herein lies a paradox and dilemma. I can only pass on my genes through my own species. Indeed this is what determines the biological definition of a species – if you can reproduce with an organism, you are of the same species as that organism. The dilemma is this: to pass on my genes I have to cooperate as well as compete, both with my own sex and the opposite sex. This is the 'moral' of the Prisoner's Dilemma: *human nature rests between the two poles of 'collaboration' and 'cheating', or cooperating and competing.*

This, in simple terms, is the picture biology offers of our condition. There are details to the picture. In mammals, herbivores are the least competitive species. You do not have to compete for grass, you just have to spread out and eat it, as sheep do. You remain in groups (collaborative behaviour) because this affords you the best protection against predators.

Carnivores are the most competitive species (cheating behaviour). Resources are few and when a prey is caught, there is intense competition for that prey. There is also, inevitably, intense competition for reproductive rights. A dominant male lion (abetted by brother or cousin lions) will take over a pride, fight off the other males, kill the cubs (infanticide is a common aspect of highly competitive species), then assert his reproductive rights – typically over a hundred times in a 48-hour period. Lest this portray the male gender as solely responsible for this bleakly competitive landscape, it is worth adding that the dominant female actively encourages competition between the males. Her game is maximum sperm collection and may the best sperm win!

Human nature lies somewhere in between – we share some of the characteristics of both herbivores and carnivores. Cooperation increases with kin (known as 'kin altruism') and decreases with complete strangers (though we can demonstrate a highly developed sense of 'hospitality' with complete strangers). We, in common with all primates, form versatile and flexible groups or tribes. With humans the degree of flexibility is astonishing. We can change behaviour – violent gang members can become reformed religious zealots, move jobs (swap a lucrative city job and work for a charity), or change countries (emigration). We can belong to a football team, sailing club, join a political party, or form a trade union. We are the incredible animal, but we still follow the rules.

What are the rules? We may now return to the Prisoner's Dilemma. If I must both cooperate and compete, which is the most successful strategy in the long term? First you must understand the rules of the Prisoner's Dilemma game, which are deceptively simple. Each player is given two cards. One reads 'Collaborate' and the other reads 'Cheat'. The two players must each place one card face down. The banker then turns the cards over, takes the score, collects the cards, shuffles them, and deals out two cards again to the two players. The game continues in this manner for 30 rounds. At the end of the final round the banker adds up the scores and the winner is the player with the highest score. The scoring is as follows:

If both players play the 'Collaborate' card: both players collect three points.

If one player plays the 'Cheat' card, one player plays the 'Collaborate' card: the player who plays the 'Cheat' card gains five points. The player who plays the 'Collaborate' card gains no points.

Both players play 'Cheat' card: both players are fined one point.

Played over more than one round, the Prisoner's Dilemma is a 'non-zero sum' game. The question is – *how can I end up with the maximum points possible, no matter what my opponent plays?*

The mathematician, Anatol Rapaport, provided the solution to this problem. His solution is known as Tit-for-Tat, and is deceptively simple. You initially play the 'Collaborate' card. After that you play whichever preceding card your opponent played. So, if he played 'Cheat' you play 'Cheat in the next round, and so on'. This approach results in an 'evolutionary stable strategy' (a term coined by the British biologist Maynard Smith).

However, this model fails to predict behaviour in some situations. In the ultimatum game, two players are given some money to divide between them in one round. The first player decides how to split the money and the second player can either accept, in which case the money is shared according to the first player's proposal, or reject, in which case, neither of them receives anything. Reciprocation does not become an issue because there is only one round to the game. Culture seems to have a significant affect as in some cultures a 50:50 split is typically offered and in all cultures offers of less than 20 per cent are usually rejected. According to game theory, any offer should be accepted because getting some money is better than none.

If you have followed the game so far, you may still be wondering what relevance this holds for you at your desk, planning tomorrow's meetings, or auditing recent sales figures. We – at home, at work, at play – are continually making this simple choice between compete or cooperate. Our lives are a mesh of all the moments that we cooperated and all the moments that we competed. We made those decisions, consciously and mostly subconsciously, to try and win for ourselves (or, as a biologist might observe more precisely, for our genes). Whether in the mundane act of offering a cup of coffee (reciprocal favour behaviour), or in the dramatic act of a corporate takeover (resource aggrandisement behaviour), we are playing out versions of the Prisoners' Dilemma.

We cannot escape our natures – but we can be wise about our natures and we can harness them. One would be a dodo (evolutionarily speaking) if one did not recognize that everyone else in the firm is one's enemy, as well as one's friend – competing for roles, promotion or resources and collaborating to achieve objectives – together we are strong and divided we are weak. It is in all our best interests to act as kin, to cooperate as if we were family.

The effective leader plays the 'Collaborate' card, and wants his or her team to do the same. But the leader is not naïve either. He or she recognizes that the instinct to play the 'Cheat' (or 'Compete') card is strong. We would not be human otherwise. So the leader harnesses the compete card, both within the firm and against other firms.

We may now usefully return to the military world where it all began and draw some lessons that are applicable to all organizations. An army does something that few civilian enterprises succeed in doing: it creates highly cooperative and cohesive units (The Regiments), which have a highly competitive edge (they want to be better than every other Regiment). And within a regiment, competition is harnessed (through inter-platoon skill-building competitions and rivalry) in a manner that is *beneficial* to the whole. Furthermore, The Regiment creates mechanisms in which employees (the soldiers) truly believe they are family – it does this through unique totems such as regimental 'Colours' and cap-badges, links to geographical recruitment areas, unique regimental customs and traditions and so on. As a consequence the army triggers kin altruism (although arguably this was stronger in the old structure of county infantry regiments when the British Army was larger than it is now – the recent unit amalgamations has eroded this considerably).

This is why a soldier will lay his or her life down for another – the supreme act of altruism (because you are guaranteeing your genetic extinction). Soldiers, biologically, act as if fellow soldier were kin (the phrase 'brothers-in-arms' is not accidental), and by laying down their life, they will at least guarantee that half the genes are saved – despite the fact that the other soldier is a genetic stranger! The nobility of this act of martial self-sacrifice is compelling – it is universally admired and rewarded in human society.

Civilian organizations might not believe that they are engaged in life or death struggles, and the outcomes of success or failure in civilian society differ to those experienced on a battlefield – but the rules are the same. We alternately collaborate and cheat to achieve our aims, because our 'nature' compels us to do so.

In summary then, the story of the Prisoner's Dilemma provides us with a popular metaphor for 'human nature'. Competition and cooperation are the horns of the dilemma. We don't have to escape human nature – we can use it! To succeed, an organization must harness both competitive and cooperative behaviour in a manner that benefits both the individual and the collective entity. Finally, it is worth linking these fundamental drives back to Freud and Jung. They are a useful pair because they fairly neatly fall into the compete/cooperate dichotomy. In very simple terms, Freud believed we are animals (compete) and Jung believed we had a spiritual nature (cooperate)!

This is the theory. Sometimes, though, the reality can be disappointing. People may back-stab, crawl, lie, cheat, flatter themselves, take credit for other people's work, blame others for their failures, treat people badly and so on. Sadly it happens, and we all know that 'bad and toxic leaders' get to the top doing all these things and worse. They play the 'cheat' card against a group of people, most of whom are continually and forlornly playing the 'Collaborate' card, and they win. This is another expression of the 'binary' mode of leadership thinking that we looked at towards the end of Chapter 4.

Numerous recent examples from the world of banking show us that it is possible to play 'casino capitalism', with ruinous consequences for broader society, and still be personally rewarded for long-term organizational failure. Perceived excessive and greedy corporate behaviour like this has engendered protest groups like the 'Wall Street movement', and prompted the UK Prime Minister to open discussion on board room remuneration.

The choice is yours – you can do it. You can be a bad leader, the times have never been better since the early period of capitalism in the 19th century, and clearly you may win. Or you can do the right thing – and perhaps shareholders will start demanding that boards look for leaders who are inclined to play the collaborate card rather more often.

How the brain works

The neurology student will know that the brain has five divisions – not three as is described in many of the best-seller 'popular psychology made easy books':

1 The myencephalon, the base of the brain that connects with the spinal cord.
2 The metencephalon, just above the base, and including the cerebellum (the bit that looks like a squashed lettuce at the back of your head).
3 The mesencephalon, also just above the base but forward.

4 The diencephalon, the 'middle' of the brain that contains most of the limbic ring structures.

5 The telencephalon, the cortex or 'grey matter'.

The popular triune brain model simplifies this and lumps the first three divisions together, calling them the 'old reptilian brain', it re-names the diencephalon the 'emotional brain', and it categorizes the telencephalon as the 'reasoning brain'.

As far as the left and right hemispheres of the brain are concerned, these may be thought of as superimposed on the divisions of the brain. With few exceptions (the three collosi, or neural joins running down the middle of the brain) we have two of everything in our brains: two thalami, two amygdala, two olfactory lobes, and two hemispheres. This is true of almost all our organs – it is a successful evolutionary gambit. In human beings, it is the hemispheres that are most interesting: the telencephalon (ie your cortex or grey matter) that has developed specific functions in specific areas.

Although the two sides of the brain are similar in appearance, they have different functions. Neither is the brain perfectly symmetrical – it is slightly skewed to the right. This is known as lateralization. In the pre-natal stage, the right side develops first. In neonates, between 1 and 2 years of age, the left hemisphere 'catches up', and by the age of 5 we have fully lateralized brains. The corpus callosum, which divides the two hemispheres, is not fully developed (myelinated), however, until the age of 10. The 'quirkiness' of a child's way of looking at the world is in part attributable to the non-lateralized brain functions.

The catching up of the left hemisphere is due to the language learning spurt that infants make between 1 and 2 years old. By 5, a child will have established his or her handedness, though some children continue to display ambidextrous traits beyond this age. At 10, it is common to set children intelligence tests – this is a reflection of the full myelination of the corpus callosum allowing the child to cognate far better than in his or her infancy – the beginning of adult reasoning.

The function of the corpus callosum is to transfer information from one side of the brain to the other. There are two other major connections: the anterior callosum and the thalamic callosum. The two sides of the brain can function independently, but in most cases, the two sides cooperate.

Left brain and right brain thinking is a controversial subject and one that has suffered from popular misconceptions. Let us dispel some myths. First, there is no such thing as a right brain or a left brain thinker. All of the brain, or many parts of the brain, are used in both hemispheres when we cognate, perform tasks, receive sensory stimuli and so on. Lateralization of function is the exception rather than the rule. When statistically significant hemisphere differences are found, they tend to be slightly biased in favour of one hemisphere or other, not absolute differences – we appear to lean towards using one side more than the other, in the same way that we are left- or right-handed (to determine which side you are biased towards, there are two common tests – the sodium amatyl test and the dichotic listening test, if you want to research these).

The only true left brain or right brain thinkers are split brain patients (usually epileptics) whose corpus callosum (the bundle of nerves joining the two hemispheres) has been severed to alleviate their condition – and there have only been 50 or so such patients since the 1970s. True split brain patients literally have two minds that think independently and cannot communicate with each other (a weird proposition).

Second, the principal and uncontroversial difference between the two brain hemispheres is that the left hemisphere contains the two language function areas, and the right does not (though a 'shadow' language ability exists in the right hemisphere). These two areas are known as Broca's and Wernicke's areas (after a French and an Austrian neurologist, respectively).

It was this fact (established by the mid-1800s) that led to the general belief that the left hemisphere was 'superior' and led the right hemisphere. Nowadays, ironically, in some quarters it is more fashionable to say that you are a right brain thinker because, in popular literature, right brain equals holistic, intuitive, sensitive and so on. Factually incorrect, but a popular belief nonetheless.

A 'shadow' language learning area exists in the right side because:

- almost all functions in the brain are duplicated;
- left-handed people (sinistrals) obey the contralateral rule and engage the right brain predominantly; and
- some people just appear to prefer the right 'shadow' side for language functions; typically, these may be 'creative' thinkers or simply ambidextrous people.

For right-handed people, the right half of the brain contains visuo-spatial and 'face-reading' areas, the left contains two language function areas; left-handers obey the contra-lateral rule – the opposite of the above, possible because almost all functions are duplicated, there is a shadow on the opposite side (nature's redundancy). So to talk 'left brain/right brain', or 'right brain is the emotional brain' is a gross oversimplification and clearly wrong for left-handers – you could say that only left-handed people are in their right minds!

Every time you learn something or develop a skill, neural circuits are altered in your brain as new connections and pathways are made between neurons. These neurons communicate with one another through synapses – communication nodes or junctions. These paths and the efficiency of the synapses become stronger as we practise new skills; we find things easier to do. For example, a musician learning a new tune will have to make new connections in the brain to deal with it: some neurons recognize the notes on the sheet music, others hear the tune, and so on. To learn this new tune, you practise playing it, and this selects and strengthens the connections among these various circuits in your cortex. It is this new association that forms your memory of the tune. The better you have learnt it (lots of practice), the longer your memory of it will last. When we learn new skills we create new neural pathways or links between neurons in our brain. This is why 'self-talk', 'visualizations' and rehearsals can help us to prepare for events and improve our performance.

Thirdly, it is accepted that the right hemisphere is dominant in visuo-spatial tasks. Fourth, the right hemisphere is dominant in 'face reading', that is to say interpreting the emotional state of a speaker by reading the cues on his or her face. These last two facts are the root of all the holistic, intuitive, synthetic labels that are sometimes attached to people – to jump from one specific brain function (the ability to perceive form and order in space) to claims that the left and right brain represent the ying and yang in the human soul, is quite a leap. To say that the right brain is 'emotional' is another leap, and it leads over a precipice that hundreds of thousands are happy to jump, judging by the quantity of self-help books sold every year!

So what? It is possible to say – and it is possible to prove with various tests – that you may perform better in verbal tasks or in spatial tasks. These results you may, legitimately but with due caution, use to conclude that you have a preference or bias for right or left hemisphere thinking – but no more. You may legitimately claim – without reservations – that, in your employment, you may be better at certain tasks than at others, based on the results of the tests, all other things being equal (such as good or poor leadership!). You may find that you have naturally pursued hobbies, jobs, interests and so on that are suited to your bias (such as journalism), but equally you may not (prostitution, for example!). You may find, and you probably will find, that focusing your energies in one activity (crosswords) will lead to an improvement of that ability.

What of 'lateral thinking', seldom mentioned in textbooks? Why the academic prejudice? Possibly because the 'big idea' when distilled, amounts to common sense – 'Don't bang your head against a brick wall square on, walk around it; don't get fixated with a problem, think around it.' That, in a nutshell, is the idea being sold. What is being encouraged really, is what might be commonly called 'right brain thinking' (for right-handers!).

Hopefully this gives you a flavour of the sorts of assumptions that are made when left brain/right brain thinking is packaged and sold in books, courses and tests. It is responsible if it is explained, and irresponsible if it is not.

General differences in hemispheric functioning

The majority of research in hemispheric functioning has focused on language abilities and handedness. This is because the language learning areas in the brain are known (Broca's area and Wernicke's area) and because the relationship between handedness and brain asymmetry is also known. Brain asymmetry is the well-known fact that damage to one side of the brain (a severe blow to the right hemisphere), causes damage on the opposite side of the body (paralysis in the left leg) – the contralateral principle.

Dextrality and sinistrality

There are three factors that determine hemispheric functioning: your sex, whether you prefer to use your right hand (dextrality) or left hand (sinistrality), and whether there is a family history of sinistrality. All these factors are, ultimately, part of your genetic inheritance. You can't, in that sense, 'change the way you think.' You can learn thinking skills ('lateral thinking' or the appreciation in Chapter 14), but the basic structures of your brain will remain the same – you cannot shift Broca's area to the right side of the brain by reading lots of poetry! Perhaps an analogy might be that you can improve your place-kicking in rugby by practising – but if you are right-footed, you will always take that place-kick with your right foot. That doesn't mean that you can't learn to use the left foot, but it will always be the inferior foot and will feel odd.

Here are some generalizations that can be drawn about the hemispheres and their use.[3, 4] Dextrals (right-handed people) overwhelmingly use the left hemisphere for language. Sinistrals (left-handed) and ambidextrous people mainly use the left hemisphere but a third use the right hemisphere. This follows the general rule that sinistrals show a higher incidence of reversed asymmetry as well as reduced asymmetry. Reversed asymmetry and reduced asymmetry means less lateralization of the brain functions. In other words, if you were to observe a sinistral brain scan, you would see both hemispheres showing hot areas (electrical activity), more so than with dextrals. This is, of course, what you would expect, because the left hand engages the right hemisphere, so straightaway language functions are more diffused. You can also see this with hand movements when people talk. Observe yourself or others when gesticulating – the hand that gesticulates the most will tell you on which side of the brain (the opposite side) the language function is dominant. Both President Obama and Prime Minister Cameron, for example, gesticulate with their left hands.

Sinistrality is predominant in males, twins, mentally impaired people, epileptics, dyslexics and mathematicians. The last category is interesting. Most people would say that mathematicians must be left brain thinkers because mathematics is a language, it is about analysis and relationships between values. Not true – the most gifted mathematicians (and scientists) display right brain thinking (as well as some left brain thinking, it is not either/or). In MBTI language they tend to be NT. The most obvious example of this is Einstein who, when he was not busy proposing the theory of relativity, made some interesting remarks about the importance of 'envisaging' a problem (ie right brain thinking).

Hemispheric 'emotional' processing is contentious: it is generally agreed that the left frontal lobe has an excitatory function (damage causes depression), and the right frontal lobe has an inhibitory function (damage causes hypomania). This is well established and was part of the justification for carrying out frontal lobotomies – unfortunately with unpredictable results because the brain is just not an organ that permits easy surgery. A neurologist called Antonio Damasio has written a book called *Descartes' Error*[5] on the subject, which tells the story of a worker who was spiked through the skull but survived, and whose behaviour suddenly changed as a result. In simple terms, our frontal lobes act as an on-off switch for our 'emotions'. The left frontal lobe revs them up (hence damage leads to depression), and the right frontal lobe dampens them down (hence damage leads to manic, excitable behaviour). Effectively, you lose your ability to balance your 'emotions' if the frontal lobes are damaged. Car accident victims suffer from this (if they bang their heads hard enough), leading to tragic breakdowns in relationships when one partner starts acting differently ('He's not the person I used to know' – true, the brain damage is such that it leads to personality disorders).

Gender differences

Gender differences are disputed. Some physiologists argue that the only difference between a male and female brain is size, and even this difference is fallacious because the two brains are equal in size relative to body weight. What is being disputed is brain structure, not functioning. Our brains are chemical soup kitchens and the ingredients (hormones, neurotransmitters and so on) are markedly different in men and women. For example, men have 300 times the level of testosterone sloshing about in our bodies (and brains), which explains a lot, from male predominance for violent crime to those awful G-strings that muscle-bound poseurs wear on Bondi Beach. Men and women, in this sense, do think differently – it's just plain scientific fact. Just as it is fact that during a part of the menstrual cycle, the chemical balances in the female brain are altered. Experiments do appear to have demonstrated that males and females think differently in some ways, although some men think in what is often thought to be female ways (the feeling preference in MBTI) just as some women think in male ways (thinking preference in MBTI):

- Dextral women with no sinistral family history display less lateralization of functions. Nobody is really sure why, but this is the origin of the claim that women, generally, think more holistically than men, ie they use both hemispheres.
- Sinistral women with or without a sinistral family history display the most lateralization of functions. Again, nobody is really sure why. It is as if left-handedness in women (engaging the right hemisphere) exaggerates the lateralization.
- Men generally have better spatial abilities (right hemisphere). There are several (mostly evolutionary) theories for this – men are hunters so they need to find prey, men tend to be predominantly polygamous so they need to find females and so on.
- Women generally have better language abilities (left hemisphere). Theories explaining this tend to focus on women as nurturers requiring social skills to teach their young and keep the 'troop together'. Cynics (or men) say that women just love to gossip.
- Women generally have better perception of facial expressions (emotions – right hemisphere). Again, theories explaining this focus on women as the 'emotionally intelligent' gender. Critics would say a man wrote the ballet Swan Lake, a male playwright wrote *Romeo and Juliet*, and a man painted the Mona Lisa – all tangible evidence of emotional intelligence. 'Ah,' feminists would say, 'that's because we never had the opportunity in the past.' 'Ah,' the counterblast would come, 'but you have now, and men still predominantly excel in these fields.' 'Ah,' the feminists would retort, 'that's because the judges are white males.' The debate goes on.

The cerebral lateralization of functions

Although there is some dispute as to the nature and extent of functional lateralization, there is broad agreement that the functions shown in Table 8.1 are represented in the cerebral hemispheres.[6] This is a useful summary of the main left and right brain functions. Just to give you one example: under 'language' it states that the right hemisphere has the emotional function. This is true. There is a condition known as 'aphasia' that affects the language functions. Some aphasics can read and comprehend language, but because the damage is in the right hemisphere, they cannot invest emotional content in the words. So you can ask them to read a poem, and they will

TABLE 8.1 Left and right hemisphere functions

	Left Hemisphere	Right Hemisphere
Vision	Words Letters	Geometric Patterns Faces Emotional Expressions
Audition	Language Sounds	Non-language Sounds Music
Touch	Unknown	Tactile Patterns Braille
Movement	Complex Movement	Movement In Spatial Patterns
Memory	Verbal Memory	Non-verbal Memory
Language	Speech Reading Writing Arithmetic	Emotional Content
Spatial Ability	Unknown	Geometry Direction Distance
Processing	Verbal Sequential Analytic Temporal Rational Digital Intellectual	Visuo-spatial Simultaneous Synthetic Spatial Intuitive Analogue Emotional
Inferred Preferences from the Above	You tend to be conforming • prefer structured assignments • prefer to discover systematically • recall verbal material • look for facts • look for sequences • look for outline • think logically • try to improve	You tend to be non-conforming • prefer open-ended assignments • prefer to discover by exploring • recall spatial material • look for main ideas • look for relationships • look for summary • think intuitively • try to invent

read it without emotion. They simply cannot tell the difference between a passage of poetry and the football results. The 'type of mental processing' by hemisphere[7] has also been added to increase understanding.

So what does this mean?

What this means to us as leaders is that:

- There are differences in the way people think and these are determined by the balance of functions in the left and right hemispheres. This is not uncommonly manifested in the choice of interests and jobs, as well as in cognitive tasks (from language ability to map reading, for example).
- Dominance in one or other hemisphere is genetic and is determined by three factors: sex, handedness and family history of handedness.
- We have a preference to use a dominant side, left or right style of thinking, but the other side is used as well. That dominant side is going to affect how we approach problem solving – our style of thinking. In neuro-linguistic programming terms it will also affect our sensory preferences and thus communication and language (word) preferences (see the perception section and visual, auditory, kinaesthetic senses).
- A right hemisphere dominant thinker prefers to use the right hemisphere, a left hemisphere dominant thinker prefers to use the left hemisphere. A right hemisphere dominant thinker also prefers to be addressed in the right hemisphere, and a left hemisphere dominant thinker prefers to be addressed in the left hemisphere. A right hemisphere dominant thinker is therefore more likely to be 'truthful', 'accurate', and responsive when addressed in the right hemisphere, and vice-versa.
- Males and females think differently, and this is largely due to the different chemical balances in the male and female brains.
- When learning occurs or skills are developed, new connections are made between neurons in the brain. This is why 'self-talk', visualization and rehearsals have a place in coaching and development (or in self-coaching).

Human behaviour and emotional intelligence

Now that we have an understanding of the concept of personality, the mechanics of the brain and the nature of human nature, we will look at behaviour and emotional intelligence (EI). Our 'preferred behaviour', that is to say the behaviour that we typically display, is the manifest part of personality. We will start this section by looking at the influences and drivers of human behaviour for two reasons: 1) to enable us to understand the people who work around us, so that we may lead and develop them more effectively; and 2) to better understand what makes us tick as individual leaders, so that we may develop ourselves and lead others more effectively – that is to say, developing our EI.

FIGURE 8.1 The components of emotional intelligence and the drivers of behaviour

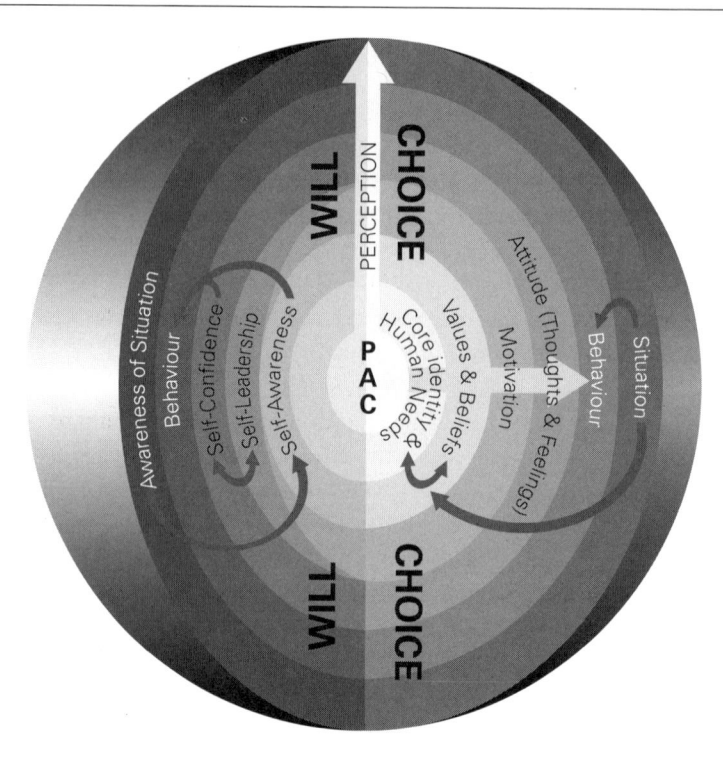

After Tozer, Oliver & Larcombe | © Jeremy Tozer & Mark Oliver, 2007

To do this, we will use the spherical model of Figure 8.1 and its onion-like layers. The right-hand side of this sphere illustrates the drivers of human behaviour; the left-hand side contains the components of emotional intelligence. The shading of Figure 8.1 relates the EI components on the left, to the behavioural drivers on the right. Thus, EI self-awareness relates to core identity, values and beliefs, and motivation; and EI self-leadership and self-confidence to attitude, and so on.

We will begin by looking at the right-hand side of Figure 8.1, starting at the outer layer and working in towards the centre. When we have grasped the nature of the drivers of our behaviour, we will then explore the concept of emotional intelligence.

Understanding others: the layered drivers of behaviour

Personality is like an iceberg; the majority of it lies hidden from casual view beneath the surface. Understanding what drives people to behave as they do requires 'human appreciation': value attached to people, together with the application of keen observation and astute deductive thought (please excuse the pun on the word 'appreciation' which is also the name of the problem solving process introduced in Chapter 14).

> - All behaviour has meaning
> - We see behaviour...
>
> ...but what drives behaviour is deep below the surface

We do not behave in a vacuum, we behave in an environment, a situation; and our behaviour does not occur automatically in response to environmental stimulation. Behaviour has to be triggered (either consciously or subconsciously) by a behavioural intention – an intention to behave in a particular way. That situation influences our behaviour just as we influence the situation, and, through this, the behaviour of others. Our behaviour is also driven by many other things:

- Our attitude – our thoughts and feelings which shape behavioural intention, which is shaped by –
- our motivation – our desire to act which usually has either a selfish or selfless focus, which is shaped by –
- our values and beliefs – beliefs may be facts or limiting opinions that we hold to be true, values are subjective beliefs to which we attach weight, which are shaped by –
- our core identity and human needs – our genetic inheritance, early influences and learnt experiences.

So there are many influences on the drivers of our behaviour which we shall now explore in a little more detail, using Figure 8.1 is a guide.

Choice

The first point to make is that our behaviour is a choice. You might hear people say things like, 'Jo makes me so angry when he does that', but Jo has not forced anyone to react angrily. The reaction – the behaviour – is a choice made in response to a feeling or emotion. Presumably that is why the old adage is to count to 10 before responding has evolved, when a different choice of behaviour may be made as the intensity of the emotion is likely to have subsided.

Situation

There are many variables within the situation or context that contribute to shaping our behaviour directly. These may include:

- Beliefs about the consequences of behaviour, which create an incentive for us to behave in a certain way or to limit our behaviour.
- Social pressure or cultural norms, the accepted way of behaving. This is especially potent when emphasized verbally or by example by key people within an organization.
- Beliefs about factors that may help or hinder performance of the behaviour.

These external variables are more likely to have a short-term effect upon a person's 'preferred behaviour', that is to say the behaviour that person typically displays. When we are removed from that context, or the sticks and carrots are removed, then behaviour may well revert 'to type'.

A mind that is stretched by a new experience can never go back to its old dimensions.
(Oliver Wendell Holmes)

Experience is not what happens to you but what you make of it.
(Aldous Huxley)

There is much to be learnt in any situation if we are open to its influence. The environment or climate can and does shape our behaviour. The question is, how much and to what degree? High-impact experiences and stressful or testing environments can reframe our beliefs. Such situations may deliver powerful 'learnt experiences' that result in reframing or recalibrating our beliefs and values; which have an ongoing influence on our behaviour. A common example is the long-term positive impact of challenging and adventurous training on people's levels of self-confidence and self-esteem that results from overcoming one's limiting beliefs. Kurt Hahn, the pioneering educator and founder of 'Outward Bound' knew this, as do all those who have been engaged in conducting any form of adventurous training, me included.

Behaviour

Behaviour is what we observe: we see behaviour and we witness and/or feel its impact. It is the preferred behaviour of both ourselves and others that we seek to develop.

Past behaviour is a good predictor of future behaviour because the beliefs underlying the attitude, underlying the behaviour, remain consistent over time – until challenged. However, what happens if we focus only on behaviour? This provides descriptive data only; it does not necessarily provide clues as to what is needed to bring about lasting change.

We may miss the opportunity to explore and influence all the other dimensions that lie behind behaviour – we are only working 'above the waterline' in the iceberg metaphor. Changing behaviour without addressing beliefs that underlie attitudes is very difficult: it requires encouraging or enforcing new behaviour in the hope that attitudes will then be shaped accordingly. Challenging beliefs and attitudes on the other hand sets the scene for sustained behavioural change.

We may ignore the link between thinking and feeling. Considerable experimental evidence shows that thoughts are mediated, even determined, by emotional processes. People make interpretations based on information they perceive from their environment and from past experiences. We have a need to understand our experiences (or try to explain what we are feeling). These interpretations help shape our behavioural responses.

For a leader aspiring to lead change, some important implications can be elicited from these statements:

- We should clarify the positive consequences of new behaviours and negative consequences of staying the same.
- We should create a normative environment where key people send clear signal messages explaining the new direction.
- We should link new behaviours to acceptance, reward and status in the organization.
- We should provide training in new skills and knowledge so that the person *believes* he or she can assume new roles and role requirements and adapt his or her behaviour.
- We should provide an environment that supports rather than blocks required behaviours.

Bringing about change (or development) is what leadership is about. But manipulating behaviour is unlikely to produce long-term change – when the circumstances change (less vigilance) the person is free to return to his or her preferred mode of operating.

For performance management, behaviour is important – but many organizations ignore more chronic attitudinal problems. Attitudinal performance problems are the most difficult to deal with and may be considered the by-product of a systematic bias in the way the person views the world. In these circumstances it is not enough to simply challenge the person at the behavioural level.

Behaviours do not occur automatically in response to environmental stimulation. They have to be triggered (either consciously or automatically) by a behavioural intention – an intention to behave in a particular way. It is now time to look at attitude.

Attitude (thoughts and feelings)

When we describe the way a person acts we often refer to his or her attitude. Our attitude in any situation is a choice if we are sufficiently controlled and reasoned.

Our attitude is influenced by inner layers in our 'onion', together with our perception of the environment and of the situation; this influences our thinking and resulting feelings (emotions). The greater our ability to understand and manage our emotions, the greater we will be able to choose the attitude we adopt in a particular situation.

In simple terms a person's attitude to life and work is the direct result of his or her past experiences, filtered through a perception of the current situation, and weighted by that person's beliefs and values. We cannot change past experience but we can change perceptions (when we understand the nature of perception) and we may influence beliefs and values. As a result we can change attitude. For leaders, this is of crucial importance and to achieve this, we must also know something about the mechanisms of persuasion, which is discussed in Chapter 11.

Attitude[8,9] may be defined as the evaluation of an object, concept or behaviour along a dimension of favour/disfavour, good/bad, like/dislike; and that evaluation can shift as a result of changing circumstances or perspectives. Across a broad spectrum of domains, ranging from satisfaction with consumer products to general life satisfaction, evaluative judgements are found to be more favourable in happy than in sad moods. When participants see no connection with their mood (which may have been induced – perhaps by clever ad agencies!) these evaluative judgements may be even more powerful (although when people become aware of the possible effect of mood, they may take steps to counteract it).

People have only limited information-processing capacity and we tend to examine matters we consider to be important closely and carefully (systematic mode). Less weighty issues are dealt with more quickly (heuristic mode). When people have a low level of motivation or limited cognitive capability, receivers of persuasive communication usually rely on simple cognitive heuristics (superficial cues) to form opinions (for example, the speaker's attractiveness). Only where individuals have the motivation and capacity to invest cognitive effort are they found to engage in deliberate, systematic thought and be influenced by the quality of the argument, which may lead to the formation of new beliefs.

Yet beliefs are a prime contributor to, or influencer of, attitude and for people of low motivation or cognitive capability, attitudes are found to be based on a small number of beliefs and, at very low levels, beliefs and attitudes can be influenced by heuristic cues that require a minimal degree of processing. Irrespective of the number of accessible beliefs on which they are based and independent of their strength, attitudes are capable of 'automatic activation'. In general, the more favourable the attitude and the greater the perceived control that a person has, the stronger should be the person's intention to perform a behaviour. Given a sufficient degree of actual control over the behaviour, people may be expected to carry out their intentions when the opportunity arises. Intention is therefore an immediate antecedent of behaviour – it guides behaviour.

Although the beliefs people hold may sometimes be unfounded or biased, their attitudes are believed to follow spontaneously from these beliefs and produce a corresponding behavioural intention that leads ultimately to behaviour broadly consistent with the underlying beliefs. Theories of reasoned action and planned behaviour assume human social relations are reasoned, controlled or planned in the sense that they take account of the behaviour's likely consequences, normative expectations and factors that may hinder performance. However, when motivation or the opportunity to process information is limited, the controlled processes cannot be used. Under these conditions attitudes can only guide behaviour if they become activated automatically and effortlessly. Automatic attitude-behaviour is usually characterized as:

- unintentional;
- occurring outside awareness;
- uncontrollable;
- unstoppable once started;
- effortless and efficient (does not interfere with other cognitive processes).

Past behaviour and habit are another line of research on automatic behaviour. The idea is simply that frequent performance of a behaviour leads to formation of a habit. Once established, the habit controls later behaviour without conscious cognitive effort. Frequency of past behaviour is an indicator of habit strength and can be used as an independent predictor of future behaviour.

Strength is an important characteristic of attitudes. Strong attitudes tend to be highly 'accessible' and bias perceptions and influence behaviour. Attitudes and behaviour are guided by the beliefs that are accessible, in the context in which attitudes are expressed and the context in which the behaviour is performed. So a strong attitude–behaviour correlation may be expected only if the beliefs in the two contexts are the same or similar. Experiments indicate that attitudes based on direct experience are significantly more stable than attitudes based on second-hand information (which is a powerful argument for experiential learning).

E-motion, or energy in motion, can be an extremely powerful influence on attitude and behaviour, and the successful leader will harness this energy. We all have emotions or feel strongly about some subjects, and the influence of this emotional 'wiring' is plain to observe at work and at play. Our emotional reactions to a given situation might have no basis in logic or rationality, but they are no less important to us because of that. Some subjects do not generally create strong feelings in us one way or another. For example, a person usually reacts rationally when dealing with such subjects as mathematics, chemistry or physics, but might react on a purely emotional level when discussing politics, religion, football teams, trade unionism, motor cars, and so on.

Emotions almost always find a means of expression – whether it is through adding to the stress felt by those who bottle up their emotions, or in the outbursts of those who do not contain them. Emotions also tend to have less impact when they have been 'brought out into the open' and discussed. For example, it is common for soldiers who are about to launch a deliberate, planned assault on the enemy to feel emotions of fear, anxiety and worry. This is quite natural, and everyone will be feeling it whether they care to admit it or not. To leave these emotions 'in the closet', is to add to their insidious and destructive power. If the leader discusses these emotions, the tension in the atmosphere is palpably reduced, and the unhelpful nature of these emotions is reduced.

Emotions can be such powerful influences on thought and behaviour – such as the way we approach problems and make decisions – that we cannot hope to control them. We can only strive to contain them.

Nobel Prize winners Kahneman and Tversky developed the prospect theory,[10] which describes decisions between alternatives that involve risk where the probabilities of outcomes are known. They suggested that people's decisions are influenced less by the final outcome and more by the potential value of losses and gains, which are evaluated using heuristics.

We can regulate our response to emotion, not the emotion itself that mediates our thoughts. Our success or failure at any task often depends upon on our relative success or failure at regulating our response to the emotions that arise in us.

There are two basic groups of emotions: love and fear. Love (selflessness) emotions are very powerful and the states they induce can motivate people (eg, enthusiasm, happiness, devotion, hope, loyalty). Fear (selfish) emotions include anxiety, hate, jealousy, shame, cockiness, conceit, sadness, worry, dread and blame. There is a link between fear and anger. Angry people are often afraid. Anger is often the fierce front we put up when we are afraid – often as a defensive behaviour. Common fears in organizations are:

- fear of powerlessness;
- fear of rejection;
- fear of failure;
- fear of conflict.

The typical way people deal with fear is to use defence shields rather than confronting fear directly. Common defence mechanisms include:

- withdrawal (either physically or emotionally);
- avoidance;
- projection (attributing feelings, actions, blame, etc to someone or something else, instead of acknowledging our own actions);
- rationalization (justifying rather than accepting responsibility);
- denial;
- intellectualization (talk about ideas rather than feelings);
- repression (pushing uncomfortable feelings deep into the unconscious);
- blaming;
- attack (physically, emotionally or mentally discrediting the source of the discomfort).

We cannot eliminate fear. But we can learn to tolerate it and to respond clearly despite its presence. Brave people typically experience enormous fear but they have the ability to tolerate the fear and respond to the situation. Confronting fear tends to defuse it. We need to manage fear rather than allowing it to control us. Recognition of fears involves bringing fears that lie 'beneath the surface' up to consciousness. This involves being introspective – going inwards and exploring (which may be harder for the extraverts out there).

In narrative therapy, fears are thought to:

- Increase in strength in direct proportion to the amount of time taken to confront them.

'The only thing we have to fear is fear itself.'

Franklin D Roosevelt

- Require a 'fear support system' to keep them alive.
- Be crushed by laughter – they have no sense of humour.

The wise leader will understand the characteristics of emotion and emotionally charged situations and take appropriate action:

- Our feelings are unique to us; other people may have similar but never identical feelings.
- We are reluctant to accept that our thoughts are influenced by emotion and we insist that we are thinking rationally, yet thoughts based on emotion probably outnumber logical thoughts.
- We find it very easy to make associations between an emotional view and other unrelated subjects. For example, a proud new father can easily relate any subject to his baby.
- Emotions may be 'creative' if harnessed and directed.
- Emotions insist on being expressed: they simply refuse to lie dormant. They continually influence our perceptions, thinking and actions, though sometimes they may be disguised from others.
- When emotions have been expressed and 'vented', they often have less effect.

Motivation

Man is not a finite resource. When motivated he can achieve a great deal, but when badly motivated he'll achieve nothing. (Anon)

The level of motivation in a team – the willingness to expend effort in pursuit of an objective – can be sensed and felt by everyone around that group, including people who come into contact with the team such as the customer. Everyone is touched by the aura – the energy, sense of urgency, enthusiasm and tangible sense of purpose that a well-motivated team exudes. Whether they know it or not, leaders who have built companies like this are true to the Latin origins from which the word 'company' is derived – *companis*, 'with bread'. In Roman times, 'company' described a group of associates who 'broke bread together'; it is also the source of our word 'companion'.

Equally well, the lack of care and attention demonstrated by people who are less motivated is even more apparent to everyone, including the customer, with corresponding bottom line impact! If you were to ask your colleagues how many believe that they could be more effective at work, you might be surprised at the result. Many people only work as hard as they have to, to keep their jobs, many are not working at full capacity, and most could be more effective or could contribute more if they were encouraged to do so.

Symptoms of poor motivation include absenteeism, poor quality work, sick days, lateness, poor customer service, and high staff turnover. Motivation is the crucial difference between winners and losers whether on the sporting field, the battlefield, or in the ruthless warfare of modern business that sometimes is masked by a thin veneer of respectability. Motivated companies are not just pleasant to work for and deal with; they are almost always the most profitable in their industries.

It is common for junior leaders to be told to motivate so-and-so by their boss, and is usually an impossible task. This superficial and casual instruction underestimates the complexities of motivation. If we consider the ACE conditions for success once again, we will see that motivation lies in all three areas:

- Ability: people must fundamentally want to do the job (because it meets their needs) and be confident that they have the skills and knowledge necessary for success.
- Clarity: people must have clear tasks and objectives (which while stretching, nevertheless must be possible), together with authority to match their level of accountability.
- Environment: they must have a supportive environment in which the boss sets an example, the minimum necessary (rather than desired) resources at least are provided, and the organizational culture is a 'positive' one.

In this section, we will examine the needs of individuals and their satisfaction and the resulting motivation. Once you have read this section, it will be worth revisiting the functional leadership checklist in Chapter 4 and the things that the leader needs to do to satisfy and develop the individual.

Needs, behaviour and goals

Humans are needy creatures: we want things, we want to be loved, we want to be happy, we want our rights, we want food, or sex or air, we want to belong. Everywhere you go you find that we humans are demanding things. If you think about it you will see that it is the non-fulfilment of our demands that channels our behaviour and forms our attitude. It is the presence of these unfulfilled needs that is known as motivation. Superficially motivation is simple – but like the iceberg there is more depth beneath; it requires careful thought if it is to be effective, for if ill-considered attempts are made leaders could look foolish and incompetent and that does not build confidence.

No one is unmotivated. A perceived lack of motivation is simply an indicator of another, perhaps unconscious influence that is winning the internal struggle for control of decisions and actions. Our behaviour can be governed by unfulfilled needs. Our desire to satisfy these needs is the source of our motivation. At the deepest level, all motivation relates to our primal instinct to compete (survive) or to collaborate (reproduce). That is, our motivation in all situations is for either self-preservation (a selfish focus based on binary thinking) or self-replication (a selfless focus, a feature of ternary rethinking).

For example, if you are in a meeting in which you perceive the presence of some threat (perhaps there is a colleague or more senior person present who you find to be intimidating), your reaction is to stay quiet or hold back suggestions and comments, your motivation for self-preservation is stronger than your motivation for self-replication (to share your ideas). Your need to survive created a behaviour (staying quiet) to achieve a goal (avoid a threat) that satisfied your need to survive. This triangular relationship is shown in Figure 8.2.

It is a fact of life that some people apply more discretionary effort at work in achieving goals than others do. There are plenty of people with very high levels of

FIGURE 8.2 The needs-behaviour-goals relationship

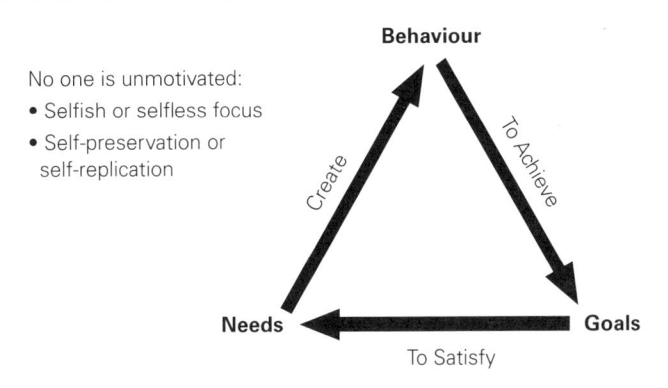

No one is unmotivated:
- Selfish or selfless focus
- Self-preservation or self-replication

Behaviour → (To Achieve) → Goals → (To Satisfy) → Needs → (Create) → Behaviour

© Jeremy Tozer and Mark Oliver, 2006

intelligence and skill whose lack of engagement in their work means that their contribution is far below their potential. Motivation is a willingness to expend effort in pursuit of an objective. The degree of effort expended (behaviour) will reflect the importance of the objective in meeting individual needs. In an organizational sense, it is clear that there must be some consistency and compatibility between organizational goals and individual needs.

Maslow's Hierarchy of Needs

Maslow's Hierarchy of Needs is one of the earliest and best-known theories of motivation. Abraham Maslow[11] suggests that our needs are organized in a series of levels – a hierarchy of importance, in an ascending order (Figure 8.3). When one level of need is satisfied, the next level is of importance. More modern research suggests that this hierarchy of needs has some cultural variations; a full appreciation and knowledge of each individual team member combined with empathy, awareness and sensitivity should overcome most discrepancies between cultures.

Although we are discussing this theory while considering the motivation layer of our layered model of the drivers of behaviour in Figure 8.1, we take the view that

FIGURE 8.3 Maslow's Hierarchy of Needs

Maslow's Hierarchy of Needs
Lower order needs must be satisfied before we progress up the hierarchy.
Position on the hierarchy changes frequently.

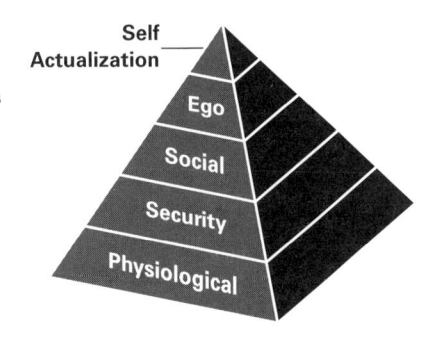

Pyramid (top to bottom): Self Actualization, Ego, Social, Security, Physiological

many of these needs are core to the individual (in simple terms, the basic human or lower order of Maslow's needs), with the higher order needs being shaped by those other 'layers' in Figure 8.1 – needs may change over time with circumstance.

According to Maslow, five needs are related to one another as a hierarchy. The satisfaction of a lower need results in greater concern with a higher one. We are motivated by unsatisfied needs, rather than those that have been gratified. Maslow, in fact, contends that the 'average person' is most often partially satisfied and partially unsatisfied in all of his or her wants.

Subsequent research suggests that different kinds of motive may be important at different levels and with different people in an organization's hierarchy. For instance, high needs for achievement seem to be particularly important for success in junior and middle management jobs. Those high in achievement motivation appear to be stimulated to greater efforts by both success and failure.

The key point here is that it helps to understand what factors in the work environment are likely to be important for most employees. While pay and conditions are important they do not make up the whole picture. Maslow points out that employees' commitment would increase if they received more feedback, the opportunity to work where they could develop friendships and be developed to realize their full potential.

Physiological needs. At the lowest level, but of enormous importance when they demand satisfaction, are the physiological needs. Indeed the way to a man's heart is through his stomach, when he is hungry. For, other than in exceptional circumstances, a person's need for security, love, even status count for nothing if he or she has been without food for a while. The picture and stories that came out of Africa in the 1980s and 1990s of families trekking hundreds of kilometres to find food, of turning up at camps even if there were no accommodation or shelter just to get food, demonstrates clearly the strength of this drive. On the other hand, when we eat regularly, hunger is no longer an important need driving us on to satisfy it.

Remember, 'a satisfied need is no longer a motivator of behaviour'. This simple statement is of profound importance, but it is often forgotten or ignored. Think about your own need for air. It is only if you are deprived of it that the need for it has any motivating effect on your behaviour. One cannot wilfully commit suicide by holding one's breath.

Security needs. Once physiological needs are reasonably satisfied, needs at the next higher level come into play and start to dominate our behaviour. These Maslow calls 'safety needs'. These are needs for protection against physical danger, threat and deprivation. Not, as many have tried to interpret Maslow, the need for feeling secure in a financial sense. The need is for 'the fairest possible break'. When a person is confident of this he or she is more than willing to take risks. But when someone feels threatened or dependent on someone or something else, the need is for guarantees, for protection and for physical security. Another example of this can be seen in the ways that some people reacted after the Chernobyl nuclear accident – the demands that all nuclear programmes be halted, that power stations be closed down, and the constant demands for more and more information; demands for guarantees, for physical security from the dangers of radiation.

Social needs. Once a person's physiological needs have been satisfied and that person is no longer fearful for his or her safety, the needs for social intercourse come into play. We need to belong, to be accepted by our fellows, to give and receive love and friendship. These are many of the factors that are discussed in group behaviour. Leaders should harness these forces for the development of teams. Thwarting social needs can lead to individuals becoming resistant, antagonistic and uncooperative. Be sure to remember, though, that exhibited behaviour by any members of the team is the result, not the cause. Think for a moment about the most 'difficult' person in your team and consider: is he or she really well integrated into the group? Has that person had difficulty in being accepted by others?

Ego needs. These can be classified into two groups: those that relate to a person's self-esteem, the need for independence, for achievement, for skill and competence; and those that relate to recognition by others, the need for status, for application, for the respect of our fellows. Unlike lower needs these are rarely satisfied and they continually drive us on to strive to 'make it', but when we get there, we inevitably find another mountain to climb.

Self-actualization needs. Finally, at the top of the pyramid, is the need for self-actualization or self-fulfilment; the requirement to realize our own potential, for continued development of our own creative ability. This is the level at which many successful business people have become engaged with philanthropic activity.

It is important to understand that the operation of the hierarchy is not a rigid stepping up and down the pyramid as life progresses. There is, in fact, a constant moving up and down the hierarchy as an individual's situations and circumstances alter – and sometimes this can be from moment to moment.

Herzberg's Two-factor Theory

Another American, Herzberg,[12] conducted a study in the late 1950s on employees in the United States to try to discover more about why they worked. He found that there were really two sets of factors; he called them *motivators or satisfiers*, because they actively worked towards satisfying a person's needs, and *hygiene or maintenance* factors. He called them hygiene factors because he said they were in the same relationship to satisfiers as hygiene is to health: that it is useful to have hygiene, but it is not crucial for good health. When present they were unimportant, it is when they are absent that they are the cause of dissatisfaction.

Herzberg discovered that satisfiers, the things that really drive people, are responsibility, achievement, opportunities to exercise their skills, variety, the possibilities for promotion, growth and recognition. The hygiene factors turn out to be things like pay, conditions of work, the quality of leadership, company policy, administration and interpersonal relations.

Compare the two. There is a degree of similarity between Maslow's bottom two layers and Herzberg's hygiene factors, while satisfiers can be equated with the top three layers of Maslow's hierarchy. Indeed, it is sometimes said that Maslow's top three layers are 'brain needs' and the bottom two are 'belly needs'.

If we consider that it is rewarding to a person to satisfy a need then we can be said to be offering 'carrots' to induce the behaviour wanted. But, beware of imagining that the same carrot works with everyone. It is the individual's perception of the value of the reward that induces the behaviour. For example, where the offer of an afternoon off may induce many people to work more quickly, there may be those with domestic problems to whom the extra time at home is no reward at all! However, relying on carrots and incentives is effectively to rely on bribes. When the carrot is removed, the desired behaviour stops. It must be the task of leadership to create the conditions in which motivated behaviour occurs as the norm.

These theories enable the leader to understand the different human responses and behaviours demonstrated at work:

- Offering people more money as an incentive does not necessarily motivate them to work harder. If the current salary is enough for their lifestyle they may not want the extra responsibility and workload that accompanies the higher salary. Most people gain job satisfaction from success, teamwork and a sense of purpose or direction. Money is no substitute for these. Continually complimenting and congratulating people devalues compliments for real achievements from leaders and lowers the respect in which they are held.
- If the lower needs are not satisfied then motivating people by addressing higher level needs does not work; for example, if people expect to be made redundant (security needs) then appealing to their self-actualization needs is unlikely to be very successful.
- The needs can vary as people change. Young people with families and mortgages may be motivated by money in their early years, but in middle age, with independent children and no mortgage, needs may change and higher level needs become more effective motivators.
- Meeting the higher level of Maslow's needs is hard compared to those of the lower order because it depends on effective working relationships – good leadership.
- Social events after hours, playing games on 'teambuilding' away days, and so on can contribute to building personal relationships and understanding, but fail to build motivation where basic leadership is lacking and the ACE conditions for success are ineffective.
- Too many coffee breaks during the working day disrupt well-motivated people who wish to get on with the job. Extra breaks in the day may not help build morale or motivation since they erode efficiency.
- Job rotation does not necessarily raise motivation. It always does this initially when there is something new to learn, but if frequent rotation means that all jobs are kept simple then all jobs can become boring and that is the cause of lack of interest and demotivation.
- Team spirit satisfies a security need, and people are rejected by the team when they let the team down by failing. Building team spirit, therefore, assists motivation.

Dan Pink[13] has considered an alternative view of incentives, compared to the traditional 'carrots offered by management'. It is based on research funded by the US Federal Reserve Bank and conducted at the Massachusetts Institute of Technology (MIT). Typically, a financial incentive is given for better performance, and the MIT research required the student participants to undertake a whole range of challenges and tasks with three levels of reward: a small monetary reward for satisfactory performance, a medium level reward, and a high cash reward for excellent performance.

The result was that as long as the task required only basic mechanical skills, performance levels met expectations in line with the incentives. But as soon as cognitive skills were required, larger rewards led to poorer performance. Not what was expected! So they tried the experiment somewhere else where the same cash incentives might have more importance – they went to rural India, and used three levels of incentive: two weeks' salary, one month's salary and two months' salary to office workers. The people offered the lowest reward performed at the same level as those offered the mid-level reward, and the people offered the highest reward performed worst of all.

In a nutshell, financial incentives only work for very basic, mechanical tasks. When work requires cognitive processing, conceptual thought and creativity – money acts like a hygiene factor. The research suggested that money is best used as an incentive when it is taken off the table – when people are paid sufficiently well that they do not think about money at work, so that they think about the work instead. The real motivational drivers for people engaged in work requiring any form of cognitive processing are autonomy, mastery (getting better at something), and having a meaningful sense of purpose (making the world a little bit better, while also making profit).

Autonomy is the desire to be self-directed. Traditional management required people to do what they were told to do, which might have worked for simple tasks but does not work in the complex modern world we inhabit. Work today requires virtually everyone to think, to innovate and to be engaged. In his RSA YouTube video, Pink quotes the example of Atlassian, an Australian software company, which every quarter gives its developers 24 hours to work on anything they want, with anyone with them they want to work with. After 24 hours, they report back with their results in an informal, social setting. The results are surprising – in that one day of free thinking, a whole array of valuable bug fixes and new product ideas are produced that no one had previously conceived. The approach is a case of realizing the fact that people generally want to do something interesting, and the organization had removed the obstacles that were in the way.

Mastery is getting better at doing things. People have all sorts of hobbies and interests that they pursue in their free time – playing musical instruments for example. Part of the reason that people do these sorts of things is that it is fun, and part of the reason is that they like to get better; they hear or see themselves making progress. Volunteers put lots of time and expertise into developing things that are given away, like Linux for example. Volunteers undertook work which was very probably more complex than the work that they were being paid to do 9 to 5, Monday to Friday, and it has been put out there for people to use – Linux powers one in four corporate servers. Challenge, mastery and making a contribution are behind this use of discretionary time to undertake significant voluntary work, as is 'purpose'.

Purpose is what creates meaning for people: it makes waking up early and going to work more than satisfying. More and more organizations are thinking about what they do in terms of a transcendent purpose. It attracts talent, and it cements the organization's place in the society in which it is based. When the profit motive becomes separated from the purpose motive, illegal and/or unethical things happen. In the last two years, we have all felt the effects of that happening at the strategic level within the banking and financial services sector operating under a 'light touch' regulation regime. At the tactical level, it results in poor customer service, or poor-quality products. The evidence suggests that people in general are both purpose maximizers and profit maximizers, but perhaps with an inclination towards purpose, and making the world just a little bit better.

Universal Hierarchy of Motivation (UHM)
Another means of gaining insight into the motivation of people is to use the Universal Hierarchy of Motivation (UHM) developed by my friend and colleague Mark Oliver[14] (with whom I have worked very closely for many years with many clients in many countries and cultures). He shows that there are seven possible motivations that can drive us, and at any one moment of the day we are at one of these levels. We may move quickly between levels or stay at a level for some time. However, we are always at one of these seven levels and therefore there is no such thing as an unmotivated person: just a person not motivated at the level we want them to be! UHM is both an holistic and an holographic model, and provides excellent insights into life and leadership for several reasons, including the following.

1. Motivation is not so deep that it is beyond conscious awareness and control, yet it is deep enough to have a profound effect on your life. It also connects the deeper aspects of yourself, such as your values, beliefs and needs that are too difficult to work on directly. With UHM, you can work more deeply on your attitude (thoughts and feelings), which directly affects what you decide. Therefore, you can impact your life because life is largely the result of cause (the decisions you make), and effect (their consequences). Denis Waitley, considered by some to be the world's leading performance coach, highlighted the importance of motivation when he said, 'Everything an individual does, whether positive or negative, intentional or unintentional, is the result of motivation. Everyone is self-motivated. For too long... it has been wrongly assumed that motivation is extraneous (externally driven).' In other words, nothing can motivate you; things can only help you be motivated.

2. Your success in life derives from your motivation. Success is linked to performance, and a significant amount of performance usually comes from your behaviour. But your behaviour comes from what you can do (skill) combined with what you want to do (motivation). Your skill is highly developable, and modern research is showing that we all have the potential for genius. Your demonstrated IQ can be raised greatly, and neuroscience is showing that people are generally not performing mentally anywhere near their peak, while epigenetics[15] also supports this conclusion from another perspective. So, although skill is what you may do, motivation determines what you do do and therefore has the bigger impact on your life.

UHM is the basis of a rational theory, and it is formed from the seven levels shown in Figure 8.4. It is represented as the six floors and one basement of a house. The motivations have been identified from a widely researched understanding of human motivations.

So UHM defines real leadership as altruistic behaviour, behaviour motivated out of the top four levels of UHM, while the bottom three levels may be better understood as influencing, they are the levels that typically drive management. This means there are three fundamental ways to manage (although they are often called 'leadership') and four fundamental ways to lead.

FIGURE 8.4 The Universal Hierarchy of Motivation (UHM)

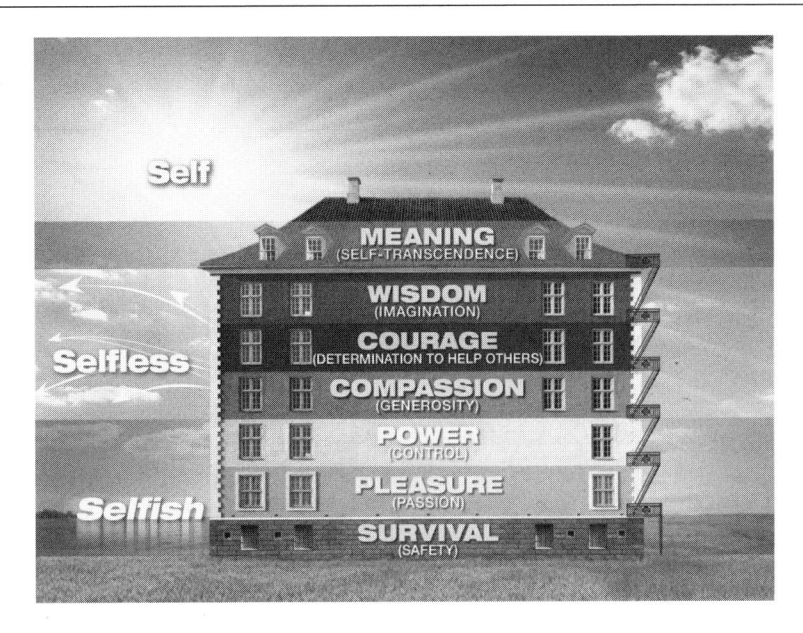

Self — MEANING (SELF-TRANSCENDENCE)
WISDOM (IMAGINATION)
Selfless — COURAGE (DETERMINATION TO HELP OTHERS)
COMPASSION (GENEROSITY)
POWER (CONTROL)
Selfish — PLEASURE (PASSION)
SURVIVAL (SAFETY)

© Mark Oliver, 2007

TABLE 8.2 UHM Drives and Leadership Approaches

UHM Level	UHM Drive	Leadership/Management Approach	Focus
7	**Meaning**	Inspiration	Self
6	**Wisdom**	Coaching (not the same as teaching)	Selfless
5	**Courage**	Chivalry (and endurance)	
4	**Compassion**	Service	
3	**Power**	(Thought leadership)	Selfish
2	**Pleasure**	(Charismatic leadership)	
1	**Survival**	(Autocratic leadership)	

No motivation is better or worse, or wrong or right, as there is a time for any one of these motivations. But to be a mature adult, and leader, we have to spend more time at levels four to six. As Confucius said, 'to become a leader you must first become a [complete] human being'. The UHM predicts that the higher the level you operate at, the more impact you will have in your own life and those of others.

TABLE 8.3 Exemplars of UHM drives

UHM Level	UHM Drive	Famous Leaders Who Typified the Styles	Approach to Leading
7	Meaning	Mahatma Gandhi (1869–1948)	Example
6	Wisdom	Socrates (470–399 BC)	Example
5	Courage	Sir Ernest Shackleton (1874–1922)	Example
4	Compassion	Mother Teresa (1910–97)	Example
3	Power	Henry Ford (1863–1947)	Persuasion (intellectual)
2	Pleasure	John Fitzgerald Kennedy (1917–63)	Persuasion (emotional)
1	Survival	Josef Stalin (1879–1953)	Compulsion

The human brain undergoes more changes from birth than any other organ, and these can be broadly split into four stages that correlate directly with UHM.

While this does not mean that a child cannot show courage or operate from other higher levels (and many do), it does mean that these higher motivations tend to become more common as people mature. But there are always exceptions and often the environment or situation affects the level driving us. For instance, we have asked thousands of participants around the world on leadership courses, at what level are politics and politicians typically operating. Almost 100 per cent have said 'power' (level 3). Therefore, the model would predict that we should expect to see a lot of adolescent type behaviour from politicians and very little leadership (as that starts at level 4)!

Beliefs and values

Our beliefs and values are the filters through which all behavioural decisions pass. Our beliefs are based on assertions (facts), or assessments (opinions) that we hold to be true. Values are subjective beliefs to which we attach weight and importance (principles, such as the principles of leadership or organizational design and so on, are objective beliefs).

Acquired early and deeply held, our beliefs and values can be the unknown architects of our lives. We come to believe many things about ourselves, others and the world.

TABLE 8.4 UHM drives and stages of brain development

UHM Level	UHM Drive	Stages of the Brain[1]	Brain Characteristics
7	Meaning	Old age	Brain cells are lost in important areas in the mid-60s, but brain flexibility can compensate significantly.
6	Wisdom	Adulthood (up to 60s or 70s)	The brain's processing speed (memory in particular) starts to decline from mid-20s.
5	Courage		
4	Compassion		
3	Power	Adolescence (up to early 20s)	The brain remains highly flexible, but prunes itself, losing 1 per cent of its brain cells per year until early 20s, but an increase in speed of neural function offsets this.
2	Pleasure		
1	Survival	Childhood (from birth to 11 years for females or 14 years for males)	The brain is at its most energetic and flexible. It is 95 per cent of its adult weight by 6 years old.

[1] The Five Stages of the Brain, *New Scientist*, April 4, 2009.

Our families and schooling model and instil certain belief systems, they nurture and reward some and punish others. Our own 'what works' experience (heuristics) also has an influence but unfortunately we do not always recognize when the situation or context changes and the belief system ceases to be useful. Our beliefs are also shaped by the cultural context in which we live. There are a range of culturally prescribed beliefs that often go unchallenged – beliefs about gender, for example.

Our beliefs are also either negative or positive; that is, they either limit our growth, confidence and performance or support it. We have thousands of beliefs just about ourselves; though many psychologists would say that it is just a handful of beliefs that really define us.

Our beliefs, acquired as we grow, may have originated from a source outside ourselves, usually a person who is important to us, such as a parent or an authority figure, whom we trust and take note of. The problem starts when they give us assessments (opinion), that we take to be assertions (fact) and believe them, but the assessments are wrong. Too many young children have been told by a parent, in effect, that they will never amount to much and have grown up shy and devoid of self-confidence as a result, which has hamstrung them at work when they are older. Such parents have psychologically damaged their child and limited his or her future.

Beliefs relating to the emotional intrapersonal (inside self) and interpersonal (between people) domains are more powerful and more difficult to change than other more objectively defined beliefs. The most powerful beliefs are those that are so entrenched that they are seen as truths, not beliefs. We tend to attend to information that has meaning for us, which means that information that is inconsistent with deeply held assumptions goes unnoticed (it may be distorted to fit existing frameworks, or ignored). Belief systems make a profound impact on how people interpret the world, how they interact with the world and, in turn, the response they evoke from the world.

Each of us carries images, assumptions and stories in our minds of ourselves, other people, institutions and every aspect of the world. They determine what we pay attention to, otherwise we would be overwhelmed with data. They also determine how we act. We navigate using our mental maps, but none of these maps can fully represent the territory. Belief systems, maps, or mental models (as they are variously known) exist below the level of awareness therefore we do not usually bring them out to examine and test them. Instead we usually assume:

- Our beliefs are the truth.
- The truth is obvious.
- Our beliefs are based on real data.
- The data selected is the real data.

It is the underlying pattern of beliefs and assumptions that allows two people to look at the exact same situation and come up with different interpretations that in turn lead to quite different responses. They determine what we attend to out of all the available data, how we interpret what we attend to, and they are influential in how we respond to the information we receive. What people often don't realize is that the way we behave often invites others to respond in ways that confirm our beliefs.

Belief systems usually work in this way:

1 Information is gathered, filtered and interpreted with reference to the belief system.
2 This interpretation guides or dictates action.
3 Feedback and/or responses from others strengthen the belief system.

Example: Jack's belief is that Jill is an untrustworthy member of the team he leads:

1 Information is selected that confirms Jill's untrustworthiness (she missed a deadline), other (contradictory) information is filtered out (Jack changed the due date and forgot to tell Jill).
2 Jill is kept out of discussions, even though the issues affect her area of work.
3 Jill's response is to pass on less information to Jack, bad-mouth Jack around the organization, and be openly critical of Jack during a team meeting.
4 Jack's belief that Jill is untrustworthy is confirmed.

Example: I am presenting to an executive group and my belief is that I am a poor speaker:

1 My mind focuses on examples of past 'failure' (unable to explain a complex concept in a clear, succinct manner) (filtering).
2 This develops anxiety symptoms (rapid speech, trembling); attending to these internal stimuli gives rise to negative feelings rather than focusing on the audience, so the presentation is stilted, hesitant and lacks conviction (action).
3 Audience is clearly unimpressed, disengaged and talk between themselves (response).
4 I am a poor presenter (belief confirmed).

Values are the subjective beliefs that we hold to be true and important. Values are beliefs that guide behaviour, and are often so deeply held that they are not subject proof. The values that most determine our personality stem from learnt experiences that are absorbed from people and events in closest proximity to us during childhood, and the earlier in life that a value is acquired, the more deeply it will be held.

As we grow, we develop a value hierarchy that both supports and grows out of our personal belief system. Our values are those states, situations and experiences that are most important to us. The lives we design are a reflection of our values. What we build satisfies our beliefs and the emotional needs associated with those beliefs. Our values can shift in the hierarchy from time to time, depending on what beliefs are being challenged or fulfilled at that particular moment. The ease with which the trade-off occurs is related to how deeply the value is held and the belief and emotional need with which it is associated. It is possible for us to have values that conflict with each other and these are resolved within us by an in-built 'sensor' that only allows congruent values to appear at any one time. You may have met leadership consultants who value integrity, but will compromise the integrity of their training and development service (ie they promise to achieve in two days what really needs a week or more) in order to meet their value of security (closing a sale to pay the bills).

Values and beliefs often come in related clusters, colouring our perception and triggering our emotions, and may be viewed as the prime determinants of success. It is usually difficult to prove that one set of values is better than another – just compare differing political ideologies. Yet the strength of values and beliefs can drive countries to war, or to self-destruction.

For example, if someone were to say that he is a Conservative (in the UK) or Liberal (in Australia) or a Republican (in the United States), we could assume that that person believes in capitalism and the profit motive based upon self-interest, and is likely to have a low opinion of egalitarian policies perceived to stifle initiative and reduce everyone to the same level. Here are examples of beliefs clustered around a common 'macho' belief theme that 'strength comes from control and independence':

- Men don't and shouldn't 'feel' in the way that women do.
- Men should conceal their feelings in the way that women don't.
- Public displays of emotion are socially unacceptable.
- Revealing feelings is a sign of weakness and others will gain power.

- Real men are independent, women are not.
- Men are either winners or losers.

These sorts of beliefs can give rise to dichotomies, in this case divided along gender lines – the rational, emotionless, separate male, and the irrational, emotional, connected female. Why is it not possible to have both? Connectedness helps create an environment where autonomy can flourish. The more confidence we have, the stronger our sense of our own self-worth, the easier it is to stand separately. An alternative belief might be: 'strength comes through connectedness rather than control'.

Clarifying values provides a solid consistent base from which individuals can make decisions and judgements. Values provide an extra check, complementing logic and analysis to keep the person on his or her own right track. Values promote consistency in decisions and judgements. It is important to identify conflicting values (eg, between the organization's and the individual's value set) as this is a source of tension and stress – and ultimately separation.

How do we know when we need to change our beliefs? When they are working against us rather than for us. Whenever we encounter a problem that occurs repeatedly, we need to look to our belief system. How might deeply held assumptions be contributing to keeping the problem alive?

The core identity

Genetic inheritance

We all start life with a set of characteristics created by the biological inheritance from our parents; no two people have the potential to grow up into the same person, not even identical twins. That certain aspects of our genetics affect our experiences and so influence our personalities is beyond doubt. To take a gross generalization, think of how many people of short stature seem to be aggressively inclined, perhaps to compensate for lack of height! Bonaparte, Hitler, and various contemporary high profile people are such examples!

Each of our physical characteristics and our basic intelligence, aptitudes, muscle coordination and dexterity, and so on, can all be attributed to our genetics. It is how we develop and exploit these endowments that we determine. For example, someone with a superb physique will only become an expert athlete by putting sufficient effort into training under the right conditions – willpower, self-discipline and opportunity. Consequently, there are many with the physical potential of becoming great athletes who do not develop the capability because they do not wish to, or because their environment does not support it. Conversely, some of us will overcome physical shortcomings by sheer determination to succeed. This is well demonstrated on the 'sailors with disabilities' yacht seen racing offshore from Sydney, or athletes in the Paralympic Games.

The most significant of the physical endowments is the brain. It is our mental capacity linked to the versatility of our bodies that provides us with the almost limitless variety of responses to our surroundings. The capacity to reason and to analyse is a more powerful asset than our physical abilities. It is through these capacities that we have been able to overcome the physical limitations of our bodies to conquer space and to walk on the moon, and to explore the depths of the oceans.

Our biological drives and instincts (two primary drives are the need to compete (survive) and the need to collaborate (reproduce)), part of our genetic inheritance, remain important determinants of behaviour. However, the ways in which we seek to satisfy (and manage) these drives is influenced and shaped by our early life experiences.

Genetic inheritance can explain differences in performance and capability in the context of human achievement. But why do individuals often act so differently from each other in similar circumstances? The answer is that we each exist with and develop a unique core identity based on our early environmental influences and learnt experiences, with the result that we each think differently. Our mental processes provide us with a wide range of different options for actions, based on our thoughts, our feelings and our responses to past experience. Though we all share the deeply rooted instinctive evolutionary and biological drives to compete and collaborate, we each have a unique way of being in the world we encounter.

Environmental influences and learnt experiences

From the moment of birth we are influenced by our surroundings. Some psychologists suggest that we are not born with our minds completely blank with only the instincts to breathe and feed, but rather we are born with a whole range of primitive instincts. It is the cultural climate and home environment in which we experience early infancy and childhood that suppress and modify these instincts so that we learn and develop our own personal ways of coping and thus each of us becomes an individual with our own unique approach to life.

As we grow we learn from our personal experiences in life. This learning – a change in behaviour, based on experience – is largely subconscious and it affects the way we think, feel and act, and determines our basic values and beliefs. Whether we are aggressive, passive or assertive and so on is based on our learnt experiences. Our biological drives and instincts remain important, but the way in which we fulfil our needs is affected by our learning.

This then is an explanation for why two brothers can turn out very differently. There is plenty of evidence that first-born children are different from subsequent children and this is very likely since the new parents' experience of having and bringing up the first infant is likely to be considerably more stressful for them than for second-born and later children. And, of course, the environment for the subsequent children includes the presence of the older sibling(s). For example, a high percentage of first-born children become CEOs. New parents think that little baby Johnny is very fragile and they jump to his every squeal, meanwhile clever little Johnny gets used to the idea that if he makes enough noise people will jump. The second child gets a raw deal in comparison – the parents have worked out how babies work and don't jump quite so high when ordered.

One of the great controversies of modern psychology has been among those who believe that genetics and environment are the foundations of personality and those who believe that a genetic and environmental mix has nothing to do with it and that personality is based wholly upon what each of us learns as we experience life. As in many great theoretical arguments, it is impossible to prove one way or the other, but what is certain is that as we as individuals grow up we learn from our personal experiences in life. Through learning we form, in large measure, a concept of self and of the world in which we live.

Transactional Analysis

To make sense of our core identity, how it exists, how it has developed and its capacity for change, the work of Dr Eric Berne[16] in the development of Transactional Analysis (TA), provides us with a remarkably accessible model. Originally developed in the early 1960s as a 'new' model of psychotherapy, it is based on several key accepted truths:

- Every grown-up was once a child.
- Every human being with sufficient functioning brain-tissue is capable of adequate reality-testing.
- That every individual who survives into adult life has had either parents or someone *in loco parentis*.

Drawing on the work of Dr Wilder Penfield, exploring the field of memory and cognition in the 1950s, the model's development was based on further scientifically evidenced findings[17] that indicated that:

- Everything that we think, feel and do is recorded in us from the moment we are born: past events recorded in detail, critically, along with the feelings associated with them.
- The brain functions as a high-fidelity recorder: able to record and retain past events and then replay sets of thoughts, feelings and behaviours in the present.
- The replay button for this high-fidelity recorder is effectively an array of triggers, again unique to each individual: sights, sounds, smells and situations.

Berne developed two models to facilitate understanding and working with core identity: a 'structural' model that gives us the framework to make sense of how we exist and a 'functional' model to explain how we work.

The structural model: how we exist

Acknowledging the accepted truths previously stated and drawing on the evidence presented by Penfield, Berne identified three distinct sets of thoughts, feelings and behaviours, shown in Figure 8.5. In TA these are referred to as 'ego states', but in reality these are merely distinctly identifiable groups or sets of thoughts, feelings and behaviours. Arranged in the now famous three circles in a vertical line, traffic light style, the first of the three is the 'parent ego state'. This set incorporates thoughts, feelings and behaviours that we have 'ingested' from the past. These are the unchallenged and unquestioned recordings made of all the thoughts, feelings and behaviours we encountered in our early growing up, particularly up to the age of 5 years. Highlighting the significance of social learning, these are recordings made of all those we

FIGURE 8.5 The three Transactional Analysis Ego-States

Transactional Analysis: How we exist

Parent Ego-State
Behaviours, thoughts and feelings copied from parents or parent figures
PAST

Adult Ego-State
Behaviours, thoughts and feelings which are direct responses to the here-and-now
PRESENT

Child Ego-State
Behaviours, thoughts and feelings replayed from childhood
PAST

After Berne, 1961 | © Amanda Larcombe & Jeremy Tozer, 2007

were dependent on during this period: our parents, grandparents, significant adults, teachers, anyone that we relied on in any way. In so doing, this is where we find the foundations for many of our belief systems, values, views on the world and ourselves. Once aware of this, this is where we can find ourselves routinely replaying ways of being and seeing the world that don't in fact belong to us: when we hear ourselves sounding 'just like my mother!' or behaving 'just like my father!'.

The third circle (the equivalent of the green traffic light!) was given the label of 'child ego state'. Again coming from the past, and those significant formative years of development, this set includes all the thoughts, feelings and behaviours associated with the strategies we developed to get our needs met (emotional, physiological and social). Underpinned by those instinctive drives, these thoughts, feelings and behaviours are developed within us, as distinct from the parent ego state where they are taken in from outside or socially learnt. In both ways, however, they highlight the environmental influences that are at play in the development of our core identity and personality. Importantly, because these strategies are developed with a view to ensuring that our most basic needs are met – to be loved, to be fed, to feel safe, to know we exist – they become part of a set of highly prized ways of being: ones that we may be reluctant to let go of.

Finally, we have the middle circle, the set of thoughts, feelings and behaviours that were given the label of the 'adult ego state'. This is the part of us that works in the present, the here and now. This is the reality-checking, objective, analysing and 'reacting to the now' part of us. Present in us from birth, these are the thoughts, feelings and behaviours that have informed and influenced the development of our child ego state: assimilating the information given to us from the environment, remembering previous experiences and how we responded, and then informing our decision making as to what course of action to take next: either reinforcing our approach or bringing about some level of modification. In the context of developing emotional intelligence, it is the part of us that can distinguish the difference between the thoughts, feelings and behaviours that might have been given to us, those we have learnt and those that truly belong to us in the present moment.

A direct development of the 'structural model', the 'functional model' gives us a framework to understand more about 'how we work': the ways of being associated with each ego state and, important in the context of knowing ourselves as leaders, the styles of thinking, feeling and behaving that are associated with each.

Berne identified distinctive sub-sets of thinking, feeling and behaving in two of the three ego states: the parent and child, shown in Figure 8.6. In both cases the intention was not to suggest that a person can have one or the other: in all cases the aim is first to recognize their existence and then to find a balance that works for the individual. Remember that both the parent and child ego states come from the past, and are therefore open to being developed or changed.

In the parent ego state, the sub-sets identified were labelled 'critical parent' and 'nurturing parent'. In critical parent lie all the recordings of thoughts, feelings and behaviours strongly associated with maintaining control: for example, setting boundaries, what can and cannot be done; what is right and wrong; what is and is not considered safe; all our social rules, what should, ought and must be done. This is where the 'this is how we do it' resides. Significantly for leaders, this is also where we form our sense of what 'control' looks, feels and sounds like: patterns that can then be replayed routinely as part of our own leadership style.

By contrast, nurturing parent is concerned more with growing, nurturing and protecting. Here are the recordings of thoughts, feelings and behaviours associated with how it was to be looked after and developed as a human being. This is where we identify what patterns of thinking, feeling and behaving are associated with

FIGURE 8.6 Transactional Analysis ego-state sub-sets

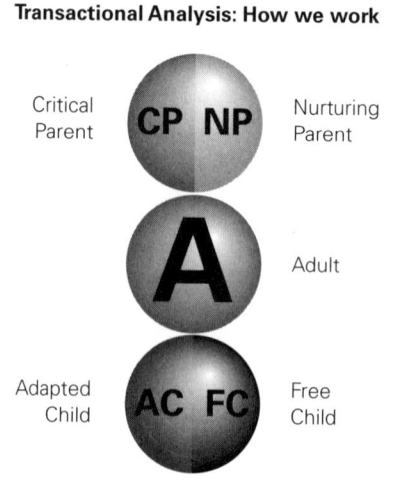

Transactional Analysis: How we work

Critical Parent — CP NP — Nurturing Parent

A — Adult

Adapted Child — AC FC — Free Child

After Berne, 1961 | © Amanda Larcombe & Jeremy Tozer, 2007

enabling and protecting another. In the context of leadership styles and abilities, this is our reference point when we are looking for collaborative behaviours, coaching and development of others. These patterns also relate to ourselves: where the replayed recordings from the past either give us permission to 'take care of ourselves' or not; pay attention to and attach value to 'developing ourselves' or not.

Moving to the child, again two sub-sets of thoughts, feelings and behaviours were identified by Berne: 'adapted' or sometimes referred to as 'compliant' child and 'rebellious' or 'free' child. Remembering that the thoughts, feelings and behaviours in child are the set of learnt patterns of being developed in response to our environment, those that enable us to get our needs met, the most significant difference between these two sub-sets is the frame of reference taken by the child in the past. For the adapted or compliant child the frame of reference developed as a small child was essentially 'external': where the child has developed approaches to relationships that rely on meeting the needs of others in order then to meet their own. As a result, a strongly adapted child is predisposed to often 'pleasing others'. As leaders these repeated patterns of thinking, feeling and behaving often manifest themselves in types of roles and sectors they choose to work in – the caring professions, service industry, marketing – and the skills they are found to excel in: listening, empathy, understanding and meeting the needs of others. By contrast, in the development of strategies for the rebellious or free child, the frame of reference is very much the 'I'. In this instance the child's needs were effectively met by doing it 'my way'. In leadership terms the resultant patterns of thinking, feeling and behaving are often associated with life's free thinkers, risk takers, creative people and often inspiring leaders: found in the world of exploration, the creative industries, research and entrepreneurial activity.

Transactional analysis as a development model

Taking both the structural and functional models of Figures 8.5 and 8.6 together, TA as a development model (see Figure 8.7), is seeking to achieve balance and positive

FIGURE 8.7 Transactional Analysis as a development model

Transactional Analysis: How we exist

Parent Ego-State: Critical Parent/Nurturing Parent
Behaviours, thoughts and feelings copied from parents or parent figures
PAST

Adult Ego-State
Behaviours, thoughts and feelings which are direct responses to the here-and-now
PRESENT

Child Ego-State: Adapted Child/Free Child
Behaviours, thoughts and feelings replayed from childhood
PAST

After Berne, 1961 | © Amanda Larcombe & Jeremy Tozer, 2007

integration: where the ego states complement and work together such that they meet the needs of an individual in the present. By acknowledging and understanding what we have gained from our past – our recordings of those around us, our learnt strategies to get our needs met – and using our 'adult' to distinguish between these, we are able to consciously realize our full potential as human beings and as leaders.

Perception

Perception is reality

Now we have looked at each of the layers in our model of the drivers of behaviour in Figure 8.1; we must consider something that runs through each of these layers: our perception. The way we perceive is both part of the drivers of our behaviour and an important factor in our approach to problem solving and decision making. The appreciation process in Chapter 14 is designed to minimize the distorting effects of personality and perception in decision making and so these paragraphs are also a precursor to reading that chapter.

Our view of the world is our 'perception'. To assume that everyone around you sees the world as you do, and will react similarly to people, events and information, is to invite misunderstanding and communication breakdown. To avoid this it is important that we understand the nature of perception and the way in which we, and those who we lead, perceive information. The key to understanding perception is to realize that it involves an interpretation of a situation.

Perception is the process by which we become aware of what is happening around us. Our senses – visual, auditory, kinaesthetic, olfactory and gustatory – provide us with information about our surroundings, but what we believe is happening, our 'perception', is a result of selecting, organizing and interpreting this information in a very personal and unique way. Neuro-linguistic programming refers to sensory preferences and thus language preferences. To people with a visual sensory preference, questions like, 'Do you get the picture?', 'Does it look clear to you?' mean more than the auditory, 'Does that sound ok?', 'Have you heard what I've said?', or the kinesthetic 'Does it feel right?'

Clearly personality and perception are very closely linked. Any organization should focus on its people and on the demanding circumstances surrounding a competitive market. On neither count is there room for perceptual misinterpretation – 'getting the wrong end of the stick'. Both people, including your competitors, and the flow of the battle for market share, are unpredictable. Effective answers to problems are never reached unless leaders think widely and deeply; it is not enough merely to look at one point of view or just to look superficially at an issue and then gloss over it. Here we consider the nature of perception, principally by using visual illusions, to make the point that things are not always what they seem.

This individual view, or perception, of life grows from our past experiences and from what we have learnt at home, in school, with friends and enemies, in our current organization and in previous jobs. Our current situation also has major influences on how we see the world. Ambitions, expectations, age, status and health all play an important part in the way in which we respond to our surroundings.

Understanding People 181

FIGURE 8.8 When you look at this image, what do you see first?

Do you see the vase or the faces? Why?

FIGURE 8.9 When you look at this image, what comes to your attention first?

The old crone or the young lady? Why?

Our immediate environment, including the people with whom we live and work, has a very significant effect on our perception of both people and events. Many of these influences are the same as those that shape our personalities.

To assume that everyone around you sees the world exactly as you do is to invite, at the very least, misunderstanding and, at worst, to lead to a total breakdown in communication. Here are some fairly common examples of this:

- An employee who may be viewed by one manager as confident but by another as arrogant.
- The same sports team may be considered to be beyond criticism by one person while another person might think of it as being just lucky.
- A junior manager walking around the factory floor may believe that it is a very pleasant organization to be a part of, but a trainee apprentice with domestic problems that need his attention may view it as being similar to a prison.

People at lower levels of an organization usually always have a very different perception of matters compared to their leaders.

Leaders who seek to understand, influence, control and motivate those around them should be aware of the nature of perception. Try to understand and anticipate why individuals tend to see things differently from each other and from you; and through this understanding and anticipation try to avoid unnecessary misunderstandings, mistakes and breakdowns in communication and trust.

As we have said, the key to understanding perception is to realize that it involves an *interpretation* of a situation. We all are, to some extent, like artists who paint pictures of the world that represent their own views of reality. In many cases these pictures may be abstract or emotional in nature and bear no resemblance to reality.

How perception works

We perceive when our attention is drawn to something in any way – visually, by listening, or by reading. We then select, organize and interpret the information we receive and then we act upon that interpretation, if necessary. But what is it that catches our attention? We notice things when their form or shape makes them stand out from their background. Although it may not be possible to identify what the shape is immediately, once the object has been identified it always seems to be clearly demarcated. There are times when we are faced with situations where there are two equally understandable interpretations; however, the perceiver is unable to disentangle the shape from the background. Look at the illustrations in Figures 8.8 and 8.9. How do you view the different representations in the same image? Why is your view more correct than someone who sees the other image?

Because of the many and varied things that happen all around us, for much of the time we are forced to be selective about what we choose to take notice of when dealing with a given situation. Things tend to come to our attention for many reasons, and advertising agencies know this well. Some are properties or characteristics of 'the object', others are to do with 'our personality'. These 'properties' tend to emphasize how easily it is distinguished from its background and help us to perceive it:

- *Intensity or degree of attentiveness.* An observer's attention is always quickly focused on 'bright' objects.
- *Size.* The larger an object the easier it is to make it stand out from its background. Try looking for a needle in a wisp of hay, never mind a haystack; however, a steel bar is quickly distinguishable from the strands of hay.
- *Contrast.* Things that are unexpected stand out and are noticed.
- *Motion.* A moving object in an otherwise still environment ensures that it stands out from the background and is readily recognized. Many wild creatures, hares, for instance, freeze when danger approaches in the hope that they are not spotted.
- *Novelty versus familiarity.* New objects in a familiar setting or familiar objects in a new setting tend to be picked out quickly.
- *The degree of threat.* People always tend to notice things that appear to threaten them, for example a competitor launching a new product. We return to 'threatening circumstances' later under the 'ostrich syndrome'.
- *Grouping.* If we are not very careful there could be a tendency to consider similar people as identical and put them into convenient categories: for example, ethnic groups, trade unionists, 'management'. It is important to remember that each person is an individual. The tendency to stereotype is very evident in the way many of us think of foreigners (however, the stereotype probably exists because many people have shared some characteristics! Just don't assume that those characteristics will be shared by all).
- *Context.* You recognize the background so well that the object stands out. Broadly speaking, it is important to be aware of what is going on around you so that you can quickly identify something out of the ordinary.
- *Halo or horns effect.* Sometimes we make overall (blanket) judgements about people that are based on insufficient evidence. For example, an attractive female job applicant may be thought of as ideal simply on the evidence of her looks to a male hiring manager – sexism in action. Equally, an otherwise ideal applicant may be rejected by a public sector interview panel simply because he happens to be white and male.

There are also a number of influences within the individual that affect the way he or she interprets what is seen; things that may indeed distort his or her vision:

- *Previous learning or experience.* Very often we see or hear what we expect to as a result of previous experience, rather than what is actually to be seen or is being said.
- *Motivation.* Sex, survival, ambition and social needs all influence the degree of importance we attach to things. What page of the newspaper do you turn to first and why?
- *Beliefs and values.* Our learnt experiences and upbringing gives each of us an individual set of beliefs and values about a job, spare time, our families, friends, morals and so on. All these are likely to influence the way we interpret and react to any situation.

- *Manner of presentation.* For example, an appealing advertisement or speech, or effective merchandising of a product attracts our attention and influences our thinking and our decision making.
- *Defence.* Now for the 'ostrich syndrome' – we often prefer to ignore, deny or reject information that we should sense as threatening to our position or to our idea (refer back to Freud's ego). There has been more than one managing director who has rejected well-founded market intelligence and research reports because these did not match his or her own interpretation of the situation. At a more mundane level, some people buy houses in highly unsuitable locations under airport flight paths, on the edge of motorways and so on, because they do not accept the evidence of their eyes and ears if the property seems ideal in other respects, and they sometimes live to regret it.

You might be wondering why time is spent discussing visual perception when clearly perception, in general, should concern itself with all the senses. There are two reasons for concentration on vision. First, a high percentage of the information we obtain about the world around us comes to us through the eyes (for instance non-verbal communication), thus, visual perception is clearly a vital sense to all sighted people. Second, it provides an easy means of demonstrating perception effects.

Deliberate distractions

The unconscious distortions of reality by the perceiver are challenging enough but they can be made worse by the deliberate distortion of reality. An artist can set out to deliberately distract the eye of the perceiver, either by distorting the perspective, or the contrast (as in Figure 8.10). Artists can visually distort logic in a much more subtle way; this is the visual equivalent of the film director's portrayal of events – something that one can accept while in the cinema but which cannot exist in real life.

For us, a much more real problem is the tactic of deception as practised by a competitor. At the simplest level, this amounts to just good camouflage. Will we be fooled by it, or will our perception enable us to see through the deception? Can we 'think competitor'?

What can the leader do about perception?

You can see that perception is a complicated matter. You might think that life would be a lot easier if we all perceived things in the same way – your way. However, that will never happen. At the same time, because individual perception lies at the heart of everything that we do, and consequently at the heart of many problems, we cannot ignore it.

If you understand the nature of perception it is possible to influence situations to avoid misunderstandings. Leaders must strive to present a picture of the world that is as close as possible to reality. This means checking and clarifying that information you receive has not been distorted by someone else's perception. At the personal level, knowledge of your own personality and its effects on your perception will help you not to distort information before you act on it or transmit it to others.

FIGURE 8.10 Deliberate distortions, after the artist Escher

As far as other people's perceptions are concerned, a thorough knowledge and understanding of those with whom you work should enable you to understand and even anticipate their ways of perceiving information. And leaders can to some extent control external factors that influence those around them such as the time and place of meetings together with the language and tone you use to communicate.

In summary, remember that:

- perception is unique to each individual;
- situations are many sided;
- few things are as simple or as straightforward as they seem.

Therefore:

- be open to multiple possibilities;
- be intentionally curious;
- pass on information as accurately as possible;
- look, listen, question and think before you speak or act!

Emotional intelligence: the enabler of adaptable and appropriate leadership style

One who knows much about others may be learned, but one who understands himself is more intelligent. One who controls others may be powerful, but one who has mastered himself is mightier still.

(Lao-Tzu)

EI defined

Emotional intelligence (EI), according to Mayer, Salovey and Caruso,[18] is the ability to reason and problem solve on the basis of emotions. This includes the capacity to recognize and assimilate emotions, understand the data from these emotions and manage them. We would describe it as applied social radar in which the reactions, emotions, moods and feelings of an individual or a group are recognized by a leader, who adapts and controls his or her own behaviour to lead that group to best effect. It thus combines interpersonal intelligence (situation awareness and understanding of others), with intrapersonal intelligence (self-awareness of behaviour and impact, and self-control) – hence the previous section with the explanation of the drivers of behaviour.

EI is the key part of the broad-band intelligence introduced in Chapter 4, which prevents us from engaging the environment in a closed and guarded way. The more self-aware and thus in tune with the environment we are, the more able we are to allow the environment to reveal itself to us in a particular situation. That is, the more self-aware we are, the easier it is for us to confidently engage without preconceived notions and to interact without emotional reactivity.

Being emotionally intelligent does not imply being 'nice' or 'emotional'. In fact, there would be many situations where being emotionally intelligent would involve being tough or restrained, either with ourselves or others. This is one common example of confusion about what it means to be emotionally intelligent.

Our level of EI impacts on performance at both organizational and personal levels:

- By removing blocks (limiting beliefs and unhelpful 'preferred behaviour') that inhibit performance, enabling us to make the best possible contribution to the organization. A sense of personal and professional effectiveness is energizing and can stimulate further performance improvement.

- By changing our patterns of interaction with other people and, hence, the subsequent behaviour and performance of all those who come into contact with us. The interdependence of team or work group members means that a change in one person will cascade throughout the group, from a leadership perspective. In simple terms, this is the ripple effect; psychologists might refer to it as 'emotional or mood contagion'.

- By changing mindsets (individually at the start of the process, and eventually collectively).

- By improving other aspects of life such as health and family relations. An unhappy or distressed personal life negatively impacts work performance.

EI is not a substitute for the essential knowledge and skills required to execute leadership functions (the 'what' of leadership). Rather, EI is the core of 'the character that inspires confidence and trust' (the 'how' of leadership).

Let us take a brief look at the history of EI. Until 1970 or so, research on intelligence and emotions was done separately. From 1970, these two areas were integrated into a new field of research, 'cognition and affect'. In 1990 Salovey and Mayer[19] reviewed the literature and then developed a theory of EI. In 1995, Daniel Goleman[20] published *Emotional Intelligence*. Goleman's theory was based on the work of Salovey and Mayer but he also stretched and developed the concept, and in 1998 he produced another book[21] that focused more on EI in the workplace, including skills and personality traits.

Goleman's writing has done much to put EI on the agenda. However, along with this new-found prominence has come a plethora of new tests, rebranded tests (many of which are actually measuring personality attributes rather than EI itself), programmes and loosely founded claims about the benefits of EI – a lot of 'pop psychology'. Another problem with some of the available EI tests is that many use self-judgements and/or observer judgements to measure EI, which research has shown to be not especially accurate – these judgements are subjective perceptions, not objective measurements of actual 'ability'. A behaviour is an observable action. An ability is what someone is capable of or shows potential in and is best measured by a practical performance test with pre-determined objective scoring criteria.

The elements of EI

The left-hand side of Figure 8.11 shows the components and the interaction of the dimensions of EI: self-awareness, self-leadership and self-confidence, situational awareness and will. These dimensions may be considered to be 'meta-abilities' – they enable all other leadership and management functions and team-working skills and abilities to be executed effectively. They are displayed in our ability to manage relationships, 'read' social situations and build networks. They are the core of our ability to 'communicate': to build rapport and find common ground, persuade, influence, engage, negotiate, coach and resolve conflict. To understand how this model works, we will start from the inside and work outwards.

Self-awareness

The starting point toward developing higher interpersonal intelligence (understanding and interacting with others more effectively) is to grow in intrapersonal intelligence. The cornerstone of high intrapersonal intelligence is self-awareness. Self-awareness is a prerequisite for any change – we must become aware of our impact and therefore the need to change.

We develop self-awareness, or personal clarity, by entering into an ongoing process of self-reflection and self-discovery, assisted by feedback given by others, the feedback that we can observe as inherent in the system (recall the example in Chapter 4 of feedback provided to the obnoxious banker who was always given the worst

FIGURE 8.11 The components of emotional intelligence and the drivers of behaviour

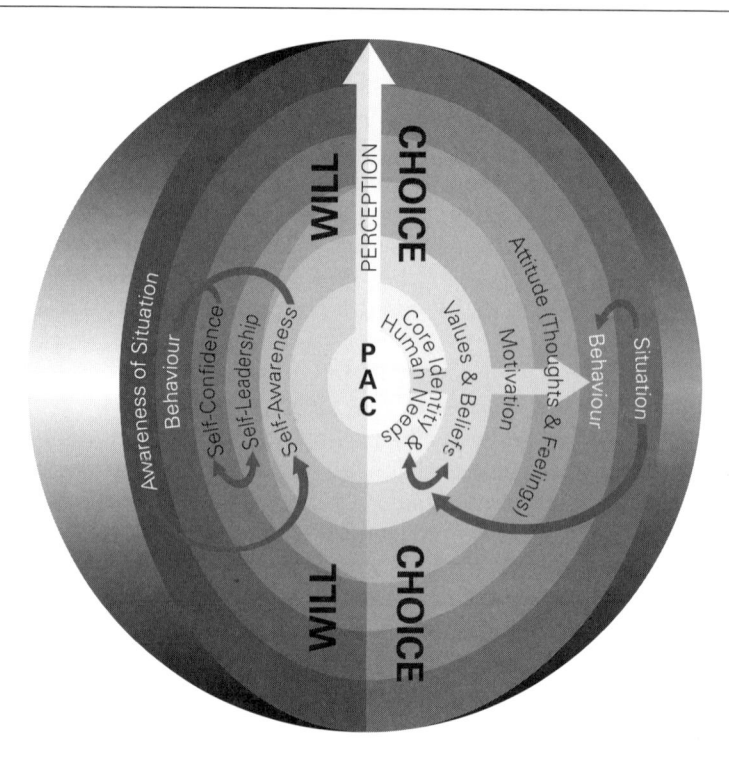

After Tozer, Oliver & Larcombe | © Jeremy Tozer & Mark Oliver, 2007

meeting rooms in the building for client meetings by the mistreated secretary), and through personal development conversations with coaches, which aid our self-disclosure and self-discovery.

We need to become aware of all the drivers of our behaviour, which were discussed in the previous section:

- Our core identity formed by our genetic inheritance, early upbringing and learnt experiences.
- Our beliefs and values.
- Our motivation, our goals and needs that drive behaviour.
- Our purpose, a powerful self-belief and internal compass. It is what we believe we are here to accomplish that influences decision making and behaviour. A sense of purpose provides direction and meaning for our lives.
- Our attitude and the thoughts, feelings and emotions (and their triggers) that help shape it.
- Our manner of perception: what do we pay attention to and what do we overlook?

- Aspects of 'the situation' we are blind to. Why are we blind to them?
- Our preferred (typical) behaviour, and especially our behaviour under stress, the impact that it has both on people (and the way they engage with us or not), and on task (help or hindrance).
- Our behaviour and its impact 'in the moment' – in TA language, are we behaving as the child's parent or as adult?

Clarity of these aspects of who we really are allows us to more accurately interpret our behaviour and assign meaning to our experience. Our self-awareness can also be enhanced by being sensitive to the reactions of others to what and how we do and say what we do. Understanding the key influences on our personal development helps us to identify 'hot spots' or emotional triggers. It provides an opportunity to question which beliefs (assessments or assertions) are no longer useful and may be 'written out' of our life story from this point. It shows which influences have been particularly validating of the person and can continue to be drawn on in times of trouble or stress.

How do we know when we need to change our beliefs? When they are working against us rather than for us. Whenever we encounter a problem that occurs repeatedly, we need to look to our belief system. How might deeply held assumptions be contributing to keeping the problem alive?

What can we do about problem beliefs? Both self-awareness and self-leadership require surfacing these mental models to explore and question their usefulness. We need to be open to questioning our own mental models and be aware that the mental models of others also impact on their perception and behaviour. Two types of skills are required: reflection (slowing down and teasing out our thinking processes to become more aware of our mental models) and inquiry (holding conversations where we openly share views and develop knowledge about each other's assumptions).

Self-awareness: the Johari Window
According to the framework created by Joseph Luft and Harry Ingham,[22] there are some characteristics that people know about themselves. This known-to-self area is the knowledge of the way one is perceived – self-awareness of preferred behaviour and impact on people and tasks. At the same time, a part of one's 'personality' is unknown to self; in some dimensions people are unaware of how they are perceived by others.

We can also look at the personality (behaviours and attitudes) known to others in an organizational setting, as well as areas that are unknown to others. In terms of what is known and unknown to self and known and unknown to others, we can create four quadrants that comprise the total window, as depicted in Figure 8.12.

The arena that is known to self and also known to others in any specific organizational setting is called the 'public arena' – it is known to all. The arena that is unknown to self but is known to others is referred to as the 'blind spot'. It is unknown to the person either because no one has been willing to share feedback, or it may be that feedback is there (in terms of non-verbal communication), but the person is not alert enough to sense it or does not wish to 'see' it.

FIGURE 8.12 The Johari Window

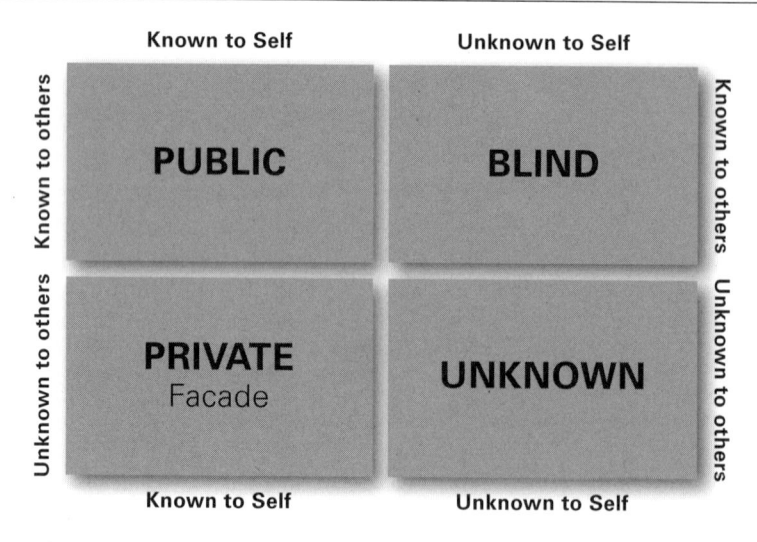

	Known to Self	Unknown to Self	
Known to others	PUBLIC	BLIND	Known to others
Unknown to others	PRIVATE Facade	UNKNOWN	Unknown to others
	Known to Self	Unknown to Self	

After Joseph Luft & Harry Ingham | © Jeremy Tozer, 2007

The arena that is known to self but unknown to others is referred to as the 'private arena' since it is only known to the subject. Again, it may be private because the subject has been unwilling to share or disclose this to others in the organizational setting, or it may be private because the others in the system are not picking up the non-verbal and verbal clues that are available from the subject in the system.

The last arena, unknown to self and unknown to others, is called the 'unknown'. In Freudian psychology, this is the subconscious or unconscious. This is that part of the personality iceberg which is beneath the surface, and unless we make conscious efforts to probe and understand, we will never really have any insight into it. Yet, much of that part of a subject's personality referred to as the unknown may be having a significant impact on others in terms of the preferred behaviours a person displays.

Feedback

There are two processes that affect the shape of the Johari Window (the configuration of the four arenas). The first is called feedback (Figure 8.13) and it reduces the size of the blind spot by making things that are known to others also known to the subject. This is the extent to which others in the organization are willing to discuss matters with the subject. It is also the extent to which the subject is asking for feedback and attempting to perceive the verbal and non-verbal feedback that exists in the system.

Disclosure

The other process that affects the shape of the Johari Window is disclosure (Figure 8.14). This is the extent to which people are willing to discuss information about themselves with others in their organization. In a coaching situation, careful questioning

Understanding People   191

FIGURE 8.13   Feedback and the Johari Window

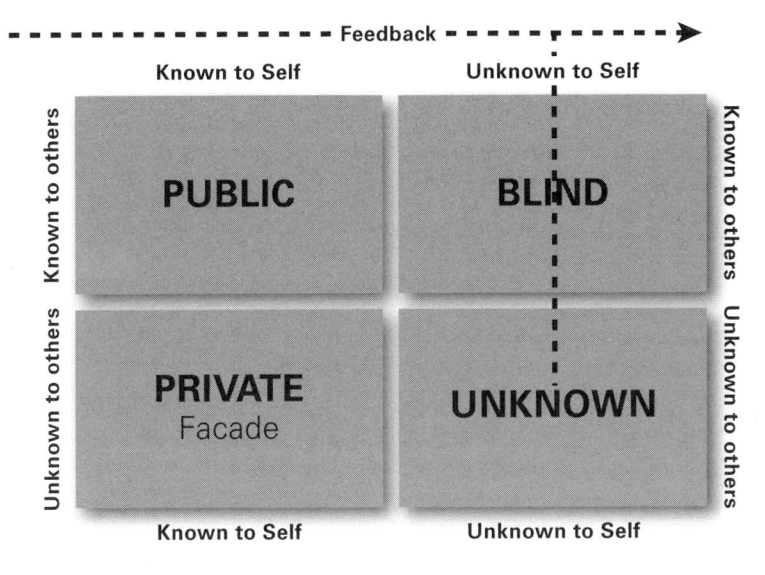

	Known to Self	Unknown to Self	
Known to others	PUBLIC	BLIND	Known to others
Unknown to others	PRIVATE Facade	UNKNOWN	Unknown to others
	Known to Self	Unknown to Self	

After Joseph Luft & Harry Ingham | © Jeremy Tozer, 2007

FIGURE 8.14   Disclosure and the Johari Window

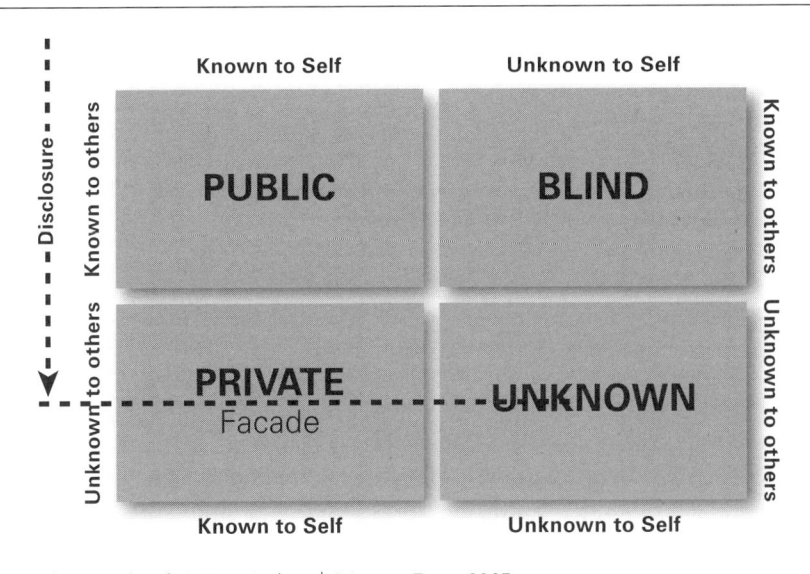

	Known to Self	Unknown to Self	
Known to others	PUBLIC	BLIND	Known to others
Unknown to others	PRIVATE Facade	UNKNOWN	Unknown to others
	Known to Self	Unknown to Self	

After Joseph Luft & Harry Ingham | © Jeremy Tozer, 2007

FIGURE 8.15 Feedback, disclosure and the Johari Window

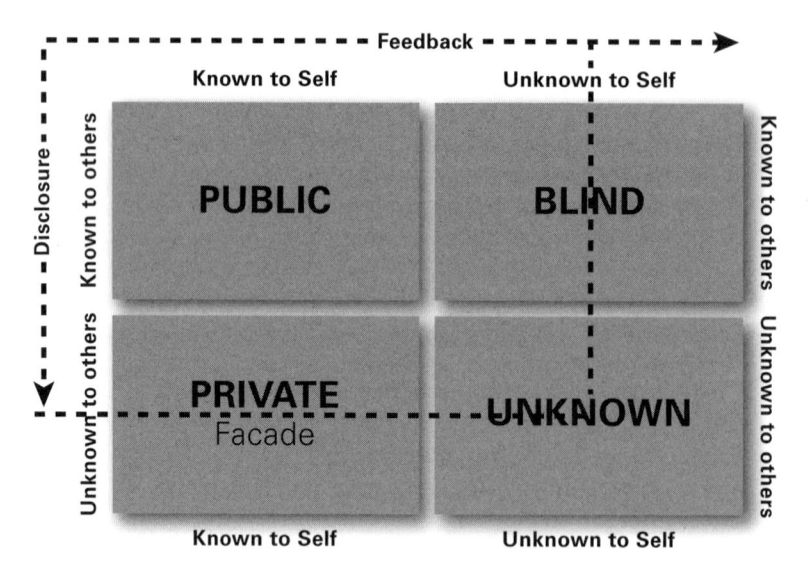

	Known to Self	Unknown to Self
Known to others	PUBLIC	BLIND
Unknown to others	PRIVATE (Facade)	UNKNOWN

After Joseph Luft & Harry Ingham | © Jeremy Tozer, 2007

may well assist people to clarify their own beliefs, values, motivators, etc, generating self-awareness. This is the first step to self-leadership.

The most relevant disclosure is not what people say about themselves but rather their behaviour. If you want to understand people better, you really have to look at the behaviour those people display to gain relevant insights into their values and what this behaviour represents.

Figure 8.15 illustrates the combined effects of these two processes. The implications should be obvious to leaders: to maximize your own effectiveness, you need to minimize your own blind spot – increasing your own self-awareness by seeking feedback (and developing the skill to give it to others), and discerning non-verbal feedback that is in the system around you. Likewise you need to maximize the public area of others around you if you are to understand them, particularly in a leadership capacity. 'Disclosure' discussions with a trusted coach or mentor will also assist in developing the self-awareness that enables your own self-leadership and EI.

Identifying the early stages of emotional arousal provides the opportunity to intervene before emotions escalate and cause problems (out of control emotions can make smart people act stupidly). Feelings, when identified and used positively, can serve as catalysts for change. For example, truthful but unpalatable assessment centre or 360-degree feedback often leads to a strong emotional response – sadness, anxiety, grief, anger – and that response can serve as the fuel that drives change.

Understanding preferences provides insights into one's own perception, decision making and judgement and provides information on potential blind spots. It brings to the surface some significant areas of difference that have the potential to create conflict within teams or groups. It will assist us to appreciate the value of difference or diversity (which is the real value of diversity, not diversity for the sake of political correctness). It clarifies what energizes us and what drains us. Once we understand our preferences we may begin to practise developing complementary patterns of perception, decision making and judgement to increase flexibility so that we may tailor our approach to the needs of the situation.

We can intervene to break the cycle at two points: at the level of the beliefs (to then shape behaviour) or at the level of the action (behaviour). Sometimes though, we have to start by changing the behaviour so we can generate data to challenge the belief. New/different behaviour:

- provides different feedback/responses;
- weakens existing belief system and strengthens alternative belief system;
- opens the way for new or different information to be selected for attention;
- strengthens alternative actions, and so on.

The more reflective we become, the better able we are to contain our emotions with our thought processes and thus approach problems and make decisions that are less reactive and more responsive. All emotions will be expressed. The challenge for each of us is to develop our ability to regulate our response to emotion to enable a more appropriate expression of our emotions.

Fact: I cannot change another person. The paradox: When I change myself, the other person changes.

I change myself, I change my world.

(Gandhi)

Will

Self-awareness is vital to our developing EI and leadership intelligence; but self-awareness is not enough. We must have the will to act upon what we have discovered about ourselves and transform ourselves. It is a courageous and heroic act to intentionally seek to deepen and expand our human experience. Nietzsche called this 'will to power'. An ability to lead ourselves (and ultimately others) grows out of a strong will that is formed on a foundation built of self-awareness. EI 'will' enables the choice of behaviour.

Self-leadership

Self-awareness and the will to grow empower us to lead ourselves and to display self-confidence; it is self-determination.

Self-leadership involves self-discipline and self-control – the ability to keep our TA child and parent 'under control', so that we might behave as the adult. Self-discipline is the ability to adhere to values, and to display appropriate behaviour when it is not your natural 'preferred behaviour'. It enables you to apply yourself to work and to follow-through despite distractions, fears or obstacles because you know that it is the right and proper thing to do. Self-discipline enables us to 'motivate' ourselves using self-awareness of our drivers and preferences. Self-discipline also enables us to have constructive conversations with ourselves: self-talk to develop self-efficacy (or self-belief). Such conversations enable us to make connections between neurons in the brain and to strengthen their pathways, which is what happens when learning and development occurs (see the previous section on the mechanics of the brain).

Self-control is the ability to contain any emotional interference that may seek to intrude and pull us back into a self-protective mode. While our emotions continue to influence us, we determine our thoughts and actions. It is thinking before acting, redirecting disruptive moods or emotions. Self-control enables us to:

- Contain and channel emotional energy in the service of our values-based goals.
- Manage turbulence and frustration.
- Stand by our convictions.
- Persevere.
- Be increasingly and appropriately flexible.
- Act with greater self-confidence.

Self-leadership and the will to say or do what needs to be said or done are the cornerstones of moral courage ('the daily choice of right and wrong') and they enable us to take calculated risks.

Self-confidence

We are all better than we know, if only we can be taught to realize this then we may never again settle for anything less.

(Kurt Hahn, founder of Outward Bound)

Our self-confidence grows in correlation to our ability to lead ourselves with greater self-awareness. The relationship between self-leadership and self-confidence is reciprocal. Each is caused by the other and each is the effect of the other. The more we can self-lead, the more we grow in confidence and the easier it becomes to self-lead. For example, if you have ever parachuted, you were probably extremely nervous prior to the first jump at the proposition of leaping out of a perfectly serviceable aircraft. However, your self-leadership kicked in and you told yourself that you had been properly trained, that your parachute had been checked and properly packed, and you knew what to do. Your self-leadership enabled you to make the first jump. When you landed safely, and probably during the descent, you felt exhilarated. As a result of your successful first descent, your self-confidence, self-belief and self-esteem grew considerably, making it very much easier to make the next jump, easier to self-lead. This is the reciprocal relationship between self-leadership and self-confidence.

Associated with self-confidence is self-efficacy and self-reliance, a positive self-belief in one's capability to overcome challenges or perform a given task without needing excessive support or mollycoddling. This develops when positive feedback is received as a result of performing various tasks, or through the observation of others completing tasks successfully. Training, properly delivered feedback (rather than inconsiderate, general or threatening criticism), coaching and recognition for gradual improvement are all important mechanisms for improving self-efficacy. If you as a leader do not believe in yourself, it is very hard to persuade your team to believe in you. Equally you should be building your team members' self-confidence.

Optimism is also linked closely to self-confidence and self-leadership. Optimism in leadership is not the unbridled zeal and groundless belief in the achievement of the clearly impossible. It is a combination of the positive 'glass half full' (rather than half empty) approach to life in general, the belief that properly thought through decisions may be effectively implemented and plans may be achieved (see Chapters 14 and 15), and a tactic to use when faced with setbacks and challenges.

Self-esteem, self-assurance and self-confidence are vital attributes of any effective and successful leader. They underpin everything that the leader does and how he or she does it. A lack of self-confidence leads to a sense of insecurity, helplessness and failure to accept responsibility. This underpins many undesirable or negative behaviours and attitudes, such as bullying, actively avoiding and not listening to feedback (however well-intentioned it is), avoiding decisions, or making snap, autocratic (wrong) decisions to avoid the possibility of conflict during discussion.

I once worked extensively with an organization whose board appointed a new female CEO who was, to the casual observer, extremely confident. She spoke extremely well in presentations to large audiences of the people in her organization. However, her actions and behaviour were rarely congruent with the organization's espoused values, and it was impossible to have a rational conversation with her on any subject that conflicted with her view of the world. She would not and could not listen, and bullied senior executives who very quickly learnt that the way to survive in the organization was to nod their heads in agreement, even when they knew that the wrong decision was being made. I remember a conversation about self-assurance and self-confidence with one of the most able business unit heads. After I had described the symptoms of a self-assurance and self-confidence deficit, he remarked, 'So you've met the new CEO.'

People with high self-esteem are more likely to assume an active role within social groups or working teams, and they usually express their views more frequently and with greater assertiveness and effect than others do. People lacking self-confidence and self-esteem frequently view themselves as helpless and often inferior as well, unable to improve their situation and lacking the mental robustness and resilience to tolerate stress and minimize the anxiety caused by many everyday events, changes in work, pressures and so on. Many people who are plagued by self-doubt, lack of self-confidence and self-assurance experience problems in forming 'normal relationships' with other people because they are frightened that such exposure will reveal their inadequacies.

Executives deficient in these two attributes are often far less likely to employ the best candidates available for a job because they feel threatened and lack peace of mind about the security of their own jobs. They do not realize that by hiring the best available talent they can bask in the reflected glory of their team. By hiring inferior candidates this syndrome cascades through the organization, resulting in a spiral towards oblivion.

People lacking self-confidence and self-esteem, in spite of whatever 'skills' training they may receive, find it difficult to face change because they do not trust in their capacity to manage the unknown – they have no faith in their ability to succeed. They are, therefore, unable to stretch beyond their comfort zone. Conversely, when people have high self-esteem and self-confidence, they usually have high levels of energy, initiative and flair. It is essential that leaders have these characteristics if followers are ever going to follow out of confidence and not curiosity. It is, therefore, essential to develop these attributes in everyone within the organization if they were not developed earlier in life.

While head-hunting, I often noted the correlation between high self-esteem and self-confidence and the activities pursued by candidates in their free time or earlier in life. Without exception, those who pursue an adventurous or demanding team-based activity, such as ocean-racing, climbing, rugby, hockey and so on, are particularly aware of 'people' in general, aware of their environment, and are at ease with themselves.

Self-confidence is also a social 'quality' that is attractive to others; people with an innate self-confidence and self-assurance generally manage to network effortlessly when meeting a group of people for the first time. Self-confidence underpins social skills.

Situational awareness

The way we think, feel and act develops in and is shaped or maintained by a broader sociocultural context and displayed through social customs, societal values and beliefs and so on. In an organizational sense we work both with national and organizational culture, and we also have to understand complex role relationships: different functions, business units, supply partners, customers, agendas, priorities and so on. Reading the environment in the broadest sense enables us to anticipate the need for change.

Situational awareness includes actively 'listening': sensing moods and emotions, questioning (either to yourself or openly if appropriate – 'I sense you feel this is not the right thing to do. If I'm right, why do you feel that?') and interpreting behaviour and language accurately to identify how others feel. This knowledge is used to respond appropriately and with empathy not sympathy (via your body language, facial expressions, voice tone and the words that you use). In TA terms, situational awareness means recognizing when others are acting the part of the parent, adult or child. Our self-awareness and self-leadership will then help us to respond appropriately.

Understanding emotions involves having insight into people and why they feel, react and behave as they do. Having an understanding of how emotions change over time is also an important aspect of this element of EI. People who need to develop in this area are often surprised by people's reactions and claim that they 'didn't see it coming'. They tend not to register that a feeling can progress to a stronger emotion over time if underlying issues are not addressed. In the workplace, it is important to understand people's responses to your decisions and behaviour so that you can take effective action. This may not always translate into changing your mind but certainly has implications for how you go about doing things.

Our ability to perceive emotions during meetings is useful. It can also be helpful when preparing for meetings, whether performance management meetings, interviews or more regular forums. We often prepare for meetings by reviewing content and/or predicting questions and obstacles but we tend not to so readily prepare from an emotional perspective – which includes time, place, layout as well as the 'message' and language to be used.

Some workplace applications of this ability include:

- Finding common ground and building rapport through empathy and sensitivity to others' feelings, needs, perspectives and concerns.
- Reading people accurately and listening for what lies behind the words during meetings and decision-making forums – the verbal and non-verbal communication and signals. (As much as 80 per cent of information about our emotional state is communicated non-verbally.)
- Assertiveness to express our views constructively if we disagree, to give constructive criticism or praise, to deal effectively with 'put-downs' and to address difficult issues as they arise. Ensuring that your communication is perceived as assertive and not passive nor aggressive. How you are perceived is subjective and based on others' perception; some people might think your preferred behaviour is assertive, yet for others it might be passive and for others aggressive.
- Reading clients' and customers' needs, intentions and attitudes.
- Demonstrating reciprocity in working relationships. Reciprocity (give and take) is essential in sustainable relationships otherwise people may feel used, exploited or manipulated.
- Recognizing employees' concerns, needs and attitudes to their work, to you and to the organization.
- Being sensitive to our impact on people and to their needs (how they feel about us and what we say and do), as well as our impact on 'the task' at hand – do not be shy in asking for feedback: people are waiting to be asked. Just don't react negatively if it is not what you want to hear!

Behaviour

We can learn to recognize and imitate appropriate observable behaviours and assimilate some useful tools to help us be assertive and so on. But without really developing the dimensions of EI that lie beneath the surface we will always be acting and risk being seen as insincere – we will lack authenticity.

Each of the dimensions of EI contributes to increased behavioural effectiveness. Self- and situational awareness, self-leadership and self-confidence are manifested in our ability to manage relationships and our flexibility in asserting ourselves effectively (see Chapter 9): our ability to 'read' social situations, adapt our thinking and style, empathize and build networks. They are reflected in our ability to influence, coach, motivate, persuade, influence, resolve conflict and negotiate with others.

What does it all mean?

Our journey of self-discovery, new-found self-awareness, and enhanced self-leadership and self-confidence (intrapersonal intelligence) enable us to understand and 'appreciate' those around us with greater sensitivity, accuracy and competency (interpersonal intelligence). EI is an awareness of self and emotions that allows us to self-manage so as to pick up on environmental cues and connect more effectively with others.

Our awareness of the world in which we live and work can be radically altered by our development of increased EI. Enhanced EI enables us to expand our appreciation to a wider context, most immediately in terms of organizational or national culture. The way we feel, think and act develops and is maintained in a broader sociocultural context (displayed through social customs, societal values and beliefs, institutions, and so on).

In an organizational sense, increased competency regarding EI can enable us to understand and appreciate the complex role relationships (differing functions, business units, supply partners, customers, etc) without emotional interference. This ability to 'read' the environment in a broader sense enables us to anticipate the need for change.

The environment gives us constant feedback as to how we are interacting with it (successfully, partially, dismally, etc). If we develop our EI, we develop our capacity to learn from the situation and engage our will to bring this new knowledge into our self-awareness, incorporate it, and lead ourselves into a new and even more effective way of interacting with the world.

EI is rich with a history of research that clearly shows that our emotions and our thinking processes are far more linked than we thought they were. Indeed, Damasio's work[23] shows that without feeling and emotion, it is almost impossible to make good decisions!

Notes

1. Sigmund Freud, *New Introductory Lectures on Psychoanalysis* [1933], Harmondsworth: Penguin Freud Library 2, pp 105–06.
2. Jung, C G and Baynes, H G, 1921, *Psychological Types, or, The Psychology of Individuation*, London: Kegan Paul.
3. Neil R Carlson, 1998, *Foundations of Physiological Psychology*, London: Pearson.
4. Mark R Rosenzweig and Mark Leiman, 1982, *Physiological Psychology*, London: DC Heath.
5. Antonio R Damasio, 1994, *Descartes' Error: Emotion, reason and the human brain*, New York: Putnam Publishing.
6. John Pinel, 2009, *Biopsychology*, London: Pearson Allyn and Bacon.
7. Simon Green, 1987, *Physiological Psychology*, London: Routledge & Kegan Paul.
8. Icek Ajzen and Martin Fishbein, 1980, *Understanding Attitudes and Predicting Social Behavior*, Englewood Cliffs, NJ: Prentice-Hall.
9. Fishbein, M and Ajzen, I, 1975, *Belief, Attitude, Intention, and Behavior: An introduction to theory and research*, Reading, MA: Addison-Wesley.
10. Kahneman, Daniel and Amos Tversky, 1979, Prospect Theory: An analysis of decision under risk, *Econometrica*, XLVII, pp 263–91.
11. A Maslow, 1954, *Motivation and Personality*, New York: Harper.
12. F Herzberg, 1959, *The Motivation to Work*, New York: John Wiley.
13. Dan Pink, 2009, *Drive: The surprising truth about what motivates us*, Harmondsworth: Riverhead Books (Penguin).

14 Mark Oliver, 2012, *The Seven Motivations of Life – Taking leadership to a higher level*, Melbourne: MarkTwo Consulting, **www.marktwoconsulting.com**.

15 The study of changes in gene activity that do not involve alterations to the genetic code but still get passed down at least one successive generation.

16 Eric Berne, 1961, Transactional Analysis in Psychotherapy, Grove Press Inc., New York.

17 Harris, T A, 1973, *I'm OK, You're OK*, London: Arrow Books.

18 Mayer, J D, Salovey, P and Caruso, D R, 1999, Emotional Intelligence meets traditional standards for an intelligence, *Intelligence*, 27.

19 Salovey, P and Mayer, J D, 1990, Emotional intelligence, *Imagination, Cognition, and Personality*, 9, 185–211.

20 Daniel Goleman, 1995, *Emotional Intelligence: Why it can matter more than IQ*, New York: Bantam Books.

21 Daniel Goleman, 1998, *Working with Emotional Intelligence*, New York: Bantam Books.

22 J Luft and H Ingham, 1950, The Johari Window, A graphic model of interpersonal awareness, in *Proceedings of The Western Training Laboratory in Group Development*, Los Angeles, CA: UCLA.

23 Antonio R Damasio, 1994, *Descartes' Error: Emotion, reason and the human brain*, New York: Putnam Publishing.

09
Interpersonal communication: the currency of leadership

> Leader–team communication
> The communication process
> Building rapport
> Listening
> Questioning
> Inferences
>
> Style of communication and assertiveness
> How to assert yourself
> Non-verbal communication
> Eye accessing cues
> Assertive communication

The majority of any leader's time is spent involved in communication, whether talking, listening, reading or writing. Communication between people is what enables the work of individuals to be combined and coordinated, so effective communication is absolutely vital to success.

Successful communication does not simply mean talking, writing reports and memoranda, sending e-mails and making telephone calls. Communication must be sent to a receptive audience, the message must be clear and unambiguous, sent in terms that the audience can understand, and must reach its intended destination with the intended effect.

There are many excellent books on the subject of communication, and it is not the intention of this book to compete with those. However, since communication is the currency of leadership and the lubricant of the leadership engine, this book would be incomplete without some discussion of the subject. While writing and reading skills are essential, this chapter focuses on oral communication and what we have found to be the essential interpersonal communication tools for use in routine 'communication engagements' and in formal briefings and presentations and so on, with your team members, other colleagues, partners and customers, etc.

Leader–team communication

First, communication is a two-way process. Spoken information requires concentration on the part of the listener as well as consideration of certain principles and techniques by the speaker. An inability to listen is a failing among some people in positions of authority.

Another failing, often very evident in hierarchies, is that we sometimes speak or write without much consideration for the recipient. It is not enough to communicate in the same style and at the same 'level' to everyone. We should vary our pace (when speaking) and our vocabulary in accordance with our audience. We should not address senior executives, peers and team members in exactly the same way – we need to communicate in terms which are relevant and that they will understand. Self-evident, you may say; but to be able to adapt our communication style to such widely differing recipients is essential and it is still an ability that is overlooked; this may be a matter of ignorance or arrogance. To try to understand the other person's situation is good sense. It is also good manners. Good communication is often simply a question of courtesy.

A major failure of leadership is the tendency of team leaders to lose touch with their team members by concerning themselves only with bigger issues. Communication then becomes a one-way street in which trust is damaged, and team members pass upwards what they think the leader wishes to hear. This starts a vicious downwards spiral of dysfunctional dynamics and leads to a complete breakdown in trust.

It may be beneficial to evaluate the quality of team communication by asking a number of questions:

- Do team members divulge information easily?
- Are other's viewpoints considered by all team members?
- Do team members willingly offer information?
- Are one another's feelings considered by team members?
- Do team members remain guarded, keeping their conversations restricted to the job?
- Do team members know what their colleagues think about their contribution?

Provided that the leader remains objective, honest and open; and ensures that personal likes and dislikes do not interfere with communication, a regular flow of effective communication will contribute to effective teamwork.

A two-way flow of ideas and information that is understood and interpreted as it was intended, which leaves all involved feeling engaged, is the goal of most communication. In two-way communication, the receiver actively responds to the sender's message, ie sends a return message. In this manner, the sender may confirm immediately whether his or her message has been clearly understood. Another advantage of two-way communication is that it enhances receptivity. Most people respond better to communication made 'with' them rather than 'at' them. Two-way communication provides scope for clarification of ideas, can signal respect for the receiver and can allow the contribution of ideas and opinions by the receiver.

The communication process

Basically, communication involves the imparting of an idea or opinion from one person to another, or to a group of people. Communication can be thought of as a process of exchanging information, beliefs and feelings with people; it may be verbal, written or non-verbal, and can be transmitted up, down and across any hierarchical structure. All communication involves:

- a sender: the initiator of the communication; and
- a receiver: the person (or persons) for whom the communication is intended; and
- a process, shown in Figure 9.1.

The sender wants the receiver to understand the idea, opinion or mental image that he or she is trying to communicate. This message is encoded into either written or

FIGURE 9.1 The communication process

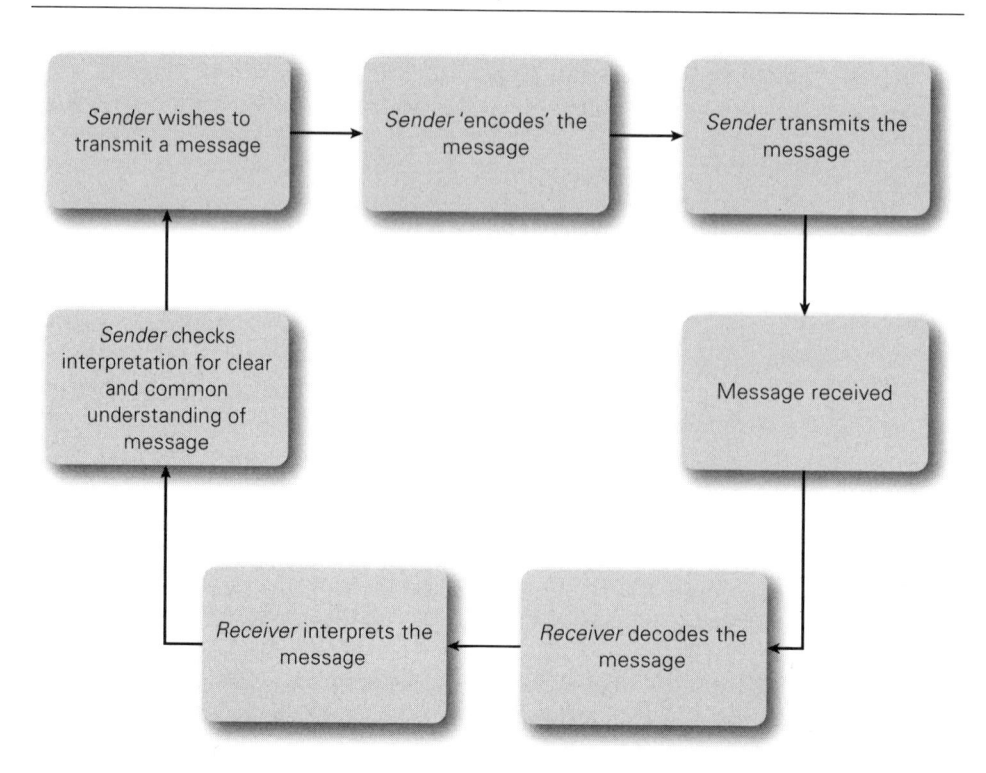

```
Sender wishes to     →    Sender 'encodes' the    →    Sender transmits the
transmit a message         message                      message
       ↑                                                    ↓
Sender checks
interpretation for clear                              Message received
and common
understanding of
message
       ↑                                                    ↓
       ←    Receiver interprets the    ←    Receiver decodes the
            message                         message
```

spoken language. The method of communication transmission is chosen by the sender. Upon receipt the receiver decodes the message but subconsciously applies his or her own perceptual filters during interpretation. The sender knows that this will occur and therefore checks for clarity to ensure a common understanding of the message by re-entering the process and asking open questions or by asking the receiver to become a sender and repeat the message in the receiver's own words. Sadly, this last step is often over-looked with unfortunate consequences!

The human backdrop

Part of the purpose of the previous chapter was to lay the foundations for understanding – understanding how the brain works, how people think, how they perceive and therefore how they interpret communication. It is a very human need to seek meaning and make sense of information and events; just look at Figure 9.2.

FIGURE 9.2 Completing the incomplete to achieve meaning

© Jeremy Tozer, 2011

It is very likely that you have tried to complete the partial words – we have a predisposition to 'completing' the incomplete. It is therefore essential to keep in mind that the interpretation of your communication will be influenced by its style and manner of delivery, and the feelings, conditioned and unconditioned responses and perceptions of both yourself as 'sender' and others as 'receivers'.

It is common in communication skills development to refer to the communication that people pay attention to as having the following composition:

Body language – non-verbal communication	55 per cent
Voice – rhythm, speed, volume, pitch (RSVP)	38 per cent
Words – choice of language	7 per cent

This is based on the work of Albert Mehrabian[1] and is often misquoted or misused. As he says on his personal website:

My findings on this topic have received considerable attention in the literature and in the popular media. Silent Messages *contains a detailed discussion of my findings on*

inconsistent messages of feelings and attitudes (and the relative importance of words, versus nonverbal cues).

Total Liking = 7% Verbal Liking + 38% Vocal Liking + 55% Facial Liking

Please note that this and other equations regarding relative importance of verbal and nonverbal messages were derived from experiments dealing with communications of feelings and attitudes (i.e., like-dislike). Unless a communicator is talking about their feelings or attitudes, these equations are not applicable.

What this means to us in practical terms is that the disproportionate influence of voice, tone and body language has most effect when the situation is ambiguous, especially when the words spoken are inconsistent with the tone of voice or body language of the speaker.

Fundamental principles

In keeping with the rest of this book, there are six principles which we suggest underpin all forms of effective communication. We call them the ABCDSS of communication and they are shown in Figure 9.3.

FIGURE 9.3 The ABCDSS of communication

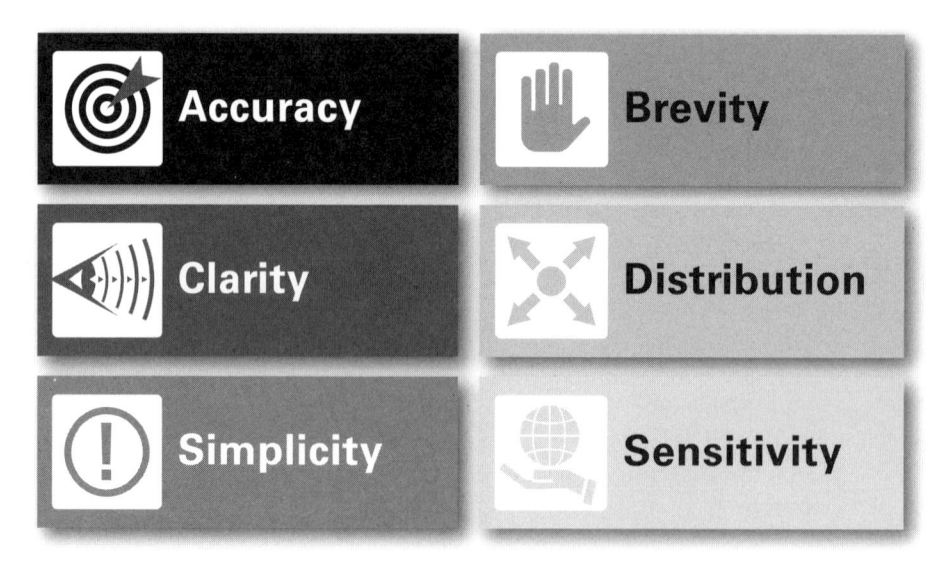

- Accuracy
- Brevity
- Clarity
- Distribution
- Simplicity
- Sensitivity

© Jeremy Tozer, 2007

Accuracy

Unless you are aiming to deceive, then self-evidently the message must be accurate, and it must not imply things to be true that are not true. When I was trained to write intelligence reports and summaries about future intentions and events, the message was forced home that a very clear and careful distinction should be drawn between the use of words such as 'possible' and 'probable', 'may have' and 'will have', 'likely' and 'could', and so on.

Brevity

Unless something is brief, it is unlikely to be properly read or listened to. And if it is not listened to or read with care and attention, then it will not be understood. And if it is not clearly understood, subsequent thought and action are likely to be misaligned.

I would have written a shorter letter, but I did not have the time.
(Blaise Pascal, 1656)

The challenge of being brief, particularly if we are to observe the principles of accuracy, clarity, simplicity and sensitivity, is that it takes far longer to write (or to prepare what we are going to say), than if we were to 'waffle'. When members of the Privy Council meet the British Sovereign the meetings are conducted standing. A wise monarch realized that this would help ministers avoid repetition and deviation, while also reducing meeting duration! The custom continues!

Clarity

Great emphasis has been placed on clarity within just about every aspect of this book. Nothing can ever be too clear, and if there is no chance for a confirmatory dialogue between the individuals receiving your communication, then it will take time, effort and incisive though – to 'draft' your message.

There is nothing in life like a clear definition. (The Duke of Wellington)

Distribution

This means ensuring that the message is disseminated to all those who need to know, and in the appropriate format(s). In organizations that have ill-defined matrix structures, a surplus of 'dotted lines' and unclear role relationships, to circumvent the problem of not knowing to whom a message need be distributed it is common practice to inform a significant percentage of the organization. This clogs e-mail inboxes, and induces information overload, which in turn often leads to the message being deleted by those who really do need to read it. It also results in people feeling obliged to attend more meetings than they really need to. These meetings involve too many people, and consequently become highly ineffective. The other reason for inappropriate inclusion of addressees in distribution lists is indulgence in corporate politics. While sometimes this is a necessary evil, it is spotted by all and does little to enhance the sender's 'perceived trustworthiness'.

A source of continual amazement is the number of people who do not realize the difference between a 'To' and 'cc' e-mail addressee. Recipients of the former should be people who actually have to do something with the information sent – they must know. The latter category of people are those who should know, because the information may impinge on their plans and actions. Military written communication is more explicit and clear – the distribution list for letters is divided into 'Action' and 'Information' addressees. The distribution lists themselves are clearly defined (and derived from the organizational structure), thus reducing the margin for error.

Simplicity

Brevity and simplicity contribute to clarity. If things are not simple, there is increased potential for confusion and misunderstanding. And, where there is misunderstanding or misinterpretation, then there is the likelihood of misalignment of subsequent thought and action. KISS (keep it simple, stupid!) applies both to plans and communication.

Sensitivity

This means ensuring that the communication is 'appropriate'. Depending upon whether 'the message' is the subject of conversation, announced in meetings, written or broadcast, the following need to be considered:

- The recipient(s) and 'personality', or the addressees.
- The actual words to be used.
- Voice tone.
- Non-verbal communication and body language.
- Time, place and setting.
- Likely perception and interpretation by recipients.

Communication preparation

Communication preparation entails consideration of these elements:

- *Aim, purpose and effects:* What is the aim of the message and why does it need to be sent? What effects do you wish the message to have and on whom?
- *Content:* What does the message need to contain? How will it be structured so that it is accurate, clear, brief and simple?
- *Audience:* Who is to receive it, what is their 'emotional state or frame of mind', how do they 'perceive', and what are their needs and interests? How will sensitivity be achieved?
- *Environment:* Where is the message best transmitted and received?
- *Timing:* When is the message best delivered? Is the receiver ready for it?
- *Medium:* By what means is the message most appropriately transmitted?
- *Distribution:* Who needs to know what the message contains?
- *Confirmation:* How will reception and correct interpretation be ensured?
- *Follow-up:* What should happen next? How will I check the effectiveness of my communication and maintain or improve it in future?

Building rapport

People like people who are like themselves. (Anon)

Rapport may be described as an harmonious accord, understanding and empathy between people – or, in short, a connection or being on the same wavelength. Building professional rapport is building liking and respect. It is essential to have rapport between sender and receiver if meaningful communication is going to occur. This applies equally to presentations, one-to-one leadership conversations, or sales situations. Increasing 'liking' is achieved by reducing differences; and we may reduce differences by mirroring and matching, and using 'universals' and 'truisms' to cover all bases, as explained below.

Mirroring and matching

Given that most people like people who are like themselves, we can start to build rapport by matching their language, voice RSVP, and physiology or body language. Creating a state of rapport is something that happens quite naturally between people on a regular basis without any conscious effort, particularly between friends. However, it does not always occur in work situations, because we do not usually appoint every person to the roles that they occupy. So, with many people at work, we have to make a conscious effort to develop rapport – but if we try too hard, or if the other person becomes aware that we are actively trying, we may fail.

Around 93 per cent of communication that relates to attitudes and feelings is based on body language (and posture) and voice tone. By subtly matching and mirroring that of the person with whom we are communicating, we can make ourselves more like them – subtlety is the key. The other person would be conscious of your using the same words and language as they do, but judicious use of some of the same language will add to the rapport – particularly if you are reflecting back their issues, needs or concerns.

Posture: is the other person/s leaning in a particular direction, slouching, tilting their head in a certain direction, keeping their arms or legs in a particular position, crossing their arms or legs, using small or large gestures and so on? Voice: is the other person/s talking quickly or slowly, raising the pitch at the end of the sentence, talking softly or loudly, using short, simple words or long words, and so on?

Universals and truisms

Universals and truisms are particularly useful when starting conversations with people whom we do not know well, or whom we have never met before. Universals are statements that are applicable to everyone and which create 'sameness'. You could refer to news, the weather, the market dynamics, change and so on. They could relate to things that everyone may be thinking or feeling. For example, at the start of a presentation to an unfamiliar audience, you might open with something like: 'I imagine that you are all wondering what I'm going to talk about, and how I will structure what I'm going to say, how long I am going to take and what breaks are planned.' It is highly likely that most if not all people in the audience are thinking just that.

Truisms are verifiable 'here and now' statements and may directionalize thinking. These might include people's common role in the business or common expectations. A truism is based on fact, and therefore a conversational piece that is not disputable. For example, if a workshop you are running is taking place on a very cold and wet day, you might have this as a truism in your introduction: 'It's cold and wet outside, so you will probably be glad to know that, although there are some practical activities to make some points, all of this workshop today will be conducted inside.'

Never assume participants all think the same way or have the same opinions as you and don't exclude people for example by only referring to 'he or him' and never 'she or her'.

We can also use different language to make the same point repeatedly in order to appeal to people who have a visual, auditory, or kinaesthetic communication preference.[2] For example, the questions, 'What uses can you see for this idea?', 'How do you feel that you can use this idea?' and 'How does this sound as a useful idea?' all mean pretty much the same thing, but appeal to those different preferences. Words such as 'see', 'look' and 'show' appeal to the visual preference; 'feel' and 'touch' to the kinaesthetic, and 'sound', 'listen' and 'hear' to the auditory preference.

Listening

It is common when discussing communication skills to use the term 'active listening'. Arguably the most powerful and complete explanation of what this means is conveyed by the Mandarin character for listening, shown in Figure 9.4. In common with many characters, it is made up of smaller elements, which mean:

- *Ear*, I must listen to the words spoken.
- *King*, I must treat the other person with respect.

FIGURE 9.4 Listening

© Jeremy Tozer, 1997–2006

- *You*, it is the other person and his or her message that are important to me.
- *Eyes*, what are your eyes telling me that I am not hearing?
- *Undivided attention*, if I do not pay attention, then I cannot listen effectively. (Multitasking is a dangerous fallacy – you can only do one thing well at a time!)
- *Heart*, what are the feelings and emotions that lie behind your words, what do you really mean?

Like many 'soft skills' listening is a science to be studied and an art to be practised. It requires self-discipline at times to remain silent despite one's emotional inclination to speak. The first step in 'learning to listen' is to make a conscious decision to take note of what is being said – to become an active listener. Effective listening is both hearing what is said and understanding what is meant. The major barrier to mutual understanding is the effect of perception on our interpretation of what we hear.

When we listen to people, if we are to be effective we must encourage people to speak openly and honestly, to cover issues that are personally important to them, to give the listener an understanding of their perception of a problem. To listen effectively it is necessary to understand the barriers to effective listening and take suitable precautions:

- Tiredness and stress, personal problems and minor illness or pain, which cause distractions.
- Having had similar or totally dissimilar experiences to those of the person you are trying to listen to, which cloud judgement.
- The value and respect that you attach to people in general, without which you will not concentrate as much as perhaps you should.
- Allocating an appropriate amount of uninterrupted time.
- Ensuring the use of a suitable environment. This includes the place (room) that you choose to use, and its furniture and layout, which will send 'signals' and influence the dynamic of the conversation.

Whatever you do, don't:

- Argue.
- Interrupt.
- Pass judgement without due consideration.
- Make false assumptions and jump to conclusions.
- Let the speaker's emotions have undue influence on your own.
- Direct the speaker by leading a conversation to meet your own ends.
- Hear only what you want to hear.
- Make light of other people's problems.

There are some other common conversational tendencies that may also create barriers:

- The reassurer – 'Don't worry, it will all turn out all right.'
- The advice-giver (often based on limited understanding of the facts) – 'If I were you, I'd...'.

- The rationalizer – 'Of course, whenever that happens, it's just a sign of...'.
- The interrupter – 'You don't need to say any more. I can guess.'
- The autobiographer – 'I remember when that happened to me, I approached it by...'.
- The deflector – 'Oh, it sounds awful, let's not think about that. Let's change the subject...'.

There are some general guidelines that should be borne in mind to ensure that listening is effective:

- There must be a purpose for listening.
- The good listener searches for meaning in what is being said even if it is of no interest to them personally.
- Snap judgements about the message must be avoided. Good listeners will consider the entire message.
- The listener must focus on the speaker and prevent anything from distracting him or her.
- Empathy should be shown towards the speaker and the listener must show interest in what is being said.
- The listener should pause and think before offering a response.
- The message should be clarified and rephrased to ensure mutual understanding.
- If discussing problems, the listener should look for the real cause of the problem, not just the symptoms. The leader should then help the speaker to develop the confidence and ability to solve his or her own problems.
- The listener should cultivate the ability to be silent when appropriate to do so.

In effective listening, we must remember that:

- Decisions and beliefs are often only as good as the information on which they are based.
- No one knows everything; there is always more to learn.
- We need to listen with intensity, observe with awareness and react with empathy.

Paying attention

Paying attention is part of both building rapport and listening. It covers a range of ways that lets the other person in a conversation know that you are listening and builds the rapport necessary for a free flow of dialogue. In a well-led team where people know and trust each other, the rapport building done in any meeting may be no more than a greeting – but you still need to pay attention. With people who are not well known, a conscious effort to build rapport and pay attention has to be made; contributors to this are shown in Table 9.1.

TABLE 9.1 Building rapport by paying attention

Your demeanour	Sincerity
Relaxed, unassociated conversation	Note taking – where appropriate
Stated purpose and time frame	Unbiased attitudes
'Connecting' with the applicant, forming a human bond	Use of appropriate vocabulary
	Vocal clarity, inflection and tonal range
Eye contact – about 20–30% of the time	Facial expressions, posture and body language
Friendliness	Pace of speaking
Enthusiasm	Showing approval where appropriate
Appropriate use of humour	Preserving the other person's ego
Body language	Showing respect

Questioning

Questions need to be asked for many reasons, including: to ensure clarity, to provoke thought and discussion, to draw on people's experience, to encourage participation and to explore opinions and attitudes. It is a combination of active listening and questioning that enables you to gain understanding of people. Questioning, like listening, is a basic leadership necessity, yet is so often done badly – watching some of the questioning of the Murdochs by the House of Commons Culture, Media and Sport Committee inquiry into phone-hacking was excruciatingly painful. Part of the reason so little real information was gained in the first meeting must surely be due to the ineffective questioning of some of the committee members. Figure 9.5 illustrates how to use questions.

FIGURE 9.5 Questioning

Questioning

Use a funnel of questions:
- Open *(When, Where, What, Why, Who, How)*
- Probing
- Focusing
- Closed – usually to confirm (yes/no)

Avoid:
- Leading
- Multiple

Questions, generally speaking, should create a funnel that leads to concrete and definable answer. The funnel starts with open questions (questions that usually begin with *when, where, what, why, who, how*). Open questions give you the best possible chance of an answer that tells you more than you knew at the start. A closed question, a question that may be responded to with a yes or no, usually gets just that. Having asked an open question, and received an answer, further open questions may be used to probe the issue and focus discussion. At the conclusion of the open questioning and discussion, it may be appropriate to use a closed question to gain a confirmatory 'yes' (or 'no').

Leading questions may be dangerous. These are apparently open questions, but they may direct a particular response, or course of action, for instance: 'Why don't you do...?' Leading questions may simply be questions that have been clumsily constructed, or they may be designed specifically to lead responses. The latter usually results in a feeling of manipulation in the person who has been asked the leading questions.

Multiple questions are very simply a number of questions that are asked in the one sentence. Stereotypically, on your return from a late night out, your partner might ask, 'What time do you call this, where have you been all this time, what have you been doing?' Which question will you answer first? If you ask multiple questions at work, it is likely that the easiest question will be answered, and very probably the others will be ignored.

A doctor might use this funnel of questions in his or her surgery:

- What appears to be the problem?
- What sort of pain are you experiencing?
- How often?
- Where does it hurt?
- What triggers it?
- Where exactly is the centre of the pain?
- Is it here? (The doctor asks as he or she pushes on the epicentre, causing brief but searing agony!)

Other things to consider when asking questions include:

- Use short questions. An elaborate question is more likely to influence the answer.
- Ask one question at a time – do not be ambiguous.
- Use silence or neutral responses effectively. Silence allows time to think and can encourage people to talk more freely and clarify or add information.
- Use reflective statements. These indicate that you require further information or elaboration; for example a team member says, 'I enjoyed that project', and the team leader responds: 'You enjoyed that project?'
- Persistent probing questioning. Continue with a question until it is answered to your satisfaction: get the facts.
- Comparison of inconsistencies. Ask people to clarify apparently inconsistent information gained from a previous question or discussion.
- Use of affirmation. Show you understand through body language (nodding), 'uh huhs', etc.

- Assess non-verbal communication:
  - handshake;
  - gaze;
  - eye contact;
  - posture and attitude;
  - facial expressions.
- Listen attentively to each response, then decide on your next question. It is critical not to rush as you may not fully appreciate a person's response and miss valuable clues. Consider each answer carefully, ensuring that you have gathered the information you need.
- Stimulate value judgements. Asking a person how he or she feels about conduct on the job; personal commitment to a task or relationships with co-workers provides insight into that person's value system.
- Probe 'choice points'. Choice points are situations that require a person to explain why he or she opted for a particular course of action and rejected another. Listening to the reasoning behind a selected option can help provide insight into the individual's beliefs and values system.

Clarifying

Clarifying brings vaguely expressed ideas, plans and views into sharp focus, and enables the listener to understand how others perceive a particular subject; it is closely connected to questioning. Not only facts, but people's emotional states need to be clarified and appreciated since for many people their emotions will dictate their behaviour. Methods of clarifying include:

- Questioning: as above, to gather more information, and listening.
- Paraphrasing: rephrasing the main themes of a speaker's statement (addressing both facts and emotions, passing the message back to the speaker) and using open questions to confirm understanding.
- Summarizing: providing the speaker with a précis of what has been said as understood by the listener at regular intervals, and using questions to confirm understanding.

Hints when asking questions

- As a leader at meetings, pose the question, pause then nominate a person to answer if no one volunteers – nominating a person first encourages others to 'switch off' (Pose-Pause-Pounce!).
- Avoid asking 50/50 or rhetorical questions.
- Don't ask questions that show your own bias or leanings.
- Put a question in context – set the scene or explore the situation before asking the question.

FIGURE 9.6 The ladder of inference

Get Off the Ladder of Inference

1. Reflect on your reasoning (self-awareness)
2. Make your reasoning transparent to others
3. Question the reasoning of others
4. Be willing to be mistaken
5. Provide and request data and concrete examples
6. Challenge mental models, both yours and theirs
7. Share underlying assumptions, perception and beliefs
8. Validate inferences – yours and theirs

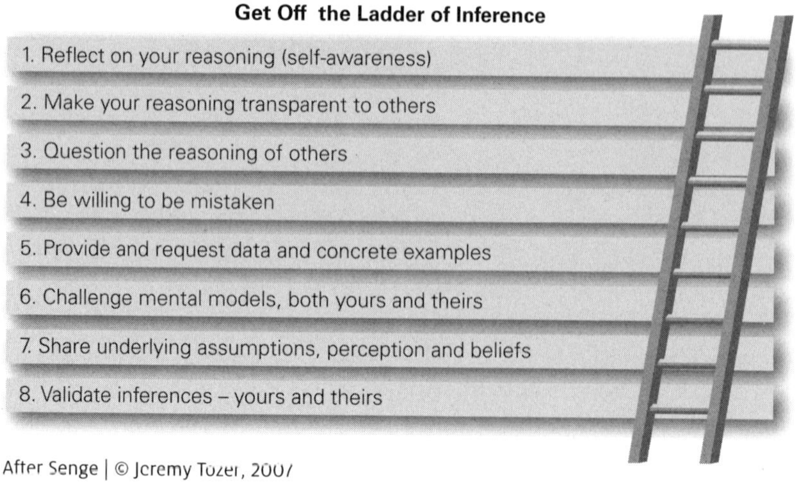

After Senge | © Jeremy Tozer, 2007

Inferences

An inference is a deduction or interpretation that you have assigned to the actions taken or the words used by someone else. In other words, you have attributed meaning to what they have said or done. Such inferences are usually influenced by your own perception of the situation and often lead to misunderstanding. The combination of active listening and questioning, and EI self-awareness usually help you climb back down the ladder of inference[3] shown in Figure 9.6.

Style of communication and assertiveness

We are all well aware of the biological response to stress: the fight or flight tendency. When we are under threat, our natural defence mechanism prepares us to cope with that threat by:

- Increasing pulse and breathing rates.
- Diverting the blood to the heart and muscles.
- Heightening awareness and concentration.

Our body is thus prepared to react instantaneously to the threat by either fighting it or fleeing from it. In modern society we rarely display such extreme behaviour; rather, we tend to respond aggressively or passively – the adapted equivalents.

Fight (aggressive) or flight (passive), are natural reflex behavioural actions (see Figure 9.7). So when you or others are reacting aggressively or passively it is an indication that someone feels threatened in some way. Often people behave aggressively

FIGURE 9.7 Aggressive, passive and assertive communication style

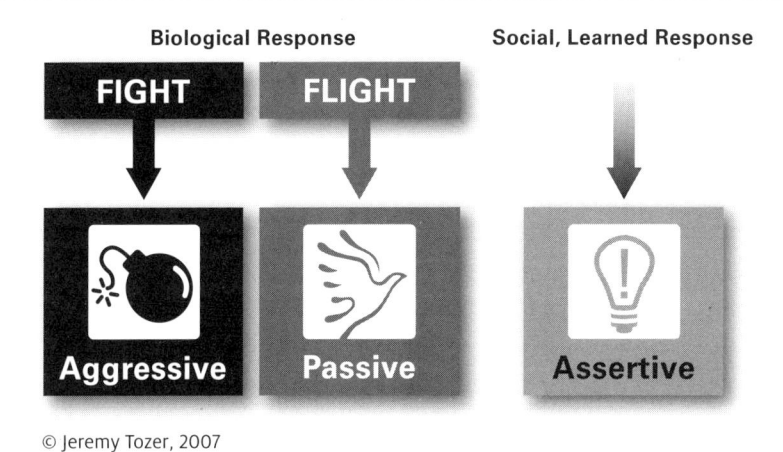

© Jeremy Tozer, 2007

or passively because they are choosing their response from a limited number of options. Assertiveness is not a reflex action – it does not come naturally. Assertive responses are a learnt ability. Over time you can school yourself to summon up an assertive response when threatened – however, you will always have to think about being assertive. It is important to remember that you have a choice of how you interact with your environment and with others. Statements like: 'He made me get angry' and, 'I had to shout because he wound me up so much' are invalid because the speaker had a range of options to choose from. We are all responsible for our own behaviour and the choices we make.

Aggressive behaviour involves believing that one's own needs, opinions, thoughts and feelings are more important than others', and showing a lack of respect for the needs of others. Aggressive behaviour ranges from interrupting others, 'telling' and being autocratic, to extreme aggression, making threats and being hostile; 'passive aggressive' is that killer look! When you behave aggressively, others will either respond in a like manner, leading to conflict, or they will acquiesce. Either way they will probably:

- resent your behaviour,
- not respect you,
- be uncooperative (or limit cooperation, doing only exactly what you ask, they will not show initiative),
- experience strong emotions,
- possibly 'retaliate' or undermine you later.

Passive behaviour involves believing that one's own needs, opinions, thoughts and feelings are less important than others, and deferring to the thoughts and needs of others. Passive behaviour ranges from saying yes when we really want to say no, through not participating in team discussions, to sulking and isolation. When you behave passively, others are likely to:

- feel sorry for you, look down on you and feel frustrated that you do not assert yourself;
- leave you to the consequences of your own behaviour;
- take advantage of your acquiescence;
- railroad you, whether this is intentional or not.

Assertive behaviour involves believing that one's own needs, opinions, thoughts and feelings are as important as anyone else's, and showing respect for the needs and thoughts of others. When you behave assertively, others will likely:

- feel respected, involved, valued;
- respect you, and your views;
- work constructively with you.

Each of the three behaviour types can be recognized by:

- the words people use;
- the voice tone people use;
- gestures and facial expressions (body language);
- outcomes or consequences, the impact on people and their feelings.

It is an inappropriate generalization to label people because, in reality, most of us demonstrate all three styles at different times, and depending on both the situation and the perception of the observer the style will differ. The major challenge in 'being assertive' is that the behaviour one person might perceive as assertive could be perceived as aggressive or passive by someone else. Stereotypically, army officers (who tend to be self-assured, self-confident and used to accepting responsibility and expecting others to do the same) may be perceived by others of a similar position to be assertive, whereas the 'cog' in the great civil service machine of government will see that same person as aggressive.

People often pay more attention to the non-verbal elements of others' communication, especially in charged situations. It is therefore possible for your interactions to be interpreted as passive or aggressive even though the words you have chosen are assertive. Because we react to what others do in terms of the whole message they send out – words, voice tone and body language – it is really important that you are in control of all these channels of communication when you are responding assertively.

Think about how you come across to others. Do you look confident, overly confident or timid? People who tend to behave aggressively or passively often flag their tendencies in their physical appearance. The message is clear. In situations where you are not confident your non-verbal communication may betray you even before you speak. Fortunately the opposite is also true – if you manage your non-verbal messages so that you look and sound confident, you will have more impact and you will give the impression of confidence. Many researchers have commented that there is a strong link between your physical state and your mental state. For instance, you may have felt down one day. Going into work smiling and being cheerful (putting on a brave face) often makes you feel better. This is because a positive approach will elicit a positive response from others. That helps you to feel better.

How to assert yourself

Assertive behaviour increases your feelings of self-confidence. You can change:

- your appearance – hairstyle, what you wear;
- your posture – upright, confident, relaxed;
- your hand gestures – open, inviting but also controlling when appropriate;
- your facial expression – receptive, friendly, interested;
- your eye contact;
- your mental state;
- your voice;
- your emotional control;
- your beliefs (EI self-awareness).

Beliefs

It is helpful to determine what you believe is important about the way you interact with others. Often we let our beliefs and opinions about ourselves and others get in the way of our communication. Sometimes this can set up self-fulfilling prophesies in which our worst fears become true. If you think through the criteria for making your choices this will guide you when you are facing difficult situations. Helpful and unhelpful beliefs are shown in Table 9.2.

TABLE 9.2 Helpful and unhelpful beliefs

Helpful beliefs	Unhelpful beliefs
- All behaviour of others has a positive intent - Trust people until they show they cannot be trusted - It's ok to express your opinions - I will listen to others and they will give me a fair hearing - I can ask questions to ensure understanding - We all make mistakes from time to time - I can say no without feeling guilty - I respect others and they will respect me - I can choose how to behave	- Every behaviour others display has a hidden agenda behind it - It's dangerous to trust people - Keep your thoughts to yourself - It's dangerous to question others - It's rude to say no - If I hold a different view I will be thought of as aggressive or unhelpful

Controlling emotions

It is often difficult to remain calm, particularly when faced with aggressive behaviour. You can do it, though, if you are prepared. Think back to a situation when you felt threatened. How did you know that you felt like that? Did you feel a certain tightening of the chest? Knots in your stomach? Sweaty palms or a dry throat? Identify precisely what you experienced and make a note of it. Next time you feel challenged by a situation:

- look out for those tell-tale indicators;
- acknowledge those responses to yourself;
- concentrate on those areas and mentally relax them, breathe steadily;
- don't let your mind race or panic – choose to keep calm!

Assertive voice tone

Consider the rhythm, speed, volume and pitch (RSVP) with which you speak. Raising your voice tone at the end of sentences, in the UK, may make you sound like you are asking a question rather than making a statement, which can undermine your confidence as perceived by others. This is a common habit in Australia and does not necessarily indicate a question! Does your RSVP convey emphasis and confidence? An even rhythm with low volume and clearly articulated words can be more emphatic or even more aggressive than shouting! Practise using different RSVPs.

Non-verbal communication

Like most if not all carnivores, our eyes face forward and in normal situations we rely more on sight than on any of our other senses. Often we try to concentrate on verbal and written communication, but observing and 'listening' to body language can provide useful clues that indicate whether people are receptive or not to your position. Similarly, other people are observing your body language. Non-verbal communication is not a substitute for clarity of language; it is part of the whole communication 'big picture'. Sometimes people write about body language as if two people were meeting in a perfectly white, noiseless room with two chairs and nothing else. That is clearly not the case. It would be wrong to infer that because the girl opposite the man sat next to me on the London underground has crossed her legs, she is subconsciously rejecting him. She could be doing it for any reason (a full bladder, for example). *We must remember that body language gives us clues – but no more – about emotional states.*

The term 'sympathetic motor mimicry' holds the clue. Outside the mating season (for most animals), and even in the case of those that mate all year (such as primates... that includes us, folks), animals, intra-species, cooperate. Competition is an exhausting, energy-hungry, time-consuming activity – so most of the time we cooperate. To facilitate cooperation we use body language – as well as verbal language – to tell the other person: 'It's ok, I'm your friend.' In a nutshell, that is what dogs do when they wag their tails at each other, when birds preen each other, and when we shake hands and do all the other things that we do to demonstrate cooperation.

The important thing to remember is that it is sympathetic – which means, in biology, you cannot help but do it. This is why, unconsciously, we copy each other's body movements and postures. It is a way of harmonizing with the other person. You can observe this in any number of ways. Next time you are in a group of people drinking, observe what happens when one person in the group lifts the glass to drink. The rest follow – especially if there is tension in the group (incidentally, this is one way to get a contact drunk quickly – that is presupposing that you have a high tolerance to alcohol!). The ritual form of this behaviour is 'toasting' in whatever form it takes.

The New Zealand All Blacks rugby team 'Haka' is a good example of reversed sympathetic motor mimicry. Why don't teams simply ignore the Haka? Or why do they find it so difficult to ignore? The Haka is competitive (non-cooperative) body language performed by one group of men against a second group of men. Competitive body language is also sympathetic. It is 'natural' to want to respond to the challenge. Not responding leaves you frustrated, which is why the Haka is good psychological practice (if you support the All Blacks), and why the All Blacks often have a flying start against other teams (their other advantage is that they are also very good at rugby).

You can demonstrate sympathetic motor mimicry to yourself by repeatedly folding and unfolding your arms when you are talking to someone. Wait until they have copied your posture, then unfold your arms. Repeat the exercise the other way and watch them follow again.

What we often describe is *asexual* body language, that is, simple body language that can be observed between same-sex people. But we are sexual beings, however un-politically correct that is. The body language that is typical of same-sex people is not necessarily the same body language that will be generated between two people of the opposite sex. Body language, of course, is also influenced by culture. At school in some countries, children may be seen shaking hands with classmates every day; that is not usual in England. What is 'proper behaviour' in a New Age commune would be out of place in a Pall Mall London club. People send and receive body language from most parts of the body. In order of expressiveness and reliability they are:

1 Facial expression and eyes.
2 Arms and hands.
3 Legs and feet.
4 Torso.

Most information comes from the face and eyes. Because humans primarily look at the face during communication, people have evolved being able to read the face best. The general rule for arms, hands, legs and feet is that closed postures signal resistance and open postures signal receptivity. The torso is much harder to read as many of the gestures are a matter of individual habit. In any case it is often very difficult to see torso gestures during a discussion. Some gestures are natural and worldwide, for example crying and anguish are recognizable no matter what culture a person is from. Other gestures are cultural, learnt gestures: for example in India and Bulgaria a headshake movement can mean 'yes'.

So we need to ensure that our body language reflects the message we wish to send. If you lack energy (for example in the middle of the afternoon) or are tired, your body language can send a 'couldn't care less' message. Similarly, if you are preoccupied with another problem your lack of concentration can be reflected in your body language. Both these circumstances could send the wrong message to colleagues.

Sometimes conflicting messages will be sent – the non-verbal communication is not congruent with the verbal communication. A very common example is the nervous laugh. A laugh that is not the result of something humorous signals nervousness or discomfort. Conflicting verbal and non-verbal messages generally indicate one of three things:

1. The person is unaware of his or her effect on others.
2. The body language is expressing a hidden agenda.
3. The person is tired or confused.

Body language can be used for emphasis. A raised voice can underline strength of feeling, the verbal equivalent of underlining. The key to emphasis is a change from the norm – save such gestures for when you really need them. A more sophisticated approach is to use conflicting messages to appropriately emphasize your point. An example is to use a very soft voice and explicit gestures to express your feelings. Table 9.3 illustrates the different body language of receptive and unreceptive listeners.[4]

Table 9.4 shows indicators that may reflect a shift in an opponent's acceptance levels.

TABLE 9.3 Non-verbal communication

	Receptive	Unreceptive
Face	Eye contact Smiling	No eye contact or squinting Tense jaw Head turned away – sideways glance
Arms and hands	Arms and/or hands open and in relaxed position Hands touching the face (but not masking the mouth)	Hands clenched Arms crossed Hand over the mouth Rubbing the back of the neck
Legs and feet	Sitting: Legs together, or one in front of the other slightly Standing: Weight evenly distributed, hands on hips, body tilted toward speaker	Sitting: Crossed legs, pointing away from the speaker. Sitting or standing: Legs and feet pointing toward the exit
Torso	Sitting on the edge of the chair Body tilted toward the speaker	Leaning back in the chair

TABLE 9.4 Indicators of acceptance or resistance

Acceptance Indicators	Resistance Indicators
Cocking the head	Fidgeting nervously
Taking off or otherwise playing with spectacles	Reducing eye contact
	Placing hands behind one's back
Pinching the bridge of the nose	Placing a hand over one's mouth
Leaning forward, uncrossing legs	Gripping one's arm or wrist
Increasing eye contact	Crossing arms in front of chest
Putting hands to chest	Squinting eyes dramatically
Touching the forehead or chin, as in the statue *The Thinker*	Making fist-like gestures
	Twisting the feet or the entire body so that they point to the door
Touching you (if the movement is to reassure, and not to interrupt)	

Eye accessing cues

Memory retrieval provokes characteristic eye movements that may give us clues or cues about a person's emotional state. This is radically different to other forms of body language in one respect. Body language, or sympathetic motor mimicry, is about external sensations. Eye accessing cues are about recall, or internal sensations. Information is gathered by our senses, and all sensory information is relayed via the thalamus in the brain. There are three nuclei in the thalamus:

1. Lateral geniculate: visual.
2. Medial geniculate: auditory.
3. Ventrobasal complex: the central nervous system.

Other organs within the limbic system have a role in memory. These are:

Hippocampus: general memory retrieval.

Amygdala: 'instinct' memories, 'fight or flight' memories.

Hypothalamus: homeostatic balance, sex, aggression, hunger, pleasure.

With the emergence of cognitive psychology (the psychology of how we think), memory has become an important subject and there are three aspects to memory: registration, storage and retrieval. Within these functions there are also three memory 'processes' (a way of explaining what happens):

- Sensory memory – milliseconds (iconic, echoic).
- Short-term memory (STM) – 15–30 seconds.
- Long-term memory (LTM) – unlimited (episodic, procedural, semantic or factual).

Iconic (visual memory) and echoic (auditory memory) are the immediate memory – or imprint – which our brains receive and order, without which we would be besieged by meaningless, random stimuli. An analogy would be a still in a film spool – the brain freezes a scene, cognates it, then spools on to the next scene. This happens instantaneously, without our having to think about it consciously.

STM is what we can remember in a 15–30 second period. George Miller – an American psychologist – came up with the famous rule that we can hold in our STM seven bits of information, plus or minus two. You can prove this to yourself by doing memory tests with numbers.

Lastly, there is LTM, which is what most of us mean when we talk about memory. The three types of LTM are:

Episodic memory = 'I first rode a bike when I was 7.'

Procedural memory = 'I know how to ride a bike.'

Semantic or factual = 'I know that a bike has two wheels.'

Memory retrieval or the working memory (WM)

For memory to be useful to you, it must be retrievable. The term used to describe the retrieval of memory to the conscious mind, so that it can be 'worked', is 'working memory' (WM). There are four components to WM:

1. The central executive (allocates attention and controls memory retrieval).
2. The visuo-spatial scratchpad – inner eye.
3. Primary acoustic store – inner ear.
4. Articulatory loop – verbal rehearsal system.

For example, if I were to ask you how many windows there are in your house, you would:

1. Use the visuo-spatial scratchpad to generate an image of the front of your house.
2. Use the articulatory loop to count the windows.
3. This process would be controlled by the central executive.

Memory retrieval provokes characteristic eye movements. These are:

- Visuo-spatial – upper eye movements.
- Acoustic – sideways eye movements.
- Articulatory – downwards eye movements.

Eye movements are clearest in children, as well as in adults behaving 'naturally'. They are not empirical, but they can be used as guides. Put simply, visual recall provokes upward eye movements, audio recall provokes sideways eye movements, and articulatory recall (talking to yourself) provokes downward eye movements.

For reasons that are not clear, if the recall is accurate or 'truthful', for right-handed people the movement is to the left. Test yourself by trying to remember the colour of your first car – your eyes will flick up in an involuntary movement. However, if the recall is not accurate (if you are having difficulty remembering, or if you deliberately or even unconsciously modify or 'edit' the memory, ie lie consciously or unconsciously) the movement will be to the opposite side. Typically, your eye will flick from left to right. You are constructing a memory, not recalling a memory. The uses of this by interrogators and interviewers is obvious; it is also useful in other walks of life – trying to assess a client, or quizzing your partner after he or she has been out all night!

The 'rule' left = truth and right = lie (for right-handed people) is not absolute. Left brain/right brain dominance influences our eye movements. You have to test people (by asking neutral questions), see which way they go when telling the truth, then drop a few difficult questions that might prompt them to 'edit' the truth. It is, as you might expect, reversed with left-handed people, but again, you have to test first.

The audio recall is similar to the visual recall. You can best observe this in TV programmes about musicians. Musicians are overwhelmingly interested in sounds, obviously. Turn the sound on the TV down and just watch the eyes of the musician being interviewed about his or her music. The sideways eye movements are very obvious (or should be if they take the shades off!).

The downward eye movements are more problematic. The general rule is this: when we are talking to ourselves (the articulatory loop), right-handed people look bottom left. Next time you are sailing or gardening, and thinking about something, notice your eye movements. When we are recalling a memory that has strong feelings attached to it, right-handed people look bottom right. So next time you think: 'That sod Sergio, what the heck was up with him anyway?', again, notice your eye movements. 'Downward-looking' people have been labelled 'kinaesthetic' in NLP circles, which is a pity, because it is a coined word that doesn't mean what it says (*kines* = motion towards, *aesthetic* = sensuous perception).

From this follows another NLP belief that people are dominant in one of three 'modalities' (auditory, visual or kinaesthetic), and that if you use the right words (ie, 'Do you see what I mean' to a visual person, or 'Can you hear what I am saying' to an auditory person, or 'Do you feel this' to a kinaesthetic person) you will 'tune in' to that person. Such words may help you cover all bases, but we all have visual, auditory and kinesthetic loops in our memory function. Which one you use depends entirely on what you are recalling. A musician asked to remember the colour of his underpants will not look sideways. He will look up, unless he can't remember, in which case he might look down to check.

So what is the use of eye accessing cues? They are another tool. If you are alert enough you can spot someone's eye movements. You can, over the period of an interview, for example, begin to tell when that person is being open, frank and truthful, and when that person is being closed, guarded and perhaps untruthful. It does take practice, though.

Assertive communication

Assertive responses

Now think about the ways in which other people may be assertive or aggressive when talking to you. The ways tend to fall under the headings of generalizations, distortions and selected assumptions. These are briefly explained below, and are provided with a suggested method of response:

- *Definites.* This is when people use words 'can' and 'cannot', 'possible' and 'impossible', 'I must' or 'I must not'. Such words create constraints, often false constraints that limit action. The response to statements in this form is: 'What would happen if you did/didn't?'
- *'Universal generalizations'.* Generalizations use words like 'all', 'every', 'always', 'never' and 'none'. They deny the possibility of exceptions and so are easily challenged by stating known facts and asking open questions. When giving feedback generalizations convey little impact.
- *Linked statements.* This is where two statements are linked in such a way that they are taken to mean the same thing, for example: 'You are not smiling… you are not enjoying yourself.' This can be questioned by asking, 'Why or how does this x lead to y?'
- *Beliefs and declarations.* These are where the speaker's basic assumptions are revealed in what they say, for instance, 'Why don't you take more care?' presupposes that the other person did not take care. This is challenged by asking 'What leads you to believe that…?'
- *Cause and effect.* This is where an external stimulus (cause) is held responsible for an internal response (effect). Cause and effect is heard where people do not accept responsibility for their own feelings or actions by saying, 'His response really wound me up.' This can be questioned by asking, 'Why or how does this X lead to Y and what choices could you exercise in your behaviour?'
- *Predictions.* When people presume they know, without having asked, about another's thoughts, feelings or intentions, they are making predictions: 'You wouldn't be confident doing that.' The response to 'mind reading' is to ask how someone knows what you were thinking.
- *Incomplete comparison.* When a comparison is made that is left open-ended, for example, 'The lease-back option is better.' The response is to ask, 'Better than what?'
- *Judgement.* When a judgement is made that has no explicit basis, eg: 'This woman is the ideal candidate for the job.' The response is to ask, 'Who is making this judgement and on what grounds are they making it?'
- *Incomplete demands.* A request is incomplete when something specific and measurable is replaced by something that is not, or an unspecific request is stated, for example: 'Every customer should get good service.' Simply ask, 'What specifically do you mean by…?'

Self-talk, rehearsals and visualizations

Each day, most of us talk to ourselves or we visualize possible situations. We think about what we are experiencing and what we should do. If you are thinking about

FIGURE 9.8 The ladder of assertiveness

Climb the Ladder of Assertiveness

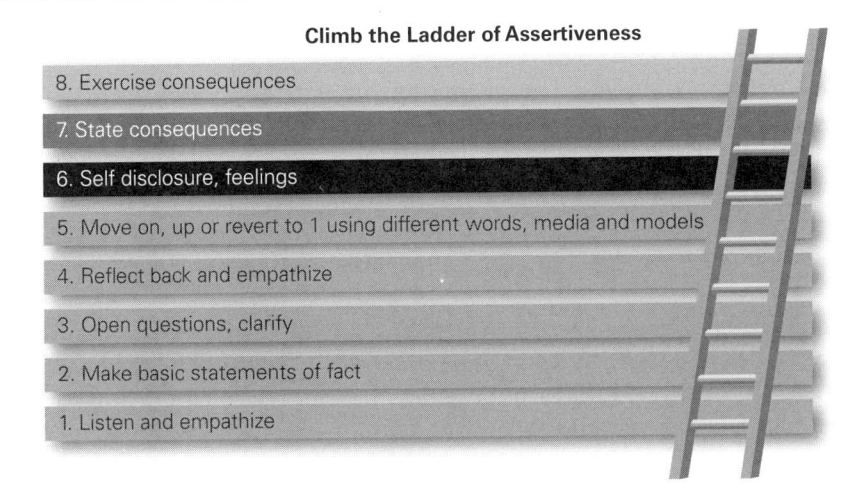

8. Exercise consequences
7. State consequences
6. Self disclosure, feelings
5. Move on, up or revert to 1 using different words, media and models
4. Reflect back and empathize
3. Open questions, clarify
2. Make basic statements of fact
1. Listen and empathize

© Jeremy Tozer, 2007

assertiveness there is a chance that your self-talk is either leading you to be overconfident and aggressive or you are undermining yourself. By telling yourself that 'you can't', your inner voice is ensuring that you won't! It is denying you choices and worrying you with unreal or improbable outcomes. As a result you may choose either to behave aggressively – perhaps by denying others choices, or by expressing your views with unnecessary force; or behave passively, denying yourself opportunities and agreeing to things that make you feel uncomfortable.

If you recall, in Chapter 8 when we looked at the mechanics of the brain, the point was made that learning new skills involves making new connections between and improving pathways for neurons. Positive self-talk, mental rehearsals, full dress rehearsals and visualizations all assist in doing this.

Positive self-talk involves thinking about a past occasion in which you were assertive, and reminding yourself about what it looked, felt and sounded like; telling yourself that problems are simply challenges that you have the capability to overcome, and reminding yourself of the benefits of following through with your plan.

Rehearsal means planning what you are going to do and say, and then doing it, or visualizing and thinking about it. Before a potentially challenging encounter, rehearse what you might say and picture yourself saying it with the right voice tone and body language – describe how you will feel when you have asserted yourself. Turn this into a mental video clip and rerun it over and over again.

When you need to be assertive, there is a ladder that you may climb during the conversation; this is shown at Figure 9.8.

There are seven progressive levels you can use in escalating your assertiveness, and you may choose to use these as appropriate. As a general rule, if you find yourself going around the loop several times, it becomes more appropriate for you to raise your assertion to the next level:

1 *Listen and empathize.* This is exactly what it says on the tin! Review the Mandarin character for listening and its meaning. Empathy is appreciating the other person's perspective. To empathize effectively you need to enter their world so that you can understand what is important and why they feel so strongly about things that are not important to you. Your words and your voice tone should demonstrate that genuine understanding. Saying, 'I understand but' generally means that you do not understand!

2 *Make basic statements of fact.* Basic assertion means simply that you articulate your needs, views and feelings or state known facts. You may consider restating facts like a broken record and standing your ground – persistence often pays off.

3 *Ask open questions.* Open questions are the ones that are most effective because they generate dialogue. Hypothetical questions (what ifs) may be used to preview performance challenges. Listen to the answers to your questions and clarify understanding.

4 *Reflect back and empathize.* In doing this, use the words and phrases that the other person has used. This serves three purposes:
   - it builds common ground between you;
   - it demonstrates that you have listened and heard;
   - it gives you time to think and collect your thoughts.

5 *Self-disclosure.* Self-disclosure means revealing your thoughts and feelings. People generally are wary of discussing feelings and to reveal yours is quite disarming. One consequence of self-disclosure is that it encourages the other person to disclose their thoughts. This helps build common understanding.

6 *State the consequences.* If something continues against your wishes or better judgement, then state the consequences that will follow, or are likely to follow and why that is the case.

7 *Exercise the consequences.* If you are in a leadership position, to maintain your credibility and to ensure consistency of expectations for people, you must exercise the consequences.

Overcoming objections

There is a very similar escalating approach to overcoming objections, shown in Figure 9.9. Listen and empathize, as has been explained elsewhere in this chapter. Then clarify to ensure mutual understanding. This means asking open questions, and reflecting back and paraphrasing the 'objector's' own words to ensure common understanding, and then asking what questions the objector has. Then answer those questions and check for understanding. Hopefully you are now able to move on, but if not then revert to step 1 but using different words, models, examples and media to make your point and overcome the objection.

FIGURE 9.9 Overcoming objections

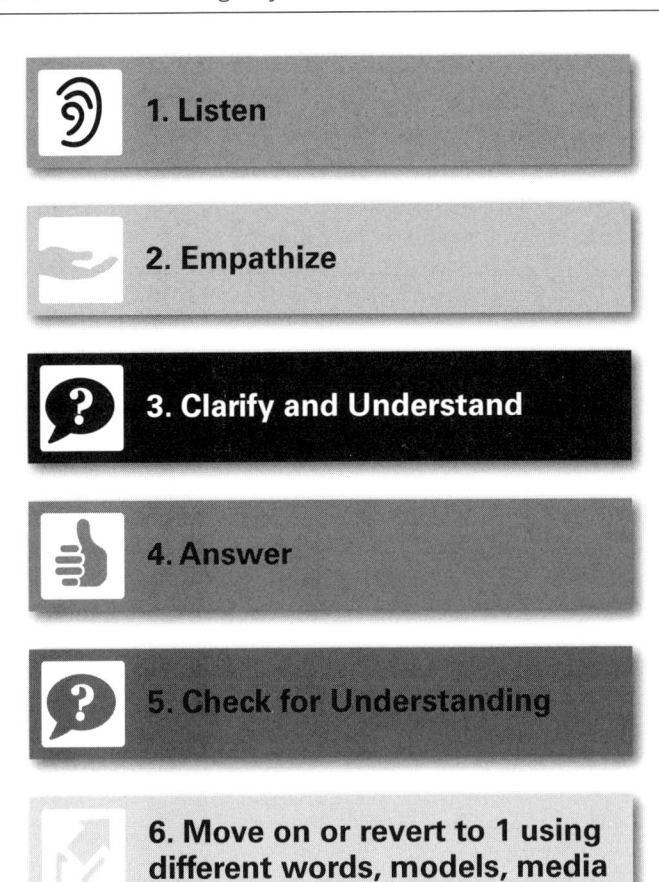

1. Listen
2. Empathize
3. Clarify and Understand
4. Answer
5. Check for Understanding
6. Move on or revert to 1 using different words, models, media

© Jeremy Tozer, 2007

Notes

1 Albert Mehrabian, 1981, *Silent Messages: Implicit communication of emotions and attitudes*, Belmont, CA: Wadsworth.
2 Richard Bandler and John Grinder, 1975, *The Structure of Magic Vol 1: A book about language and therapy*, and 1976, *The Structure of Magic Vol 2: A book about communication and change*, New York: Science & Behavior Books.
3 Peter Senge, Art Kleiner, Charlotte Roberts, Richard Ross and Bryan Smith, 1994, *The Fifth Discipline Fieldbook*, London: Nicholas Brealey.
4 Donaldson and Donaldson, 1996, *Negotiating for Dummies*, New York: IDG Books Worldwide.

10
Coaching

> Introduction to coaching
> The coach's position
> Coach's toolkit
> Path to mastery
> Coaching conversation agenda
> Developing behaviour
> Changing attitudes
>
> Building skill
> Promotion and maintenance of the desire to learn
> Confirmation that training has been assimilated
> Question technique
> Fault checking

Chapter 3 made it clear that a leader's role was to create or develop the team's ACE conditions for success. That includes:

- developing the ability of team members, as well as
- creating the optimal environment for growth (leadership example, and the warmth, empathy and genuineness of EI described in Chapter 8), and
- the optimal environment for performance, the balance between a culture of entitlement or fear, that was described in Chapter 3.

There seems to be some confusion between the meaning of the terms training, feedback, coaching, mentoring and performance management. So let us start by creating clarity of meaning (that word clarity again!).

Training (or instruction – corporations avoid the term 'instruction', yet many senior executives are happy to pay sailing or scuba diving instructors!) is the vehicle for imparting new knowledge (lectures, presentations and theory/case study lessons), and new skills (a skills lesson involves teaching, practice and feedback). *Feedback* is the development of awareness of personal impact. This involves the specifics of what was said or done (or not done), and how; and the outcome or the impact on task and people or relationships. Coaching takes things further by discussing why and how to develop, creating commitment to and defining a plan. Feedback is thus an essential part of coaching; indeed it is a prerequisite to any development but it is not coaching in itself.

Coaching is a leadership tool or 'process' for developing the ability of a person or of the team: the application of knowledge, the improvement of skill and/or development of behaviour, and the shaping of attitude. It is usually conducted in the context of a particular task or role. Effective coaching will include feedback. There appears to be no proper term for a person being coached, so we will use the expedient but inelegant term 'coachee'. There is a fine line between coaching and counselling. It is very possible in a coaching conversation focused on behavioural development and the reasons for behaviour to touch some raw nerves. The good leader will sense the point at which he or she should stop, and a qualified psychologist is engaged.

Mentoring, as far as we are concerned, is a form of coaching more to do with career development and individual growth and maturity than with day-to-day performance. It is usually best undertaken by a senior or seasoned person who is not in the same 'chain of command' as the mentee (another word lacking elegance!).

Most organizations have some form of *performance management* system. Many are thought of as annual reviews of performance when bonuses are handed out – or when people are told that they are not 'sparking' which, when questioned, leads to some vague response about something that was done or not done months before that no one can remember in detail. Performance management, as far as we are concerned, involves:

- Briefing teams about plans and their roles in them.
- Agreeing individual tasks, objectives and priorities derived from plans.
- Tracking progress, and providing feedback and coaching as appropriate.
- Reviewing plans, their progress and re-briefing teams as appropriate.
- Rewarding and/or recognizing performance and celebrating success (or holding to account) in a timely manner.
- Ensuring personal development plans (PDP) are created and implemented for individual team members. PDPs should span personal, professional (functional skill) and career development (linked to succession planning and talent management).

Introduction to coaching

Coaching is developing the ability of the team (and the individuals within it) to function effectively without constant direction and close supervision (and most team members want less interference!), their collective ability to meet likely future challenges and organization needs. The leader also needs to ensure that a leadership succession plan exists. As part of that capability development, an effective leader will conduct a programme of individual and collective coaching as well as formal collective development.

Coaching is unlocking the potential and motivation to maximize performance. Coaching involves helping people to clarify their own thinking and derive meaning (purpose), question their own, sometimes limiting, beliefs and more effectively apply their skills and knowledge. It means helping people to learn and improve (mastery) and to create their own solutions (autonomy), giving them the confidence and self-belief to stretch. The coach acts as a catalyst to improve the performance of others. The coaching relationship is a mutual process: coaching occurs with someone or with a team – it is not done to someone. Coaching therefore is much more than simply giving advice and touches three important elements of motivation: mastery, autonomy and purpose (review the motivation section in Chapter 8).

The coach who is a subject expert can provide wise counsel, advice and tuition – but most of the time this is needed more by novices than experienced people, and giving advice is not really coaching. The coach need not necessarily be an expert on the subject under discussion. Indeed, being an expert in the same subject area as the person who is being coached may be a barrier to effective coaching. The coach may find it hard not to take ownership of the situation and simply 'tell' and provide solutions; this is not coaching and certainly not what an experienced team member wants or needs. When the coach is not a topic expert but is an expert in coaching then true self-awareness of impact in the coachee, new insights on process and performance and new options and opportunities will result.

People can only do three things: think, feel and act. Coaching needs to recognize this fact and reflect it.

Patterns of behaviour and the ripple effect

All people have patterns of behaviour. When we receive certain stimuli we may react in ways that others come to expect; we become 'known' to others. Whatever we do has an impact on the people around us and we create a ripple effect. If we feel particularly happy or angry, our mood will influence the collective mood of the group we are in – we may stifle or stimulate constructive thought and actions.

By changing an individual's pattern of interaction if their behaviour is not as we would wish, we may influence the subsequent behaviour and performance of all those who come into contact with that person. The interdependence of team or work group members means that by changing one individual, a flow-on effect is possible. As leaders we must seize this opportunity; we must also recognize that our patterns of behaviour also have a 'mood contagion' effect on people – but given that we occupy leadership positions it is a more powerful one. Therefore as leaders we need to seek feedback, and develop ourselves and our emotional intelligence, and not just think of developing our team members.

Coaching: review and preview

Coaching is a tough, analytical business tool that enables leaders and their teams to honestly and openly discuss performance, both success and failure, and to learn from it for both the coachee and for other colleagues – in order to repeat success and to avoid future failure. The true power of coaching lies in previewing performance – setting people up for success; yet so many leaders think of coaching only in the sense of reviewing performance, sometimes when it is too late.

Coaching can be both formal (planned conversations) and informal (ad hoc discussions, when the need is clearly seen, or indeed when a colleague or team member asks for help). It can be leader to team member, peer to peer, or even team member to leader (managing upwards with a subtle flow of questions!), leader to team or any other combination. Through a process of dynamic interaction the coach enables people being coached to help themselves.

Generally, the best time for review coaching is 'as things happen', a conversation planned for very soon after the event. But this is top-down coaching; you might be intercepted by one of your team who says, 'Boss, I have a problem...' and you need to coach on the spot. So leaders need to have the 'coaching conversation agenda' at their fingertips and need to be able to access it at a moment's notice.

Coaching for performance, for growth and to enable

There are three styles of coaching conversation that we may have in our leadership careers:

1 *Coaching for performance*, when the leader wishes to raise the level of someone's performance from below standard to an acceptable level. This may be a planned and well-structured conversation, or series of conversations, and while a conversation may start out in the collaborative style, it may need to become directive.

2 *Coaching for growth*, when the leader is coaching as part of a planned process of capability building, to take people to the next level, when the style will be entirely collaborative (unless there are moments in which advice or knowledge need to be transmitted).

3 *Coaching to enable*, when an employee seeks assistance by effectively asking, 'Boss, I have a problem – how do you suggest I approach this...?' This may be an ad hoc, unplanned conversation.

All these conversations may follow the same coaching conversation agenda or sequence of 'headings' or steps in the conversation. It is really only the leadership style that may need to differ to suit the situation – the degree of assertiveness and 'telling' with which a point is made and the amount of time spent discussing any agenda heading.

The coach must be capable of achieving progress based on the appreciation of past lessons and the anticipation of future opportunities. The process should be a joint problem-solving process that may be adapted to both previewing and reviewing performance in formal and informal situations.

The main benefit of taking a consistent approach to structuring coaching conversations is that as people get used to 'the coaching agenda' they will start to ask themselves the questions that the coach would ask, and take appropriate action before they have spoken to the leader. This develops 'self-help'. Additionally, a consistent approach to the conversation format sets expectations and enables coaching to become embedded across an organization – a way of life in the organization, a very healthy cultural norm.

Instruction vs coaching

If you were to ask a group of novice parachutists what they would look for in the person who was going to take them through their first 'static line' jump (a static line

TABLE 10.1 Coaching versus instruction

The Instructor for Novices	The Coach for Experienced Practitioners
• Is very experienced • Radiates confidence • Is organized and structured • Gives clear, firm directions and explanations • Demonstrates required skills • Ensures skills are practised and feedback is given • Questions individuals to ensure understanding • Shows understanding, respect and empathy for individuals • Gives encouragement and recognition • Maintains high standards	• Recognition of practitioner's experience • Active listening • Open questioning • Generates options from the practitioner • Respect • Empathy • Affirmation • Support • Encouragement • Optimism • Adaptability • Patience • Creates belief

pulls the rip cord for you), and a team of skilled skydivers what they wanted in the person who was going to enable them to win an aerial performance competition, you would probably get the two answers similar to those in Table 10.1.

There is naturally some overlap between the two, but the spectrum spans 'directive instructor – questioning coach'. Figure 10.1 outlines the investment and benefit characteristics of instruction and coaching.

The coach's position

Being an effective coach at work is analogous to the role of the coach to a sports team. During a match there are three possible positions that may be adopted by the coach: on the field, in the stand, or on the touchline. Similarly, the leader at work may choose which position to adopt, although you will find that you will need to move around for best effect with your team.

On the field

In this position, the coach runs onto the field and takes over from the players to rescue what the coach believes is a dangerous situation. Too often this causes interference

FIGURE 10.1 Investment and benefit of coaching and instruction

Instruction		LEARNING	Coaching	
Directing	Advising	STYLE	Suggesting	Questioning
High for inexperienced people, if task is simple/unfamiliar all may benefit.		'Quality' of Output	High for experienced people.	
Novices learn quickly, the experienced may not develop.		Learning	Deeper learning by coachee, coach may also learn.	
Lower, unless trainee is new to the subject.		Motivation	Higher.	
Relatively low.		Time Investment	Relatively high.	
Inexperienced people or people facing new tasks.		Suitability	Experienced people where development and minimum supervision are desirable outcomes.	

After Landsberg | © Jeremy Tozer, 1997–2006

and disrupts the game. Many leaders are tempted to do this, especially when they are experts in the technical issues that their people are dealing with. There may of course be times when the leader has to do this, particularly when the team is under pressure, but it should not be the norm or default setting.

In the stand

In this position, the coach retreats into the stand and adopts the role of spectator, watching the game from a distance. The spectator will still have strong feelings about performance, often venting them in anger or applause (emotions finding an outlet). But when the game is over the spectator simply turns around and walks away. Some leaders do this too, misinterpreting what they believe to be delegation when it is actually an abdication of responsibility. It is desirable for a leader to be able to take an overview, to get a clearer, strategic picture, but the leader cannot abdicate responsibility for the performance and development of the team.

On the touchline

The third position is usually the most effective to take. The coach stands on the touchline, not taking over from the players, but sharing in the pleasure and pain of their performance and ready to help when needed. The coach's main work is

Coaching

FIGURE 10.2 The coaching zone

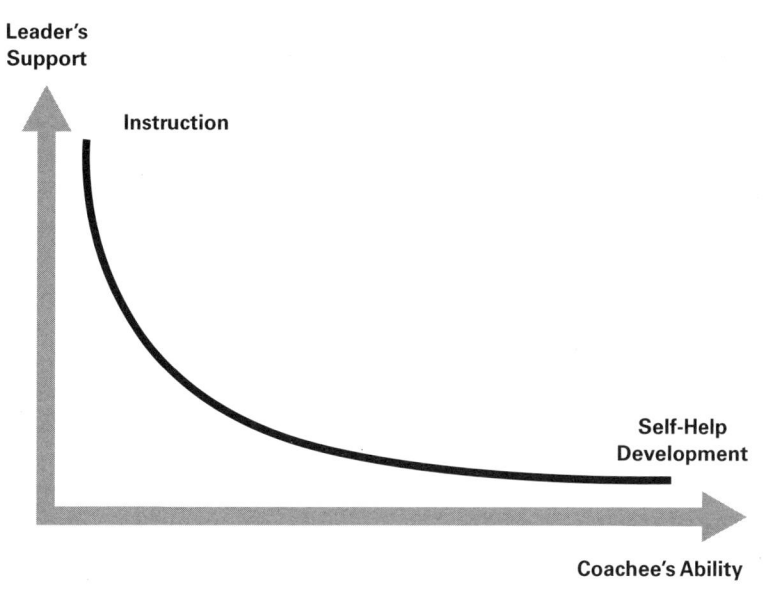

Leader's Support (y-axis) — *Coachee's Ability* (x-axis)

Curve decreases from **Instruction** (high support, low ability) to **Self-Help Development** (low support, high ability).

© Jeremy Tozer, 1997–2006

undertaken before the game when objectives are clarified, actions are anticipated and improvements planned, and afterwards when lessons are learnt and the next match is prepared for.

It is the commitment to learning and improvement that fuels better business performance and creates competitive edge. Coaching is win, win, win: people gain genuine satisfaction because they achieve their potential; the leader gains by developing the respect and loyalty the team have for him or her; and organizations gain because business performance is improved.

Leaders have to be able to vary their style considerably because developing people is not a simple matter of either coaching or instructing: there will inevitably be moments in the same conversation when the leader needs 'to instruct'; and times when the leader needs to coach with the emphasis reflecting people's level of development and their personality. The coach therefore moves fluidly around the coaching zone shown in Figure 10.2.

Coach's toolkit

The effective coach needs to have quite a few tools in the toolkit, which may be accessed at a moment's notice. Some of those we have already covered in preceding chapters. They are:

- Understanding the drivers of human behaviour, the nature of emotional intelligence, self-awareness, and the Johari Window (Chapter 8).

- Human emotions experienced during the four stages of change (Chapter 6).
- Communication, listening, questioning and assertiveness (Chapter 9).

The other essential tools are outlined below.

Path to mastery

It is worth understanding the four steps, or levels of competence, that a person experiences when developing any new skill as this will inform your approach to coaching (see Figure 10.3). The first level is really one of ignorance – you don't know what you don't know. As self-awareness is generated, people become aware of their low level of competence and inability. Provided they have sufficient motivation to develop (development must meet a personal need), they learn and improve, and consciously strive to apply new skills. When mastery has been achieved, a high level of competence may be demonstrated effortlessly, and unconsciously.

Behavioural observation

To create genuine self-awareness of personal impact in team members, the leader-coach needs to have 'behavioural evidence' – facts – at his or her fingertips. The leader-coach therefore needs to develop a sharp eye for observing behaviour and must learn to record and classify examples for use in coaching. The elements that need to be recorded are shown in Figure 10.4.

FIGURE 10.3 The path to mastery

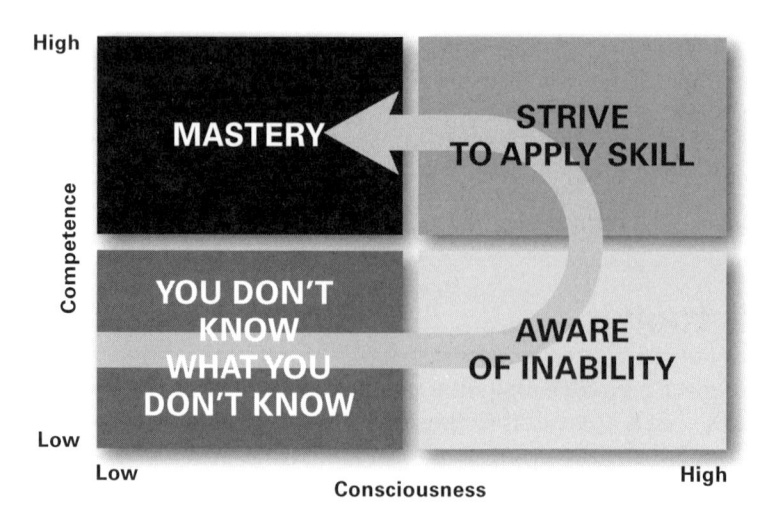

© Jeremy Tozer, 1997–2007

FIGURE 10.4 The elements of behavioural evidence

What was said and how: words, tone, body language, volume, confidence-presence

What was done and not done and how: body language, actions, process

Impact on achieving task and engaging people

© Jeremy Tozer, 1997–2007

In essence, the observant coach 'looks at and listens to' the whole person to gather specific examples of behaviour – what was said (and how), what was done and how (or what was not done), and its impact – on people and their engagement and relationships, and on task and progress towards its completion.

When observing people, be careful not to be influenced by:

- *Primacy* – you remember the first thing that was done in a situation and that influences you above all else.
- *Recency* – you remember the most recent example and are influenced in your overall assessment of a person by that.
- *Halo or horns* – there is something so strikingly attractive or so awful about the person that you fail to notice anything else.
- *Leniency* – do not make allowances, 'So and so would have done ABC if...'.
- *The outcome* – failure to complete a task may not be as a result of ineffective behaviour, rather a lack of 'clarity', skill, knowledge or an ineffective environment, and developing these are the leader's responsibility.

You might be effective in observing behaviour, but you also need to record specific examples to be used in giving feedback. Make a few notes on the context or situation and try to capture some of the actual words used, as well as a few adjectives to describe tone, body language and other's 'engagement' as well as the result – the impact on both people and task. Note what could have been done more effectively and/or what behaviour should be continued and what developed.

Feedback

All too often when people hear the work 'feedback' they think something negative is coming their way. The two parts of the word 'feed' and 'back' imply giving something back that nurtures. It does not mean hammering people into the ground:

TABLE 10.2 Description of feedback

Ineffective Feedback	Effective Feedback
• Broad sweeping statements	• Focuses on facts
• Focuses on the person	• Focuses on behaviour
• Focuses on blame, points the finger	• Acknowledges others' feelings
• Belittles and demeans	• Enables growth
• Appears judgemental	• Appears logical and rational
• Leads to defensive behaviour and conflict	• Leads to learning and forward progress
• Creates confusion	• Clarifies expectations
• Erodes self-confidence	• Increases mutual trust and confidence
• Does not improve ability	• Develops ability

once they have been pushed beneath the surface, it is very difficult for them to re-emerge!

If you think about feedback that you have been given, both effective/constructive and ineffective/destructive, (let's avoid saying 'good' or 'bad' feedback – feedback on 'bad behaviour' is still 'good' if the way it is delivered moves the receiver forward), it probably looked, sounded and felt something like the description in Table 10.2:

Types of feedback

Feedback can fall into two categories: motivational feedback – recognition of good performance, positive reinforcement that builds self-esteem and sustains desired behaviour or performance levels; and developmental feedback – used in performance improvement conversations to shape future behaviour. This enables the person to understand their impact, what needs to improve and why.

Giving EIC feedback – example, impact, commit

Whatever the type of feedback being given, the 'handrail' shown in Figure 10.5 applies – what will vary, as ever, will be 'style' – the extent to which the conversation about examples of behaviour and perceived impact uses open questions or employs emphatic statement of facts, requirements and consequences if no change is observed.

First, remember that feedback is not just intended for increasing poor performance and developing behaviour but also for maintaining or repeating high levels of performance. To start with, you need to establish a licence to give feedback.

Most people want more feedback than they get otherwise they will never be aware of 'the blind spots' that everyone else sees in their Johari Window. Yet so many people seem frightened of giving it! This is usually due to the mistaken belief that they will cause offence or 'it's not my job' and responsibility is passed to the HR department, a lack of confidence or moral courage, or simply people do not know how to give it.

FIGURE 10.5 EIC feedback

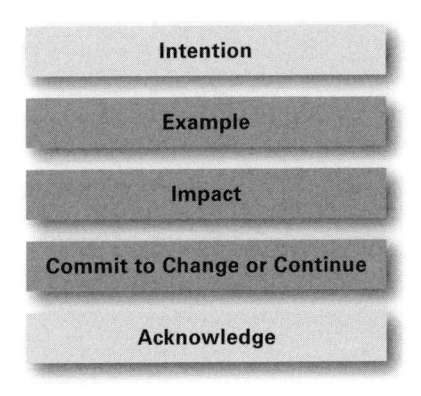

```
Intention
Example
Impact
Commit to Change or Continue
Acknowledge
```

© Jeremy Tozer, 2007

If feedback is given using the sequence shown in Figure 10.5, it will be non-threatening and will truly be of great value to the individual receiving it. Simply ask, 'May I give you some feedback?' – if the answer is no, which it seldom is, you should think about asking, 'Why not? What are you afraid of?'

1 *Intention*. Clarify in your own mind what you want to achieve; prepare to set the right tone by choosing the right words and the right examples to achieve your aim. Do you wish to belittle someone, or engage the person in a useful conversation?

2 *Example*. Ask open questions about what occurred, what was said, done or not done and how. For example, 'Do you remember what you said in the meeting? What did you say? How did you say it?' If the person you are talking to is trying to avoid confronting specific examples of the behaviour, you can escalate from asking open questions to 'filling in the blank spaces' in the other person's answer to making assertive statements of fact. For example, 'During the meeting you said abc. Your tone and body language were xyz.'

3 *Impact*. Ask open questions about the impact that this has had on the task, customers, people and relationships. For example, 'What reaction did you observe, what was the expression on Bill's face? How did this help to achieve the task?' Similarly, you may need to describe the impact and make assertive statements such as, 'The impact on the group was abc – I felt like xyz' (disclosing your feelings is powerful).

4 *Commit*. Seek commitment to the change required for improvement, or commitment to continuation of the same effective behaviour. A closed yes or no question may be asked here.

5 *Acknowledge* – when offered feedback by colleagues say thank you, it encourages a flow of feedback, or thank the recipient of your feedback for taking it on board.

If you are giving motivational or reinforcing feedback, there is probably no need to labour each of these stages – common sense must apply – the whole conversation may only be 30 seconds.

If several different actions that collectively form a pattern of behaviour are being addressed, then the conversation might include example 1 and impact 1, example 2 and impact 2 and so on. At this point the coach might suggest that a pattern of behaviour exists and it warrants a change.

If it is avoidable, do not tell! Whenever possible ask open questions that invite self-assessment and prompt thought. Example questions include:

- What was the situation?
- What were you thinking?
- What did you do/what happened? Tell me more about that.
- What exactly did you say? How might it have been perceived?
- Why did you do/say that?
- What was the impact on the task?
- What was the impact on the customer?
- What was the reaction of other people in the team?
- What body language did you observe among your colleagues?

When people answer these types of questions they are more likely to own the answer than if the facts are simply given to them. However, do state the full facts about examples and impact if they are not fully appreciated or lightly touched upon when raised by the feedback recipient – use an appropriate degree of assertiveness.

Feedback should be objective; be hard on the facts (what happened and impact) but not on the person. Focus on facts: assessment should relate to results not efforts; the results must be within the job holder's control. Don't get distracted by arguments not related to the issue.

Seek acknowledgement and agreement. In a 'performance improvement' situation, enable the employee to accept that the issue and its cause(s) exist. While you should start with open questions, you may need to steer thought with more specific questioning – a questioning funnel, linked to facts and impacts. If the coachee is in denial it is quite appropriate to state the facts relating to examples and the full impacts, and to state the consequences of a continuation of the same behaviour. You can then use closed questioning to ensure that the message is understood. Then if the coachee wishes to commit to changing you may resume discussion on 'reasons for performance'.

After the examples and impacts have been discussed seek commitment to the change needed or continuation of good performance. A question like, 'What do you think is a better way to work?' may start discussion on exactly what is needed and gains agreement to change or development. Use a closed question or statement at the end of this phase such as, 'Do you agree that this behaviour has negative consequences and xyz is required?' Be hard on the facts but open on the reasons for them.

FIGURE 10.6 The coaching conversation agenda

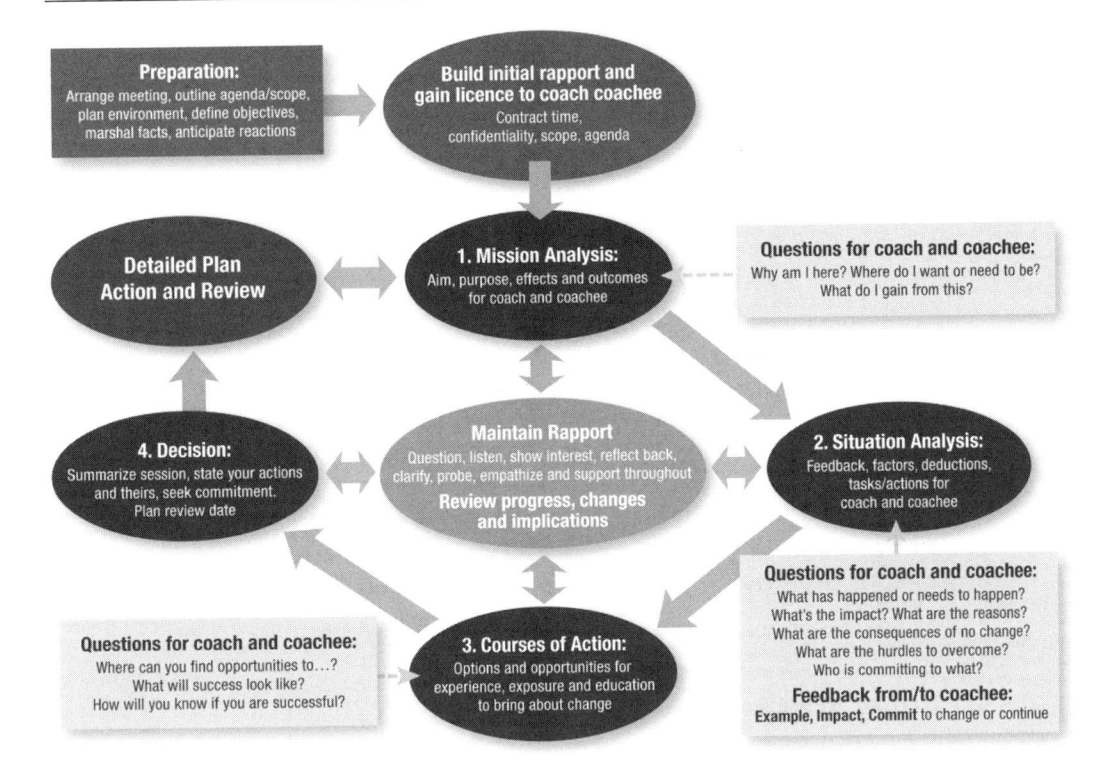

Preparation: Arrange meeting, outline agenda/scope, plan environment, define objectives, marshal facts, anticipate reactions

Build initial rapport and gain licence to coach coachee Contract time, confidentiality, scope, agenda

1. Mission Analysis: Aim, purpose, effects and outcomes for coach and coachee

Questions for coach and coachee: Why am I here? Where do I want or need to be? What do I gain from this?

Detailed Plan Action and Review

Maintain Rapport Question, listen, show interest, reflect back, clarify, probe, empathize and support throughout **Review progress, changes and implications**

2. Situation Analysis: Feedback, factors, deductions, tasks/actions for coach and coachee

4. Decision: Summarize session, state your actions and theirs, seek commitment. Plan review date

Questions for coach and coachee: What has happened or needs to happen? What's the impact? What are the reasons? What are the consequences of no change? What are the hurdles to overcome? Who is committing to what?
Feedback from/to coachee: Example, Impact, Commit to change or continue

Questions for coach and coachee: Where can you find opportunities to…? What will success look like? How will you know if you are successful?

3. Courses of Action: Options and opportunities for experience, exposure and education to bring about change

Coach = Facilitator, supporter, enabler, motivator   **Coachee** = Person responsible for change

© Jeremy Tozer, 2007

Coaching conversation agenda

The 'coaching conversation' agenda (the what) shown at Figure 10.6 is a handrail that may be applied to any formal or informal coaching situation; only style (the how) will need to be adapted to suit the occasion. You might want to use this as a template to plan a coaching conversation. (You will notice it has a similar flow to the problem-solving process called 'the appreciation' described in Chapter 14.)

The agenda is a handrail, it is not a purely clockwise linear sequence and you may find that you need to go back a step or two then proceed forward again. This process may be applied a number of times consecutively when different, unconnected issues are being addressed.

Preparation

Hopefully it is stating the obvious, but a scheduled coaching session needs to be prepared, as opposed to the impromptu session when someone knocks on your door or leans over your work station divider and asks for your help! The things that you need to consider and facts that you need to have at hand include:

- Identify the opportunity, problem, skill or behaviour that you need to address.
- Define objectives. What do you plan to accept as a leader?
- Review past performance data.
- Consider the personality, perception, ability level and learning style of the person you will coach; and his or her likely reaction.
- Plan to keep an open mind – and don't prejudge or form preconceived ideas.
- Plan to set a positive tone.
- Consider where and when the session is best held.
- Agree the meeting time and day (not 4 pm on the Friday before a long weekend!).
- Ensure there are no distractions – switch your mobile phone off.
- Create a comfortable environment – think of the room and seating.

Learning styles

Recognizing the basic learning styles that influence the way in which people learn most effectively can assist you in tailoring training and coaching to the people you are working with. Honey and Mumford[1] studied people's different ways of learning. These styles are summarized in Table 10.3.

Rapport and licence to coach

It is essential that for any coaching to be effective, the person being coached must want to be coached, and the coach needs to build some rapport with that person to facilitate conversation. This means some 'idle banter' which is anything but idle – it should enable you to learn something about the person you are talking to and show interest in him or her – background, wants, fears, aspirations, and so on. Depending upon the relationship and the context, you might need to ask 'for a licence to coach', or offer coaching and wait for the person to ask for it. In the normal leader/follower relationship you will probably organize sessions as a matter of course with all your team members. If you know people well, building rapport may simply be a quick exchange of a few words that leads straight into the next step.

Attention needs to be paid to the physical environment: the time of day, the location, the furniture, interruptions. If you wish to show the coachee that he or she is valued and that this is a genuine coaching session, then block out time, divert calls and find a quiet place with a round table or low coffee table. Sitting either side of

TABLE 10.3 Honey and Mumford's learning styles

Activists – like new experiences, are open minded, will act first and think later, tend to avoid detail and get bored easily	**Pragmatists** – like to get straight to the point, to apply new ideas which are immediately useful and relevant, and to have role models
No lengthy explanations Minimal detail Do not give precise instructions Do not 'sell' the task Let them do it themselves Involve them with other people Give them 'limelight' Let them generate ideas Don't repeat activity	Ensure high 'face validity' in the learning activity Explain the relevance of required action to their performance Be authoritative in the subject matter Ensure practise and feedback from experts Provide some form of reward for learning Tend to favour expedient solutions
Reflectors – like research, to learn from the experience of self/others, require time to think and may be risk averse	**Theorists** – like to understand a concept before acting, are logical and integrate facts and value planning and intellectual stretch
Let them observe someone Allow reflection time for their own activities Structure training to include exchange of views Give them time to prepare Brief them carefully, they listen and assimilate information Let them decide for themselves Don't force them into the limelight	Prepare and plan the session together with him or her if appropriate Explain techniques Give time to explore the idea methodically Ensure structured situations with a clear purpose Allow time for questions Avoid shallow or contradictory techniques and disorder

a rectangular desk with the 'coach' in a higher chair does not exactly create the atmosphere most conducive to successful coaching.

Mission analysis: aim and purpose of the coaching session

Work with the person you are coaching to establish clarity about the overall aim, specific objectives (the effects that you wish to have and on whom or what) and the purpose of the coaching session(s) – collectively these address what needs to be achieved and why this is so.

The aim, effects and objectives may relate to the person's own needs, to your needs as a leader, and/or to the needs of the business and the demands of the role that the coachee occupies. Purpose relates to both business needs and to the person's motivation. If the person is not motivated to develop, coaching will make slow progress. You may need to challenge perceptions and question beliefs here in order to create a desire to grow.

Questions to ask in this phase will include:

- What, overall, do you want to achieve from coaching? (both coach and coachee) – How does this relate to your work, career and other personal goals?
- What effects do you wish to have and on whom or what and why?
- What other specific objectives do you have for coaching – skills, understanding, behaviour? (both coach and coachee)
- What future challenges will you face; what is needed to meet those challenges?

Situation analysis: ACE, feedback and self-awareness as factors

In this phase you need to discuss, assess and agree what has happened or is happening if you are in review mode; or what needs to happen if you are previewing performance. Then you should identify and discuss the 'factors affecting performance' – the reasons behind what has occurred or the factors that will enable future success. Once the factors have been identified, then deductive thinking – asking, 'So what does this mean, what are the implications, what can we do about this?' – will enable specific tasks or actions to be identified.

In this phase, you can use ACE as a diagnostic tool to identify factors. Since ability is a factor (and behaviour is one part of ability), in a coaching session this is where feedback should be discussed using the EIC techniques already described. It is also important to understand the drivers of human behaviour as these will include some of the factors that need to be addressed.

Other factors and related questions might include:

- What has happened or needs to happen?
- What was the impact?
- What are the reasons for this?
- What do you understand is the higher intent (vision or aim) and plan?
- What is your role in achieving this?
- What are your objectives and priorities and how do they link to the higher intent?
- What is the purpose of your role? How do you feel about it?
- What effects are you trying to have and on who or what?
- What is in the environment around you that impacts your performance? (Systems, processes, resources, workplace, structure/authority, and possibly the leader's behaviour!)
- How could the environment be improved?

- What skills, knowledge or behaviour do you need to develop?
- How do you feel about your work?
- How does your work align to your personal goals (life goals or career development objectives)?
- What values and beliefs underpin the way you work (attitude that drives behaviour)?
- What do you need to stop, start, and carry on doing?

Reasons for performance are likely to be found in more than just the ability area (which itself consists of the three elements of skill and knowledge, behaviour and attitude and intellect to manage the level of complexity faced). Remember that clarity, environment and provision of the necessary training in knowledge and skill and feedback on behaviour are primarily the leader's area of responsibility. Listen, question and probe – do not think that the first answer is the only thing that you need to consider. Invite and then offer deductions after questions. Ask open questions to clarify both your understanding and the coachee's understanding. Separate fact and deduction from assumptions and guesses since any assumptions may well be false!

When coaching for performance you need to generate the desire to learn and improve. Poor attitude or commitment may be due to boredom, conflicting fit to role (preferences, values, beliefs, motivators, own sense of purpose, aspirations), lack of challenge, resentment, lack of confidence. Be hard on the facts but not on the person, be open on the reasons for performance. You first have to understand the person before you can take appropriate and effective action. (Review Chapter 8 on human behaviour.)

The output of this step is a discrete 'task list' – a shopping list of things to do – for both coach and coachee. As you conclude this step, agree and note a summary of actions with the coachee.

Courses of action open: options and opportunities

In this phase of the conversation, the options and opportunities for improvement – the ways in which the tasks and actions from the previous step may be implemented – are discussed. The most useful opportunities occur when people align their development needs to the priorities of their organization and environment.

Questions to ask might include:

- Where can you find opportunities to...?
- What will success look like?
- How will you know if you are successful?

Options generally fall into the categories of:

- *Experience* – practice and feedback on the job, perhaps using specific assignments or projects as a vehicle, perhaps through peer 'buddy' coaching.
- *Exposure* – to the example and scrutiny of others, perhaps through mentoring and executive shadowing or formal programme alumni networks that may encourage the formal sharing of case studies and examples.

- *Education, formal training, self-study programmes and online resource libraries* – but remember that formal training is often the easy option for developing 'problem people' but often the least effective route unless specific skills, knowledge or processes need to be taught.

Work with the employee to identify options to fix specific problems; questions might include:

- How can your everyday work environment be a 'classroom' that builds on your strengths and develops or manages your weaknesses?
- What opportunities exist in your day-to-day work when you could do X? What other opportunities exist?
- How will you know if you are being successful?
- How can you gain additional feedback?

If the coachee has recently returned from a formal training programme, you might ask:

- When and how will you apply what you have learnt on the programme to work?
- What exactly will you apply these new skills to?
- How will you know if you have applied them successfully?
- How will you share successes with others to build a learning/adoption culture?

As a leader-coach, ensure that the coachee:

- Starts with a commitment to achieve excellence, which is most easily achieved in areas in which he or she has a natural aptitude or talent.
- Seeks opportunities to practise skill strengths while attending to the weaknesses that interfere with performance.
- Plans for reflection on the learning that occurs.

Decision and commitment – setting objectives

To select the priorities, ask the coachee, 'What options will most assist you to close the gap between where you are and where you want to be?'

For the chosen option for each of the 'task list' actions you need to formalize development objectives. These are statements about the level of expertise you want to develop for a particular skill, and the results you want to achieve. Objectives should be SMART; see Figure 10.7.

Again, open questions are essential to result in the coachee not just accepting objectives, but to effectively set them for him or herself.

FIGURE 10.7 Performance objectives

> **Performance Objectives – SMART**
>
> Specific and stretching
> Measurable
> Achievable and agreed
> Relevant, Reviewed and Resourced
> Time-constrained

Plan, document and review the meeting

You may now combine the development objectives and actions that you need to take as leader, with the selected options to create a workable plan.

Assess and reflect on your own performance in this coaching session:

- Did you follow your conversation plan?
- Did you achieve the objectives?
- Did you find the real causes behind the issue?
- Do you need to lead differently? How?
- What would you improve on next time?

Document and record the action plan and give the employee a copy – and make sure that you implement the plan.

Leadership coaching style

While the 'process' of coaching and the 'conversation structure handrail' remain valid for most, if not all, coaching situations; how the process is applied – your style – will always need to vary to suit the coachee and the circumstances – and this may change from moment to moment depending upon context and the reactions of the coachee.

Coaching style is discussed as part of understanding the nature of leadership in Chapter 4.

Developing behaviour

Change is implicit in developing a person's behaviour. The emotions that a person feels when he or she experiences change are shown in Figure 10.8. These emotional stages and blocks to change were explained in Chapter 6.

It is important that leaders are aware of this, so that they may recognize the phase that individuals and groups are in, and meet people where they are at in the

FIGURE 10.8 Emotions experienced in change

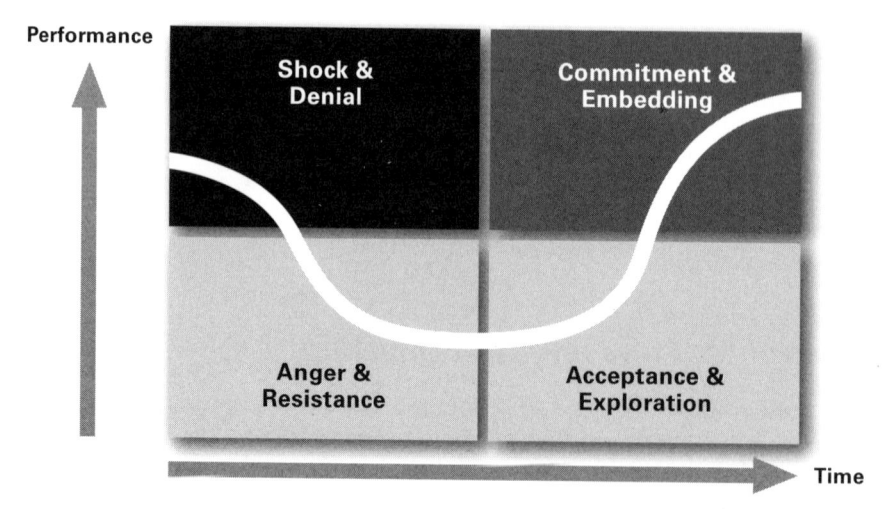

After kübler-Ross, 1969 | © Jeremy Tozer, 2007

appropriate manner. For example, if people are in the first phase of shock and denial, it probably will not be too useful to talk in detail about what is going to happen – rather, people need to understand why things are happening.

Shock and denial

The first stage that people go through is initial shock and denial. When we are faced with trauma or bad news, we often experience initial disbelief or denial that we now have to live in a new reality. We think there must have been some mistake, that what we are told is going to happen is not actually intended and can't happen. Denial is a defence mechanism used to protect the ego. Denial doesn't last long, and if leaders have been regularly briefing their teams, taking questions and checking for understanding about the 'drivers of the operating context' and the organization's intentions, then most of these reactions can be minimized or eliminated because there will be no surprise that something has to change.

Anger and resistance

From shock and denial, people move into the stage of anger (the emotion) and resistance to change (emotion reflected in behaviour). This might take the form of passive resistance, or overt acts of sabotage. Within this phase, bargaining might be observed in which suggestions to do things differently are put forward, but which often amount to leaving everything as it was. Depression might also be observed in this phase in which people give up, or become lethargic or uninterested or melancholy –

they feel sorry for themselves. Organizationally this is reflected in a drop in morale and probably a loss of productivity.

Maslow's hierarchy of needs indicates the need people have for security. Change threatens their level of security. Change takes people out of their comfort zone and may induce defensive actions from real or imagined threats. Some of the common barriers and hindrances are outlined below.

Perceptual blocks

The nature of perception, and the problems it causes generally, is discussed in Chapter 8. In relation to change, people may be inclined to stereotype, look for ulterior motives in all leadership decisions and behaviour, encounter difficulty in defining the exact nature of a problem, limit the scope a problem's examination, and so on.

Emotional blocks

Emotional blocks to change include the fear of failure (largely based on low self-confidence and self-esteem), lack of trust and confidence in others, the inability to cope with apparently conflicting information, a predisposition to be judgemental and to reject ideas without consideration, and the inability to devote time to considering problems and situations dispassionately. The lack of confidence in plans for the future is an emotional block, itself caused by a cognitive block.

People fear change, and fear underlies much resistance. It is not really a fear of change, per se, but rather a fear of anticipated or potential loss associated with the change. This may include:

- Loss of security as previous certainties end and the future is perceived as uncertain.
- Loss of confidence as people worry about their capacity to learn new skills and new ways successfully.
- Loss of relationships due to restructuring and the resultant change in working relationships, and possibly friends being made redundant.
- Loss of direction as people seek clarity in the organization's aim, purpose and objectives, and the direction their own career will take.
- Loss of territory and/or status, which may be due to a change in physical space (for example losing an office to move into an open plan space) or a change to 'perks' that accompany status.

Organizational blocks

A common organizational block is lack of clarity – people may be able to recite the vision, but they lack understanding of what it means for their day-to-day activity and priority of work. Another clarity block is the oft-seen lack of consistency in messages, or mixed messages, that come from different senior executives – a reflection of their own lack of understanding. Cultural blocks to change may include historical precedent, ingrained habits and norms, taboo subjects that are never discussed, the conflict between reason based on logic and facts, and reaction based on experience and feelings, and the effect of inflexible tradition. Environmental blocks to change include a lack of support for individuals within the organization, the inability of leaders to cope with constructive criticism, and leaders failing to listen to their people and their ideas.

Cognitive blocks

The cognitive blocks to the implementation of change include the use by leaders of inappropriate or imprecise language and terminology that is not commonly understood, mental inflexibility in the use of new methods, processes and procedures, and insufficient or inadequate information and understanding of 'what, why and how'. Unless these barriers are moved by effective leadership and communication, programmes and priorities can easily become derailed without apparent cause. Attitudinal shifts can only be created through positive, consistent and frequent articulation of direction and its benefits by leaders in language that is understood by all, meaningful two-way conversation and feedback, and by the example of leaders' behaviour.

Exploration and acceptance

Next people move into the phase of exploration and acceptance. People emerge from depression, they explore new ideas and new ways and, accepting that change is inevitable, look towards the future with a positive attitude. Deciding to accept and explore change is one thing. However, it takes lots of self-discipline and support to adjust and to solve problems and change habits that have been shaped over a long period of time.

Commit and embrace

The support of the leader and others that the individual respects will help build commitment. Finally, as the new order is seen to be more effective, best practice is shared and success (individually and collectively) is recognized (reinforcing feedback) and rewarded, people commit to and embrace the new.

The change paradox

There is an apparent paradox here. People may become bored surprisingly quickly, and experiments on sensory deprivation and solitary confinement have shown the need for the stimulation of change. If that is the case, you would imagine that people would not merely enjoy change but actively seek it out and promote it. It is the areas of change, the depth or extent of the change in those areas and one's immediate leader's 'quality of leadership' that limit this readiness to change. In simple terms, we like both change and stability at the same time.

Behaviour is influenced by many factors, as explained in Chapter 8; some of these are internal and personality-based, others are situational. The organizational or situational factors include:

- Clarity of expectations.
- Leaders' example.

- Environmental systems (for example, reward, recognition, performance management).
- Beliefs about the consequences of behaviour.
- Organization culture and social pressure (normative beliefs – these are particularly potent when emphasized by key people in the organization).

When positive feedback is received following improved/changed behaviour, then self-esteem is raised and the behaviour may be continued because 'good' feedback feels good. Over time this may succeed in changing attitude by reframing the underlying belief system in operation, but it may not. Some people may choose to display different 'behaviour' (the result of systemic influences), without necessarily changing their underlying beliefs. As soon as the systemic influence (the carrot and stick) are removed, behaviour may revert to type. This is why past behaviour is a good predicator of future behaviour: the beliefs underlying the attitude (the behavioural intention) that give rise to the choice of behaviour remain consistent over time – until challenged.

Changing attitudes

Focusing only on observed behaviour does not necessarily provide clues as to what is needed to bring about real, enduring change. We may miss the opportunity to explore and influence all the other dimensions that lie behind behaviour (we are only working 'above the line') – the internal personality-based factors.

Changing behaviour without addressing the elements that underlie attitudes is very difficult. It requires encouraging or enforcing new behaviour in the hope that attitudes will then be shaped accordingly. Changing beliefs and attitudes, on the other hand, sets the scene for sustained behavioural change. Attitudinal performance problems are the most difficult to deal with and may be considered the by-product of a systematic bias in the way the person views the world. In these circumstances it is not enough to simply challenge the person at the behavioural level.

We must not ignore the link between thinking and feeling. Considerable experimental evidence suggests that thoughts are mediated, even determined, by emotional processes. People make interpretations based on information they perceive from their environment and from past experiences. We have a need to understand our experiences (or try to explain what we are feeling). These interpretations help shape our behavioural responses.

When we describe the way a person behaves, we often refer to his or her attitude. A person's attitude to life and work is the direct result of his or her past experiences (the genetic inheritance, early upbringing and learnt experiences), weighted by that person's beliefs, emotions, motivation and perception of the current situation. So attitude is a function of a number of things, all influenced by perception.

Recall from Chapter 8 that perception itself is influenced by a number of factors, shown here in Table 10.4. Now while many of these also shape 'attitude', some do not. Those that do not are the levers that we can use to challenge beliefs and shape a more favourable perception of the world, as shown in Figure 10.9.

The ACE Conditions for Success: Ability

TABLE 10.4 Factors influencing perception

Personality-based Factors	Characteristics of 'The Object' Perceived
Early upbringing	Intensity or degree of attentiveness
Learnt experiences	Size
Beliefs and values	Contrast
Emotion	Motion
Motivation	Novelty/familiarity
Degree of threat	The degree of threat
Grouping	Grouping
How things are presented	Context
Defence – the 'ostrich' syndrome	Halo or horns effect

FIGURE 10.9 Influencing perception to change attitude

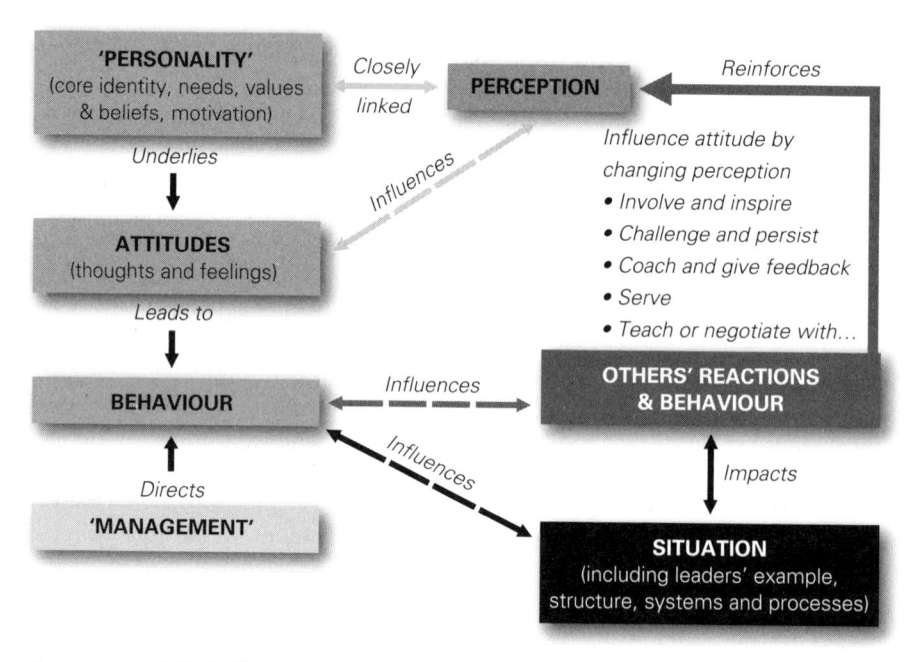

© Jeremy Tozer & Mark Oliver, 2007

So while we cannot change people per se or their past experience, we can change current perceptions and we can therefore influence values and beliefs through involvement, recognition to build self-esteem, constant education, and challenging but non-aggressive questioning and empathetic discussion. We can therefore influence attitude;

although attitudes formed from personal experience are far harder to change than those formed from second-hand information.

For a leader aspiring to practise change leadership, some important implications can be elicited from these statements:

- We should clarify the positive consequences of new behaviours and negative consequences of staying the same.
- We should create a normative environment in which key players send clear messages explaining the new direction.
- We should link new behaviours to acceptance and status in the organization.
- We should provide skills and knowledge so that people believe they can take on new roles and adapt their behaviour.
- We should provide an environment that supports and enables rather than blocks and suppresses required behaviours.

Bringing about change (or development) is what leadership is all about. But manipulating behaviour is unlikely to produce long-term change – as we have said, when the circumstances change (less vigilance) people are free to return to their preferred mode of operating. We therefore need to shape attitudes by doing all of the following:

- Understanding people's core identity and the way they perceive things.
- Meeting their motivational needs.
- Challenging 'undesirable' perceptions and limiting beliefs.
- Shaping the environment.
- Giving positive feedback on new behaviour.

Building skill

You may find as leaders that you have to plan and deliver training (a form of learning and development) to your team. It goes without saying that you must therefore have a thorough knowledge of your subject if you are going to be able to teach it! The key to successful instructional training lies in the imaginative and common sense application of three principles, which are:

1. To make good preparation and planning (the lesson plan).
2. To promote and maintain the desire to learn.
3. To confirm that training has been assimilated.

These principles can be further enhanced by three techniques which are:

1. The use of audio-visual aids.
2. Question technique.
3. Fault checking technique.

Preparation and planning

All training must be planned and follow a logical progressive sequence. You must therefore be clear at the start what the aim and purpose of the lesson is as it will affect the design of the lesson, the training aids used and the method by which you test your participants' learning. The aim and its purpose must be clear to your participants too.

You will also need to define your learning objectives. These are precise statements of what participants will achieve during the lesson(s). They are more concrete than the aim and usually a number of learning objectives combined will enable you to achieve your aim – typically learning objectives will reflect what you expect your participants to actually achieve.

The numerical size, ability and previous knowledge of your class will indicate to you the time required to achieve a particular objective and how you might approach a plan that creates maximum learning and practice with minimum 'downtime'. You must choose the time, place and training aids that will best enable participants to learn.

It is most important to be clear what exactly you wish the participants to do at the end of the lesson and/or the programme. Do you want them:

- To demonstrate their understanding?
- To demonstrate application of learning?
- To carry out some task?

The nature of your final 'test' of learning may dictate both the sequence and nature of the lesson and the equipment you will need.

The lesson plan

A lesson plan simplifies your preparation and will help you to deliver any form of training in an effective manner. In outline every lesson needs a beginning, a middle and an end.

The beginning

Build rapport: this means reducing the differences between you and the class at an unconscious level – see Chapter 9. The beginning breaks naturally into three parts:

1 *Preliminaries.* These are preparations that cannot be made until the class assembles. For example, the roll call, buddy pairing, the obligatory health and safety caveats, timings of breaks, meals and so on, and other 'housekeeping' points, issuing any materials and so on.
2 *Revision.* This checks relevant learning from earlier sessions and also gets the participants thinking.
3 *Introduction.* Here you should state the aim and purpose of the lesson, explain why it is important and relevant, how it links to past and future sessions ('signposting'), set out the format or flow of the session and timings, and give an incentive to generate participant attention. You might also ask what participants would like to achieve and ask them to set the 'ground rules' for the session.

FIGURE 10.10   Developing skill

> **Developing Skill – EDIP**
>
> Instructional/Training lesson format:
> Explanation
> Demonstration
> Imitation
> Practise – Feedback – Practise

© Jeremy Tozer, 1997–2006

The middle

This is the main teaching part of the lesson. It should start with an overview and break into a logical sequence of stages, with some sort of check or test at the end of each stage to establish whether or not the participants are learning before progressing to the next.

The stages of a 'skills' lesson have a sequence designed to ensure a maximum of practical work. There are four phases (shown in Figure 10.10):

1 *Explanation* – You must explain to the class in simple and clear terms what the concept, model or equipment is and how it works.

2 *Demonstration* – Demonstrate how to use the concept, model or equipment, perhaps using a case study, worked example or live task.

3 *Imitation* – You should now ask participants to imitate you by giving them practice with an example under careful control, while you check how they progress with each stage to prevent participants developing faults, or bad habits, and to correct misunderstanding.

4 *Practice* – This is where you give the participants more opportunity to develop skill while providing them with feedback and guidance. Practice might form the final test and thus give confirmation that learning has taken place.

The end

There is a logical way in which to close a lesson and to ensure also that the desired objective has been achieved. The sequence is as follows:

1 Take questions from the class to enable them to clear up any doubts.

2 Test for confirmation to see whether the learning objectives have been achieved by asking open questions.

3 Ensure participants complete any learning logs or buddy pair action plans – share some of these.

4 Define and agree any actions to be taken after the lesson.

5 Seek feedback from the class on the lesson and your performance.

6 Give a summary to emphasize the main points.
  7 Pack up the room.
  8 Look forward to interest the class in the next lesson in the programme.

Rehearsal

You should, wherever possible, rehearse your lesson to ensure that your timings are realistic and to iron out any snags that may occur. Preparation and planning are vital to successful training. Do not be taken in by the 'gifted amateur' who claims just to walk into the class and 'get on with it'. If he or she is any good he or she will have prepared the lesson, and is quite likely to have taught it many times before. Inevitably, at first you tend to feel constrained to teach lessons in a rigid and formal way, with frequent reference to your plan. As your skill and confidence develop you will find a style of your own, which will enable you to be more relaxed. A relaxed performance generally allows participants to learn more than a rigid one, especially in discussion periods.

Promotion and maintenance of the desire to learn

To optimize learning it is essential to arouse participants' interest and help them want to learn. Having gained their interest, you must do your best to maintain it. There are a number of actions you may take that will help.

Before the lesson

- Discomfort with the status quo and awareness of the need to learn and develop.
- A look forward from a previous lesson.
- An interesting programme designed to attract attention.
- Advertisement – any display that will arouse curiosity and promote interest.
- Publicizing past 'alumni successes' and incentives.

At the beginning of the lesson

Develop the interest of the class during the introduction by giving:

- The aim, a clear statement of what is to be achieved.
- The purpose, a relevant reason why it is important that the class learn it.
- An incentive, if there is any 'reward' to be gained from learning the subject.

Maintenance of the desire to learn

This is concerned with keeping every member of the class wanting to learn, and therefore interested, throughout the period. These things help in this respect:

- Variety. No more death by PowerPoint!
- Effective training aids.
- Maximum activity in and involvement by your class.
- Use of all the senses.
- Realism and relevance.
- Simplicity.
- Avoidance of distractions.
- Pace and tempo.
- The rhythm, speed, volume and pitch of your voice.
- Laughter.
- Pauses for reflection.
- Silence, which can create some constructive discomfort.
- Hand gestures.
- Being enthusiastic.
- Recognition for learning.

Confirmation that training has been assimilated

Confirmation at several stages in a lesson is designed to ensure that the learning objectives are achieved by its completion. It checks that at each stage of a lesson learning has taken place and allows a pause so that participants may clear up any doubts. Confirmation may take place at any time during a lesson to see if the class is still with you and alert. There are, however, times when it must be done:

- At the start of a session to confirm the previous session within a programme.
- At the end of each stage to ensure that learning is taking place.
- At the end of the lesson to ensure that the learning objective has been achieved.

There are many ways in which it can be done that give variety and generate interest:

- revision periods;
- quizzes;
- discussions;
- exercises;
- competitions;
- participants 'teaching' and 'supervising' each other.

Generally speaking you will be testing or confirming three aspects of development:

- *Knowledge.* This is usually confirmed by asking questions and obtaining answers orally or in writing/online.
- *Behaviour and skills.* These are best tested by asking the participant to perform a task that requires use of the skill and/or behaviour.
- *Attitudes.* Attitudes are measured in two ways:
  - by asking questions about situations and requiring the participant to give an opinion or explanation;
  - by observing the participant's behaviour, interpreting it and possibly discussing it.

Question technique

Questioning, coupled with a comprehensive knowledge of the subject, will enable you to keep your participants active and alert. To apply the technique effectively, you should understand:

- The purpose of questions.
- How to put questions to the class.
- How to deal with questions from the class.

Questions may be used to:

- Teach by making the class reason out answers for themselves.
- Test by checking knowledge.
- Create activity by keeping the participants mentally alert and engaging them.
- Encourage adoption by asking about actions that individuals will take to apply what they have learnt.

Direct questions to the class as a whole give time for the whole class to think out the answer and then nominate the participant who is to give the answer: pose the question – pause – nominate (or pose, pause, pounce!):

- Do make sure that the question is clear so that it is easily understood by the class.
- Don't ask questions that encourage guessing – avoid 50/50.
- Don't ask questions that require a verbal answer to test a skill.
- Don't ask questions that test the participants' powers of expression where this is not intended. These are unfair and may cause confusion or embarrassment.

Questions put to you by your participants will fall into three categories: relevant, irrelevant and those to which you do not know the answer:

1. *Relevant questions.* If the question covers a point already taught, put it back to the class. This checks whether the point was missed generally. It may even disclose a weakness in the training. In any case it will help the class activity.

Should the question be on a point still to be taught, tell the participant that the point will be dealt with later in the lesson. If the question discloses an omission or a deficiency in the lesson, you must take steps immediately to rectify this.

2 *Irrelevant questions*. If the question is genuine, you must deal with it constructively. The rule should be: 'give encouragement but don't waste time'. If the question is a deliberate attempt to mislead, stop the question firmly with the least waste of time!

3 *When the answer is not known.* Do *not* try to bluff it out. Admit that you do not know and tell the class you will give them the answer at a future time. Ensure that this is done.

Fault checking

As a trainer, you must expect and look for mistakes. Correcting them will raise standards of knowledge and skills. Most people learning a new subject will make mistakes. You should aim to treat faults individually. Some faults are due to neglect. Others are made by people who are trying too hard and these mistakes deserve encouragement, not rebuke.

There are a number of things that will help you spot faults:

- Know the subject well, and anticipate mistakes.
- Try to see what everyone is doing.
- Use the class to mark each other's answers, or spot each other's faults.

Tolerate mistakes. They are quite normal when people are learning. Correct them in a constructive way and be fair – people are usually trying. Be firm at the first sign of idleness – an idle attitude will affect the motivation of the other participants; they will expect you to deal with it!

Note

1 Honey, P and Mumford, A, 1992, *The Manual of Learning Styles*, 3rd edn, Maidenhead: Peter Honey.

11
Influence, persuasion and conflict resolution

> Means of influence
> Persuasion
> Conflict
> Conflict resolution

Chapter 9 provided a succinct outline of the essential tools and techniques of interpersonal communication, which when combined with the 'people' knowledge of Chapter 8 and the coaching techniques of Chapter 10 should stand you in good stead for most of the communication challenges that you may face. This chapter takes communication a stage further and provides some basic frameworks to assist you with influence, persuasion and conflict resolution.

Means of influence

The *OED* defines influence as an action exerted imperceptibly or by indirect means, by one person or thing on another so as to cause changes in conduct, development, conditions, etc. It is useful to think of 'influence' as having two forms: indirect and direct or face-to-face.

TABLE 11.1 Indirect and direct influences

Indirect Influence	Direct Influence
• System, process and structure and consequences • Lobbying other influencers • Written appreciations and papers • Moral obligation • Social proof	• Reciprocity • Liking and relationship (emotional intelligence) • Persuasion: facilitated discussion • Persuasion: formal presentation • Persuasion: conversation

Indirect influence

System, process and structure

Chapters 3 and 5 made the case that the design of systems, processes and organizational structure and other environmental conditions lead to corporate culture and 'behavioural consequences'. The appreciation process explained in Chapter 14 is an ideal tool to use in designing the environment in which people work. The design of these 'levers of behaviour' needs a high level of holistic thought and deductive reasoning, and takes time to introduce.

Lobbying and association

In the Houses of Parliament there is a hall known as the Central Lobby where Members of Parliament meet non-members who are usually seeking to persuade the MPs to use their influence, hence the term 'lobbying'. To lobby successfully, you need to develop your network and understand who (subject matter experts, key groups, 'successful people') might be in a position to influence the person, people or things that you want influenced. You might also want to consider why they will influence things on your behalf and what political sensitivities are involved – what's in it for them? Could things backfire on you – will you be seen as manipulative?

Written appreciations and papers

A written appreciation is a structured paper that defines a problem or task, the factors that affect achieving that task or solving that problem, and the options available. It compares the advantages and disadvantages of each option and makes a recommendation. The essence of an appreciation is rational, logical and holistic thought. Provided that it is circulated to the right people, and that it is read and understood, it is an effective aid to influencing. The problem with papers is that they do not take into account emotions, which unfortunately are an inevitable part of decision making for very many people – executives included.

Moral obligation

Moral obligation means doing favours for other people, and building up a 'bank account' with a large balance of favours owed that you may draw on. When people feel morally obliged, they often repay you with a bigger favour to avoid feeling that they are in debt.

Social proof

The basics of social proof come down to the idea that if you see someone doing something or using something, and the method or product works for them, then it's fairly safe to assume that it will work for you too. Many people are risk averse and do not wish to be guinea pigs, so if you are pushing a new idea, you need to find some willing volunteers to test it, who can then become the basis of your social proof. The bandwagon effect takes off when lots of people do things just because other people are doing those things, without thinking about it – it becomes assumed wisdom. Many disastrous decisions have been made because of the bandwagon effect, including at least one totally inappropriate acquisition and merger of two very different banks in Australia a few years ago (one paper-free, the other almost devoid of electronic files): the board rationalized it away, but the fact remains that the acquired bank was sold at a substantial loss a few years later.

Face-to-face influence

Reciprocity

Reciprocity is at one level give and take: what goes around comes around. It is a result of the social conditioning that exists in most cultures. If you have not 'given' to people, it will be difficult to expect them to give to you. Reciprocity in your relationships is built up over time: it is impossible to suddenly think that you require a reciprocal relationship with someone today, and create it!

Liking and relationship

People comply with requests from people they know and like – people like people who are like themselves. Physical attractiveness, grooming and 'similarity' to the other person count in liking – Chapter 9 explains how to reduce differences and increase rapport. 'Relationship' is more than liking and reciprocity and has been dealt with in Chapter 4 (leadership style) and Chapter 8 (emotional intelligence). A strong relationship is characterized by mutual trust, confidence and respect, and integrity.

Persuasion

Persuasion is a direct means of influence used by leaders to enable others to engage with the leader's aim, objectives and preferred course of action. It usually entails overcoming resistance to objectives and involves understanding the audience, awareness,

FIGURE 11.1   The persuasion continuum

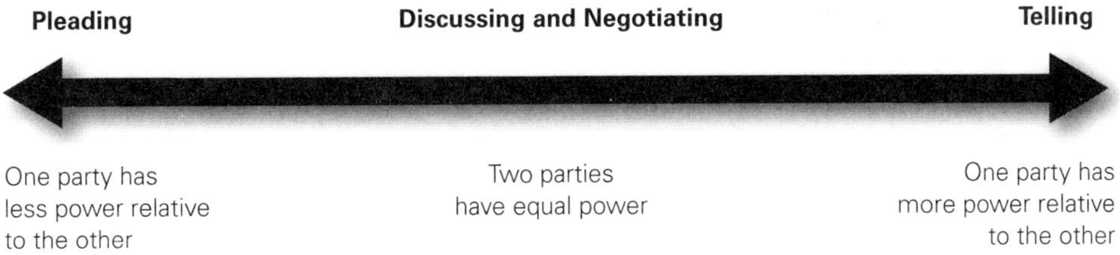

Pleading	Discussing and Negotiating	Telling
One party has less power relative to the other	Two parties have equal power	One party has more power relative to the other

© Jeremy Tozer, 2007

sensitivity, questioning, active listening and assertiveness. Bear in mind that people are usually unwilling to back down on a position that they have taken for a variety of reasons – pride, not wishing to appear weak, or just plain obstinacy, and so on. So obtaining an initial commitment to an idea, or at least to consider an idea usually facilitates future compliance.

Persuasion is of special interest to everyone (whether persuading a child to eat dinner, or persuading a CEO to pursue one policy over another). For the leader, persuading people to adopt an idea is another problem to solve, and it may occur on a continuum that has pleading and telling as its two extremes, as shown in Figure 11.1. The following paragraphs should give you a useful framework to help with your persuasiveness when combined with the basic communication tools and concepts of Chapter 9 and the 'knowledge' of people you will have gained from Chapter 8.

The message

The aim and purpose of the message

As ever, you need to be clear in your own mind about what you are trying to achieve and why in 'delivering the message'. That goes beyond achieving acceptance of the actual content of the message itself, and extends into the resulting emotions and impact on relationships that are the consequences of most, if not all, meaningful conversations.

Who – the source of the message

The source of the message, or possibly the source of the information contained within the message, is a significant factor in gaining its acceptance. The key factors in this are:

- *Status and/or credibility.* In an organizational setting, more attention will be paid to a message delivered by the CEO than by junior manager. A subject matter expert, or a person talking from a significant base of experience will have more credibility than a novice.
- *Attractiveness.* Attractiveness is not about physical beauty! Being courteous and pleasant, interested in the audience, and using humour may all help to make the person delivering the message attractive.

- *Trustworthiness*. This will be largely based on the source's track record – how often has the source played the 'collaborate' or the 'cheat' card? What is the motivation that lies behind the sending of the message?
- *Non-verbal cues*. Body language can either enhance or detract from the persuasiveness of a message. Hiding behind notes and talking to your shoes is unlikely to be as effective as engaging the listener openly and boldly.

Who – the recipient of the message

An audience analysis, even the briefest consideration, will help you shape your message and make it more effective. To persuade the person or persons you need to consider their needs, fears, wants, personality (what triggers their reactions?) and likely perception, their motivation and agenda, and so on.

A consideration of the audience will influence how you are going to persuade them – formally or informally, engaging other influencers, using primarily an emotional appeal (selling to their fears or discomfort) or the logical thought of an appreciation (Chapter 14), or indeed carefully combining all of these mechanisms.

What – the message itself

Your message content is not the only thing that is important in persuasion, so is its packaging. The packaging may take a number of forms, which are briefly outlined here.

Explicit or implicit message

An explicit message effectively states clearly what it is you wish people to know and consider. This might be appropriate when dealing with an audience that lacks knowledge or experience about the subject. An implicit message effectively sets the scene and allows the audience to draw their own (and hopefully your) conclusions, and this is sometimes more suitable when dealing with expert audiences or with people in senior positions of authority.

One-sided and two-sided arguments

Similar to the explicit or implicit message, a one-sided argument states your point of view, whereas a two-sided argument presents both cases and their pros and cons. A one-sided argument is more likely to succeed with audiences who lack knowledge and experience, or with those already converted to your cause. However, it may cause those who disagree to view your argument as biased and not credible. In presenting both sides, it is possible that those who previously agreed with you may realize that they did not have all the facts and they may adopt another position. Equally, it can arm supporters of your view with counterarguments to use against dissenters. Generally though, two-sided arguments fare better as long as counter-arguments are anticipated and neutralized.

Emotional appeal

It is very difficult to persuade if you do not – at some level – engage people at an emotional level. Chapters 8 and 9 should assist you in doing this by developing your emotional intelligence, building rapport and enhancing the effectiveness of your face-to-face communication.

Order of presentation

People tend to remember the first and last points made in presentations best, and this is known as the primacy and the recency effects, so your conversational presentation should cover your key points in your introduction and in your summary. If your message is structured with a beginning, middle and end, you will effectively:

- tell them what you're going to tell them;
- tell them what you said you were going to tell them – but in more detail,
- tell them what you told them!

Where – the context of the message

Assessing where you deliver the message is also important in persuading people to adopt it. Do you choose a formal or informal setting? An important message is often more likely to be accepted and acted on if delivered in a formal setting. The environment can also be shaped to assist with developing emotional appeal if you believe that that is necessary to help your case. You can engage all the senses: sight with posters and visual layouts, sound with appropriate 'mood music', touch with models, materials or the furniture, taste and smell with refreshments. At a very basic level, it should be designed with comfort in mind – so hot unventilated rooms, uncomfortable chairs and tea made with a tea-bag filled with dust dipped into lukewarm water are not exactly conducive to creating an effective environment!

Facilitated formal discussion

If you decide to do this with either an individual or a group, you are effectively in a planned coaching conversation. By asking open questions, in essence, you are helping people to arrive at their own sensible conclusions. Chapters 9 and 10 should enable you to do this on most occasions.

If the subject of the discussion includes problem solving to reach a decision or recommendation for a decision, then facilitating or coaching people through an appreciation (see Chapter 14) is a very powerful and effective means of persuasion that will arrive at an answer with its base in logic and reason while engaging people in the process. The thought process of the appreciation is structured, contains objective detail and its output is based on deductions as opposed to assumptions (and there is a difference between the two – the former may be treated as fact, the latter is usually little more than a guess). Care should be taken in using this thought process to ensure that it is not seen as simplistic or rigid and inflexible, and that it is not used to justify a preconceived idea. That would be situating the appreciation, rather than appreciating the situation and identifying all possible effective courses of action. How this thought process is applied and followed can be tailored to ensure emotional engagement; 'thought process' applied with 'social process'.

Bear in mind that if your own idea has not been carefully thought through, this approach will result in commitment to a rational course of action that may be very different to your own initial idea!

Formal presentation

A presentation that is intended to persuade requires considerably more preparation than a presentation intended to simply inform. The planning for the presentation is best made by making an appreciation (see Chapter 14), which will clarify the effects that you wish to have and on whom, the audience (the decision maker, influencers and others) and their needs, wants, fears, agendas, hooks to engage their interest, likely objections and 'emotional triggers' and so on, politics and blockers, and key messages. Your key messages for the presentation, which should be kept to around three to five, should be repeated throughout the entire pitch. You should anticipate objections and plan how you will respond to them. Your pitch needs to be rehearsed so that it flows effortlessly. If the words can be spoken without your having to concentrate on what you are saying excessively, you will be able to devote some concentration to looking at the reactions of the audience and adapt what you intend to say and how you intend to say it. During your preparation and rehearsals, bear in mind that buying decisions from external suppliers are often based 40 per cent on the products and services offered, with the remainder split equally between rapport created, organizational politics, and your demonstrated understanding of the context and business needs. You might apply this as a rough rule of thumb for other types of proposal.

The 'pitch', is usually enhanced by combining your understanding of Chapters 8, 9 and 10 with the following presentation structure used to 'sell' a course – action itself identified in an appreciation (Chapter 14 again!).

The beginning

Opening remarks – express gratitude for the opportunity, explain how you wish the presentation to run, when you prefer to take questions, and so on.

The middle

- Statement of aim and purpose.
- The agenda – essentially answering the questions why, or what and how.
- Why? The context or situation and its implications to hook your audience.
- What? The aim and purpose (to do something in order to achieve something) – the concept or idea.
- How? The execution, in general outline, with highlights on key areas.

The end

Summary of the why, what and how, and conclusion – a call to action or agreement of the next steps.

Throughout your presentation you should consistently repeat your three to five key messages (perhaps using different words, media or examples). Persuasive messages have three components in them: a feature or benefit and its impact, some proof or evidence of its efficacy, and its relevance.

Indulge me with this simple and not very subtle example of a persuasive message with those three persuasive components intended for an executive in the pharmaceutical industry:

Tozer Consulting guarantees to improve the quality of your business transformation strategy development and its execution by aligning activity and engaging people. By clients' own measures in change programmes, we have increased new revenue streams by 50 per cent, reduced actual investment versus budget by 40 per cent, and more than doubled service level agreement quality measures. Given the leadership, the mindset and cultural challenges that you are facing in changing from a pharmaceutical 'block-buster drug' and generics manufacturer, to the key partner in a health outcomes ecosystem, when can we discuss your needs and how we might approach meeting them?

Protecting against persuasion

It will help your persuasiveness to be aware of the two main methods that may be used to protect people against your persuasiveness. The first is inoculation. By being exposed to a weak argument in favour of a point of view, the ability to later refute a more powerful 'attack' may be strengthened. The second is forewarning. If people expect that their view is going to be challenged, they may prepare counter-arguments to preserve it.

Other dos and don'ts

- Minimize differences and build rapport with the audience.
- Ensure that the message is relevant to the audience.
- The message, if adopted, should make the receiver 'look good'.
- Do not forewarn those likely to be resistant to your message.
- Adapt your pace – sympathetic audiences will think about what you are saying.
- Repeat your key messages: it creates the illusion of truth.
- Provide social proof: people often like to feel safe and conformity assists.
- Ensure that you hold people's attention: if they do not pay attention they cannot think about your argument.
- Prevent distractions from occurring.
- Messages with a positive frame around them are usually more persuasive than those without.
- Messages may be more persuasive if they do not appear to be or feel as if they are intended to persuade.
- Tailor the message to the psychological preferences of the audience.
- Confidence counts – ensure that you are confident, and build the confidence of the audience.
- Avoid challenging core beliefs.

Persuasion has been described as an 'art', and most people would probably agree that some are better persuaders than others. It is hoped that this section has shown that even artists need 'tricks', and these are available to anyone willing to learn and implement good practice.

Conflict

Conflict is an inevitable fact of life, and it may be either a constructive or destructive process. Conflict might exist between individuals or between teams and is essentially another problem to be solved – arguably all leadership work is just a series of concurrent, consecutive and layered problems to solve and decisions to make, which is why problem solving and decision making, examined in Chapter 14, are such important subjects for leaders to come to grips with.

Leaders can prevent many conflicts from arising by simply fulfilling the functions of leadership described in Chapter 4, particularly during planning, briefing and coaching. There are other measures that can be taken to minimize the chances of conflict occurring. Such preventative actions might include the leader recognizing symptoms of conflict in their early stages and not letting them get out of hand, ensuring participation, and building a climate in which team members feel able to discuss their thoughts openly.

While 'prevention is better than cure' it is unlikely that all potentially damaging conflict situations can be prevented. Therefore, it is helpful to the leader to have an understanding of conflict and other tactics that may be applied.

The outcomes of all conflict can be thought of as falling into one of four categories:

1 Lose-Lose. This is when neither side gains from the conflict and usually results in resentment.
2 Lose-Win. This is when one party is unassertive and lets the other benefit despite the cost.
3 Win-Lose. One party imposes a solution on the other resulting in the loser feeling resentful and defeated.
4 Win-Win. Both parties will gain from the resolution with improved relationships.

The first three of these outcomes are usually destructive and encourage dysfunctional behaviour; they:

- prevent the team achieving its objectives;
- prevent cooperation;
- create dissatisfaction;
- reinforce differences of perception, opinion and tension;
- demoralize the team members;
- prevent effective decision making;
- lead to distrust and ill-will.

The win-win resolution is constructive and promotes trust, enables creative solutions, stimulates development of people involved, and improves communication.

Types of conflict

Conflict normally can be thought of as one of the following types: intrapersonal, interpersonal or inter-team.

An intrapersonal conflict is a one that occurs within the person. For example, a person may know something would be good for the team, but sees it as counter-productive to his or her own personal interests, or it may be a conflict between organizational values manifested in decision making and personal values.

Interpersonal conflicts are conflicts between individuals. These can be destructive to teams and can stem from a number of sources: personality, unclear roles and interdependencies, conflicting work priorities, different ideas about solutions to problems, and so on. If not dealt with effectively, they may get out of hand. These types of conflicts must be dealt with as soon as possible to prevent a total breakdown in relationships.

Inter-team conflict is, very simply, conflict between teams. The reasons for this usually come under the heading of 'clarity', although such conflicts may arise from interpersonal conflict between the leaders of teams. Some of the responses that you may observe within a team involved in this sort of conflict are:

- People close ranks, and cohesion, loyalty and conformity to norms increase.
- The team protects its turf, its area of responsibility, and identifies the other team as the enemy.
- This internal focus reduces external task effectiveness.

Causes of conflict

The causes of conflict give us some fundamental clues about the actions teams can take to convert them into positive forces for improvement. In general terms, conflict may emerge from the team's objectives, priorities structure, systems or processes (often from the wider organization) or from individuals themselves, as shown in Figure 11.2.

FIGURE 11.2   Causes of conflict

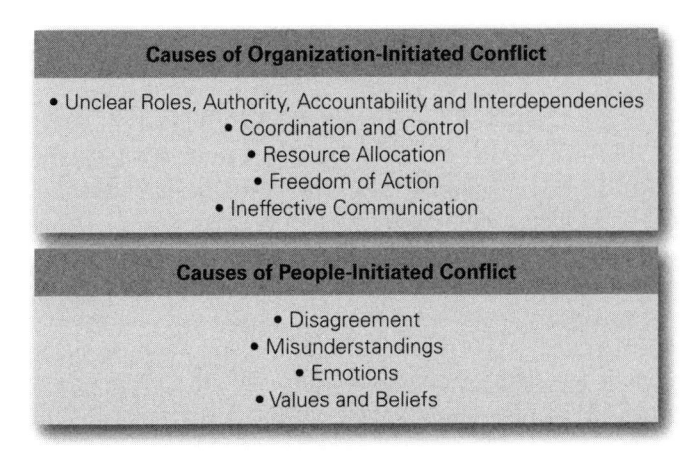

Causes of Organization-Initiated Conflict
- Unclear Roles, Authority, Accountability and Interdependencies
- Coordination and Control
- Resource Allocation
- Freedom of Action
- Ineffective Communication

Causes of People-Initiated Conflict
- Disagreement
- Misunderstandings
- Emotions
- Values and Beliefs

After Thomas, 1976 | © Jeremy Tozer, 2007

Organization- (or team-) initiated conflict

This is caused by inadequacies in organizational conditions such as unclear or inadequate structure and process (design failure), environment, team size, communication routes and methods, ill-defined objectives, roles, working relationships and interdependencies.

Conflict often arises due to gaps (people think others are responsible for something) or duplication (several people think they are responsible for the same thing). Conflict can also result from coordination or control mechanisms – when these become more important than the task itself, they can lead to the battle for control. Rewards, status and resources all have the potential to give rise to conflict through destructive competition. When resources are limited, both individuals in teams and the teams themselves often compete for what is available. If this is not dealt with reasonably, conflict is likely to result, as individuals and groups identify inequities in allocation and take retributive action.

How much scope team members are granted in completing a task and how much they are involved in decision making can also affect the level of conflict. If people are given complete freedom to do as they wish, conflict is probably more likely to eventuate; so give team members as much scope to use their initiative as is consistent with the need for coordination.

People-initiated conflict

Team-initiated causes of conflict can often be controlled by the team's leader or the wider organization; people or human conflicts are more difficult to control. Differences of opinion and power struggles among competing people and simple personality clashes give rise to conflict:

- Disagreement over facts – misunderstandings in which people are aware of the facts but interpret them in different ways.
- Disagreement over objectives where team members disagree over the direction of the team's efforts and the specific targets they are expected to achieve.
- Disagreement over methods where members fail to agree on the plan.
- Disagreement over values where there are fundamental differences about what is right and wrong.

Many conflicts arise from misunderstanding between two or more people. Conflict results when a person misunderstands what is expected. This usually comes about through a lack of adequate communication and the distorting influence of perception. The team leader or members may assume their colleagues know what is expected but may fail to fully delineate responsibilities and requirements.

An event or issue is not necessary to give rise to conflict. Emotional conflicts, for example, can be caused by people's personal feelings about others. Emotions tend to last longer than any particular conflict-initiating event. Such conflicts are common in teams and can be insidious. People may refuse to talk to one another or to work together, and the conflict may continue for long after the original cause of the relationship breakdown. It is perhaps more likely that emotions will become focal in interpersonal conflicts rather than in conflicts between teams.

Influence, Persuasion and Conflict

A divergence in viewpoints between team members about objectives and how they are to be achieved will give rise to conflict. Such differences may have a base in perception, previous experience, or insufficient information. Closely related to the viewpoints issue is that of differences in values or fundamental beliefs. People's values are reflections of their personality and what they believe and, as such, they are difficult, if not impossible in some cases, to change. Behaviour is the outward manifestation of values and beliefs.

Positions in conflict

When conflict or disagreement is experienced, particularly under stressful conditions, it is very common to see people lock themselves into the 'first position'. In this position, the more an idea is discussed, the more entrenched and hotly defended a person's own view or position becomes – an irrational escalation of commitment. This is due largely to the ego's defensive response to perceived threat – the primeval fight or flight response that is part of human nature. A topical irrational escalation of commitment is that displayed by many EU politicians and unelected technocrats in positions of authority in relation to the euro (which is arguably intellectually flawed in design and morally deficient in its anti-democratic operation, which tries to overcome its conceptual flaws).

The 'second position' involves understanding the situation from the other party's perspective. However, the wise leader will strive to adopt the third position (Figure 11.3) – the helicopter view that neutral outsiders would perceive and which enables dispassionate thought and the reframing of the situation and problems. The 'first position' can only be avoided and the 'third position' adopted when one has a strong degree of emotional intelligence.

FIGURE 11.3 Positions in conflict

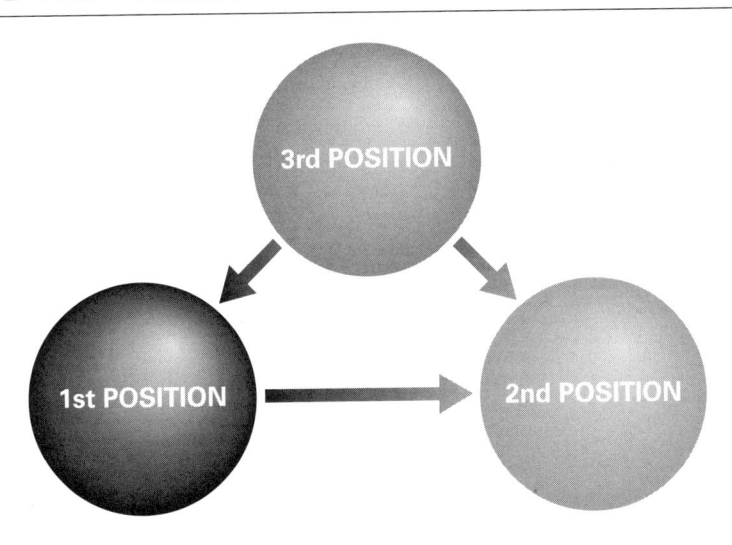

After Potter | © Jeremy Tozer, 2007

Optional responses to conflict

A person's response to a conflict situation will generally fall into one of five categories: competing, accommodating, avoiding, compromising and collaborating. Thomas[1] places these responses on two dimensions, reflecting varying degrees of assertiveness and cooperativeness. An assertive response to conflict refers to the extent to which someone tries to satisfy his or her own concerns. Cooperativeness refers to the extent to which an individual attempts to satisfy the other person's concerns. This is illustrated in Figure 11.4, with the uses and risks of each option shown in Figure 11.5.

FIGURE 11.4   Responses to conflict

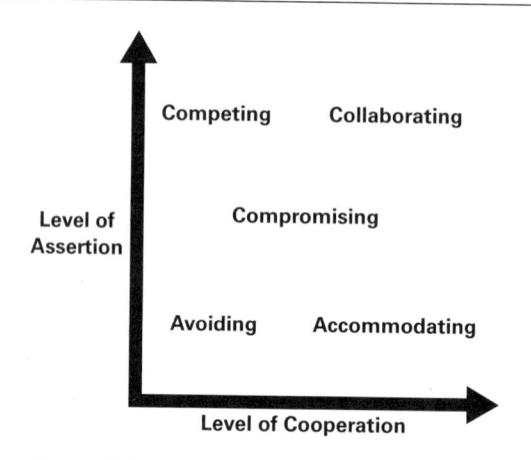

```
         ▲
         │  Competing      Collaborating
         │
Level of │       Compromising
Assertion│
         │  Avoiding       Accommodating
         │
         └─────────────────────────────▶
             Level of Cooperation
```

Thomas, 1976

Avoiding

The most natural response to a conflict situation for many people is to avoid it in some way, but it does not resolve the matter. Avoidance might take the form of postponing, ignoring, isolating or withholding the problem.

One method is to postpone dealing with the conflict. This may be to give time to acquire more facts and information because an ill-informed reaction may be counterproductive, or it might be the excuse for doing nothing. Where a person wants to broaden conflict to suit his or her personal agenda, he or she might ignore it. Another avoidance tactic is to isolate the conflicting people so that they do not interact with each other. This is often impossible within a team situation. When two people in conflict cannot reconcile their differences, a less drastic option is for them to withhold their feelings and control themselves.

If conflict is regularly avoided, things festering beneath the surface become worse. For this reason, avoidance is only a useful tactic as a temporary or survival measure.

FIGURE 11.5 Uses and risks of optional responses to conflict

Conflict Resolution Options

Option	Uses	Risks
Avoiding (low cooperation, low assertiveness)	Short-term solution, parties can be separated	Problem grows worse. Leader using avoidance as an excuse
Accommodating (high cooperation, low assertiveness)	When more important issues force you to give way	Leader seen to value others more than self/own team, leader seen to be easily swayed
Competing (low cooperation, high assertiveness)	Values issues, there is a need to make a stand	Leader seen as inflexible, unwilling. No solution if other party is also competing
Compromising (mid-range cooperation and assertiveness)	Acceptable outcome. Achieves acceptable result and builds relationships	Acceptable, concessions may decrease efforts to find collaborative solution.
Collaborating (high cooperation, high assertiveness)	Desired but rare outcome, both sides win	If no collaborative solution exists, this may prevent pursuit of other options

SOURCE: Thomas, 1976 | © Jeremy Tozer, 2007

Accommodating

Accommodating involves one party sacrificing their own interests to satisfy another party's. The approach can be useful in some situations, but is probably unhelpful if it is used too frequently. It may result in one being seen as weak and constantly taken advantage of. Accommodation may be a good means of escape for a person who finds out that he or she is wrong about something.

Competing

Competing is the opposite response to accommodating. A person considers only his or her own interests and ignores those of the other. The approach, if used too frequently, may promote acrimonious challenges or suppressed animosity. Communication will probably break down, trust and support may well deteriorate, and hostilities result.

Compromising

Compromising, which can include arbitration, negotiation and bargaining, is an attempt to provide both conflicting parties with at least a reasonably satisfactory result. Compromising is a search for middle ground when the conflicting parties have mutually exclusive objectives and relatively equal power. Compromise, if used too frequently, will result in a leader being seen as someone who is more interested in simply keeping everyone happy rather than in solving problems – a weak leader.

Collaboration (integrative solutions)

Collaboration views conflicts as constructive problem-solving situations. It is a process in which conflicting parties confront the situation and attempt to resolve it through collaborative or creative problem solving, such as following the steps of the appreciation, which is explained in Chapter 14. The process encourages conflicting people to channel their energies into a problem-solving process, rather than into fighting with one another. Both or all parties play a constructive role.

Conflict resolution

For a leader to resolve conflict, the first thing to do is to understand the situation and the causes and symptoms of the conflict. The majority of conflicts stem from a lack of clarity, therefore creating clarity often resolves the conflict.

If the conflict has its basis in the behaviour of one person causing an impact on others, then a very effective approach is to combine behavioural observation with feedback to initiate change, as explained in Chapter 10. The feedback handrail enables individuals to resolve conflict with each other in an adult conversation and involves stating facts, remaining impersonal and calm, not apportioning blame or attacking the other person's personality, and stating preferred personal outcomes without setting expectations. It has five stages:

1 *Situation* – agree the state of your current 'working relationship'.
2 *Objective* – agree how your working relationship should be.
3 *Example* – agree indisputable facts that are anchored in time: 'You did/said/did not do/looked like'.
4 *Impact* – describe the impact on the team, business, customers and you; disclose feelings.
5 *Commit to change* – state the change that you would like and seek commitment to it; for example: 'I would like xyz to happen in future. Will you do that? How can we ensure this?' 'What do I need to do differently?'

The resolution of more complex conflict requires negotiation and an understanding of distributive and integrative solutions.

The best resolution to a conflict is one that satisfies all parties. Such solutions are rare. More often resolutions end in trade-offs where each party gives up something of lesser value to them in return for something of greater value. Trade-offs can speed up and improve a conflict's resolution.

A distributive agreement usually only involves one issue – a 'fixed pie' – in which one side gains at the expense of the other. In most complex conflicts there are multiple issues that each party values differently, so the scope of options is considerably expanded. There is no longer a fixed pie; rather, there will be multiple solutions that the parties may identify and compare. Such solutions are known as 'integrative solutions':

- They create better agreements than purely distributive ones.
- They are the only option available where no distributive solution can be reached.

- The beneficial atmosphere of deriving integrative agreements from joint problem solving strengthens relationships.

However, parties in conflict sometimes fail to find integrative solutions because each assumes its interests directly conflict with the other party. Even when both sides want the same outcome they are sometimes unable to reach a solution. Evaluate the relative importance of each interest to you and, by identifying your priorities before you start, you will be better able to reach a solution by trading the interests that are less important for the ones that are more important.

Avoid the win-lose mentality and do not impose fictional barriers around a conflict. Think laterally and try to establish what is important to each party without making unfounded or irrational assumptions about their interests. Rather than considering issues separately, consider packages that allow the simultaneous discussion or resolution of multiple issues. If you are, or represent, one of the parties involved in the conflict (as opposed to being an independent third party) beware of your own biases and the effects of perception on your ability to develop or evaluate integrative solutions to conflict.

Planning conflict resolution negotiations

The appreciation is a powerful thought process that enables you to fully appreciate a situation and make a decision about what is the best course of action to pursue. It may be used to plan your approach to resolving conflict and negotiating. The appreciation is explained in detail in Chapter 14, where its focus is on defining strategic, project and operational plans.

The appreciation starts with defining exactly what you want to achieve (the aim) and why (the purpose) by considering higher level intentions, your objectives, desired outcomes and effects. The appreciation then considers all the factors that affect achieving your defined aim and its purpose. A useful way of developing integrative options in conflict resolution is to complete a Stakeholder Analysis Chart (see Table 11.2) in the factors analysis step of the appreciation of the conflict situation.

While negotiators often have several interests they sometimes fail to evaluate the relative importance of each. Analysing the underlying interests in a negotiation and the relative importance for both parties allows you to avoid the 'fixed pie' and make beneficial trade-offs. To be fully prepared to negotiate you must clearly identify your priorities so that less important interests may be conceded, in order to obtain the most important ones. Equally you should assess others' interests.

You may not have enough information to assess others' true preferences. It is important to recognize this and use the discussion as an opportunity to obtain information. It is far more valuable to recognize that you lack important information than to make an uninformed or false assumption.

The bargaining zone is the overlap between what 'a seller' will accept as a minimum and what the 'buyer' is prepared to give as a maximum. If there is no overlap then there is no distributive element in the potential solution. The endpoints of the zone are identified as the reserves of the parties involved. To be a 'tough' negotiator you must have a thorough knowledge of your opponent's reserve without disclosing your own.

TABLE 11.2 Stakeholder analysis chart

Stakeholder	Us	Them
Purpose, aim and objectives		
Wants, interests and relative importance		
Needs and BATNA		
Fears		
Distributive elements		
Integrative elements		
Their assumptions		
Our assumptions		
Hidden agendas		
Common ground		
New insights and different perspectives		
Problems to be solved in order of priority		

BATNA: Best alternative to a negotiated agreement – the best you can expect to get with no agreement.
Interests: What each side really wants even if it is not publicly stated.
Position: The stated requirement that one side demands of the other.

Identify the options and evaluate. Identify complete integrative packages not separate solutions to each problem. Compare the advantages and disadvantages of each option in your eyes and theirs.

Finally, decide. Relate options to your BATNA (see Table 11.2) and decide upon acceptable options.

The conflict resolution/negotiation meeting

Offer to act as 'facilitator' – you need the conversation to flow in a structured manner – and follow the ACCoRED agenda:

1 Acknowledge and agree that 'the conflict' exists and agree the meeting aim and purpose.
2 Clarify ground rules.
3 Clarify the situation.
4 Reframe the issues.
5 Explore options.
6 Decide what to do.

1. Acknowledge

Acknowledge a conflict exists and agree the meeting aim and purpose.

2. Clarify ground rules

Involve those present by brainstorming the ground rules for the meeting; eg listen for meaning, no interruptions, see things from the third position, participate, put ego aside, respect, follow the ACCoRED agenda and so on. You might want to list things on a flipchart as a reference point for use later on.

3. Clarify the situation

Start by stating the facts as they would be seen from the third position. This is the first step to move things from competition to collaboration.

Discuss each party's perception and the impact of the facts on each party; this way everyone will feel 'heard'.

4. Reframe the issues

Discuss each party's interests and the position(s) that fulfil them. Positions are normally declared, and behind opposing positions you may find shared interests. Open questions may reveal the true interests – reflect these back, empathize and confirm.

Identify common ground. Use open questions to identify common ground, reflect back, empathize and confirm:

- Turn negatives into positives, be objective and neutral. Turn statements like, 'You never...' into, 'How can we ensure...'.
- Enable multiple solutions. Don't say, 'This is how to do it...' say, 'Let's look at the... process'.
- Separate issues from people.

Recognize problems to be solved and their order of priority.

5. Explore options

People generally have a preconceived idea of the solution, which is their own ideal solution. Explore other options. Taking a problem-solving approach – 'mission analysis, factors/deductions, options open' gives room to negotiate (the bargaining zone).

6. Decide

Compare the advantages and disadvantages of each option, relate them to your BATNA and decide upon acceptable option(s). You may withdraw from a meeting to compare the pros and cons of each and determine what is acceptable and then return to the meeting with a decision.

Common mistakes in conflict resolution and negotiation

Many discussions fail to reach an agreement because the parties involved are unable or unwilling to think hard and wide about potential solutions. On other occasions, negotiations may reach an agreement that is more disastrous than not having an agreement at all. This section looks at common mistakes and how to avoid them.

1. Irrational escalation of commitment

Negotiators can fail to realize when a course of action is no longer the best option or even rational and they still continue to pursue it. They do this for a number of reasons:

- The most common reason is that time and money have been invested in pursuing this option and to change will mean losing money. What must be realized is that the money already spent is a sunk cost and can have no bearing on the successful outcome of, or withdrawal from the negotiation. However, people do not want to admit failure (by changing a course of action or withdrawing), they want to appear consistent, particularly as most organizations reward consistency ('nobody was ever fired for buying IBM'). The consistent course of action is to increase commitment to previous actions.
- People tend to select the information that supports their point of view or course of action (confirming) rather than seeking to question it (disconfirming). Therefore they remain committed to a deal because they fail to assess accurately what the deal is worth or what the opposition will do.
- They fail to consider what the opposition will do and enter an opportunity that is in fact a trap.

2. The mythical fixed pie

The best discussions end in a resolution that satisfies all parties. Such solutions are rare. More often they end in trade-offs where each party gives up something of lesser value to them in return for something of greater value. Trade-offs can speed up and improve a conflict's resolution.

A distributive agreement usually only involves one issue, 'a fixed pie' in which one person gains at the expense of the other. In most conflicts there are multiple issues that each party values differently; this was discussed above.

Parties in a negotiation often don't find an integrative solution because each assumes its interests directly conflict with the other party. The 'what is good for them must be bad for us' attitude is also known as the 'incompatibility bias'. Even when both sides want the same outcome they are sometimes unable to reach a solution. Evaluate the relative importance of each interest to you and, by identifying your priorities before you start you will be able to reach a solution by trading the interests that are less important for the ones that are more important.

3. Anchoring and adjustment

In a negotiation both sides adopt a starting position and then adjust their positions, eventually arriving at an agreement or an impasse. The starting positions act as anchors that subsequently affect the rest of the negotiation. Usually final agreements in a negotiation are more affected by the initial positions (anchors) than by any subsequent concessionary activity on the part of an opponent. It is better to walk away from a negotiation than to legitimize an offer that is too extreme. To do this you must have enough knowledge of the disputed issues to recognize an unrealistic anchor.

To use anchoring to your advantage you must decide on an initial offer that is sufficiently attractive to attract the attention (and counter-offer) of the other party while at the same time being to your advantage. It cannot be so extreme that it will not be considered. Do not place too much importance on an initial position too early in the process and do not allow any anchor to prevent you thinking deeply or laterally about the possible solutions.

4. Framing negotiations

The way the options in a negotiation are presented or framed can strongly affect a manager's willingness to accept them.

Framing the situation. On the assumption that the quality of the product is the same and the discount can only be achieved after a 10-minute walk to a different store, would you make the effort for: 1) £30 discount on a £70 purchase, and 2) a £30 discount on an £800 purchase? Statistically 90 per cent of people would make the effort for the first purchase but only about 50 per cent for the second. The main reason given is that a 43 per cent discount is a far more attractive deal than a 4 per cent discount. In fact, the options have been framed in terms of the percentage discount. Instead of considering whether the percentage discount is enough to make you walk an extra 10 minutes you should consider whether the extra 10 minutes is in fact worth the £30 you expect to save. Therefore, rationally, the decision to save £30 should be the same in each case.

Framing the outcome. Consider the situation of the 'half-empty' vs 'half-full' analogy. You can define a negotiator's behaviour as risk-averse, risk-neutral or risk-seeking. In a situation where you have a 50 per cent chance of winning £10 million in a lottery, a risk-neutral behaviour would be to accept £5 million in lieu of the lottery ticket;

a risk-averse behaviour would be to accept, say, a guaranteed £3 million versus a possible £10 million; and a risk-seeking behaviour would be to accept £7 million in lieu of a possible £10 million and to relinquish the thrill of gambling itself. The way a negotiation is framed can have significant impact on the negotiator's preference for risk and lead them to make irrational choices because their preference for risk can change, particularly when they are uncertain about future outcomes or events.

To negotiate rationally, you must remember that how an offer is framed can dramatically affect its perceived value. If an offer is made that is a modest improvement on a previous reference point it can be perceived as a modest gain. If an offer is made that is a modest shortfall to your opening position it can be perceived as a loss, even if it is the same offer.

Frames in negotiations can make the difference between agreement and an impasse. Both sides typically talk in terms of a certain outcome that they must get and any compromise is perceived as a loss. Risk-seeking negotiators may achieve greater gains but are more likely to fail to reach an agreement. Negotiators who maintain a risk-neutral or risk-averse position often obtain more profitable results. Finally, a risk-seeking negotiator (one who pushes for a better deal) would only be consistently successful when facing a risk-averse opponent.

5. Availability of information

When we evaluate information and options we often select some facts and ignore others. For example, people often rely on information that is more easily available regardless of its relevance. Something easy to recall seems more important than something that is less easy to recall. People tend to overestimate the probability of unlikely events if the memories associated with them are particularly vivid and thus easier to recall. In negotiation, presenting information in colourful or vivid ways can exert much greater impact on decisions than equally informative but dull presentations. Be aware of the power and influence the control of information can have on a negotiation's outcome.

Certain types of information can be more prominent and therefore available because of the way they are stored in the memory. For example, ask an accountant, a marketer and a human resources manager from the same firm what its problems are and you will get a different answer based on the information most readily available to each person. To negotiate rationally, managers must draw on past experiences as well as present information to assess various options. This is not always easy, as present information is more prominent. Good negotiation and decision making requires you to use reliable not just available information. You will have to distinguish what is emotionally familiar to you from what is reliable and relevant.

6. The winner's curse

Consider this situation. You are travelling overseas and you meet a merchant who is selling a very attractive gem. You have purchased one or two gems in your life but are far from expert. After some discussion, you name what you are sure is a fairly low price. The merchant accepts and the gem is yours. How do you feel? Most people feel uneasy. This is called the winner's curse. Yet why would you make an offer that you would not want accepted?

This situation is common to many negotiations. One side has more information than the other. Perhaps the gem isn't as valuable as you thought. Perhaps the merchant knows more about the market and the true condition of the gem. Having better information, the merchant is most likely to accept your offer when it is higher than the gem's true value.

An ongoing relationship between parties can help solve or reduce the winner's curse since the seller may not wish to take advantage of the buyer. Obtaining unbiased information about a market or situation can help adjust the balance of knowledge between the negotiating parties. Some negotiators may feel that purchasing expert information to confirm what they already know is a waste of money. They would be acting more rationally by using independent appraisals as insurance against accepting a poor settlement or making a poor purchase. In a negotiation, if each side understands and can explain the viewpoint, motivation and preferred outcomes of the other it increases the chance of a negotiated settlement.

7. Excessive confidence and negotiator behaviour

We have discussed how a number of biases can affect both decision making and outcomes in a negotiation. One of the reasons that so many people perform badly in a negotiation is overconfidence.

Most people are overconfident about their ability to estimate what their opponent wants to achieve, the strength of their own position and their ability to persuade others to accede to their point of view. Few managers concede that uncertainty exists. Fewer still seek information that contradicts their chosen viewpoint.

Overconfidence may inhibit the variety and scope of possible and acceptable settlements. When a manager is overconfident that his or her particular position will be accepted it reduces the incentive to compromise. However, with a more accurate assessment an executive is likely to be uncertain about the chances of success and will therefore search for and/or accept compromise.

People tend to hold certain beliefs and ignore information that contradicts them. Managers are likely to enter negotiations with one strategy for reaching agreement. They assume success and develop their strategy accordingly. A different and more rational view is to realize that your initial strategy may not work and seek to disprove it by searching for new information. If you are not open to disproving information you will have a harder time adapting when confronted by unexpected circumstances in a negotiation.

Note

1 K W Thomas, 1976, Conflict and conflict management, in M D Dunnette (ed), *Handbook of Industrial and Organizational Psychology*, pp 889–935, Chicago, IL: Rand-McNally.

PART TWO
Developing the ACE Conditions for Success

Section 2: Clarity and Engagement at Every Level

Note: Throughout these chapters, 'problem' is used in its most general sense, ie a task, challenge, obstacle, project, opportunity, threat – anything requiring a decision and subsequent action.

12
The leadership work of creating clarity and engagement: problems, decisions and plans

> Problems to solve, decisions to make
>
> A trio of recurring, cascading and iterating processes

Problems to solve, decisions to make

You will recall the 'ACE conditions for success' introduced in Chapter 3 (see Figure 12.1), with 'clarity' being the area in which most performance improvement may be gained, and the priority for consideration before any future activity is undertaken. The prime requirement of leaders is to create clarity in order to align the work of their people; and to do it in such a way that they engage their people.

One way of looking at work, any type of work, is to think of it as a series of consecutive, concurrent and layered problems to solve (the activity) and decisions to make (the output of that activity). Depending on the type of problem being addressed the decision (course of action to be adopted) may or may not require a more detailed plan to be put together.

For example, in 'solving the problem' about whether to make a 'yes or no' business acquisition decision, the decision is itself not an outline plan. However, the decision to acquire or not, and its reasons, need to be communicated to those who need to know. Whereas, if a decision to acquire is yes, then how to integrate that acquired business is a problem to be solved, and a plan will result from that activity. Both the

FIGURE 12.1 The ACE conditions for success

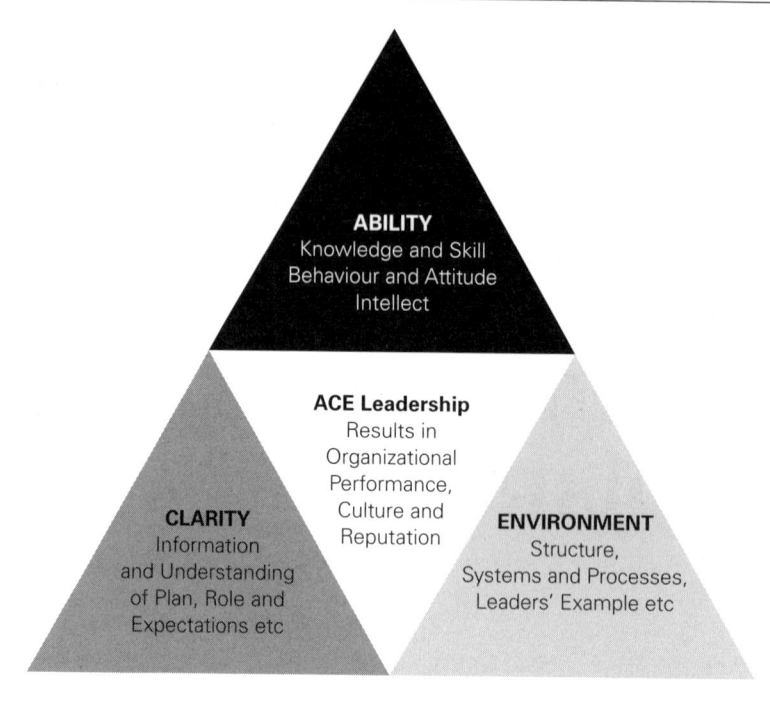

```
                        ABILITY
                    Knowledge and Skill
                   Behaviour and Attitude
                          Intellect


                      ACE Leadership
                        Results in
                       Organizational
                        Performance,
        CLARITY         Culture and      ENVIRONMENT
      Information       Reputation         Structure,
    and Understanding                 Systems and Processes,
      of Plan, Role and                Leaders' Example etc
       Expectations etc
```

© Jeremy Tozer, 1997–2007

acquisition decision and the integration plan, if conducted effectively, will result in clarity within the acquiring and the acquired organizations.

A problem at one level may consist of several smaller problems at a lower level and/or itself be part of a more complex higher level 'problem' or 'project'. In this sense business operations are one long project with no set end and with many changes, challenges and opportunities to make improvements along the way. So leadership work really is just a series of consecutive, concurrent and layered problems to solve and decisions to make.

Thus there is a requirement for all leaders to be able to think clearly, solve problems, make decisions and create and communicate plans, whatever their level of work, in order to overcome challenges, seize opportunities and complete tasks. In other words, to turn a vision, idea or strategy into reality, and to do it in such a way that alignment is maintained with the organization's higher intent and with people who are engaged, committed and unified in their endeavours. If this does not happen then innovation and initiative will be stifled, change will never be realized and a reactive workforce will have to wait on the boss's decision to deal with every little piece of 'niff naff and trivia'.

Problems might be relatively low level issues (simple problems) that may be tackled with 20 seconds thought (how best to progress a telephone residential customer's complaint). They might be deterministic problems; the sort of problems that can be solved by applying a formula, process or 'SOP' (standard operating procedure).

However, that process or SOP has to be determined in the first place, and will need review and improvement (or possibly out-sourcing or 'in-sourcing'). Problems might be indeterminate, complex 'wicked problems' with complex answers, such as the global supply chain/channel partner 'change problem' in Chapter 14, or the review or development of a strategic business or organizational transformation plan, or discrete project plans.

This section of the book pays most attention to problem solving and decision making, which arguably are applicable to every person in every organization, not just to its leaders, and reflects the earlier comment that all work is just a mass of concurrent, consecutive and layered problems to solve and decisions to make. It also looks at turning decisions into robust and adaptable plans, and the effective cascade and execution of those plans with inbuilt dynamic review and adaptation.

Training and experience can enable intuitive decision making when there is little time for reasoning and analysis. However, this can be very dangerous because although situations may look familiar, few are identical and while a preconceived or rehearsed solution may work, it may well not be the most effective solution and it may fail miserably. Intuitive decision making is arguably more suited to tactical situations than the more complex problems found at strategic levels of operation, but unless the discipline of clear thinking is inculcated early (when junior leaders work at the tactical level), it will be difficult to develop later in life – and if the skill of clear thinking is developed to a high standard it can be used instead of or to assist intuition in tactical, time-pressured situations. I read somewhere that, on average, the longest period of undisturbed thought that issues receive from the responsible executive is 12 minutes, which reinforces the need to develop clear thinking.

You will also recall the concept of effects-based leadership (EBL) that was introduced in Chapter 1, illustrated in Figure 12.2. The concept is of leaders delegating tasks, objectives, authority and resources and trusting the junior leader to work with the team to decide how best to achieve those tasks and execute his or her plan. This is a formal reflection of the leadership work that we have just mentioned: the layered, concurrent and consecutive problems to solve and decisions to make and communicate.

This section of the book has been written to introduce the individual leader to a proven and effective suite of scalable and universally applicable leadership processes for problem solving and decision making, planning and briefing; and a system or common operating platform that is proven to create an agile, responsive, engaged and focused organization. These processes break strategy into smaller component parts that flow down through the organization; and the review mechanisms and notably the process of back briefing flow back up through the organization, integrating these small pieces into the bigger strategy.

The following pages describe the tools that enable the doctrine of EBL to be realized, whether or not that philosophy is formally introduced to the organization with that name tag or any other. These methods have been proven in organizations spanning the private, public and third sectors in the UK, Europe, the United States, and across Asia and Australasia – from an internetworking company in Japan, to a charity in South Africa, Mexico and the UK, and a bank in the UK and Australia.

It is not essential that an entire organization adopts these ideas simultaneously for the tools and methods to work. The individual leader who sees value in them may

The ACE Conditions for Success: Clarity

FIGURE 12.2 Creating clarity with effects-based leadership processes

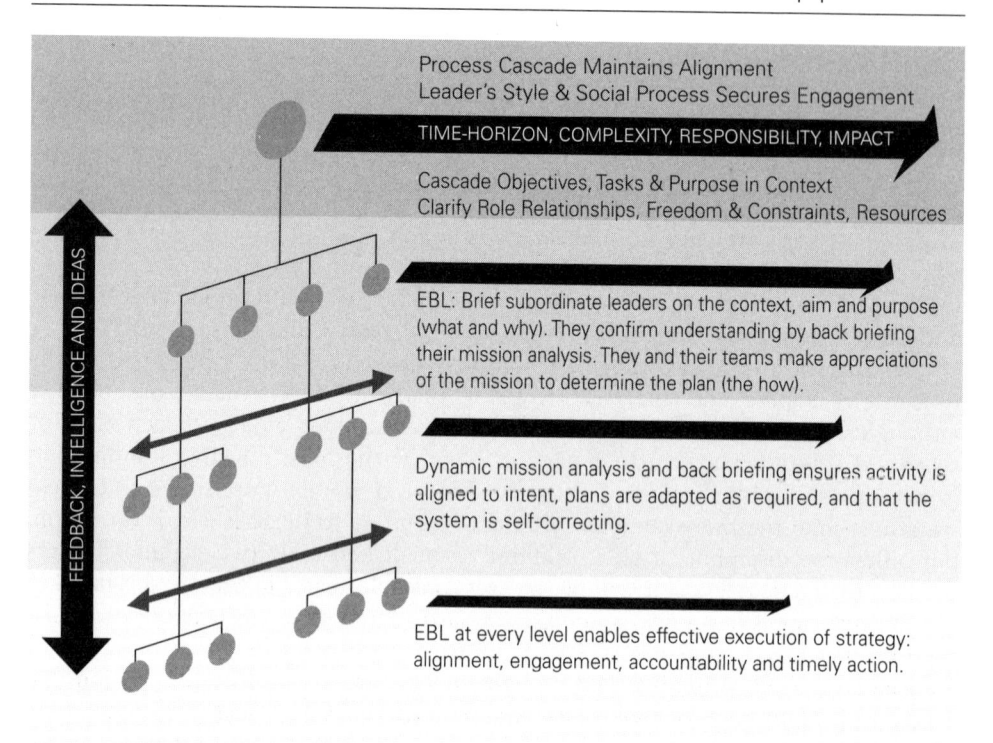

Process Cascade Maintains Alignment
Leader's Style & Social Process Secures Engagement

TIME-HORIZON, COMPLEXITY, RESPONSIBILITY, IMPACT

Cascade Objectives, Tasks & Purpose in Context
Clarify Role Relationships, Freedom & Constraints, Resources

EBL: Brief subordinate leaders on the context, aim and purpose (what and why). They confirm understanding by back briefing their mission analysis. They and their teams make appreciations of the mission to determine the plan (the how).

Dynamic mission analysis and back briefing ensures activity is aligned to intent, plans are adapted as required, and that the system is self-correcting.

EBL at every level enables effective execution of strategy: alignment, engagement, accountability and timely action.

FEEDBACK, INTELLIGENCE AND IDEAS

© Jeremy Tozer, 1997–2007

introduce them him or herself and enjoy the benefits of doing so – the case studies cited in subsequent chapters show how they have been used in parts of organizations rather than across an entire organization for that very reason. Their full power and potential to add value, however, is realized when the methods become common currency among the leadership population within a unit or an entire organization.

This system of adaptable and flexible leadership processes, when intelligently applied with 'social process', creates 'clarity, alignment, engagement and accountability' across an enterprise (no matter what size, location or culture), which combine to deliver outstanding results. It is a system that promotes rational thought yet includes within in it assessment of the emotional factors that are so important in decision making, especially those that rely on people's support and engagement for their successful implementation.

Compared to 'the usual' approach to leadership in organizations, the method outlined here takes more of a disciplined, project management approach to getting things done. It is applicable whether the work in hand is operational and routine, a discrete project, a programme (series of projects), or the development and execution of a strategic plan such as a merger, acquisition and integration, transformation, divestment or change. The method involves a trio of recurring, cascading and iterating leadership processes.

A trio of recurring, cascading and iterating processes

CASE STUDY A reason to read on!

Leaders at every level learnt and applied common processes for decision making, planning, briefing that build alignment, trust and flexibility. The results are impressive:

- An anticipated change time was halved: a planned two-year change project has been implemented in 12 months with constant headcount reduction and minimal angst.
- Measures: applications processed within service level agreement turnaround times have risen from 40 to 80 per cent.
- Measures: a fully functional quality control system is in place; vetting rose from 37 to 100 per cent.
- Leaders now lead their teams in difficult times, taking change in their stride.
- A full multi-skilling programme has been implemented in the last six months across all disciplines.
- Morale is high and retention has increased.
- 'Best practice' procedures implemented and enhanced.

Mike Begg, National Manager, Capital Finance (now HBOS Australia)

Decision making and planning is often thought of as one amorphous, dreary process. Planning also suffers from a surplus of 'strategies' (which are often tactics by a pompous name) with little or no ownership, understanding or commitment to execution – 'implementation inertia'. How many glossy strategy documents have you seen (especially in the public sector) which are little more than statements of hope and aspiration and contemporary management mantras, with no executable detail, the sole purpose of which appears to be to decorate coffee tables in the reception area?

To develop strategy effectively and then turn it into reality (via high quality execution), we need a mechanism that enables 'conversations' that define, align and agree objectives at every level of the organization – from the strategic, through the operational to the tactical level – in a time-effective manner; a mechanism that creates 'line of sight' from corporate strategic objectives down to the individual tasks of the operator on the front line. Such a mechanism is the iterative, recurring, cascading cycle of discrete, rigorous and engaging leadership processes, decision making (the appreciation), planning and briefing shown in Figure 12.3.

FIGURE 12.3 The cycle of strategy to reality

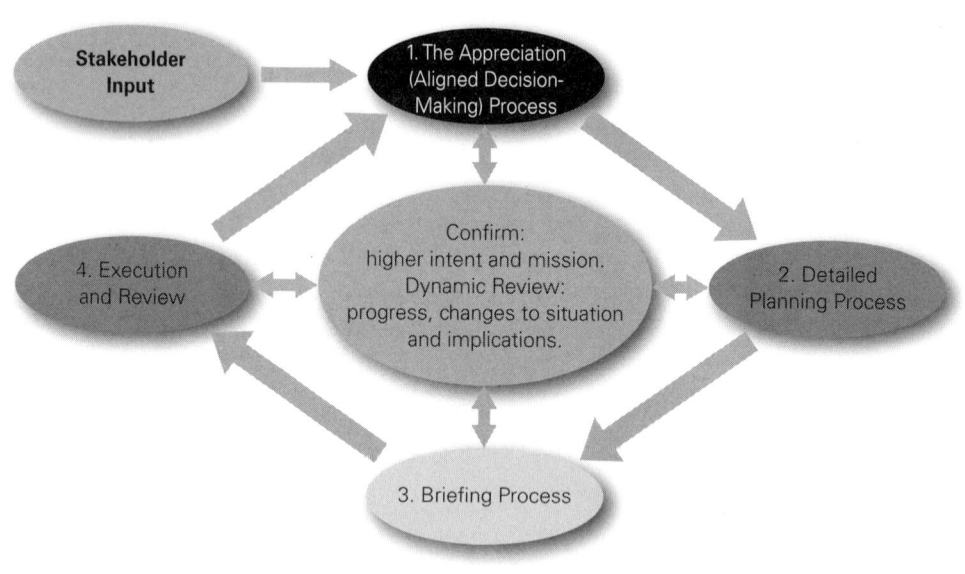

© Jeremy Tozer, 1997–2007

1. The appreciation[1] (or aligned decision-making process)

This is a mix of problem solving (the activity) and decision making (the output) in which the mission (or aim (vision) and its purpose (reason why)) is clarified through the process of mission analysis, deductions made about factors affecting achievement of the mission, overall options or courses of action (CoA) identified and compared, and a decision made on which CoA to pursue. When the leader acts as facilitator, participation in this process creates ownership of the resulting decision. This may be done collectively and/or in a series of meetings and conversations with different stakeholders.

A very important feature of mission analysis is that it concludes with the back brief to your leader. This provides an opportunity for you to confirm your understanding of your task's priorities and the effects that you intend to have; your leader may learn more about the implications of the direction given, and alignment is ensured, both laterally and vertically.

2. Detailed planning

The chosen CoA, which is an outline plan, is turned into a detailed plan. Again, this may be facilitated collectively in one or more meetings, and with different people. Participation in a facilitated process creates ownership of the resulting plan or particular aspects of it.

3. Briefing

People may have been involved in planning over days or weeks, but it would be wrong to assume that they have the clarity needed for optimal effectiveness during its execution. So the next step is to create clarity before implementation by briefing the team on the final plan and, during this, instilling a sense of confidence in the team and questioning their understanding of it. This process can also overtly create accountability. Without a clear, concise brief before work starts, something will inevitably go off the rails.

4. Execution

Delegated tasks within the brief are then the subject of the sequence of appreciation, planning and briefing (as appropriate) by the owner of that task, but at a lower level; this results in the actual 'doing'.

Dynamic reviews

Progress reviews, front line visits (and conversations with people at the sharp end), regular 3D feedback and progress evaluation are conducted and re-planning and re-briefing may result. Thus there is an iterative, recurring cascade of aligned thought and action.

These tools and methods (leadership processes) are not intended to slow you down! Rather, intelligent and appropriate application of these methods will enable you to make more effective and efficient use of the time and resources you have available so that you can make good decisions when faced with time-critical 'wicked problems'. The effects that this approach delivers internally are seen at three levels:

> *First order effects* include improved clarity, alignment, accountability and autonomy, engagement and sense of purpose (motivation).
>
> *Second order effects* include improved speed and quality of execution, teamworking and cross-boundary collaboration.
>
> *Third order effects* include increased interoperability (common language and methods), adaptability and use of initiative, and 'team discipline' (or predictability).

Experience shows that in many organizations there is little linkage between big bold strategies and the people who created them, and the tactical actions and operational work required and the people who have to do that. When these leadership processes are common to leaders at all levels, that problem is overcome.

Step 1, the appreciation, is usually conducted with the least amount of rigour – if it, or something like it, is conducted at all. Yet it is the key to success as it influences everything that follows by gaining clarity and buy-in to a clear defined 'mission'. If one was a cynic, one would say that Step 2 (detailed planning) in many places produces a thick document the quality of which is assessed by paper weight or electronic file size. Step 3, the collective briefing, seems to be virtually unheard of, with many executives and managers preferring to send e-mail links to intranet sites for people to find and read plans! In recent years UK governments and public sector organizations have shown themselves to be particularly adept in assuming that because a decision has been made, the plan has been implemented and the policy objective has been successfully achieved.

The lack of this integrated, dynamic, iterating, recurring and cascading cycle is why, in so many organizations, initiatives and strategies remain documents that are not understood, and adoption and implementation do not occur – the thought process to make these big ideas meaningful and translated into action is missing. Thus all leadership effort is undermined, and resources are squandered as people continue to work in a blanket of fog. This whole sequence of leadership process is cyclic, with every step the subject of a dynamic review of the situation and progress made, which enables a rapid change of direction whenever it is necessary.

When reading these notes, bear in mind that what separates the junior leader's work (the supervisor or corporal) from the senior executive's work (the general or the director) is complexity, time horizon, felt responsibility and impact over time. Many of the functions performed by leaders remain the same at all levels (problem solving, decision making, planning, briefing and so on), as does the requirement for behavioural flexibility in one's chosen leadership style (although executive behaviour has greater impact on corporate culture). What changes is the level of complexity faced, the degree of ambiguity, the time horizon and corresponding cognitive power required in the leader, the leader's felt responsibility, authority and influence and the attention paid to leadership behaviour.

Recognition of this enables these leadership processes to be used across an entire enterprise. This cascading, recurring and iterative approach to leading organizations integrates the leadership structure and builds organizational leadership capacity – the doctrine of EBL. This approach creates a common operating platform that transcends individual leaders and their arrivals, departures and foibles, and gives an organization the capability to change and react with great agility. It ends reliance on personality and specific individuals. When embedded into the organization, these processes enable continuous change, innovation and optimal performance, and they help to perpetuate a culture of leadership as they remain long after people have moved on.

These processes have universal application. However, the way in which they are employed by the leader (on the continuum of 'facilitated to given') will influence people's level of ownership, commitment and engagement and therefore the quality of the results delivered.

It is a system that builds organizational leadership capacity through common, cascading, iterating and recurring leadership processes, as shown in Figure 12.4. The process steps (the 'what') are universal and apply to any situation to create clarity and alignment. The manner in which these processes are applied (the 'how' or 'social process') will determine the level of stakeholder and employee engagement. This is the challenge for the leader: to develop not just an understanding of process, but dexterity, confidence and flexibility in its use.

If a common approach is adopted and applied to all decision making, planning and briefing, which you and others become familiar with, then important items will not be overlooked when decisions are made and plans put together under time pressure. Equally, when people contribute to, read or review papers in a common format, they will absorb the information more easily, and understanding, contribution quality and interoperability are enhanced.

FIGURE 12.4 Cascading, iterating and self-monitoring processes for alignment and engagement

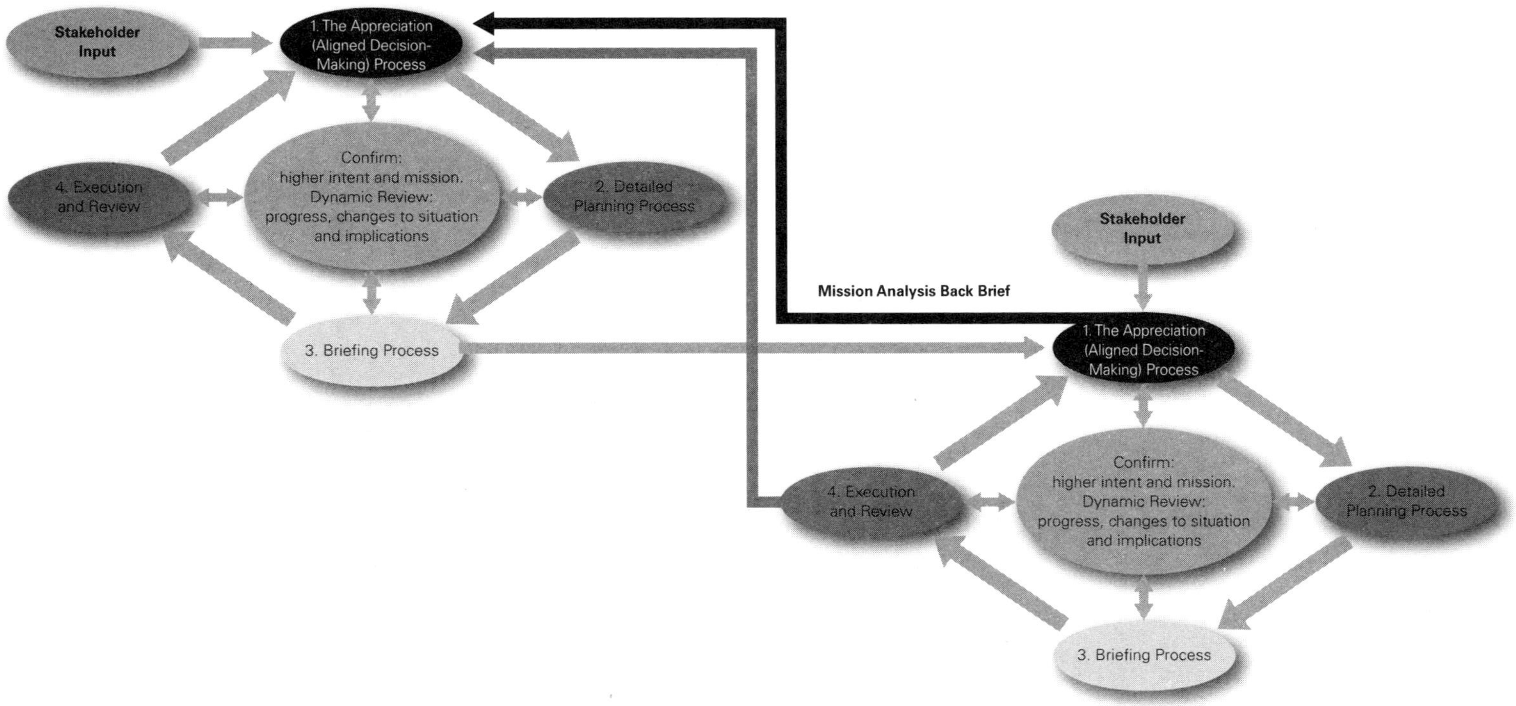

© Jeremy Tozer 2010

It is also worth pointing out here how these methods for decision making, planning and briefing may improve the quality and effectiveness of meetings, reduce meeting frequency and duration, and reduce e-mail volume – this should attract your attention, because the chances are very high that you spend much of your working life in meetings that you consider to be ineffective or a waste of time! Most meetings are held for the purpose of solving problems (the activity), making decisions (the outcome of problem solving), and/or making recommendations for decisions, and/or conveying information on one or more subjects. If the framework and techniques of the appreciation are applied to those subjects that come under the headings of problem solving and decision making, and the framework and techniques of the briefing are used to convey information, subject by subject, the result will be:

- increased clarity and alignment;
- increased ownership and accountability;
- increased trust and confidence;
- reduced meeting duration and frequency;
- reduced volume of e-mail.

An investment bank with which we worked extensively trained all the managers and executives in its IT department in these common tools and techniques. After three months when performance was reviewed, it estimated that the leadership population had reduced time spent in meetings by approximately 60 per cent. I also worked with the management population of the IT department of a university. A 'micro example' of the effectiveness of these tools is that the usual four-hour weekly management team meeting was completed in two and a half hours on the first occasion on which these tools were used. The cost of the management time that was saved alone (based on their hourly rate of pay) more than paid for their training. More than this, they had a degree of cohesion, unity and clarity that they had seldom experienced, which had a very positive second-order effect on their subordinate team members when they in turn were briefed.

EBL ensures the creation of a winning strategy and effective execution of that strategy on a sustainable basis; it creates collective agility and perpetual change-readiness. Effective leadership process (and with it, effective leadership 'culture') becomes embedded in the organization, integrating different levels, functions and business units, and aligning business objectives and processes across the enterprise – competitive advantage results. When extended to business partners and the supply chain, even more significant gains will result.

Note

1 Tozer, J, 1997, *Leading Initiatives*, Sydney: Butterworth Heinemann Australia.

13
People, personality and decision making

Cognition

Ways of thinking

Group dynamics

Decision-making biases

Cognitive dissonance

Understanding

Before the tools, methods and processes for creating clarity and effects-based leadership (EBL) are examined, it is worth understanding the psychological context in which they will be used, for this context forms part of the justification for doing something that may look and feel very different from past or current practice. The other part of the justification is the nature of the operating context (information proliferation, compression of time and space, and VUCA) described earlier.

Reflect on the 'nonsenses' that you have witnessed at work. You will observe that much unnecessary stress and waste of resources is caused by a lack of foresight, anticipation, over-simplified solutions to complex problems or poorly conceived or preconceived ideas: a lack of clear thinking.

Most of us think we are problem solving (thinking clearly) all the time. In reality we are looking through the files of experience in our brain, and seeking something similar that can be selected and adapted. Such an approach may work on occasion, but every situation is unique and requires a unique solution (to which past experience may be brought to bear). Favourite preconceived solutions may work but will probably not be the most effective solution to a new problem and, quite often, solutions based purely on past experience fail badly. Repeating past actions does not encourage improvement or innovation; it relies on so-called 'leaders' simply telling people what to do because they know the solution.

So why do we not think clearly? We all like to think we do but we suffer from the effects of stress and personality. So it is useful to have some understanding of the impact of personality on thinking. Thinking allows us to understand and to reason but thinking is not always as effective as it could be. A basic grasp of psychology, neurophysiology and group dynamics helps a leader maximize the effectiveness of his or her own thinking and that of the team. It also helps the leader to understand the value that an effective decision-making process can add.

Cognition

Cognition refers to the collection, storage, use and retrieval of information in the brain for the purposes of reasoning, interpreting, learning and making judgements. The brain has developed through the twin processes of 'nature and nurture' – genetic inheritance and experience – which influence:

- Beliefs, facts and opinions that we hold to be true and give bias to our thinking.
- Values and beliefs to which we attach weight and importance.
- Motivation, our desire to act to meet a need.
- Attention, the conscious direction of thought to assimilate detail, to apply deductive rigour or to remain aware to the wider environment and sensitive to changes within it.
- Perception, how we interpret information that comes to our attention, the subconscious filtering of data that can help us to see what we expect to see and find what we are looking for rather than discover the unexpected.
- Emotions, how we feel about things. The primitive part of the brain controls the 'fight or flight' instinct; another part of the brain is used to control our emotions and their expression.
- Intellect, in the sense of the volume and complexity of data that we can process together with the complexity of our mental processing (serial, parallel and parallel serial processing, etc).
- Heuristics, rules of thumb that we have learnt through experience and which we tend to stick to, but which are actually 'unproven theories' that may not work every time.
- Subconscious linking of thoughts to create meaning – the filling-in of blank spaces to create meaning where there was none. The resulting 'meaning' may be called intuition, creativity or incisive insight. This is the result of accumulated experience (intuition) or chance connections (the 'aha' or 'light bulb' moment).
- Ability to learn and adapt by making new connections between the neurons in the brain.

All this naturally influences our thinking, our choices and our behaviour. We will confine ourselves here to the direct impact of personality on decision making. It is not just individuals who think; perception, attitudes and so on are also shaped by the 'collective thinking' of people interacting with each other. Corporate cultures can be strong and can lead people to interpret information, think and react in institutionalized ways – which can help 'do' things and hinder rational thought.

On top of all this, the brain may suffer from information overload, caused by the proliferation of data and/or stress. It leads to either closure (we close our minds to other inputs no matter how important they are) or projection: we make false assumptions, often ones that would make our life easy if they were true, or ones that support preconceptions.

Ways of thinking

Our personality affects our thinking, and we all have preferences in the way we think, which may be accentuated under pressure and conditions of stress.

Divergent – convergent thinking

Divergent thinking involves taking problems apart and constructing and exploring ideas. It uses inductive reasoning – reasoning that makes generalizations based on individual instances and therefore allows for the possibility that the conclusion is false, even where all of the premises are true.

Convergent thinking involves combining deductions and different ideas together based on elements that these ideas have in common. It uses deductive reasoning to show that a conclusion necessarily follows from a set of premises or hypotheses: a deductive conclusion must be true if the premises are true. It follows that deductive reasoning is a method of gaining knowledge. Effective decision making requires both divergent and convergent thinking to be employed.

Conscious – unconscious thinking

This is rational, logical thinking or intuition, 'gut feel' and inspired ideas. If time allows it is worth testing 'gut feel' with rational thought to see if the same conclusion is reached. These ways are compounded by other inclinations in our thinking and decision making.

Reflective – impulsive

Very simply, some people think and ponder for a long time, perhaps never coming to a conclusion. Others rush to a decision without much thought. Both ends of the spectrum can result in carnage!

Field dependent – independent thinking

Field dependent people are those who are influenced by their perception of surrounding stimuli so that they always perceive taking into account the 'field' surrounding a 'problem'. Apart from the perception, it is also the entire mental apparatus that is affected by this dependence on the 'field' (and thus also cognitions and emotions). Essentially field dependent people are significantly influenced by context in making judgements, while field independent people pay little or no attention to context (ie, they are able to isolate their point of interest).

Decision-making biases

These different ways of thinking, when combined with core beliefs, result in certain biases when making decisions that the leader needs to be aware of.[1] These biases are:

- Social proof, the bandwagon effect, doing or thinking what others do, because others are doing or thinking it.
- Blind spot: people often fail to compensate for their blind spots even when they are aware of them.
- Confirmation: the tendency to look for support or confirmation of preconceived ideas, or to avoid new information that contradicts an established view.
- Optimism: over-estimating the positives or under-estimating the negatives. Contingency planning enables leaders to hedge their bets.
- Presentation: how information is framed and presented will influence the way that information is interpreted.
- Choice supportive: people tend to recall past decisions, choices or performance as being better than they actually were and as causes of past success but not of failure.
- Distinction is a bias to view two options as more dissimilar when comparing them simultaneously than when considering them separately.
- Extreme avoidance: an aversion to choices that appear to be extreme and a preference for an intermediate choice.
- Narrow focus: people may focus too intently on one feature of a problem or situation and ignore other important features.
- Neglect of probability: the bias to disregard probability in uncertain conditions.
- Familiarity: potentially dangerous liking for ideas because they are familiar (the comfort zone).

Open cultures and giving people explicit licence to challenge established wisdom, together with self-awareness of personal preferences help to mitigate these biases.

Cognitive dissonance

It is one of the paradoxes of human behaviour that as we get closer to making serious decisions so we become assailed by doubts. Think of a time when you have been about to make a major purchasing decision such as buying a car or a house. At those times people always question their decision and seek reassurance when writing the cheque. A logical sequence of problem solving to help identify the best course of action would have provided some security through confidence that the decision was correct or the best possible decision with the time and information available. Using such a process minimizes the negative effects of doubt and lack of confidence in the leader, which can only be reflected and magnified in his or her followers.

It is post-decision steadiness more than pre-decision certitude which carries the day.
(Brigadier General S L A Marshall, *The Armed Forces Officer*, 1950)

Group dynamics

Using the collective expertise of people to solve complex problems and to gain their 'buy-in' is essential. However, there are some group dynamics that need consideration in order to optimize this approach.

Group size affects decision making; individuals may hide in large groups, fail to recognize the importance of any one factor or task, or fail to take responsibility for decisions and outcomes. Peer pressure influences the individuals within a group to change their attitudes, values or behaviours in order to conform to established group norms. Depending on the prevailing culture, this may be positive. However, the pressure to conform can limit a team's ability to challenge understanding and to think creatively. People in groups frequently adapt their behaviour to conform to views other than their own. Contributory factors include the fear of disapproval, a lack of self-belief, conflict avoidance, high anxiety and low status, and a high need for approval from others.

Groupthink[2] may be observed in cohesive teams focused on external issues and problems: it is the tendency for individuals to go along with majority decisions or views. This often happens when team members have similar backgrounds and values and/or where they perceive a need for consensus and unanimity[3] and/or they simply wish to keep their leader happy – or they are idle and coasting! The group dynamics may induce conformity that is difficult for any individual to overcome, even if they know that the group view is wrong. Such groups are prone to short-cutting rational decision making.[4] In extreme cases, the group may begin to feel invulnerable and take excessive risks. Social prejudice is a belief that another social group is less capable than one's own. Again, very cohesive teams can reinforce such beliefs. Overcoming groupthink needs the leader explicitly to welcome dissenting views and create the open and honest environment in which individuals with different perspectives feel able to say and discuss what they are thinking.

Group cultures can reinforce cohesion under stress, but they can be destructive when disparate groups are brought together as partners in some joint endeavour. Antipathy may develop before the groups physically meet each other (the competition drive again – Chapter 8). Such a clash of cultures does nothing to aid working relationships.

One dysfunctional group trait is behaviour that prevents the sharing of information effectively, perhaps again due to competition, or the idea that 'knowledge is power'. Rather than revealing information known only to them, individual team members may talk only about things that everybody already knows.

Understanding

Information becomes knowledge when it is learnt and, as they say, 'knowledge is power'. Actually, this is incorrect. Knowledge is only useful – powerful – when its meaning is understood. In other words, knowledge has been analysed to help us gain insights into a situation (knowing what is going on and why), and when deductive thinking and judgement are applied to those insights, we may gain foresight (being able to identify and anticipate what may happen and/or what we ought to do). In sport, we may have knowledge of the rules of the game and of the players being fielded; analysis will give us insights into the game; and when judgement and experience are brought to bear we may have the foresight that gives us understanding.

> *Know the enemy and know yourself; in a hundred battles you will never be in peril. When you are ignorant of the enemy but know yourself, your chances of winning or losing are equal. If ignorant of both your enemy and of yourself, you are certain in every battle to be in peril.*
>
> (Sun Tzu, *The Art of War*)

> *Intelligence is knowing a tomato is a fruit; wisdom is not putting it in a fruit salad.*
>
> (Peter Kay)

Therefore understanding ('wisdom' in Peter Kay's quote), the ability to place knowledge in its wider context, is essential in effective decision making. It provides leaders with the insight and foresight required to make effective decisions, which includes managing the associated risks and the second- (and subsequent) order effects – the downstream implications and consequences. These decisions may span:

- the development of policy, plans and partnerships;
- shaping the operating environment and influencing events;
- developing empathy with individuals or groups and influencing them.

Understanding = Insights + Foresight

Situational Awareness + Analysis = Insight

Deductive Reasoning + Judgement = Foresight

Understanding, developing insights and foresight relating to a particular situation, are not a natural response for many people; they are something that requires conscious thought and effort. Understanding occurs at three levels:

1 At the individual level (the personal interpretation and analysis of information to create understanding).

2 At the collective level, in which a shared perspective is created by people from a discrete group with its own distinct culture and ethos.

3 Common understanding between different groups, in which people from one group understand the perceptions of other groups and establish a common foundation for thought, communication and action.

The leader needs to work at creating understanding at all three levels and the following may assist in that:

- Self-awareness, of perceptual filters, heuristics and bias.
- Processing information with collation, integration and interpretation (deductive reasoning).
- Consideration of a problem from different perspectives.
- Collating and exploiting individual understandings to develop deeper insights and collective understanding.
- Exploiting networks and relationships.

The problem-solving and decision-making process explained in the next chapter is designed to minimize the distorting or limiting effects of personality in making effective decisions.

Notes

1 Stanovich, K E and West, R F, 2008, On the relative independence of thinking biases and cognitive ability, *Journal of Personality and Social Psychology*, 94, 4, pp 672–95.
2 Irving, J, 1982, *Groupthink: Psychological studies of policy decisions and fiascos*, New York: Houghton Mifflin.
3 Brooks, I, 2003, *Organizational Behaviour – Individuals, groups and organization*, Maidenhead: Prentice-Hall.
4 McConville, T, 2003, *The War on Terrorism: A new classic in groupthink*, London: Cass.

14
Decision making: the appreciation

- Introduction
- The appreciation in detail
- Task and time schematic plan
- Appreciations at the strategic level
- Contingency planning
- Other problem-solving tools and techniques
- The appreciation and personality types
- Examples of appreciations
- Annex A: Standard Operating Procedure (SOP) for meetings and minutes
- Annex B: Appreciation template
- Annex C: Project/task outline plan template
- Annex D: Strategic plan and second-order task tracking document template

Introduction

Given that the majority of leadership work involves problem solving (the activity) and decision making (the output of problem solving), to optimize leadership effectiveness, both individually and collectively, the ideal approach to decision making will:

- Enable collective or individual problem solving and timely high quality decision making.
- Facilitate working in fast changing, uncertain and complex environments.
- Extract meaning from information and filter out extraneous 'clutter'.
- Be applicable to any problem, task, opportunity or situation at any level of complexity in which a decision needs to be made about what to do.
- Produce robust yet flexible plans that may readily be adapted as circumstances change, and actual progress is assessed.

- Encourage initiative and enable the alignment of activity.
- Raise the user's level of thought and understanding to set his or her work in context and maintain alignment.
- Enable the integration of the leadership structure and work of an organization or partner organizations.
- Engage participants and users, and induce accountability and ownership.
- Build trust when it is a common thought process within teams and organizations, because people know that others will think clearly and act with alignment.
- Minimize the distorting effects of personality on our thinking.
- Give us and others confidence that all the options have been examined and the best option chosen with the time and information available.
- Give teams a logical, adaptable handrail or thought process to follow.
- Be relevant to anyone who needs to make decisions as part of their job – only the level of complexity, time-horizon, responsibility and impact varies, not the steps in the process.

There is nothing inherently difficult in the problem-solving and decision-making process – for simple problems people do this instinctively. For example, in planning a weekend away we consider where to go, how to get there, the cost, and so on.

We tackle problems every day. Every problem derives from a situation. The solution involves an examination of the situation and it usually requires a decision on the course of action to pursue. The thought process that follows – the appreciation – may be applied to making any decision at any level in any context. It is a fundamental thought process and life skill. All that alters at higher levels of leadership is the degree of complexity, and the requirement for the output from conducting an appreciation to be captured and built upon and/or cascaded. Depending on the situation and the type of problem, the appreciation may result in an outline plan, leading to further detailed planning with and briefing of those involved, or simply a yes/no decision will result, which may or may not need to be briefed to people.

The appreciation (so named because of the analogy that serious art critics and experts 'appreciate' art, rather than simply look at it) is designed as a formal but flexible form of a logical thought process that enables leaders, their teams and individual contributors to solve problems and arrive at conclusions (decisions or recommendations to decision makers) under the stress of business and the pressure of time. While it may feel cumbersome to use at first, with practice it simply becomes a way of thinking and dealing with issues – any problem, task, opportunity, or challenge – on a daily basis.

If you can understand this decision-making process (to be precise, the first three steps of the process are problem solving, the final step alone is the actual decision making) you are becoming proficient in one of the essential skills of a leader. Some people have an aptitude for clear thought under pressure, but this is something we must all develop.

There follows a case study, which is examined as the first of the detailed examples towards the end of this chapter.

CASE STUDY

The Company's Technical Support and Documentation Website department (handling over 60,000 pages), which I led, has used this methodology for several years now. Initially, it created clarity of vision, mission, purpose and plan where we had confusion and lack of direction. The level of clarity and the buy-in obtained through the process for creating that clarity has resulted in unity, cohesion and collaboration within the team.

The appreciation is a dynamic and flexible process that we use to start all our projects and to define our business plans. My management team buys into the process wholeheartedly because of the immediate outputs and their consequences. The methodology has now become embedded within my group, building our capacity to deliver.

As a result, we have been recognized as a model of effective global cross-functional teamwork within the company, we have had our budget increased, and we have won two industry awards following the execution of our strategic plan. We have been recognized by the Service and Support Professionals Association (SSPA) with the STAR Awards for Best Practices in the Self-Service Category. We were also cited as one of the Ten Best Web Support Sites by the Association of Support Professionals (ASP). This is another prestigious award that showcases excellence in online service and support.

(Janet Ramey, Director, Cisco)

The explanation of the process will be accompanied by an example of its application (creating a business plan for a chain of estate agents). Further examples may be found at the end of the chapter together with some working document templates. These real examples which I have facilitated and led include the case study above, solving a $5 billion channel partner business model/supply chain problem for an internetworking company, and turning around a failing village pub.

The appreciation is an 'aligned decision-making process'. In outline an appreciation of a problem consists of four steps:

1 *Mission (or task) analysis.* Here you establish clarity about what you are trying to achieve and why. This step is dynamic, iterative and is called 'Mission analysis' or 'Task clarification' as it results in confirming or identifying a clear, precise aim and purpose – your mission or task. Inclusion of stakeholders' thinking (facilitated workshops and meetings in which open questions are asked) can secure engagement and support, even if they are not fully involved in subsequent steps.

2 *Factor or situation analysis.* Evaluate or reason-out all the factors that affect achieving your mission and make valid deductions about what needs to be done. Again, inclusion of stakeholders' thinking (facilitated workshops and

FIGURE 14.1 The appreciation process cycle

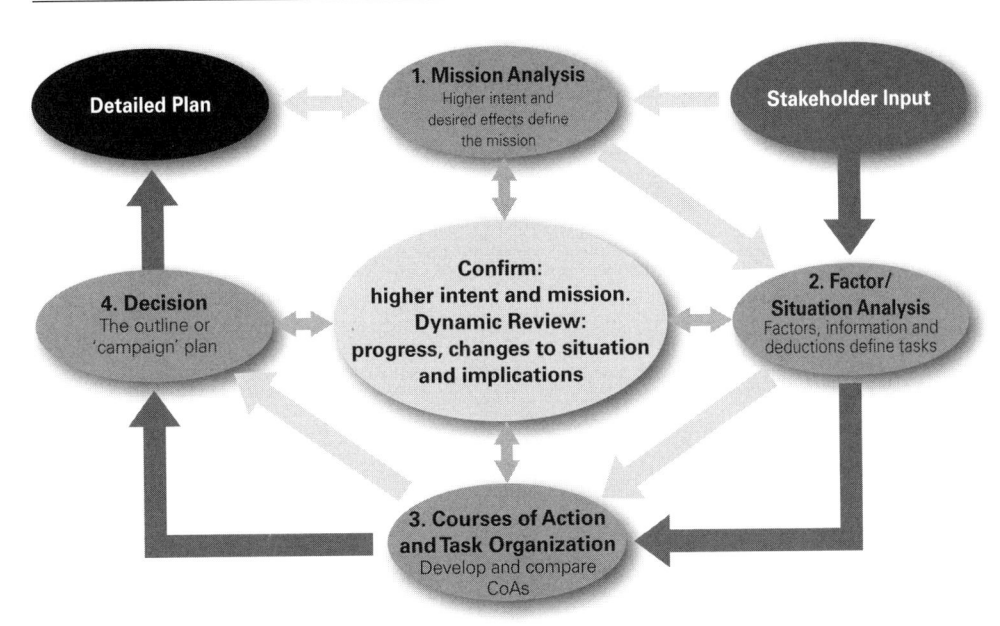

© Jeremy Tozer, 1997–2007

meetings in which factors are identified and deductions made) can secure engagement and support.

3 *Courses of action (CoA) and/or task organization.* Identify all the practical options or courses of action open to you – the different ways of completing the tasks identified in step 2, including their sequencing and grouping, and compare their advantages and disadvantages.

4 *The decision.* The selection of the best CoA (or outline plan) to achieve the aim, which forms the outline plan or concept of operations upon which a detailed plan is based.

Feedback and input

It is not intended that the leader and/or the leadership team apply this way of thinking in isolation. Think of it as the structure, or handrail, for conversations at every level of leadership informed by formal input – intelligence, research, and other sought input, feedback, ideas and so on, and informal input – freely offered ideas and thoughts elicited in ad hoc conversations and so on. Such input may be applied to each stage of the cycle.

Flexibility

The decision-making process (or appreciation) is a logical sequence of reasoning, leading to the best solution to a strategic, tactical, administrative or personal problem.

FIGURE 14.2 The appreciation: aligned decision making

The Appreciation: Aligned Decision-Making Process

Mission Analysis Involvement of all stakeholders in this stage will enable alignment to and ownership of the mission.	a. Leader's Intentions (2 up): End-state, Desired Effects, Purpose, Strategy. b. Essential Tasks: Specified and implied → concurrent activity. c. Constraints and Freedom of Action. d. Time and Space (max of 1/3 of time used for planning at your level). e. Changes to the Situation – monitor during execution. f. State your Mission – 'to do *action* in order to achieve *purpose*.' g. Back brief your mission analysis to your leader to confirm understanding, make implications of direction explicit and ensure alignment.
Factor/Situation Analysis Utilize the expertise of subject matter experts in this stage.	a. List the factors that affect achieving the mission. b. Analyse the factors by saying 'So what?', 'Therefore?' to form deductions. A factor is anything that affects the problem, task or opportunity. Separate deductions from assumptions, and make deductions from deductions. c. Assessment of tasks and priorities.
Identify the Courses of Action and Task Organization Utilize the expertise of your team members in this stage.	a. Identify the different options or complete courses of action open – how the mission may be achieved. This includes the grouping and sequencing of tasks. b. Compare advantages and disadvantages of different CoAs.

The Leader's Decision	a. Selection of the CoA that best achieves the mission.
	b. Involvement of team members in the decision stage depends upon:
	  • (Confidential) Information of higher intent that the leader alone knows
	  • Time • Importance of decision
	  • Leader's expertise • The nature of the subject under discussion
	  • Importance of 'teamwork' • Team members' ability.
	c. Brief those involved and affected.

© Jeremy Tozer, 2007

It is a process suitable for the supervisor and the CEO. What varies is only the complexity of factors and implications. The appreciation may be:

- quick (mental) or deliberate (discussed and/or written);
- individual or collective;
- facilitated or 'given';
- dynamic not linear;
- all stages completed in one session, or each stage completed, back briefed to stakeholders and iterated;
- used as the format for all papers proposing recommendations;
- used as a sales tool in 'solution-creation' with the client;
- used as the agenda for every discussion that seeks to make a decision or recommendation.

For big decisions – such as defining strategy, or planning a merger, acquisition, product launch, IT change, process outsourcing, designing a patient healthcare pathway and so on – the process may be facilitated over several days in a workshop, with the output captured and then refined. It may be conducted over a longer time frame in many meetings with the output of each meeting integrated and played back to all stakeholders – or a mix of both. It applies as much to making 'work' decisions, as it does to buying a house, deciding where to go on holiday or which car to buy.

For quick 20-second tactical decisions – in the hospital, in the call centre, in a client meeting, in the marketing department, in the distribution centre, on the police or fire brigade front line – it can be reduced to four questions answered in your head or in a quick conversation with colleagues:

1 What am I trying to achieve and why?
2 What are the key factors to consider?
3 What options exist?
4 Which option shall I choose and why?

This is where it becomes a really powerful thought process – not just using it on 'special occasions' for 'big decisions', but making it a routine way of thinking so that effective decisions are actually made about all actions, rather than just doing things out of habit.

It can also be used as a sales tool if you are selling value-added or value-created solutions. By facilitating the process with a client, you engage them personally, help them to define their needs and so on, and they generate the options from which they choose one.

It is not a linear process either; it is dynamic. It is perfectly possible to move from one step to the next and then move back a step when further information becomes available. It is in this way that the four steps increase the quality of decisions made using the best information available at the time when the decision is required.

> *The forgoing action clearly indicates that one of the most difficult things we have to do is to recognise the moment for making a decision. The information comes in by degrees. We never know but that the next minute will bring us further information that is fresh and vital. Shall we make a decision now or shall we wait a little longer? It is usually more difficult to determine the moment for making a decision than it is to formulate the decision itself.*
> (Captain Adolf von Schell, *Battle Leadership*, 1933)

When this way of thinking enters the bloodstream and influences every decision at every level, the quality of decision making and subsequent consequences are dramatically improved throughout an enterprise.

Paradox

There is a paradox in clear thinking. The discipline of clear thinking, a true appreciation of situations, creates freedom – it creates freedom of choice, freedom from unnecessary stress and freedom from cognitive dissonance, as psychologists say ('confidence wobbles' in plain English).

> *The appreciation process is probably the most valuable business lesson I have learnt in the last five years; it has significantly improved the performance of myself and my team*

> by doing the thinking up front and implementing a course of action that needs little or no re-engineering and is easy to adapt as the situation changes and evolves.
>
> I can't speak highly enough of the process – it works to great effect. The speed at which the problems are solved and the quality of the output is fantastic! People become engaged and ownership is built while clarity of what, why and how is created. The process stops people jumping to conclusions and doing things the way they have always been done. The quality of thought and ideas is greatly improved. Using the process improves the atmosphere in meetings by reducing tension in the room and focusing on a common goal.
>
> I highly recommend that every leader takes the opportunity to learn the process, use it every day for problems big and small, and experience the motivating effect of making the right decision every time.
>
> (Mawgan Wilkins, Director Global Products and Services, Cisco Systems)

An appreciation is a sequence of logical thought and sound reasoning. Whether written, mental or verbal, do not allow it to become a theoretical process; it should be a flexible means for the orderly and practical consideration of the factors affecting the solution of any problem. You can expect the situation to change after you have made your appreciation, apparently undermining the validity of your work – in fact much or most of your work will remain valid. The appreciation is designed to be a dynamic process, so simply run through the mission analysis again, address the changed or new factors, and follow through the new or amended deductions and revise your selected CoA as appropriate.

In business terms, particularly in a highly competitive market, there is often no opportunity for gaining reassurance for your own decisions. Making a decision can be painful; the bigger you perceive the decision to be, the greater the uneasiness you are likely to feel. Knowledge of this 'cognitive dissonance' should help to reassure the inexperienced leader that having doubts is natural and normal. Leaders need to be aware that doubts afflict both themselves and others, so that they may develop the confidence to minimize its effects on themselves and to be aware of the need to support colleagues at times of decision. Using the appreciation process minimizes the negative effects of doubt and lack of confidence in the leader and stops them being reflected in his or her followers.

No leader can delegate the whole appreciation of his or her mission to a 'subordinate' since only the leader is far enough removed to view the whole in perspective. Others may work on the appreciation, or indeed lead parts of the factor analysis and CoA development, but the leader should always drive the mission analysis and the selection of the CoA.

When this consideration of factors is followed by a group you have collective support, since the end result should be arrived at through logic, not through factional interests. If written, anyone reading the appreciation should arrive at the same conclusion – unless factors have been overlooked in which case it is easy for a reader familiar with the format to spot errors and it is relatively simple to make the necessary changes.

One of the greatest advantages of adopting this process is that it develops awareness of 'the big picture' – which can be termed 'vision' in the CEO. This is where part of the appreciation's power lies when instilled as a way of thinking.

The appreciation in detail

1. Mission analysis

    a Leader's intentions (two up):, end-state, desired effects, purpose, method.

    b Essential tasks: specified and implied → concurrent activity.

    c Constraints and freedom of action.

    d Time and space (maximum of one-third of time used for planning at your level).

    e Changes to the situation – monitor during execution.

    f State your mission – 'to do *action* in order to achieve *purpose*.'

    g Back brief to your leader to confirm your mission, if appropriate.

This thought process was conceived to enable Army officers to seize the initiative in the absence of specific direction – to create clarity when none is specifically given – to take action that supports the main effort rather than going off at a tangent, and waste time, resources and effort on something that is not required. It is a key part of the British military doctrine of mission command ('effects-based leadership (EBL)' in civilian speak – delegating tasks in context (the 'what') and empowering the leader to determine 'how' the task will be completed within defined constraints). This is equally relevant to business, which operates in a fast changing world (but a world that is still not as dynamic and fast paced as the battlefield – where the consequences of bad decisions and plans become so rapidly and awfully apparent!).

In mission analysis you establish clarity about what exactly you are trying to achieve and why, and what will limit your decision. In a business owner's strategic plan, I suggest that the owner's personal vision, purpose and exit must also be included.

a. Analysis of your superior's and organization's intentions, mission and your purpose

It is essential to understand exactly what the desired end-state is and/or what your boss and your boss's boss intend to achieve (ie intentions two levels up), the reasons why – the purpose – and what your part is in the higher level plan. Often, complex organizations have superficially clear ambitions or strategic objectives that do not mean much to more junior leaders. By answering the question, 'What specific effects do I want to have and on whom or on what?' (effects or impacts on the customer, the market, partners, your own organization and staff, processes and so on), you will give depth and meaning to otherwise big, bold and seemingly vague statements. This will allow you to act with alignment because you know what is wanted and you can continue to act without constantly checking back.

b. Identification of essential tasks (specified and implied)

Any tasks specified by your leader and other obvious tasks that are implicit – normally those that are required no matter what shape the final plan might take – must be considered so that maximum effort can be focused on the essential tasks and concurrent activity initiated as soon as possible.

Concurrent activity is worth emphasizing. It is not necessary to solve the whole problem and write a detailed plan before action is initiated. If other people are required to contribute in some way, warn them as soon as possible. They will then have the maximum time to do what needs to be done and they will experience less stress or panic.

c. Constraints and boundaries/freedom of action

It is important to understand what should limit your thinking and therefore your definition of your mission and the scope of your plan. It is often difficult to decide what should be set down as constraints. The rule is that constraints are those imposed upon you by your superior (not simply established habits and norms – these might need to be challenged). They are not those things you decide should limit your actions as a result of considering the factors – this would be 'situating the appreciation' as opposed to appreciating the situation. All too often people work under unchallenged false assumptions they believe to be genuine constraints until they are forced to question their beliefs. Constraints and freedoms are also factors and need to be considered in step 2 (factor analysis) as well.

d. Time and space

A good rule of thumb is that you give yourself a third of the time available before a task must be completed for planning at your level before briefing your team. They will then have sufficient time to plan and execute. This idea cascades down and the time available reduces as the problem or task itself becomes reduced in scope.

e. Changes in the situation

Has the situation changed since you received your last briefing from your boss? Sometimes, while you are carrying out your appreciation, something may change. You could have one of three answers:

1 The situation has changed but your plan is still good.
2 The situation has changed; your original mission is still possible but you need to amend the plan.
3 The situation has changed; your original mission is no longer valid. You should then consult your leader, but if you cannot you should support your superior's main effort.

f. The mission

If a specific task or mission has not been given to you, you should now be able to state your own distilled from the foregoing. This must be a statement of overall intent and its purpose, and the wording must be memorable, unambiguous, clear, concise, precise and positive. If everyone involved can remember it, they can align action to it. The wording you use must be thought through carefully as it may affect choices made further into this decision-making process.

Mission: To do something, *in order to* achieve a purpose.

g. Back brief

Now you can give a 'back brief' to your boss (especially useful in organizations where direction tends to be vague). In a back brief you confirm your mission, desired effects, essential tasks and priority of work. This enables you to check your understanding of your leader's intentions; and your leader may learn new things about the implications of the direction he or she has given (or with a vague boss, you will probably find that you have assisted his or her thinking!). This dialogue also ensures alignment, both vertically and laterally. Once your back brief has been confirmed or amended, you should then pass a 'warning order' to your team (give early warning to those involved of as much as you know about the what, why, who, when, where and how) and initiate concurrent activity.

Example

Let's imagine that a regional chain of 20 branches of a family-owned estate agency business has made a strategic decision to grow as a cohesive, flexible, but focused organization offering a full property sale and letting management service. They now need to plan how to achieve that. (The strategic decision itself will have been made as a result of a higher level appreciation.)

a. Analysis of your superior's and organization's intentions, mission and desired effects

- Become employer and service provider of choice – build referrals system and culture.
- Build and leverage brand presence, leverage profile built by winning the industry's most prestigious award.
- Create and seize new revenue opportunities that result from government legislation and value-added service offering.
- Strengthen organization capability: develop branch leadership to ensure consistency, build sales orientation and cross-selling of services while maintaining customer service ethic.
- Increase number of branches – high street presence.
- Maintain 'family company' traditional care for employees/customers and dislike for bureaucracy while also becoming more commercial and more organized as required.
- Provide a full spectrum of property buying, selling and management services.
- Engage staff to secure full commitment.

b. Identification of essential tasks (specified and implied)

- Strategic brand marketing.
- Develop branch 'brand experience' consistency.
- Develop surveying arm.
- Develop letting arm including relationships with sub-contracting tradespeople.

- Build strategic relationships with finance and insurance houses.
- Develop internal leadership capacity.
- Identify towns for new branch presence.

c. Constraints/freedom of action/risk

- Capital/cash flow.
- Control of growth.

d. Time and space

Traditional quiet period commences in three months, ideal time for training and development.

e. Changes in the situation

Review monthly.

f. The mission

To develop a first-choice, sales and full service-estate agency and property management business, in order to exceed the expectations of buyers, tenants, landlords and vendors, and to provide security to employees and shareholders.

Everything in the decision-making and planning process is now directed towards achieving that mission.

2. Factor/situation analysis

a List the factors.
b Analyse the factors by saying 'So what?', 'Therefore?' to form deductions. A factor is anything that affects the problem, task or opportunity. Separate deductions from assumptions, and make deductions from deductions.
c Assessment of tasks and priorities.

a. List the factors

A factor is anything that affects achieving the mission. Start by listing all the factors that affect achieving the mission (so you do not overlook any), and then add the deductions that may be derived from those factors. The list might result from systems thinking, brainstorming, mind mapping, system drawing, fish-boning, force field drawing and so on. Having created a list, it is useful to then form logical groupings of factors as this will make their consideration easier.

It is essential that all the relevant factors are considered otherwise problems will be oversimplified and solutions will be ineffective. If as a leader you are changing or shifting a system, you must first understand that system. For example, many years ago when Dr Beeching was reviewing British Rail in an attempt to create a cost-effective service, he closed down all the parts that, when viewed as discrete entities, did not make money. Unfortunately for the travelling public, many of these smaller branch lines fed traffic into the main lines. Without them, people could not get to the main lines, so the main lines lost passengers and became unprofitable themselves. This is a glaring example of failing to understand the problem – the size and complexity of the system that one is working with. Politicians are especially prone to this error and allow 'ideology' to dominate rational thought.

Alistair Mant[1] in his book, *Intelligent Leadership*, makes the distinction between 'frog' and 'bike' systems: the difference between these when viewed as systems lies in their relationship to the whole. You can strip a bike down, clean it, rebuild it with new parts and so on. After you have cut a frog's leg off, it tries to limp on but does not 'operate' so well. You can try to replace the amputated leg but a prosthetic is not that effective to a frog's way of life. The analogy to over-simplified yet appealing slick and polished management consultant solutions such as outsourcing or changing organizational structures is obvious: systems as a whole as well as their component parts need to be understood.

b. Analyse the factors

Each factor must be discussed in relation to the mission and should lead to one or more deductions affecting the attainment of the mission. A good test of the factor is to ask, 'What does this mean, what does it imply?' or more simply, 'So what?' to indicate what you should do about it (therefore...). If the answer to 'So what?' is 'So nothing', the factor should be discarded since it is extraneous information that clouds the issue.

The most useful words in this deductive process are 'So what?' If you enjoy being bolshie or intentionally difficult, you will find this a particularly easy expression to use! You do not need to know the answer to the question to ask it – someone from within the team will answer it if there are deductions to be made. What is important is that someone, and ideally the leader, keeps asking this question until no more deductions can be made, or there is no more planning time available.

Each factor must be examined exhaustively. Deductions themselves must be subjected to the 'So what?' test. If the answer is, 'Therefore xyz needs to be done', a further deduction should be drawn and so on until that particular line of argument is exhausted. This deductive process will produce a list of sub-tasks or lower level objectives that need to be attained if the overall mission or aim is to be achieved, and it will lead to identifying the different methods for achieving each sub-task.

The outputs of this deductive thought process may include 'critical information requirements' (questions to answer), guidance for further planning, specific tasks or projects – which may include identification of risk – and risk management plans.

Ideally, the various factors should be arranged in a logical order starting with the most important or overriding factor so that the discussion of one factor leads logically to the discussion of the next. A summary of major deductions may be a useful heading to include if the appreciation is complex.

All the relevant information must be weighted critically. Remember that factors stem from the best information available to you at the time. Factors include both the emotional and rational aspects of a problem – consider emotions as important qualitative factors upon which a decision may be based, but do not allow emotion to control decision making – rationally make a decision that might be based on emotional considerations. This requires self control and an understanding of the power of emotions.

Typical factors include constraints and freedom of action. The rule is that constraints are those limits imposed upon you by your leader or the organization. They are not those things that you decide should limit your actions as a result of considering other factors – this would be 'situating the appreciation'. Examination of constraints may provide additional essential tasks.

Other factors include risk and risk management, stakeholders (needs, wants, measures of success, etc), leadership and the leadership structure, people (morale, people's feelings, norms, numbers of people, capability, etc), the market (direction, expectations, share, etc), competitors (likely intentions, share, weaknesses, etc), customers, decisive points, tempo of work, distributors, suppliers, time, surprise, communication, logistics, strengths, weaknesses, opportunities, threats and so on.

Many people will be familiar with the SWOT technique. It helps in the analysis of problems but does not clarify your aim and purpose nor identify a preferred course of action. If the appreciation process is used with strengths, weaknesses, opportunities and threats considered as factors, you will have a far more powerful model that can be used at any stage of the organization's life, or at any level, and applied to any business problem. It creates a discipline of continuous self-analysis, and analysis of all the environmental factors influencing the market that the organization is in.

Strengths

- How strong and stable are your accounts?
- How strong is your market share?
- How stable is the market?
- How strong is your product range?
- How strong are your financial resources and reserves?
- How agile is your organization?
- How responsive, well-trained, engaged and well-led are your people?

Weaknesses

- Leadership?
- Corporate culture and norms?
- Structure, policy and processes, and behavioural consequences?
- Equipment and resources?
- Product range?
- Market share?
- Brand reputation and recognition?

Opportunities

- Increased market penetration?
- Alliances, partnerships, or voluntary mergers, to leverage strengths?

- New product development?
- Access other markets or market segments?
- New customer needs?

Threats

- Reduction in market share or profitability?
- Approaching product end of life?
- Departure of key staff and loss of knowledge?
- Government and legal restrictions?
- Technological changes and new competitors?
- Changes in customer expectations?

Weaknesses should not just be left as taboo subjects, recognized and not discussed. The root causes have to be traced back and the necessary changes have to be made which may include changing leaders' behaviour, or changing leaders if they are unable to adapt. Weaknesses may be a result of a shortage of space or insufficient capacity to meet demand, failure to meet market expectations of value and quality, unsuitable people in leadership roles and unskilled, uninterested front line employees, a mature market with a product life cycle in decline, high operating costs and cash flow problems, and ultimately poor leadership from the top.

Benchmarking is a useful process of performance comparison, part of the evaluation function of a leader. Comparison may be made to the past, numerical objectives, competitors, non-competing organizations and between internal business units. If this is done in tabular form on a spreadsheet, like Table 14.1, it is easy to share, amend and develop.

A common mistake is for people to confuse assumptions with deductions. If assumptions are treated as fact, the result is scenario planning, and a plan results that is valid only if those assumptions become fact. Additionally, people often say, 'We have to...' or 'We must...' rather than 'We could...' followed by 'What else could we do... ?' when deductions are being made. There are few deductions that result in a single option task, which a 'We must' statement implies. Raise a red flag if anyone says 'We must'!

TABLE 14.1 Factor headings

	Factor Heading	Information and Deductions	Outputs	Priority
1			Tasks, planning guidance, critical information requirements, risks, etc	
2				

TABLE 14.2 Factors for the estate agent

Factor Heading	Information and Deductions	Resulting Tasks	Priority
Sales and Marketing			
1 Strategic Marketing	Customer research suggests brand needs 'freshening' Little consistency in 'look' across branches Customers value localization	Appoint branding agency to review and refresh brand Produce 'brand equity' guidelines for branches without overdoing uniformity	1
2 Local/Tactical Marketing	Industry award created press profile and positive reaction in local markets	Develop local office marketing plans to leverage existing local press relationships	1=
3 Sales	New services to be offered will require branch staff to cross-sell rather than focus solely on their own transaction	Develop branch staff sales training programme Branch managers to be measured and to introduce measures to encourage cross selling Develop incentive programme to support cross selling	2

It may be that little is known about a factor therefore few, if any, meaningful deductions can be made. The obvious task is to gather the necessary information. This requires clear, specific questions to be constructed and the sources of information to be identified. The wrong question, or the well-intentioned but badly worded question, may result in lots of work and research that produces information – but not the information that is required. The intent of the question must be clear to those answering it.

For our notional estate agents, some of the factors might include those shown in Table 14.2.

c. Preliminary assessment of tasks

This section comes at the end of step 2. It is the assessment and prioritization of all the tasks or objectives that fall out of the deductions made in the analysis of the factors that make up the problem. In effect, it is a shopping list of 'ongoing operational work and one-off jobs to do and projects to complete' in order of priority. It is possible that each 'job to do' itself will have a number of options.

It is also likely that, when concurrent actions are totalled, there will be insufficient resources to carry them out. Two options are then open: divide the task into phases/stages; or set ruthless priorities and go for economic courses of action. It is often helpful here to group together all the discrete tasks into logical 'task groups' or projects, and those into functional lines of operation or work-streams.

3. Courses of action (CoA) and comparison

   a Identify the options or complete courses of action open – how the mission may be achieved.

   b Compare advantages and disadvantages of different CoAs.

A CoA is a phased sequence of tasks and their method of attainment, which combine to achieve the mission. A CoA may be regarded as an outline plan or 'concept of operations'. As a very simple example, a military assault on an enemy position might have six options: an attack on the left or right flank or a helicopter landing at the rear of the enemy position, undertaken in daylight or at night. Within each of these options there will be phased sequence of tasks.

Each part of a problem will have its own options for its resolution, and the different combinations of these options, or different grouping and sequencing of the identified tasks, produce the different CoAs that enable the whole problem to be solved or the mission to be achieved.

In this step, list the outline of each practical CoA open to you that you have identified. These might be visually represented, as shown in Table 14.3. Against each CoA you must also list the advantages and disadvantages. It would be very unusual (or even wrong) to arrive at this stage with only one CoA open. If this happens to you, you have probably wrongly dismissed a practical CoA. Weighting key factors, piloting and modelling, as well as judgement and experience, are methods to enable the CoAs to be compared.

If information and therefore the resulting deductions relating to factors are missing, it may still be possible to identify several CoAs in very broad outline. It is then possible to link the questions that need to be answered to each option if that option

TABLE 14.3 Weighing up the options

CoA	CoA Description	Advantages	Disadvantages
1			
2			

is to be fully understood. This is useful because you may find that higher levels of leader rule out certain options for reasons that you were not aware of. You can then expend effort in answering only those questions that are linked to options acceptable to that higher level of leader.

4. The leader's decision

a. Selection of the best CoA

This section of the appreciation is the culmination of the whole argument. Now is the time to weigh one CoA against another and make a decision. This section must finish with a definite decision or recommendation to a more senior leader on the CoA to adopt. Remember that the decision is the leader's sole responsibility – whether it is delegated, made consultatively or not.

b. Involvement in the decision

The involvement of team members in the decision making depends upon a number of factors:

- (confidential) information about the 'higher intent' that the leader alone knows;
- time;
- leader's expertise;
- importance of teamwork;
- importance of the decision;
- the nature of the subject under discussion;
- team members' level of 'skill and will'.

While these factors may influence how the decision is made, under normal conditions all team members could and should be involved in the previous three steps of mission analysis, factor analysis, and identification of CoAs.

The leader is usually the person held accountable for a decision and its consequences and may choose a style from a continuum of decision-making options based upon the above factors. If team members' ability (behaviour and attitude, skill and knowledge) is the main consideration in choosing a decision-making style, then Figure 14.3 is a useful guide.

Decision-making style:

- *Organized*. Accountable person collates information then makes the decision and informs others of it.
- *Purposeful*. Accountable person collates information with input from others then makes the decision.
- *Considerate*. Everyone is involved in making the decision.
- *Inspirational*. Accountable person delegates decision authority to others, having briefed others on situation, higher intent, constraints, limitations and freedom of action.

FIGURE 14.3 Decision-making style

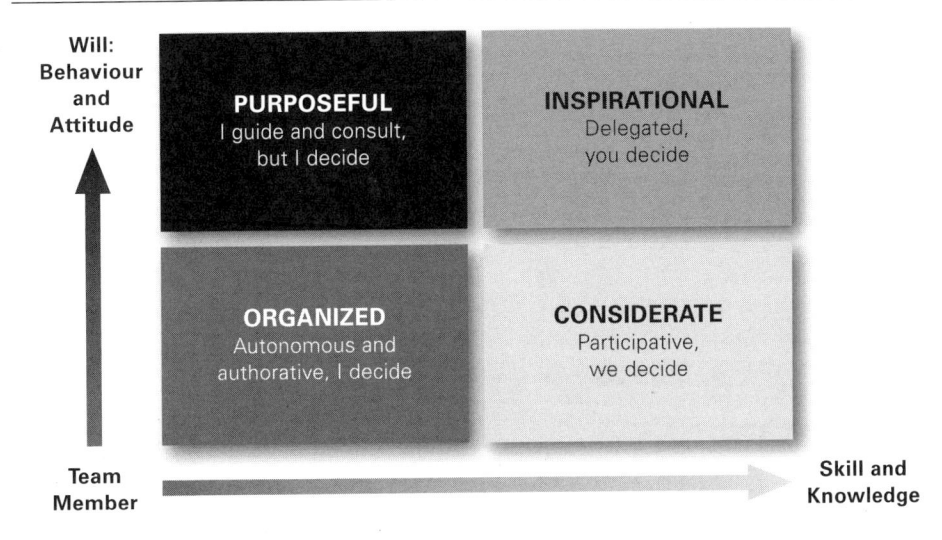

Will: Behaviour and Attitude ↑

PURPOSEFUL I guide and consult, but I decide	**INSPIRATIONAL** Delegated, you decide
ORGANIZED Autonomous and authoritative, I decide	**CONSIDERATE** Participative, we decide

Team Member → Skill and Knowledge

© Jeremy Tozer, 1997–2007

CASE STUDY Investment bank chief executive's decision-making style

I worked with the CEO of an investment bank on and off for a year, one of the sharpest and most intelligent CEOs I've met. He thought he was very participative and couldn't understand why the top team disliked him so much. I observed several meetings. In every decision that was made, he gave the impression that team consensus was sought: 'What do you think we should do?' he asked. In many cases he over-ruled their view and gave his (different) decision (which always had a good reason behind it).

All the team wanted was for him to set the right expectations for decision making – were they going to make it with consensus or did he only want their input? With his 'neck on the block' the team were quite happy for him to reserve decision-making authority after they offered him advice. It was 'being misled' in the process that annoyed them so much. Once I made this known to him it was easily rectified and working relationships improved considerably.

Note that the problem solving (mission analysis, factor analysis, develop COAs) might also be done in any of the above styles – with a different style reserved for the actual decision. What is important is that the leader sets the right expectations for how the decision is going to be made. Do not consult, let people think that the decision is theirs and then make your own decision!

The ACE Conditions for Success: Clarity

FIGURE 14.4 Schematic plan format

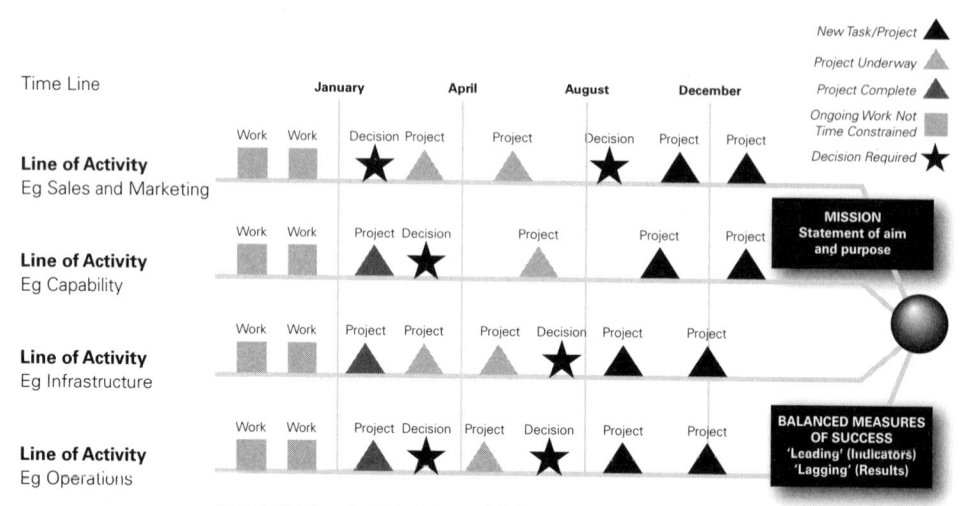

Time Line	January	April	August	December	
					New Task/Project ▲
					Project Underway ▲
					Project Complete ▲
Line of Activity Eg Sales and Marketing	Work Work	Decision Project ★ ▲	Project ▲	Decision Project ★ ▲	Project ▲
					Ongoing Work Not Time Constrained ■
					Decision Required ★
Line of Activity Eg Capability	Work Work	Project Decision ▲ ★	Project ▲	Project ▲	Project ▲
					MISSION Statement of aim and purpose
Line of Activity Eg Infrastructure	Work Work	Project Project ▲ ▲	Project Decision ▲ ★	Project ▲	Project ▲
Line of Activity Eg Operations	Work Work	Project Decision ▲ ★	Project Decision ▲ ★	Project ▲	Project ▲
					BALANCED MEASURES OF SUCCESS 'Leading' (Indicators) 'Lagging' (Results)

'Lines of Activity' are reflected in structure; each line has an accountable leader. 'Squares and triangles' represent projects or logical groupings of tactical tasks, each with an accountable leader.
Each line and 'square or triangle' will be subject to the same cycle of the appreciation, planning and briefing in order to maintain alignment and engagement.

© Jeremy Tozer, 1997–2007

Task and time schematic plan

Having chosen a CoA, it may now be summarized and disseminated on a simple, easy to assimilate visual 'task and time synchronization matrix' such as that shown in Figure 14.4. It is a form of Gantt chart, but one that results from rigorous and clear thinking rather than one that is populated at random by brainstorming, which is what often occurs. In military circles, it is often referred to as a 'campaign plan schematic'.

Here the triangles are logical groupings of related tasks (both projects and ongoing operational work), which themselves have been placed in sequence along 'lines of activity' or 'themes of work'. Each line and task group should have a leader responsible for the achievement of that line and task. Each task group leader will apply the appreciation process to clarify what their mission is and how their line and task group mission may be completed. If the structure of the organization, in broad terms, does not reflect the logical organization of tasks, then the plan is not likely to be executed effectively or efficiently. Organizational structure should facilitate making things happen, rather than prevent it. A chart such as the one in Table 14.4 provides detail to support the schematic plan.

Now revert to our mythical chain of estate agents and property managers. The 'task organization' quickly suggested a logical organization structure reflected in this organizational plan. CoAs really relate to the different ways of executing each task or project; which is the next level down in the cascade of aligned thought and action.

The visual plan, shown in Figure 14.5, is supported by a document outlining the aim, purpose, detailed tasks, by who and by when for each of the projects, 'task

The Appreciation

TABLE 14.4 Detail supporting the schematic plan

Serial	Project or Task Group Name and Mission (The 'triangles and squares')	Detailed Tasks	By Who	By When
	Determined by mission analysis of tasks resulting from the strategic appreciation	Result from appreciation applied to the project mission at left		
		a. b.		
		a. b.		

FIGURE 14.5 Example campaign plan

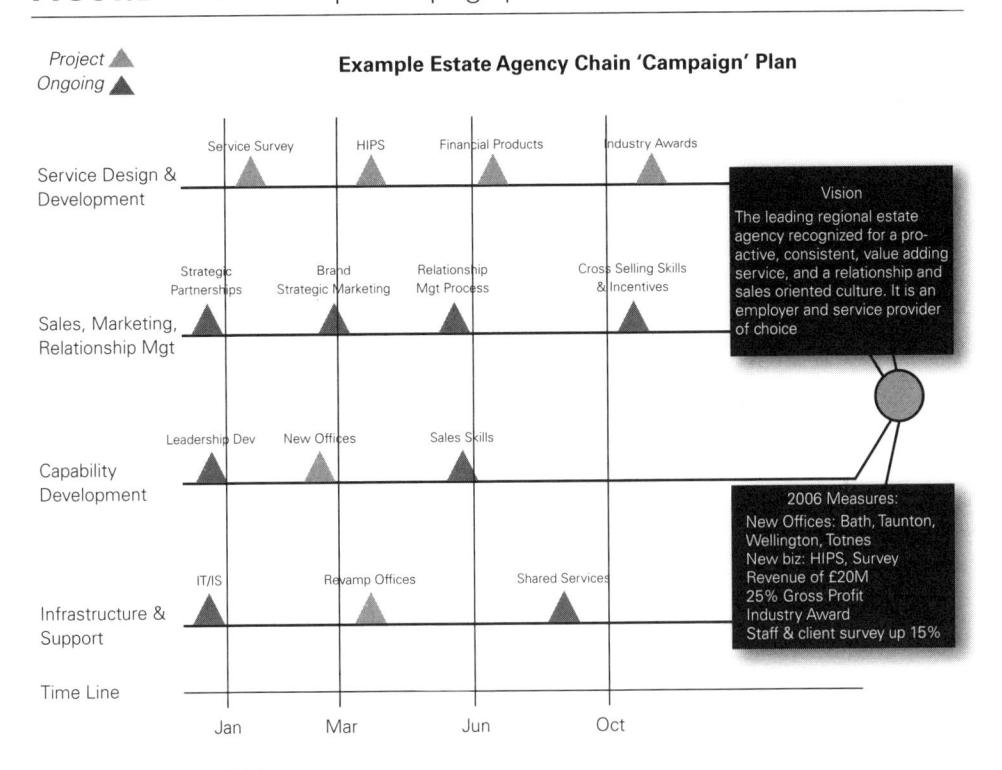

Example Estate Agency Chain 'Campaign' Plan

Project ▲
Ongoing ▲

Service Design & Development: Service Survey, HIPS, Financial Products, Industry Awards

Sales, Marketing, Relationship Mgt: Strategic Partnerships, Brand Strategic Marketing, Relationship Mgt Process, Cross Selling Skills & Incentives

Capability Development: Leadership Dev, New Offices, Sales Skills

Infrastructure & Support: IT/IS, Revamp Offices, Shared Services

Time Line: Jan, Mar, Jun, Oct

Vision
The leading regional estate agency recognized for a pro-active, consistent, value adding service, and a relationship and sales oriented culture. It is an employer and service provider of choice

2006 Measures:
New Offices: Bath, Taunton, Wellington, Totnes
New biz: HIPS, Survey
Revenue of £20M
25% Gross Profit
Industry Award
Staff & client survey up 15%

© Jeremy Tozer, 1997–2005

TABLE 14.5 Supporting document for the campaign plan

Project or Task Group & Mission (Aim & Purpose)	Detailed Tasks	By Who	By When
1 Strategic Marketing: Define and communicate brand; in order to build brand recognition, loyalty and equity	• Define differentiators and brand values • Review branding guide and toolkit for corporate and branch use • Redesign corporate website and simplify navigation, improve experience • Develop corporate brand advertising plan • Engage branches and customers in the process • etc	Marketing Director	
2 Strategic Marketing: Facilitate branch development and execution of local marketing plans; in order to build local and corporate brand equity	• Develop adaptable templates with branches for local use • Review branch office décor and customer experience • Clarify expectations for staff at branch level through branch managers • Train branch staff and coach the application of tools • etc	Marketing Director and Branch Managers	
3 etc	• etc		

groups' or lines of ongoing 'operational work' (in other words the output of appreciations made for each task or project).

Time for decision making and planning

This process is not designed to ensure that decision making and planning activity are conducted to the nth degree. It exists to assist you to make the *best possible decision you can with the time that you have available.* The very best quality decision that is made too late is less use than an 80 per cent decision that is made in a timely fashion. Do not be a slave to the process; the process is there to help you sharpen the clarity and scope of your thinking.

There is a difference between decision making and planning. Decision making as we have shown involves clarifying the mission, identifying outline courses of action and selecting one. Planning involves decision making, and adding detail to the selected course of action to produce an executable plan. This is then briefed to those who will execute it. They in turn may need to go through the same cycle of decision making, planning and briefing at their level.

If the nature of the subject about which you are producing a plan requires something to be achieved by a particular date, for instance planning the launch of a new product, then the planning rule of thumb is that you should use one-third of time available for decision making and planning at your level, before you brief other people and initiate their activity – the one-third/two-thirds rule. Within your one-third, about 30 per cent should be given to understanding the situation and the problem, 50 per cent to developing courses of action, and 20 per cent to producing and issuing formal direction (your plan and briefing).

Do not wait until the end of the decision-making and planning process to initiate activity if there are things that need to be done, whatever overall course of action is adopted, that you may initiate sooner. Warn people as soon as possible so that they might initiate concurrent activity and not suffer undue haste, and conduct their own anticipatory planning. The challenge is to strike a balance between providing too little information too late, and inundating junior leaders with a succession of evolving and possibly contradictory directions.

Balanced measures

Many readers will be familiar with the concept of the 'balanced scorecard'[2] conceived by Kaplan and Norton. This provides a measurement framework that adds non-financial performance measures that are of strategic importance to the traditional financial measures that organizations use to assess performance – part of its purpose is to ensure that financial measures are not achieved at the expense of doing things that enable long-term performance. It suggests that measures are created, and data is collected and analysed, to view the organization and its activity from four perspectives:

1. The learning and growth perspective (employee skills, knowledge, behaviour and attitudes, and corporate culture).
2. The business process perspective (efficiency and effectiveness in exceeding customer expectations and in enabling the organization to operate internally).
3. The customer perspective (the value offered to the customer, customer needs and satisfaction).
4. The financial perspective (traditional financial measures, risk assessments and cost-benefit analyses).

While this is an entirely sensible idea, these measures are not necessarily derived from an integrated decision-making and planning process. If the appreciation is used to determine an organization's strategic plan (which, if it is to be of any use, will include all those elements that contribute to an organization's success), then a schematic plan provides a sound base for deriving balanced measures. Such measures may be used to populate a four-quadrant scorecard, such as that envisaged by Kaplan and Norton or, more logically, measures and leading indicators derived from the key tasks and projects on each line of activity on the schematic plan together with financial measures.

Subsequent review of the appreciation

When you think you have finished making your appreciation of a problem, you should see if it stands up to the following tests:

- Is the reasoning valid?
- Have you 'situated the appreciation' (used preconceived ideas and false assumptions) or have you truly appreciated the situation?
- Have you made valid deductions?
- Is the sequence logical?
- Is everything relevant to the mission included; has anything been forgotten?
- Is it free from vagueness, ambiguity and prejudice and is it accurate?
- Will the plan achieve the mission?

Avoiding cognitive pitfalls

Mental hygiene and sound thinking habits can help the leader to avoid decision-making traps and pitfalls. These include:

- Maintaining an open mind.
- Embracing uncertainty and working with the grain of it.
- Using flexible frameworks, prompts and checklists to explore different ideas and perspectives.
- Separating assumptions from deductions.
- Challenging assumptions and norms.
- Always seeking more deductions and alternative CoAs; not stopping at the first good idea.
- Using competing CoAs and ideas rather than seeking evidence to support a preferred or preconceived CoA.
- Engaging in conversation with people who have different backgrounds and think differently, or are impartial observers.
- Using 'constructive conflict' to stimulate constructive thinking.
- Being emotionally intelligent, self-aware and externally aware in decision making.
- Checking for the effects of bias, habitual norms and ingrained shortcuts.

Appreciations at the strategic level

It should be borne in mind that this level of thinking is not really based upon 'scale or quantity' but on 'complexity'.

Four questions

At the strategic level, the executive leader has essentially four broad questions to answer:

Q1. What is the current situation and what are its features? (Framing the context, both internally for the organization and externally as it affects the organization.)

Q2. What are we trying to achieve and/or how should a more favourable situation be described? (Framing the problem: defining the end-state or outcome, often known as the 'vision'.)

Q3. What means do I have at my disposal? (Framing the problem: available means will limit achievable outcomes.)

Q4. How will I deploy those means to achieve specific objectives, milestones, changes or outcomes? (Balancing ends and means to define the strategic plan to achieve the end-state.)

As Lt Gen Andrew Graham pointed out in a recent discussion with me (he is the erstwhile Director General of the Defence Academy of the United Kingdom), the first question means:

understanding the situation in which you and your organization find yourselves and in which the challenges that you face are framed. Not the situation you think you are in, want to be in, hope to be in, planned to be in or wish you were in but the one you actually are in. This involves searching questions, thorough personal analysis and a recognition that the answers could be extremely unpalatable.

These four questions are not sequential and linear. Q1 will lead to Q2, but consideration of Q3 may lead to an amendment to the answer to Q2 if the ways and means available clearly are not sufficient to achieve the aim.

Strategy managers

Many commercial organizations have 'strategy managers' whose role is to work on strategic plans, almost independent of the CEO. Given their level of responsibility and authority, they will never have the same view of the organization, its operating context and so on that the CEO will have and it is wrong for a CEO to delegate all strategic planning to such managers.

The CEO has to undertake the mission analysis, or at least give sufficient direction for the planning team to conduct an initial mission analysis that the CEO will then confirm. A more effective way of using planning staff is shown in Figure 14.6.

FIGURE 14.6 Planning with a staff system

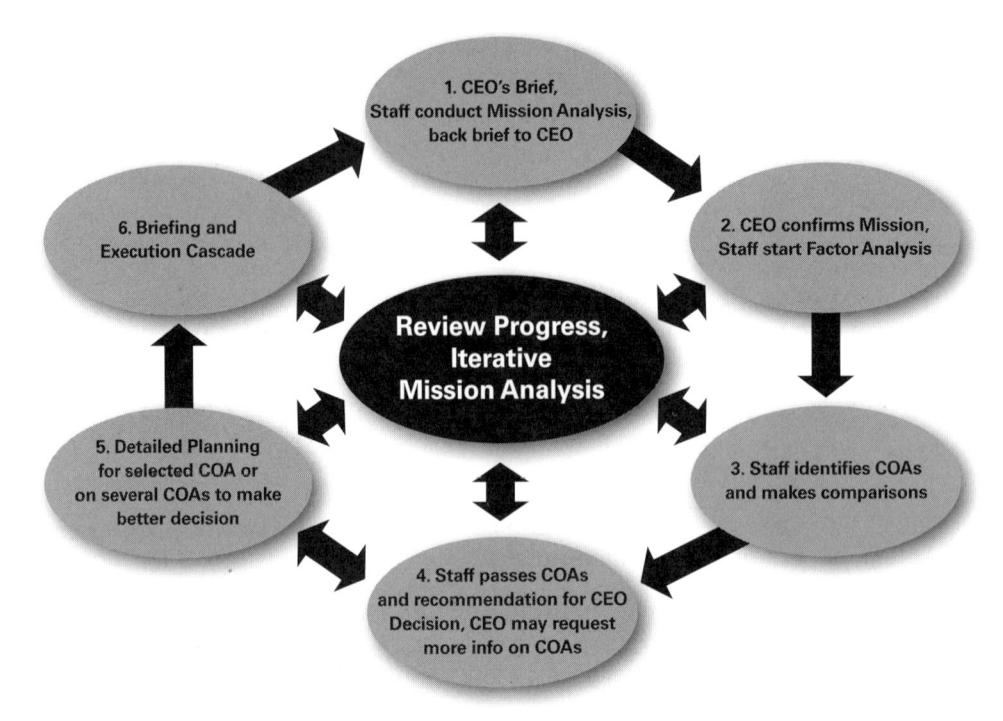

```
            1. CEO's Brief,
       Staff conduct Mission Analysis,
            back brief to CEO

6. Briefing and                    2. CEO confirms Mission,
Execution Cascade                  Staff start Factor Analysis

              Review Progress,
                 Iterative
              Mission Analysis

5. Detailed Planning               3. Staff identifies COAs
for selected COA or                and makes comparisons
on several COAs to make
better decision

         4. Staff passes COAs
     and recommendation for CEO
     Decision, CEO may request
         more info on COAs
```

© Jeremy Tozer, 2007

The sequence is effectively the same as a normal appreciation at a lower level, but a process in which more people are involved in parts of the process. When the staff identify the CoAs open, the CEO may request more information about one or more of them in order to properly understand them.

Situation analysis

Just as constraints and limitations in mission analysis at lower levels of leadership decision making help to define the mission, and then reappear as factors that lead to 'tasks', so too will an initial situational analysis that frames the context reappear under factors for further consideration at the strategic level – this is not a linear process. This framing includes a clear understanding of the (external) operating context, the competitive market (and its drivers and its direction – the shape the market is taking, how it is likely to look some years into the future), and the socio-economic and geo-political, technical, legal and governance, customer and/or consumer and risk environments.

Internally this means have a realistic grasp of your organization's strengths, weaknesses, actual capability and weaknesses (especially cultural: people and leadership) – the view that external and dispassionate consultants might take, rather than a rose-tinted internal view influenced by the ego's defence mechanisms. You also need an accurate assessment of the capability and effectiveness of any strategic partners with whom you are engaged.

Mission analysis

At the strategic level, the following questions need to be answered in defining the mission (the statement combining the aim or overall intent, and its purpose – see earlier paragraphs):

- *What is the desired future end-state or vision?* This may be an enduring and favourable situation. At the corporate level, and depending upon the nature of your business, when the organization is close to achieving the vision, it may need to be reset. All thinking and activity will then be directed towards realizing this vision, which needs to be clear and inspiring to galvanize people into action. This end-state should be determined from your analysis of the existing situation and be realistic. Visions that have a basis in 'the dreamtime' and unbounded blue-sky thinking are rarely achieved, and usually build cynicism and erode confidence – especially when resourcing is inadequate from the outset.

- *What is the organization's purpose, its reason for being?* While the end-state or vision may be achieved and changed, the organization's purpose, its fundamental reason for existing, need not change if it has been carefully thought through. A purpose should act as a perpetual beacon for people, because it is a sense of 'noble purpose' (the reason why something is to be done) rather than objectives (what is to be achieved) that really motivates the majority of people. Is the purpose of a pharmaceutical company, for example, simply to make profits for investors, or to improve the quality of life for people and in the process make a profit for both reinvestment and a return to shareholders? If you were going to work for a company, which purpose would inspire you more? This takes some soul-searching by executive teams and boards. If some of the old shipping lines had thought their purpose was to transport people rather than operate a fleet of ships, they might have invested in aviation and survived.

- *What are the organization's strategic objectives,* perhaps expressed as decisive conditions, the achievement of which, will indicate that the vision or end-state has been achieved?

- *What effects do you wish to have* on:
    - Governments and regulators?
    - Partners in your 'ecosystem'?
    - Investors?
    - Employees?
    - The communities in which you operate?
    - Customers and end-user consumers?

- *What constraints and freedom of action do you have?* Putting aside the constraints of finance, resources, regulation and so on, consider espoused organizational values. Unless you intend to develop (or reinforce!) employee cynicism, values need to be 'lived' and reflected in your decision choices. Remember constraints are also considered as factors.

Factors

There are some significant factors that may well need to be included in decision making and planning at the strategic level. Many people may be familiar with a PEST analysis (political, economic, sociological, and technical). This may be extended with legal and governance, competitors, the physical environment, risks (strategic risks and uncertainty were highlighted in Chapter 1), centre of gravity (explained on page 330), and customers, products and value (explored on pages 331–34). As stated earlier, mission analysis does not flow into an assessment of factors in a linear fashion – it is entirely possible that the ways and means that are at your disposal are insufficient to achieve your desired end-state. Therefore, either your ways and means must be increased, or the scope of your desired end-state, strategic objectives, desired effects and so on, must be scaled back. The factors to consider include:

- *Political environment.* National or local government policy, the interests of major 'power groups' and so on, can affect the rules of conducting business. The instability of a government, and the presence of corruption, can affect an organization's very viability.
- *Economic environment, finance and its management.* The dynamics of markets, capital, inflation, interest rates, currency values, state of national economies and so on, which affect demand for your product or service. Do you depend on a few major accounts, are you as recession-proof as possible, what 'shock waves' are on the way? This environment is complex and it may help categorizing the components into those that give primary and secondary effects.
- *Social environment.* The cultural patterns, values, beliefs and preferences that dictate people's behaviour and attitudes. What broad social changes or issues may affect your product's attractiveness? Increasingly communities, via the media and politicians, have influence or control over your 'licence to operate' if you are perceived not to be a responsible organization.
- *Technological environment.* Those events, trends and solutions available that can improve your capability to deliver and to add value. Technology may well assist your competitors, and may even make your product obsolete. Breakthroughs may lead to restructuring. Are you aware of the effect that emerging, or developing, technology may have on your business?
- *Legal and governance environment.* The pattern of law-making activity, existing laws and regulations, governance (or lack of) and corruption.
- *Competitor environment.* The identity, current state, likely intentions, motives, strengths, weaknesses and so on, of those that you compete with.

Competition may also be indirect. Other organizations may do things that induce customers to do less business with you.

- *Your organization's effectiveness and capability.* This includes the conceptual, moral and physical components outlined in Chapter 1. Briefly, these are the thought processes within an organization, the ability to align and engage people (leadership), and the means to operate (anything bought or hired).
- *The physical environment.* The physical surroundings of an organization – the availability of resources, proximity to population centres, and effects of local geography, climate (and change) and like matters.
- *Global risks* (see Chapter 1):
  - economic disparity and global imbalances;
  - governance failures;
  - currency volatility, fiscal crises and asset price collapse within and between countries;
  - illegal economy: illicit trade, organized crime and corruption;
  - water, food, energy, security;
  - finite limit of natural resources;
  - climate change;
  - demographic change;
  - geopolitical and societal tensions.
- *Centre of gravity.* Examining the centre of gravity (see next page) focuses attention on the decisive factor(s), which usually means exploiting specific market opportunities, specific competitor weaknesses or your own specific strengths (or minimizing your own weaknesses or guarding against specific risks).
- *Strategic partners.* A realistic understanding of the capability, strengths, weaknesses and limitations of any strategic business partners with whom you are engaged in pursuit of a common aim and purpose is also essential. This is where a jointly conducted mission analysis is essential – as soon as partners' objectives and purpose start to diverge, the harder it becomes for people at the tactical level to work effectively with partner staff and to make any headway. Remember that these partner organizations will be suffering from the same sources of internal friction that you are.
- *Internal capability.* A realistic, honest and dispassionate understanding of the capability, strengths, weaknesses, limitations and deployable assets and resources of your own organization is essential if you are to balance the means at your disposal with the definition of the end-state, aim, purpose, strategic objectives and desired effects. This includes understanding your organization's leadership capability, since it is leadership at every level that makes anything happen. It is very tempting for executives to wear rose-tinted spectacles when looking at their organization's internal capability, because anything less than ideal will inevitably reflect on what they have or have not done as executive leaders in the past.

Centre of gravity

Centre of gravity is another Clauszwitzian concept. In the business sense it is that characteristic, or capability, from which an organization derives its freedom of action, corporate power and competitive advantage. A centre of gravity may not always be tangible and, at the strategic level, may be an abstraction such as morale, confidence or brand reputation as much as a capability such as organizational agility or an asset or differentiator such as intellectual property or strong channel partner relationships and dominance of third-party referrals. An organization's centre of gravity may change as plans unfold and progress is made towards achieving whatever the end-state is.

In a bipolar competition, an enterprise should identify and undermine the opponent's centre of gravity while protecting their own. In a competitive market, an organization should exploit the advantage given by its own centre of gravity while minimizing the competitive advantage that others in the market derive from their own. A matrix such as the example in Table 14.6 illustrated with an example, may help in making deductions about centre of gravity and its implications:

TABLE 14.6 Centre of gravity matrix

Own Centre Of Gravity Product capability and reliability	**Own Critical Capabilities** R&D expertise
Competitor A: Centre Of Gravity Low-cost production	**Competitor A: Critical Capabilities** Low labour costs, and R&D cycle times and cost reduced through industrial espionage
Own Critical Vulnerabilities Offshore production security Channel partner relationships	**Own Critical Requirements** Retain technological lead Enhance brand reputation Strengthen channel partner relationships
Competitor A critical vulnerabilities Genuine R&D weakness 'Loyalty' of overseas sales force	**Competitor A critical requirements** Develop sales force and channel partner relationships Maintain production cost advantage

Let us assume that your company is a United States-based internetworking vendor whose routers have proved to be both highly effective and extremely reliable, with a working life way in excess of what was anticipated. Your product sales force is also very effective, and during the early years of your rapid growth when increases in product sales were almost exponential, your business strategy allowed channel partners, who were selling service and spare parts on your behalf, to develop strong relationships with the end user. Your major competitor is based in a large, state-controlled Asian country where the costs of production are very low in comparison to yours. Within weeks of you releasing a new product your competitor releases a remarkably similar product with a remarkably similar part number – indeed its corporate logo is also remarkably similar to yours! It would appear that it engages in reasonably sophisticated industrial espionage on a large scale.

The deductions you might reasonably draw from considering your centre of gravity as a factor in your strategic appreciation are:

- You must retain and increase your technological lead, which includes retaining key personnel.
- You must enhance and exploit your brand, and strengthen and leverage your channel partner relationships to minimize the impact of a low-cost competitor with a similar product offering. This might include ethical and legal tactics that effectively prevent your competitor's sales force from developing channel partner relationships.
- You must add increased value to differentiate your products (see the 'value-created' and 'value-captured' levels of product value below). This may include up-skilling the sales force to sell consulting services and solutions design, rather than continuing to sell at the value-offered and value-added levels.
- Your talent acquisition team might consider headhunting key individuals from your competitor's sales force.
- Your organization must take security more seriously and improve physical security, security policy and procedures, and security intelligence – one of the greatest threats to security is the failure of people to recognize that any threat to security actually exists.

Customer/consumer

This spans the identity, wants, needs, behaviours, values and so on, of those who buy from you. This includes not only the demographic/psychographic truths about end-user consumers, but recognizes that customers can include buyers who represent groups or organizations such as government departments, other companies, and so on.

The customer value model defines the value that a supplier provides from a customer's point of view. That is, what an organization needs to provide to win and maintain customer accounts. This is derived from careful customer research, and there may be one for each major customer. The value may not be inherently in the product itself or what is delivered, but rather what it can do for the customer by assisting in achieving a desired outcome. For example, in our homes we want electricity, not for its own sake, but for what it can do in creating light and power to operate appliances. Therefore, it is the total perception of value, the mindset of the customer that is important.

Karl Albrecht[3] proposed a hierarchy of customer value that is analogous to Maslow's hierarchy of needs. This hierarchy of customer value has four levels. In ascending order they are:

1. *Basic.* The fundamental components of your customer value package required just to be in business.
2. *Expected.* Features and benefits that your customers consider 'normal' for you and your competitors.
3. *Desired.* Added-value features that customers know about and would like to have, but do not necessarily expect because of the current market and your competitors' offerings. This is the first level of possible differentiation and superiority over your competitors.
4. *Unanticipated.* Added-value features that go well beyond expectations and results from the customer's experience of doing business with you. It may be unusually fast turnaround, an unusually confidence-inspiring guarantee, unusual expertise on the part of your employees, advanced features, and so on. These are 'surprise' features that can set you apart from your competitors and win you the loyalty of customers – if, of course, they really do add significant value in the eyes of your customers.

The customer value package may be thought of as having the following elements:

- *Environmental:* the physical setting in which the customer experiences buying (and possibly using) the product.
- *Sensory:* the direct sensory experiences during purchase and use. This component includes sights, sounds, taste, smell, touch, emotional reactions, aesthetic features and the psychological ambience of the customer environment.
- *Interpersonal:* the interaction the customer has with employees, partners/resellers and possibly with other customers, as part of the total experience. This includes friendliness, courtesy, helpfulness, physical appearance and apparent competence.
- *Procedural:* the procedures (and response times) that the customer experiences in dealing with your organization – such as the duplication of questions asked in dealing with call centres.
- *Deliverable:* anything the customer physically takes custody of during the buying, usage or service experience, even if only temporarily.
- *Informational:* receiving the information needed to function as a customer or product user.
- *Financial:* what is actually paid for the product value package underpinned by commitment to being the lowest-cost supplier within the concept of value offered.

Every enterprise should subject its customer value package to continual and critical scrutiny with the objective of constantly improving it. Using the components just described, enterprises can conduct a 'value audit' of the customer interface to see how well it performs. It is also important to get the direct input of customers in this audit in order to discover defects or opportunities not obvious to the leaders or their staff.

There are several ways to develop and retain customer access and the avenue or combination of avenues you choose must make sense for your line of business and the potential customers that might be interested. These are some of the common considerations:

- *Niche focus:* a narrowly defined product or service value proposition. A concentrated marketing effort may be directed and concentrated economically at a niche, but it may preclude developing a wider customer base.
- *Target customer:* a narrowly defined category, identified by common features. Existing channels may reduce the cost of reaching this customer base.
- *Product range:* a wide range of appropriate products enables a supplier to maximize the amount of business done with a single customer by exploiting the account and satisfying many different needs.
- *Wide customer base:* a mass-market approach. Proximity to customers (geographically or via the internet) and a means of brand differentiation are usually important.
- *Customer-access products:* a way of doing business that keeps the vendor in contact with the customer so that the vendor may make future sales without repeating the costs of sale.
- *Partnerships:* working with other organizations in the value chain to increase customer access and exploit strengths and investments. Partnerships usually succeed when the partners are not in competition and when each benefits directly from something that only the other partner has.
- *The account (or relationship management) system* that builds relationships and brand loyalty, seeks genuine and useful customer feedback, identifies and satisfies needs (repeat business), and retains active, growing accounts.

Products and services

Another way of looking at value is the hierarchy of product and service value reflected in the design, marketing and sale of products and services (which need to matched to the buying preferences or buying level of the customer – there is no point selling a value-creating service to a value-offered (features and benefits) junior level buyer). To paraphrase colleague and friend Dominic Rowsell:[4]

1 *Value offered.* The vendor simply makes products available, offering the value (features and benefits) to the channel partner and/or customer, who knows exactly what they want, and applies their knowledge to use and extract value from the vendor's products which they buy 'off the shelf'.

2 *Value added.* The vendor responds to a channel partner/customer who has defined their needs, and the vendor and/or partner add value to the customer by using their knowledge of the vendor's products and services, and knowledge of the customer's needs to build a 'simple' solution.

3 *Value created.* The buyer looks to the future with a sense of direction and seeks insights from a trusted supplier or vendor. The vendor creates value for the channel partner/customer by designing or facilitating the design of a unique solution to their problem (the Appreciation process is an ideal sales tool to engage a customer in solution design and to get inside their decision-making cycle). The vendor assumes responsibility for some risk.

4 *Value captured.* The buyer seeks a step-change and has sufficient confidence in the vendor to place themselves in the vendor's hands. Vendor, channel partner and/or customer capture value in a joint venture, sharing full risk and reward through next-generation products and services or organizational change (for example outsourcing call centres).

Risk

Risks and uncertainty were described in Chapter 1, and that will not be repeated here. Strategic risks are those events that impact upon or change the overall strategic context, and at worst they may prevent achievement of a strategic objective. At the time of writing, at least one media organization and one camera corporation are at strategic risk because of the actions or inaction of key executives. An operational or tactical risk may arise due to an act of ineffective planning, or ineffective execution.

In considering risks, the matrix in Table 14.7 may assist in identifying those risks that warrant the creation of risk management plans. The risk tolerance line is the lower edge of the shaded cells.

TABLE 14.7 Risk matrix

Impact	Likelihood				
	Very High	High	Medium	Low	Very Low
Very High	E	E	H	H	M
High	E	H	M	M	M
Medium	H	M	M	L	L
Low	M	M	L	L	L
Very Low	M	L	L	L	L

KEY
E Extremely high risk, mission failure likely
H High-risk, likely failure to achieve some objectives
M Moderate risk, probable mission success
L Low risk, little or no impact

Structure

When the campaign plan schematic was introduced a few pages back it was pointed out that it contained logical groupings of related tasks, sequenced along lines of activity (or themes of work). Let us repeat here that if the structure of the organization, in broad terms, does not reflect the logical organization of tasks, then the plan is not likely to be executed effectively or efficiently. Organizational structure should facilitate making things happen, rather than prevent it. The subject of organization and its design is the focus of Chapter 22.

Contingency planning

Assumptions are important in planning, particularly at the strategic level, as consideration is given to how events may evolve. There are two forms of contingency planning: branches and sequels.

A branch is a 'turning' from the main path (the original plan) that may be taken if certain conditions arise – an alternative way. A sequel is a subsequent plan that may be put into action on completion of a particular plan and/or the achievement of its objectives. A culminating point is that point during the campaign when current activity may be maintained but without the prospect of further progress. It will be necessary at this point to have a branch or sequel to follow.

In both cases, an appreciation should be conducted as previously outlined, but new or future factors are identified and assumptions made about them. The assumptions are treated as deductions to lead to the development of a recommended CoA, as shown in Figure 14.7. If the assumptions prove to be true, then the recommended

FIGURE 14.7 Contingency planning

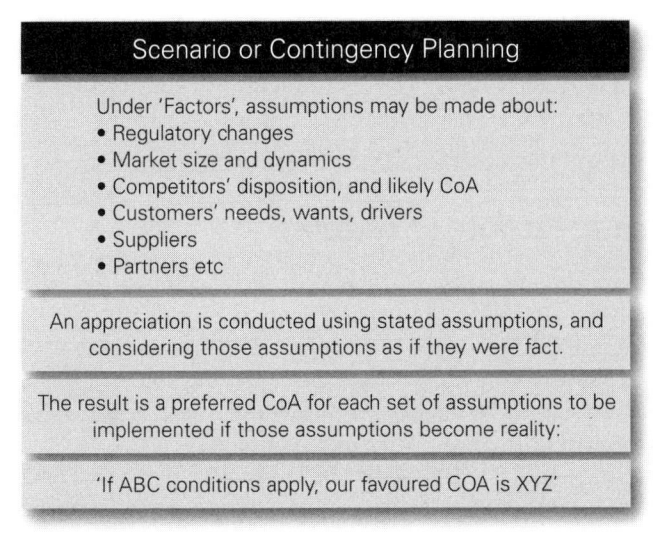

> **Scenario or Contingency Planning**
>
> Under 'Factors', assumptions may be made about:
> - Regulatory changes
> - Market size and dynamics
> - Competitors' disposition, and likely CoA
> - Customers' needs, wants, drivers
> - Suppliers
> - Partners etc
>
> An appreciation is conducted using stated assumptions, and considering those assumptions as if they were fact.
>
> The result is a preferred CoA for each set of assumptions to be implemented if those assumptions become reality:
>
> 'If ABC conditions apply, our favoured COA is XYZ'

© Jeremy Tozer, 1997–2007

CoA holds good – but only if the assumptions turn out to be 'real'. When reasonable assumptions are made, there is at least a basis for future planning and action without causing unnecessary delay.

'Selection and maintenance of the aim and its purpose' is a cardinal principal of business activity; it underpins any form of clarity and useful activity. Some schools of thought, especially in government circles, suggest that a clear aim is necessary but that it may not necessarily be maintained. The counter is that if an aim cannot be maintained then it should never have been selected in the first place. Decision making is not linear – mission analysis and deductions about ways and means are dynamic. An aim that is clearly beyond your means to achieve should never be selected; it erodes confidence and morale and leads to mission failure. Perhaps political expediency and ill-considered utterances are behind this government approach; one only needs to review how the 'mission' was changed in the Balkans and more recently in the Middle East to see political expediency at work.

Other problem-solving tools and techniques

Many people will have learnt many tools and techniques for problem solving, decision making and project management. The appreciation process does not make these redundant but is the foundation for all decision making. The four steps (mission analysis, problem/factor analysis, the comparison of courses of action open, decision) are 'basic first principles'. All that changes at different levels of leadership is that the number of variables, the unknowns and complexity of the problem increase. The process can still be applied.

Most if not all other tools for problem solving and decision making may be used within each of these four steps. For example:

- A SWOT analysis is really just a simplified and incomplete appreciation – strengths, weaknesses, opportunities and threats are just four factors.
- Brainstorming or mind mapping might be required to list the factors that need to be considered and may help to identify additional options after deductions have been made.
- CoAs may be modelled, weighted, piloted and so on.

Brainstorming – a note of caution

Brainstorming can often generate fewer ideas and less innovation than when people work individually for a period and then aggregate their individual thoughts. Working in a group environment can induce certain individuals to become intellectually idle, or 'group think' takes over, or people worry about being assessed by their colleagues. This can particularly apply to introverts, potentially some of the deepest thinkers in the group, who are less prone to projecting themselves.

Overall, 'group work' alone tends to be more effective when evaluating ideas, rather than in creating them. So leaders should ask their team members to produce their own solutions to problems (make their own appreciations) and then facilitate the integration of their individual work to produce a collective appreciation, with collective ownership of the adopted CoA.

The appreciation and personality types

In Myers-Briggs[5] typology, people's individual preferences and personality type are examined in four areas:

1. A focus on the outer world or your own inner world – how you are energized. This is called Extraversion (E) or Introversion (I).
2. A focus on 'basic information' that is absorbed, or on information to which meaning has been attached – what you pay attention to. This is called Sensing (S) or Intuition (N).
3. Do you prefer to think first about logic and consistency or people and circumstances – how you make decisions? This is called Thinking (T) or Feeling (F).
4. Do you prefer to get things decided or do you prefer to stay open to new information and options – how you live and work? This is called Judging (J) or Perceiving (P).

We all display parts of the whole model, but under pressure we have a preference for one type of each approach (sensing or intuition, thinking or feeling and so on).

Experience and typological research (including Jungian psychology) on the operation of the mind (as opposed to the brain) shows that the body and mind continuously carry out two operations – gathering information and ideas, and then evaluating them; life is just a continuous process of decision making with these two steps. The first part of gathering involves using the five senses to conduct an informal and loose form of mission and factor analysis, the second part of gathering involves using the sixth sense (the mind) to come up with ideas (a sort of 'identification of courses of action'), before evaluating them and coming to a conclusion (decision).

During the first two steps of the appreciation (mission analysis and factor analysis/deductions), the 'sensate' person relies on the five senses, while the 'intuitive' person uses a 'sixth sense' to gather information and look for patterns and meaning. In the comparison of options and decision-making steps, the 'thinking' person uses logic or IQ, while the 'feeling' person uses EQ (emotional quotient).

What the typological research warns us is that, depending on our personality type, we will have a predisposition for the types of thinking referred to earlier – this means that we may need to be reminded of our tendencies when making decisions. The appreciation, as an holistic process, helps to overcome our individual weaknesses while also giving us a collective process to follow.

In the appreciation, 'mission analysis' engages all, but especially the intuitive; 'factor analysis' naturally engages the sensate, 'Courses of action' engages the intuitive, and 'The decision' engages thinking for practical (business) consequences and feeling for the 'people' consequences. Therefore it naturally engages all types of personality (although at different stages) and the appreciation follows a 'natural process'– and could be said to be an high order process. It can thus be seen that the appreciation

TABLE 14.8 Personality types and effects

What energizes		Attracts attention	
Extroverted	**Introvert**	**Sensing**	**Intuition**
External	Internal	Five senses	Sixth sense
Outside thrust	Inside pull	What is real	What could be
Blurt it out	Hold it in	Practical	Theoretical
Breadth	Depth	Present	Future
People, things	Ideas, thoughts	Facts	Insights
Interaction	Concentration	Existing skills	New skills
Impulsive	Reflection	Utility	Novelty
		Step-by-step	Dart around

Deciding		Living	
Thinking	**Feeling**	**Judgement**	**Perception**
Head	Heart	Plan	Spontaneous
Logic	Values	Regulate	Flow
Objective	Subjective	Control	Adapt
Justice	Mercy	Settled	Tentative
Principles	Harmony	Organized	Flexible
Reason	Empathy	Decisive	Open
Firm but fair	Compassionate		

process when applied collectively will minimize any harmful effects of your own personality type that would distort your decision making, and when used by a group it is a powerful way of arriving at the 'best' decision.

Summary

Since this is arguably the most important and complex chapter in the book, and the one that makes the biggest difference to business performance, here is a short summary.

The four steps in the appreciation of a situation are:

1. Mission analysis.
2. Factor analysis.
3. CoA development and comparison.
4. Decision on the COA to adopt.

The essence of an appreciation is clear thought, critical examination and logical reasoning. Approach the task with an open, unprejudiced mind, do not 'situate the appreciation', that is, form a convenient plan from preconceived ideas and then bend the facts to fit it; rather, make a considered appreciation of the situation as it really is.

It is one of the paradoxes of human behaviour that as we get closer to making serious decisions the more we become assailed by doubts. Using this process minimizes the negative effects of doubt and lack of confidence that may affect the leader and be reflected in his or her team members.

The appreciation is designed as a formal but flexible form of a logical thought process that enables leaders and their teams to arrive at conclusions under the stress of business and the pressure of time. While it may feel cumbersome to use at first, with practice it simply becomes a way of thinking and dealing with issues, on a daily basis. If you can understand this decision-making process you are becoming proficient in one of the essential skills of a leader. Some people have an aptitude for clear thought under pressure, but this is something we must all develop.

The appreciation can be mental, oral or written. It is a logical sequence of reasoning, leading to the best solution to an operational, administrative, or personal problem. It is a process suitable for the supervisor and the CEO. What varies is the level of ambiguity, the timescale, and the number and complexity of factors and their implications – not the process itself. This assists in providing consistency, common language and understanding across an enterprise, and a process that people can grow with as their careers develop. Remember that a decision maker needs self-confidence, sound judgement and an understanding of implications as well as authority, trust and confidence in his or her colleagues to be effective and, thus, prevent bottlenecks in work flow.

As a leader you should not delegate making an entire appreciation of a task or mission given to you by your boss to a (subordinate) team member, since only you are far enough removed to view the whole in perspective. Only you, the leader, can complete the whole mission analysis – if others start it, you will need to complete or amend it and sign it off. You can delegate the factor analysis and development of CoAs to others (but again you should review them) – so people may be involved in all the steps. If mission and factor analysis and CoA development is guided and facilitated by you, you will be surprised at the level of buy-in – even from temporarily attached or virtual team members.

Since the identification of possible CoAs is arrived at through logic, not through factional interests, support is increased. If written, anyone reading the appreciation should arrive at the same conclusion unless the choice of options is a 'judgement call' or factors have been overlooked. It is therefore easy for a reader familiar with the format to spot errors and it is relatively simple to make the necessary changes to planning and actions, demonstrating the dynamic nature of the whole process.

One of the greatest advantages of following the process is that it develops constant awareness of 'the big picture' which, with maturation during a stretching career, can be termed 'vision' in the CEO. This is where part of the appreciation's power lies when instilled as a way of thinking: it continuously develops what some people call 'strategic thinking'.

The appreciation is *the* process by which all decisions should be made. The essence of an appreciation is clear thought, critical examination and logical reasoning.

Examples of appreciations

Rather than focus on corporate-level plans (which because of their scale can often be more generic in their appearance and less precise and meaningful to the reader), examples have been selected that illustrate both the appreciation process and the translation of divisional business plans into effective execution.

Strategic business and organization development plan

Situation

I was asked to assist Janet Ramey, an executive whom I had trained earlier in her career as a 'global high potential leader' in Cisco Systems in the United States, who was now promoted to lead the technical services/customer support website group (TS Web). The website contained over 60,000 pages, so not a small website! The division was newly formed by amalgamating business units and expanding the scope of their work. What was needed was a clear sense of direction, a clear purpose, and a strategic plan to clarify and align their work.

To start with, I trained Janet's leadership team and key individual contributors in the same leadership concepts, tools and techniques that she had learnt on the 'hi po' programme. I then facilitated an appreciation of their situation for three days after the training phase.

Mission analysis

In the absence of a clear briefing from a newly appointed Vice President (who was still in the process of creating clarity for himself), by pooling the collective knowledge distributed among TS Web's top team it was possible to create understanding of higher intent and so on to define their mission (to be confirmed with the VP via a back briefing). This was done through facilitated discussion following the sequence of mission analysis questions; the input from the top team was captured in real time in a spreadsheet and refined.

The parent technical services division higher intent might be summarized as:

- Enable customer 'self-help' support.
- Provide an engaging and productive customer experience.
- Improve productivity.
- Gain industry recognition and win awards.

At the corporate level the higher intent was:

- Increase customer satisfaction.
- Increase margin.
- Increase revenue.

The essential tasks were identified to be:

- Ensure effective knowledge management.
- Ensure a seamless user flow.
- Define user requirements and user experience.
- Increase margin and revenue.
- Maximize TS web capacity.

After some discussion the mission was agreed upon. This was later back briefed to the VP who was very pleasantly surprised at the level of clarity created by the mission analysis process in the absence of a clear and specific briefing being given to Janet and her team.

Factor analysis

After the mission analysis had been completed, we proceeded with factor analysis on the assumption that the mission would be signed off on back briefing (if it wasn't, the factor analysis and subsequent CoAs could be readily amended based on the outcome of the back briefing, but there was no need to delay further work).

A list of factors was brainstormed individually then collated. The factors included:

- People (capacity, skills audit, morale, development needs, etc).
- Resources (money, time, vendors, IT, etc).
- Clarity (measures, industry standards, customer satisfaction needs, etc).
- Systems.
- Stakeholders (key executives, internal business units, sub-contractors and so on).

Some of the factors and the deductions made from them, which took two days to analyse initially, are shown in Table 14.9. The final list of tasks resulting from this was then prioritized.

Course of action development

The list of about 120 tasks and projects were grouped into clusters, then further grouped into lines of activity known to the team as 'Tracks'. Several cluster and track options were examined, and the option chosen best reflected the core expertise and time-availability of the key people within each track team. The management structure was then clarified and altered to reflect these tracks to enable effective execution of the plan.

Execution

The schematic in Figure 14.8 was supported with a detailed spreadsheet containing:

- the mission analysis, 'sub-tasks' and priorities for each of the task groups above,
- the task dependencies, coordination and control measures, deadlines and leading indicators of success,
- the names of accountable people, and the resources allocated to them.

The ACE Conditions for Success: Clarity

TABLE 14.9 Factors, deductions and tasks

Factor List factors affecting the problem	Information Ask 'So what/therefore?' and record deductions and deductions of deductions	Tasks What tasks result from deductions?

Headcount	Limited, limits work we can do, forces us to choose, forces us to analyse and then communicate
	
	Global, geographically dispersed and culturally different. Communication issues exist
		1 Create rapid analysis team (RAT), ensure deployment is to most successful activities
		2 Develop communication plan:
		  a Formal cascade briefing system
		  b Face to face routine briefings
		  c Common terminology
		  d Improve e-mail usage
		3 Rollout appreciation methodology

Current capabilities and skills and staff turnover	Many people recently hired, some remain 'unknown' High use of expensive contractors High turnover largely due to lack of career and professional development	1 Make inventory of current skills and capabilities 2 Identify future needs, gap analysis 3 Create and implement professional skills and career development plan 4 Review training and development needs in conjunction with leaders' quarterly performance management meetings
Management Information System: C3	Our eyes into TS and drives our knowledge management. If we can't modify C3 or get modifications made we won't be able to meet our commitments – especially increasing customer satisfaction	1 Increase our visibility in the C3 steering committee 2 Engage VP in supporting our C3 enhancement requests 3 Analyse our plans re C3 and highlight all areas where we are dependent on C3

TABLE 14.9 *continued*

Factor List factors affecting the problem	Information Ask 'So what/therefore?' and record deductions and deductions of deductions	Tasks What tasks result from deductions?
Website search	Search doesn't meet customer expectation	1. Provide personalized search based on customer segments and profile 2. Simplify customer search to enable customer success 3. Improve ability to return appropriate content
Navigation	Navigation is not easy, it is not personalized and it detracts from the ideal customer experience	1. Provide personalized navigation based on customer segments 2. Investigate task-based navigation 3. Define information requirements, collect and process to better understand customer needs and expectations

This one-page schematic made it possible for everyone, at a glance, to understand the division's work, their team's role within that and the sequence of activities and dependencies between tasks and projects.

The results

The following were Janet's observations of the benefits of this approach to decision making and planning:

- A clear aligned plan resulted, owned by those whose job it was to execute it.
- It clarified roles and responsibilities of existing and new positions in the group.
- The simple one-page schematic made it easy to communicate (internally and externally) and raise awareness of TS Web's direction and contribution.
- It enabled identification of personnel with skills and personal goals not matched to the 'new' organization for redeployment.

FIGURE 14.8 TS Web strategic plan

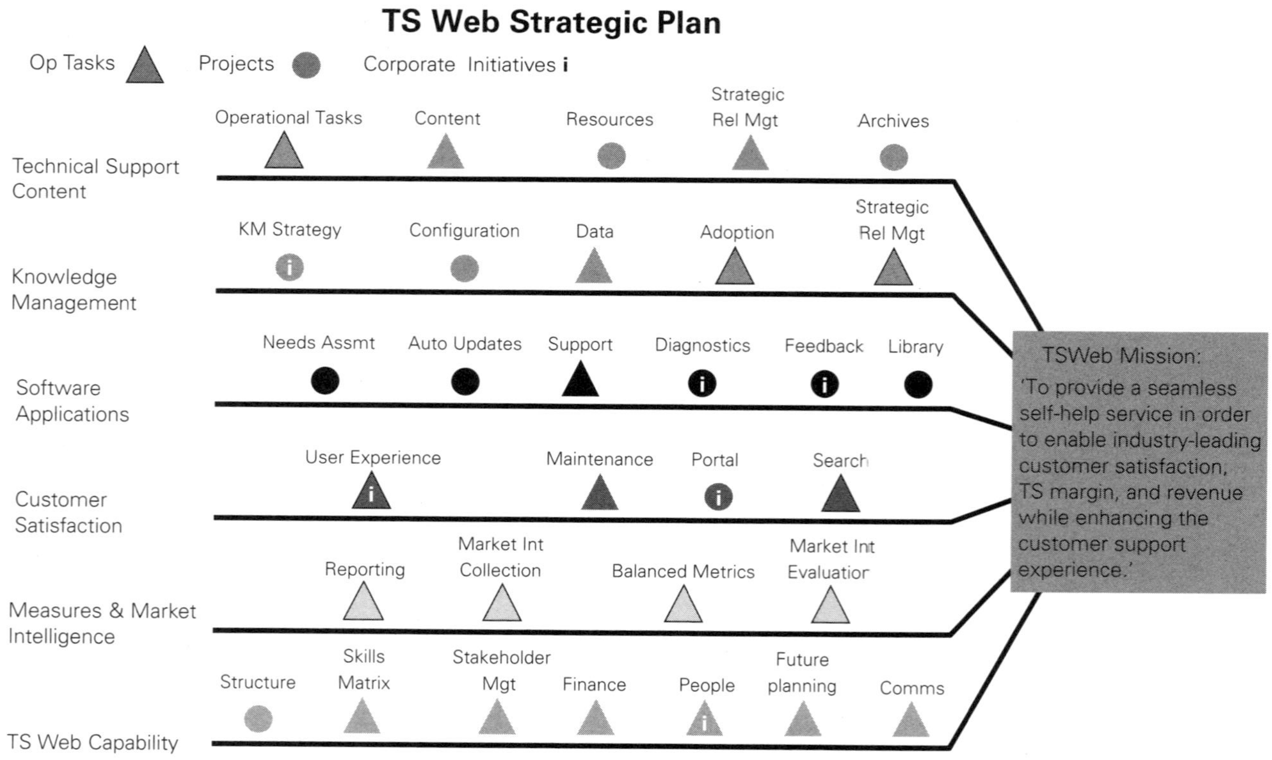

TS Web Strategic Plan

Op Tasks ▲ Projects ● Corporate Initiatives i

TSWeb Mission: 'To provide a seamless self-help service in order to enable industry-leading customer satisfaction, TS margin, and revenue while enhancing the customer support experience.'

Technical Support Content: Operational Tasks ▲ — Content — Resources — Strategic Rel Mgt — Archives

Knowledge Management: KM Strategy i — Configuration — Data — Adoption — Strategic Rel Mgt

Software Applications: Needs Assmt ● — Auto Updates ● — Support ▲ — Diagnostics i — Feedback i — Library ●

Customer Satisfaction: User Experience i — Maintenance — Portal i — Search

Measures & Market Intelligence: Reporting — Market Int Collection — Stakeholder Mgt — Balanced Metrics — Market Int Evaluation

TS Web Capability: Structure ● — Skills Matrix ▲ — Finance — People i — Future planning — Comms

- Improved reporting of key metrics and analysis of key drivers (balanced measures).
- It eliminated unaligned work: 90+ anticipated projects were reduced to around 30, saving a major investment in time, effort and money.
- Smooth transition ensured for old/new divisional directors (Janet was promoted out of this role).
- Dramatically improved the effectiveness and efficiency of the top team.

Additionally, internally the group was recognized by the division's SVP as the exemplar of effective global cross-functional teamwork, the budget was increased substantially, and they won two industry awards following the execution of the plan. Janet's group were recognized by the Service and Support Professionals Association with the STAR Awards for Best Practices in the Self-Service Category, and were cited as one of the Ten Best Web Support Sites by the Association of Support Professionals. All of this is a reflection of the group's leader, a highly capable lady who embedded an effective way of working.

Strategic business model change

Situation

I was asked to help a Director in a business-to-business ICT company who found himself appointed as the leader of a global programme charged with implementing a new supply chain/channel partner/inventory business model to resolve what was estimated to be a $5 billion 'problem'. The project team comprised 12 senior executives who had worked on the project for one year and who had got nowhere. The Director knew from past experience that the appreciation would solve the problem, and he asked me to first teach the appreciation to the executive team and then to facilitate its application – which was done over four days. This is a summary of that exercise.

Background to the project

- Historically the company had no distribution network; it sold parts to partners who serviced corporate end-users – the company concentrated on 'selling product' not solutions, which incorporated spares and service.
- The company had invested in depots around the world to supply partners and now wanted to supply end-users direct to maximize use of these assets.
- Within the next 12 to 18 months the current business model/partner programme was due to go 'end of life' worldwide, to be replaced by a new partner programme.
- The new partner programme ('Smart Parts') involved a menu of the degree of support provided by the company to partners and to end-users. The shipping by the company of parts to end-users was intended to look more attractive to all stakeholders than shipping parts to partners.

- The number of partners was to be reduced from 400 to about 50 and the remainder were due to become branded resellers.
- The company sales organization did not find it easy to sell spares – incentives were based on selling whole new equipment, and culturally they were product salesmen so they were not inclined to selling 'consulting solutions'.
- Through the old programme partners had built up large inventories of spares to support their end-user customers; estimates for the size of this inventory were up to $5 billion worldwide – there was no accurate tracking mechanism. Parts may have been assembled into product and sold at greater margin by unscrupulous partners (product at that time had no identifying serial numbers).
- Partners were requesting the company assist with the reduction of the inventory or to compensate them for losses incurred through write-offs.

This 'roadblock' was slowing down the implementation of the new Smart Parts partner programme, and until it was removed it would severely hamper the expansion of the programme as well as other aspects of the company's business.

The programme leader was asked to propose a solution(s) for conversion and/or utilization of this inventory to reduce partner inventory of spares, and to achieve this in the shortest possible time while minimizing the financial impact to the partners and maximizing the company's annuity revenue opportunity.

In the first five minutes of the workshop I showed that no progress had been made in the past year because everyone involved was solving a different problem. Furthermore, the questions about 'higher level intent' showed the need for appreciations to be made at all levels, as certain other executive decisions had been made with insufficient thought about downstream consequences and implications.

Mission analysis

Higher intent:

- Implement Smart Parts in a short time frame.
- Reduce partner inventory of spares currently blocking the expansion Smart Parts.

Desired effects:

- Increase use of depot assets and own logistic capability.
- Ensure the shipping by the company of parts to end-users would be more attractive to all stakeholders than shipping parts to partner.
- Achieve inventory reduction/removal in the shortest possible time while minimizing the financial impact to the partners and maximizing the annuity revenue opportunity.
- Minimize the partners' risk and liability for the spares inventory.
- Increase uptake of company annuity-based services to generate higher levels of annuity revenue.

Essential tasks (specified and implied, which can initiate concurrent activity):

- Identify size of partner inventory ($$).
- Analyse current booking profile for spares sales.
- Select partner champion to test concept.
- Audit age and usability of partner inventory.
- Secure support from product sales force to focus on service/solution sales.
- Assign resources and skills.
- Identify IT and business process requirements.
- Identify financial drivers/inhibitors to progress.
- Provide sales training on value proposition and solution selling.
- Review sales incentives.

After three-quarters of the day devoted to mission analysis alone, the project mission was stated as: 'To remove the inventory roadblock in order to enable the implementation of the new Smart Parts programme.' This looks so simple, it is hard to imagine the confusion and misdirected thought and effort that had been a feature of the team up until this point. However, having pursued the mission analysis question agenda in an inclusive and facilitated manner, the team was now both clear on their mission and committed to it.

Situation analysis

The factors were identified by individually brainstorming then collectively listing all the factor categories and the specific factor headings. The example factors shown in Table 14.10 were considered.

At this stage, in theory, deductions should be made about the factors affecting the problem to identify tasks and options. However, with so little information actually available, few meaningful deductions could be made.

What the group was able to do was identify the specific questions that needed to be asked and of whom, in order to obtain the information required from which to make deductions. While questions were being drafted, the team realized the importance of constructing clear and specific questions that would yield the required information. There were examples of questions which, on the surface, were relevant but if asked as they were first written, would fail. The intent in asking the question was not obvious to the reader. Time would be wasted if the right questions were not asked from the outset.

In this phase, it was necessary to prevent false assumptions being made and to ensure that a factor was fully explored before another was discussed. Control by the leader (or in this case me as facilitator) of a participative yet disciplined process is key to making an effective appreciation.

TABLE 14.10 Example factors

Factors	Information and Deductions	Tasks/Questions to ask
Inventory		
Inventory Visibility	Fair market value of inventory Potential dispositions Impact on eco-partners Partners may have varying levels of inventory management capabilities Partners might not send back the product that is actually under contract	Establish: • Age of product • Type of product • Revision level • Quantity • Quality • Location • Box condition • Inventory value – our assessment and partners' assessment using agreed accounting practices Determine partners' asset management capabilities and forecasting model Ensure returned product is what is under contract
Grey Market	'Grey market' impact on our business. (eg product appearing on eBay)	What is the impact of partners dumping inventory? Perform analysis to quantify impact of non-recovered inventory
Margin and Revenue	Ensure as far as possible neutral to positive impact on our overall margins and revenue	Calculate impact as a result of each of the inventory options
Accounting	All inventory taken on to our books must be accounted for correctly	Ensure correct reserves are in place to offset any inventory costs Ensure inventory is acquired by correct legal entity

TABLE 14.10 *continued*

Factors	Information and Deductions	Tasks/Questions to ask
System Infrastructure and Limitations	Partners' and our internal systems may not be able to support the proposed solution	Establish if partner systems provide sufficient visibility to us Engage IT to estimate feasibility of solutions from a system point of view Assess partner systems, and develop an integration strategy where necessary
Geography and Logistic Support	End user, partner and our locations Service overlap and gaps	Establish if end-users are in a location where we do not offer service. Work with partners to get end-user data Perform gap analysis on end-user locations and our service locations. Do ROI on expanding service locations for those not covered
Customs Duty/VAT	Tax implications of moving inventory	Perform analysis on which countries' parts will move to where (to one of our locations or to another partner) Analyse the feasibility of duty drawback via partners
Legal Eligibility	Legal obstacles	Work with legal department to evaluate country by country if there are any legal hurdles in our inventory solution
Communication	Communication to partners and internal departments about options and implications	Define CoAs in detail with pros and cons from our/partners'/and end-users' points of view Smart Parts team to disseminate these CoAs and seek feedback Cross-functional collaboration required and nominated leaders to be held accountable

TABLE 14.10 *continued*

Factors	Information and Deductions	Tasks/Questions to ask
Remarketing	Potential route to dispose of partner inventory Leaving the inventory with the partners may flood the grey market and compete with our remarketing programme	Identify what products are at partner/age/revision/volumes and suitability for remarketing
Risk	What is the risk of losing a partner we don't want to lose?	Assess and define parameters that would result in losing the partner Identify which partners we don't want to lose Identify the partners we would want to lose

Courses of action open

While CoAs in detail could only result from a full analysis of factors affecting the problem, several CoAs in very broad outline could be identified without waiting for answers to the questions above. Then the questions that needed to be answered for each option to be fully considered were identified. This was done so that if the CEO ruled out any CoAs, only those questions relating to acceptable CoAs would be researched.

A full and accurate comparison of CoAs can only result from making deductions about known factual information. Even with the lack of information, the team was surprised at the number of advantages and disadvantages that could be stated about the options that were identified (see Table 14.11). It was again necessary for the leader to prevent false assumptions being made. 'Red flag' phrases such as, 'We have to...' and, 'The only way to do...' were immediately challenged with: 'Yes, we could do that; what else could we do?'

Decision and further developments

The team was now able to take several courses of action forward for a decision to be made. In the event, the CEO immediately ruled out CoAs 3 and 5 in Table 14.11 and eased a constraint – a phased process over three years rather than a 'big bang' was now acceptable. Following this change, with only 24 hours' additional work, the recommended and accepted course of action became a phased buy-back or trade-in over three years with credit on a sliding scale being given for an increase in product and service commitments.

TABLE 14.11 Analysis of possible CoAs

Course of Action	Example Questions to Ask	Advantages	Disadvantages
1. Buy Back of Inventory	What size of budget do we need? How large is the spares inventory out in the field? At what price do we buy the inventory? How is the inventory valued? How do we assess the quality of the product? What are the refurbishment costs? Is there a partner willing to buy the inventory? How are we going to dispose of non-useable inventory? How do we determine eligibility of product for buy back? What is the install base the inventory is supporting? What room for negotiation is there on inventory liability? What is the overall impact to our margin/revenue for an inventory buy back? What are the customs/VAT/tax implications? What are the tax benefits of 'philanthropy'?	• Philanthropy – has tax advantages • No grey market • Immediate solution for partner • Total asset visibility • Quick adoption of Partner Programme 2001 • Long-term tie in to us is possible • Ultimately increase visibility of who end-users are	• Cost to us • Increased inventory handling • Increased logistics costs • Increased inventory levels • Impact to repair partners • Potentially most expensive/ lowest margin for us • Is this creating a 'trapped' environment for the partners
2. Partial Buy Back with Future Buy Incentives	What inventory will qualify? Who disposes of excess inventory and how? How do we prevent dumping? What future incentives are acceptable?	• As above	• Inventory handling costs and holding levels for us although they are lower than CoA 1 • Logistics costs and impact to repair partners although they are lower than CoA 1 • May not completely solve the issue for the partner • Adoption of Smart Parts may not be as quick

TABLE 14.11 *continued*

Course of Action	Example Questions to Ask	Advantages	Disadvantages
3. No Buy Back		• No cost to us • Easy to implement • Flexibility for partner to dispose of inventory as they wish • No disruption to contract repair partners	• Low adoption rate for Smart Parts • Burden for inventory disposal is on partner • Potential grey market increase • Impacting on us • Relationship/goodwill/brand/perception damaged and new product sales compromised • Not a viable solution?
4. Brokerage	As above plus Do we know how to broker inventory? What are the customs/VAT/Tax implications? What are the tax benefits of 'Philanthropy'? What are the time frames? How do we prevent dumping?	• Reduced cost to us • No disruption to contract repair partners • Opportunity to utilize inventory how we wish	• No experience of brokerage market • Potential conflict to our sales organization • Control over how/where the partners inventory is sold • Conflict with our own remarketing
5. Use of our capital financing business	What are the time frames? Is it legal/ethical to get a partner to purchase the inventory? (off balance sheet financing) Do we have budget to fund 'Cost of Funds'? What are the rules behind refinancing? Is there a third party large enough/willing to handle this and who are they?	• Allows costs to be deferred over a longer period • Extends the availability of inventory for future use • Assets are off the partners' financial books • No grey market • Immediate solution for partner • Total asset visibility • Quick adoption Smart Parts long-term tie in to us • Ultimately increases visibility of who end users are • Deferred impact to repair partners (over CoA 1)	• Possible financial reporting issues (analyst and shareholder perception) Incremental financial costs to us

The Appreciation

The holiday abroad

Situation

It is 1 January. You are an expatriate married person with two children below school age and you are working in the UK. Your home town is Hobart and you find the UK weather to be similar to that of Tasmania – often sunny, but sometimes cold and wet. However, in recent years the UK has had very good summers.

It has been a very busy period and you have been working late with pressures and stresses. Your partner (and you) need a break to wind down and relax. Your partner has been badgering you for some time to go on holiday for one week this year where, if possible, the food and weather are both good, it must be abroad, but not on any account to take the children. (The children could go to their English grandparents at any time except August when they are on a world cruise. If they cannot go to the grandparents then there are lots of couples in the company who would look after them, except during the Easter block leave period.) You agree to look into the idea and subsequently visit the local travel agent (you haven't started booking online yet!). He tells you that the only holidays now available are as in Table 14.12 (costs converted to dollars for one week for two people).

TABLE 14.12 Holiday availability and costs

Place	Total Cost before 31 May $	Total Cost after 31 May $	Remarks
Austria	700	960	Food good but dull. Weather changeable but normally better in August
Cyprus	1,400	1,800	Food unpredictable. Weather always good
France (Brittany)	1,100	1,380	Food superb. Weather similar to UK
Morocco	840	1,100	Food doubtful. Weather always good
Cornwall	360	420	Food variable. Excellent surfing and cider

You then go and see your boss and find out that the best times for leave are:

22–29 March	Easter leave.
01–14 May	Gap between two peak periods.
03–21 August	Someone else can stand in for you.

You check your bank balance and find that as a result of the financial crisis there is very little in your account and you also discover that the banks still are not lending. By living frugally, the following can be saved:

By 22 March	£500
By 1 May	£1,000
By 3 August	£1,400

Mission

What is your mission analysis and aim? What is your appreciation of the situation, what options are open, which option do you choose and why?

Mission: to go on holiday abroad this year so that we can relax without the children. *Mission analysis:* what is the intention of my superior and what is my role in the overall plan? My partner's intention is to go on holiday abroad this year so that we can relax without the children. The children (stakeholders) need to be cared for. My part in the plan is to organize the holiday.

What am I required to do, or what tasks do I have to complete to achieve the mission? The specified task is: organize a one week holiday this year. The implied tasks are:

- Organize childminders for the holiday.
- Check passport expiry dates and visa requirements.
- Check exchange rates and order travellers' cheques.
- Source guidebooks and local info.

Has the situation changed in principle? If the grandparents' cruise is cancelled after this appreciation, then the implication of it must be considered.

Factor analysis

TABLE 14.13 Holiday factor analysis

Factor Heading	Information	Outputs
		Tasks, planning guidance, critical information requirements, risks, etc
Constraints	• The holiday must be this year. • If possible the weather and food must be good. • The holiday must be without the children.	These are the criteria on which to make a decision from the options generated
Leave Dates	The 3 leave periods are: 22–29 March 1–14 May 3–21 August	• A holiday is only possible during one of these periods • August is the best choice for weather • May is the second best choice for weather • March is the worst choice for weather *Task:* Book a holiday during a leave period, dates to be confirmed.
Childminders	The children need to be looked after My wife's parents can look after the children at any time except August when they are on a world cruise Other couples in the company would look after the children at any time except during the Easter block leave	• Childminders are available for all leave periods • There are two options in May • In March the grandparents are available • In August the couples are available • The children would be happier with their grandparents Therefore a holiday outside August may be best *Task:* Book childminders

TABLE 14.13 *continued*

Factor Heading	Information			Outputs
Financing	A bank loan cannot be used to pay for the holiday. By living frugally the following can be saved: By 22 March £500 By 1 May £1,000 By 3 August £1,400			• Savings are the only source of funds • I can afford £500 by the first leave period • £1,000 by the second and • £1,400 by the third

Total Costs

Place	Before 31 May ($)	After 31 May ($)	Deductions
Austria	700	960	*Task:* Select location within savings outlined above • As Cornwall is not abroad this option is discounted • I cannot afford any overseas holiday by the March leave • I cannot afford Cyprus and Brittany for 1 May leave • I cannot afford Cyprus after 31 May, so Cyprus is discounted this year • I can afford Austria or Morocco for 1 May leave • I can afford Austria, Brittany and Morocco after 31 May for the August leave
Cyprus	1,400	1,800	
France (Brittany)	1,100	1,380	
Morocco	840	1,100	
Cornwall	360	420	

Location and Food

Place	Quality of Food	Weather	
Austria	Good but unimaginative in the past	Changeable, better in August	*Task:* Prioritize food/weather choice priorities • Austria would be acceptable in August otherwise the weather is not good • Brittany would be acceptable from July – September when the weather is better • Morocco is not preferred • Holiday before 31 May is not preferred as good food and weather are not available
Brittany	Superb	Similar to UK or warmer	
Morocco	Bad experience, not to our taste	Always good	

Summary of deductions

Timing: A holiday is possible only during:

  22–29 March,

  01–14 May, or

  03–21 August.

Funds: I can afford a holiday costing no more than:

  By 22 March   £500.

  By 1 May   £1,000.

  By 3 August   £1,400.

Affordable: The following holidays are affordable:

  Austria and Morocco before 31 May.

  Austria, Brittany and Morocco after 31 May.

Childminders: Childminders are available all year but grandparents (the preferred choice) are not available in August.

Food and weather:

  Austria is acceptable in August.

  Brittany is acceptable in August.

  Morocco is least preferable unless an alternative source of food is available; the weather is acceptable all year.

  A holiday before 31 May is not preferred because good food and weather are not available.

Preliminary assessment of tasks

- Save money.
- Book leave.
- Organize childminders for the holiday.
- Confirm travel details and hotel.
- Check passport expiry dates and visa requirements.
- Check exchange rates and order travellers' cheques.
- Source guidebooks and local information.

Courses of action

The constraints (selection criteria) are:

- A one-week holiday this year.
- The holiday must be abroad without the children.
- If possible the weather and food must be good.

The CoAs satisfying these constraints are shown in Table 14.14.

TABLE 14.14 CoAs satisfying constraints

No	CoA	Advantages	Disadvantages
1	Austria in August	Cheapest option in August Childminders from the company are available Food is good Weather is better in August	Grandparents not available Food good but unimaginative
2	Brittany in August	Affordable Childminders from the company are available Weather similar to UK with recent good summers Food superb	Affordable but expensive Grandparents not available Good weather not guaranteed
3	Austria in May	Affordable Grandparents can babysit	Food good but dull Weather changeable
4	Morocco in May	Affordable Grandparents can babysit Weather good	Food is doubtful
5	Morocco in August	Affordable Childminders from the company are available Weather good	Food doubtful Grandparents not available

Decision

I will select Course 2. The holiday will be in Brittany for one week between 3 and 21 August. A couple from the company will look after the children. I have chosen this CoA because it offers the best combination of food and weather within the time and financial constraints.

Turning around a failing rural pub

Situation

This pub had been the twice-yearly venue for an informal golf club made up of university friends who were all now successful businessmen. They had been playing golf nearby and staying in the pub for two weeks each year for 15 years when the pub was put up for sale following the foot and mouth outbreak and its consequences for the rural economy in Devon.

The golfers formed a company and bought the pub, largely to continue their golfing holidays. This is a synopsis of the plan the implementation of which turned the failing pub around – again, a plan resulting from facilitated, focused discussion.

In 2002:

- Turnover £150,000.
- Profit: £20,000.
- Business plan clarity: no plan, no clarity.
- Environment and management style: ineffective systems, processes and infrastructure, no form of advertising or promotion.
- 'Traditional' owner-occupier management and staffing of limited ability.

In 2004:

- Turnover £320,000.
- Profit: £60,000.
- Business plan clarity: to be the best pub on Dartmoor – see below.
- Environment and management style: professional practices embedded.
- Ability of owner and staff: high quality chef and front of house staff supported by effective leadership.

Mission analysis

Higher intentions:

- To maintain the pub as 'our' golf club venue.
- For 'The Ring of Bells' to be the perfect village pub.
- To grow the business by buying more pubs, or exiting the pub business, having secured our club.
- To increase capital value and realize it in 10 years.
- To have fun running the pub and the enlarged group.

Desired effects:

- To be very slick in operation.
- To provide a hub for the local community.
- To provide a great experience for our customers.
- To be seen as a role model of how to run a pub.

Essential tasks: specified and implied (initiate concurrent activity):

- Hire good front of house and chefs.
- To upgrade the accommodation quality.
- To upgrade the kitchen and dining facilities.
- To market the pub through a website, PR and local radio.
- To improve management systems and make good use of IT.

Constraints and freedom of action:

- 13th century property makes building very difficult – no straight edges on the walls!
- Grade II listed building constrains options.
- Small labour pool available.

Changes to the situation – monitor during execution: After a year, a change of ownership of the nearby hotel which owned the golf course caused the pub to re-examine its market offering when they closed the course to golfers not staying at the hotel – less focus on golf groups (there were still other golf courses within an hour's drive), more on celebrating anniversaries (exploiting the dining room and overnight accommodation).

State the pub's mission: 'To turn the Ring of Bells around in order to maintain it as a golf club venue and to provide a return to investors.'

Factors

Some of the factors, deductions and resulting tasks are shown in Table 14.15.

TABLE 14.15 The pub: factors, deductions, tasks

Factor	Information/Deductions	Tasks
Small local labour pool	Hard to recruit good local chefs so recruit from outside the area. They will need accommodation	Rent house for staff accommodation
Pub is remote – a destination pub set in a 'perfect English village'	There is no marketing at present People do not drive this far just for a drink People will drive for food, events or overnight stays Everyone has one or two anniversaries Local clubs, groups and hunts like this type of pub to host their events	Create website for cost-effective marketing and to take bookings Promote pub as 'the perfect English village pub' and as a place to celebrate birthdays, etc Build links with local clubs and groups

TABLE 14.15 *continued*

Factor	Information/Deductions	Tasks
Kitchen equipment	Cramped conditions and old equipment makes it hard to produce consistently good food. Close-down takes longer than is acceptable, costing more in staff hours.	Redesign layout and refit with new oven, chillers, hot lamps to provide separate areas for hot, cold, dessert and washing up
Accounting uses old spreadsheet system	Time-consuming to produce monthly reports which are error-strewn	Move to new system such as SAGE
Rooms	Pub is on the edge of Dartmoor which is well known to visitors Occupied rooms provide restaurant customers Rooms are tatty	Upgrade rooms to match perfect pub image Optimize website for search engines and provide easy online means of booking
Food ordering	Food orders taken at bar are physically walked to kitchen leaving bar empty, customers kept waiting and sales are lost. Some food orders are lost, losing sales and reputation	Buy new till system to print orders directly in kitchen

Identify courses of action and task organization

Various kitchen designs, IT systems and so on were compared for ease of use, functionality, durability, cost and return – ie which improvements would increase cash flow the most to fund other improvements.

The selected CoA was illustrated with the various tasks and projects grouped and sequenced as shown on the campaign plan in Figure 14.10. This was reflected in people's roles – that is, a person owned everything on a line.

FIGURE 14.10 The pub plan

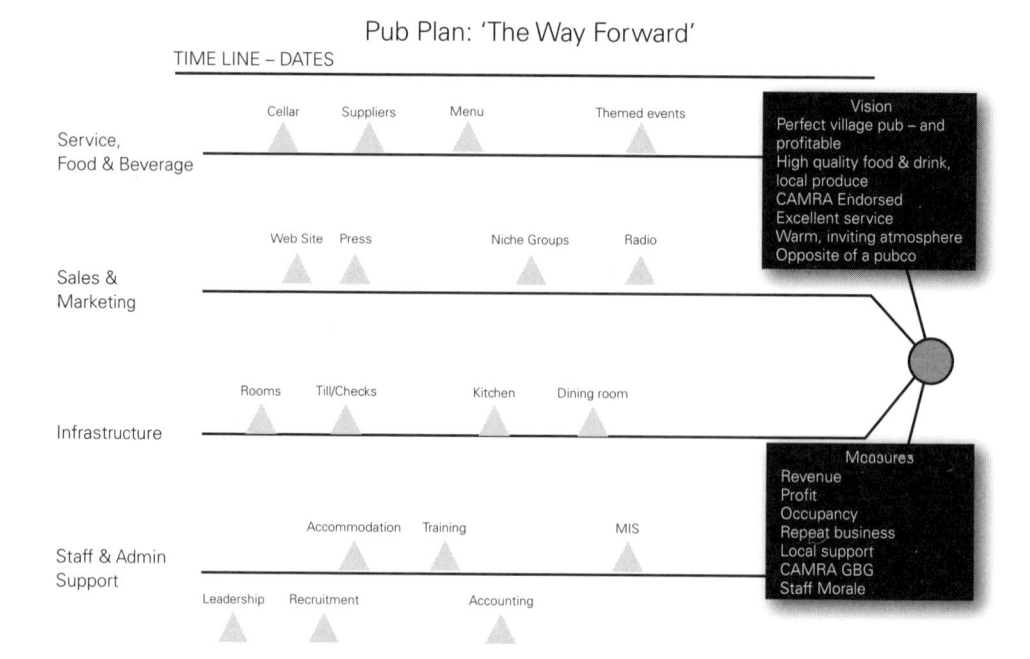

Pub Plan: 'The Way Forward'

TIME LINE – DATES

Service, Food & Beverage: Cellar, Suppliers, Menu, Themed events

Sales & Marketing: Web Site, Press, Niche Groups, Radio

Infrastructure: Rooms, Till/Checks, Kitchen, Dining room

Staff & Admin Support: Accommodation, Training, MIS, Leadership, Recruitment, Accounting

Vision
Perfect village pub – and profitable
High quality food & drink, local produce
CAMRA Endorsed
Excellent service
Warm, inviting atmosphere
Opposite of a pubco

Measures
Revenue
Profit
Occupancy
Repeat business
Local support
CAMRA GBG
Staff Morale

The implementation of this plan by an effective leader who created clarity amongst all those involved of 'what, why and how', together with a modest investment in infrastructure, has doubled the revenue and trebled the profit within a year and a half and led to a business plan for a small chain of similar pubs.

Notes

1 Alistair Mant, 1997, *Intelligent Leadership*, Sydney: Allen and Unwin.
2 Kaplan, R S and Norton, D P, 1996, *Balanced Scorecard: Translating strategy into action*, Boston, MA: Harvard Business School Press.
3 Karl Albrecht, 1994, *The Northbound Train*, New York: AMACOM.
4 D Rowsell and I Gotts, 2010, *Why Killer Products Don't Sell*, Chichester: John Wiley.
5 Myers, I Briggs, McCaulley M H, Quenk, N L and Hammer, A L, 1998, *MBTI Manual (A guide to the development and use of the Myers Briggs Type Indicator)*, 3rd edn, New York: Consulting Psychologists Press.

Annex A: Standard Operating Procedure (SOP) for meetings and minutes

Tailor these as you see fit!

Purpose and scope of meetings

- Decision making about issues within the team's control with implications and impact across the team's area of responsibility.
- Passing recommendations upwards on corporate issues with implications and impact on the team's area of responsibility.
- Reporting on matters with implications and impact across the team's area of responsibility.
- Plan progress reviews.
- Formal briefings: specific plans, information updates.

Agenda and preparation

Agenda items are either subjects to be discussed leading to a decision or a recommendation for a decision to be passed upwards, or subjects to be briefed to the team.

Sponsors should submit items for inclusion to the meeting chairman. Sponsors should provide briefing notes on accepted agenda items for circulation one week before the meeting.

The agenda format is:

- Date and location of the team meeting.
- Names of people required to attend.
- Agenda items (as per Table 14.16).

TABLE 14.16

Serial	Time	Item	Sponsor	Remarks	Briefing or Decision
1					
2					
3					

1. Agenda item: decision – team discussion required

In this situation, the team will discuss a subject and at the conclusion of discussion it will make a decision or produce a recommendation for the decision-making authority. A one-page decision background brief and draft initial appreciation are to be prepared by the item sponsor using the following structure, to be used as the basis for the appreciation. This will be amended following discussion and attached to the meeting minutes:

- Situation
  - market drivers, activity and requirements;
  - competitor activity;
  - partner activity;
  - higher intent and requirements.
- Mission analysis – initial mission analysis conducted by subject sponsor leading to mission statement.
- Factor analysis – key factors and deductions.
- Courses of action open and comparison.
- Recommendation and reasons why.

2. Agenda item: reporting and briefing

Sponsors will brief or report to the team using the following situation report (sitrep) format:

- Situation/context overview.
- Mission (aim and purpose).
- Execution
  - general outline (who is doing what and by when by phases);
  - key measures and milestones;
  - progress made;
  - obstacles and anticipatory actions;
  - future intentions, changes to plans;
  - risk management;
  - issues that may require team decisions.

Meeting conduct

Nominated individuals will be appointed to these roles:

- Chairman – to control timings, to summarize discussion, to ensure clear decisions are reached, to check individuals' understanding on actions to be taken after the meeting.
- Agenda item sponsors – to provide decision background briefing or situation report for items appearing on the agenda.

- Facilitator to drive the appreciation (aligned decision making) process for each agenda item requiring a decision or recommendation. The facilitator should be chosen from those least connected with the subject and best placed to be dispassionate and rigorous in facilitating the process.
- Scribe/minute-taker – to record summary of subjects discussed, decisions/recommendations made, with actions to be taken by who and by when.
- Timekeeper – to ensure the chairperson is aware of the clock in order to stop/start agenda items.

Minutes

- Minutes will include the time, date and place of the meeting and the names of those present.
- Minutes will be circulated within 72 hours of meetings taking place.
- Minutes will be taken for each agenda item as follows:
    - item briefed: for subjects briefed at the meeting, the item sponsor's briefing notes will be attached as an Annex to the minutes or will be made available to minutes recipients on request;
    - decisions/recommendations reached: the updated background brief/draft appreciation will be attached as an Annex to the minutes;
    - other items will be recorded (as per Table 14.17).

TABLE 14.17

Serial	Item	Sponsor	Summary	Actions	By When	By Who

Attendees at top team meetings should brief their direct reports within 48 hours of minutes being circulated.

Annex B: Appreciation template

Template for:

- Strategy development and definition
- Change management
- Project scoping and outline planning
- Process review and improvement
- Idea development
- Problem solving and decision making

Use this template to assist in making a decision or recommendation, or to define the outline plan to address any project, problem, task or opportunity.

This is a working document that creates a rationale for action. The output that is carried forward into the actual plan is taken from the mission analysis, tasks (resulting from factors/deductions) and the selected course of action.

1. Mission analysis

TABLE 14.18

Who/What	Effect
Who do you need to involve in the mission analysis?	
What are the higher level intentions and direction or given mission – think two levels up; what are the desired end-state, purpose and strategy?	
Specifically, what effects do you wish to have and on who or what?	
What essential tasks can you identify no matter the overall course of action – specified and implied tasks?	
What concurrent activity can be started now and by whom? (Brief people and start work ASAP!)	

TABLE 14.18 *continued*

Who/What	Effect
What constraints/boundaries and freedom of action do you have – what must limit your thinking and what 'constraints' are habitual norms and not real constraints? What is the scope of the task?	
Time and space: by when must the mission be achieved? How long do you have for planning before you must start the cascade/execution (rule of thirds: keep one-third of time available for planning at your level) and what geographical space must you cover?	
Has the situation or operating context changed? If so, how and what are the implications?	
State your mission (mission = statement of overall aim/intent and its purpose). In a short, simple, clear, unambiguous and memorable sentence that links action to purpose, state what you are trying to achieve and why?	'To do action in order to fulfil purpose.'

Now back brief your mission analysis to confirm your desired tasks, objectives and priorities as necessary.

2. Factor/situation analysis

- Who do you need to involve in the factor analysis?
- A deduction must end with an option and/or a defined task/role – otherwise discount the factor as 'information overload'.

TABLE 14.19

Factor	Information and Deductions?	Therefore? – Tasks
List factors affecting achieving the mission in logical groupings	What information is known about the factor? Ask 'So what/therefore?' to make deductions and deductions of deductions	What specific tasks can you identify as a result of deductive thought? Keep your language precise and clear! Re-list tasks in order of priority – 'must, should, could do'

Now compare the identified tasks to work currently in progress to determine what you stop, start and carry on doing. You may also assess the 'start' and 'carry on' activity to determine what activity is best outsourced, what is best 'insourced' and what internal activity needs review and improvement.

3. Courses of Action (CoA) open

And/or task organization (grouping and sequencing of tasks):

- Who do you need to involve in the CoA development and comparison?
- Compare the advantages and disadvantages of each option, subtask or COA.
- Select the best option(s) to achieve your aim.

TABLE 14.20

Course of Action (Brief description)	Advantages	Disadvantages

Decision

- Who do you need to involve in selecting the preferred CoA and making the decision?
- What is the decision (or recommendation) and why?

Annex C: Project/task outline plan template

When plans are created, the text in italics may be deleted by the plan author.

This document may be created most effectively by making an appreciation, which is the working document rationale for action and then cutting and pasting the appropriate output of that into this document. This same blank template may then be used by owners of sub-tasks in that higher level plan to define actions at the next level of detail downwards by:

- Adding the delegated higher level task to the higher intent section.
- Conducting mission analysis on that task and creating a mission statement for it.
- Identifying detailed tasks and selecting a course of action and filling in the relevant sections on this document.
- If the task complexity warrants, this may be repeated at lower levels again.

TABLE 14.21

Higher Intent	Direction given by your leader, other higher level plans, etc
Mission Analysis: *Desired effects, impacts and outcomes* *Define the effects that you wish to have – on whom and/or what* *Boundaries, constraints and freedom of action* *Time and space* *These assist in scoping the task and clarify overlaps or gaps with other projects*	
Project/Task Name:	**Mission:** *To do action; in order to fulfil purpose* *The mission results from the mission analysis in your appreciation of the situation. It is a two-part, clear, unambiguous statement of overall intent (aim) and its purpose, to which all thought and action are then aligned.*
Execution	**General outline:** *This is the selected course of action from your appreciation made as a result of comparing the pros and cons of the different methods of achieving your mission: the grouping, sequencing, phasing of tasks and options for completing those tasks.*

TABLE 14.21 *continued*

Tasks	Key Stakeholders	Accountable Person	Completion Date
Tasks may be immediately apparent (essential tasks, specified and implied) to initiate concurrent activity, or may result from deductions made in 'factor/ situation analysis'. A factor is anything which affects achieving the mission. Identify factors and then repeatedly ask the question 'so what?' to identify tasks which are then prioritized. That deductive argument need not be captured for the working plan, but it may be required to explain how the plan and its tasks were arrived at.			

Administration and logistics

Might include:

- Equipment and consumables provision.
- Purchase orders.
- Suppliers, etc.

Control and communication

Might include:

- Authorities.
- Reporting.
- Cross-briefings, updates and feedback.
- MIS/ICT.

Annex D: Strategic plan and second-order task tracking document template

When plans are created, the text in italics may be deleted by the plan author. This document may be created most effectively by making an appreciation which is the working document rationale for action and then cutting and pasting the appropriate output of that and into the first part of this document. Specific task owners then do the same at the next level down and their 'back briefed' missions and task outline plans and measures are then added to this document under 'Execution: Detailed Tasks'.

TABLE 14.22

SITUATION	*External drivers, 'market', competitors, internal organization, etc. This should be completed if this document is to be used for briefing*
MISSION ANALYSIS: *Higher Intent (vision, end-state, direction, ambitions) desired effects, objectives, outcomes and priorities*	
MISSION	*To do action; in order to fulfil purpose* *The mission results from the mission analysis in your appreciation of the situation. It is a two-part, clear, unambiguous statement of overall intent (aim) and its purpose, to which all thought and action is then aligned.*
EXECUTION	**General outline:** *This is the selected course of action from your appreciation made as a result of comparing the pros and cons of the different methods of achieving your mission: the grouping, sequencing, phasing of tasks and options for completing those tasks.*

The Appreciation

FIGURE 14.11 Example schematic plan

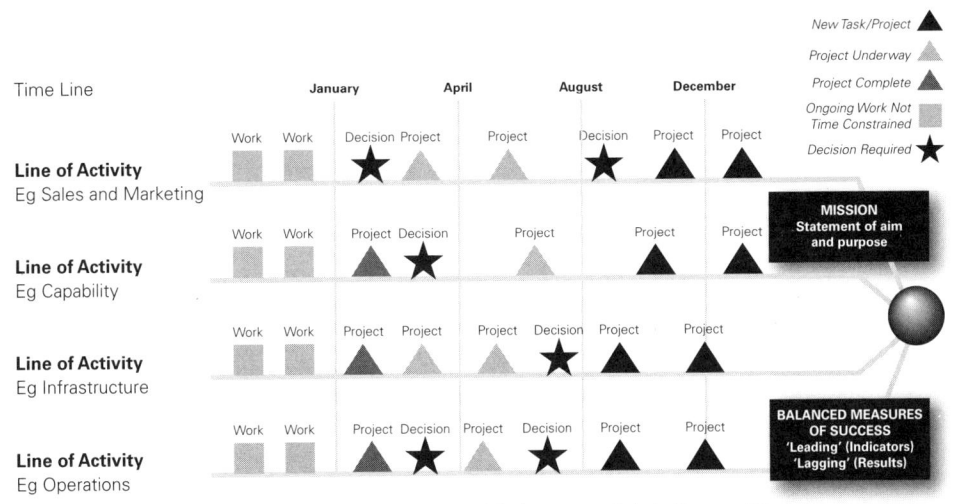

Legend:
- New Task/Project ▲
- Project Underway ▲
- Project Complete ▲
- Ongoing Work Not Time Constrained ■
- Decision Required ★

Time Line: January — April — August — December

Line of Activity — Eg Sales and Marketing
Work, Work, Decision, Project, Project, Decision, Project, Project

Line of Activity — Eg Capability
Work, Work, Project, Decision, Project, Project, Project

Line of Activity — Eg Infrastructure
Work, Work, Project, Project, Project, Decision, Project, Project

Line of Activity — Eg Operations
Work, Work, Project, Decision, Project, Decision, Project, Project

MISSION — Statement of aim and purpose

BALANCED MEASURES OF SUCCESS
'Leading' (Indicators)
'Lagging' (Results)

'Lines of Activity' are reflected in structure; each line has an accountable leader. 'Squares and triangles' represent projects or logical groupings of tactical tasks, each with an accountable leader.
Each line and 'square or triangle' will be subject to the same cycle of the appreciation, planning and briefing in order to maintain alignment and engagement.

© Jeremy Tozer, 1997–2005

TABLE 14.23

Summary of Strategic Objectives/ First-order Tasks (The squares and triangles taken from the schematic above)	Leading Indicators and Measures of Success	Accountable Person	Completion Date	Key Stakeholders

Execution: detailed tasks

TABLE 14.24

Objective/First-order Task Name **Mission:** Clarify with mission analysis	Accountable Person: Completion Date:	Leading Indicators and Measures of Success:
Second-order Tasks (Result from an appreciation on achieving the first-order task mission made by whoever is responsible for achieving that task)		

Tasks, including risk management	Outline Plan: How, with what resources	Who	By When	Remarks/ Review
1.1	These may be tracked in project management applications			
1.2				

Co-ordinating instructions (eg timings, control measures and risk management)

Administration and logistics

Might include:

- Equipment and consumables provision.
- Purchase orders.
- Suppliers, etc.

Control and communication

Might include:

- Authorities.
- Reporting.
- Cross-briefings, updates and feedback.
- MIS/ICT.

15
Planning and briefing

Planning

Detailed plan format

The briefing

Early warning

Communication: routine briefing and updates

Project management and routine leadership

Other common tools

I keep six honest serving men, (They taught me all I knew)
Their names are What and Why and When, and How and Where and Who.

(Rudyard Kipling)

Chapter 14 dealt with the appreciation, the process of clarifying what you are trying to achieve and identifying and selecting the 'best' overall course of action (CoA), or outline plan, to pursue. Depending upon the nature of the subject (problem, task, project, etc) about which you have made a decision, and the complexity of the resulting CoA, it may be necessary to produce a more detailed plan, perhaps over time and in many meetings and discussions. Once planning is complete, or when sufficient planning has been completed to launch people into action in the first phase of a plan without wasting their time and energy and your resources, it will be necessary to brief the team – do not assume that they remember the output of several planning meetings!.

This cycle of activity is shown in Figure 15.1. Briefings are essential – it is dangerous to assume that the team understands the plan in outline and their roles in detail simply because they have been involved in planning, or have been e-mailed a planning document.

Remember that this is a dynamic, iterative cycle and non-linear process; if changes occur (to higher intent, the situation on the ground, 'factors affecting', expected progress, constraints and so on) then the question 'So what?' needs to be asked. The answer may lead to re-planning, re-briefing and so on.

Remember too, that if stakeholders are involved (see Figure 15.2) and their expertise is exploited in the decision making and subsequent planning, they are going to have far more commitment to executing the plan than would otherwise be the case. Effective execution requires people's full engagement and use of their initiative; rather than paying lip-service to a 'tick box' set of instructions.

376 The ACE Conditions for Success: Clarity

FIGURE 15.1 The strategy to execution cycle

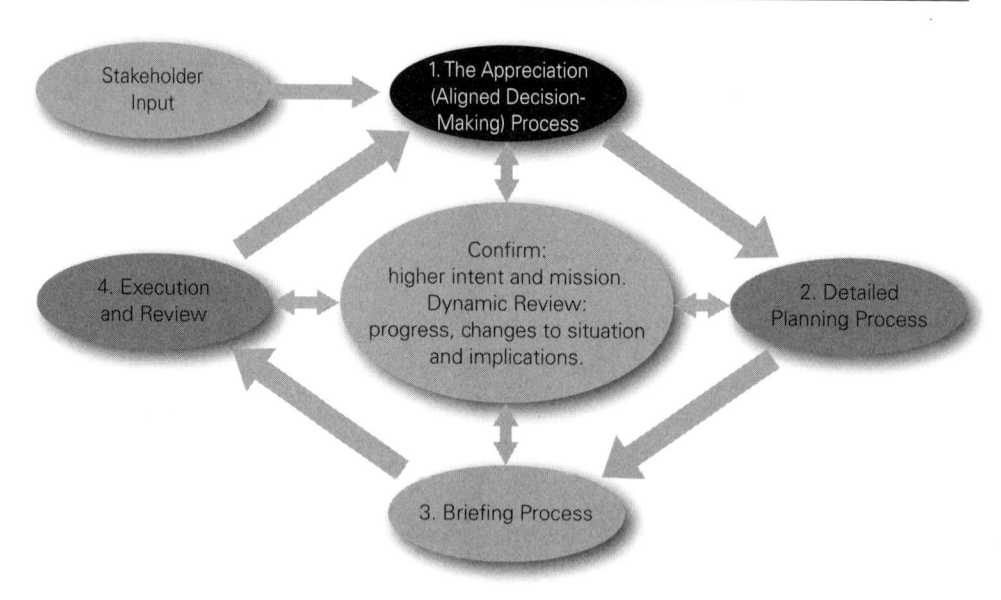

© Jeremy Tozer, 2011

FIGURE 15.2 Input into decision making

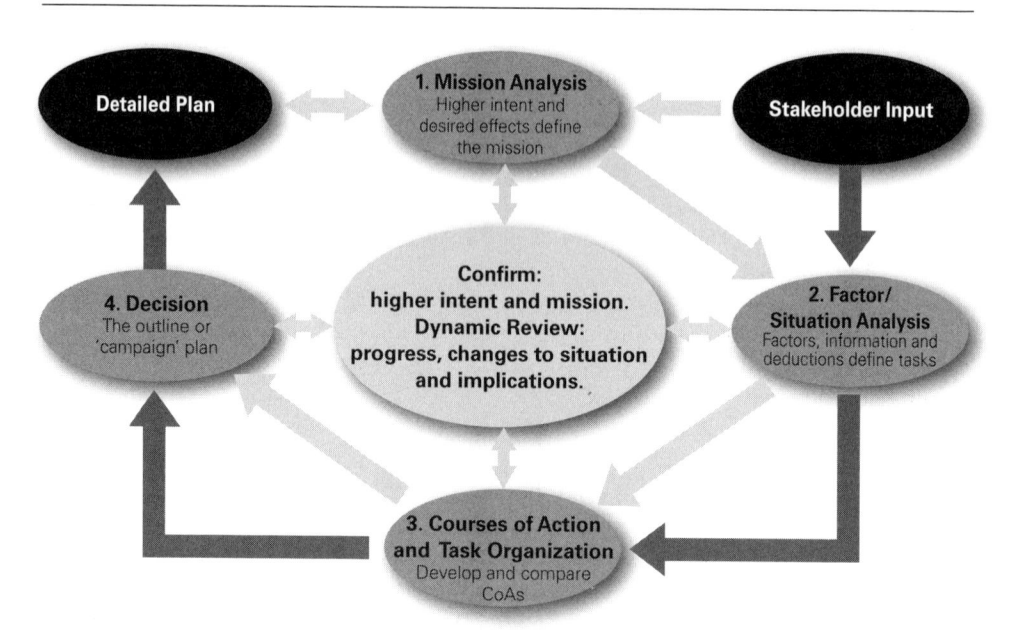

© Jeremy Tozer, 2011

Planning

The output from the appreciation that you have made is the selection of a course of action, an outline plan, a concept of operations. To turn it into an effective plan, some flesh needs to be put on to the bones; and as they say, 'the devil is in the detail'. People often struggle with what level of detail they need to drill down into. There is no hard and fast rule, but as a guide, tell your team what they need to know to understand the context and do their job. The level of detail should be kept to that which the users of the plan need to know for the level of work they are engaged in. Give people sufficient detail to enable them to understand their role, and maintain alignment. If your team members are leaders of teams in their own right, then avoid giving them the level of detail that their team members need – they should work that out as they make their own appreciations, and so on.

Over-detailed plans are time-consuming to produce, difficult to remember and stifle initiative.
Gen Sir Nigel Bagnall

Detailed plan format

The detailed plan will evolve with the collective and/or individual involvement of the team and other stakeholders over one or many meetings. It is best written in a logical progression of headings that helps you to build and develop the plan. If a common format is adopted and applied to all activities for which a plan is required, and which you and others become familiar with, items will not be overlooked when plans are put together under time pressure. Equally, when people read or review plans in this common format, they will take in the information more easily – understanding, contribution and interoperability are enhanced. The recommended format is shown in Figure 15.3. A written plan has to be brief to be remembered, and clear to be understood. The words used must be chosen carefully, with accuracy and precision in mind – they will influence choices when the plan is implemented.

Mission

This is carried forward from the mission analysis in your appreciation process that precedes detailed planning. Your mission stems from your analysis of higher intent 'one up and two up' (the intentions of your boss and your boss's boss), essential tasks, desired effects and constraints/freedom of action.

Execution

General outline

Reproduce your outline plan from your appreciation – the selected course of action. The outline plan may consist of a number of key phases: describe them all briefly. For a major, complex initiative, it may only be possible to plan the first phase in

FIGURE 15.3   The planning process sequence

The Planning Process Sequence	
MISSION	From The Appreciation mission analysis
EXECUTION	a. General outline: The CoA from own Appreciation: when and where actions take place in relation to each other b. Grouping and tasks by phases in detail (who is to do what, by when, and within what specific constraints) c. Coordinating instructions: timings, control measures, general constraints, risk management
ADMINISTRATION AND LOGISTICS	What support is being provided by whom, when, where and how
CONTROL AND COMMUNICATION	a. Authorities b. Reporting and flow of information needed

© Jeremy Tozer, 1997–2006

detail, the detail for further phases being dependent on progress, reactions and/or outcomes of the first phase.

Grouping and tasks

In this paragraph you should list any sub-teams or groups that you need to establish or that already exist within your team, by phases as appropriate. Additional individuals or groups that have been attached to your team should be included here. Allocate precise tasks for each phase (derived from the objectives that you need to attain) to each individual and/or sub-group and its leader, and include any constraints, limitations or extra authority that you are delegating. This will assist colleagues to make their own appreciations of how to achieve the tasks delegated to them.

Coordinating instructions

Include any activity, information or measures that is vital to understanding the plan and which apply to all or most phases. Timings, preparatory action, control measures, risk management and action to be taken should anticipated events occur are usually best given here. Measures might include leading indicators as well as final targets (lagging measures – when the task is complete, the target may or may not have been reached). These may be drawn from the key activities on each line of activity in your schematic plan – thereby producing a set of balanced measures directly derived from a comprehensive and holistic plan. This gives you a balanced scorecard that is clearly linked to the plan you are working to.

Administration and logistics

Detail any distribution of resources, issue of equipment or materials, administrative matters such as changes to normal routine, etc that are necessary.

Control and communication

This is designed to give clarity about who is controlling or able to authorize what, the 'chain of command' and so on. Changes to normal reporting procedures or additional reports and returns that are required (information flow upwards), changes to authority for decision making, etc should all be addressed here.

The briefing

Briefings are as critical as rigorous decision making to effective execution, yet for many leaders in business the concept is unknown. Presumably they expect their people to be mind-readers. Briefings are the means of passing on your intentions, creating clarity and building confidence.

Briefings to the team should be a regular feature in any leader's diary – whether they are routine updates in which information is conveyed on a variety of subjects, early warning briefs ahead of detailed planning for major changes, or briefings for specific plans, tasks or projects. We will concentrate on the latter since the 'template' may be adapted for the former as required.

Briefing is the critical moment at the start of any plan's implementation. It is the time when the leader must:

- Reinforce what needs to be done and why, while reassuring the team and calming nerves (in times of change).
- Convince the team that the plan they have helped to create is the plan that will work.
- Inspire the belief that the plan will be effectively executed and the mission completed.
- Provide people with the information and direction they need to make decisions, particularly if all does not go according to plan – so that they may work effectively, collectively or independently.
- Make clear the support and resources that will be provided.

For any task, the leader must ensure that everyone in the team knows at all times:

- What is going on and what is about to occur and why.
- When it is going to occur.
- How it is going to occur.
- What their part in it is.
- Guidelines for action they should take if the task does not go according to plan.

The ACE Conditions for Success: Clarity

FIGURE 15.4   Sequence of a briefing

The Briefing Sequence		
	PREPARATION	Confirm venue, date, time and attendance. Prepare handouts. Rehearse brief and use of audio visual aids.
1	INTRODUCTIONS	Ensure everyone knows who everyone is.
2	SITUATION	a. Context, market, competitors, customers, partners. b. Own organization intent and plan 2 levels up. c. Team composition: attached to/detached from team.
3	MISSION	From the Appreciation mission analysis.
4	EXECUTION	a. General outline: The CoA from own Appreciation: when and where actions take place in relation to each other. b. Grouping and Tasks by Phases in detail (who is to do what, where, by when, and within what specific constraints). c. Coordinating Instructions: Timings, Control Measures, General Constraints, Risk Management. d. Summary of Execution.
5	ADMINISTRATION AND LOGISTICS	What support is being provided by whom, when, where and how. Resources, equipment, transport, etc.
6	CONTROL AND COMMUNICATION	a. Authorities. b. Reporting and flow of information needed.
7	CONFIRM	Open questions from and then to the team.

© Jeremy Tozer, 1997–2006

The manner in which you convey this information must be clear, concise, precise, confident, unambiguous, simple and inspiring. Rehearsals are strongly recommended – if you cannot swiftly and clearly articulate your plan, do not expect anyone else to understand it!

Since you will have involved the team in the appreciation and detailed planning (a participative leadership style), and the briefing's purpose is simply to ensure clarity and build confidence; it is quite appropriate to be 'directive' during the briefing. Indeed the briefing is not another planning session and it will be ineffective if it becomes a two-way discussion. The ideal briefing will follow the logical sequence of Figure 15.4, which builds on the documented plan.

Preparation

The leader needs to make any necessary preparations to be able to give the brief. This includes ensuring the people who need to be there will be present, booking a suitable location and preparing any audio-visual aids, confirmatory takeaway notes and so on. If the leader is unused to briefing, if the brief is complex, or if other people are going to present a section of the brief (such as leaders of each phase, or the logistician), then it must be rehearsed so that those other people say exactly what you expect them to say and in the right manner. How the briefing is stage-managed is as important in creating confidence as the clarity and simplicity of the plan itself.

1. Introductions

Ensure that everybody needed is present and that everyone knows one another and why they are there. This is also a simple way of introducing relative strangers who may be attached to your team, or who may simply need to be aware of what you are doing. This is not done just out of politeness. It is a simple human fact that if one knows a face and what a person's job is, it breaks the ice and will greatly aid cooperation and enhance teamwork later on.

Conclude this section with a brief 'Description of the task'. Simply outlining in one sentence the nature of the task will help other people orientate their minds to what their part in the task is likely to be. They can 'tune themselves in' to what is about to be covered; for example, 'This is a briefing for the launch of ABC product.'

2. Situation

Explain the context in which the task will be carried out. If this is done well, people will psychologically commit to the mission before it has been explicitly stated. The situation may include geographical, demographic, economic and market influences, as well as your own organization's higher intentions as sub-paragraphs. This may be extracted from your appreciation (but there is no need to read out the appreciation in full including all your deductions):

- *Market.* State the relevant facts relating to the market in which you are working.
- *Competition.* Outline the state of play with regard to competitors, their likely plan and their expected next actions.
- *Own organization.* Brief the team on higher level organizational plans and intentions so that they understand their team's role in the 'bigger picture'. As a rule of thumb, brief two and one levels above your own. Share information: it makes the team feel involved.
- *Attachments and detachments to own organization.* For a project, outline any temporary additional people working with your team, or detached from it.

While the above includes all the things you know about the situation, it is also useful to say what you do not know that may have an impact.

3. Mission

Your mission stems from your appreciation of tasks allocated to you by your superior, their purpose and the higher intent. The mission must be clear, concise, precise and unambiguous. If you express it in the infinitive it will convey a sense of action, which is what you want to happen. This should be followed by the purpose so people understand the reason why it is going to happen.

When briefing, state it slowly and repeat it to allow it to sink in. Missions are best given as: 'To do something (action) in order to achieve (purpose).' For example, 'To launch a line extension to ABC brand in order to increase brand equity and market share.'

4. Execution

General outline
Explain your outline plan (the CoA from your appreciation) by phases in simple terms, including the objectives necessary for overall success.

Grouping and tasks by phases
Taking each phase in turn, explain the composition of any sub-teams that will work together and brief each individual or sub-group (and its leader) by stating their name(s) and looking at them while you do it – maintain eye contact. Allocate their specific tasks and include any particular constraints or additional authority and resources allocated for that particular task. Ensure that each person understands their role, or sub-team's role, by asking them before you address the next individual.

Coordinating instructions
Include timings, preparatory actions, risk management, etc – only give details at this stage that are essential to understanding the plan and that are applicable to most, if not all, of the audience and most or all of the phases.

Summary of execution
Summarize the plan to give the individuals clarity on the bigger picture and their part in it once again. Use this opportunity to stress the importance of each individual's task, generate commitment and enthusiasm.

7. Administration and logistics

The execution section should only have included details essential to understanding the essence of the plan and each team member's part in it. The detail which should be included here covers:

- equipment and materials;
- resources and logistics;
- administrative support and so on.

8. Control and communication

Ensure that the team is clear on who is controlling and/or coordinating the various aspects of work, and brief the team on any changes to normal authorities or reporting lines. Include how progress is to be measured, how feedback will be shared and what reports and returns are needed, and any delegated authorities.

9. Questions

Finally, to ensure clarity and understanding, ask those present if they have any questions and give them a few minutes to read through their notes before you expect questions to be asked. After this, ask open questions of each individual to confirm their understanding of the 'big picture' and their part in it – what they are responsible for. This is the only means you have to ensure that your intent has been understood. By asking open questions such as, 'What is your role in Phase 1?' you can enter a confirmatory dialogue. Importantly, you have also enabled people to accept accountability by stating what they will do in front of the whole team. This does much to generate commitment and mutual trust and confidence; success will be all the more probable.

Dos and don'ts

When briefing:

- Do make your briefings clear, concise and simple.
- Do tell people at the outset what the format of the brief will be, and when you wish people to ask questions.
- Do provide people with written confirmatory notes at the start so that they can listen rather than write, if it is appropriate to do so.
- Do give your team members a thorough understanding of your intentions and those of your superior.
- Do integrate all team members in coordinated action.
- Do allow team members the maximum freedom of action consistent with the need for coordination – let them make their own appreciations about how to achieve delegated tasks.
- Do convey confidence and enthusiasm, and look people in the eye.
- Do be aware that over-detailed instructions stifle initiative, restrict flexibility, are seldom remembered and are time-consuming to prepare and deliver.
- Don't try to give detailed plans and briefs covering every possible contingency.
- Don't let the flow of your brief be interrupted by taking questions throughout.
- Don't let a briefing become a discussion. If it becomes clear that something has been overlooked in planning, explicitly stop the briefing, revert to planning, then reschedule or restart the briefing.

Remember things can and will go wrong during the execution of any plan, but effective planning and briefing will have reduced the chances of that happening to the minimum, and the team will be able to continue effective work in your absence.

Early warning

As soon as you know that your team has a task to complete, or there is a change of direction, etc, you should make a quick appreciation of the situation and then warn people. This 'early warning' must be passed as soon as possible so that people can start thinking about what is to come and anticipate what is required. A warning brief should include as much of the following as possible:

- Quick description of the situation.
- Your initial mission analysis.
- Task organization/team composition (if known at this stage).
- Execution general outline – the scope of the plan (if known at this stage).
- Specific tasks and who is responsible (if known).
- Details about any collective briefings or planning sessions – who is to attend, where and when.
- Coordinating instructions including action that others should take immediately.

The issuing of a warning brief should not be delayed until the leader has made a detailed appreciation or written a full plan if the leader has information that will help colleagues prepare for or anticipate what may come next. Sub-group leaders can and should start to conduct their mission analysis and make their appreciations as soon as they have received an early warning of a future task.

Communication: routine briefing and updates

It is surprising just how few organizations have any effective mechanism to keep people properly and routinely informed of what they need to know, and early enough so that anticipatory thought may be developed. Effective mechanisms do not include reliance on corporate magazines, intranet sites and e-mails from one's leader; it means regular collective face-to-face update briefings given to you by your boss (in person or by video link). It is therefore not in the least surprising that so many employees in so many organizations are disengaged and believe themselves to be members of the mushroom club (kept in the dark and fed on the proverbial!).

Figure 15.5 illustrates the four methods or routes for communicating within organizations. Large enterprises tend to rely on 1 (especially e-mail), whereas people listen more attentively to 4. Leaders should formally brief people, whether for specific projects and tasks or with updates on a variety of issues, and back up these face-to-face briefings with a succinct written (e-mail) summary (method 1). They should then check, during conversation in planned walkabouts and so on, that the message is understood (method 2), and they should engage in chats during tea breaks, to make sure that gossip reflects routes 1 and 2 (method 4). Method 3 is the realm of strategic leaders and HR directors to shape the systems and structure that influence collective behaviour.

FIGURE 15.5 Methods of communication

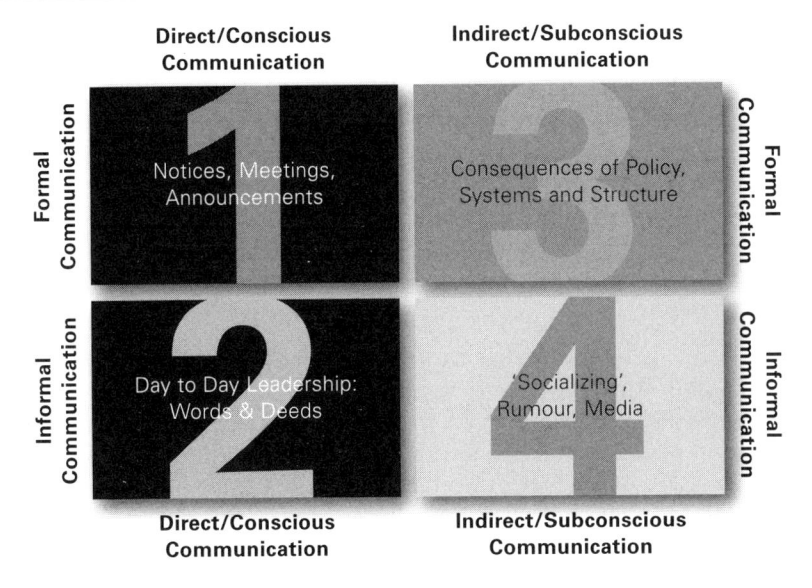

Quadrant 1 (Formal / Direct-Conscious): Notices, Meetings, Announcements
Quadrant 2 (Informal / Direct-Conscious): Day to Day Leadership: Words & Deeds
Quadrant 3 (Formal / Indirect-Subconscious): Consequences of Policy, Systems and Structure
Quadrant 4 (Informal / Indirect-Subconscious): 'Socializing', Rumour, Media

© Jeremy Tozer, 1997–2006

Project management and routine leadership

The appreciation, planning and briefing processes clearly have particular application to strategic, tactical, programme and project planning and execution. However, they should also be used in 'routine' leadership.

When asking the four key questions of the appreciation (What am I trying to achieve and why? What really affects achieving that? What are the options? Which option?) and holding formal and informal briefings become habitual and enter the bloodstream of the organization, that is when things really start to hum. Everyone can and should make daily (incremental) improvements to the way things are done; this is a form of innovation and these tools assist making it happen. The same tools enable step-change improvements to be embedded.

Other common tools

Six Sigma

An internet search of Motorola's Six Sigma reveals two project methodologies inspired by Deming's Plan-Do-Check-Act cycle, which have a manufacturing background:

'DMAIC' *is intended for projects to improve an existing business process.*

'DMADV' *is intended for projects to create or design new products or processes.*

Define the problem, and the project objectives.

Measure key aspects of the current process or product and production capabilities and risks, and collect data.

Analyse the data to establish causes of defects (DMAIC), or develop design options and select the best design (DMADV).

Improve the current process.

Control the future process to prevent defects.

Design details – optimize the new product or process design.

Verify the design.

These manufacturing tools have been adopted in some organizations for use in business planning and other types of decision making, and a superficial examination suggests that Six Sigma has most of the elements of an appreciation. However, the appreciation may have certain advantages: while you may make widgets more efficiently as a result of DMAIC, there is no explicit means of confirming that you should still be in the widget-making business.

Mission analysis provides a set of questions that enables specified and implied tasks to be understood and forces alignment by understanding intentions at higher levels. Mission analysis results in a single, clear unifying aim and purpose that enables multi-disciplinary teams to work together. The appreciation explicitly flows into the detailed planning and briefing cycle (with dynamic review); and it is the explicit use of these simple leadership processes that aids effective implementation of the decision or plan.

PRINCE2®

PRINCE2 (PRojects IN Controlled Environments) is a process-based method for project management and is used extensively by the UK government and the private sector both in the UK and abroad.

The PRINCE2 method is in the public domain and offers guidance on project management; guidance such as 'a mandate to scope or start a project is expected which defines in high-level terms the reason for the project and the outcome sought' (= mission analysis). It is suggested that the appreciation, planning and briefing tools described here are the detailed 'how to' that make working with PRINCE2 both more efficient and more effective.

16
Cascade of planning and briefing

Tasking procedure

Leadership structure

Extraction of relevant information

Communication in an organizational structure

As will be clear by now, a cascade of leadership processes is required to take corporate-level strategic plans and strategic objectives and turn them into aligned plans and objectives that are relevant and meaningful to every level of the organization (Figure 16.1). This produces line of sight from the grandest objective to the tasks that the individual performs on the front line.

The mechanism for this is the iterating, cascading and recurring cycle of processes (Figure 16.2) for the decision making (the appreciation), planning and briefing described in the preceding chapters. These processes help overcome the effects of information anarchy, the confused compression of time and space, and VUCA, discussed earlier. These processes also minimize the effect of the causes of friction and the performance gap that exists between strategy and its expected outcomes and strategy execution and actual outcomes: imperfect information, imperfect decision-making process and the imperfect transmission and interpretation of information. Of equal (if not greater) importance is the social process that is used in parallel to engage people in focused and meaningful conversations, with 'outputs' that they own and feel accountable for. Together, these mechanisms enable the alignment of activity by committed people.

Tasking procedure

'Tasking procedure' is a very simple SOP – standard operating procedure or common way of working – that every leader at every level should understand. The aim

FIGURE 16.1 Alignment of objectives, plans and activity

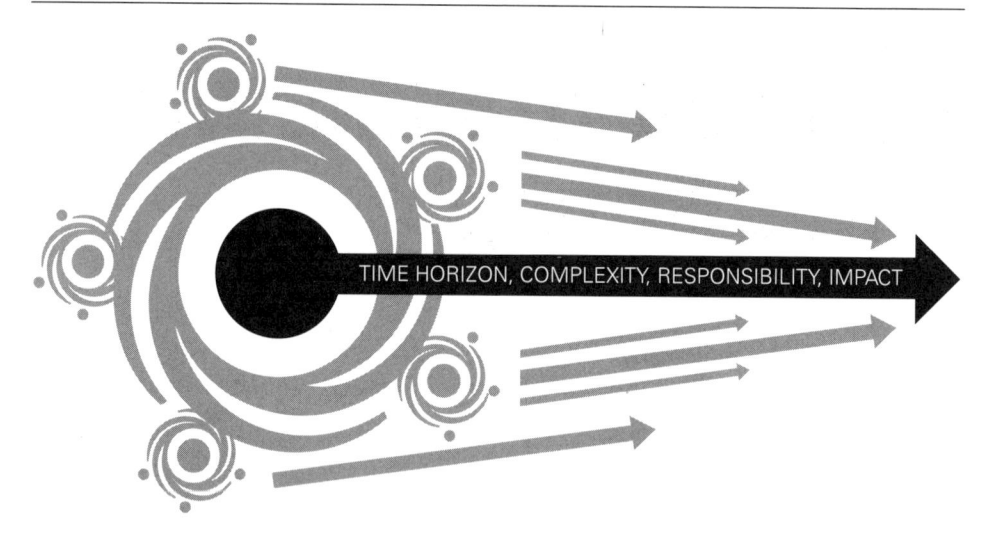

TIME HORIZON, COMPLEXITY, RESPONSIBILITY, IMPACT

© Jeremy Tozer, 2010

of the tasking procedure is to initiate activity as rapidly, efficiently and effectively as possible by ensuring that every person understands what they need to do, why they need to do it, and what they are to do it with. The principles are:

- Concurrent activity.
- Anticipation at all levels.
- Knowledge of the decision making, planning and briefing system. This means that everyone:
  - understands what briefings/meetings they must attend as a matter of course;
  - understands the sequence that these processes follow;
  - is able to extract relevant information to make their own appreciations and plans at the next level down.
- Efficient and effective SOPs for all routine action.

Leaders should embed the common, effective and flexible processes that comprise the decision making, planning and briefing system because:

- the sequence is logical, easy to follow and easy to remember;
- people know what to expect when this becomes the norm;
- it becomes habit, and tired and/or stressed leaders are less likely to omit important points;
- subordinate leaders and team members can grasp concepts and details quickly and make relevant extracts on which they can base their own decisions, plans and briefings.

FIGURE 16.2 Cascading, iterating and recurring processes to align activity and engage people

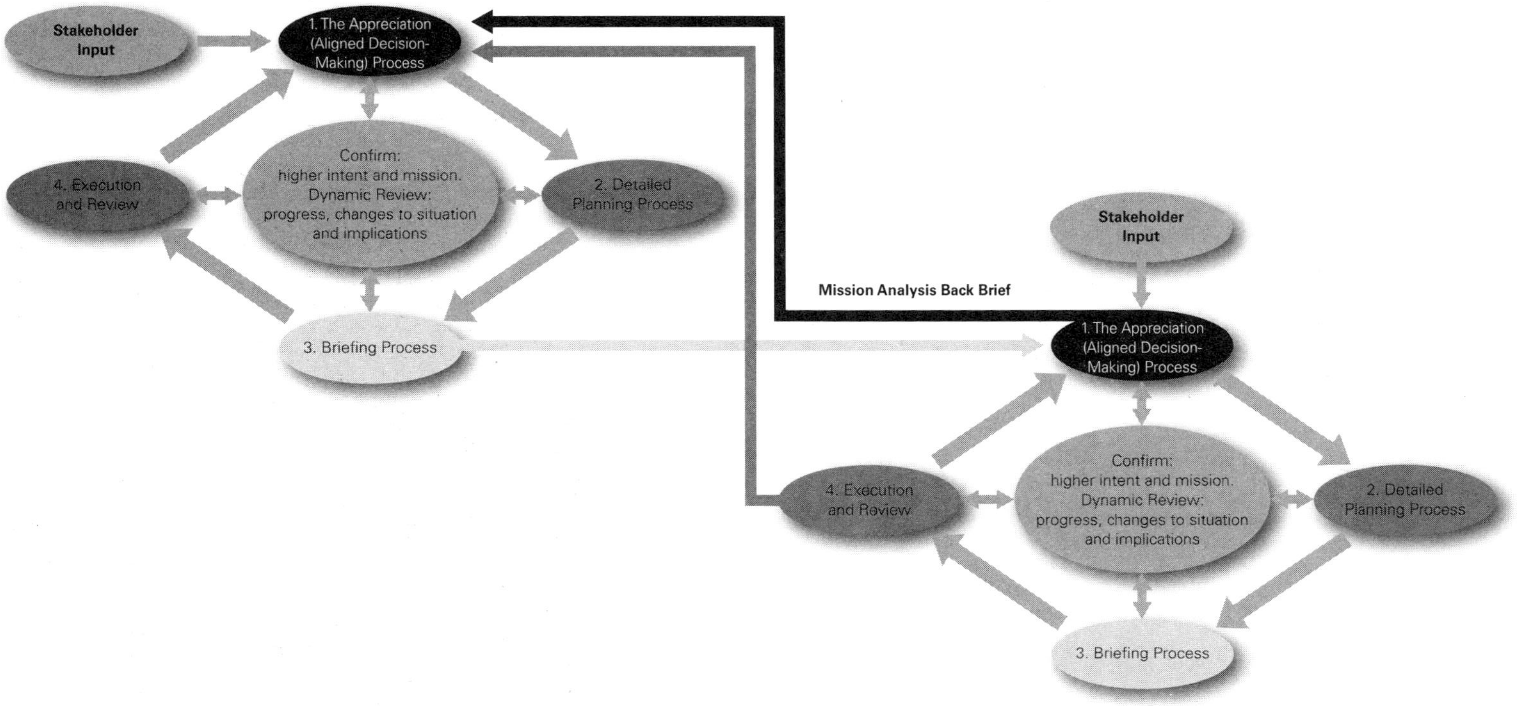

© Jeremy Tozer 2010

FIGURE 16.3 Effects-based leadership and the cascade of clarity

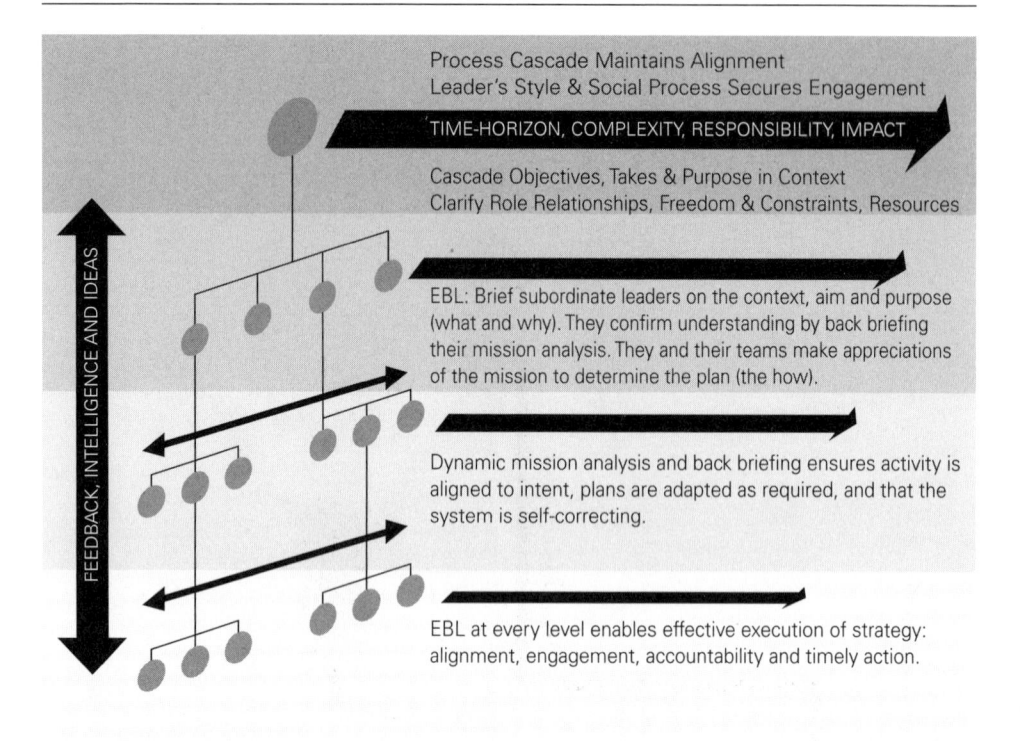

[Figure 16.3: Diagram showing cascade of clarity with hierarchical tree structure. Labels include:
- Process Cascade Maintains Alignment / Leader's Style & Social Process Secures Engagement
- TIME-HORIZON, COMPLEXITY, RESPONSIBILITY, IMPACT
- Cascade Objectives, Takes & Purpose in Context / Clarify Role Relationships, Freedom & Constraints, Resources
- EBL: Brief subordinate leaders on the context, aim and purpose (what and why). They confirm understanding by back briefing their mission analysis. They and their teams make appreciations of the mission to determine the plan (the how).
- Dynamic mission analysis and back briefing ensures activity is aligned to intent, plans are adapted as required, and that the system is self-correcting.
- EBL at every level enables effective execution of strategy: alignment, engagement, accountability and timely action.
- Vertical axis: FEEDBACK, INTELLIGENCE AND IDEAS]

© Jeremy Tozer, 1997–2007

Leadership structure

While the combined thought and social process is the method of creating clarity and engagement, the leadership structure of the organization are the veins and arteries through which these processes, and the information contained in them, flow. This is the realm of organization, which is explored in detail in Chapter 22. In a similar way that the discipline of the processes we have examined create clarity, freedom of action and ownership; there is a paradox in the discipline of applying the 'first principles' of organization structure to align accountability with authority both laterally and vertically (the prime source of stress in most organizations) which most people also find to be liberating. Figure 16.3 gives a 2D view of what is a 3D reality in most organizations.

Extraction of relevant information

As leaders, you may well have subordinate leaders reporting to you who will comprise your own briefing group. These subordinate leaders will need to be able to extract from your briefing their own task(s), make their own appreciation and detailed plans about how they will carry out the task(s) and then brief their own teams. This cycle of processes is cascaded down through the organization until the lowest team leader is briefing the front line operator.

As a rule of thumb, use a third of the available time to complete a task for the appreciation, planning and briefing at your level. As the decision and plan cascades, the size of the 'owner's' part reduces and thus less time is needed for thought. This way, there is just about enough time for every leader at every level to think about and then start execution of their part of the master plan.

People at every level need to understand the big picture relative to their own level, hence the concept of briefing people on the situation 'two levels up'. Equally as a leader you need to ensure understanding two levels down. This does not mean doing your subordinate leaders' jobs, but you ought to be talking to their team members and asking questions about objectives, purpose and so on and gauging their level of understanding, ownership and engagement. If your subordinate leaders' team members don't know what is going on, you can put them right while you are with them, and then you need to address the 'leadership problem' that exists with their team leader – has that team leader failed to create clarity and engage his or her team, or have you failed to do that with your subordinate team leaders? In this way you are assessing the quality of leadership in your part of the organization and keeping your finger on the pulse.

As a leader you will attend your boss's briefings and will be given his or her mission and you will receive your own detailed tasks. Figure 16.4 shows how you should take information received at your boss's briefing and process it to extract what you need for your planning and briefing at the next level down.

Mission analysis applied to your detailed tasks (confirmed in back briefing your leader and amending both your and his or her intentions as appropriate) will lead you to define your own team's mission. Application of the appreciation, planning and briefing processes enables you to delegate to your junior leaders their own clear detailed tasks. This cycle is repeated as they in turn convert the tasks that you have given to them into a mission, and then allocate their own sub-tasks to specific individuals. By assigning tasks (outputs) and by detailing constraints and boundaries and allocating resources, you empower people to conduct their own mission analysis and to make their own appreciations. This leads to the ownership of solutions.

The beauty of this cascading sequence of common methods that breaks strategy down into smaller more manageable pieces, is that as well as ensuring alignment, trust and confidence, people's 'level of thinking' is raised. When people use these common methods as SOP, leaders can be confident that others will think clearly, act in alignment with well thought out plans that are clearly understood and owned by those involved – leaders are then willing to delegate more tasks and authority. Organizational agility and execution speed and quality are built. These processes enable 'effects-based leadership (EBL)' to apply (see Figure 16.3). This is the philosophy of decentralizing decision-making authority to the lowest possible level to enable rapid aligned decisions and action. It requires timely and effective decision making by subordinate leaders who understand the context, the 'higher intent', and the effects they should achieve, the purpose of these effects, and who have a clear responsibility to fulfil that intent. This has been proven to be a very effective approach.

FIGURE 16.4 Extraction and cascade of briefing information

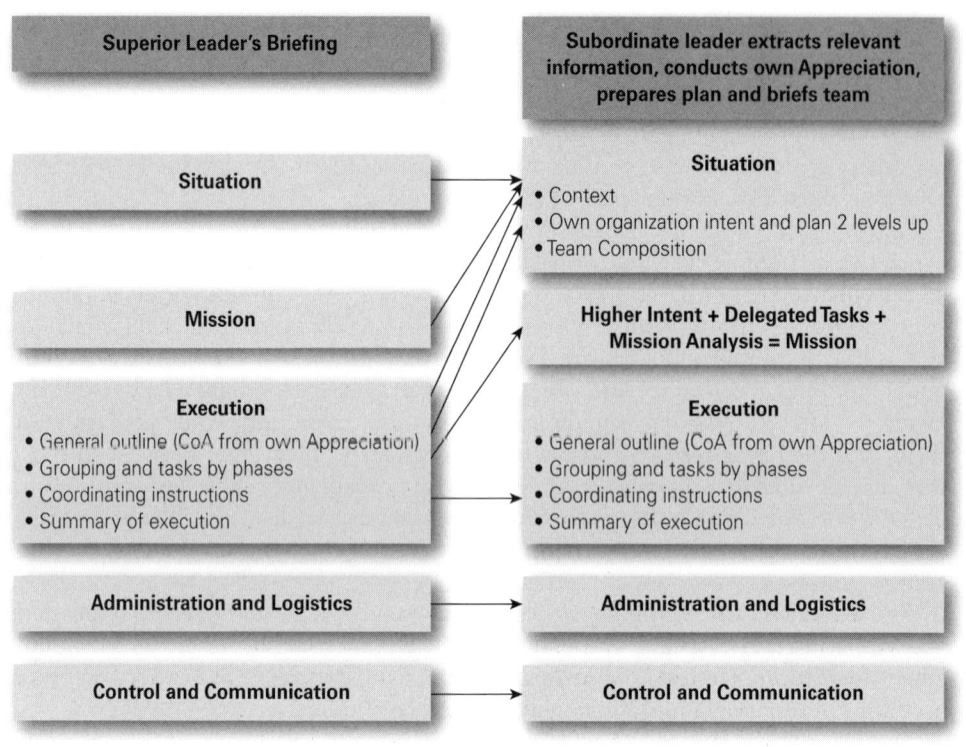

Superior Leader's Briefing	Subordinate leader extracts relevant information, conducts own Appreciation, prepares plan and briefs team
Situation	Situation • Context • Own organization intent and plan 2 levels up • Team Composition
Mission	Higher Intent + Delegated Tasks + Mission Analysis = Mission
Execution • General outline (CoA from own Appreciation) • Grouping and tasks by phases • Coordinating instructions • Summary of execution	Execution • General outline (CoA from own Appreciation) • Grouping and tasks by phases • Coordinating instructions • Summary of execution
Administration and Logistics	Administration and Logistics
Control and Communication	Control and Communication

© Jeremy Tozer, 1997–2006

Communication in an organizational structure

Again, it must be stressed that the diagrams presented here to illustrate organization structure show a hierarchy of levels of work complexity. They are not meant to promote the archetypal command and control, rigid and inflexible organization that has characterized many organizations to date.

Most organizations have some form of structure of leadership accountability, and it is this structure that can be used to facilitate the passage of information up, down and across the organization. Figure 16.5 illustrates how communication may flow within a work team which, by definition, has two levels of work within it – that of the leader and that of the team members. The leader A may, quite obviously, talk to any of his or her team members as individuals, or to the team (or a group within the team) collectively. The team members (B1 – B4) will, quite naturally, talk to each other. In this example, the leader and team in question are at the top of the organization, and this pattern of relationships repeats – B1 and B3 are both leaders of teams, and similarly, some of their subordinates are also team leaders.

Cascade of Planning and Briefing

The circle of communication shown in light shade indicates the leadership communication between the team leader and either individual members of the team, or the whole team. The dark shaded arrow indicates the communication among peer team members. The 'clarity' created by the leader A will determine how much time the leader needs to spend in resolving minor differences and clearing up misunderstandings, which is time wasted in unnecessary 'light' communication. If sufficient clarity is created, the peer team members can get on and do their jobs without delay, communicating at the 'red' level as required without having to escalate issues to the leader, thus freeing up the leader's time.

A three-level grouping is shown in Figure 16.6 – it shows a leader A of a team of subordinate leaders B1 – B4, who have teams at level C (for simplicity only two teams are shown, C1 – C3, and C4 – C6). The pattern of communication relationships in Figure 16.5 is repeated, and an additional communication loop is added. The communication loop illustrates communication between peers in different teams working across the organization.

The same comments apply to the 'light' and 'dark' communication as before. Where peers in different teams at level C are unable to agree or clarify misunderstandings,

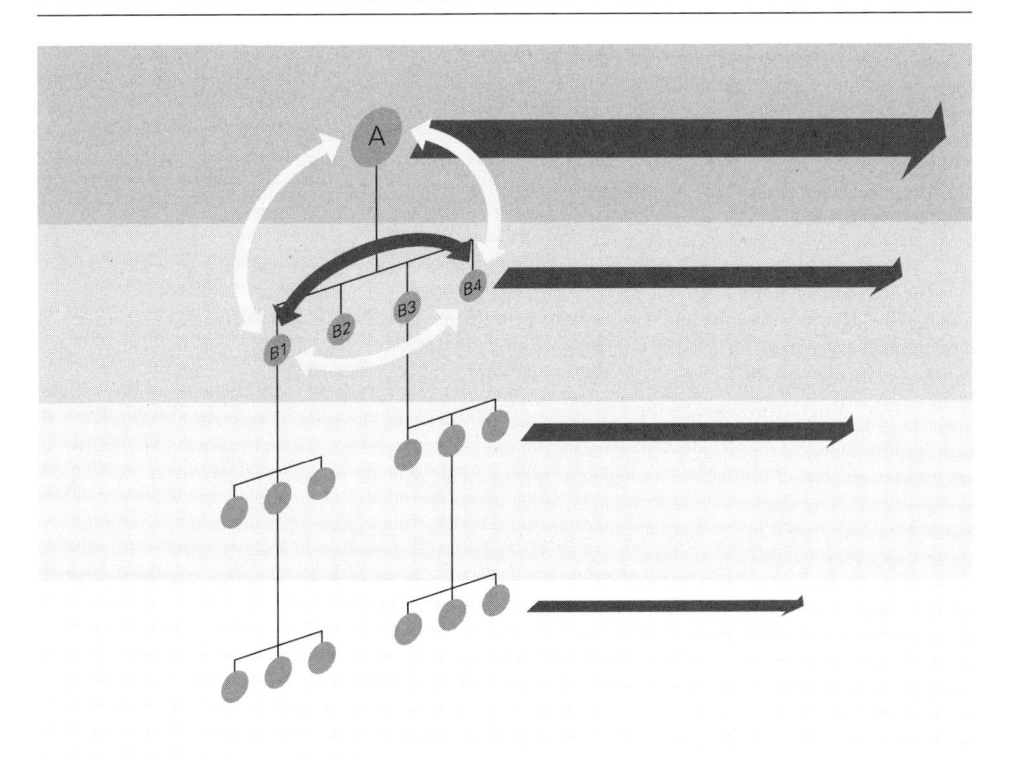

FIGURE 16.5 Communication between a leader and his or her team

© Jeremy Tozer, 2008

FIGURE 16.6 Communication between a leader of a team of leaders and their teams

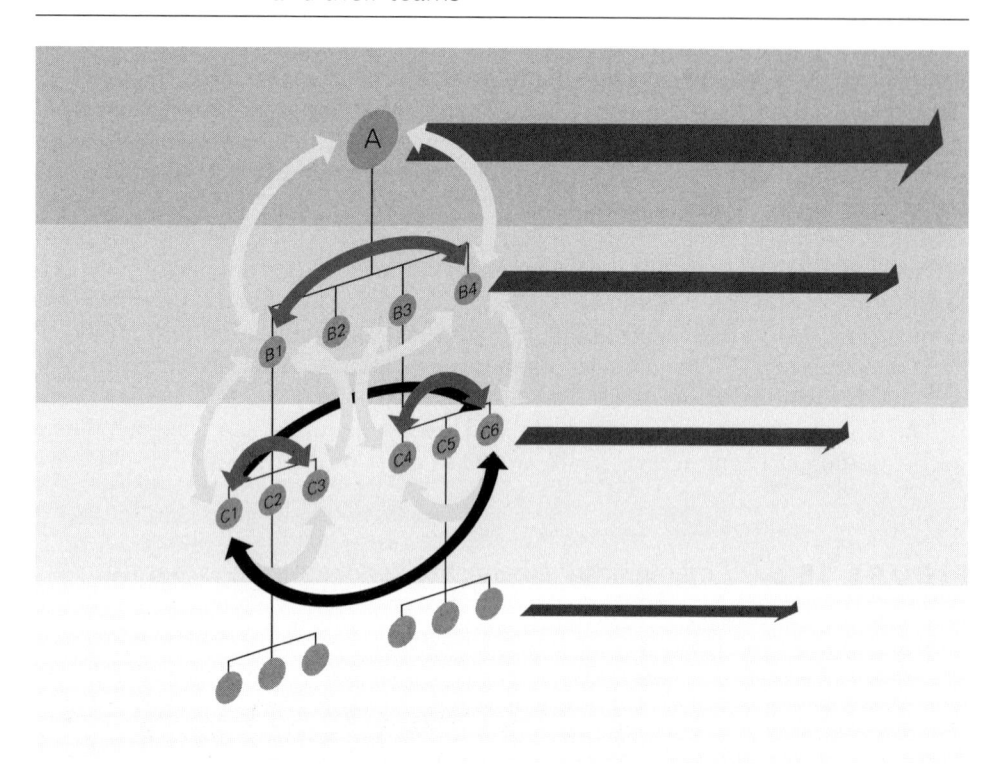

© Jeremy Tozer, 2008

they escalate matters to their respective leaders at level B. If the leaders at level B are unable to agree things between themselves, they in turn escalate the matter to the leader at level A, who is the final arbiter. However, the leader at level A will not be expecting trivial matters to reach his or her level of escalation. This shows that if the leader at level A has been really clear, then he or she will minimize the amount of unnecessary time spent in extra conversations and in dealing with 'niff naff and trivia'.

This pattern of three-level groups also recurs in any large organization structure, and the leader of a three-level group adds some checks and balances to the work of their subordinate leaders. This is explored in Chapter 22.

17
The intelligence system to inform decision making

> The intelligence cycle
> Intelligence and planning

It is not the intent of this book to provide the details on the establishment and operation of a market research-intelligence strategy. However it is worth setting 'intelligence' within the context of decision making and planning as it should be integral to effective decisions, especially at the strategic level, if you wish to anticipate what is over the horizon.

First, 'intelligence' as used here must be defined. Intelligence is that product which results from the processing of information concerning nations, markets, competitors and their products and services, customers and consumers, and business partners. It may be of strategic, operational or tactical significance. Its purpose is simply to reduce uncertainty in decision making and enhance the effectiveness with which operations are conducted in the pursuit of organizational objectives. Its essence is therefore prediction, not the presentation of recent history (although an understanding of history will assist in prediction).

There are seven principles that govern the effective organization and production of intelligence:

1 *Centralized control.* Intelligence should be centrally controlled partly to prevent duplication of effort and ensure the efficient and economic use of all resources, but mostly to ensure that prediction is based on all the information available and that nothing has been overlooked.
2 *Responsiveness.* Information is gathered and intelligence produced to meet the requirements of the leader and the organization that the intelligence function is supporting.

3 *Timeliness.* The most accurate and reliable intelligence reports are useless if they arrive too late to be considered in decision making. An incomplete report in time is more use than a complete report too late.

4 *Systematic exploitation.* Information, and the sources and agencies that provide it, must be exploited systematically.

5 *Objectivity.* Information, or the interpretation of it, must never be distorted to fit a preconceived idea; that is akin to situating the appreciation.

6 *Continuous review.* Intelligence 'products' should be reviewed and revised continuously, taking into account new information. The question 'How does this alter the current assessment?' should be asked of all new pieces of information.

7 *Accessibility.* Intelligence is of no value if those who need to know it are not told it.

In the military world, an eighth principle applies: security of sources. If a source is compromised then its usefulness ends (and if the source is a person, then that source may come to a sticky end).

The intelligence cycle

The intelligence cycle is the name for the cycle of activities that gather information and turn it into intelligence, as illustrated in Figure 17.1.

Direction

Direction is, first, that given by the organizational leader to the 'intelligence function', and secondly by the intelligence function to the sources and agencies involved in the intelligence cycle. Military leaders require their intelligence staff to answer the questions:

WHO? is going to do

WHAT?

WHERE?

WHEN?

HOW? and in

WHAT STRENGTH?

Many commercial business leaders will want answers to these questions as applied to competitors, to the market direction, to consumer or customer needs, and to risks highlighted in Chapter 1. So these questions may be rewritten as:

- WHO is going to do, need or offer
- WHAT action, product or service
- WHERE in the market and in what segment

FIGURE 17.1   The intelligence cycle

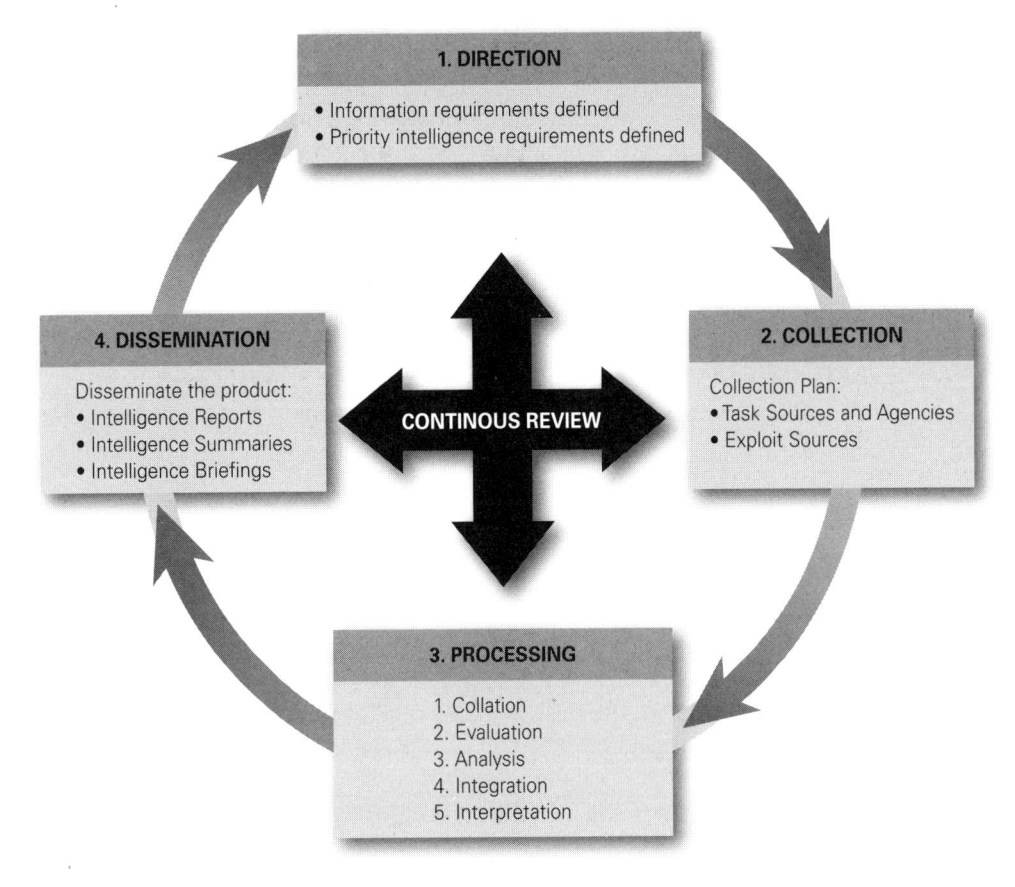

1. DIRECTION
- Information requirements defined
- Priority intelligence requirements defined

2. COLLECTION
Collection Plan:
- Task Sources and Agencies
- Exploit Sources

3. PROCESSING
1. Collation
2. Evaluation
3. Analysis
4. Integration
5. Interpretation

4. DISSEMINATION
Disseminate the product:
- Intelligence Reports
- Intelligence Summaries
- Intelligence Briefings

CONTINOUS REVIEW

© Jeremy Tozer, 2008

- WHEN
- HOW and in
- WHAT STRENGTH and with what resources?

The questions posed enable you to define your organization's intelligence requirements. A comparison of the current information and intelligence that you posses will lead you to define your knowledge gaps and the specific information that is now required – the questions that you need to ask and answer. Your questions may be structured to confirm or refute assumptions that have been made or to confirm or refute deductions that you have made from 'known' information; in order for decision-making planning to progress.

Collection

Having defined your information requirements, it is now necessary to create a collection plan. This is merely a matrix of the sources and agencies that will be tasked to provide which information or answer what questions. The sources and agencies may then be briefed (to put the questions and information requirements in context) and tasked – the task should include the time by which the information is required and the format it is required in to make its assimilation and use as easy as possible.

Sources and agencies

There are a variety of sources and agencies available to organizations – such as open source publications, market research agencies, academic experts, your customers and so on. Internally, an oft overlooked and under-utilized resource is your sales force, a good source of tactical intelligence which, if it is properly exploited, may inform your own strategy as well as indicate the strategy that your competitors are pursuing. The selection and tasking of sources and agencies will depend on a number of factors:

- reliability;
- speed and responsiveness;
- cost-effectiveness;
- area of expertise;
- risk.

Processing

Processing involves the conversion of information into intelligence. There are five steps in doing this:

1. collation;
2. evaluation;
3. analysis;
4. integration; and
5. interpretation.

1. Collation

Collation is the system for receiving, registering, sorting and recording all the information and data entering the 'intelligence office'. It enables all subsequent activities as well as the cross-referencing and comparison with other information received. An efficient collation system is a prerequisite for deriving intelligence from information already held.

2. Evaluation
Evaluation involves assessing a piece of information in terms of relevance, reliability, credibility and accuracy. A judgement of its relative value will determine the weighting given to it as it is integrated and analysed.

3. Analysis
Analysis is the step in which items of information are taken and repeatedly subjected to the questions, 'What does this mean?' and, 'So what?' until all the relevance and significance of the information is extracted.

4. Integration
Integration involves combining pieces of analysed information that support each other, preferably obtained from different sources, to construct a picture.

5. Interpretation
There are two aspects to interpretation. First there is the recognition of a complete picture. Second, interpretation means placing this picture in the context of the predictive questions asked initially: 'What is going to happen, when and how?' and so on.

Dissemination

This is the timely passage of intelligence to the 'customer' in a user-friendly form. The manner and form of dissemination are governed by these principles:

- *Timeliness*. Intelligence must be received in time to be of use for planning or decision making.
- *Accuracy*. All facts that are reported as facts must be true, and care should be used in the use of language, especially with the words 'likely', 'possible' and 'probable' used in predictions.
- *Brevity*. Reports must be kept as brief as possible, but at the same time include everything that the customer or decision maker needs to know.
- *Interpretation*. Again care should be used in the language used ('likely', 'possible', 'probable', etc) and a clear distinction should be maintained between facts and deductions made from them.
- *Standardization*. Reports will be understood more quickly if presented in a logical, progressive and familiar sequence under appropriate standard headings, for the same reasons that plans and briefs should have a standard sequence.
- *Distribution*. Intelligence staff must ensure that everyone who needs to know is in the know and when they need to know.

Methods of dissemination
Intelligence may be disseminated verbally (formal briefs or impromptu updates), in writing (formal full briefs, periodic intelligence summaries, and immediate intelligence reports), graphically or pictorially.

Intelligence and planning

Figure 17.2 shows the place of the intelligence system in the execution cycle that develops strategy and turns it into reality.

FIGURE 17.2 Intelligence and the execution cycle

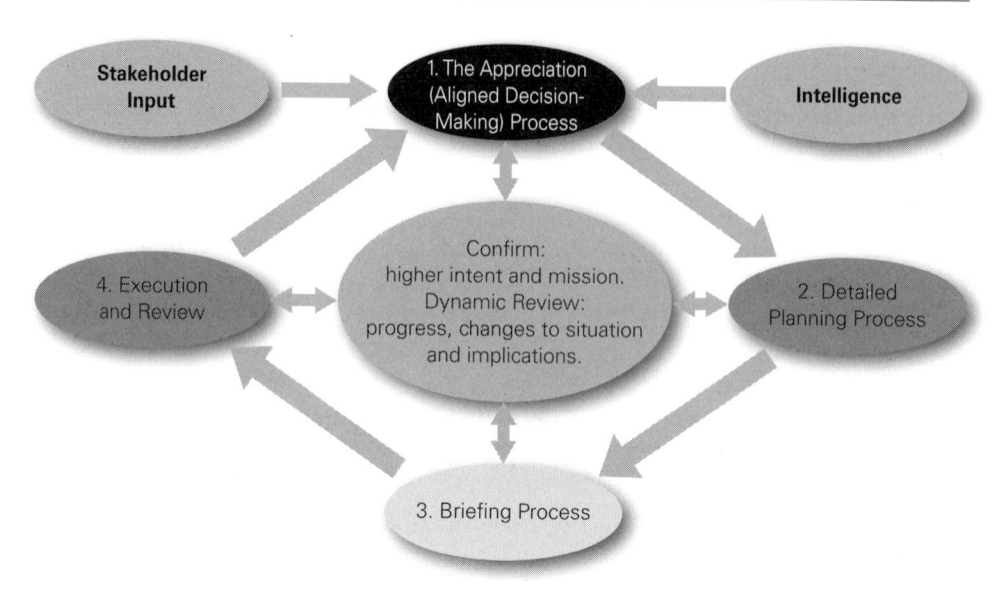

© Jeremy Tozer, 2011

While a steady stream of intelligence may inform the fine details of a plan, its primary use is in the initial appreciation (decision making) phase and particularly during mission and factor analysis, as shown in Figure 17.3. The place of intelligence in the cascade of decisions and plans is shown in Figure 17.4.

FIGURE 17.3 Intelligence-informed decision making

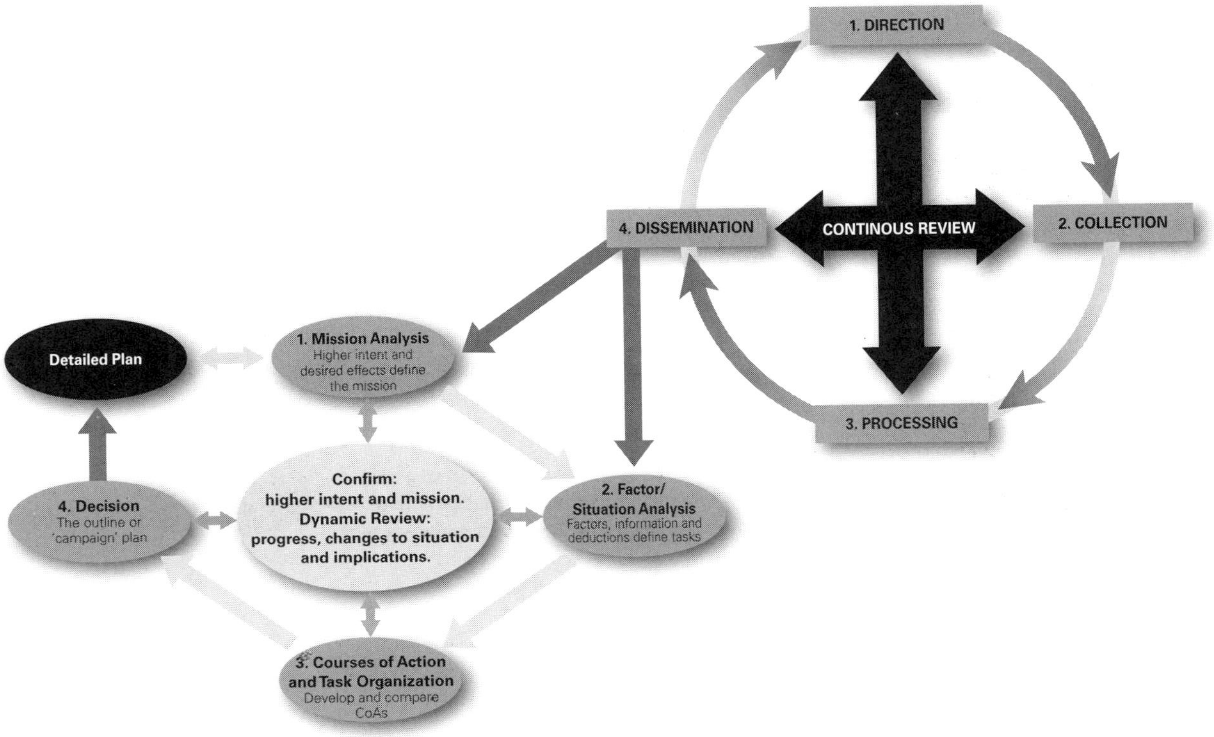

© Jeremy Tozer, 1997–2006

FIGURE 17.4 Intelligence in the decision making, planning and briefing cascade

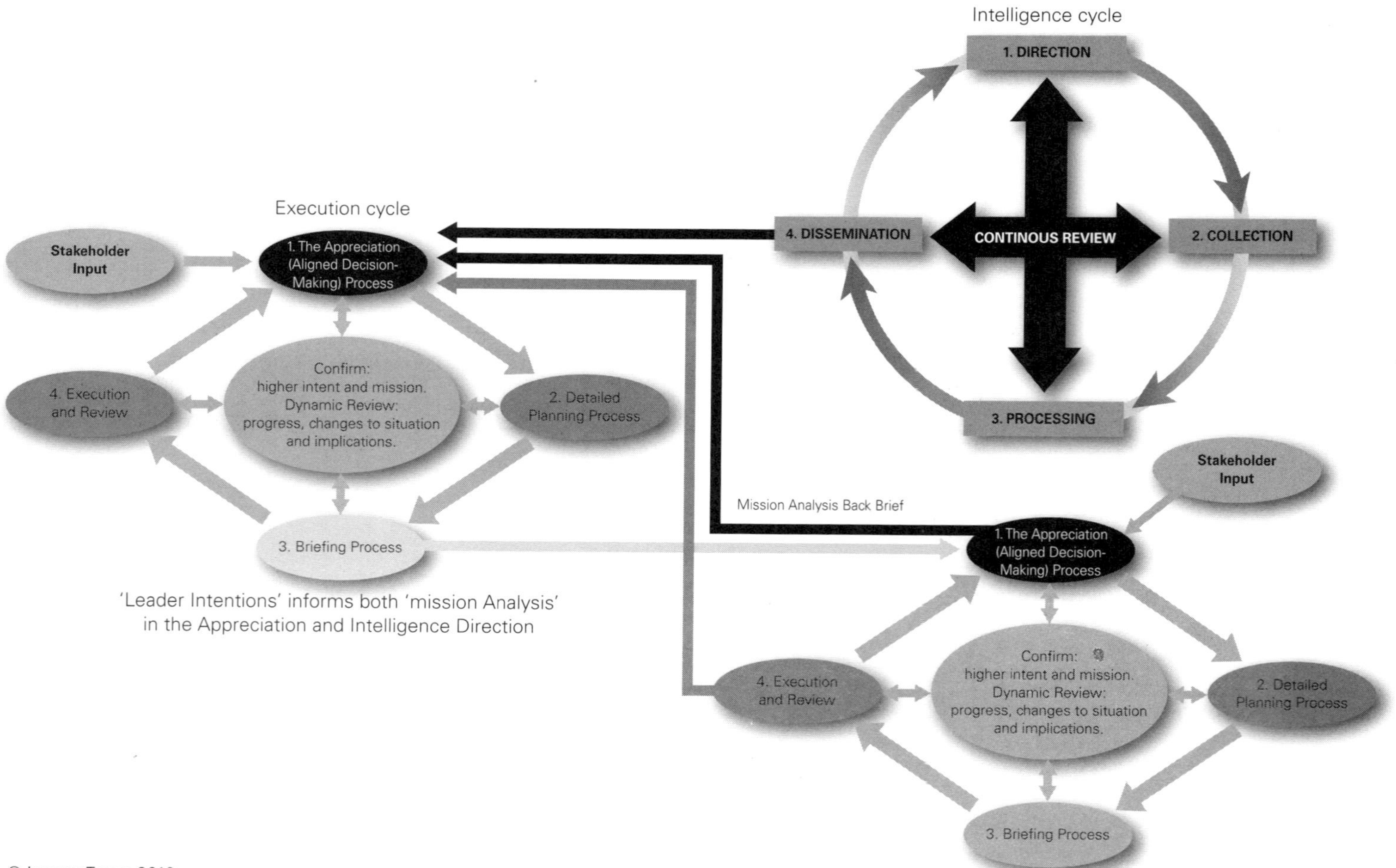

© Jeremy Tozer, 2010

18
Directing, coordinating, controlling and evaluating progress

Directing

Coordinating

Control (and influence)

Evaluating progress

We should start by being clear on the meaning of some terms:

Directing. Directing means establishing through effective two-way communication with your colleagues what is required to be done and why, giving any necessary guidelines that relate to how it is to be done – although as far as possible this should be left to people's initiative. The communication may be through an informal chat, or at a formal briefing or meeting.

Coordination. Coordination is concerned with lateral relations within an organization. The aim of coordination is either to seek the cooperation of people not in the leader's own team and therefore over whom the leader has 'vertical authority', or to link actions by two or more groups within the leader's team.

Controlling. Some contemporary writers have given the word 'control' an unpleasant taste so let us be clear that we mean it not in the interfering and domineering sense, but being able to influence events and outcomes. The control function exists to ensure that what ought to be done is done.

Evaluating. Evaluating is a process by which the leader judges progress in a task against its plan, and results in part from the control measures. Continuous evaluation will bring the leader back to the (re)planning function and on through the other functions of briefing, controlling/coordinating, supporting, informing and back to re-evaluating.

Directing

Except in emergencies or when the occasion demands, it is unlikely that the stern, strict and autocratic leader who continually barks out his or her orders will achieve much in the long run. People quite naturally resent being pushed around, and such 'techniques' cannot guarantee their effective cooperation.

The direct 'order' that something be done by someone in a certain way by a certain time is certainly not the best method of gaining wholehearted commitment. Better results can be obtained by requesting or suggesting that something is done – always explaining the reason why. This gives subordinates leeway in using their own initiative, which will gain their commitment.

Whether suggesting or requesting (and only on occasion telling) the leader must ensure that the individual team members clearly understand what is to be done. Leaders should talk in terms that their team members will understand and explain their wishes and intentions clearly and concisely. Many terms and situations that are clear to the leader may convey an entirely different meaning to the people working for him or her – ask open questions to ensure that everything has been completely understood and that the message you intended to be received has been received without 'corruption' by perceptual filters.

As a general rule, written instructions are best when making them a matter of record is required; when precise figures or complicated details are involved; when a particular team member or group has to be made especially accountable; or when a bulletin board is used for general direction, tasking or work assignments.

Oral requests are always best for giving simple instructions affecting routine tasks and for clarifying the details of a written order. The face-to-face nature of the communication allows the leader to inject his or her personality and inspiration into the request or direction, clarify the meaning and identify any assistance the subordinate may need. A voice- or video-phone is the next best means of communication; e-mail is the most dangerous as it does not allow the leader to gauge response to the message (has the message been perceived as intended?) and is the cause of so many conflicts.

In directing, the leader is charting a delicate course between too little supervision and too much. If it is insisted that all instructions are documented, the enterprise will be bogged down with administration, and the pace of work will slow down. If team members feel that their leader is 'breathing down their necks', their initiative and interest will be stifled. The amount of direction given to subordinates should always be the minimum necessary to ensure alignment and efficient completion of the task. Direction as a function of leadership is at the heart of ensuring that people get the job done. Even the best planning and organizing will fail if the direction given is unsuitable, or is given in an inappropriate manner.

Direction will be effective if the leader can honestly answer yes to these questions:

- Are my intentions clear to my team members?
- Are my intentions clear enough to avoid ambiguity?
- Do all my team members have a common interpretation of the task or plan?
- Have I avoided over-directing people; do they want and need greater freedom of action?
- Have I allocated sufficient resources to the task?

For directive leadership to be successful, a number of prerequisites are necessary:

- *Standardization.* A common business doctrine, common systems, processes and terminology that enhance clarity in all activity and communication.
- *Reliability of response.* Action must be aligned to a clear understanding of the 'higher intent'.
- *Trust.* A mutual understanding that impossible tasks will not be set, and the minimum necessary support will be provided.
- *Risk.* Direction and trust imply that the superior is willing to accept an element of risk.

Coordinating

A leader's responsibilities extend in three directions: upward to his or her superior, downward to his or her subordinate team members, and laterally to a team or person, not working directly for that leader but who may be involved in, or affected by the leader's work. The coordinating function of leadership is concerned with the leader's lateral relations within the organization.

The aim of coordination is to seek the cooperation of people not in the leader's own team, or to link actions by groups within his or her team. No team in an enterprise is so independent or self-contained that it does not rely on other teams for help in accomplishing its mission. A leader needs to work out joint problems with other groups, by person-to-person contact, by planned and effective meetings and liaison visits.

Effective coordination is best achieved by advising those involved well in advance about what help is required – a suitably constructed warning brief. The leader, though having control over his or her own team's activities, cannot control to the same extent the work of others whose help and assistance is sought. It is wise to give them as much time as possible to organize the assistance requested, in the knowledge that they will have their own priorities to fulfil and may plead that pressure of work makes them unable to help, especially when help is requested at short notice.

If the leader wishes to seek the willing cooperation of other departments, it is important that requests are made in a personable way. Gratitude must always be expressed for help given, and help should be given willingly in return when it is requested by those who have assisted in the past. Such cooperation secures good relations for the future, since few people are prepared to help the type of leader who consistently refuses or fails to help them.

It must be emphasized that 'control' in the sense defined here is essential. Let us be quite clear that it is meant not in the interfering and domineering sense, but in the sense of being able to influence events and outcomes and manage risk. The most effective planning and preparation will be to no avail unless it can be translated into action that accurately reflects the work needed to achieve the original objectives of the plan. This is where the requirement for control and evaluation arises: to ensure that what ought to be done is done.

Perhaps one of the greatest fears that newly promoted or inexperienced leaders have is that they will not be able to control a subordinate leader, perhaps a foreman or supervisor, who may be a lot older and probably far more 'street-wise'. The concern is, 'How will I get him or her to do what I need done willingly?' Provided one is sensible in one's approach and follow this advice, those fears have little or no substance and one will soon become comfortable in the leadership role. Nevertheless there are some techniques that may be used to help keep ahead of events rather than merely reacting to them.

Timely, effective control and prompt evaluation by the leader, helps to maintain momentum in an activity. The skill is in recognizing that any given task or activity could be improved, and implementing effective control measures in good time to ensure that it is. The development of this skill will assist you to become more effective.

Several conditions must exist before effective control can take place:

- *Plan.* A good plan that expresses clear objectives to be achieved within a precise framework is an absolute necessity. It must include detailed tasks, or what is expected of subordinates and how their part fits into the overall plan – the subject of earlier chapters.
- *Standards or objectives.* All performance objectives should be set using the mnemonic SMART:
  - Stretching. Most individuals and all teams will rise to a significant performance challenge.
  - Specific. Objectives have to be clearly stated and understandable.
  - Measurable. Everyone must be able to assess when an objective has been achieved, and the criteria used in measuring performance must be defined.
  - Achievable. The objective has to be achievable – objectives that cannot possibly be met demoralize and demotivate.
  - Agreed. The individual or team must agree and commit to achievement of the objective.
  - Relevant. Objectives must clearly contribute to achieving the team's plan and be relevant to the needs of the business, and not just to those people who wish to achieve them.
  - Regularly reviewed. Ongoing evaluation is necessary to ensure that the objective remains relevant and 'on track' for successful achievement.
  - Resourced. Sufficient resources must be allocated for the objective to be achieved.
  - Time-constrained. A completion time for objectives, and for each phase if applicable, must be clearly defined at the outset.

- *Information.* A constant two-way flow of information must be maintained. It can take many forms:
  - personal observation;
  - face-to-face communication;
  - verbal and written reports, both qualitative and quantitative. These should be simple and kept to the minimum.
- *Influence.* The way to effective control lies in having the ability or means to exert influence on the course of events to be controlled – in other words being able to effect things when the occasion demands.

Control (and influence)

There are various means available to you as a leader to help you control and influence events:

- *Formal authority/position.* Your position should provide you, as a leader, with the minimum authority needed to make decisions for which you are accountable – but it does not mean that you have 'real power'. That is given to you by those you lead when they accept you, when you have won their trust and confidence and earned their respect.
- *Expertise.* Having recognized ability in a particular field.
- *Communication.* The ability to argue, persuade or inspire convincingly and change the attitude of others – see the chapters on communication and coaching.
- *Obligation.* By building up a reputation for being caring, helpful and cooperative it is possible to establish a credit balance of obligation with others: when you need goodwill or assistance it is likely to be more forthcoming if you have given the same in the past.
- *Personal traits or style of leadership.* Behaving in a manner that accords with the highest standards of the team and 'espoused values' will generate a tendency to listen to what you say and respect for your judgement. The leader alone sets the standards the team will conform to – high or low.

Timing of control

Control is an ongoing function but it is possible to identify particular types of control according to when it is exerted:

- *Before the event.* Obviously the best form of control is anticipation during decision making and planning that prevents problems arising in the first place. Hence the time-effective rigour built into the cycle of decision making, planning and briefing already examined in detail.
- *During the event.* In other words dealing with problems as they occur. Clearly this reduces efficiency and can be disruptive, but it can prevent disasters.

Hence the need for the iterating, recurring and ongoing cycle of decision making, planning and briefing.

- *After the event.* While control at this stage cannot prevent or deal with problems it can ensure that the same mistake is not repeated. How often do you debrief activities and record and share learning both within your team and beyond?

Evaluating progress

The earlier problems are identified, the quicker they may be resolved. Under ideal conditions this should be unnecessary because everyone should know their job and do it as best they can. However, people are human and can make mistakes, standards may slip, and the unexpected can occur and stop everything. Therefore leaders must keep a constant check on progress to ensure the achievement of the task.

Having set objectives it is necessary to ensure that they are met. Evaluation should be an ongoing and progressive process. It is dependent on the task and overall plan but progressive evaluation allows you the flexibility to alter a plan or the approach to ensure efficient completion of a given task; it is not usually particularly effective to wait until the end of a task to evaluate. You can achieve this in a number of ways:

- Set objectives, the completion of which is reported to you.
- Regular physical checks by you to see how the task is progressing.
- Qualitative and quantitative discussion with all stakeholders in the task.

The key is to ask oneself: could the task be done any better, and could anything else be done at the same time? The answers will indicate to you the control measures or changes of plan that are needed.

Failure to meet objectives

When you see that an individual is failing to meet set objectives you need to find out why (the ACE model of Chapter 3 may be used as a diagnostic in doing this) and then perhaps set new objectives. Performance and coaching are dealt with in detail in Chapter 10. In outline, by questioning and listening you should:

- Establish that the individual understands the objectives.
- Ensure that the individual is aware of the gap between actual performance and agreed objectives.
- Explore ways in which that gap may be closed.
- Ensure that any external factors that may be influencing performance are explored and dealt with.
- Agree the next review date.

PART TWO
Developing the ACE Conditions for Success

Section 3: Shaping the Environment

19
Introduction to shaping the environment

The last of our ACE conditions for success to consider is environment. As we said in Chapter 3, the environment comprises the infrastructure of the workplace – its systems and processes, its approach to organization, structure and the definition of role relationships, facilities, resources, products and services, the external market (or operating context) and its 'philosophy' or approach to its business – and importantly, the example of its leaders, which all influence culture.

The example of one's immediate leader, at any level, is one of the most important environmental influences on the behaviour of the team. A good leader can, to a certain extent, insulate the team from environmental 'nonsense' – although the leader will in effect only be papering over fundamental design cracks.

Many of these elements of environment are the preserve of strategic leaders to design and shape. It is unfortunate that in many organizations insufficient rigour and clarity of thought are employed in designing the framework in which people work. The consequences of these deficiencies in executive thought are seen in dysfunctional behaviour within the organization. A simple example is the technology company that wishes to sell solutions (a consultative sales approach, which combines product sales with spare parts and maintenance service), but then structures the organization with two competing sales forces (product sales and service sales) supported with financial incentives that do not encourage those two sales forces to work together in the best interests of both their own company and the customer.

In this section we will explore the framework that people working within, the essential intangibles of morale, loyalty and trust, organizational ethos and culture (incorporating purpose, values and principles of business), and organization and structural design principles. The design of the workplace layout, products and services that employees and customers have confidence in, IT systems, business processes, and HR policies and processes and so on fall outside the scope of this book, although the appreciation process explained in detail in Chapter 14 is an ideal tool to assist with designing or reviewing such matters. Similarly, the external market and operating context that your organization works in is beyond the scope of this book, although some of the generic strategic drivers set the scene for us in Chapter 1.

20
Teams and groups

Characteristics of groups and teams
Types of teams
Group dynamics
Stages of team development
Maintaining the team
Advice to leaders

Understanding teams and groups is fundamental to leadership. Leaders need to understand the dynamics of teamwork to be able to harness the strengths and energy of their teams and to know how to minimize the effects of their likely weaknesses. We all know the value of teamwork from our personal experience and from observing the example of successful sports teams, yacht crews, orchestras, and the armed services. We see the way these teams react to support each other and to accept as normal their dedication to training and discipline to maintain their effectiveness.

From the moment of birth we are all vitally affected by the influence of other people. Initially it is our parents with whom we have contact, but gradually, as we develop we need to expand our contacts and to be able to interact socially with others. The family is probably the first group to exert its influence upon us and our behaviour and gradually the horizons expand as friendships and more formal groups such as school classes and working groups come to exert their influence on our lives. In this chapter we will consider group dynamics, the characteristics of teams, and the stages of team development, so that you may understand and better lead your own teams, whether at work or on the sports field.

Characteristics of groups and teams

People join groups because membership satisfies their need for companionship, affection, friendship, status and, sometimes, power. The formation of groups depends on such things as the ability of members to communicate and to get on with each other. The fact that all members are substantially in agreement about important matters, makes it possible for the group to develop rules or norms on acceptable behaviour.

Consider for a moment how the development of a group evidences itself in a Hell's Angels Chapter and a church choir. A group can be said to exhibit the following characteristics:

- It has a definable membership of two or more people.
- The members share a sense of comradeship and loyalty to the group and to each other.
- Members share common interests.

We have all experienced membership of groups. We also know the frustrations in trying to organize, say, a night out or a 'pub crawl' for a group of friends – people have different ideas of where to go, when and what to eat and so on. The same frustrations are not found in an efficient and high-performing team. There are, therefore, some additional minimum characteristics a group must have to become a team:

- A specific aim and purpose, or mission, around which the team can unite and direct its efforts.
- A leader (elected, appointed, or de facto) to direct, coordinate, resolve conflict and control, as necessary.
- The imposition of restraint on behaviour – discipline or rules, whether from an internal or external source.

The mission

The existence of a mission or an aim and purpose is what primarily defines a team. In industry, all groups are faced with a constant stream of differing tasks. To cope with these, the members of a team must create an atmosphere of cooperation and trust, so that the basis of a team is formed. This is not sufficient, however, because, for a team to continue to work together in happy cooperation, it must perceive itself to have more successes than failures in the tasks undertaken. To ensure this success all the evidence indicates that the team needs effective leadership.

Leadership

There are no results without leadership and if you are reading this book, you will probably accept that fact of life. All teams look for leadership and if it is not present because no leader has been appointed, then a natural leader will emerge to fill the vacuum (which is why organizations have known 'go to' people – the extant organization – in addition to the names of team and department leaders on organizational charts). Each team needs someone to:

- Take responsibility for looking after the interests of the individuals within the team.
- Create the conditions in which the team can be successful and take responsibility for the continuation of the team, to build its identity and ensure the team's survival.
- Take responsibility for achieving tasks and objectives.

Chapter 4 made clear the role of the leader, and also illustrated how shared leadership operates. The concept of 'effects-based leadership (EBL)' introduced in Chapter 1 is, in effect, distributed leadership. The leader must look to the good of the team and the wellbeing of its members by always putting the interests of the team before the leader's own. Effective leaders are selfless rather than selfish.

The once fashionable notion of self-directed teams as an OD panacea ignores a fundamental fact of work and human nature. First, no team that is part of a bigger organization is truly self-directed since this implies that it works in isolation and has no requirement to align its work to anything else. Aspects such as rosters, leave planning and allocation of minor duties or tasks may be self-managed by agreement, but in every organization a team has to be coordinated with others in their work. They cannot be inwardly focused or they would only attempt to satisfy their own needs.

Second, no one can say 'you are empowered' and expect to see 'empowered' people. 'Empowerment' occurs only as a result of developing all three ACE conditions for success. This is only developed and promoted by effective leadership.

Third, from experience, four people is the maximum number that true democracy seems to operate in and that only applies when all the members are highly trained, highly motivated, and of reasonably equal intellect and ability – and even with four, a casting vote might be necessary. This feature of human nature was the reason that the Special Air Service's founder, David Stirling, decided that the SAS structure should be based on teams of four, since they operate in very tough conditions behind enemy lines with little support and they need each team member to be fully committed to a course of action. This phenomenon has also been observed by Dr Belbin (of team roles fame), formerly the chairman of the Industrial Training Research Unit, University College, London.

It is not possible for a large team of, say, 12 to operate without a formal leader or, in the case of two companies that we have encountered, with leadership actively suppressed to encourage 'self-directed teams' (a brewer and consumer health business – they both abandoned this fad after productivity took an entirely predictable nosedive). Teams need leaders who can ensure that tasks are achieved, roles and plans clarified, capability developed, work coordinated, healthy norms inculcated and that administration is sound.

Each team needs someone to take responsibility both for looking after the interests of the individuals within the team and for the continuation of the team to ensure the team's survival. An effective leader will undertake all these responsibilities. That person must see that the job gets done and must look to the good of the team and the wellbeing of the members by always putting the interests of the team before his or her own. When an individual's personal objectives coincide with those of the team, then individual commitment and motivation will always be higher. So leaders must know individual team members' needs, aspirations and values and, where possible, link them to those of the team.

Discipline

The word 'discipline' is not fashionable in many quarters and has a somewhat unpleasant connotation attached to it. For example, one frequently hears BBC newsreaders talk about incompetent civil servants and medical staff 'being disciplined'; this attaches 'punishment' to the concept of discipline. Such use of language illustrates ignorance of the true nature of discipline and its foundations, which underlie civilian life and business, just as much as it is a military necessity.

The basis of collective 'team' discipline is self-discipline, subordination of self for the benefit of the team. It therefore has a moral and social foundation. Self-discipline may come from within, based upon a person having a concept of duty and exercising self-control, or may be imposed from without – but it is the development of self-discipline from within, which leaders must strive for.

Liberty implies discipline

Slim uses the example of choice:[1]

> *You can take out your car or bicycle, you can choose where you want to go, your own destination. That's liberty! But, as you drive or ride through the streets towards your destination, you will keep to the left side of the road. That's discipline... if you think for a moment, you will find that there is a connection between liberty and discipline.*
>
> *First of all, you will keep to the left for your own advantage... if you drive on any side... you will end up on a stretcher... So you accept discipline. Other people have as much right... as you have... . So for their sakes as well as your own you keep to the left... . But it's no use keeping to the left unless others... do the same. You rely on their discipline. Lastly, even supposing you are tempted to go scooting about on the wrong side... at the back of your mind will be the thought 'if I do the police will be after me'.*
>
> *There are, thus, four reasons why you keep to the correct side of the road:*

1 *Your own advantage.*
2 *Consideration for others.*
3 *Confidence in your fellows.*
4 *Fear of punishment.*

> *Whenever we put a curb on our natural desire to do as we like, whenever we temper liberty with discipline, we do so for one or more of those reasons. It is the relative weight we give to each of these reasons that decides what sort of discipline we have. And that can vary from the pure self-discipline of the Sermon on the Mount to the discipline of the concentration camp – the enforced discipline of fear.*

The road safety analogy gives a clear indication of the vital importance of having clear rules to get everyone in the team working together effectively to achieve whatever task has been set. Leaders should ensure that the 'rules' (norms) are kept and these norms assist them in keeping teams together. If you lack moral courage to apply the rules to all the members of your team consistently by letting things slip, you will lose respect of the team members who do maintain the standards and you risk the disintegration of the team. It is this personal acceptance of 'intelligent rules' and your commitment to the group that, as leader, you must strive to obtain from every single member of your team.

Other characteristics of teams

If the team had a single task to complete then mission (aim and purpose), leadership and discipline might be all that the team requires to be successful. However, in business, there is a never ending stream of tasks – as soon as you see the summit of one 'Everest', the next appears. So to sustain success, a number of other defining characteristics of the ACE conditions for success are required in the team:

- Competence in the requisite skills and knowledge for the role that any individual occupies.
- Adherence to values, abiding by a defining code of behaviour.
- Motivation, a genuine desire within the individual to do the job, whose interest is stimulated and whose needs are satisfied by the type of work undertaken and the environment in which it is conducted.
- Defined membership: the team must know who is in it! It must also have enough people to do the job.
- Effective communication, which includes regular team briefings and meetings (not a reliance on e-mail and paper notices), frequent interaction between team leader and team members, and the effective use of communication systems. It also means open, honest and clear communication that prevents misunderstandings and promotes trust. Implicit in this is the moral courage and confidence to face up to weaknesses and say what needs to be said without fear.
- Defined role relationships to align accountability with authority and ensure that jobs are tenable, and to remove a major source of stress – which is having to rely on influence and personal relationships to overcome structural deficiencies.
- Effectively designed and commonly understood processes and systems to get things done, using a common language.
- A clear and commonly interpreted team plan, and defined individual roles, tasks and objectives with regular reviews.
- Development of team and individual capability, with regular feedback.
- Team identity – people tend to identify with smaller groups rather than entire organizations (one of the reasons why the British Army developed its county-based regimental system).
- Reciprocal confidence and trust among members.

Types of teams

It is very fashionable to refer to all types of groups as teams: the business leadership literature of recent years, popular press and television's obsession with sport have contributed to this. But there are many types of teams, with their own characteristics, which need consideration if the team is to be properly designed and developed.

The leadership team

This may be the top (executive) leadership team in an organization, or it might refer to a team of peer mid-level leaders. In both cases they work directly for the same leader, the CEO for the top team. When they come together, they need to work with the cohesion and interdependence of any closely knit team, with the common purpose of developing the collective capability and performance of the teams and groups that they represent. However, particularly in top teams, they are likely to have strong characters and personalities, possibly with a tendency to pursue independent action. Indeed they will probably be leading business units or functions and therefore be undertaking activities that (they may feel) have a less interdependent nature on a day-to-day basis.

The project team or task force

These groups are established with multidisciplinary members to assume responsibility for a specific programme, project or task that may cross boundaries. Their performance is usually assessed by task completion. Membership may be a secondary (part-time) role for people within the group, or they may be assigned from other teams to work on the project full-time. The team may also have members in it who are consultants on short-term interim employment contracts.

The functional work team

This is a coordinated group of people with similar and complementary skills who work together for the same leader with a high level of interdependence, a sense of mutual accountability and shared leadership. Both common and individual outputs and objectives will be defined in pursuit of the common aim and purpose (or mission) of the team.

The work group

This differs from the functional work team in that the work undertaken by people is, inherently, of an individual nature – there is not the same level of interdependence that is found in the team, they just happen to work for the same leader, and consequently the group has a less well-defined aim and purpose or mission than the work team. The people working in such groups may be referred to as 'individual contributors'.

Quality circles and networking groups, etc

These tend to be groups whose leader is in a secondary (part-time) role, and whose members are usually volunteers with a particular interest that they wish to pursue.

Group dynamics

Whenever a number of people are thrown together, whether by accident or design, as in a team, it is inevitable that friendships are formed. Those with similar interests or background get together and within the formal organization of the team there are informal groups whose membership and, often, interests change over time, but that settle into patterns of behaviour acceptable to each other. Recall these groups from your own experience in business, at school, or at university? This development of informal groups of association is known as 'group dynamics' and in a well-led team the leader who understands group dynamics can take advantage of them because:

- The informal groups can blend well into the formal organization to get jobs done by interpreting 'rules' in a practical, rather than a slavish, way.
- They can accept delegation and thereby lighten a leader's load.
- They may be useful as unofficial communication channels.
- They can encourage cooperation among individuals.
- They can be helpful in the planning and introduction of change.

You will recall from Chapter 8 that there are two fundamental drives in people: competition and collaboration. Leaders need to ensure that informal groups can recognize and identify with the aim, purpose and objectives of the team. In this way the informal groups will cooperate to get the task in hand completed. Competition drives us to improve standards. Competition is natural among groups and one way for leaders to harness this competitive spirit is to identify to teams an 'outside enemy'.

Competition or a healthy rivalry among teams within the same organization can be used to raise standards and business results, but cooperation among these teams is vital, so the leader must ensure that constructive competition does not become destructive or hinder progress – for example by sharing best practice that has been used to raise standards or achieve results. There is a fine line that leaders must be aware of between constructive and destructive competition. Remember that ultimately you are competing against an external business rival, not each other. In poorly led teams, informal groups can create problems by:

- *Resisting change.* You must be aware of a certain resentment you feel when, for whatever reason, a new routine or working practice is imposed upon you. Whatever it is, until you have settled into the new routine you feel resentful. Badly handled group dynamics can lead to resentment growing rather than diminishing.
- *Developing conflicting objectives.* The informal groups provide members with social satisfaction. These social groupings can develop objectives that conflict with the organization's own. For instance, group members may find their own social interaction so rewarding that they begin returning late from tea breaks and so on.
- *Spreading rumour.* Informal groups often set up a 'grapevine' to communicate with one another and this can lead to the circulation of rumours and distorted information.

Working in teams in which participation by all is encouraged and discussion is welcomed produces the best results in certain kinds of situations, such as:

- Solving problems that have many different facets, or that require different skills, information, knowledge and the pooling of ideas.
- Making decisions that require judgement, rather than factual analysis.
- Gaining acceptance to a decision and commitment to its implementation. (Chapter 14 shows that there are four steps in making a decision, the first three of which are problem solving to clarify the aim and purpose, consideration of factors that affect achieving the aim, and identification and comparison of options open. Team members certainly can and should be involved in those three steps. It may or may not be appropriate to include the team in the final step, selection of the best option – the decision.)

The excessive participation of all the individuals in a team in problem solving and decision making may be less productive for:

- simple routine tasks or problems;
- problems that have a 'correct' solution;
- problems where it is difficult to demonstrate the solution to team members.

When poor leadership abounds, people tend to want to be consulted in all matters: they have no confidence in their leaders. When an effective and capable leader has the trust and confidence of his or her team it is quite natural for team members to be happy to participate less in minor decisions – indeed, they often do not wish to waste their time on trivial matters because they have confidence that the boss will make the right decision. This reduction in discussion makes the team more efficient. So what might be described as a benevolent dictatorship can work, but only with highly effective, well-trained leaders who have earned the trust and confidence of everyone within their teams.

Cohesiveness

Cohesiveness, in essence, is the attractiveness of the team to its members. It determines the extent of the members' contributions to the team and the efforts that they will make on the team's behalf. The factors affecting cohesion are:

- *Contact and communication.* The opportunity to make regular contact with one another, their physical proximity in relation to each other, and the flow of understood, open and clear communication, based on facts not assumptions or rumours.
- *The similarity of the work.* Similar work produces similar challenges around which people can unite and bond.
- *The incentive system (individual or team).* The way people are remunerated and are recognized may stimulate self-centred or team-centred behaviour.
- *Compatibility of individuals.* People like people who are like themselves. Homogeneity of values, social expectations and so on adds to compatibility – but may lead to 'group think'.

- *Size of team.* Too large a team (usually more than 10 to 12) makes activities impersonal and does not lead to or assist in 'the tribal identity' of smaller teams.
- *External threat.* A common threat always unites a group of people. Consider the effect of disparate people in the USSR or UK in the Second World War.
- *Leadership.* The magic word that this book is all about.

Highly cohesive teams support and protect their members, especially against any influence from outside the team. They also have more influence over the behaviour of team members as the general level of conformity to norms increases with the level of cohesiveness. This cohesion may show itself in united team action that can be used to the advantage or disadvantage of the organization. It is possible for a team to be too cohesive, too concerned with its own maintenance, membership and priorities, and focused solely on its own needs. It can become dangerously blinkered as to what is going on around it and may confidently forge ahead in completely the wrong direction. The leader has to watch for such signs and take corrective action. Some of those signs are:

- Destructive competition or negative thoughts about other teams in the organization.
- Complacency and a sense of invulnerability – blindness to the risk involved in 'pet' strategies, or repeating 'proven' formulae.
- Rationalization of inconsistent facts, blaming others for mistakes regardless.
- Moral blindness – the 'might is right', the 'we are never wrong' sort of attitude.
- A tendency to stereotype non-team members as 'enemies'.
- Strong team pressure to squash dissent and anything 'different'.
- Self-censorship by members – not 'rocking the boat', refusing to say what is right and what needs to be said.
- Perception of unanimity – filtering out divergent views that question what is the accepted 'norm'.

Conflict between teams

Inevitably there are times when differences in perception, poor communication, or some other failure of leadership allow conflict to arise between groups, between the sub-groups within a team or between teams themselves. This conflict can be heightened through excessive competition among teams and a breakdown of trust. Such a breakdown can be catastrophic because mistrust leads to poor communication which, in turn, produces greater mistrust and so a vicious cycle has been established. Within a team that is in conflict with another, Adair[2] and Argyle[3] suggest the following characteristics may be observed:

- Conflict increases the degree of cohesion and loyalty once an outside 'enemy' has been identified.

- Perception of other teams becomes distorted as the team tends to see only its own strengths and the faults in others.
- When a threat is perceived the team wishes to guard its own existence and space – it becomes territorial. It may cut itself off from communication with other groups.
- Under threat, a team tends to demand more conformity from its members than the established norms and may accept more control from its leaders. There is a greater emphasis upon unity.
- The team is likely to devote more effort to maintaining its own existence at the expense of directing its energy to the task.

In essence then, a team closes ranks and places more value on itself than other groups – it pursues win/lose resolutions to situations. As a result, 'winners' become more cohesive, may experience a release of tension, and may become complacent and, therefore, less productive. At the same time the losing team may fragment and reorganize, experience a rise in tension and deterioration in morale, and may blame the organization or its leaders.

Group cultures can reinforce cohesion under stress, but they can be destructive when disparate groups are brought together as partners in some joint endeavour. Antipathy may develop before the groups physically meet each other (the competition drive again). Such a clash of cultures does nothing to aid working relationships. A dysfunctional group trait that might be seen is behaviour that prevents the sharing of information effectively, perhaps again due to competition, or the idea that 'knowledge is power'. Rather than revealing information known only to them, individual team members may talk only about things that everybody already knows.

Decision making

Using the collective expertise of people to solve complex problems and to gain their 'buy-in' is essential. However, there are some group dynamics to consider, in order to optimize this approach.

Group size affects decision making; individuals may hide in large groups, fail to recognize the importance of any one task, or fail to take responsibility for decisions and outcomes. Peer pressure influences the individuals within a group to change their attitudes, values or behaviours to conform to established group norms. Depending upon the prevailing culture this may be positive. However, the pressure to conform can limit a team's ability to challenge understanding and to think creatively. People in groups frequently adapt their behaviour to conform to views other than their own. Contributory factors include the fear of disapproval, a lack of self-belief, conflict avoidance, high anxiety and low status, and a high need for approval from others.

Group-think[4] may be observed in cohesive teams focused on external issues and problems. It is the tendency for individuals to go along with majority decisions or views. This often happens when team members have similar backgrounds and values and/or where they perceive a need for consensus and unanimity[5] and/or they simply wish to keep their leader happy – or they are idle and coasting! The group dynamics will induce conformity that is difficult for any individual to overcome, even if they know that the group view is wrong. Such groups are prone to shortcutting rational decision making.[6] In extreme cases, the group may begin to feel invulnerable and take excessive risks. Social prejudice is a belief that another social group is less capable than one's own; again very cohesive teams can reinforce such beliefs.

Overcoming group-think needs the leader explicitly to welcome dissenting views and create the open and honest environment in which individuals with different perspectives feel able to say and discuss what they are thinking.

Stages of team development

The task of building and maintaining a high performing team is made much easier if we are aware of how they develop over time. All teams are living entities or organisms; they are dynamic, continuously developing and changing in response to certain factors. Those factors are either internal or external and include:

External factors	Internal factors
Changing markets and business needs	Changes in team purpose, role and objectives
New organizational structures	Changes in team membership – people leaving or joining
New technology	Changing relationships within the team

The personal growth or maturation of team members

Tuckman and Jensen[7] investigated this developmental process and suggest that any group or team usually evolves through several well-defined stages from initial formation to maturity; this is shown in Figure 20.1. Only when a team reaches its mature stage can it be fully effective in successfully achieving task requirements through the coordinated efforts of committed team members – it is performing because the ACE conditions for success (Chapter 3) have been created. This process repeats since leaders always want to improve performance or personnel change, and that means the ongoing evolution of the team. At each of these stages the team must resolve issues about both the task and their social relationships. The stages of development that a team goes through in its evolution of the ACE conditions for success are:

Forming

Storming

Norming

Performing

Mourning (and then reforming).

Think of this as continuous evolution, not in a circular or cyclical fashion, but following an Archimedes' spiral with time as the axis along which these processes are taking

FIGURE 20.1 The stages of team development

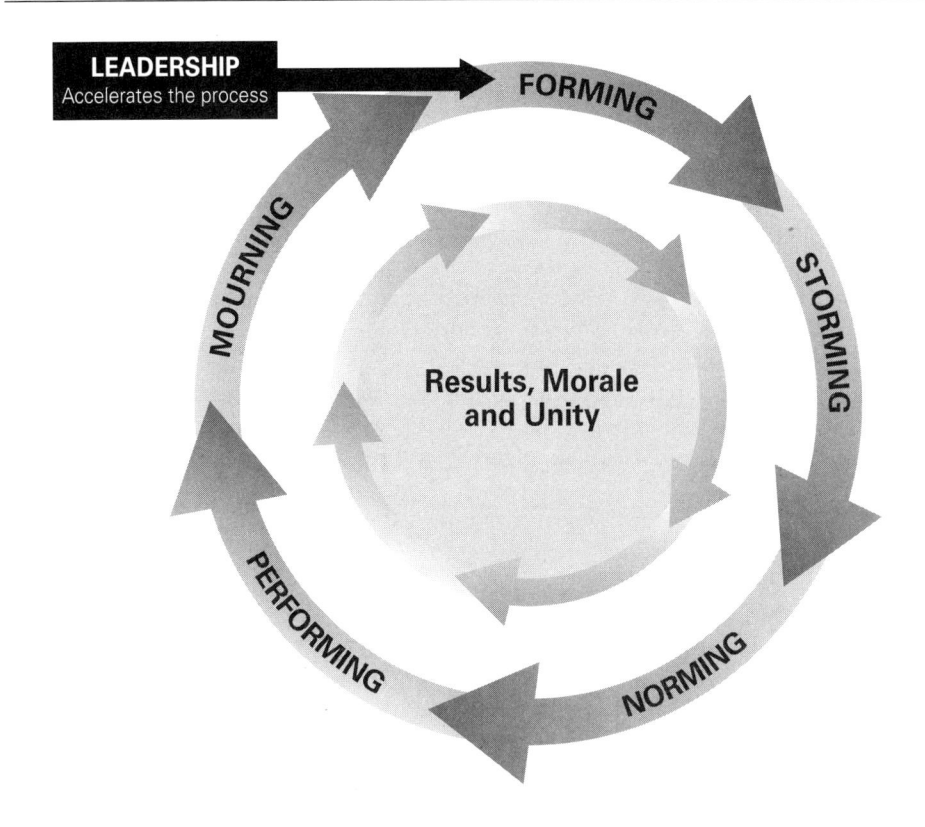

Stages shown in cycle: FORMING → STORMING → NORMING → PERFORMING → MOURNING, with LEADERSHIP accelerating the process, centred on Results, Morale and Unity.

After Tuckman & Jensen 1977 | © Jeremy Tozer, 1997–2006

place. The team is a living organism that is constantly evolving and none of these processes are static for long. The speed of evolution is largely influenced by the quality of leadership within the team, both from the team's appointed leader and from the leadership that other members of the team themselves display.

Results and 'the spirit of teamwork'

It is worth noting that business results and a tangible level of high morale and unity – the spirit of teamwork – within the team are the outcome of evolving to the performing level. This is why so many 'team-building away days' in which a work team or group undertake a new activity together, such as crewing an ocean racing yacht, fail to deliver any lasting business benefits on their return to work. In the context of crewing the yacht, the team or group will progress to the performing level – it is the job of the sail training instructors to ensure this. Knowledge of each other as people and interpersonal relationships undoubtedly benefit from such activities, but a day on a yacht does not in itself develop a clearer business plan, align activity and clarify roles, priorities and objectives. Nor does it provide the leader of the team with the conceptual processes to do that. Leadership is what accelerates team development and the delivery of results.

Forming

During the forming stage the leader brings the individual team members together (or inducts a new team member to an established team). When an individual's personal objectives coincide with those of the team, individual commitment and motivation will always be higher; this is a factor in recruitment. So the leader must know individual team members' needs, aspirations and values and, where possible, link them to those of the team.

Frequently, some people will want to impress his or her personality on the team (watch for the drive to compete or collaborate!) while the team's mission (aim and purpose), objectives, processes, organization and roles and so on are being clarified. Individuals try to 'size each other up', learn about each other's abilities, background and experience, and may try to learn about any established norms of the team. Many people are cautious about introducing new ideas and respect the established way of doing things; they do not want to appear radical or unacceptable to the team (the drive to conform).

During the 'forming' phase of team development the leader must lay the foundations of teamwork by creating an atmosphere of mutual trust, confidence, support and inter-group relations (relate this to the functional leadership checklist in Chapter 4). In this first phase you, as leader, must get to know everybody as well as possible – learn about their attitudes, beliefs, needs and personality – what makes them 'tick' (see Chapter 8). It's helpful to maintain a notebook with a section for each team member, to record everything you know about them – their birthday, work experience, qualifications, hobbies and interests, strengths and weaknesses, summary of all interviews and discussions, hopes and aspirations, development needs, spouse and children's names, and so on. Usually the team operates as a collection of individuals and it is quite likely that some individuals try to impress others with their knowledge or experience and they may be rather more assertive, dominant or exuberant than is usual for them. This often passes when they settle in.

Team roles

Belbin[8] has identified nine team roles that are required to be performed across and within the team – roles that are not 'functionally specific' (see Table 20.1); this may be a factor in recruitment and selection.

Arguably, the 'specialist' role is not really a role since, depending on the team's work, experts in a number of subjects may be required. The above is interesting when one looks at leadership teams – teams of people who are also leaders of their own teams. Within such a leadership team, the presence of a 'completer' helps the team, but surely that completer also needs to be a 'shaper' within his or her own team?

TABLE 20.1 Team roles

Roles and Descriptions – Team-Role Contribution	Weaknesses
Plant: Creative, imaginative, unorthodox. Solves difficult problems	Ignores details. Too preoccupied to communicate effectively
Resource investigator: Extrovert, enthusiastic, communicative. Explores opportunities. Develops contacts	Over-optimistic. Loses interest once initial enthusiasm has passed
Coordinator: Mature, confident, a good chairperson. Clarifies goals, promotes decision making, delegates well	Can be seen as manipulative. Delegates personal work
Shaper: Challenging, dynamic, thrives on pressure. Has the drive and courage to overcome obstacles	Can provoke others. Hurts people's feelings
Monitor evaluator: Sober, strategic and discerning. Sees all options. Judges accurately	Lacks drive and ability to inspire others. Over-critical
Teamworker: Cooperative, mild, perceptive and diplomatic. Listens, builds, averts friction, calms the waters	Indecisive in crunch situations. Can be easily influenced
Implementer: Disciplined, reliable, conservative and efficient. Turns ideas into practical actions	Somewhat inflexible. Slow to respond to new possibilities
Completer: Painstaking, conscientious, anxious. Searches out errors and omissions. Delivers on time	Inclined to worry unduly. Reluctant to delegate. Can be a nit-picker
Specialist: Single-minded, self-starting, dedicated. Provides knowledge and skills in rare supply	Contributes on only a narrow front. Dwells on technicalities. Overlooks the 'big picture'

Team size

A critical aspect of team composition is its size. 'Management' (whoever that is!) often decides team size in organizations, influenced by the nature of the work, current 'fads' and financial considerations. Such thinking often does not permit leadership and teamwork to flourish. Team size presents three tendencies:

1. The larger the team, the greater the range of knowledge, skills and experience.
2. The larger the team, the more difficult communication and providing effective leadership to each team member becomes.
3. The smaller the team, the greater the danger of over-supervision.

The second point carries the risk of overlooking valuable contributions from some members or them not being put forward. A common trait of larger teams is their tendency to fragment into smaller units naturally. People often find it more satisfying to work in smaller teams where they can relate to others on a more personal basis. It is usually the case that morale is higher and absenteeism lower in small teams than in larger ones.

Storming

The storming stage often involves some conflict, open or concealed, among individual team members. There is likely to be disagreement within the team about some issues. People might question the mission, objectives, 'rules' and norms. There could even be a split within the team. In a new team, or on a new project, this can be beneficial since more effective mechanisms may emerge and trust starts to develop among team members.

In the storming phase the leader may well be resolving conflict between individuals, sub-teams, or external teams, amending or changing rules, procedures and systems and so on. The following are possible problem areas that the leader may need to address:

- *An atmosphere of tension, indifference or boredom.* The leader needs to cut through this early on, before it becomes a major issue. Everyone immediately recognizes such an atmosphere, team members and visitors alike, and it will lead to a deterioration in the level of morale and esprit de corps within the team if it is not dealt with quickly.
- *Unclear roles, role relationships (accountability and authority) or objectives.* Energy and resources are channelled into unnecessary diversions, and lead to a breakdown of unity and trust if there is a lack of clarity. Clarity of tasks and priorities will stem from business planning (Chapter 14).
- *Over-dominant individuals whose continued 'noise' disrupts other team members.* Leaders should present such people with 'behavioural evidence' (see coaching and feedback, Chapter 10) and that requires confidence and moral courage. If such a situation is not resolved, stresses will be induced within the team and your credibility as a leader will be in doubt – trust will deteriorate.

- *Meetings that digress and do not remain focused on their purpose.* Most of us would agree that far too much time is wasted in meetings that have no clear agenda or reason, which degenerate into discussion of a multitude of trivial issues. Meetings need to be planned in advance with the aim and objectives of the meeting and an agenda forwarded so that all parties can prepare for it. Only those people who are essential to the meeting should be there. Too frequently managers invite the world when often only part of the world needs to know the result. Timings need to be indicated and should usually be adhered to. The leader, or chairperson if the leader has abdicated this responsibility, must keep the meeting on track and interrupt those who deviate, digress, or repeat things unnecessarily. Simple, accurate and clear expression is called for with the aim of the meeting always kept in mind.
- *Disagreement and dissent.* This may be based on differing perceptions about the importance of issues, inflexibility or plain 'bloody-mindedness'. Chapter 8 and will assist with this.
- *Perceived unclear reasons for decisions, etc.* Communication and an effective decision-making process are the key (see Chapters 9 and 14).
- *Disagreement expressed after the event, not during discussion.* This sort of 'noise' serves no purpose. The level of trust has to be such that people feel free to express their concerns at the appropriate time. Just asking people is often not enough – they have an in-built mistrust and cynicism towards 'management', based on years of down-sizing, right-sizing and management fads failing! If the leader truly knows his or her people, he or she can anticipate their reactions and allow for those in the initial stages, thus preventing problems from occurring.
- *Criticism, sarcasm and sniping at people.* This is based on mistrust, lack of mutual respect and/or confidence, and probably an inclination towards cynicism, 'playing' politics, back-stabbing and the lack of courage to speak directly to the 'target'. This has to be addressed by the leader and, if continued despite 'an interview without coffee' and the example of others, it may be a reflection of the basic signs of a malcontent. The continued presence of such people in the team must, therefore, be questioned.
- *Lack of awareness of the current situation and progress made.* The leader needs to constantly update everyone on the situation and plans. Remember that 'informing' was the fifth of the six key functions of a leader in our checklist in Chapter 4.

Norming

After the storming, as mutual trust and confidence grow, the team starts to settle in and the team's identity begins to form. People identify with the team and consider themselves to be 'full members'. With good leadership, norms of devotion, pride, efficiency, ownership, loyalty, etc develop, which shape the team's distinct identity. Higher standards, new and more effective procedures and roles may evolve and become accepted. These enable the team to carry out its task and enable its members to work in harmony as a cohesive team. Communication permits an open exchange of ideas and members are willing to listen and to respect the views and perspectives of others.

Norms

The norms are the shared and accepted rules or standards that define what is and what is not acceptable in terms of the values, behaviour, attitudes and beliefs of the team members. Norms may be explicit when imposed on the team by the leader or the organization. The implicit and unwritten norms are determined by the behaviour of established team members who ensure they are complied with by new members and also by outsiders working with the team. Team identity is based on the norms established by the group, and the leader must prevent unhealthy or undesirable norms from emerging before they grow into larger problems. Argyle,[9] Anantaraman[10] and Robbins[11] suggest that there are different kinds of norms that have different functions:

- Demonstrating team core values.
- Promoting team continuation and survival.
- Encouraging reliable responses and behaviour by team members.
- Minimizing conflict and differences.
- Promoting team identity.

Work norms or performance-related norms

There are norms about the most efficient, simplest or easiest (but not necessarily the best) method of working. These represent the team's solutions to problems encountered or their attitude to work, and when leadership is lacking they can often differ from those preferred by more senior or more effective leaders. This may be the front-line solution to inflexible or unnecessary bureaucracy, a better practice that has not been recognized by superiors whose finger is not on the pulse or, in badly led companies, a lazy way of getting the job done with little attention to detail and lip-service paid to quality.

There are norms about the time and effort that people put into their jobs, the quality and quantity of work done, their speed of operating, their personal standards, attitudes to matters like absenteeism and sick leave and company standards, safety and organizational values. The leadership provided directly influences the level to which these norms exist. In badly led companies these norms are kept to the maximum level that makes life comfortable without incurring any penalty.

Undesirable norms reflect the quality of leadership provided and it will be difficult for the leader who has allowed this to happen can sort it out. It therefore, poses a challenge for the next leader, particularly if the team is cohesive. Sometimes efforts to overcome these norms can lead, albeit temporarily, to disruptive action from the team. The new leader will need the unfailing support of more senior leaders and the HR system (which in one past public sector client has too often kept the organization out of court by paying poor performers to leave the enterprise, signalling 'why bother?' to everyone else).

Norms are not, however, necessarily negative. Many teams sustain a high level of output to satisfy their own needs. It is the leader's job to see to it that the team links its needs to those of the company. This is often the case for both groups of professionals and production teams, who may identify with, and firmly believe in, their work, its purpose and company values, and display high standards of behaviour.

The key norms that a leader needs to influence and shape as early as possible are those processes and methods that create clarity: the approach to problem solving and decision making, planning, briefing and clarifying role relationships; and the attributes of collaboration and initiative.

Attitudinal and belief norms

The individuals who make up a team often develop common thoughts and feelings – attitudes – about their working environment and conditions of employment. This includes company policy, procedure, economic and technical matters, and even views about other parallel teams in the same organization. For example, a sales team that spends its life on the road facing occasional rejection by customers might feel that the marketing department have an easy job.

Some of these beliefs are based on inaccurate information and are, therefore, untrue. Leaders need to see that rumours are squashed immediately and that only accurate information is circulated. In this way leaders can influence beliefs and, therefore, behaviour.

Interpersonal behaviour norms

Personal conduct and social behaviour are usually more restrained at work than at home. Work becomes easier and energy is better used if team members agree to act in a predictable and reliable way – to adhere to their company or work team values or code of behaviour. For example, the members of a team may decide to share the workload of a sick team member. There may also be norms that relate only to social activity such as celebrating certain events like birthdays or milestones in the team's own development. These norms contribute to satisfaction, harmony and the avoidance of conflicts by making the behaviour of others more predictable.

Appearance norms

Teams or whole companies may develop norms about physical appearance that can result in both the style of clothing 'encouraged', physique and personality, or style of everyone in the enterprise. This can result in a personality cult in which the ability and experience of candidates during recruitment is overlooked in the search for a like-minded person to join the cult.

Language norms

Many teams or organizations often develop their own language that is difficult for outsiders to understand. It may include 'jargon' related to their tasks, abbreviations for processes and equipment, nicknames for people and the use of slang. This private language certainly eases communication, and serves to reinforce the team identity – the negative effect is that outsiders are excluded.

Conforming

We tend to conform to established 'norms' for several reasons:

- Because we agree with the norms and believe them to be valid. Beliefs are not easily challenged.
- Because team membership is valuable to us, it confers 'status' and satisfies affiliation needs.
- To avoid being 'different' and being singled out for attention.
- To 'fit in' and gain the cooperation and support of our colleagues.
- To strengthen our beliefs and attitudes that make us feel less vulnerable.

Many of these reasons may be attributed to a lack of self-confidence, lack of self-esteem and/or lack of moral courage in the individual. This is why personal growth and maturity is so important in maintaining a healthy team. An effective team satisfies both the needs of the task (and, therefore, the organization of which it is part) and the needs of the individual (the Adair three circles model; see Chapter 4). This is teamwork. Unlike morale that cannot be measured, there are some measurable indicators of team performance:

- output and/or productivity versus set targets and time scales;
- quality/standards maintained;
- absenteeism and staff turnover;
- interruptions to work flow.

Organization environment

Few teams perform their tasks in isolation: they are usually part of a much larger organization, a team of teams. The company's objectives, policies and procedures, structure, culture, technology and physical surroundings, all ultimately determined by the CEO's leadership (and through him or her, by the example of other leaders), very strongly influence team norms.

These organizational factors cannot be considered separately since they are interdependent and interrelated. In industry where there is commercial pressure to operate at the lowest possible cost and at maximum productivity, rigid and inflexible jobs to meet specified targets performed by semi-skilled people were (and still are) common. Organizational systems have imposed tight constraints and have limited the freedom of action, use of initiative, and the personal communication among people. Teamwork has been stifled and the contribution that individuals can make has been restricted.

These factors are generally under the control of 'senior management', a vague term that promotes anonymity and does nothing to project leadership – who is 'senior management'? If it is a person let us see him or her! These factors have a direct influence on the way in which the team functions and, in turn, lead to the results achieved and the degree of satisfaction of members.

Performing

By this stage the team, or rather its leader, has resolved both task and working relationship issues, and has established a flexible and functional way of doing things – shaped and developed the ACE conditions for success. Personality clashes, if not reconciled, are understood: not everyone likes everyone else, nor do they have to; mutual respect, however, is necessary. The leader can now channel all the team's energy into the task.

Mourning

Mourning (which is also referred to as 'adjourning') occurs when a project team completes its task and is disbanded, when people depart from a permanent team, or when a permanent team changes its purpose, role and normal activity. At this point, the team and its members are likely to experience the emotions associated with change and go through the change cycle described in Chapter 6. The team will then re-form, or its members will be inducted into new teams – and the cycle repeats. If the team is effectively re-forming with a new member(s), then if the leader has established healthy norms, the team will reach the performing level very much faster and more smoothly.

In this fifth stage, the leader will need to be sensitive to people's emotions and vulnerabilities – especially if the team has been particularly cohesive. If the leader chooses this moment to celebrate success (whether that is the successful completion of a project which is the prelude to the team's disbandment, or the recognition of past performance and efforts, prior to the departure of individual team member), then recognition of the past can be linked to an optimistic and enthusiastic look forward to the future.

By establishing a culture or daily way of thinking that promotes learning, continuous improvement, innovation and change, the negative impact of this fifth stage may be minimized or eliminated and ever higher standards can be reached.

Maintaining the team

It is not so easy to discuss the leader's role in maintaining the team as it is not nearly as clear-cut as the steps a leader takes to either achieve the task or to satisfy individual needs. Adair[12] suggests that it is easier to think about teams that are threatened from without by forces aimed at the team's disintegration such as internal political 'empire building' or external competition, and from within by disruptive individuals or ideas.

The leader may then observe how the team allocates priority to maintaining itself and resisting these pressures to break up. For instance, one way is to use competition and identify an external opponent to cement relationships within the team. The expression, 'United we stand, divided we fall' is applicable to all teams. For the leader the task is to build on this phenomenon of the team 'personality'.

It is universally accepted that nothing succeeds like success or, conversely, fails like failure. A team that has tasted success is likely to have generated the morale and confidence that will carry it to further success, to punch above its weight. Ideally, this means giving a new team an early taste of success by starting with a relatively simple task – one at which their chances of success are high – so that confidence and high morale enables them to succeed at the more difficult tasks they meet later. But watch out for failure: once the team has failed it must be given a chance to redeem itself, or it may collapse. Giving a team a task that it feels is beyond its capabilities is likely to so demoralize it that it will disintegrate into a collection of individuals.

Identification is another important element in building up esprit de corps and generating success. Everyone likes to be associated with success. Armies, football teams and clubs all have identifying emblems and colours. Wearing some form of uniform or team identifier may appear to the 'politically correct' view to be futile and irrelevant gestures, but they can touch some of the most primeval chords in the human mind.

Advice to leaders

- As a leader, you and your followers are all part of the same team; their successes and failures are yours.
- When you speak or write never say 'you' – always say 'we'.
- Put the team's interests first, yours last.
- Your interest in them as individuals must be sincere.
- Be your team's champion and at the same time their chief critic.
- Your loyalty to them must be genuine.
- Be accessible at all times to discuss problems or concerns.
- Say what you mean and mean what you say.
- Understand your people.
- Criticize constructively.
- Give praise, publicly, when it is due.

Notes

1. Field Marshal Sir William Slim, 1957, *Courage and Other Broadcasts*, London: Cassell.
2. John Adair, 1986, *Effective Teambuilding*, Aldershot: Gower.
3. Argyle, M, 1974, *The Social Psychology of Work*, Harmondsworth: Penguin.
4. Irving, J, 1982, *Groupthink: Psychological studies of policy decisions and fiascos*, Houghton Mifflin.
5. Brooks, I, 2003, *Organizational Behaviour – Individuals, groups and organization*, Englewood Cliffs, NJ: Prentice-Hall.
6. McConville, T, 2003, *The War on Terrorism: A new classic in Groupthink*, London: Cass.

7. Tuckman, B and Jensen, M, 1977, 'Stages of small group development revisited', *Group and Organizational Studies*, pp 419–27; see also Tuckman, B, 1965, 'Development sequence in small groups', *Psychological Bulletin*, 63, pp 384–99.
8. Meredith Belbin, R, 1993, *Team Roles at Work*, Oxford: Butterworth-Heinemann.
9. Argyle, M, 1974, *The Social Psychology of Work*, Harmondsworth: Penguin.
10. Anantaraman, V, 1984, 'Group dynamics and the human relations organization model', in V Anantaraman, C Chong, S Richardson and C Tan (eds) *Human Resource Management: Concepts and perspectives*, Singapore: Singapore University Press.
11. Robbins, S, 1991, *Organizational Behavior: Concepts, controversies and applications*, Englewood Cliffs, NJ: Prentice-Hall.
12. Adair, J, 1986, *Effective Teambuilding*, Aldershot: Gower.

21
The essential intangibles: morale, loyalty and trust

Morale

Loyalty

Trust

Morale

'Morale is to the material as three is to one', said Napoleon Bonaparte. By this he meant that high morale counts for much more than simply having enough physical resources for a task. 'Morale', as far as we are concerned, is 'the mental attitude or bearing of a person or group as regards confidence, resolve and zeal.' There are many intangibles, such as morale, that lead to business performance. While this cannot be quantified on the balance sheet, it is reflected in the market capitalization of stocks and shares.

Morale is vital to all organizations and is especially visible in service organizations because if it starts to wane it becomes very apparent to customers, which is usually reflected in customer loyalty. Call centre staff talking to customers on the telephone are leading the relationship with those customers, so making sure that their frame of mind and approach are positive and that they are able to mould solutions is vital. If morale is low people will usually seek to undermine 'process' and take shortcuts. Implicit in high morale is a motivated and cheerful workforce. Not only does this produce the climate that encourages innovation, cooperation, productivity and efficiency; it reduces staff turnover ('knowledge' loss), boosts customer loyalty and, therefore, raises profitability.

People often refer to the level of morale in organizations and the divisions and departments within them; but morale is rarely defined or analysed. There is very little that has been written on the subject by either business leaders or academics; indeed the most incisive examinations seem to be found in the writing of military leaders. Armies worldwide realize the value of high morale and its absolute necessity for success. It is true that 'battles are won in the hearts and minds of men' and there are many examples of engagements in which numerically superior, better equipped forces have failed in the face of determined action by small, relatively poorly equipped groups of soldiers, but whose leaders maintained high morale.

Soldiers, like their civilian counterparts, are in many ways a reflection of the society from which they come. The soldier comes from the same background as the person in industry – people are people whatever their jobs, and they respond in similar ways to the same stimuli. The understanding that armies have of morale stems from hard and bloody experience, and armies have to sustain morale for longer periods in more extreme conditions of stress and discomfort. It is, therefore, not surprising that business can improve its understanding of the nature of morale from studying the profession of arms.

Morale is certainly not contentment or satisfaction evolving out of good material conditions and an easy job. Morale is essentially a state of mind. To quote Slim:[1] 'It is that intangible force which will move a whole group of men to give their last ounce to achieve something, without counting the cost to themselves; that makes them feel they are part of something greater than themselves.' It is more than happiness. Morale is the ability to rise to challenges and to overcome them, to carry on with the job with confidence and determination. It is the product of a mind with a conscience. It contributes to the motivation of the individual and a team's esprit de corps. Morale cannot be built by a quick fix or bought with parties and presents.

It is the result of good leadership, and superficial attempts to build it breed cynicism and mistrust. In the packaged goods company that I joined as a salesman on leaving the army, there was a general malaise and lack of interest in boosting sales and distribution of our products among the state sales force. People were often bored, uninterested and took no pride in their work. One day a competition was started, the scene was set, its importance communicated and the sales force issued cameras and asked to take photographs of displays of their products that they had built in their stores. While the prizes were insignificant, this sudden apparent surge of interest in the humble sales rep, briefings on our importance in building the brand presence in stores, and the issue of a camera by what was a fairly parsimonious company had a very positive effect on morale and hence sales. Unfortunately the interest that was taken in each sales rep's work, display of leadership and emphasis on teamwork was short-lived and a couple of months later the malaise had returned. Twenty per cent of the state sales force found jobs elsewhere within the year.

Foundations of morale

Field Marshal Slim took command of 14th Army in Burma in 1943, an army shattered by continuous defeat, exhausted by a relentless 800-mile retreat, convinced of the supremacy of an invincible enemy. In the list of global priorities, 14th Army was at the bottom after the armies in Europe and North Africa, it was thus deficient in the most basic necessities.

Slim[1] considered that the most serious danger he faced was that morale was threatened. This is how he analysed the problem:

> *Morale must, if it is to endure – and the essence of morale is that it should endure – have certain foundations. These foundations are spiritual, intellectual, and material, and that is the order of their importance. Spiritual first, because only spiritual foundations can stand real strain. Next intellectual, because men are swayed by reason as well as feeling. Material last – important but last – because the very highest kinds of morale are often met when material conditions are lowest.*
>
> *I remember sitting in my office and tabulating these foundations of morale something like this:*
>
> **1** Spiritual
>   **a)** *There must be a great and noble object.*
>   **b)** *Its achievement must be vital.*
>   **c)** *The method of achievement must be active, aggressive.*
>   **d)** *The man must feel that what he is and what he does matters directly towards the attainment of the object.*
>
> **2** Intellectual
>   **a)** *He must be convinced that the object can be attained; that it is not out of reach.*
>   **b)** *He must see, too, that the organization to which he belongs and which is striving to attain the object is an efficient one.*
>   **c)** *He must have confidence in his leaders and know that whatever dangers and hardships he is called to suffer, his life will not be lightly flung away.*
>
> **3** Material
>   **a)** *The man must feel that he will get a fair deal from his commanders and from the army generally.*
>   **b)** *He must, as far as humanly possible, be given the best weapons and equipment for his task.*
>   **c)** *His living and working conditions must be made as good as they can be.*

It was one thing thus neatly to marshal my principles but quite another to develop them, apply them, and get them recognised by the whole army.

At any rate our spiritual foundation was a firm one. I use the word spiritual, not in its strictly religious meaning, but as a belief in a cause...

The fighting soldier facing the enemy can see that what he does... matters to his comrades and directly influences the result of the battle. It is harder for the man working on the road far behind, the clerk checking stores in a dump, the headquarters' telephone operator monotonously plugging through his calls – it is hard for these and a thousand others to see that they too matter. Yet everyone had to be made to see where his task fitted into the whole, to realise what depended on it, and to feel pride and satisfaction in doing it well.

Now these things, while the very basis of morale because they were purely matters of feeling and emotion, were the most difficult to put over... I felt there was only one way to do it, by a direct approach to the men themselves. Not by written exhortations, by wireless speeches, but by informal talks and contacts between troops and commanders. There was nothing new in this; my Corps and Divisional commanders and others right down the scale were already doing it... And we all talked the same stuff with the same object...

I learnt, too, that one did not need to be an orator to be effective. Two things only were necessary: first to know what you were talking about, and, second and most important, to believe it yourself. I found that if one kept the bulk of one's talk to the material things the men were interested in, food, pay, leave, beer, mail, and the progress of operations, it was safe to end on a higher note – the spiritual foundations – and I always did....

It was in these ways we laid the spiritual foundations, but that was not enough; they would have crumbled without others, the intellectual and the material. Here we had first to convince the doubters that our object was practicable... A victory in a large scale battle was, in our present state of training, organization, and confidence, not to be attempted.

All commanders therefore directed their attention to patrolling. In jungle warfare this is the basis of success. It not only gives eyes to the side that excels at it, and blinds its opponent, but through it the soldier learns to move confidently in the elements in which he works. Every forward unit... chose its best men, formed patrols, trained and practised them, and then sent them out on business. These patrols came back to their regiments with stories of success.

Having developed the confidence of the individual man in his superiority over the enemy, we had now to extend that to the corporate confidence of units and formations in themselves. This was done in a series of carefully planned minor offensive operations. These were carefully staged, ably led, and, as I was always careful to ensure, in great strength... we could not at this stage risk even small failures... the individual superiority built up by more successful patrolling grew into a feeling of superiority within units and formations. We were then ready to undertake larger operations. We had laid the first of our intellectual foundations of morale; everyone knew... our object was attainable.

The next foundation, that the men should feel that they belonged to an efficient organization, that Fourteenth Army was well run and would get somewhere, followed partly from these minor successes.

A most potent factor in spreading this belief in the efficiency of an organization is a sense of discipline. In effect, discipline means that every man, when things pass beyond his own authority or initiative, knows to whom to turn for further direction. If it is the right kind of discipline he turns in the confidence that he will get sensible and effective direction. Every step must be taken to build up this confidence of the soldier in his leaders. For instance, it is not enough to be efficient; the organization must look efficient...

Thus the intellectual foundations of morale were laid. There remained the material... Material conditions, though lamentably low by the standards of any other British army, were improving. Yet I knew that whatever had been promised... from home, it would be six months at least before it reached my troops. We would remain, for a long time yet, desperately short...

These things were frankly put to the men by their commanders at all levels and, whatever their race, they responded. In my experience it is not so much asking men to fight or work with inadequate or obsolete equipment that lowers morale but the belief that those responsible are accepting such a state of affairs. If men realise that everyone above them and behind them is flat out to get the things required for them, they will do wonders, as my men did, with the meagre resources they have instead of sitting down moaning for better.

> *I do not say that the men of the Fourteenth Army welcomed difficulties, but they grew to take a fierce pride in overcoming them by determination and ingenuity. From start to finish they had only two items of equipment that were never in short supply; their brains and their courage. They lived up to the unofficial motto I gave them, 'God helps those who help themselves'.*
>
> *In these and many other ways we translated my rough notes on the foundations of morale, spiritual, intellectual, and material, into a fighting spirit for our men and a confidence in themselves and their leaders that was to impress our friends and surprise our enemies.*

There is a clear link between the practical leadership demonstrated by Slim and his subordinate commanders and the morale of the army, but what is the link between motivation and morale? Remember that morale is the mental attitude of a team, and motivation is that which stimulates interest in a job and induces a person to act in a particular way (behaviour that satisfies a personal need). Slim's analysis places the 'spiritual' over the 'intellectual', which is in turn superior to the 'material'. There is an apparent paradox when this is compared with Maslow's hierarchy of needs that places basic physiological needs (the material) first then security, affiliation, self-esteem and self-actualization needs.

Perhaps the answer lies in the following: physiological needs are all relative, and people usually want more than is necessary for survival; and people can change their perspective. A cohesive team, unified around a common challenge and purpose, satisfies security and affiliation needs. Leadership may persuade people that their physiological needs have been satisfied (to a minimum acceptable level that permits human endeavour), that their security needs can best be met by achieving the aim and fulfilling the purpose that ensures their survival, and that each person is vital to the success of the plan (self-esteem is satisfied). Self-discipline and a sense of duty reinforce acceptance of what needs to be done to ensure success. Thus, self-actualization is achieved by making these supreme efforts.

Montgomery[2] expresses his view of morale in a different way. He identifies four basic factors that are essential:

1. Leadership (although arguably this is the factor that ensures all others).
2. Comradeship.
3. Self-respect.
4. Discipline.

Leadership

> *Morale is, in the first place, based on leadership. Good morale is impossible without good leaders.*
>
> (Field Marshal Montgomery)[2]

The aspects of leadership that he particularly identified were decision in action, calmness in crisis, the ability to relieve people of their burdens, and the ability to instil self-respect in people.

Comradeship

Morale cannot be good unless men come to have affection for each other; a fellow-feeling must grow up which will result in a spirit of comradeship. Men learn to have faith in each other according to the abilities of each... Friends will prevent a man from feeling lonely... He will derive strength from their presence and strive not to let them down.

(Field Marshal Montgomery)[2]

All organizations are composed of people and however inspiring a leader is or however perfect the cohesion and discipline in the team, the morale will be 'cold' and 'harsh' if the warmth of comradeship is lacking. It is assisted by esprit de corps and pride in the organization and its identity.

Self-respect

No man can be said to possess high morale if the quality of self-respect is lacking... Self-respect implies a determination to maintain personal standards of behaviour. Efficiency is inseparable from self-respect... A man who feels he is trusted will feel that he is efficient, and he will at once begin to respect himself... He will have confidence in his own ability... Men who are trusted gain self-confidence.

(Field Marshal Montgomery)[2]

Arguably, self-respect develops concurrently with, or as a by-product of, comradeship, discipline, achievement and development of one's ability. However, it is not a term often heard at work and for this reason Montgomery's analysis of it has been included here.

Discipline

Discipline was introduced in Chapter 20, but let us now look at it in more detail.

All organizations require discipline if they are to be both effective and efficient. For example, retailing is about providing customers with a consistent experience over time and a wide geographical area. You cannot provide this without having a disciplined organization. Discipline ensures success by minimizing and hopefully eliminating unpleasant surprises for the customer. For discipline to be effective, you need to work out exactly what has to be 'tight' and what can be left 'loose' – what has to be controlled and what can be left to initiative and originality.

True discipline is not someone shouting orders at others. That is dictatorship, not discipline. The voluntary, reasoned discipline accepted by free, intelligent men and women is another thing. To begin with, it is binding on all, from top to bottom.

(Field Marshal Sir William Slim)

Unless the lesson of duty be first well learned, the lesson of discipline can be but imperfectly understood.

(Sir John Fortescue, 1927, *A Gallant Company*)

As Slim said (see Chapter 20):[3]

You can take out your car or bicycle, you can choose where you want to go, your own destination. That's liberty! But, as you drive or ride through the streets towards your destination, you will keep to the left side of the road. That's discipline.... if you think for a moment you will find that there is a connection between liberty and discipline.

Whenever we control our desire to do as we like – temper liberty with discipline – we do so for one or more of these reasons: for our own advantage, consideration for others, confidence in others, or fear of punishment. It is the relative weight we give to each of these reasons that decides what sort of discipline we have, which varies from self-discipline to the enforced discipline of fear.

> *Discipline is teaching which makes a man do something which he would not, unless he had learned that it was the right, the proper, and the expedient thing to do. At its best, it is instilled and maintained by pride in oneself, in one's unit, and in one's profession; only at its worst by a fear of punishment. Discipline is a vital component of high morale, and it is required to some degree in all but an anarchic community.*
> (Field Marshal Earl Wavell)

> *Training in self-discipline consists in analysing a man's character and then in developing the good points while teaching him to hold in subjection the bad points. This leads on, automatically, to collective discipline, in which the outstanding factor is the subordination of self for the benefit of the community.*
> (Field Marshal Montgomery)

In all organizations, there are times when we need to subordinate ourselves – our interests and desires – for the benefit of our colleagues and/or our organization (in the Army this is a permanent requirement). This involves a voluntary self-discipline that recognizes and respects the rights of others, and the requirements of our employers. At the same time, the organization should recognize the importance of the individual and only impose those restraints that are necessary for the communal good (which includes the good of the organization – not just its other employees). Therefore discipline has both a moral and a social foundation.

Discipline is a state of mind that produces a readiness for willing, intelligent and appropriate conduct. It is essential to distinguish between discipline and punishment. They are not the same, and punishment or disciplinary sanctions are means that can be used to influence the action of people – their discipline. Resorting to punishment is a negative approach to developing discipline, but there are occasions when it needs to be used without hesitation, for example, gross breaches of integrity and dishonesty; acts that cannot and should not be tolerated (despite the appalling 'example' set for us by some of our political leaders).

In Chapter 20 we introduced discipline as a necessary part of effective teamwork because an efficient organization needs to know and rely on the actions of the people within it. This organizational stability can only be achieved by a high degree of self-discipline. We may consider discipline under three headings: imposed, self and collective.

Imposed discipline

This is a type of discipline that armies apply to recruits and it is a popular civilian conception of discipline in the armed forces. It is simply the first step in developing self-discipline within recruits. It is through the imposition of discipline that new recruits learn the basic standards of behaviour that are expected in army life, what is the right and proper thing to do, and they learn to maintain mental alertness and perseverance in adversity through demanding training. This requires a directive style of leadership. As training progresses and the recruits can meet the physical and mental challenges set and gain satisfaction and a sense of achievement, they start to carry out their tasks because they want to – their own self-discipline is asserting itself, and imposed discipline is relaxed. Thus imposition by others gives way to imposition by oneself.

Self-discipline

The basis of all order and efficiency is self-discipline. People need to have an inbuilt set of standards that govern their behaviour and conduct. This varies from person to person and the level depends on a number of factors, including the influences on people in early life. When people see the need to maintain certain standards and adhere to them, self-discipline has been achieved and its essence is mental self-control and restraint, and awareness of the need for a sense of duty towards others. Self-discipline does not only assist with performance of the duties in one's role, it assists with the display of emotional intelligence. Trust is linked to self-discipline, for trust is only given when there is confidence in our reliability and consistency; self-discipline is implicit in trustworthiness.

Collective discipline

This is discipline within a group or team and is founded upon the self-discipline of individuals. This is the discipline that ensures stability under stress and consistency in the team's or organization's performance. Such discipline only develops with effective leadership and through individuals accepting and aligning themselves to team objectives and methods. This inevitably requires a degree of sacrifice of personal interests in favour of the group, and that is why self-centred people never really become full members of any team to which they belong; they are members on paper only.

If you ponder on it for a moment, discipline can be linked to motivation. Security as we have seen is one of our basic needs, as is 'belonging' to a group. Knowing the rules, the norms of the group can further add to the sense of satisfaction of that need when people realize that the 'rules' exist purely to ensure an environment of mutual support and act as an aid to effectiveness. To be self-disciplined we strengthen our minds so that we can overcome any negative influences that may surround us. Through it, we learn to restrict our thoughts or behaviour within definite limits and, through this habit, self-discipline is strengthened, enabling us to display fortitude in the face of fatigue, stress or discomfort.

The fact that psychologists can offer an explanation for observed behaviour does not in any way diminish the behaviour or the person exhibiting it. Our needs are common to most, if not all people and act as 'goads' to behaviour. It is, therefore, extremely important that we understand that people under stress experience a heightened need for the support of others, and often they want to merge themselves into the corporate body of which they are a part. We learn to gain confidence and encouragement from working with our colleagues; we can derive strength and satisfaction from their company; and our own identities merge into the larger corporate identity. There is, however, a price to be paid for this sense of 'belonging': to be a member you have to accept that you have a 'duty' towards the organization and its other members.

Signs of low morale

Many people, especially those with limited experience or understanding of morale, believe that high morale is found only in a successful organization – or that high morale is directly the result of success. While success helps to build morale to a higher level, the foundations of morale can be firmly established in very adverse conditions, as has been proved by many great leaders.

So how can you recognize that morale is low? These tell-tale signs should trigger concern in the leader:

- High staff turnover. While some staff turnover can be healthy and people may need to leave to satisfy personal needs that an organization, or their leader, cannot meet, an abnormally high turnover of staff is indicative of poor morale and, therefore, poor leadership. This is obviously very costly to organizations in terms of lost expertise, costs of hiring and retraining, and lost opportunities that are not quantifiable.
- Uncooperative, unhelpful attitudes, lack of commitment and lack of enthusiasm. These all contribute to 'atmosphere' and are noticeable by anyone with any sensitivity walking into the environment, even for the first time. Do people go out of their way to assist you, or do things grudgingly? Does routine bore them and would they rather do something more stimulating? Has their leader kept them informed of the reasons behind major decisions, have they been involved in low-level decisions, do they know that they play an important role in the organization? Has communication and the passage of information failed? If the answer to any or all of these is 'yes', leadership is lacking.
- Is cynicism, doubt, complaining and finding fault with everything on the increase? Is negativity pervading the air? Again, these are signs of poor morale.
- Are standards falling in product quality, work area cleanliness, personal appearance, or timeliness, punctuality, and so on? These all result from a lack of self-respect, itself a part of morale.
- You know things are really bad when people openly talk about how bad things are – you then have a major problem to sort out.

The causes of low morale are all the result of leadership failing to 'grip':

- Clarity of purpose and role.
- Unrealistic and constantly moving goal posts.
- Inconsistency in values, discipline, standards, priorities and ever-changing decisions and direction.

- Poor communication and feedback.
- Failure to meet expectations, or giving rise to false expectations.
- Failure by leaders to keep promises or meet commitments.
- Dysfunctional organizational structure.
- Lack of effective performance management, especially the reluctance to remove 'dead wood' while others work hard.
- Lack of organizational pride and esprit de corps.
- Poor administration.

There are many conscious steps that you can take to promote and improve morale among your team members – review the ACE conditions for success and leadership in Chapters 3 and 4!

Loyalty

Loyalty was discussed in depth in Chapter 4. Loyalty is being faithful or true to allegiance and, as a leader, your loyalty extends upwards, downwards and sideways. Loyalty in the leaders at every level of the organizational hierarchy develops loyalty within the remainder of the enterprise and this is reflected in loyal customers, as we see below.

The loyalty effect

Josiah Royce,[4] Professor of Philosophy at Harvard University in 1908, suggested that loyalties arrange themselves in a hierarchical group. At the bottom of the pyramid is loyalty to individuals, above that loyalty to groups, and at the top of the pyramid loyalty to principles. He maintains that loyalty per se could not be judged but that the principles that one is loyal to may be. He suggests that loyalty to those principles is what determines when a person should end his or her loyalty to an individual or a group.

Leadership that generates loyalty is not only about loyalty to individuals and groups, but about loyalty to a set of principles that enables an enterprise to sustain performance over time. Implicit in this is a preference for a partnership approach to business and careful selection of people, whether customers, employees or shareholders. Frederick Reichheld[5] examined how the concept of loyalty affected businesses:

- Loyal customers spend more rapidly and easily over time, generating repeat sales and referrals. This minimizes a company's cost of sales and produces more profitable accounts.
- This assists an enterprise to recruit and retain the best talent. As employees become more knowledgeable about their company and their customers they are better able to exceed customer expectations and hence, add greater value. Their consistency and service delivery reinforces customer loyalty and helps to sustain growth.

- Customer-focused and loyal employees anticipate customer needs, challenge assumptions and innovate, also reducing operating costs and improving customer value. This leads to better productivity and more loyal customers yet again. (But beware the loyalty that creates 'blind obedience and complacency'.)
- The ease and efficiency of working as a partner with loyal customers generates both the cost and value advantage that is difficult for competitors to match.
- The sustained performance of a company produced by these effects attracts loyal shareholders, ready to invest in measures that will further sustain long-term performance and help to stabilize the company.

At the time, research by Bain & Company International showed that disloyalty stunted US corporate performance by 25 to 50 per cent and businesses that located and retained loyal customers and investors displayed superior performance. Where there was a high incidence of disloyalty among staff, teams were dysfunctional, and staff turnover high. In contrast, a high retention rate of customers assisted in building company morale, and reduced the costs of sales and operations.

Building a base of loyal accounts surely is integral to any company's business strategy. For this approach to business to be successful, a company's leaders have to believe in, and display, the leadership practices consistent with building loyalty. Sound, effective leadership generates innovation, a focus on customer needs and service, and loyalty within the company. This is reflected in creating value for the customer and, hence, loyal accounts. Those companies that focus solely on the current year's profit are likely to do so to the detriment of loyalty. Short-term expedient decisions, particularly those that directly affect employees, assist in eroding loyalty and while short-term gains may be seen on the bottom line that year, performance is not sustainable over time. Then both employees and shareholders suffer. If the focus is on developing long-term sustainable performance and customer value, profit is a welcome by-product of building customer, employee and shareholder loyalty. This means a paradigm shift from 'we exist to generate immediate profit and make short-term decisions' to 'we exist to create value for all stakeholders and as a result generate sustainable profits'. Which paradigm does your organization reflect?

Few companies would deny that their people are their most important asset, and almost every chairman's opening address in a corporate annual report alludes to this. However, there are few accounting systems that take note of the assets created by loyal customers, loyal and experienced employees and loyal shareholders.

Trust

Trust in organizations, has both a personal and an organizational or systemic dimension.

Extending trust is both an emotional and logical act. We trust people because we feel that they are trustworthy, but as leaders we know that the example of trusting others builds confidence and loyalty, and ultimately leads to higher levels of performance.

TABLE 21.1 Factors inducing trust or paranoia (after Jaques)

Trust-inducing	Paranoiagenic
• Equitable system of pay differentials related to differentials in levels of work and output • Clear definition of role purpose, tasks, objectives and priorities • Clear definition of freedom of action, and constraints and limitations • Clear definition of accountabilities and authorities in lateral working relationships • Leaders one-stratum higher from immediate subordinates in the level of work and capability • Mentors assisting with career development • Regular coaching and feedback • Employees well-informed about the context of their work, company intentions and likely changes • Vertical authority in line with accountability • Level of work in line with a person's capability • Provision of timely personal, professional and career development • Loyalty displayed by leaders • Recognition of performance	• Power bargaining over pay, or unfair bonus 'incentive' systems • Leaving people to sort out their lateral working relationships by means of manipulation, personal networks, or force of personality • Leaders more or less than one stratum removed from subordinates and 'breathing down their necks,' or being 'pulled down into the weeds' • No mentoring, no career development, no real awareness of employee's potential capabilities • Employees in the dark about what is likely to happen, what they are currently doing and why they are doing it • Accountability without commensurate authority; and being told to influence difficult people • Under-recognition and under-utilization of capability • Absence of feedback from manager and lack of any performance or progress reviews • Development plans that are never implemented • 'Empowerment' as a phoney gimmick in place of clarity of accountability and authority • Undefined dotted line relationships in multiple directions • More than one leader to set priority of work • Policies, processes and procedures that have dysfunctional or undesirable outcomes

The trouble with trust is that we might be let down and it is the risk aversion so prevalent in many managers that prevents trust being extended. Unfortunately, if we wish our people to trust us as leaders, first we have to extend that trust to them – that means taking a risk – and second, we have to be seen as trustworthy. Being trustworthy inspires positive expectations of us in others – and that comes down to the integrity, loyalty, confidence in others and leadership competence that we display. Good leaders have a tendency to trust rather than distrust people, but qualify that extension of trust with sound judgement about a person's abilities. Trust and confidence go hand-in-hand: it is hard to trust people unless you are confident in them, and if you have confidence, then it is easier to trust.

At an organizational level, the framework in which people work – the organizational structure, clarity of role relationships, and the systems and processes people work in and with – can assist in inducing trust across the organization, or they may induce paranoia and distrust. Table 21.1 illustrates this

Notes

1 Field Marshal Sir William Slim, 1957, *Defeat into Victory*, London: Cassell.
2 Field Marshal The Viscount Montgomery of Alamein KG, GCB, DSO, 1948, *Forward from Victory: Speeches and addresses*, London: Hutchinson.
3 Field Marshal Sir William Slim, 1957, *Courage and Other Broadcasts*, London: Cassell.
4 Professor Josiah Royce, 1908, *The Philosophy of Loyalty*.
5 Frederick F Reichheld, 1996, *The Loyalty Effect: The hidden force behind growth, profits, and lasting values*, Boston, MA: Harvard Business School Press.

22
The role of organization and structure in leadership

> Principles of organization

Bureaucracy
My Lord, if I attempted to answer the mass of futile correspondence that surrounds me, I should be debarred from all serious business of campaigning... So long as I retain an independent position, I shall see no Officer under my command is debarred by attending to the futile drivelling of mere quill-driving from attending to his first duty, which is and always has been, so to train the private men under his command that they may without question beat any force opposed to them in the field.
(Wellington, writing from The Peninsular to the Secretary of State for War)

'Organization' has various meanings. We can say 'I'll organize lunch' meaning to take responsibility for ensuring that it happens; we can use the word in the sense of giving order to and making arrangements for an activity; or it can be used in the sense of a structured, systematic and disciplined collective body. So far we have been concerned mainly with the leadership of people to achieve tasks that have been planned. However, in most circumstances, people need to be grouped into permanent or temporary teams, usually within a wider structure, their actions directed and coordinated, and resources deployed to support them. So we need to consider the role of organization in enabling leaders to lead people in the successful execution of strategy and achievement of objectives.

All relationships take place in some sort of social structure, and it is the known structure that sets the limits and expectations and defines the roles that shape our behaviour towards each other. Structure lies in the pattern of relationships among roles in any organization. Have you suffered from restructures that result in another matrix that does not work? How many reorganization fads and panaceas have failed, each building cynicism among the workforce? It is not the concept of a matrix or hierarchy that is wrong, nor the product-led versus customer-led structure that is wrong; it is the unclear interdependencies and roles, unaligned accountability and authority, and lack of 'requisite structure' that is at fault.

The usual approach to redesigning or restructuring organizations is to present imaginative proposals based on perceived future requirements and/or current management fads. Many ideas have been put forward to eliminate hierarchical structures under the names of leaderless or self-directed teams, quality circles, matrix management, etc. However, none of these have ever got rid of hierarchy because some form of hierarchy is essential to every efficient organization – hierarchy is a means of breaking 'big tasks' into smaller, more manageable pieces; hierarchy makes complexity manageable.

It is because many organizations have grown with too little thought about the principles that should be applied in designing them that the desire to replace hierarchical structures has arisen – hierarchy is not inherently bad. It is not the removal of the concept of hierarchy that is important but removing the causes of the stifling of initiative, imposition of bureaucratic 'red tape', indecision and risk aversion, inertia, lack of clarity, decision-making authority in the wrong places and authoritarian and micro-management behaviour.

The right structure will facilitate the speedy and effective completion of tasks and provide the framework in which clarity of role, authority and accountability helps to promote sound working relationships and trust. In thinking about structure we should bear in mind that over-flat structures often lead to:

- Poor direction and lack of clarity of task and role for everyone because leaders have too broad a span of control and have no firm grasp of the issues facing a diverse team.
- Insufficient time spent developing subordinates.
- Insufficient incisive thought, planning and anticipation leading to relentless crisis management.
- Lack of career paths for those with leadership ambitions, which leads to staff turnover (when the local economy is healthy).
- Too large a gap between the complexity of work and the context that the leader has to deal with, and that of most of the team members.

On the other hand, excessive numbers of organizational layers leads to:

- Lack of 'headroom' and freedom of action for subordinates.
- Stifling of initiative.
- Slow decision making.
- Inefficient communication channels.
- A bureaucracy that hinders rather than facilitates.
- Unnecessary costs of employment.

Ill-defined matrix structures (meaningless dotted line relationships on a chart) generally erode trust because:

- They fail to align accountability with authority and allow people to hide because no one appears to be accountable for anything.
- Gaps in responsibility are usually created – so work remains incomplete and issues are not followed through.
- Duplication is often created resulting in people feeling that someone is doing their job, 'treading on their toes' or checking up because they are not trusted.

It is therefore essential to get the balance right. Balance is stressed because downsizing and re-engineering seem to have swung the pendulum too far to the lean flat style that has resulted in poor morale, high staff turnover and loss of knowledge and experience, higher stress, more crises, and less learning and development due to lack of time.

An interesting fact of large industrial organizations is that there is always a nearly unanimous clarity amongst those involved at lower levels about who is actually keeping the thing going.

(Sir John Harvey-Jones)

There are four types of organization relevant to an enterprise. First there is the formal or manifest organizational structure that appears on organization charts, showing the reporting structure. Second there is the informal or extant organization. In healthy enterprises with leadership and teamwork at every level this is merely a preferred social grouping; in inefficient organizations lacking leadership this is the collection of personal relationships that actually gets things done. Third is the assumed organization. This is the organization as people assume it to be. There are as many of these as there are people in the organization! Fourth there is the 'deliberate' organization that you would have if the whole thing was properly thought through and designed, rather than allowed to grow in the usual haphazard manner.

Organization, the structural and procedural concepts, is something that effective armies have constantly been studying (but until relatively recently more usually evolving through experience, because of the need to rapidly deploy mobile units over long distances that can operate effectively immediately in the absence of communication). They need enough leaders to provide adequate command in action but not too many so that leaders get in each other's way. Business has the same needs but they are not so obvious since the consequences of failure are not so immediate and bloody and people may hide from the connection. An intriguing fact is that many armies have evolved, quite independently, a remarkably similar approach to structure. Even more intriguing is that many of these would closely match the design that would emerge if the work of the late Dr Elliott Jaques were used as its conceptual base.[1] Indeed in conversation with me, Dr Jaques said that the British Army was a perfect match to a requisite organization – and I do not think anyone in the Army has ever heard of Dr Jaques! Dr Jaques, a Canadian and author of more than 20 books on the social sciences, psychology, complexity of work and human capability, is best known for objectively measuring the complexity of work in roles (time span of discretion) and an objective understanding of the nature of human potential capability and its maturation throughout life. Dr Jaques' concept of 'Requisite organization' (reflected in principles 1, 5 and 6 in Figure 22.1) is the ideal vehicle on which effects-based leadership (EBL) should travel.

People do not have to like each other to work together effectively, but they do need to respect and trust each other. Trust is the social glue that holds organization together and effective organization should be tested against the criterion: does this structure or process induce and enhance people's ability to trust each other and the organization?

Principles of organization

The principles that we shall look at derive from observation of dysfunctional phenomena and consideration of the nature of things: the purpose of a managerial leadership accountability hierarchy, the components of tasks, the complexity of work, the capability of the mind to cope with complexity, and so on.

There are certain principles of organization that should be employed consistently within an organization. These do not exist to produce an inflexible bureaucracy but to assist the speedy and successful completion of tasks and rapid reconfiguration of a business and its units to meet new challenges. The paradox of discipline and freedom described in Chapter 2 applies here.

All interpersonal relationships occur within a social system and a dysfunctional system will produce dysfunctional working relationships; the right organization will stimulate the growth of healthy and effective relationships. These ideas should be viewed as first principles to be considered in all situations and applied as the leader's judgement and wisdom see fit.

This is the part of the book that will probably feel most uncomfortable to most people – probably people working in the public sector and in some HR departments, given our experience – but invest the time to think about these ideas – they work (they normally resonate with line managers who actually do have accountability for results). With thought and discussion, they have been embraced by leaders (deans and heads of school) in one university client; and a month after adoption in an investment bank, with some resistance from some of the top team, the whole top team said that they found these ideas 'liberating'. While this approach to structure facilitates the use of EBL and the appreciation, planning and briefing tools we have examined, these tools may be used in any approach to structure and will improve business performance. This approach to structure just helps make leading people easier!

We are all, to some extent, creatures of habit and victims of our experience – don't let this close your mind to thinking about new ideas.

1. A requisite hierarchical structure

If you have ever heard statements or questions like, 'I'm too big for this role', 'He's out of his depth in that job', 'I need more headroom', 'She's outgrown that job' then read on. What do these statements refer to – what is the 'size of role'? The answers lie largely within an understanding of the work of the late Dr Elliott Jaques.

FIGURE 22.1 Principles of organization

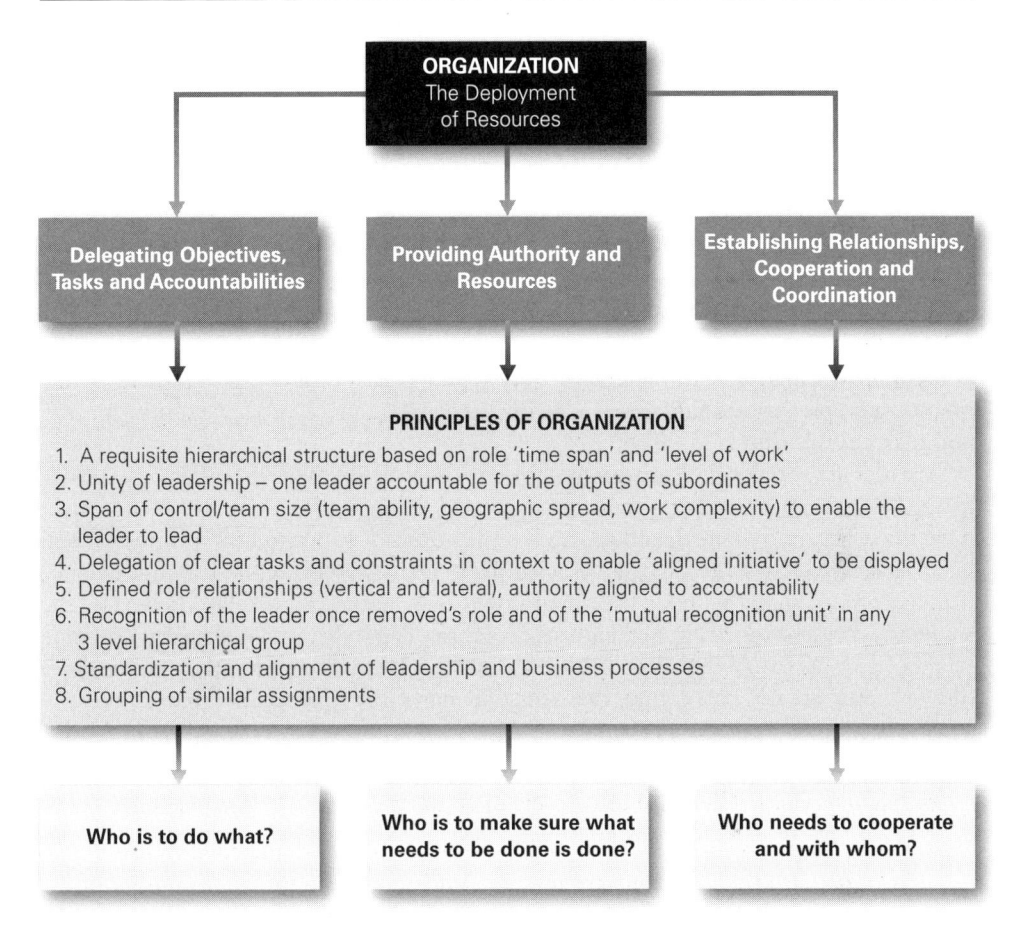

ORGANIZATION
The Deployment of Resources

- Delegating Objectives, Tasks and Accountabilities
- Providing Authority and Resources
- Establishing Relationships, Cooperation and Coordination

PRINCIPLES OF ORGANIZATION
1. A requisite hierarchical structure based on role 'time span' and 'level of work'
2. Unity of leadership – one leader accountable for the outputs of subordinates
3. Span of control/team size (team ability, geographic spread, work complexity) to enable the leader to lead
4. Delegation of clear tasks and constraints in context to enable 'aligned initiative' to be displayed
5. Defined role relationships (vertical and lateral), authority aligned to accountability
6. Recognition of the leader once removed's role and of the 'mutual recognition unit' in any 3 level hierarchical group
7. Standardization and alignment of leadership and business processes
8. Grouping of similar assignments

- Who is to do what?
- Who is to make sure what needs to be done is done?
- Who needs to cooperate and with whom?

© Jeremy Tozer, 1997–2007

Leaders who can cope with their level of work – summary of Jaques' research

Over 55 years of research by Jaques and his colleagues builds on effective patterns that are repeated through hierarchy's 3,000-year history. His research spans human capability (time-horizon[2] and the mental processes to manage complexity), and effective hierarchy (levels of work[3] defined by role time span[4] and complexity).

Human cognitive power, which defines a person's time-horizon, follows a predictable pattern of growth or maturation of one day, three months, one year, two years, five years, 10 years, 20 years and 50 years. This is based on a person's cognitive processing of information of different orders of complexity. The pattern is predictable but people do not mature at the same time or age.

Real boundaries of managerial hierarchical layers or 'strata' exist in the most effective organizations at time spans of one day, three months, one year, two years, five years, 10 years, 20 years, and 50 years. These time spans coincide with the desired number of strata in any large organization and these hierarchical strata reflect the stratification of human cognitive capability, which may be measured in terms of levels of abstraction and time-horizon.

The levels of work or strata of an organization, measured by time span, are based upon the level of task complexity (itself affected by the level of information complexity), with each strata containing roles of the same level of work faced by leaders and individual contributors within it.

The greater the time span of a role – or level of work – the greater the level of responsibility and the greater its felt level by the incumbent and subordinates – the role's scope. To be effective, the occupant of a role needs to have the time-horizon and cognitive capability to match the time span or level of work in that role. These quantum steps may be addressed by considering cognitive processes, information and task complexity.

A leader at every level or stratum within an organization must be sufficiently greater in capability than his or her subordinates to add value, set the context for the work, have the wisdom to judge the effects and implications of subordinates' proposals, and be sufficiently self-assured to get on with his or her own job while leaving the subordinates to do theirs without breathing down their necks. To do this effectively, the leader must be one quantum step higher in cognitive capability and managing work one strata of complexity higher than his subordinates. (Note that these strata define level of work, they are not pay grades; there may be many more pay grades than strata.)

Complexity of cognitive processes, information and tasks

Cognitive processes. There are four levels of cognitive (or mental) processing:

A Declarative processing (DP) in which information is organized and direct associations and assertions are made in immediate situations. A number of reasons may be given or statements made about a subject, which are not connected – they are individual bits of information.

B Cumulative processing (CP) in which significant pieces of information, none of which are conclusive on their own, are combined and conclusions drawn. For example, in interviewing, the interviewer builds a collection of clues from which he or she makes a judgement on the suitability of an applicant.

C Serial processing (SP) in which information is combined in a linear and logical sequence, cause and effect studied, and predictions made, eg, 'X will lead to Y which will lead to Z'.

D Parallel processing (PP) in which separate serial processes or lines of thought are held in parallel and viewed in relation to each other. A number of scenarios and options will therefore be considered.

As we mature we progress up these four levels of processing, which are used to make sense of data and turn it into useful information. Just as we can employ more complex cognitive processes, there are more complex variables to apply them to – information complexity. It is possible to assess a person's capability by observing their intellectual arguments.

Information complexity. Let us now consider information itself and the five orders of information complexity:

Pre-verbal, information expressed in pre-verbal infancy – gestures.

1. *Concrete verbal* (CV). Thinking and language in children. The variables are clear and unambiguous; they are not tangled with each other and are relatively unchanging.
2. *Symbolic verbal* (SV). Adult's thought and language. This allows work to be discussed and briefings given, which enables products to be made, sold and marketed, accounts and information systems maintained, etc. It is the combination of a myriad of concrete things.
3. *Conceptual abstraction* (CA). Ordinary symbolic verbal language is used to express concepts of ever-changing variables and to discuss intangibles by senior executives. To mean anything, these concepts have to be illustrated with concrete examples, eg corporate culture change, the effects of corporate 'values', the effects of government policy and foreign exchange rates, the bringing together of wide-ranging accounting categories on balance sheets and so on.
4. *Universal abstraction* (UA). Combining conceptual abstraction to make universal concepts for whole societal change, philosophies and ideologies, etc.

With maturity we apply the four levels of cognitive processing in turn to increasing levels of information complexity – that is we apply more complex processes to more complex information. Our thinking moves from A1 through the categories of A2, A3, A4, B1, etc and the mode in which a person operates may be termed his or her category of potential capability. This may be evaluated by the way a person behaves, approaches and discusses work. Different people will mature at different times of their lives, so while the pattern is universal the timing is not. By the end of childhood, we generally have moved through the four cognitive processes applied to first-order complexity information (A1–A4) and start again at the second-order complexity (B1) – this is where the world of work starts.

Problem complexity. Jaques also found that there are four types of problem complexity:

A. Direct action and immediate situational response. (Problems dealt with as they arise.)
B. Diagnostic accumulation. (Problems anticipated and resolved by collection, collation, and evaluation of information.)
C. Alternative serial plans. (Possible courses of action based upon cause and effect are evaluated and the best course chosen.)
D. Mutually interactive programmes. (A number of interactive or parallel serial plans are implemented and adjusted with regard to timing and resources to keep the whole plan in line with the aim.)

These four types of problem complexity are overlaid with the four levels of information complexity to produce categories of task complexity, which again we may label A1, A2, A3, A4, B1, B2, B3, etc.

The key to success in any role is that a leader's cognitive capability must be equal to the category of task complexity, the level of work (LoW) faced. Therefore a person with B1 level of cognitive capability has a role that involves B1 level of task complexity. This match partly defines the selection criteria for people, and also separates the strata of an organization.

Thus the strata of an organization are based upon the category of task complexity, with each stratum containing roles of the same category of task complexity held by both leaders and individual contributors (IC – technical experts) within it who share the same category of cognitive capability. Remuneration is based on level of work, not the number of subordinates one has, and this ensures that ICs feel valued.

Jaques' work has shown that a maximum of eight levels are necessary in most large commercial organizations, with less in smaller enterprises (in answering the question 'How many layers?', one starts with the vision and purpose to define the LoW of the most senior role and then one work downwards). The levels are: B1, B2, B3, B4, C1, C2, C3 and C4.

The starting point for establishing an effective hierarchy is at the top of the tree, and the acknowledgement that the more complex the task, the greater the cognitive power required to do it.

2. Unity of leadership

Who reports to who is the wrong way to look at structure. You can report to any number of people about any number of things. What matters, from the perspective of getting things done (leadership), is no one has more than one 'boss'. Thus at every level, one person is responsible for an area of work – for the people, their deployment, their tasks and priority of work, and their outputs, and everyone knows who their boss is. The often ill-defined matrix structures are inherently dangerous as no one can effectively 'serve two masters' as conflicts of interests and priorities of work are bound to arise. Unity of leadership is the basis of any effective organization.

Providing effective leadership is a full-time role in itself, and no leader who is required to invest excessive time in selling, researching or designing products or services can be expected to provide effective leadership to the team. This is particularly so when part of a leader's remuneration is based on his or her own 'functional productivity' (eg sales activity) rather than solely on the leadership of people and their resulting outputs.

If a person is temporarily detached from his or her permanent team and its leader and attached to another team and its leader, then the two leaders' accountabilities must be defined and understood by the person being detached/attached as well as the two leaders concerned. If this division of duties is constantly adhered to, then everyone knows what to expect. Usually the temporary team leader should be responsible for:

- task delegation and work prioritization;
- routine performance feedback; and
- discipline within the project team.

TABLE 22.1 Strata, level of complexity and role

Strata	Level of Task: Mental Processing and Information Complexity	Role Description
(1 day – 3 months)	B1: SV, DP Direct judgement	Shop Floor Operator
(3 months – 1 year)	B2: SV, CP Data accumulation and diagnosis	First Line Manager or Team Leader/Supervisor
(1 year – 2 years)	B3: SV, SP Construct alternative routes to goals	Second Line Manager or Unit Manager or Unit Specialists
(2 years – 5 years)	B4: SV, PP Parallel processing and trade-offs	Site/Functional General Manager (GM) or Business Unit Specialist Managers
(5 years – 10 years)	C1: CA, DP Judge downstream system consequences	Business Unit Managing Director (MD) or Group Specialist Directors
(10 years – 20 years)	C2: CA, CP Worldwide data accumulation and diagnosis	Strategic Business Unit Group MD or Head Office Specialist Directors
(20 years – 50 years)	C3: CA, SP Strategic options, alternative routes to make or transform whole systems	Executive Chairman or Chief Executive Officer (CEO)
(50 years +)	C4: CA, PP Worldwide parallel processing and trade-offs	Super Corporation Chairman/CEO

SOURCE: Elliott Jaques, 1996, *Requisite Organization: A total system for effective managerial organization and managerial leadership for the 21st century*, Cason Hall.

The permanent leader remains responsible for:

- assessment of potential and management of all career development;
- ensuring development is planned and delivered;
- welfare and routine administration (unless otherwise agreed);
- formal annual performance assessment;
- pay reviews and other forms of recognition and reward; and
- any other disciplinary matters.

The permanent leader should seek input into the annual performance assessment from the temporary leader during and after the assignment. If the project has been lengthy an 'insert' for the review should be written by the temporary leader. Naturally, the permanent leader will take an interest in detached subordinates and talk with them frequently.

3. Span of control

There are limits to the amount and quality of 'overseeing' that a leader can exercise effectively for his or her team members. Those factors are number of personnel, distance and time.

Personnel

The number of direct and indirect relationships multiplies as the number of team members increases: having seven subordinates produces over 100 combinations of relationships within the team for a leader to manage. It would be hard indeed for any leader to effectively have more than seven subordinates and not only be able to manage the number of relationships, but also devote enough time to understand in detail what is happening in each subordinate's area of responsibility, and therefore be able to resolve conflict or make decisions from the whole team perspective while planning ahead and ensuring that the team members get a regular flow of feedback and coaching. Fewer than three subordinates can often lead to over-supervision, which in turn leads to frustration on the part of the team members. A student of group dynamics will have observed that people are often happier working in smaller groups (often four to eight people) rather than in large groups, and if no sub-group leader is appointed, one frequently emerges who will represent the group to the team leader.

Additionally, the ability of the individual team member will affect the total span of control. Obviously a leader will need to spend more time with less able subordinates, which will impact the maximum span that may be effectively led.

Distance

Personal contact is vital to effective leadership and if subordinates are spread out over a large geographical area, it stands to reason that the leader cannot exercise effective leadership over a large group. Therefore he or she may only be able to lead a smaller span of control.

Time

Some tasks/functions are excessively time-consuming, and again the leader may not have time to do justice to a full 'span of control'. This depends entirely on the nature of the work being done.

This principle may be summarized by saying that the span of control decreases as the number of variables, the complexity of situations and the absence of the leader from his or her subordinates increases.

4. Delegation of clear tasks in context

A good sign of a healthy organization is the way that both tasks and authority are delegated within it. The larger the organization, the greater is the need to set up a clear and efficient delegation system, which will enable the leader to exercise his or her influence overall.

What is a task? A task is an intention to turn an idea into reality through work. As MacDonald[5] has made clear, a machine may be 'programmed' to carry out a task in terms of quantity and quality (within tolerances), time to completion and resource inputs. But people are not machines and if they have no opportunity to exercise discretion in the path followed to complete the task, then the organization will not realize the potential value that they can add by understanding the purpose of their work, how it relates to the work of others, and adapting their work by exercising judgement as circumstances change, and by conceiving innovative and improved ways of achieving the same outcome or better outcomes.

So when the leader delegates tasks, that leader must make clear the context and purpose of the task (the reasons why it is important), how it relates to the work of others, the outcomes or effects that are expected, and the priorities of those effects – which means the leader must also be clear about his or her own work. The other components needed to define a task, which have to be appreciated by the person to whom the task is delegated, include:

- the quantity or quality of the output;
- the date by which the task must be completed;
- the resources available;
- the requisite authority (and other people need to know authority has been delegated);
- the freedom of action (or the boundaries limiting freedom of action) that exists for the person to whom the task has been delegated, so that subordinates will know when and when not to refer to the leader;
- specifying with whom he or she should cooperate or seek assistance as appropriate;
- the system of progress assessment and evaluation if the task is lengthy.

Curiously enough, these features of task delegation are also parts of EBL! If a person is to exercise discretion in achieving a task, then at least one of the elements of quantity/quality, resource use or time should be left open or given with an upper or lower limit. Allowing people to exercise discretion and do their own thinking not only engages them, but provides leaders with the mechanism for assessing performance in a meritocracy.

As a leader, you will be delegated tasks by your leader. Some of them you will wish to carry out personally; others you will wish to delegate to your team members – but you cannot escape or abdicate your responsibility for completion of the task. As a leader of a team, you have responsibility for everything done by members of that team, including the complete outcomes and results of their combined work. Individual team members can only be accountable for areas under their direct control. This acceptance of responsibility by leaders is the key to building trust, confidence and loyalty. The buck therefore stops with the leader.

5. Defined role relationships (authority aligned to accountability)

In most organizations, a major cause of unnecessary stress, duplication of effort or gaps in the execution of plans, time wasted in meetings and so on is the lack of clarity that individuals have about how their role relates to their peers around them. This is especially so in ill-defined matrices with their multitude of dotted lines, which permeate many organizations. This allows people to hide by creating places where no one anywhere is accountable for anything. Or this creates avoidable conflict when people try to establish the authority they need to meet their accountabilities to their bosses. If structural ground rules are not established, people will naturally invent their own to their best advantage, causing unnecessary conflict and generally resulting in a huge waste of time at meetings. There are few organizations that do not need to operate some form of matrix structure; matrixes are not inherently wrong. What is wrong is leaving them as unclear as they tend to be.

The problem is a lack of alignment between the accountabilities that people have to their boss and the authority that they have to meet those accountabilities. All too often people are told to use their influence to get things done, which is usually their boss's excuse for failing to properly consider the framework in which their people are being forced to work. While authority should be the last resort to make things happen, if a person's role is not legitimized by the clear delegation of authority, their role is fundamentally untenable. Authority is usually considered only in the vertical hierarchical sense, with little attention paid to lateral role relationships. Equally, little attention is paid to the role of the 'leader-once-removed' in any organizational structure, which is where we shall start to explore this aspect of structure.

In considering role relationships, too many people and too many HR departments are obsessed with who reports to whom. One can report to many different people about many different things, but from the perspective of making sure that things happen, only one person can give any other person the priority of work and then be held accountable for their outputs. And if no leader is held accountable for the work of others, then there is no leadership structure and nothing will ever get done. This is where the design of structure needs to start, with the recognition of the fundamental principle of 'unity of leadership': only one leader can define a subordinate's priority of work if that leader is to be held accountable for the work of that subordinate.

FIGURE 22.2 A leadership hierarchy based on levels of work

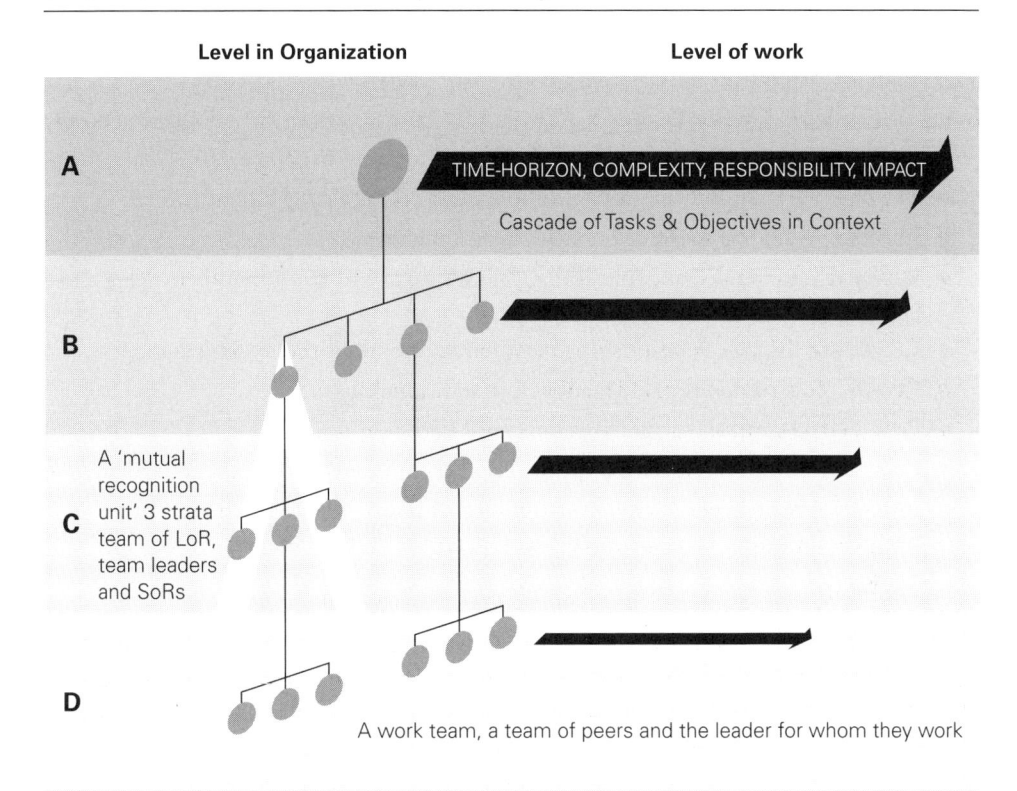

Level in Organization   **Level of work**

A — TIME-HORIZON, COMPLEXITY, RESPONSIBILITY, IMPACT

Cascade of Tasks & Objectives in Context

B

C — A 'mutual recognition unit' 3 strata team of LoR, team leaders and SoRs

D — A work team, a team of peers and the leader for whom they work

LoR = Leader once Removed, SoR = Subordinate once Removed

After Dr Elliott Jaques, 1988/1996 | © Jeremy Tozer, 2008

We shall now consider some basic principles, which intuitively resonate with and make sense to most readers who have endured the pain of being held accountable for work that they had no authority to influence.

In most organizations of any size, 'three-layer hierarchical groups' will be seen at the same level across the organization and/or recurring down from the top of the organization. A three-layer group consists of a leader (the Leader-once-Removed – LoR), a team of peer leaders, and their team members (who are the Subordinates-once-Removed – SoR) from their leader's leader. This is represented by levels ABC and BCD in Figure 22.2. Ideally, the number of people involved in such a grouping permits everyone to know everyone else by name (to create what Jaques calls a 'mutual recognition unit' – MRU).

So in this structure, the types of role that need clearly defined accountability and authority, include the following:

- The leader of a team.
- The leader of an MRU (the LoR in a three-strata grouping).

- Lateral role relationships among peers at the same level within an organization.

Vertical authority: the leader of the team

If Senior Leader A holds a Leader B accountable for the outputs of subordinates C1, C2 etc, then Leader B must have the authority to:

- Veto any new appointment of a subordinate to the leader's team.
- Induct and set the work context for team members.
- Delegate clear tasks, accountability and authority to team members C1, C2, etc.
- Clarifying the role relationships between members of the leader's team.
- Coach and provide regular feedback to team members.
- Provide recognition for performance and verbal appraisal.
- Contribute to performance appraisal and recommend any grade awarded.
- Initiate or recommend removal from role of team members who are not performing to the level required for which expectations have been set.

Vertical authority: the leader-once-removed

While the leader A at the top of a three-strata MRU has the same responsibility to develop and create the ACE conditions for success for his or her immediate team of peer leaders at B as they do with their teams at C, he or she also has additional responsibilities as the LoR:

- Ensuring that a consistent quality of leadership is provided to the teams of SoRs by their leaders across the group.
- Ensuring equality of opportunity and work conditions across the group.
- Establishing clear working relationships between all teams of SoRs across the group. In cases where the SoRs' immediate team leaders have been unable to agree amongst themselves, this is escalated to the LoR.
- Talent pool analysis, development of SoRs and succession planning for subordinates. This is because only the LoR has the broader perspective of levels of performance and potential across the group, and it eliminates the effects of conflicts of personality that may occur between a competent team leader and a competent SoR.
- Final decision making in relation to dismissal, removal from role, promotion, transfers, appeals and pay reviews (the SoR's immediate leader may recommend but should not decide).
- Building and sustaining the three-strata MRU team.

In addition to the LoR, leader and SoR authority and accountability relationships described above, there are the relationships between a supervisor or a project team leader and their team members to consider, and the relationship between a project leader and a peer colleague on the project. All of these accountability and authority relationships are suggested in Figure 22.3.

FIGURE 22.3 Vertical authority and accountability

Leader – Subordinate					
Leader once Removed – Subordinate once Removed					
Supervisor – Subordinate					
Project Team Leader – Subordinate					
Project Leader – Peer Colleague on Project					
D = Decide, **R** = Recommend					
Veto appointment	D	D	R	D	D
Induct and set work context	D	D	R	R	D
Determine task type	D	D	R	R	D
Assign task	D	D	D		D
Coach	D	D	D		D
Verbal appraisal (recognition)	D	D	D	D	D
Recorded appraisal (recognition)	R	R	R	D	R
Pay change and bonus within band				D	R
Transfer from role	R	R	R	D	R
Assess potential and career counsel			R	D	R
Change pay band			R	D	R
Promote/Demote			R	D	R
Dismiss			R	D	R
Appeal				D	

© Jeremy Tozer, 1997–2006

Lateral role relationships

Lateral role relationships occur when C1 has accountability to his or her leader for causing C2 to take action, but C2's leader is accountable for the C2's output.

Here is a summary of the types of lateral role relationships that exist:

- *Collateral.* Collateral relationships exist only between a leader's immediate peer subordinate team members.
- *Adviser.* All team members have advisory relationships with their leader; advisers must use their initiative to freely offer advice.

The ACE Conditions for Success: Environment

- *Service-receiver.* Service receivers must know what services they are authorized to receive and from whom (ie support for their PC).
- *Coordinator.* Coordinative roles exist when people not subordinate to each other need to work in concert with one another to get things done.
- *Monitor.* Monitors ensure standards are adhered to.
- *Auditor.* Auditing is a stronger form of monitoring and prescribing is the strongest.
- *Prescriber.* Prescriptive roles (ie safety roles) need to have stop/start type authorities delegated.

When a person, C1, has had the nature of his or her role relationship with his or her peers clarified, then C1 requires the lateral authorities shown in Figure 22.4 to meet his or her accountabilities to the leader, and the other people at level C need to know that C1 has been delegated these authorities. If a level B leader cannot agree the lateral authorities for his or her Cs among peer level B leaders, then he or she needs to escalate the decision to the LoR, Leader A.

FIGURE 22.4 Lateral authority and accountability

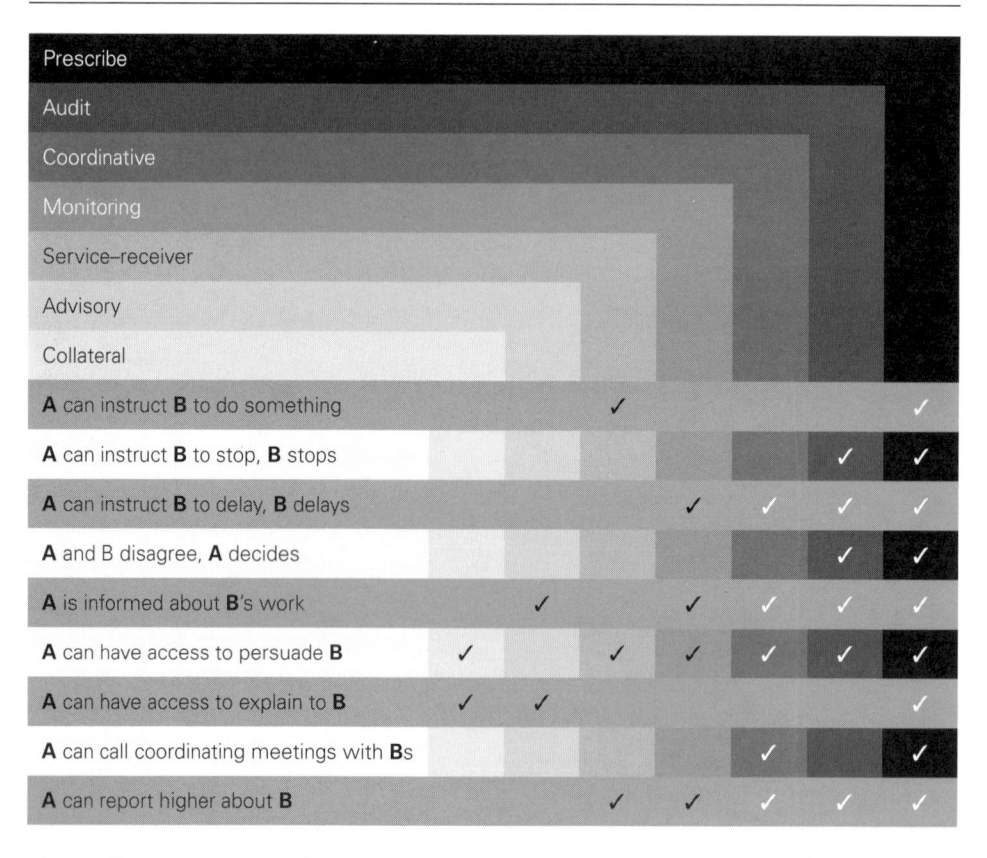

	Collateral	Advisory	Service–receiver	Monitoring	Coordinative	Audit	Prescribe
A can instruct **B** to do something				✓			✓
A can instruct **B** to stop, **B** stops						✓	✓
A can instruct **B** to delay, **B** delays				✓	✓	✓	✓
A and B disagree, **A** decides						✓	✓
A is informed about **B**'s work		✓		✓	✓	✓	✓
A can have access to persuade **B**	✓		✓	✓	✓	✓	✓
A can have access to explain to **B**	✓	✓					✓
A can call coordinating meetings with **B**s					✓		✓
A can report higher about **B**				✓	✓	✓	✓

After Dr Elliott Jaques, 1988/1996 | © Jeremy Tozer, 1997–2006

6. Recognition of the role of the leader-once-removed

The three-layer group leader's role must be recognized. The authorities that this person should have were outlined in the previous 'principle', but given the importance of this role and the general lack of understanding of it, it has been highlighted as a principle in its own right. The LoR (your boss's boss) is the only person who can undertake a number of vital leadership tasks effectively:

- Ensure equilibration of the quality of leadership received by SoRs from the peer leaders in the LoR's team (the 'same deal' across a department).
- Conduct talent pool analysis with a detached and holistic view and ensure timely career development (leaders may be threatened by capable 'subordinates' or personality clashes may exist between an otherwise competent leader and competent subordinate).
- Ensure equality of opportunity and work conditions across the group.
- Establish clear working relationships between all teams of SoRs across the group. In cases where the SoRs immediate team leaders have been unable to agree amongst themselves, this is escalated to the LoR.
- Final decision making in relation to dismissal, removal from role, promotion, transfers, appeals and pay reviews for SoRs (the SoR's immediate leader may recommend but should not decide).
- Build and sustain the three-strata MRU team.

The SoR may assess the quality of leadership provided by a subordinate leader by:

- 'Walking about' and asking the SoRs to explain where they fit into the higher level plans and to describe their role and that of others in their team.
- Observing and considering the frequency and quality of briefings.
- Determining how much crisis management rather than planned work happens.
- Determining the quality and frequency of coaching, feedback and recognition.
- Assessing the quality of administration of employees.
- Assessing the level and quality of delegation.
- Assessing the willingness of a subordinate leader to lose a team member to another team and role if it is in the career interests of the SoR who has the ability needed for the new role and who wishes to pursue it.

If LoRs are to exercise these responsibilities, there are implications for the maximum size of the three hierarchical layer group, ie leader once removed, subordinate leaders and subordinates once removed. The LoR has to know each individual in the entire group personally. Jaques suggests that the limit for this MRU is 300 people.

These LoRs should refuse to accept and certainly not solicit views on their subordinates from the SoRs. This will break the trust that should exist between the LoR and his or her team of leaders.

7. Standardization

Standardization must not be confused with rigidity and unthinking slavish adherence to a tick-box procedure. Standardization applies to the conceptual framework underpinning thinking and action and in the meaning of terminology in use. Processes (for intelligent application) and standard operating procedures, reporting formats, types of equipment procured and deployed, application of policy for pay, promotion, etc all contribute to making an organization efficient. This efficiency combined with the effectiveness of the people employed is what makes an organization agile, responsive and adaptable. In this way consistency across the company is achieved and new teams or groupings can be formed that require the minimum settling-in period to become operationally effective.

> As a sales rep with a major consumer packaged goods company, the State Sales Manager tried to show how our results compared to other States. This proved very difficult because we all used different forms and often measured different things. How did the National Sales Manager know what was being achieved?
>
> (Tozer)

What separates the junior leader's work (supervisor) from the senior executive's work is the level of complexity of work, the time horizon required in the leader, the level of responsibility felt by the leader, and the greater attention paid to the silent messages sent by a senior executive's behaviour and non-verbal communication. In brief, many of the functions performed by leaders remain the same at all levels, as does the requirement for behavioural flexibility (leadership style); what changes is the level of complexity faced and the 'time horizon' or cognitive capacity required. Recognition of this enables a common doctrine of leadership to be used across an organization. This includes embedding common leadership processes at all levels for decision making, planning and briefing to create 'clarity'. The social process with which this is done (leadership style) is what engages people and shapes part of their environment. The case for such an approach (effects-based leadership (EBL)) has been made in various preceding chapters.

8. Grouping of similar assignments

It makes obvious sense to group similar or closely related tasks together in an organization. However, this must be balanced against the need both to develop agile business units capable of working independently with little need for additional support, and the need to develop leaders' breadth of vision and leadership capacity by giving wide-ranging responsibility over as many functions as possible as early as possible.

Notes

1. Notably Elliott Jaques, 1996, *Requisite Organization: A total system for effective managerial organization and managerial leadership for the 21st century*, Cason Hall; Elliott Jaques, 1964, *Time Span Handbook*, Cason Hall; Elliott Jaques and Kathryn Cason, 1994, *Human Capability: A study of individual potential and its application*, Cason Hall.
2. Time-horizon: the maximum period that a person is able to anticipate ahead, to plan, organize and achieve his or her task.
3. Level of work: the weight of responsibility felt in roles as a result of the complexity of the task and information relating to the task, and measured by the time span of the role.
4. Time span: the targeted completion time of the longest task or task sequence in a role. Time span measures the level of work.
5. I MacDonald, C Burke and K Stewart, 2006, *Systems Leadership: Creating positive organizations*, Aldershot: Gower.

23
Organization ethos and culture: built to adapt and to last

> Core identity
> Business doctrine
> Mythologies
> Cultural norms
> Envisioned future

Organizational ethos and culture is an interesting subject. Because in some ways it is so difficult to define or describe – but you know it when you see it or feel it – one could ramble on for pages with reams of fluffy material, as plenty of books do, and not make much of an impression. This will be a relatively short and succinct chapter for these reasons:

- If you have made it this far into the book, then you are unlikely to need long, warm and fluffy explanations!
- An organization's real ethos and culture (as opposed to that which it might trumpet in recruiting and marketing blurb) is the result of lots of people demonstrating some similar behavioural and attitudinal tendencies. This is the result of effective leadership at every level. If all your organization's leaders are doing the sorts of things that all the preceding chapters have been about, then you do not need to worry too much about how your culture is developing.
- If all your leaders are doing this good leadership stuff, then a short, succinct chapter is all you need to codify how you wish your culture to continue.
- If your organization and its leaders are not demonstrating, across the organization, the type of behavioural flexibility, or using the types of tools we have discussed so far, then there is little point in reading this chapter. Building an effective leadership culture starts with getting the basics of leadership right

at every level (starting top-down if you do not wish your subordinates to show you up) and then developing executive leaders' understanding of organizational development issues from a sure foundation. (I always wonder why so many senior executives attend strategic leadership programmes at expensive business schools; when they lack the basics that we have been discussing they will have no means of implementing their wonderful new nuggets of strategic knowledge!)

A six-year research project by Collins and Porras, described in their seminal work, *Built to Last*[1] showed that companies that were 'built to last' had outperformed the general stock market by a factor of 12 since 1925. Their research compared a selection of companies built to last to similar well-performing competitors. The research showed that if, in 1926, you had made a $1 investment in general stock in a comparison company and the same investment in the stock of a company built to last, and reinvested all dividends, the 1990 values would be $415, $955 and $6,356 respectively. In their view, a company that was built to last and enjoy enduring success had two paradoxical features kept in balance, a yin and yang of business.

Those two features were core ideology (which we prefer to call a 'core identity' – it includes but is bigger than ideology) and an envisioned future. What that means in simple terms, is a core purpose and core values that remain fixed, while business strategies, structure and practices continually adapt to a changing world. The dynamic of preserving the core and stimulating progress is what has made those 'built to last' companies élite in comparison to their competitors. Preserving the core provides security, continuity and stability; stimulating progress ensures renewal and adaptation – which fits with the thoughts on change outlined in Chapter 6.

FIGURE 23.1 Balancing core identity with envisioned future

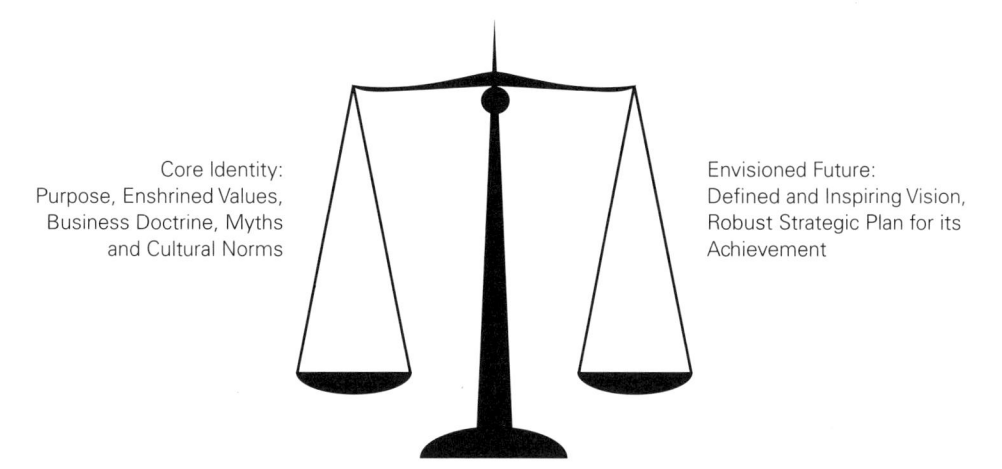

Core Identity:
Purpose, Enshrined Values,
Business Doctrine, Myths
and Cultural Norms

Envisioned Future:
Defined and Inspiring Vision,
Robust Strategic Plan for its
Achievement

After Collins & Porras, 1994 | © Jeremy Tozer, 2010

Truly great organizations understand what must never change and what is open for change; they ensure both continuity and progress – the same paradox of discipline and freedom that has been evident in several chapters in this book. Success for companies built to last comes from the underlying processes and dynamics embedded within the organization, woven into its fabric through its core ideology – not from reliance on a great idea, technological advantage or a charismatic leader. This paradoxical state enables companies to:

- Pursue a clearly defined vision and plan and cope with unexpected change and opportunities.
- Maintain identity-creating traditions and customs, and use them to support progress and change.
- Balance conservatism and prudence with bold, daring ideas.
- Exploit the benefits of common procedures and methods, and ensure operational autonomy.
- Pursue a purpose beyond profit (which is more meaningful for most people), yet make more profit.
- Maintain a tight, define culture, and yet be highly adaptable and agile.
- Be organized around core ideology, and organized to suit the environment.
- Have leaders steeped in the core ideology, who are catalysts for change.

The research showed that companies that are built to last:

- More thoroughly indoctrinate employees into the core ideology.
- Attain consistent alignment with core ideology by making it pervasive; it transcends individual leaders.
- Have an envisioned future that fosters change and innovation and discourages complacency.
- Do not have shareholder returns as the primary driving force, yet they make more money than purely profit-driven companies.
- Everything can change – but not the core ideology that is the guiding light and driving force.
- Make bold decisions and pursue audacious goals.
- Only employees who fit with the core ideology last and succeed.
- Focus on beating themselves not the competition. The pursuit of excellence ensures that they beat the competition.
- Do not rely on 'words', rather they pursue thousands of steps.

If most of the these features of companies built to last are compared to the characteristics of organizations, or those parts of large organizations, that embrace effects-based leadership (EBL), or to the philosophy of EBL itself, you will see there is a very high degree of overlap.

Core identity

It is vital not to confuse core identity with strategy, operational effectiveness, policies or procedures. As time goes on systems, policies and procedures will inevitably need to change as will strategy, people, and products and services.

Core identity defines the enduring character of an organization – a consistent identity that transcends product and market lifecycles, technological change, individual leaders and management fads. It is the glue that holds organizations together as it grows, decentralizes, diversifies, expands and develops diversity. Collins and Porras suggested that it had two parts: core purpose and core values. We have added business doctrine, myths and cultural norms.

Purpose

An organization's purpose is its fundamental reason for existence, it is why it does what it does, which gives meaning to people's work (see Chapters 8, 14 and 21). Meaning is what people seek and find fulfilment from, and it is purpose and meaning rather than vision which inspires most people as it touches 'the spirit' (forgive the brief foray into fluffiness, but it matters!).

As Collins and Porras showed, the most successful companies have an altruistic reason for existence beyond simply making money, and they give many examples. Purpose, therefore, underpins 'vision'. As you will have noted in Chapters 14, 15 and 16 – which covered 'hard skills' about decision making, planning and briefing – every mission statement at every level should include a what (aim or vision) and why (the reason or purpose), which sets context as well as providing meaning.

Purpose should not be confused with the vision or an objective. You may achieve a goal or implement a strategy but you cannot fulfil a purpose – it will always be there to fulfil and thus guides. The primary role of purpose is to inspire employees by giving them meaning – a guiding star. It is not necessarily there to differentiate a company from its competitors – although thinking customers may find that a company's purpose resonates with them.

A few years ago we worked with one leading second-tier bank on some of this organizational-level leadership 'stuff', and during the course of that week, the executives defined their bank's purpose as 'securing your financial future'. This was quite a powerful statement because it was relevant to whoever read it – customers, employees, investors, business partners – it should have been incorporated into the logo! Of course, the trick is to ensure that this is not used as a marketing gimmick (which will only give rise to cynicism and ultimately be counter-productive), rather that it is something that underpins decision making at all levels.

Values

These are the organization's essential, timeless and enduring tenets – a small set of guiding principles or beliefs that are held to be important; not to be confused with operating practices and not to be compromised for short-term gain or expediency. They have intrinsic value and require no rational or external justification; nor do they sway with fads and trends, nor changing market conditions. Values may have an external focus (usually customers, but increasingly 'the community') or an internal focus (employees and product quality). For example, Nordstrom valued customer service eight decades before customer service became fashionable and was seen as vital. Procter & Gamble has valued product excellence for 15 decades. There is no universal set of right values: what matters is that you have them and 'live them'.

It is also interesting to note how similar the value statements are in organizations – both commercial and public sector. That is hardly surprising: they buy goods or services from people to provide goods or services to people – and since human nature has not changed in the last three millennia, it is hardly likely to change in the next few years! In 1997, I suggested a set of values that reflected what most people seek in organizations. MacDonald, Burke and Stewart,[2] employing much greater rigour than I did back then, proposed that all people, societies and organizations share the same core values. It is pleasing that their list of core values has remarkable overlap with my 1997 attempt! They contend that to maintain productive relationships, people must demonstrate behaviour to be found at the positive end of the core values continua:

Honest – Dishonest

Trustworthy – Untrustworthy

Courageous – Cowardly

Respectful and Dignifying – Disrespectful and Undignifying

Fair – Unfair

Loving – Unloving.

These core values enable:

- The display of moral courage, doing the right thing not simply what is expedient.
- Clear, effective and sensitive leadership at all levels.
- Institutional intolerance of incompetence and dishonesty, that is no carrying of 'dead weight' or untrustworthy people.
- Security, if not guaranteed employment, then guaranteed employability from personal growth and development.
- Recognition and reward for contribution and effort.

John Harvey-Jones[3] wrote an interesting piece on 'values', which is abridged here:

> *The value system is one of the prime means of transferring the ownership of problems to your people. The integrity of the system will then be enforced by the people themselves. Values are also an invisible recruiting sergeant... likely to attract people who share your basic values... A value statement is... a personality profile of the company, and hence of the people in it... values are... codes of belief and behaviour and involve making hard choices clearly and unambiguously... you need to check that you are prepared to reject the opposite of what you are selecting for the basis of your future business.*

It is fashionable now, and has been for some years, to articulate your values in written form. It is often the rule that the more places there are in which values are written down (coffee mugs, backs of security passes, etc), the less they are taken seriously – especially by executives. Conversely, some of the places with the most clear and tangible values do not write them down, you just know them. This was certainly my experience in the army; everyone knew what the values were at Sandhurst from day one – they were strong, powerful and tangible, but they were never written down!

British Prime Minister (by default, rather than election) Gordon Brown attempted to define 'British values', and was not very successful. On the radio recently I heard the profound statement, 'If you don't know what the values are of a decent society, it's the fault of bad parenting.' Does this mean that there is no point in defining values? It is a moot point, but what matters is that the example is set from the top and they are seen to be lived and adhered to; it is leadership example that matters, not glossy brochures in the reception area. In recent years it has been very trendy to deride people who have commented on a collapse of moral standards in British society – recognition that 'rights' have obligations attached to them, personal behaviour and use of foul language in public, sense of community and caring neighbours and so on. Yet the evidence shows that this is happening, and much of it started at the top in the Blair government – with the manipulation of the truth or outright lies, influence for favours, unhealthy relationships with the media (especially the Murdoch news empire), the politicization of areas of the higher levels of civil service and the police, and so on. This amorality and complete disregard for any maintenance of integrity spread to MPs, resulting in the public revulsion and anger that came with the exposure of the expenses scandal. Is it any wonder that with such an example to follow, the University of Essex Centre for the Study of Integrity has just published a report finding that Britain has become a more dishonest and cynical country in the past decade?

The essence of a values statement is that there can be no compromise: the values are the arbiter in all decision making. Leaders must live and work by their stated values 24 hours a day or they will give rise to cynicism and mistrust. An interesting set of values are those of the British SAS. Its founder, David Stirling, wrote these values in 1941 and they still apply:

1 The relentless pursuit of excellence.
2 Maintenance of the highest standards of discipline in all aspects of life.
3 No sense of class.
4 Humility.

They are remarkable because this organization was considering values decades before most business enterprises had ever heard of the word. Not only have these values endured, but few people would associate them with a rigid hierarchy and a tradition of 'officers being gentlemen' that was so often the case in 1941!

Chapter 8 explored the nature of individual beliefs and values and showed how these influence individual choices, decision making and behaviour. Like individuals, organizations can have a value system that helps to define the corporate culture and influence decision making in the organization. Corporate values, if they are to be effective, should represent the interests of its customers, employees, investors and the reasonable expectations of society at large (and it is society through elected government that grants organizations their licence to operate). In the ideal corporate situation all members share and agree to one code of behaviour because people whose personal values match those of their employer are more likely to be productive and satisfied, and behaviours are the outward manifestation of values and are usually viewed by observers as the 'truth' about an organization.

Business doctrine

Dogma is 'what to think'.

Doctrine is 'how to think' effectively.

In Chapter 2, we introduced the concept of the three elements of commercial effectiveness: moral, physical and conceptual. The conceptual component of commercial effectiveness is a formal expression of the concepts and knowledge that an enterprise accepts as being relevant at a given time. It is the doctrine, or philosophy if you prefer a softer word, that considers the nature of current and likely future business and provides the basis on which all plans and work are based. The guidance of doctrine is not to be confused with slavish adherence to dogma. It is the fundamental principles, concepts and tools that guide how people are organized and carry out their work. It provides a foundation for common understanding and sets common expectations for leaders and the led throughout an organization.

Doctrine must be an intellectually rigorous, clearly articulated and experience-based 'understanding' that gives competitive advantage to an organization. This common understanding is designed to guide and requires intelligent application by leaders who exercise their discretion and judgement to suit the local conditions; it is therefore 'elastic' and adaptable, and will evolve through trial, exercise, the advance of technology, availability of resources and (if they ever happen) developments in human nature. It is not intended to 'reduce risk' for managers by providing rote recipes for predictable and unthinking action, nor is it there to constrain.

It is good practice to distinguish between what constitutes the fundamental doctrine that leads to strategy development and what is simply 'management by fad' as such techniques can be dangerous. Operating with 'zero inventory' or 'just-in-time' processes might assist cash flow and reduce investment in 'physical stuff', but it makes companies in developing areas highly vulnerable to the vagaries of logistic supply. Mistaking these techniques for strategy also brings with it the risk of competitive convergence, rather than competitive differentiation. Thus, these techniques must be viewed as nothing more than techniques that might assist with the execution of plans where it is appropriate to do so. Hopefully you have accepted these caveats, so these thoughts are offered to influence the development of your enterprise's own 'business doctrine'.[4]

There are three approaches to undermining your competitors' ability to seize the initiative and, therefore, to seize your customers: pre-emption, dislocation and disruption:

1. *Pre-emption.* To pre-empt a competitor is to seize an opportunity before it does in order to deny it competitive or strategic advantage. The purpose of pre-emption is initially negative since it seeks to frustrate the courses of action open to a competitor.

2. *Dislocation.* To dislocate a competitor is to deny it the ability to bring its strengths and competitive advantage to bear on a particular situation by forcing it to react elsewhere. Unlike pre-emption, which is opportunistic, dislocation is a deliberate action and critically depends upon sound market research and intelligence. The purpose of dislocation is more far-reaching than pre-emption in that it is designed to reduce your competitor's effectiveness or corporate power at a strategic level. In this way you are not forced to compete on your competitor's terms.

3. *Disruption.* To disrupt is to selectively throw into confusion plans, projects and business units that give coherence of your competitor's own strategy. Like dislocation this is a deliberate action that requires sound information and it is designed to reduce your competitor's effectiveness to less than the sum of its constituent parts. It is creating the inverse of synergy.

Your competitor may well be employing any, or all, of the above against you and the best defence is cohesion. Cohesion is unity; it is what holds together the constituent parts of an organization and, therefore, produces resilience to dislocation and disruption. It minimizes a company's vulnerability and the adverse effects of missed opportunities.

The bedrock of cohesion is leadership and adherence to the fundamental principles of business that are described below. These principles are not merely a theory to adhere to, nor are they simply a model to follow. These principles are ideas to be understood and used to inform your decisions and actions.

The principles of business

A study of both military and commercial history reveals that these principles are valid and timeless. Indeed Richard Luecke[5] has devoted an entire book to drawing on the lessons of history of change, technology, innovation, planning and uncertainty, and global management, and applying them to the present.

That these principles were first written by leaders of armies and nations, rather than by business executives, is merely an indication that the science and history of war is considerably older and perhaps better understood and hence valued than the history of business. The principles employed by Gideon and the 300 Israelites in the successful repulse of the Midianites, who were 'as innumerable as the sands of the sea shore' make for interesting study. The actions of Alexander, Xenophon, Hannibal, Gustavus Adolphus, Frederick the Great, Prince Eugene, Napoleon, Wellington, Nelson, Montgomery, Patton and Slim show that they all adhere to some common enduring and universal principles – like the laws of physics. Indeed, the most successful and prominent leaders in history have all studied their predecessors and the lessons that they have taught. As the historian John Laffin[6] demonstrates, Patton and Sultan Mahomet (15th century) both studied Alexander; Napoleon studied Cromwell who studied Gustavus Adolphus who studied Hannibal, Alexander and Julius Caesar.

The principles of business that form part of the conceptual component of commercial power are described below. With the exception of the prime principle that is placed first, do not place undue emphasis on the order in which the others appear.

Selection and maintenance of the aim and its purpose

It is essential in the conduct of all activity to select and to define the aim and its purpose (together, the mission), and derived or contributing objectives, clearly, unambiguously and precisely – all thought and action should then be directed to achieving these. Once decided these must be communicated as widely and repeatedly as possible so that all can direct their efforts towards achieving it.

Maintenance of morale

Morale is an essential element of corporate effectiveness. High morale fosters the competitive spirit and the will to win and engenders energy, enthusiasm, and determination. It inspires organizations from the highest to the lowest levels. Although primarily a moral and intellectual aspect that depends on leadership, it may be affected by material conditions and leaders should endeavour to ensure that the best conditions of work possible are provided.

Aggressive (proactive) action

Proactive or aggressive action is the chief means open to leaders to influence the outcome of business competition. It confirms the initiative on the proactive organization, granting the freedom of action necessary to secure decisive business results. When forced on the defensive this must be followed as soon as possible by proactive action. Proactive action embodies a competitive state of mind that breeds the determination to gain and to hold the initiative; it is essential for the creation of confidence and to establish a moral ascendancy over competitors and, thus, has an effect on morale. Good people do not want to wait to do things; they want to get on with it!

Surprise

The potency of surprise as a psychological weapon and a tactic should not be underestimated. It causes confusion and paralysis in competitors' senior levels and can erode the cohesion and morale of competing organizations. It may be achieved through the use of intelligence and information, technology, new doctrine, timing, audacity, simplicity, speed and quality of execution, originality, secrecy or concealment and (legal) deception about intentions.

Concentration of force

Success normally results from the concentration of force – superior resources concentrated on a narrow front and reinforcing success – at a decisive time and place.

This does not preclude 'dispersion' of some resources that may be valuable for the purposes of deception and for avoiding discovery.

Economy of effort

The corollary of concentration of force is economy of effort. It is impossible to be strong everywhere and if decisive strength is to be concentrated at the critical time and place there must be no wasteful expenditure of effort where it cannot significantly affect the issue. To gain substantial advantage leaders have to take calculated risks in less vital areas.

Flexibility

Since no plan will ever be executed as originally conceived, and although the aim and purpose might (should?) not alter, leaders need to exercise judgement and flexibility in modifying their plans to meet changed circumstances, taking advantage of opportunities or shifting points of emphasis. Flexibility depends upon openness of mind on the one hand, and simple plans that can easily be modified on the other, underpinned by an inherently agile organization (which requires the approach to EBL, planning and briefing, and structure already described). A balanced reserve of resources is usually a prerequisite for flexibility at any level.

Cooperation

Cooperation is based on team spirit, goodwill and communication, clear tasks and role relationships, and it entails the coordination of the activities of all departments and branches for the optimum combined effort. An understanding of the capabilities and limitations of others is essential for cooperation, and unity of leadership is a means of achieving cooperation.

Sustainability

Sustainability is a prerequisite for the ongoing success of any business and foresight is its key – it refers to the holdings, allocation and transfer of resources, logistic support, financial management, personnel administration (pay, welfare, etc), facilities and so on. A clear appreciation of logistic, human and other constraints is as important to leaders as their ability to make sound appreciations of situations. No business plan can succeed and be sustained without administrative support commensurate with the aim and purpose of the plan: it follows that leaders must have a degree of control over the administrative plans proportionate to the degree of their responsibility. Scarce resources must be controlled at a high level: the administrative organizations must be flexible enough to react to changes in situations with the most economic use of the available resources.

Integrity and ethics

A business perceived to lack integrity or to operate in an unethical, immoral, or irresponsible manner soon loses the support of customers, suppliers and the community at large.

Mythologies

Macdonald et al[7] have shown that mythologies influence organizational culture and behaviour. As they say, myths are the rules of thumb that have been learnt through experience – an underlying assumption and current belief as to what is positive and valued behaviour, and what behaviour is negatively valued. Mythology is a combination of a story with emotional content and some rational thought. Here is an example. The boss does not hold regular briefings for the team or the individuals within it. His boss brings forward the date by when something that you are working on is needed, but your boss doesn't tell you until hours before. You feel kept in the dark and increased pressure as a result of the changing deadline. This happens a few more times and the pattern has become a law: boss David does not tell anyone anything and induces stress and crisis management. The mythology that this starts to create is that the boss is untrustworthy and unfair. Now that the mythology exists, people tend to look for examples that reinforce it, the mythology is extended to other leaders, and it becomes part of the culture.

To change the mythology, first the mythologies and associated leadership behaviour need to be identified. Second, leaders need to overtly and explicitly accept the mythology and its behaviour (which may be painful, but has to be done without arguing or disputing the mythology) and then explicitly and overtly behave differently. Consistently behave as you did in the second step, and eventually a new positive mythology will be created.

Cultural norms

Cultural norms in this context have two parts. First there is the commonly observed behaviour and attitude of people within an organization. Second is the use of visible symbols, traditions, customs, ceremonies and events that express or embody the desired behaviour and attitude of people, the organization's values and its purpose.

Developing desirable norms of behaviour was dealt with in Chapter 20. As an example of the use of visible symbols and tradition to assist with developing cohesive units, and to develop competitive spirit and high levels of performance, let us look to the 'green machine'. It is no accident that unlike many other armies in which one infantry battalion looks and feels the same as most others, the British Army is very different – especially the infantry. In just about every army of the world, the infantry has the most mentally and physically demanding and frightening role, usually conducted in the most unpleasant environmental conditions. The British infantry is a collection of smaller regimental 'tribal groupings' that work very effectively alongside other infantry units and with supporting arms and services, and as part of larger formations, primarily because they use a common language and methods, and common and consistent approaches to structure and defining role relationships (business doctrine).

Each regiment has, as its visible symbols, its own unique identifiers such as its cap badge, and other ways of adding differences to standard uniform. Regiments have their own customs such as the way in which the loyal toast is drunk, the celebration of specific battles and moments in history, regimental parades, family and sporting events. Regiments have their own 'Colours', the flags under which soldiers used to rally, emblazoned with the regiment's own and unique collection of battle honours. The Colours are viewed as the living embodiment of the regiment's spirit and are accorded the highest compliments. In 'the infantry of the line' a Company Sergeant Major (CSM) is addressed by Officers as 'Sergeant Major', and the Regimental Sergeant Major in a battalion is addressed as such or as Mr so-and-so. In the five Regiments of Foot Guards, the Regimental Sergeant Major is addressed by Officers as Sergeant Major, and all the CSMs are addressed as Company Sergeant Major. There is a myriad of differences between infantry regiments which helps to create 'identity' because its value is understood, and this is inculcated in all new recruits and preserved at all costs (except under government cuts imposed by politicians and civil servants who frequently know the cost of everything and the value of nothing).

Envisioned future

The envisioned future has two components: the vision or desired end-state, and strategic plan by which the organization will achieve it.

Vision

Many visions in organizations are so far 'out there', so far removed from reality, and so based on 'blue sky thinking' from a workshop with some fluffy consultant guru, that they do nothing but induce cynicism and depression in employees because they are seen to be unattainable. In 1960 President Kennedy stated, 'I believe that this nation should commit itself to achieving the goal, before this decade is out, of landing a man on the moon and returning him safely to earth.' That speech electrified the Apollo team and the United States into action by informing a clear, compelling and achievable mission for them. (You will recall that in mission analysis at the strategic level described in Chapter 14, the mission is informed by the vision.)

Vision should be a definable end-state, an enduring and favourable future situation. And when you get close to achieving it, you may need to reset it – if it is clear that you will never reach it, it will be one of those unachievable, confidence-sapping visions that induces cynicism and lethargy and erodes confidence. The vision needs to be a clear, focused and ambitious concept that everyone may picture and understand, and which avoids vague platitudes and ambiguity. It should incorporate some sense of a genuine 'noble purpose' because this is a contributing factor to morale (see

Chapter 21). People have to believe that it is achievable, and they need to understand how their day-to-day work contributes to achieving it. If the vision lacks meaning for people, the nature of work itself seems to lose its value and lethargy starts to creep in.

The vision is made meaningful for people and informs decisions, plans and work priorities and so on through the whole approach to EBL that has already been described at length.

Plan to achieve the vision

For this, reread Chapter 14; especially the section on appreciations at the strategic level.

Notes

1 James Collins and Jerry Porras, 1994, *Built to Last*, Sydney: Century Hutchinson Australia.
2 Ian MacDonald, Catherine Burke and Karl Stewart, 2006, *Systems Leadership: Creating positive organizations*, Aldershot: Gower.
3 John Harvey-Jones, 1994, *All Together Now*, Oxford: Heinemann.
4 Jeremy Tozer, 1997, *Leading Initiatives: Leadership, teamwork and the bottom line*, Sydney: Butterworth Heinemann Australia.
5 Richard Luecke, 1994, *Scuttle Your Ships Before Advancing and Other Lessons from History on Leadership and Change*, New York: Oxford University Press.
6 John Laffin, 1966, *Links of Leadership: Thirty centuries of command*, London: Harrap.
7 Ian MacDonald, Catherine Burke and Karl Stewart, 2006, *Systems Leadership: Creating positive organizations*, Aldershot: Gower.

Conclusion

In writing this book, this has been the chapter I have most looked forward to, but it has also been the one that I thought would pose the most challenges. At 486 pages long, how can I possibly summarize the book succinctly? I am not sure that I should try!

I have endeavoured to produce a book that can be used in two ways: as a total system for designing organizations, their systems, leadership processes and structure, or as a collection of discrete components that may be used independently of the others, each of which will add value in their own right, but will add more value as other components are added.

In Part One of the book the scene was set with an examination of:

- the operating context and the capability requirement of effective organizations;
- core propositions about people and the nature of work;
- the conditions people need if they are to be successful;
- the role of the leader, and the nature of leadership;
- communication as the lubricant of the leadership engine; and
- the leadership of change.

The intent of this part of the book was, in very basic terms, to suggest what it is that leaders should actually be doing and how they should be doing it.

The intent of Part Two was to provide you with the necessary conceptual tools, in detail, the application of which will enable you to create those ACE conditions for success:

- to develop people's Ability;
- to create Clarity; and
- to shape the Environment.

As I hope that I made clear in Chapter 3, of the three conditions for success, clarity must come first. If you are really clear about what you are trying to achieve, why and how, then you will know from that what 'ability' needs to be developed or acquired, and what is required in the environment.

If there is a single thread running through most if not all of this book, it is the paradox of freedom and discipline, of autonomy as a result of clarity. And if there is a single chapter that is more important than any other, it is Chapter 14 – The Appreciation, aligned decision making – the power of which still never ceases to amaze me. All work is a series of concurrent, consecutive and layered problems to solve and decisions to make, whatever your industry, whatever your level. The 'problem' may be a project, the review or design of a system or process, or the creation of a business plan, the resolution of a conflict or the launch of a new product. If nothing else, it absorbs these questions into your bloodstream:

- What are you really trying to achieve and why?
- What are the key factors which affect you achieving that?
- What are the options open to you?
- Which is the best option?

So with that last thought I shall conclude this book.

You might be interested in our series of A5-sized full-colour thin plastic desktop aide memoire cards which cover the key concepts and tools in this book. You may view and order them from the leadership toolkit page at **www.tozerconsulting.com**. Bespoke versions may be produced for your organization.

You might also be interested in 'ACE Insights,' our organizational effectiveness diagnostic which may be seen on its own page at **www.tozerconsulting.com**. If you would like to discuss how to use and embed any of the concepts and methods described in this book in your organization, then please contact the author at **jeremy.tozer@tozerconsulting.com**

GLOSSARY

A word on language. While language can assist in defining culture and words mean different things to different people, the language used here is precise to assist in the creation of clarity and is not intended to imply anything other than that which it is defined as. Thus, when the term 'superior' is used it means a manager or leader at a higher level in an organization; it is not intended to imply that such a person is 'better' in any way. Likewise 'subordinate' is meant in the sense of a person who is accountable to a superior leader; it is not meant to demean that person as an inferior being, it merely indicates that he or she is subordinate to someone else in the company's authority structure.

Ability   The combination of skill, knowledge, behaviour, attitude and intellect or cognitive power.
Accountability   Those features of any role that the incumbent is required to do by virtue of the role.
Agency   In intelligence usage, an individual or organization engaged in collecting or processing information.
Aim   The aim is a positive, clear, concise and unequivocal statement of overall intent.
Appointment   A position or role held by an individual and distinguished by a specific title.
Appreciation   The logical process of reasoning by which a person or group clarifies and defines the aim and purpose in relation to a problem or task, considers all the relevant factors affecting the achievement of that aim and purpose to deduce the courses of action open, and arrives at a decision upon the course of action to be taken.
Attitude   Thoughts and feelings that shape behavioural intention.
Authority   The features of a role that enable the incumbent to legitimately carry out the work necessary to meet the accountabilities of the role.

Balanced measures   Leading indicators and lagging (historical) assessments of vital activities specified within a plan, balanced to ensure that the achievement of one desired effect or outcome is not at the expense of another.
Beliefs   Assessments (facts) or limiting assertions (opinions) that are held to be true.
Benchmark   A process of comparison between one product, system, process, or result and another within the same company, or among companies in the same or different industries.
Briefing   The formal communication of information or a plan to those affected by it, normally carried out face-to-face, collectively, and following a standard sequence or format to ease the assimilation of information by those receiving the briefing. Briefings may take several forms: *Information briefs* in which updates are presented quickly, clearly and concisely; *Decision briefs* are a summary of the staff work completed in making an appreciation; *Back briefs* are opportunities for subordinates to brief their superiors on their mission analysis and agree their intentions and plans; *Plan briefs* in which a discrete project or strategic plan, etc is communicated by a leader to his or her subordinates.

Campaign   A sequence of planned, resourced and executed operations designed to achieve a strategic objective within a defined time scale and geographical area, usually involving the synchronization of different business units or divisions.

Centre of gravity That characteristic, or capability, from which a competitor derives its freedom of action, or corporate power and competitive advantage. A centre of gravity may not always be tangible and may be an abstraction such as morale, confidence or brand and may change.

Cognitive power The potential strength of a person's cognitive processes and, therefore, the maximum level of task complexity that can be managed by that person.

Cognitive processes The mental processes by which a person is able to organize information to do work.

Command The lawful authority vested in personnel in the UK's armed services by which direction, coordination and control may be exercised by a commander over those subordinates in the unit or sub-unit, together with responsibility for the actions of those subordinates. Command combines the leadership of people and the management of resources to achieve a mission with responsibility for both the mission's outcomes and the conduct of troops under command.

Contingency planning Contingency planning is the process by which other courses of action are considered and options built in to a campaign plan to anticipate opportunities, reverses or changes to the situation or context.

Control The continuing oversight, direction and coordination of assigned people in accordance with the leader's intent.

Coordination The coordinating function of leadership is about leaders' lateral relations within organizations. The aim of coordination is either to seek the cooperation of personnel not in leaders' own teams or under their authority, or to link actions by two or more of their own sub-teams.

Course of action An option in outline or overall plan which may be adopted to achieve a defined mission or aim and purpose.

Decisive points Specific events that must be successfully completed or achieved, the combination of which are necessary for overall success.

Directing Establishing through effective two-way communication with subordinates what is required and providing any guidelines, boundaries, constraints or measures that are necessary that relate to how it is to be done – although as far as possible this should be left to individuals' initiative. The communication may be through an informal conversation, or at a formal briefing or meeting.

Discipline A person or group's state of mind that leads to a readiness for willing, intelligent and appropriate conduct and the subordination of self for the benefit of the wider organization and its objectives.

Doctrine The framework of common understanding that provides the foundation for the coherent, integrated, practical and intelligent application of fundamental principles and procedures by which an organization guides its actions in pursuit of organizational objectives.

Effective The considered and balanced combination of the most efficient means to achieve a task with regard to wider effects and consequences. This may include retaining the capacity to undertake the unexpected.

Effects-based leadership (EBL) The descriptive term for the approach to leadership which adapts the relevant parts of the British Military Doctrine of Mission Command for civilian use.

Efficiency Timely, integrated, streamlined and productive systems, methods and procedures. At its extreme, efficiency allows no spare capacity for response to the unexpected. Efficiency focuses on task, not people.

Emotional intelligence The social radar and behavioural flexibility that allows a person to sense and understand the moods, reactions and feelings of others, the person's own behavioural preferences and impact, and to adjust behaviour to have the desired impact on others.

Evaluation A continuous process by which the leader judges progress in a task against its plan.

Flexibility The ability to adapt to changing situations and amend plans without the negative influences of preconceived and rigid ideas.

Initiative The combination of seeing the need to take action and then taking appropriate action without reference to a superior authority.

Integrated leadership The capability that results from integrating leadership between and within levels, business units and locations through common methods for communicating, enabling timely decisions by those best placed to make them, and aligning activity in a manner that engages people and encourages the display of initiative, and by aligning accountability with authority both laterally and vertically to define role relationships.

Integrity The combined virtues of honesty, sincerity, reliability, unselfishness and loyalty, and a person's adherence to a moral code of values.

Intellect The ability to reason and to recognize and understand the significance of information concepts, trends, the capacity to reduce problems to their fundamental elements on which plans are based.

Intelligence Information that has been processed to infer or deduce meaning and predict future events.

Intelligence cycle The cyclic production of intelligence from information: direction (definition of requirements), collection (tasking sources and agencies), processing (collation, evaluation for reliability, analysis, integration and interpretation) and dissemination (reports and briefings).

Judgement The maturity and wisdom to balance conflicting advice in arriving at decisions and to adopt simple, pragmatic and effective solutions.

Knowledge a) Knowledge in the context of leadership comes in four forms: industry-specific knowledge, knowledge of subordinates (strengths, weaknesses and abilities, etc), knowledge and understanding of self, and knowledge of the organization and its capabilities and business doctrine. b) A combination of facts, concepts and information learned from an accepted body of knowledge. c) Self-generated knowledge that has been learnt heuristically (through experience).

Leader A person responsible for achieving objectives through the work of others by creating the conditions in which they may be successful, and for building and maintaining the team of which he or she is a member.

Leader-once-Removed (LoR) The relationship between the leader of a three-layer or three-strata grouping in an authority hierarchy, and the subordinates of a subordinate team leader.

Leadership The capacity and will to rally people to a common purpose willingly and the character that inspires confidence and trust.

Level of work The weight of responsibility felt in roles as a result of the complexity of the task and information relating to the task, and measured by the time span of the role.

Loyalty Being faithful and being true to allegiance to a person or institution; this allegiance is to superiors, subordinates and peers.

Management The allocation, coordination and control of resources and the administration of people (pay and claims, welfare, posting, leave and so on).

Manoeuvre To move into a position of advantage within the market and with competitors from which corporate power may be applied.

Mission A clear, concise and unequivocal statement of overall intent and the purpose it is designed to achieve pertaining to a particular grouping of people, best expressed as 'to do (something) in order to (achieve something)'.

Mission analysis A logical process for extracting and deducing from a superior's briefing the tasks necessary to fulfil a mission or, in the absence of a specific briefing, the dynamic and continual process of consideration or review of a task or mission. It ensures that the chosen courses of action remain consistent with the 'higher intent' and takes into account changes that occur to the circumstances within which the mission is being pursued.

Mission command The British military doctrine of command that enables organizational agility and alignment of activity with leaders committed to their work. It conveys understanding to subordinate leaders about the intentions of the higher commander and their place within this plan, enabling them to direct their units and sub-units to achieve tasks and accomplish missions (specified or implied) with the maximum freedom of action and appropriate resources and without having to wait for detailed direction from above.

Moral courage Moral courage is the daily choice of right instead of wrong; it is what makes a person do something because it is the right, correct and necessary thing to do no matter that it may be difficult, unpopular or distasteful to implement.

Morale The mental attitude and bearing of a person, team or unit.

Motivation A desire to act for which there is a selfish or unselfish focus for behaviour.

Mutual Recognition Unit (MRU) The three-strata grouping within an authority hierarchy consisting of LoR, SoRs and intermediate leaders and within which the LoR knows all the SoRs.

Objective A precise statement of a measurable, concrete goal that needs to be attained if the aim or mission that gave rise to the objective is to be achieved. It is usual for a number of objectives to be essential to achieving an aim or mission. Objectives apply at the strategic, operational and tactical levels.

Operational level Campaigns and major initiatives are planned and directed at the operational level to achieve the aim of a strategic directive. It is the level that provides the gearing between strategic objectives and all tactical activity within a geographical area of operations.

Operational pause Operations cannot be conducted continuously without inducing excessive human stress. Therefore, there may need to be periodic pauses during which the initiative has to be maintained through other means.

Organization The deployment of resources, delegation of authority and tasks, and establishment of role relationships.

Organizational leadership capacity The collective leadership capability that results from developing leadership in depth and breadth within an organization primarily through embedding common methods for communicating, enabling timely decisions by those best placed to make them, and aligning activity in a manner that engages people and encourages the display of initiative.

Preferred behaviour The behaviour that a person typically displays, especially under conditions of stress.

Responsibility Those features of any role that the incumbent is held accountable for by the organization and his or her superior, whether or not the work has been delegated to a subordinate for action. Unlike tasks, accountability and authority, responsibility cannot be delegated.

Self-confidence This is belief and faith in oneself and in one's ability to achieve delegated tasks, and to overcome challenges and obstacles encountered particularly when faced with the unknown of change. Self-esteem, self-respect, self-discipline and moral courage are contributory factors.

Self-discipline The subordination of self for the benefit of others and ability to do what is known to be the right and proper thing to do. Self-discipline is a person's state of mind that leads to a readiness for willing, intelligent and appropriate conduct and underpins consistency.

Sequencing The arrangement of activities within a campaign in the order most likely to achieve the desired conclusion.

Skill The ability to apply learnt techniques, processes and methods in a role.

Social process The ability to read social situations, build and manage relationships, and resolve conflict to influence and engage people in their work.

Source In intelligence usage, a person from whom or thing from which information may be obtained.

Stakeholders Those individuals, teams or organizations with an interest in, or who may be affected by, the activities carried out by a person or team.

Strategic concept of operations The course of action accepted as a result of an appreciation of the strategic situation. It is a statement of what is to be done in broad terms, sufficiently flexible to permit its use in framing all the activity that stems from it.

Strategic level The level at which an organization, or group thereof, determines its aim, purpose and objectives and deploys the full range of resources available to achieve them.

Strategy The overall plan to achieve a long-term aim and fulfil its purpose.

Stratum A level within the hierarchical structure of an organization containing roles of the same level of work.

Subordinate A person at a lower level in an organizational hierarchy with less authority and fewer responsibilities than the superior to whom that subordinate reports.

Subordinate-once-Removed (SoR) The relationship between the subordinates of a team leader in a three-layer or three-strata grouping, and the team leader's own superior.

Superior A person at a higher level in an organizational hierarchy and with greater authority and responsibilities than the subordinates reporting to that superior appointment.

Superior-once-Removed The relationship between the superior of a team leader in a three-layer or three-strata grouping, and the team leader's own subordinates.

Tactical level Activities within an operation or campaign are planned and executed at a tactical level to achieve the operational objectives of that campaign. This level is characterized by the application of integrated and coordinated units and people at the point of main effort to secure an objective. It is at the tactical level that most people are directly employed in business.

Tactics The skill and art of deploying people and resources to achieve a mission with the maximum economy of effort and maximum effectiveness, which furthers progress towards achieving operational and strategic objectives.

Task A precise action to be carried out by a person or sub-group whose efforts contribute to achieving the mission of the parent grouping. An objective becomes a task when a leader delegates it to a specific person or sub-team as part of his or her plan.

Task organization The composition of a team or larger grouping of people, dedicated to a specific task or project.

Tasking procedure The standard operating procedure that has the aim of launching employees into action as swiftly and as efficiently as possible, understanding what they have to do and why, and with what support, and with a sense of ownership of their part in the wider plan.

Team A grouping of people in either a permanent or temporary arrangement who report to the same leader.
Tempo The rate or rhythm of activity.
Time-horizon The maximum period that a person is able to anticipate ahead, to plan, organize and achieve his or her aim.
Time span The time span is the target completion time of the longest assignments (tasks or projects) that may be encountered in a role.

Values Beliefs and ethics to which weight and importance are attached, that guide behaviour and dictate moral standards for thinking and judging.
Vision A statement of what an organization aspires to be, its desired 'end-state'.

Willpower The enduring will to win and to see a task through to its completion through good times and bad. It requires determination, stamina, tenacity and self-discipline. It is a part of courage, decision and initiative.

INDEX

NB: page numbers in *italic* indicate figures or tables

ability, developing through   129–32, *130*
   education and training   130
   experience   131
   exposure   131–32
ability   37, 39, *39*, 46
   elements of   129
ACE conditions for success   37–52, *39, 41*, 134, 166, 285, 408, 416, 422, 443, 460, 479
   see also ability; clarity *and* environment
   essentials of concept of   42
   Insights   45, 118
   in NHS Primary Care Trust (PCT)   45
   and organizational conditions: integrated leadership   48–52, *49*
   as leader's job description   38, *38*–42, *39, 41*
   as leadership and organization effectiveness diagnostic tool   45–47
      case study for   46–47
   as organizational and leadership effectiveness assessment and diagnostic tool   42–45, *43, 44*
action-centred leadership (Industrial Society)   62
Adair, J   62, 64 *see also* circles of need model
Albrecht, K   332 *see also* customer value
Allport, G W   141
   Trait Theory   141
anger   160, 192, 248–50
   and resistance   123–24
Apple   6
appreciation(s)   *see* decision-making
appreciation examples   340–63
   holiday abroad   353–55, 358–59, *354, 355–57, 359*
   strategic business and organization development plan   340–41, 343, 345, *342–43, 344, 345*
   strategic business model change   345–48, 350–51, 353, *348–50, 351–53*
   turning around a failing rural pub   360–63, *361–62, 363*
assertiveness (and)   102, 17, 195, 197, 214–18, 215, 223–26, *225 see also* communication
   beliefs   217, *217*
   controlling emotions   218
   tone of voice   218
Axelrod, R   143

balanced scorecard   323–24, 378
behaviour   7, 129, 153–74, *154, 155, 163, 169, 170, 171*, 197 *see also* assertiveness
   aggressive   215
   development   247–51, *248*
   passive   215–16
Belbin, M   414, 424
benchmarking   315
beliefs
   as influencers of attitude   158
   and values   188–89
Bennis, W   32
Berne, E   176, 178–79 *see also* transactional analysis (TA)
blocks – cognitive, emotional, organizational and perceptual   123–24
body language   38, 103, 196, 204, 206, 207, 212, 216–21, 225, 237, 239, 240
   conflicting messages of   220, *220, 221*
   of different cultures   219
brain, gender differences of   150–51
brainstorming   277, 312, 320, 336–37
BRIC economies   6
briefing   379–84, *380 see also* communication; planning and briefing *and* planning and briefing cascade
   administration and logistics   382
   control and communication   382
   dos and don'ts of   383
   execution   382
   introductions   381
   mission   381–82
   questions   383
   situation   381
Briggs, K C   141
Built to Last   125, 467
Brown, G   471
Burke, C   113, 114
business doctrine   472–76
   administration   475
   aggressive (proactive) action   474
   concentration of force   474–75
   cooperation   475
   economy of effort   475
   flexibility   475
   integrity and ethics   476

Index

maintenance of morale 474
principles of business 473–74
selection and maintenance of aim and purpose 474
surprise 474

Cameron, D 150
capability requirement as future agenda 12–16, *13*
case studies for
  ACE conditions for success 46–47
  decision-making 304
  leadership work of creating clarity and engagement 289
Cattell, R 141
  16PF (primary factors) Questionnaire 141
change, emotional responses to 122–24, *122*
  anger and resistance 123–24, 248–49
  blocks
    cognitive 123–24, 250
    emotional 123–24
    organizational 123–24, 249–50
    perceptual 123–24
  commitment 124, 250
  and change paradox 250–51
  exploration and acceptance 124, 250
  shock and denial 122–23, 248
change, roadmap for 116, *117*, 118–22
  build confidence 120–21
  build powerful guiding coalition 118–19
  consolidate improvements 121
  embed and institutionalize change 121–22
  empower others to act 120
  frame the context 118
  frame the problem
    define end-state 119
    define plan 119–20
  maintain momentum 121
change 113–25 *see also* change, emotional responses to *and* change, roadmap for
  exponential rate of 7
  and human unpredictability, stress and emotion 7
  journey of 119
  paradox 125
  planning as holistic 119–20
  reasons for failure in 115–16
  resisting 418
chapter notes/references 20, 36, 52, 98–99, 125, 198–99, 228, 301, 363, 432, 446, 465, 478
charisma 31, 92, 94, 468
China 6
  as largest English-speaking nation 6
  skilled labour in 6
Churchill, W 76, 88

circles of need model (Adair) 62–64, *63*
clarity 18–20, 27, 34, 37–42, *39*, 46–47, 115, 134, 162, 205–06, 340–41
  and aligned communication channels 106–07, *107*
  of communication 12, 39, 416, 419
  creating 13, 14, 16, 32, 41, 57, 78, 81–82, 108, 111, 120, 274, 285, 291–92, 309, 363, 379, 390–91, 393, 429, 479
  and engagement 285–88, *286*, 390
  lack of 15, 45, 67, 124, 249, 274, 426, 448, 458
  of purpose 104, 442
  of thought 323, 411
Clausewitz, K von 8, 330
Clement, S 54, 56
coaching (and) 131, 229–59
  behavioural observation 236–37, *237*
  building skill 253–56, *255 see also* skill, building
  changing attitudes 251–53, *252*
  conversation agenda *see* coaching conversation agenda
  coach's position 233–35, *234*, *235*
    on the field 233–34
    in the stand 234
    on the touchline 234–35
  coach's toolkit 235–36
  confirmation of assimilation of training 257–58
  developing behaviour 247–51, *248 see also* behaviour development
  fault checking 259
  feedback 237–40 *see also* main entry
  vs instruction 232–33, *233*
  path to mastery 236–40, *236*, *238*, *239*
  patterns of behaviour/ripple effect 231
  for performance, for growth and to enable 232
  promotion and maintenance of desire to learn 256–57
  question technique for 258–59
  review and preview of 231–32
  self- 153
coaching conversation agenda 241, 241–47
  actions open: options and opportunities 245–46
  decision and commitment – setting objectives 246, *247*
  leadership coaching style 247
  learning styles 242, *243*
  mission analysis: aim and purpose of coaching session 243–44
  plan, document and review meeting 247
  preparation 242
  rapport and licence to coach 242–43

situation analysis: ACE, feedback and
 self-awareness 244–45
cognition 139, 176, 187, 296–97
 and cognitive dissonance 298–99, 307
 and four levels of cognitive process 452
collaboration and competition *see* Prisoner's
 Dilemma
Collins, J 125, 467, 469
communication 106–12 *see also* communication
 process
 aligned channels of 106–07, *107*
  see also clarity
 assertive 215, *215*–16, 223–27
  see also assertiveness
  and overcoming objections 226, *227*
  responses 223–24
  self-talk, rehearsals, visualizations 224–26,
   225
 eye access cues for 221–23
  and working memory 222–23
 formal and direct/conscious 107–08
 formal and indirect/subconscious 109
 informal and direct/conscious 108–09
 informal and indirect/subconscious 109–10
 interpersonal *see* interpersonal
  communication
 leader–team 201–02
 non-verbal 218–20, *220*, *221 see also* body
  language
 in an organizational structure 110–12, *110*,
  111, 392–94, *393*, *394*
 routine briefing and updates 384, *385*
 style of 214–16, *215*
communication process 202–06, *202*, *204*
 fundamental principles of 204–06, *204*
  accuracy 204–05
  brevity 205
  clarity 205
  distribution 205–06
  sensitivity 206
  simplicity 206
 human backdrop to 203, *203*
 and preparation 206
confidence 94, 115, 230, 267, 416, 427,
  441–42
 building 18–19, 32, 45, 76, 91, 120–21,
  379–81, 444
 excessive 281
 lack of 245, 249, 339, 430
conflict 67, 90, 192, 215, 268–84, 429, 458
 avoidance 299
 causes of 269–71, *269*
 and compromise 138
 constructive 324
 positions in 271, *271*
 responses to 272–74, *272*, *273*

between teams 420–21
 types of 268–69
conflict resolution 51, 57, 103, 187, 197,
  274–81, 413, 426, 456, 480
 ACCoRED agenda for 277–78
 and common mistakes in resolution/negotiation
  278–81
 planning negotiations for 275–76, *276*
conflicting objectives 418
contingency planning 298, 335–36, *335*
control 14, 29, 32, 75, 87, 116, 119, 158,
  173–74, 178, 182, 270, 350, 403, 413, 421
 autocratic 78
 amd communication 379, 382
 conditions for effective 406–07
 span 456–57
 timing of 407–08
coordination 78, 270, 383, 403, 405–07, 475
core identity (and) 154–55, 174–80, 469–72,
  467 *see also* transactional analysis
 core values 467, 469–70
 environmental influences/learnt experiences
  175–76
 genetic inheritance 174–75
 purpose 469
courage *see* moral courage
cultural norms 156, 232, 469, 476–77
customer value 331–33, 444
 Albrecht's hierarchy of 332

Damasio, A R 150, 198
Darwin, C 137
 and theory of evolution 143
De Gaulle, General 26
de la Billière, General Sir P 75
decision-making (and) 7, 302–74 *see also*
  appreciation examples; intelligence *and*
  intelligence cycle
 aligned process for 304–05, *305*, *306*
 the appreciation 303–4, 309–19, 338–40
  courses of action (CoA) and comparison
   317–18, *317*, 338
  factor/situation analysis 312–17, *315*, *316*,
   338
  leader's decision 318–19, *319*, 338
  mission analysis 309–12, 338
 the appreciation and personality types
  337–38, *338*
 appreciations at strategic level 325–35
  see also value
  centre of gravity 330–31, *330*
  customer/consumer 331–33
  factors 328–31
  mission analysis 327–28
  products and services 333–34
  risk 334, *334*

Index

situation analysis 326–27
strategy managers 325–26, *326*
structure 335
approach to 302–03
biases 298
case study for 304
contingency planning 335–36, *335*
feedback and input 305
flexibility 305–07
group dynamics 299
intuitive 287
paradox 307
problem-solving tools, techniques and brainstorming 336–37
task and time schematic plan 320, 322–24, *320, 321, 322*
   avoiding cognitive pitfalls 324
   balanced measures 323–24
   decision making and planning 322–23
   subsequent review of the appreciation 324
decision-making, annexes to
   appreciation template 367–69, *368, 369*
   project/task outline plan template 370–71, *370*
   Standard Operating Procedure (SOP): meetings and minutes 364–66, *364, 366*
   strategic plan and second order task tracking document template 372, *373, 374*, 374
defence mechanism(s) 118, 138, 160, 214
   denial as 123, 248
   of ego 118, 137, 327
definitions (of)
   attitude 158
   courage 88
   influence (OED) 260
   integrity 89
   leader 31, 55
   leadership 31, 53–56
   style 78
delegation/delegation of tasks 72–76, *73*, 120
   direction of 74–75
   problems with 75
   reasons for 73–74
   and what should not be delegated 74
Descartes, R 136
dextrals/dextrality 149–50 *see also* brain
directing 82, 403, 404–05
   prequisites for success of 405
   questions for leader on 405
discipline 16, 415, 439–42, 471
   of clear thinking 287, 307
   collective 441–42
   of effects-based leadership (EBL) 19–20
   and freedom paradox 27–28, *28*, 68, 116, 450, 468, 479
   imposed 440–41
   self- 88, 99, 124, 174, 193, 209, 250, 438, 441

doctrine 23–24 *see also* business doctrine *and* effects-based leadership
   of leadership 29–30, 464

effects-based leadership (EBL) 15–20, *17, 19*, 87, 287, *288*, 294, 309, 391, 414, 450, 457, 468, 475
   doctrine of Mission Command 15
ego 92, 118, 123, 137–38, 184
   denial as defence mechanism for 248
   needs 165
   states 176–80, *177, 178, 179*
   and super-ego 138
e-mail 4–5, 7, 54, 107–08, 205, 294, 384, 404, 416
E-motion (energy in motion) 159
Emotional Intelligence 187
emotional intelligence (and) 15, 17, 18, 29–30, 39, 56, 96, 120, 151, 153, 186–90, 192–98
   behaviour 153–74, *154, 155, 163, 169, 170, 171*, 197
   defined 186–87
   elements of 187–93, *188, 190, 191, 192*
      see also Johari Window *and* self-awareness
   self-confidence 194–96
   self-leadership 193–94
   situational awareness 196–97
   will 193
emotional quotient (EQ) 337
emotions 7, 123, 156, 160–61, 313–14
   expression of 193
empathy 77, 103, 120, 134, 163, 179, 196–97, 207, 210, 226, 227, 300
employee engagement 292
   and mobility and cynicism 7–8
English, Lt Col John 16
environment 37, 39, 40–41, 47
   and danger in the comfort zone 41, *41*
envisioned future 477–78
   plan to achieve vision 478
   vision 477–78
essential intangibles *see* loyalty; morale *and* trust
evaluating 64, 404
   ideas 336, 337
   and monitoring 102–03
   progress 51, 408
expectations and desires 35–36
Eysenck, H 141
   four types 141
   Personality Inventory (EPI) 141

facilitation and training methods 130
fear (of) 41, 143, 159, 160–61, 229, 406, 440
   change 118, 119, 123

disapproval 299, 421
failure 123, 249
 and narrative therapy 160–61
feedback 22, 35, 40, 51, 62, 70, 77, 84–86, 91, 102, 105, 124, 130–31, 164, 172, 187–90, 191, 192, 192–98, 224, 229–31, 244–46, 250–51, 255, 274, 305, 333, 382, 416, 456, 460, 463
 example, impact, commit (EIC) 238–40, 239
 types of 238, 238
figures
 ABCDSS of communication 204
 ACE conditions for success 39, 286
 ACE insights assessment of conditions for success 43
 aggressive, passive and assertive communication style 215
 aligning complex organizational activity to clear aim and purpose 13
 alignment of objectives, plans and activity 388
 the appreciation: aligned decision-making 300
 the appreciation process cycle 305
 areas of need for a leader to satisfy 63
 balancing core identity with envisioned future 467
 behavioural evidence, elements of 237
 briefing, sequence of a 380
 cascading, iterating and recurring processes to align activity and engage people 389
 cascading, iterating, self-monitoring processes for alignment and engagement 293
 coaching conversation agenda 241
 coaching and instruction, investment and benefit of 234
 coaching vs instruction 233
 coaching styles 86
 coaching zone 235
 communication between a leader and his/her team 110, 393
 communication between a leader of a team of leaders and their teams 111, 394
 communication channels in organizations 107
 communication methods 385
 communication process 202
 completing the incomplete to achieve meaning 203
 components of emotional intelligence and drivers of behaviour 154, 188
 components of leadership ability 57
 conflict, causes of 269
 conflict, positions in 271
 conflict, responses to 272
 conflict, uses and risks of optional responses to 273
 contingency planning 335
 decision-making style 319
 developing skill 255
 effective ACE conditions 41
 effects-based leadership 19, 288
 effects-based leadership processes 17
 elements of ability 130
 emotional responses in change 122
 emotions experienced in change 248
 extraction and cascade of briefing information 392
 feedback, description of 238
 feedback, EIC 239
 functional leadership checklist 65
 functional leadership checklist self-assessment 67
 hierarchy of 'complexity' and 'level of leadership work' 30
 influencing perception to change attitude 252
 intelligence cycle 397
 intelligence in the decision making, planning and briefing cascade 402
 intelligence and the execution cycle 400
 intelligence-informed decision making 401
 integrated levels of leadership 49
 Johari window 190
 Johari window and disclosure 191
 Johari window and feedback 191
 Johari window – feedback and disclosure 192
 ladder of assertiveness 225
 ladder of influence 214
 lateral authority and accountability 73, 462
 leadership hierarchy based on levels of work 459
 leadership hierarchy based on levels of work complexity 69
 leadership structure 390
 leadership style quadrants 79
 leadership style quadrants in detail 80
 leadership styles, balancing 84
 leadership styles: follower level and leadership coaching 85
 listening 208
 Maslow's hierarchy of needs 163
 needs–behaviour–goals relationship 163
 organizational effectiveness 22
 overcoming objections 227
 path to freedom 28
 path to mastery 236
 perception illustrations 181
 perception: deliberate distortions 185
 performance objectives 247
 planning with a staff system 326
 persuasion continuum 263
 principles of organization 451
 pub plan 363
 questioning 211

schematic plan format   320
schematic time and task synchronization chart   345
sources of power and results obtainable   93
strategy to reality cycle   290
strategy to reality gaps   10
strategy to reality performance gap   9
team development, stages of   423
transactional analysis as a development model   179
transactional analysis ego-state sub-sets   178
the three-transactional analysis ego-states   177
TS Web strategic plan   344
Universal Hierarchy of Motivation (UHM)   169
vertical authority and accountability   71, 461
Foch   26
Freud, S (and)   137–38
   beliefs and personality model of   137–38
   the ego and defence mechanisms   137–38
   the super-ego   138
   the unconscious   190
friction   8–9, 387
   internal   10–11, *10*, 329
functional leadership and checklist   64, 66, *65, 67*

Galen   136
gaps, strategy to reality   10–11, *10*
Gardner, H   95–96
genuineness   50, 56, 94, 105, 120, 134, 229, 432
global risks   6, 329
globalization   135
   and fragmentation   5
Goleman, D   96, 187
Graham, Lt.Gen, A   325
group dynamics   63, 296, 418, 421–22, 456
   and groupthink   299

Hackett, General Sir J   25, 59–61
Hahn, K   156
Hamilton, W   143
Harvey-Jones, Sir J   25, 449, 470
Health Service Journal: Primary Care Organization of the Year   45
Henderson, Col G F R   26
Hobbes, T   137
honesty   77, 89, 201, 416, 470
   and dishonesty   440, 470
Honey, P   242, *243*
human nature   142–46 *see also* Prisoner's Dilemma

inference/ladder of inference   214, *214*
influence   260–62, *261*
   face-to-face   262
   liking and relationship   262
   reciprocity   262
   indirect   261–62
   lobbying and association   261
   moral obligation   262
   social proof   262
   system, process and structure   261
   written, appreciations and papers   261
influence, persuasion and conflict resolution *see* conflict; influence *and* persuasion
information complexity   97–98, 452–54, *455*
   five orders of   453
information proliferation   395
Ingham, H   189 *see also* Johari Window
intellect   39, 40, 56, 245, 296
   and mode of thinking   129
intellectual capabilities   95–96
   bodily–kinaesthetic   95
   interpersonal   96
   intrapersonal   96
   linguistic   95
   logical–mathematical   95
   musical   95
   spatial   95
intelligence   *see also* intelligence cycle
   and planning   400, *400, 401, 402*
   principles governing organization and production of   395–96
intelligence cycle   396–99, *397, 400*
   collection   397–98
   direction   396–97
   dissemination   399
   processing   398–99
intelligence quotient (IQ)   168, 337
   test   135
Intelligent Leadership   313
integrity   35, 77, 89–90, 173, 262, 446, 471, 476
interpersonal communication   200–228
   see also assertiveness; communication; listening; questioning *and* rapport, building
   eye accessing cues   221–23
   inferences   214, *214*
   non-verbal communication   218–20, *220, 221*

Jacques, E   24, 35, 54–55, 56, 69, 450–54, 459
   and Requisite Organization   96, 449
Johari Window   189–90, 192–93, *190, 191, 192*
Jung, C (and)   137, 138–39, 141
   archetypes   139
   Jungian psychology   138, 337
   structure of personality   139

Kahneman, D   160
Kaplan, R S   323–24
Kay, P   300

Kennedy, President 477
knowledge 31, 39, 54, 56, 95, 130, 245–46, 258, 416, 472 *see also* leadership knowledge and skills
  of customer needs 50, 333
  inside 94
  management 104, 341
  psychological 136
  and skills 85, 100, 129–30, 162, 187, 229, 230, 253, 259, 426
  and understanding 300
Kotter, J P 116
Kübler-Ross, E 122

Laffin, J 473
Landsberg, M 85
leader/follower relationships 59–60, 87–88, 93, 242
leader-once-removed (LoR) 35, 69–72, 69, 71, 108, 459–60, 462, 463
leaders
  strategic 49, 51
  at tactical level 50
leadership *see also* effects-based leadership
  ability 39
  accountability 110
  action-centred 62
  as an art 26
  behaviour 120
  change 253
  learning pyramid 28–29
  flexible style of 39
  and management 58
  nature of 25
  organizational 21, 25, 40, 107, 116, 292
  and people and work 24–26
  self- 193–94
  shared 58–59
  tactical 52
  tactical/episodic 48
  transforming 84
  unity of 454, 456
leadership, leaders and teams (and) 33–34
  leadership as full-time job 33
  power of personal example 33–34
leadership ability (and) 53–105 *see also* definitions; leadership; leadership knowledge and skills; leadership role profile: critical behaviours for *and* leadership thought
  clarifying role relationships 67–72, 69, 71 *see also* role relationships
  the how of leadership *see* leadership style and behaviour
  leader and shared leadership 58–59
  leader/follower relationships 87–88

leadership and leader defined 53–57, 57
power, authority and leadership behaviour 92–94, 93 *see also* power
relationship between leader and follower 59–61
leadership differences and similarities 29–32, 30
  leaders vs managers 31–32
  leadership vs leader 31
leadership knowledge and skills 61–67, 63, 65, 67
  action-centred leadership 61–62
  dealing with task needs 62–63, 63
  and functional leadership checklist 64, 66, 65, 67
  meeting individual needs 64
  satisfying team needs 63
leadership role profile: critical behaviours for 100–105
  building relationships and influencing 103
  coaching and developing others 101–02
  determination and drive for performance 104
  monitoring and evaluating 102–03
  personal example 104–05
  planning and briefing 101
  problem-solving/aligned decision-making 100–101
  self-development 105
  teamwork and team development 103–04
leadership style and behaviour 76–87, 79, 80, 84, 114 *see also* definitions
  autocratic 78
  coaching 85–87, 85, 86
    delegate 87
    direct 86
    excite 86
    guide 86
  collaborative 81–82
  directive 78, 81
  effective 78
  flexible 39
  incentive-based 83
  selection of appropriate 80–87
  strategic/transformational 79
leadership thought 95–98
  binary and ternary mode of 95–96
    see also intellectual capabilities
  and cognitive power/level of work 96–97
  implications for structure 97–98
leadership work of creating clarity and engagement (and) 285–94 *see also* clarity
  case study for 289
  dynamic reviews 291–92, 294
  problems and decisions 285–88, 286, 288
    see also decision-making
  recurring, cascading and iterating processes 289–92, 294, 290, 293
    appreciation/aligned decision-making 290
    briefing and execution 290

detailed planning 290
Leading Change 116
leading transformation and change *see* change *and* systems
listening 208–11, *208*, 226, 227
  active 208, 209, 211, 214, 263
  barriers to effective 209–10
  guidelines for 210
  and paying attention 210–11, *211*
Locke, J 136
Looking for Trouble 75
loyalty 7–8, 63, 76–77, 84, 90–91, 104, 105, 413, 446, 458
  brand 333
  customer 434, 443
  and effect on businesses 443–44
  lack of 89
  research on 444
Luecke, R 473
Luft, J 189 *see also* Johari Window

MacDonald, I 72, 113, 114, 457, 470, 476
Mant, A 27, 54, 55, 78, 96, 313
Maslow, A 83–84, 123
  and hierarchy of needs 84, 123, 163–64, *163*, 165, 166, 249, 332, 438
Mayer, J D 186, 187
Maynard Smith, J 144
Mehrabian, A 203
memory, working (WM) 222–23
mentoring 229, 230, 245
military analogy 145–46
mission analysis 17–18, 75, 114, 119, 131, 243–44, 278, 290, 204, 308, 309–12, 325–29, 336–37, 339, 340–41, 347, 355, 360–61, 365, 367–68, 377, 384, 386, 391
Montgomery of Alamein, Field Marshal the Viscount 31, 54, 55–56, 57, 129, 438–40, 473
Moran, Lord 88
moral courage 77, 88–89, 102, 104–05, 194, 416, 426, 470
  lack of 238, 415, 430
morale (and) 64, 72, 314, 330, 411, 434–43
  comradeship 439
  discipline 439–42
  drop in/erosion of 123, 249, 336, 421, 426
  foundations of 435–38
  high 423, 426, 432, 434–35
  leadership 438
  low 120, 434, 449
  maintenance of 474
  self-respect 439
  signs of low 442–43
motivation 23–24, 37, 39, 56–57, 64, 95–96, 134–35, 158–59, 166–67, 183, 188, 231, 244, 251, 259, 264, 281, 296, 416, 424, 435, 441
  incentive-based 83
  and morale 438
  and needs, behaviour and goals 162–65, *163*
  universal hierarchy of (UHM) 168–70, *169, 170, 171*
Mumford, A 242, *243*
Mutual Recognition Unit (MRU) 35, 69–71, *69*, 108–09, 459–60, 463
Myers, I B 141
Myers-Briggs Type Indicator (MBTI) 139, 150
  four areas of preferences and personality types 337
mythologies 72, 476

Napoleon 26, 31
narrative therapy and fears 160–61
Newton, I 137
Nordstrom 470
Norton, D P 323–24

Obama, B 150
Oliver, M 168
operating context *see also* capability requirement; change; effects-based leadership; employee engagement; friction *and* strategy to reality
  ICT, information and time/space compression 4–5
optimism 77, 104, 195, 298
organization ethos and culture *see* business doctrine; core identity; cultural norms; envisioned future *and* mythologies
organization and structure in leadership 447–65
  see also principles of organization
organizational effectiveness 22–23, *22*
  conceptual component of 23
  moral component of 23
  physical component of 22
organizational leaders 11, 50, 79, 109, 396
organizational transformation 118–19
  see change

paradox: discipline and freedom 27–28, *28*
Penfield, W 176
people, personality and decision-making 295–301 *see also* cognition; decision-making; group dynamics; thinking *and* understanding
perception (and) 7, 139, 158–59, 165, 173, 180, *181*, 242, 244, 249, 251–53, *252*, 270–71, 296–98, 420–21
  deliberate distractions 184, *185*
  gap 45
  how it works 182–84

inferences   214
the leader   184–85
overcoming ill-founded   119
perceptual blocks   123
understanding preferences   192–93
performance management   23, 33, 100, 109, 116, 120, 196
and importance of behaviour   157
lack of effective   443
systems   230
personal values and standards   88–92 *see also* charisma; integrity; loyalty; moral courage *and* self-discipline
humility and respect for others   91
selfless commitment   91–92
personality   140–42
classification of   140–41
defining   142
idiographic approach to   140, 142
nomothetic approach to   140–41
questionnaires for defining   141–42
and religious/philosophical beliefs   141
personality questionnaires
16PF (Primary Factors) Questionnaire (Cattell)   141
Eysenck Personality Inventory (EPI)   141
Maudsley Medical Questionnaire (MMQ)   141
MBTI matrix of psychological types   141–42
personality types   337–38, *338*
A Perspective on Infantry   16
persuasion (and)   262–67, *263*
aim and purpose of message   263
content of message   264
context of message   265
dos and don'ts   267
facilitated formal discussion   265
formal presentation   266–67
order of presentation   265
protecting against   267
recipient of message   264
source of message   263–64
PEST analysis   328
Pfizer   19
Philips   19
Pink, D   83, 166–67
Plan-Do-Check-Act cycle (Deming)   385–86
planning (and)   289–90, 375–86, *376*
see also briefing
communication: routine briefing and updates   384, *385*
contingency   335–36, *335*
detailed plan format for   377–79, *378*
administration and logistics   379
control and communication   379
execution   377–78
mission   377

early warning   384
PRINCE2   386
project management and routine leadership   385
Six Sigma   385–86
planning and briefing cascade   387–94
communication in an organizational structure   392–94, *393*, *394*
extraction of relevant information   390, 392
leadership structure   390, *390*
tasking procedure   387–88, *388*, *389*
Plato   136
Porras, J   125, 467, 469
power (of)   92–94, *93*
access and the network   94
attraction   94
expertise   93–94
information   94
respect, trust and confidence   94
role or authority   93
PRINCE2   386
principles of organization   450–64
defined role relationships   458–62, *459*, *461*, *462 see also* role relationships
delegation of clear tasks in context   457–58
grouping of similar assignments   464
recognition of role of leader-once-removed   463
requisite hierarchical structure for   450–54, *451*
and cognitive processes, information and tasks   452–54, *455*
and Jacques' research   451–52, *453*
see also Jacques, E
span of control: personnel, distance and time   456–57
standardization   464
unity of leadership   454, 456
Prisoner's Dilemma   143–46
collaboration and cheating   144–45
military analogy of   145–46
moral of   143
Rapaport's Tit-for-Tat solution to   144
rules of   144
used for war-gaming   143
problem-solving processes   82, 232, 241, 274, 278, 295, 303, 336–37
Procter & Gamble   50, 470
progress, evaluating   404
and failure to meet objectives   408
propositions about organizations, leadership, people and work   21–36 *see also* leadership *and individual entries as detailed on contents pages*
impact of 'organization' on behaviour   34
leadership differences and similarities *see main entry*

prospect theory (Kahneman and Tversky) 160
psychology 134–42, 175–76, 190, 296
  see also Freud, S and Jung, C
  behavioural 7, 139
  cognitive 139, 221
  evolutionary 140
  humanistic 139–40
  neurological 139
  and personality see personality
pyramid of leadership learning 28–29

questioning/questions 211–13, *211*, 214
  and clarifying 213
  considerations and hints for 212–13
  leading 212
  multiple 212

Ramey, J 340–41
Rapaport, A 144
rapport, building 207–08, 254
  by mirroring and matching 207
  by paying attention 210, *211*
  using universals and truisms 207–08
references/notes 20, 36, 98–99, 125, 132, 198–99, 228, 259, 281, 294, 301, 363, 432–33, 446, 465, 478
Reichheld, F 443
report on dishonesty and cynicism in Britain (University of Essex Centre for the Study of Integrity) 471
Requisite Organization 96
requisite organization 449
research on
  cognitive power (Jacques) 96
  'built to last' companies 467–68
  financial incentives 83
  loyalty/disloyalty (Bain & Company International) 444
risk 5–6, 81, 87, 160, 164, 179, 299, 300, 313–14, 328–29, 334, *334*, 396, 405–06, 422, 475
  assessment 323
  averse 262, 279–80, 446, 448
  avoidance 31, 75
  calculated 194
  global 329
  seeking 279–80
role of a leader see ACE
role relationships 67–71, *71*, 458–62, *459*
  lateral 72, 461–62, *462*
  MRU three-layer units: LoRs, SoRs and peer leaders 69–71, *69*, *459*, 460
  peer leaders 459
  subordinates-once-removed (SoRs) 69, 70–71, *69*, *71*, 108, 459–60

vertical authority – leader of team 70–71, 460, *461*
vertical authority – leader-once-removed 70–71, 459, 460, 463
Rousseau 137
Rowsell, D 333
Royce, J 443

Salovey, P 187
Samsung 6
security, need for 123, 164, 166, 195, 249, 438, 441
self-awareness 84–85, 187–90, 192–93, *187*, 214 see also Johari Window
self-confidence/self-assurance 75, 80, 91, 118, 123, 154, 156, 172, 187, 194–97, 339
self-discipline 88, 91, 124, 174, 193–94, 209, 250, 415, 438, 440–41
self-esteem 121, 165, 194–96, 238, 251–52
  lack of/low 123, 195, 249, 430
self-talk 148, 153, 193, 224–25
sinistrals/sinistrality 149–50 see also brain
situational awareness 187, 196–97
Six Sigma 385–86
skill, building 253–56
  by defining learning objectives 254
  lesson plan for 254–56, *255*
  by preparation and planning 254
  rehearsal for 256
skills
  and knowledge 129
  training 130
Slim, Field Marshall Sir W 58, 91, 116, 120, 415, 435–40
Stewart, K 113, 114
SMART/SMART objectives 246, *247*, 406
stakeholder analysis chart 275, *276*
standard operating procedures (SOPs) 48, 114, 286–87
Stirling, D 414, 471
strategy to reality – the execution gap 9–12, *9*, *10*
strength as characteristic of attitudes 159
stress 7, 16, 41, 56, 57, 60, 159, 189, 209, 297, 435, 441
  biological response to 214
  of responsibility 91
  sources of 15, 34, 67, 115, 174, 303, 390, 416, 458, 476
Strong, J 55
structures
  ill-defined, matrix 449
  and organizational layers 448
  over-flat · 448

Index

subordinates-once-removed (SoR) 69, 70–71, 69, 71, 108, 459–60, 463
SWOT analysis 314–15, 336
systems
  of differentiation 114
  of equalization 113–14

tables
  ACE: the generic question areas 44
  agenda items 364
  analysis of possible CoAs 351–53
  building rapport by paying attention 211
  campaign plan, supporting document for 322
  campaign plan: example 321
  centre of gravity matrix 330
  CoAs satisfying constraints 359
  courses of Action (CoA) open 369
  detail supporting schematic plan 321
  example factors 348–50
  execution: detailed tasks 374
  factor headings 315
  factor/situation analysis 368
  factors, deductions and tasks 342–43
  factors affecting (RWC) team success 38
  factors for the estate agent 316
  factors inducing trust or paranoia 445
  helpful and unhelpful beliefs 217
  holiday availability and costs 354
  holiday factor analysis 355–57
  Honey and Mumford's learning styles 243
  indirect and direct influences 261
  inhibitors of acceptance or resistance 221
  input into decision making 376
  left and right hemisphere functions 152
  minutes items record sheet 366
  mission analysis 368
  non-verbal communication 226
  perception, factors affecting 252
  personality types and effects 338
  planning process sequence 378
  project/task outline plan template 370
  pub factors, deductions, tasks 361–62
  risk matrix 334
  road map for change 117
  stakeholder analysis chart 276
  strata, level of complexity and role 455
  strategic plan and second order task tracking document template 372
  strategy to execution cycle 376
  team roles 425
  UHM drives and leadership approaches 169
  UHM drives and stages of brain development 171
  UHM drives, exemplars of 170
  weighing up the options 317

task complexity, four types of 453–54
team development stages 422–24, 426–31, 423
  forming: team roles and size 424, 426, 425
  mourning/adjourning 431
  norming 427–30
  performing 431
  storming 426–27
team/group characteristics 412–16
  discipline 415
  leadership 413–14
  the mission 413
team/group dynamics 418–22
  cohesiveness 419–20
  conflict between teams 420–21
  decision-making 421–22
teams and groups 412–33 *see also* team development stages; team types *and* team/group dynamics
  advice to leaders on 432
  characteristics of *see* team/group characteristics
  and maintaining the team 431–32
  trust 44, 446, 445
  types of 416–17
'three-layer group' and its leader 35
  and leader-once-removed (LoR) 35
  and subordinates-once-removed (SoRs) 35
thinking 56, 129, 139, 142, 337 *see also* cognition; core identity; emotional intelligence; leadership thought *and* psychology
  blue sky 327, 477
  clear 205, 287, 295, 307–08, 320, 323
  conscious – unconscious 297
  deductive 244, 300
  divergent – convergent 297
  and feeling 157–58
  impact of personality on 296
  reflective – impulsive 297
  field dependent – independent 297–98
  strategic 339
  systems 312
Trait Theory (Allport) 141
transactional analysis (TA) 134, 176–80, 177, 178
  as development model 179–80, 179
  structural model for 176–79
transforming behaviour 83–84
transformation *see also* change
  organizational 118–19, 287
trust 34, 444, 446, 445, 449, 470
Tversky, A 160

UK Army Act (1955) 77
uncertainty 15, 29, 121, 281, 395, 473
  see also risk
  and complexity 5–7
  embracing 324

understanding   300–301
  leadership ability   *see* leadership ability
  three levels of   300–301
understanding people, behaviour and emotional intelligence   133–99 *see also* emotional intelligence; human nature; Prisoner's Dilemma
  basic psychology – study of mind and behaviour *see* psychology
  core identity   174–80, *178, 179*
  how the brain works   146–53, *152*
  perception   180–85, *181, 185*
  what is personality?   140–42
universal hierarchy of motivation (UHM)   168–70, *169, 170, 171*

value(s)
  core   428, 467, 469–70
  customer   331–33, 444
  product and service   333–34
values   469–72
Venn diagram   62, 63
visualization   148, 153, 224–25
Vroom, V H   82
VUCA (volatility, uncertainty, complexity, ambiguity)   6–7, 10, 295, 387

Wavell   440
Wilkins, M   308